THE HISTORY OF
THE SYNOPTIC
TRADITION

RUDOLF BULTMANN

THE HISTORY OF
THE SYNOPTIC
TRADITION

Translated by
JOHN MARSH
Principal of Mansfield College, Oxford

Revised edition

OXFORD
BASIL BLACKWELL
1972

© in this translation 1963
BASIL BLACKWELL OXFORD
Second edition 1968
with corrections and with additions from
the 1962 Supplement
Reprinted 1972

Translated from the second German edition (1931)
by agreement with
VANDENHOECK AND RUPRECHT, GÖTTINGEN

ISBN 0 631 11350 9

PRINTED IN GREAT BRITAIN BY
WESTERN PRINTING SERVICES LTD., BRISTOL

In Memoriam

WILHELM HEITMULLER

TRANSLATOR'S PREFACE

To translate this important work of New Testament into English has been a labour, but a labour of love, and of appreciation for much that I owe to Professor Bultmann. I was privileged to be in his lectures and seminar at Marburg in 1931–2, and he made a very considerable impression on me then, for which I have been increasingly grateful. It has been one of the misfortunes of the English-speaking world that this outstanding contribution to Form Criticism has not been put into English before. I hope that, despite the faults of the translation, many more English readers will now discover Bultmann at first hand. I cannot do other than thank Messrs. Blackwell, and particularly Mr. Schollick, for their not inconsiderable patience, and three of my pupils at Mansfield College, Oxford (Messrs. McPherson, Moth and Wren) for their kindly help in preparing the index of Gospel references.

JOHN MARSH

Mansfield College, Oxford

Pages for which additional material is given in the Supplement are distinguished by an asterisk alongside the page number

CONTENTS

III. The Editing of the Traditional Material

THE MATERIALS AND THE TASK

WHEN Synoptic criticism reached the conclusion that Mark was the oldest Gospel and that it also lay behind the structure of Matthew and Luke, the critics, happy about their conclusion, quickly and readily jumped to another, and found in Mark's presentation of the life of Jesus—'perhaps with some adjustment in detail'[1]—the actual course of historical events. The great epochs and changes of the Galilean Ministry and the final catastrophe in Jerusalem—according to Holtzmann's typical judgement[2]—could be shown to be the well-ordered and consistent principles of Mark's presentation. The backbone of the historical development was the revelation of the Messiahship step by step, or even the developing confession of his Messiahship by Jesus himself.

It was Wrede's work on the Messianic Secret which did most to call into question this traditional attitude which went far beyond what could be established by a cautious analysis of Mark, such as Weizsäcker had undertaken. Wrede's work constituted a quite annihilating criticism of a seemingly clear picture of historical development in Mark. This picture is an illusion; Mark is the work of an author who is steeped in the theology of the early Church, and who ordered and arranged the traditional material that he received in the light of the faith of the early Church—that was the result; and the task which follows for historical research is this: to separate the various strata in Mark and to determine which belonged to the original historical tradition and which derived from the work of the author.

Johannes Weiss, who set himself this task, in his work *The Earliest Gospel* (1903), had considerable confidence in what Papias has to say about Mark being the interpreter of Peter. He therefore thought he would be able to discover fairly easily beneath the work of the Evangelist a certain amount of reliable historical material, namely, Peter's reminiscences. Since then it has become generally recognized that the problem is much more complicated, the strands of traditional and editorial material more numerous, the conditions under which

---

[1] Wrede, *The Messianic Secret*, 1901, p. 11. Cp. O. Cullmann, *R.H.Ph.R.*, 5, 1925, pp. 459ff.; B. S. Easton, *The Gospel before the Gospels*, 1928, pp. 3ff.
[2] E.g. *Lehrbuch der histor.-krit. Einleitung in das N.T.*[2], 1886, pp. 368f.

the material was shaped very different, and the modifications more widespread than J. Weiss had believed. E. Wendling's[1] ingenious attempts at analysis of Mark have admittedly not met with general acceptance, and certainly his claim to have discovered sources is untenable. For all the brilliance of many of his literary and critical observations, and however right he was to undertake his analysis, his ignoring of the Synoptic problem, his mechanical idea of the way an editor works, his unjustified use of his knowledge of literary history as if it were itself literary criticism, has prejudiced his whole work.

The most important and far-reaching work in the field of Synoptic research since Wrede, has been done by Wellhausen.[2] His work is more comprehensive than Wrede's for he has shown how the theology of the early Church has influenced the traditional material, not only in Mark, but also in Matthew and Luke, and therefore in Q, which, like Mark, lies behind them. Wellhausen stated very clearly the fundamental assumption that the tradition consists of individual stories or groups of stories joined together in the Gospels by the work of the editors; and he also showed how pieces of primitive tradition alternated with secondary material,[3] but he did not reach a final, comprehensive and detailed conclusion. But he did see the complexity of the problem, though he could go no further than to say: 'it is not enough to think that it was simply an oral tradition that the editors used. . . . And there is no reason to dismiss the suggestion offhand that once the Mark we know was written down it was itself the subject of editorial review. In any event, the most important thing is to recognise that unquestionably secondary material has found its way into the tradition. Whether it is literally secondary is quite another question. The first thing we must do is to stop looking for the pure Ur-Markus and fixing the various stages of its redaction.'[4]

In these circumstances it was inevitable that the analysis of the Synoptics into literary sources should give way to an attempt to apply to them the *methods of form-criticism* which H. Gunkel and his disciples had already applied to the Old Testament. This involved discovering what the original units of the Synoptics were, both sayings and

[1] *Ur-Marcus*, 1905. *Die Entstehung des Marcus-Evangeliums*, 1908.
[2] His commentaries on Mark, Matthew and Luke, 1903–4 (Mk.[2] 1909). *Einleitung in die drei ersten Evangelien*, 1905; [2]1911.
[3] This had already been observed by D. F. Strauss and the Tuebingen school; cp. esp. Ed. Zeller, *Vortr. u. Abh.*, 1865, pp. 448ff. There was a noteworthy reaction in the work of K. Holl, *Urchristentum u. Religionsgeschichte*, 1925, pp. 23ff. In a justifiable desire to treat the content of the Synoptic tradition as a unity Holl too readily identified the spiritual with the literary unity and so contested the opinion that the Synoptic tradition originated in particular units.
[4] *Einleitung in die drei ersten Evangelien*[2], p. 48.

stories, to try to establish what their historical setting was, whether they belonged to a primary or secondary tradition or whether they were the product of editorial activity. Looked at like this, it is a matter of indifference in what source any particular unit happens to be found. Naturally such a method cannot be confined to Mark, but must be applied to the whole range of Synoptic material. But just as naturally such a task cannot put aside literary nor yet historical criticism. Not only is the result of Synoptic study such as the Two-source theory presupposed, but even the distinction between tradition and redaction could not be made without literary analysis. Form-criticism cannot possibly perform its task in opposition to literary criticism although it rejects the particular ways in which literary analysis has been transcended in the writings of E. Wendling, F. Spitta[1] and W. Haupt.[2] But, on the other hand, form-criticism has readily learnt[3] much from literary inquiries, such as those of B. H. Streeter[4] and W. Bussmann.[5]

A start has already been made with this work.[6] The distinction of traditional from editorial material is the real subject of K. L. Schmidt's *Der Rahmen der Geschichte Jesu* (1919). His work is a thorough-going and conclusive discussion of the earlier position especially Spitta's ingenious but misleading suggestions. But more than anybody else, M. Dibelius in his *Formgeschichte des Evangeliums* (1919) has subjected the different units of the Gospel tradition to form-critical inquiry. Admittedly, he has not examined the whole content of the Gospel material, but has contented himself with certain types of material essentially narrative, and brilliantly shown how fruitful the method is for discovering the stages in the development of the tradition as well as for the Gospels as a whole.

The following investigation therefore sets out to give an account of the history of the *individual units of the tradition*, and how the tradition passed from a fluid state to the fixed form in which it meets us in the Synoptics and in some instances even outside them. I am entirely in agreement with M. Dibelius when he maintains that form-criticism is not simply an exercise in aesthetics nor yet simply a process of

[1] *Die synoptische Grundschrift in ihrer Ueberlieferung durch das Lukas-Evangelium*, 1912.
[2] *Worte Jesu und Gemeindeueberlieferung*, 1913.
[3] Unfortunately the same cannot be said of E. Meyer's analysis of Mark in his valuable work *Ursprung und Anfaenge des Christentums*, I, 1921, where he has not made proper use of Wellhausen's work. For the rest I am almost completely in agreement with J. Schniewind's judgement of recent works in literary criticism (*Th.R.*, N.F. 2, 1930, pp. 134–61).
[4] *The Four Gospels*, 1924. It is much to be regretted that this scholar worked without dealing with the researches of the form-critics.
[5] *Synoptische Studien*: I *Zur Geschichtsquelle*, 1925; II *Zur Redenquelle*, 1929.
[6] Naturally such work is not absolutely new; E. Fascher has shown how its themes have played some part in earlier research, *Die formgeschichtlichen Methode*, 1924, pp. 4–51.

description and classification; that is to say, it does not consist of identifying the individual units of the tradition according to their aesthetic or other characteristics and placing them in their various categories. It is much rather 'to rediscover the origin and the history of the particular units and thereby to throw some light on the history of the tradition before it took literary form'.[1] The proper understanding of form-criticism rests upon the judgement that the literature in which the life of a given community, even the primitive Christian community, has taken shape, springs out of quite definite conditions and wants of life from which grows up a quite definite style and quite specific forms and categories. Thus every literary category has its 'life situation' (*Sitz im Leben*: Gunkel), whether it be worship in its different forms, or work, or hunting, or war. The *Sitz im Leben* is not, however, an individual historical event, but a typical situation or occupation in the life of a community. In the same way, the literary 'category', or 'form' through which a particular item is classified is a sociological concept and not an aesthetic one, however much it may be possible by its subsequent development to use such forms as aesthetic media in some particular literary product.[2] But in the literature of primitive Christianity, which is essentially 'popular' (Dibelius) in kind, this development had not yet taken place, and it is only possible to understand its forms and categories in connection with their 'life situation', i.e. the influences at work in the life of the community.

It is no objection to the form-critical approach, but rather a demonstration of its fruitfulness, to find that one piece of the tradition is seldom to be classified unambiguously in a single category.[3] For just as in real life we are able to convey a number of different ideas in a single saying, so it is with literary forms. And the analysis that form-criticism undertakes seeks to discover the influences which have been active in the formation of the tradition. But it often has to deal with the fact that in literary composition—however primitive it may be—traditional forms are used as technical devices; and in so far as form-criticism can detect the suitability or unsuitability of the form, its purity, and whether it has been subject to

[1] *Th.R.*, N.F. 1, 1929, p. 187. Dibelius is right in criticizing P. Fiebig, who thinks of form-criticism as almost entirely a formal inquiry.

[2] This view is misunderstood by M. Albertz (*Die synoptischen Streitgespraeche*, 1921) and E. Fascher (*Die formgeschichtliche Methode*, 1924) though it is clearly developed in O. Cullmann (*R.H.Ph.R.*, 5, 1925, pp. 459–77 and 564–79). The dominant idea of form-criticism has been excellently stated in the essay 'Zur geschichtlichen Betrachtung der Poesie' in J. Burckhardt's *Weltgeschichtlichen Betrachtungen*, pp. 69–80. This shows quite clearly that the methods of form-criticism are by no means confined to so-called 'popular literature'.

[3] This is the opinion of Fascher, op. cit.

modification or not, it will serve to throw light on the history of the tradition.[1]

It is essential to realize that form-criticism is fundamentally indistinguishable from all historical work in this, that it has to move in a circle. The forms of the literary tradition must be used to establish the influences operating in the life of the community, and the life of the community must be used to render the forms themselves intelligible. There is no method of regulating or even prescribing the necessary interplay and mutual relationships of both these processes, no rule to say where the start must be made. When M. Dibelius pursues his 'Constructive Method', i.e. when he reconstructs the history of the synoptic tradition from a study of the community and its needs; and when, contrariwise, I proceed from the analysis of the particular elements of the tradition, we are not opposed to each other, but rather engaged in mutually complementary and corrective work. Dibelius can no more get a clear idea of the motives of the life of the community without first making some inquiry about forms, than I, in my analysis, can dispense with a provisional picture of the primitive community and its history, which has to be turned into a clear and articulated picture in the course of my inquiries. J. Schniewind has shown very clearly how the study of form-criticism can lead us to a fruitful understanding of the primitive Christian community.[2]

In distinction from Dibelius I am indeed convinced that form-criticism, just because literary forms are related to the life and history of the primitive Church not only presupposes judgements of facts alongside judgements of literary criticism, but must also lead to judgements about facts (the genuineness of a saying, the historicity of a report and the like). Hence an essential part of my inquiry concerns the one chief problem of primitive Christianity, the relationship of the primitive Palestinian and Hellenistic Christianity.[3]

Since the first edition of this work appeared in 1921 research has made further progress. I need only refer to the comprehensive review by Dibelius in the *Theol. Rundschau*, N.F. 1, 1929, pp. 185–

[1] On the question of mixed forms see M. Dibelius, *Th.R.*, N.F. 1, 1929, pp. 202f.
[2] *Th.R.*, N.F. 2, 1930, pp. 161–89; cp. also O. Cullmann, *R.H.Ph.R.*, 5, 1925, pp. 468ff., 564ff.
[3] I have no wish to deal with my much-criticized scepticism in detail. I need only refer to M. Kaehler and his book *Der sogenannte historische Jesus und der geschichtliche biblische Christus*[2] (1896). He saw quite clearly that of the life of Jesus 'we have reports, but none that demonstrably are assessable as original sources in the strict sense of these words.' (p. 22), and that it was essential to see that 'there is no comprehensibly clear distinction between oral tradition and the saga; not even with full certainty and unexceptionably even if the generation following the eye and ear-witnesses is concerned' (p. 36.1: cp. p. 88). Many are ready to admit that, though thereafter, thinking they have paid enough service to criticism in such a general concession, struggle against criticism where it is applied in particular cases.

216, as I shall be referring to individual works in what follows.[1] Neither shall I fail, on occasion, to deal with criticisms, which have not been lacking.[2]

What *tools* then are provided for us outside the analysis of literary criticism?[3]

1. For the most part the history of the tradition is obscure, though there is one small part which we can observe in our sources, how Marcan material is treated as it is adapted by Matthew and Luke. If we take fully into account the connected question of an Ur-Marcus, and the problems of textual criticism which do not always lead to firm judgements, we may still discern a certain regularity in the way Matthew and Luke use Mark. In the case of Q admittedly, we are dependent upon a reconstruction from Matthew and Luke; but even here it is possible on occasion, by comparing Matthew and Luke to recognize what laws governed the development of material from Q to Matthew and Luke. If we are able to detect any such laws, we may assume that they were operative on the traditional material even before it was given its form in Mark and Q, and in this way we can infer back to an earlier stage of the tradition than appears in our sources. Moreover it is at this point a matter of indifference whether the tradition were oral or written, because on account of the unliterary character of the material one of the chief differences between oral and written traditions is lacking. Such considerations are reinforced through the expansion of the material, in so far, that is to say, as the same observations can be made on the stories that are found outside the Synoptics, and particularly on the later gospels—though less in the case of John than in the apocryphal tradition—and then, quite fundamentally, on the history of the text.

2. The aim of form-criticism is to determine the original form of a piece of narrative, a dominical saying or a parable. In the process we learn to distinguish secondary additions and forms, and these in turn lead to important results for the history of the tradition.

3. There are analogies to hand both for the form and history of the tradition. For the former we may take especially the sayings and stories of the Rabbis, but also Hellenistic stories, and for both there are the traditions of proverbs, anecdotes and folk-tales. Fairy stories are instructive in many respects, and in some ways folk-songs are even

---

[1] Cp. also in addition the review by O. Cullmann already mentioned (p. 5.1), the discerning essay by H. J. Cadbury in *H.T.R.*, 16, 1923, pp. 81–92.

[2] In addition to the book by E. Fascher, cp. esp. L. Koehler, *Das formgeschichtliche Problem des N.T.*, 1927, and B. S. Easton, *The Gospel before the Gospels*, 1928.

[3] On this question cp. also O. Cullmann, op. cit., pp. 569ff.

more so, because the characteristics of primitive story telling are even more firmly preserved in their set form. There are also some extraordinarily instructive analogies to the history of the Synoptic tradition in the history of the Jataka collection of the Buddhist canon.[1]

[1] Cp. the Introduction by H. Lueders to the Buddhist Fairy Stories (Maerchen der Weltliteratur), 1921.

I. The Tradition of the Sayings of Jesus

A. Apophthegms

I DO not think that it is possible to have a scientific discussion as to whether the stories about Jesus or the tradition of his sayings first attained a fixed form. The needs of the Church giving rise to both traditions would have made themselves felt at the same time. In any case, the important and compassable problem is to get to know those needs. But even then I hold it wrong to proceed one-sidedly and simply deduce the forms of the tradition from the pre-supposed needs of the community, even if it were rightly recognized. Instead, construction and analysis must go hand in hand (see above, pp. 4f.). And as to the starting-point, my preference is to proceed analytically and draw conclusions from the material of the tradition, as to its *Sitz im Leben*, its point of origin and conservation in the community, for that, too, is to be sure, the way in which the forms become fully intelligible.

It also seems to me a secondary matter whether one begins with sayings or stories. I start with sayings. But I should reckon as part of the tradition of the sayings a species of traditional material which might well be reckoned as stories—viz. such units as consist of say-ings of Jesus set in a brief context. I use a term to describe them which comes from Greek literature, and is least question-begging— 'apophthegms'.[1] The subsequent course of this present inquiry will justify my taking the apophthegms before the sayings of Jesus that are not placed in a particular framework. The chief reason is that many apophthegms can be reduced to bare dominical sayings by deter-mining the secondary character of their frame, and can thus be com-pared, in the following part of the book, with other sayings of Jesus.

I shall proceed first by analysing the particular instances of a species of apophthegms individually, and then go on to discuss their form-history in a brief review. Much of what is first stated in the course of particular analysis will find its confirmation or its sure foundation in the light of a general review.

[1] Cp. P. Wendland, 'Die urchristlichen Literaturformen' (*Handbuch zum N.T.*, 1, 3), 1912, p. 261. Similarly Herder (according to Fascher, p. 85) and Ch. H. Weisse, *Die evangelische Geschichte*, I, 1838, p. 454. W. Gemoll, in *Das Apophthegma*, 1924, has given us much useful material for the history of the apophthegm, but his work lacks conceptual clarity.

1. Controversy Dialogues and Scholastic Dialogues

(a) *Occasioned by Jesus' healings*

Mk. 3[1-6]: *The Sabbath healing of the man with the withered hand.* This is compact in structure. There is no special introduction by the editor, but only the insertion of πάλιν[1] to link it with the context. But we have some editorial trimmings in the concluding v. 6 which reveal a biographical interest otherwise alien to the conflict and didactic sayings, and which is not relevant to the main point of the story[2]—the principle involved in healing on the Sabbath. On this point οἱ δὲ ἐσιώπων in v. 4 and the healing in v. 5 are the natural ending. We cannot avoid asking the question whether the logion in v. 4 was originally an isolated element in the tradition. But the interrogatory form by itself is a typical form of a reply to the charge contained in v. 2, and so we cannot substantiate the supposition of an originally isolated tradition. It is much more likely that what we have here is an organically complete apophthegm. Its language[3] confirms what its content suggests as probable, that its formulation took place in the early Palestinian Church. It is characteristic for the history of the tradition that Luke introduces the opponent who appears at the end of Mark's story right at the beginning of his (6[7]), and that Matthew has added an isolated saying about the Sabbath (12[11f.]).

Lk. 14[1-6]: *The Sabbath healing of the man with the dropsy.* This is a variant of the preceding story. The point of v. 5, which Matthew has introduced into Mk. 3[1-6] (Matt. 12[11f.]) was evidently an isolated saying, and apparently a stock argument in the early Church's disputes about the Sabbath. The scene was thus composed as a framework for the saying, on the analogy of Mk. 3[1-6]. It is compact in structure and Luke has only added v. 1, which in any case has to serve as an introduction to the following section as well.

Lk. 13[10-17]: *The Sabbath healing of the crippled woman.* This is a further variant on the theme of Sabbath healing, perhaps, like the previous example, composed on the basis of an originally isolated saying (v. 15). It shows manifestly the least skill in composition of all three Sabbath healing stories; for here, in distinction from 14[1-6] and Mk. 3[1-6], the healing precedes the discussion, a fact which renders impossible any organic connection of the story with its con-

---

[1] πάλιν is a simple connecting formula, not referring back to any particular episode, as e.g. 1.21. The formula could well have been in use at the stage of the oral tradition.
[2] Cp. A. Meyer, *Festgabe f. A. Juelicher*, 1927, pp. 37f.
[3] Cp. Wellhausen, *Einleitung in die drei ersten Evangelien*, [2]1911, p. 21. We are not obliged to think that the form of words is a Semitism. Blass, § 245, 3.

clusion (v. 17), since the account of the miracle has to be followed by the report of the shame and confusion of the critics. For the rest, perhaps 17b is the work of the editor (Luke), since the rejoicing of the multitude is a theme which originally would be placed at the end of the miracle story proper. In any case, in the stage of oral development, the style of the miracle story could very well have influenced that of the apophthegm.

Mk. 3^{22-30}, cp. Matt. 12^{22-37}//Lk. 11^{14-23}: *The dispute about exorcism.* Mark has inserted this material between vv. 20f. and 31–35,[1] and the likelihood is that he has not been able to keep the beginning intact. For the discussion presupposes an exorcism preceding it, and no story original to the tradition would be likely to begin[2] with a reference to some activity of Jesus in quite general terms. These considerations suggest that the form of the story which Matthew and Luke found in Q could well be more original than that of Mark. But there is no unity in the composition of either Q or Mark.[3] The basic section is Matt. 12^{22-26}//Lk. $11^{14f.,17f.}$: cp. Mk. 3^{22-26}: the accusation and the twin images of a divided kingdom and a divided house as the answer, an answer in a form typical in Jewish debates. Admittedly it is possible that the saying in Mk. 3^{23b-25} (as also the Q parallels) could have existed originally in isolation; yet there are no positive reasons to support this hypothesis, and it seems much more likely that the basic section is a unity. Only the beginning of v. 22 is Marcan editing: the ὅτι Βεελζεβοὺλ ἔχει (lacking in Q) is a doublet of ὅτι ἐν τῷ ἄρχοντι τῶν δαιμονίων ἐκβάλλει τὰ δαιμόνια. If the latter construction is really a Semitism[4] expressing the original idea of a miracle worked by the power of the name, then the former construction expresses the Hellenistic conception of a demon-possessed magician[5]; the construction is intended to form a link between the accusation of possession (v. 21) and of league with the devil (v. 22b). The saying about plundering the strong man's house had manifestly been attached to the end of the story—the form that Mark knew. But we may conclude that this saying was originally unattached because the same tendency to coalescence had combined it with the original apophthegm also in

---

[1] Cp. D. F. Strauss, *Leben Jesu*, I, p. 692; A. Meyer, *Festgabe f. A. Juelicher*, pp. 41f.

[2] After the section 3^{9-12} Mark can take it for granted that in the situation as described in 3^{20} Jesus wrought miracles of healing, so that the appearance of the critic in v. 22 is to some extent properly motivated. Cp. A. Fridrichsen, *Le problème du miracle*, 1925, p. 70.

[3] Klostermann, writing on Matt. 12^{22-24} thinks that Matt. 9^{32-34} is a more accurate reproduction of the common source. Yet in Matt. 9^{27-34} he writes that these two pieces are secondary variations.

[4] Cp. A. Schlatter, *Der Evangelist Matthaeus*, 1929, p. 405, on Matt. 12^{28}.

[5] Cp. Jn. 7^{20}; $8^{48f.,52}$; 10^{20}. G. P. Wetter, *Der Sohn Gottes*, 1916, pp. 73–79.

Q (Matt. 12[29]//Lk. 11[21f.]), though only after two other originally unattached sayings had been added (Matt. 12[27, 28]//Lk. 11[19, 20]). The former of these two sayings compared the exorcisms of Jesus with those of the Jewish exorcists, while the second argued from his victory over the demons to the coming of the Kingdom of God. Finally Mark adds to what has gone before the saying about the sin against the Holy Spirit (vv. 28f.), as something cognate in meaning, and links it up with an editorial note in v. 30.[1] He needs nothing else to bring the section to a close, because the second half of the contextual story (vv. 31–35) serves that purpose for him. In Q however, instead of that saying, was added the logion about for and against (Matt. 12[30]//Lk. 11[23]) and further, to serve as a conclusion, the saying about the clean-swept house (Matt. 12[43–45]//Lk. 11[24–26]: in Matt. displaced). Luke thereafter brings the story to its end with a new apophthegm, 11[27f.] (Blessing of the Mother of Jesus), while Matthew inserts other sayings (12[33–37]) and the passage about the demand for a sign (12[38–42]), so as to finish the story in Marcan fashion (12[46–50] following Mk. 3[31–35]). So we can clearly trace the process of expanding an original apophthegm by the addition of particular sayings right back behind Q and Mark. Material considerations confirm the formal analysis: Jesus' reply in Mk. 3[23–26] (no more than Matt. 12[27]//Lk. 11[19]) brings no positive counter-charge, but simply the accusation that his opponents are talking nonsense, that is to say, an indirect charge of wilful blindness. Mk. 3[27], like Matt. 12[28]//Lk. 11[20] argues from the eschatological consciousness, i.e. it makes the demand that from the works of Jesus we have to draw the conclusion that the Kingdom of God has drawn nigh. If the connection between Matt. 12[27] and [28] were original, it would follow that the Jewish exorcists also cast out demons by the Spirit, and that their activity also demonstrated the coming of the Kingdom.[2] Finally, it is quite characteristic for the history of the tradition that originally the opponents were described in general terms as τινές (Lk. 11[15] following Q, see below) while Matthew substitutes 'the Pharisees' (12[24]) and Mark 'the Scribes' (3[22]) (see below).

Mk. 2[1–12] par.: *The healing of the paralytic.* Vv. 1f. is Mark's editorial transition, but it also contains the original beginning of the section, since the story that follows presupposes ἐν οἴκῳ (or εἰς οἶκον). The story itself has two points: 1, the miracle; 2, the saying about forgiveness, and obviously the second is somewhat extraneously inserted

---

[1] Perhaps Mk. 3[28]f. was not in the text of Mark which Luke used, for Luke has nothing corresponding to it. Cp. W. Bussmann, *Synoptische Studien*, I, 1925, pp. 22f.
[2] Cp. the analysis of Fridrichsen, *Le problème du miracle*, pp. 70–75.

into the first: vv. 5b–10 are a secondary interpolation. For the πίστις of the paralytic and his friends, which is demonstrated so clearly in vv. 3f. and is verified by Jesus in v. 5a, disappears in vv. 5b–10 and vv. 11f. is the conclusion organic to a miracle story: documentary evidence of the healing by the carrying of the bed and the impression created on the observers. There is no real congruence between vv. 11f. and vv. 5b–10. After vv. 5b–10 one wants to ask: 'What is the impression on the opponents? Are they to be counted among the δοξάζοντες in v. 12?' It is much more likely that their silence would be reported, as in 3, 4, etc.! So the discussion in vv. 5b–10 is interpolated.[1] Clearly constructed for the miracle story, it is not originally an independent unit. It has manifestly arisen from the dispute about the right (ἐξουσία) to forgive sins, a right which is to be attested by the power to heal miraculously.[2] When it is stated here that the υἱὸς τοῦ ἀνθρώπου has the ἐξουσία to forgive sins, we are meant, without doubt, to understand that the Son of Man is Jesus. The only question that can be raised is whether ὁ υἱὸς τ. ἀνθρ. is a wrong translation for 'man', and whether therefore originally a universal authority of men to forgive sins was affirmed at this point (Wellhausen). Yet that is highly improbable (in spite of Matt. 9[8]); for if it were so, there would be no force in the inference from the ἐξουσία to heal to the ἐξουσία to forgive sins.[3] It is much more likely that 'Son of Man' is a circumlocution for 'I'.[4] In any case, it is the ἐξουσία of Jesus that is the subject of discussion. There is no other reference in the tradition (apart from Lk. 7[47]) to Jesus pronouncing forgiveness of sins.[5] Mk. 2[5b–10] has manifestly been given

---

[1] This position was adopted by W. Wrede, *Z.N.W.*, 5, 1904, pp. 354–58; also D. Voelter, *Jesus der Menschensohn*, 1914 (*Th.R.*, 17, 1914, p. 439); A. Fridrichsen, *Le problème du miracle*, p. 91; cp. further Loisy and Klostermann. Also Bousset, *Kyrios Chr.*, 2, p. 40.3, inclines to this view, after previously considering a solution by deleting vv. 7b and 10. The objections of L. Koehler, *Das formgeschichtliche Problem des N.T.*, 1927, p. 18, and M. Dibelius, *Th.R.*, N.F. 1, 1929, pp. 211f., have not convinced me.

[2] So rightly Fridrichsen, *Le problème du miracle*, pp. 92f. He further thinks that v. 9 is a further interpolation, which, with a fine irony, corrected the original meaning of vv. 5b–10: the only miracle is the forgiveness of sin to which by contrast the healing is subordinated, and is only there at all because of their unbelief. But it is possible to understand v. 9 quite strictly on its context. The presupposition is *either* that it is easy enough to pronounce forgiveness of sins, because it is so difficult to verify; in that case the more difficult saying of the healing proves Jesus' ἐξουσία to forgive sins. *Or* (since it is difficult to put such emphasis on εἰπεῖν, and since v. 10 continues with δέ and not with οὖν) the meaning is: it is equally difficult to forgive sins and to heal; if Jesus can do the latter, he proves in so doing his ἐξουσία for the former.

[3] This was the position of Wrede, op. cit.; cp. E. Meyer, *Ursprung u. Anfang des Christent.*, I, 1921, p. 104.

[4] Thus A. Meyer, *Jesu Muttersprache*, 1896, pp. 96f., and F. Schulthess, *Z.N.W.*, 21, 1922, pp. 248f. G. Dalman, *The Words of Jesus*, 1902, p. 263, takes the opposite view.

[5] Hence C. G. Montefiore is right when he maintains in *The Synoptic Gospels*, 1[2], 1927, p. 43, the peculiar character of Mk. 2[1–12]. Cp. also L. v. Sybel, *Z.N.W.*, 22, 1924, pp. 187–89.

its place because the Church wanted to trace back to Jesus *its* own right to forgive sins. And indeed the language shows, and the analogies in Matt. 16¹⁹, 18¹⁸ prove, that the Palestinian Church demonstrates by her possession of healing power that she has the right to forgive sins. In this way she traced her authority back to an original action of Jesus to which further analogies were added immediately. Matt. 9⁸ must be understood in this same way: ἐδόξασαν τὸν θεὸν τὸν δόντα ἐξουσίαν τοιαύτην τοῖς ἀνθρώποις: in the plural τ. ἀνθρ. is expressed the conviction 'that the authority of Jesus to forgive sins has become the possession of the Church'.[1] It is significant for the history of the tradition that Lk. 5¹⁷ᶠ· prepares for the opponent who appears unheralded in Mk. 2⁶.

(b) *Otherwise occasioned by the conduct of Jesus or the disciples*

Mk. 2²³⁻²⁸ par.: *Plucking corn on the Sabbath*. The point is that Sabbath-breaking to satisfy hunger is defended on scriptural grounds. The composition—defence by counter-question—is stylistic. But the composition is the work of the Church: Jesus is questioned about the disciples' behaviour; why not about his own? i.e. the Church ascribes the justification of her Sabbath customs to Jesus. It is a likely conjecture that the scriptural proof was used apart from its present context in the controversies of the early Church; possibly also the other proof text which is added in Matt. 12⁵ᶠ· just as the polemical saying with proof text from Hos. 6⁶ which in Matt. 12⁷ (as in 9¹³ᵃ) is inserted into the Marcan narrative (unless it derives from Matthew's distinctive learning in the law). Stylistically the debate finishes with the counter-question, and the typical connecting formula καὶ ἔλεγεν αὐτοῖς shows clearly that a saying which was originally isolated has been added in Mk. 2²⁷ᶠ·[2] The question whether v. 27 belongs to the original text or not is only important for our purposes, in so far as the same tendency to include unattached logia which, we have already noticed a number of times, is manifested in a later insertion. Meanwhile, it is my view that it is overwhelmingly probable that v. 27 really belongs to the original text of Mark (cp. Wellhausen ad loc.). If that be so, then v. 28 is either the natural continuation of v. 27, in which ὁ υἱὸς τ. ἀνθρ.

---

[1] A. Schlatter, *Der Evangelist Matthaeus*, p. 301.

[2] The analysis remains essentially unchanged, even when Klostermann prefers to understand v. 27 as the original answer to vv. 23f., and to explain the Rabbinic proof of 25f. as an insertion. In any case M. Albertz completely misunderstands the character of scriptural proof in Judaism and early Christianity when in *Die synoptischen Streitgespraeche*, 1921, p. 10, he reckons Mk. 2²⁵ᶠ· as irony and on p. 74 thinks it quite ridiculous if hungry people have to justify the satisfaction of their hunger by an appeal to so ancient a precedent as David.

originally meant 'man', and for the first time was distinguished in meaning by the translator who differentiated it from ἄνθρωπος in v. 27; or v. 28 must be recognized from the start as an addition to v. 27.

Mk. 7[1-23] par.: *The dispute about 'clean' and 'unclean'.* The point of the story lies in the polemic against the Scribes. Use is made of a passage from Isaiah which contains no argument of its own, and so the more surely was derived from the traditional polemic of the Church. From the absence of an argument belonging to the passage as such it can be seen that the structure has not been determined on stylistic grounds, and possibly it derives from Mark himself. The basic section is vv. 1–8. Some (Dibelius, A. Meyer) have tried to argue that vv. 6–14 are an insertion by Mark into his text and have consequently seen the specific answer of Jesus in v. 15. But this is unsatisfactory for two reasons. First, because v. 15 is obviously dealing with the question of unclean food.[1] Second, because it is like Mark to enlarge apophthegms by such additions. So it is probable that vv. 9–13 are an additional saying of our Lord, introduced by Mark with the usual formula καὶ ἔλεγεν αὐτοῖς and derived by him from the tradition.[2] This saying has all the characteristics of pure polemic, not being an answer to a particular attack, and from its use of a scripture passage appears to be a piece of community polemic. Mark next adds another item from the tradition in v. 15. But because he himself understood this as metaphor he followed his usual custom and introduced the ὄχλος (v. 14) as the uncomprehending public. He then added the commentary (vv. 18b, 19) that had come down to him along with v. 15, making use of a transition in keeping with his theory (vv. 17–18a; v. 16 is a gloss). He further linked to it an even later expansion with ἔλεγεν δέ (vv. 20–23). Perhaps vv. 20–23 come from Mark himself (in which case ἔλεγεν δέ would mean 'and he meant thereby'), but in any case, as the catalogue of vices shows, from an Hellenistic author. On the other hand, v. 15 could belong to the oldest tradition (see below). The Pharisees and Scribes are meanwhile forgotten, and the scene has no ending of its own, though one is given to it in Matt. 15[20b] by a special construction, after the introduction of two other unattached sayings

---

The desire to have food protected from defilement by unwashed hands may admittedly have been the origin of the custom of ritual hand-washing (W. Brandt, *Die juedischen Baptismen*, 1910, p. 39). But Rabbinic discussion of this παράδοσις shows that this motive (even if it were ever the operative one) was no longer the dominant one, cp. Strack B. I, pp. 695–704; A. Schlatter, *Der Evangelist Matthaeus*, p. 478; I. Abrahams in Montefiore, *The Synoptic Gospels*, II[2], pp. 662; I, 663, 667.

[2] M. Albertz, *Die synoptischen Streitgespraeche*, p. 37, also thinks vv. 9–13 are a doublet of vv. 6–8, and his analysis of what follows is as above.

(vv. 13, 14) into the story. In addition Matthew changes round Mk. 7⁶⁻⁸ and ⁹⁻¹³, thus giving much more life to his dialogue: Jesus answers the question of his opponent with a counter-question;[1] (see below on Mk. 10²⁻¹²). The basic section Mk. 7¹⁻⁸ is an artistically stylized construction, with its origin in the community. That is shown above all in the fact that Jesus has to defend the disciples' behaviour (v.s. on Mk. 2²³⁻²⁸ and see below), and further in the fact that the γραμματεῖς come from Jerusalem particularly to see the disciples eating. Yet it is obvious that the section comes from the Palestinian Church, for it was there that the problem of the relation of the παράδοσις to the law was a living issue (v. 8; the same holds for vv. 9–13). The related motif in the introductory v. 1, which states that the Scribes from Jerusalem had some sort of inspectorial right in Galilee, is in keeping with the Palestinian setting.[2]

Mk. 2¹⁵⁻¹⁷ par.: *Eating with Publicans and Sinners*. The point of the story, expressed in Jesus' words in v. 17, has no very close connection with the situation described. The saying was thus originally unattached, and v. 15 is simply a story designed for it. The situation comes about through the quite impossible appearance of the γραμματεῖς τῶν Φαρισαίων[3] and the fact that the disciples are questioned and Jesus answers. The meal seemed to be a suitable occasion, since Jesus' use of καλεῖν would be understood as reflecting its use in an invitation to table fellowship, and since table fellowship in general is used symbolically for fellowship as such. A primitive sensitiveness would not feel that it was the wrong place for the saying in v. 17. It is instructive for the history of the tradition to note that copyists like Matthew and Luke take pains to make the incomprehensible situation of vv. 15f. somewhat more understandable; and equally that Matthew at this point uses the quotation from scripture that he also inserts into Mark's text at 12⁷.[4]

Mk. 2¹⁸⁻²² par.: *The Question of Fasting*. The saying in v. 19a shows very clearly by the argumentative nature of the question that

---

[1] We must not therefore suppose that Matthew's copy of Mark is other than our text of Mark. This is shown e.g. by W. Larfeld, *Die neutest. Evangelien*, 1925, p. 57.

[2] Cp. A. Schlatter, *Der Evangelist Matthaeus*, p. 476; Strack-B. I, 691.

[3] The situation is quite impossible. Whence and why do the Pharisees come? Do they arrive during the meal, or when it is over? It is unthinkable that they should be part of the company sitting at meat! Moreover the article in οἱ γραμματεῖς shows 'that they are the enemies of Jesus who were well known to the hearers of the story' (K. L. Schmidt, *Der Rahmen der Geschichte Jesu*, 1919, p. 85. Cp. Strauss, *Leben Jesu*, I, pp. 546f.).

[4] V. 17 is in no wise a 'secondary composition', certainly not a 'sermonic saying' added to vv. 14, 16b. How could one in that case understand the connection of vv. 14 and 16b? Besides the peculiar character of the call in 2¹⁴ is misunderstood (see below) if what follows is taken as belonging to it as its crown.

it originated in a debate. But it is another matter whether it was originally associated with the situation depicted here. That can hardly be the case, for (1) the description of the situation is quite indefinite.[1] If v. 18a means that they kept the custom of fasting, then no particular situation is given at all, nor does it in any way correspond to the style of the controversy dialogues. If it means that they were fasting at that particular time, then it is clear that the failure of the disciples to fast provides no motive for a controversy dialogue unless some specific time were mentioned. Now 18a could be a later addition fashioned on 18b by Mark or some copyist (cp. Matt. and Lk.) and then it would be irrelevant for the question of the original form of the apophthegm. Originally there would not be any specification as to who the enquirers were, and v. 18 sufficed as the introduction to the story.[3] But (2) we must consider that it is the conduct of the disciples that is questioned, and that Jesus defends their action, not his own, i.e. in reality, the Church appeals to Jesus in defence of its conduct and the description of the situation is the work of the Church. In this case the logion would have been originally unattached (unless, which I cannot believe, the Church found it complete with the situation) and was worked up into an apophthegm, at a time when the relationship of the Church to the Baptist sect was acute. The continuation in v. 19b (omitted, surely erroneously, by D) and v. 20 is a secondary development of 19a[4] corresponding neither to the style of an apophthegm nor to the situation of the Church, which is evidently the origin of vv. 18b and 19a.[5] Perhaps this expansion comes from Mark himself, and in any case it is probable that he adds the traditional metaphors of vv. 21f. which he means to be understood in the light of vv. 18f. At this point Luke thought himself free to introduce a suitable unattached saying, 5[39].

Mk. 11[27-33] par.: *The Question of Authority.* By its manipulation into the context the apophthegm has been transformed. There is no

---

[1] Mark and Luke for this reason have made their own alterations.

[2] Hence the exegetes frequently discover some particular occasion, e.g. Beyschlag: day of the feast in v. 15; H. J. Holtzmann, a special funeral fast by John's disciples on the death of their master. Cp. K. L. Schmidt, op. cit., pp. 87f. A somewhat different treatment, e.g. in Rabbinic history, in Fiebig, *Altjuedische Gleichnisse*, p. 20, which provides a good analogy: 'On one occasion the disciples kept a fast in Jabne on a Sabbath. But the Rabbi Jehoshua did not keep the Sabbath as a fast. And when his disciples came to him he said . . .' This is to provide a concrete, clearly conceivable situation.

[3] I think that in the question the words καὶ οἱ μαθηταὶ τῶν Φαρισαίων are a badly conceived analogy to the οἱ μαθηταὶ 'Ιωάννου and οἱ σοὶ μαθηταί. Cp. Wellhausen, K. L. Schmidt, op. cit., pp. 87f. contents himself by saying in connection with v. 18, *non liquet.*

[4] Cp. Wellhausen, ad loc.: Bousset, *Kyrios Chr.*[2], pp. 40f.

[5] Dibelius in my view misconceives the style of argumentative dialogue when he says that the unit of tradition could not have ended with v. 19a.

antecedent for ταῦτα ποιεῖς in v. 28, for it cannot refer to περιπατεῖν in v. 27.[1] We cannot say to what extent v. 27 comes from Mark,
but it is probable that he introduces the ἀρχιερεῖς etc. as the
opponents for the sake of the context. The conjecture has often been
made that the apophthegm was originally associated with the
cleansing of the Temple. That could very well have been the case
in an earlier edition of Mark,[2] but whether it could have been so
originally is very questionable, for the cleansing of the Temple does
not seem to be appropriate as the cause of a rabbinic debate like this.
For the conclusion of the argument has also been transformed.
Originally it would have closed with the counter-question, as was the
fashion in Rabbinical polemics (v. 1). The question had to be both
an answer to and a refutation of the attack, and this is in fact to be
found in v. 30: 'Just as the Baptist received his ἐξουσία from God
and not from men, so also do I!'[3] The author of v. 31 failed to
understand this, or else he would not have made the hierarchy think
διὰ τί οὐκ ἐπιστεύσατε αὐτῷ, but rather would he have written
'If we say, From heaven, then will Jesus claim this same ἐξουσία
for himself!' So v. 31 is an addition. While v. 30 argues ex concesso,
namely against those who acknowledge the Baptist's divine ἐξουσία,
the author of v. 31 takes the view that the opponents (the hierarchy)
did not 'believe' on the Baptist—i.e. he takes the Christian point of
view. The word πιστεύειν also shows that vv. 31f. derive from an
Hellenist (perhaps from Mark himself). In distinction from this
there is a genuine Palestinian apophthegm in vv. 28–30, about which
we can only ask whether it is an historical record or a creation of the
early Church, designed to disarm its opponents of their weapons.
Whenever the antagonists appealed to the Baptist, this passage provided the opportunity to say: If you recognize the Baptist's ἐξουσία,
you must likewise acknowledge the ἐξουσία of Jesus.

Lk. 7[36-50]: *The Sinner at the Feast.* An analysis of this passage is

[1] If one can add to the guesses of the exegetes but one more conjecture, it is in my
view most likely that Jesus' answer indicates that the ταῦτα ποιεῖς referred to Jesus' (or
the Church's) practice of baptism. We can no longer perhaps settle the question as to
whether Jesus himself baptized, as Jn. 3[22,26], asserts. But if it were the case, then it is
easily understood how the Synoptic tradition, which has obliterated every trace of it,
should have also cut off the original beginning of Mk. 11[27-33]. There is noticeable
analogy to the question of authority in the Mandaean John where (Lidzbarski, II, pp.
82, 24f.) Jahja-Johana himself is asked of the seven: 'In whose power standest thou
there, and in whose praise dost thou preach?'
[2] Favouring this is perhaps the fact that in Jn. 2[13-22] the (admittedly transformed)
question of authority is directly linked with the Cleansing of the Temple. Perhaps John
also used Mark's source. Cp. M. Goguel, *Jean-Baptiste*, 1928, p. 49.1.
[3] A. Merx is correct in *Die Evangelien des Markus and Lukas*, 1905, p. 377, on Lk. 20[4]:
'Jesus' counter-question in v. 4 contains the answer to the High Priest's question. They
would have to reply to the counter-question: John acts from divine impulse—and then
Jesus would say: I act from the selfsame impulse.'

both difficult and uncertain. The point in any case is to be found in v. 47. But v. 47 is manifestly meant to defend some position which has been attacked, not to prepare for something to follow. This means that vv. 48–50 are a secondary appendage (a position taken as long ago as Juelicher, *Gleichnisreden*, II, 299f.), especially as a quite new motif is imported in v. 49 there (exactly as in Mk. 2^{5b-10}), without being carried to its conclusion. But this leaves the question: Are vv. 44–47 to be understood in terms of vv. 41–43—that the woman's demonstration of love is the ground for knowing that she had already received forgiveness of sins; or are vv. 41–43 a supplement, leaving vv. 44–47 as original, reporting the woman's love as the actual ground for the forgiveness of sins announced then and there. If that be so, then v. 47b from ᾧ δὲ onwards must be accounted secondary.[1] Actually the οὗ χάριν in v. 47a creates the strong impression that forgiveness of sins is promised to the woman in thanks for her demonstration of affection, especially when seen in connection with the previous story in vv. 36–38. But now we have to add that the story of the anointing is a doublet of Mk. 14^{3-9}, and that what is peculiar in Lk. 7^{36-50} is contained in vv. 41–43 and 47 only (cp. Juelicher). The more probable conclusion thus seems to be that in those passages, the basis consists of the parable and its application (whose beginning is thereafter worked over), and that everything else has been constructed as realistic background on the basis of Mk. 14^{3-9}, a passage Luke there omits (Juelicher's view approximates to this). It is hardly possible to say how much of the basis has been omitted from the composition for the sake of the background situation that was introduced. In any event Wellhausen's basic proposition, that the sayings must be interpreted in terms of the story, is false. In general the sayings have produced a situation, not the reverse. Moreover, it is no longer possible to say how old the basic material is.[2]

(c) *The Master is questioned (by the disciples or others)*

Mk. 10^{17-31} par.: *The Rich Young Man.* Mk. 10^{17-22} stands out from the whole context right away as the genuine apophthegm.

---

[1] It is not permissible to appeal to the evidence of D in support of this, for what it omits begins with ὅτι.

[2] According to L. v. Sybel (*Z.N.W.*, 23, 1924, pp. 184–93), Lk. 7^{36-50} is a refashioning of Mk. 14^{3-9}, undertaken because of the Church's belief in the forgiveness of sins. However, even if it be right that the anointing (vv. 37, 38 and 46) is an irrelevance in Lk. 7^{36-50}, imported from Mk. 14^{3-9}, it does not therefore follow that Mk. 14^{3-9} is the basis of Lk. 7^{36-50} with vv. 41–47 therefore secondary. Thus Klostermann assumes that vv. (40) 41–43 (47) are an independent unit of tradition, for which the story of the anointing has been used as a realistic background.

Mark's editorial work has gone into the introduction (v. 17a), and for the rest it is accurately constructed and conceived as an unity: the sayings of Jesus are significant only as answers to the questions. Mark has provided supplementary material: 10²³⁻²⁷, a saying (or two) about riches with a subsequent discussion with the disciples: and in vv. 28–30 a saying about rewards in the Kingdom of God, which comes in answer to a question by Peter: and finally, v. 31, the saying about the first and the last. In the section 10²³⁻²⁷, 23b and 24b are doublets. If 10²³⁻²⁷ were an unity, and consequently v. 24, which emphasises the universal difficulty of entering the Kingdom of God, an intensification of v. 23, which speaks only of a difficulty for the rich, then we should have to delete ἢ πλούσιον—εἰσελθεῖν in v. 25 as a spurious addition.[1] Yet Matthew and Luke both read it. Actually v. 24 is interpolated between 23 and 25 which properly belong together, and manifestly constitute an old apophthegm which Mark probably found already joined with vv. 17–22. In between (or after) them the editor (very likely Mark himself) has added v. 24 and v. 26.[2] In vv. 28–30 either Peter's question in v. 28 is an editorial connecting link, deriving its form from the traditional saying in vv. 29f., or v. 28 is the original introduction to an ancient apophthegm, in which the original saying of Jesus has been substituted by vv. 29f. This latter view is held by Loisy, who finds Jesus' original answer in Matt. 19²⁸. By comparison of the Synoptics it is noticeable that in this passage Matthew has not only increased the element of dialogue (19¹⁷ᶠ·) but also introduced a further saying (19²⁸): the promise of authority to the Twelve.

Mk. 12²⁸⁻³⁴ par.: *The Chief Commandment*. Once again we have an organic and unitary composition. Only v. 28a and v. 34b (καὶ οὐδεὶς κτλ) need be reckoned as editorial. Mark and Luke have themselves seen this in regard to v. 34b, for they reproduce it in another context. Synoptic comparison shows that Matthew and Luke are no longer able to portray the questioning γραμματεύς as well-intentioned. They maintain that he questioned him (ἐκ)πειράζων αὐτόν, and omit Mark's conclusion recounting the Scribe's recogni-

---

[1] Thus Wellhausen; only thus is the astonishment of the disciples v. 26 to be explained who indeed were scarcely able to apply to themselves this saying about the rich. But the astonishment of the disciples is but an editorial alteration to illumine the harshness of the saying.

[2] Since v. 24 appears in D after v. 25, and since Matthew and Luke fail to reproduce it at all, we may conclude that it is altogether secondary in Mark's text. This is the view of J. Weiss, *Z.N.W.*, 11, 1910, p. 81. However this is very uncertain. The comparative περισσῶς in v. 26 presupposes v. 24, from which it is meant to be clearly differentiated; and the new statement Matt. 19²⁴: πάλιν λέγω ὑμῖν in all probability shows that Matthew had read Mark's v. 24. This is the view also of M. Goguel, *R.H.Ph.R.*, 8, 1928, p. 269, though I cannot accept his analysis of the whole section (pp. 264ff.).

tion. In addition, Luke has used the story to introduce the parable of the Good Samaritan. It is possible that such a combination had already been made in Luke's source; for the formulation of the question and counter-question (Lk. 10²⁵ᶠ·) seem to show that another version of the text is being used than in Mark's edition.

Lk. 12¹³⁻¹⁴: *The Dispute over the Inheritance.* An unitary composition, since Jesus' saying is intelligible only in reference to the question. It is characteristic that Luke has made the apophthegm serve as an introduction to the story of the rich fool by the composition of v. 15.

Lk. 13¹⁻⁵: *The Slaughter of the Galileans.* An unitary composition, which Luke again puts to a further use as an introduction to another section, this time to a parable.

Matt. 11²⁻¹⁹//Lk. 7¹⁸⁻³⁵: *John the Baptist's Question.* The actual apophthegm embraces only Matt. 11²⁻⁶//Lk. 7¹⁸⁻²³; then in both cases, evidently following Q, sayings about the Baptist are added: Matt. 11⁷⁻¹¹//Lk. 7²⁴⁻²⁸ and Matt. 11¹⁶⁻¹⁹//Lk. 7³¹⁻³⁵. Between these sayings Matthew has inserted another saying in vv. 12, 13 (Luke gives them in Lk. 16¹⁶) and enlarged it in vv. 14f.—which is perhaps his own composition. Luke on his part has introduced a saying in vv. 29f. which appears in variant form in Matt. 21³². The point of Matt. 11²⁻⁶ par. is found in vv. 5f., and these verses could have been very well handed down as an independent element in the tradition. But is that really a justifiable assumption? It is: for in all probability the Baptist's question is a community product and belongs to those passages in which the Baptist is called as a witness to the Messiahship of Jesus. In favour of this point of view, apart from the question whether the Ministry of Jesus did not start until after the death of John (see below on Mk. 6¹⁴⁻²⁹), is not only the fact that nothing at all is said about John's reactions to Jesus' answer, but above all the fact that the saying, if it is to be reckoned as an answer to the Baptist's question, cannot be other than an appeal to his miracles, a point which Luke has made quite clear by his addition in vv. 20f. But it should be clear that the saying is intended simply to take the colours of (Second) Isaiah and use them to paint a picture of the final blessedness which Jesus believes is now beginning, without any need to relate particular statements with particular events that have already happened. In that case the saying would have been originally independent, and used by the community in the composition of an apophthegm. A. Fridrichsen has shown very clearly what motive would lead to such a composition:[1]

[1] *Le problème du miracle*, pp. 64–69; cp. M. Goguel, *Jean-Baptiste*, pp. 63–65.

In discussions between Jesus' disciples and those of John the messianic character of the ἔργα, i.e. the miracles performed by Jesus, was denied. The disciples of Jesus replied that messianic prophecy was being fulfilled in their master's miracles. Whether it is possible to go further and assume that the prophecy of Isa. 35 [5f.] had already been applied by John's disciples to the Baptist must remain open to doubt. That stories of John's miracles were in circulation is in itself quite credible; for the assertion that he performed none (Jn. 10[41]) is obviously a piece of polemic. And does not Mk. 6[14] imply that reports of the Baptist's miracles were current?[1]

Mk. 10[35-45] par.: *The Question of the Sons of Zebedee.* In the first place vv. 41–45 can be separated out as a supplementary piece of the sort which Mark so often introduces into scenes from the tradition. For while vv. 35–40 treat of precedence in the Kingdom which is yet to come, vv. 41–45 deal with precedence in the Christian community; moreover Lk. 22[24-27] shows that vv. 41–45 were originally an independent item. Yet even the apophthegm vv. 35–40 is not really an unitary composition. The request in v. 37 is twice answered: vv. 38f. (the way to exaltation lies through martyrdom) and v. 40 (rejection of the request without any reference to 38f.). And no doubt vv. 38f. (a manifest *vaticinium ex eventu*) is the secondary element,[2] which in any case could hardly have had a separate independent circulation at any time, but is manifestly designed for this particular place. The remainder, vv. 35–37 and v. 40, appear to be an unitary composition, and only need to be thought of as a community product if the way in which the Messiahship of Jesus is spoken of here as something quite self-evident is thought to be possible only in the Christian Church. And that, at any rate, is my own belief.

Mk. 9[38-40] par.: *The Rival Exorcist.* It appears to me that it is impossible to see the point in v. 40—whatever reading be adopted—

---

[1] In the Mandaean Book of John, ch. 76 (Lidzb., II, p. 243), Anôš-Uthra maintains: 'I opened their blind eyes, and I healed the lepers. I made the deaf and dumb to speak and hear, and the lame and crippled to walk again.' The same thing is reported about Enos in both versions of the Mandaean Apocalypse which are to be found in Ginza R., I and II, 1 (Lidzb., pp. 30 and 48) though here the descriptions of miracles of raising from the dead and by preaching have been multiplied. Reitzenstein who earlier held the view (*Das mand. Buch des Herrn der Groesse und die Evangelienueberlieferung*, 1919, pp. 60ff., cp. *das iran. Erloesungsmyst.*, 1921, p. 111, 1) that the Mandaean text derived from a source which was older than Q on which Q itself depended, now (*Z.N.W.*, 26, 1927, pp. 55f.) thinks of their relationship in this way: the text which we find in the Book of John is the oldest, and Q depends on that, and in its turn the texts in Ginza are dependent, in a polemical sense, upon Q. I do not think that the proof succeeds. The discussion can only be carried out in a larger context. Cp. Allgeier, *Th.R.*, 20, 1921, p. 181; Gressmann, *Z.f.K.*, N.F. 3, 1922, p. 188. Schaeder, in Reitzenstein-Schaeder, *Studien zum antiken Synkretismus*, 1926, pp. 332ff.; M. Goguel, *Jean-Baptiste*, 1928, pp. 124-8.

[2] Cp. Bousset, *Kyrios Chr.*[2], p. 8.1.

which could well be a secondary addition and perhaps even a variant of the saying in Matt. 12 ^{30} par. The point can surely only be in v. 39. But that clearly implies that the apophthegm is an unitary composition. It can very well be a community product, since the use of the ὄνομα Jesus in the exorcism of demons could hardly have antedated its use in the Church. Apart from that, in v. 38, 'The subject of v. 38 is not following Jesus but association with the Apostles' (Wellhausen). I think it highly unlikely that the whole section derives from Matt. 7 ^{22} (Wendling, *Entstehung des Mk-Evgl.*, pp. 104f.); but perhaps the story of Eldad and Medad (Num. 11 $^{26-29}$) has influenced its conception.

Lk. 17 $^{20-21}$: *The Coming of the Kingdom of God.* If, as I think, one can rightly argue from the form of this saying of Jesus to its Palestinian origin, and so regard it as a genuine dominical saying, then here it is particularly clear how a saying originally handed down independently comes to have a secondary form. For the wording of the introduction is fashioned after the manner of a species of Greek philosophic apophthegms: (ἐπ)ερωτηθεὶς ὑπό . . . εἶπεν; examples can be found in G. v. Wartensleben, *Begriff der griechischen Chreia*, 1901, and W. Gemoll, *Das Apophthegma*, 1924, p. 2. There is also an Hellenistic construction here (very possibly Luke's own) like that, e.g., in Ps. Arist. §10; 2 Clem. 12 ^{2}. We have to treat the apophthegm in Lk. 6 ^{5D}, on Sabbath labour, in the same way. It is an unitary composition, which is, as a whole, Hellenistic in form, as is shown by the introduction again exhibiting the structure of the Greek philosophic apophthegm (θεασάμενος . . . εἶπεν, cp. loc. cit.) and further, by the ingenious formulation and the crisp concept εἰδέναι.

Mk. 11 $^{20-25}$ par.: *The Cursed Fig Tree.* This is a peculiar case, about which this much is clear: the dominical sayings in vv. 22f. 24 and 25 (is v. 25 genuine in Mark?) originally circulated independently, since vv. 22f. are parallel to Matt. 17 ^{20}//Lk. 17 ^{6} and in the same way v. 25 is parallel to Matt. 6 ^{14}. And yet, on the other hand the setting provided has not been composed from the contents of the sayings: rather the sayings are attached to a miracle story already in circulation whose original significance is uncertain. It is probable that the attachment took place by degrees and was continued in the history of the text (at least in v. 26).

Lk. 9 $^{51-56}$: *The Inhospitable Samaritans.* There is no distinctive apophthegm here, since there is no saying of Jesus forming the point of the story. The deficiency was recognized in the history of the text and such a saying was added to v. 55. In any case we have no

B

ancient tradition here, for the journey through Samaria is Luke's construction. But it is possible that in this instance he had in front of him some unit of the tradition deriving from the missionary activity of the Church.

(d) *Questions asked by opponents*

Mk. 12$^{13-17}$ par.: *The Census*. It is hardly possible that the saying of Jesus in v. 17 ever circulated independently. It is much more likely that we have an apophthegm here which was conceived as an unity and excellently constructed. Only in v. 13 can we discern any of Mark's editorial work. There is no reason, in my view, for supposing that this is a community product.

Mk. 12$^{18-27}$ par.: *The Sadducees*. This is an exceptionally instructive dialogue for recognizing the way in which the community influence was exercised. In any event, 12$^{26f.}$ is an addition, and yet clearly not the addition of an originally independent saying, as in Mk. 10$^{11f.}$, but of an argument only in place in a debate. But if this debate was not current as one element in the literary tradition, it is all the more certain that it was circulated as part of the theological discussions of the Church. In other words, an argument from the theological material of the Church has been introduced here, one which betrays its origin by its thoroughgoing Rabbinic character (cp. Sanhedr. p. 90b in Strack-B. I, 893). So the debate in 12$^{18-25}$ simply reflects the theological activity of the Church. The Sadducees figure as the opponents because it was traditional for them to deny the resurrection. If one can be rid of the traditional notion that the Sadducees were the Priestly party and see in them, with G. Hoelscher,[1] a scribal school, like that of the Pharisees, though admittedly less influential, it is by no means inconceivable that the Church should have had controversy with them, as with the Pharisees. On the other hand, it is not likely that the Sadducees would have picked on the Church's belief in the resurrection as the point of their attack.

Mk. 10$^{2-12}$ par.: *Divorce*. It is clear what Mark has done: he has made a transition by v. 10 to an originally independent saying, vv. 11f., which is also in Q (Matt. 5^{32}//Lk. 16^{18}), joining it on with καὶ λέγει αὐτοῖς. Matthew has also added to the story by a dominical saying (19^{12}) in the middle of his transitional passage (19$^{10f.}$). The apophthegm itself, vv. 1–9, gives the immediate impression of being a parallel to Mk. 7$^{1ff.}$, indeed it is a parallel. That Mk. 10^2 has to start with a question without any reference to any act is

---

[1] G. Hoelscher, *Gesch. der. israelit. u. jued. Religion*, 1922, § 93, pp. 218ff.

simply due to the fact that the disciples' questions about divorce were not so easily used as a basis for interrogation as was their eating with unwashed hands. But as in that passage the debate here certainly derives from the Church; it is set out in an unified way, though use is made of material from the polemics of the Church. The awkwardness of the construction shows its artificiality. Jesus replies with the counter-question in v. 3: τί ὑμῖν ἐνετείλατο Μωϋσῆς; that is indirectly with a quotation from scripture, though neither counter-question nor quotation is in place at this point. The counter-question is in no sense a counter-argument, and the scripture reference does not really answer the opponents, but is subjected to their criticism! In other words, vv. 3f. really belong to the opponents. The formulation of v. 4 is completely impossible, for in any real debate this is the point at which the conditions of divorce must be stated. They are missing because the pronouncement is so framed as to make Jesus reject divorce altogether! For the rest, Matthew who, in my view, has used his scribal learning, has again made an excellent formal correction in introducing κατὰ πᾶσαν αἰτίαν in 19³. That is to say he reckoned the question about the conditions of divorce to be necessary, and by a transposition gave the scripture quotation to the Pharisees as a counter-argument (19⁷); v.s. on Mk. 7¹⁻³³.[1] Admittedly in doing this he has deprived the discussion of its radical character. For while in Mark Jesus radically rejects divorce (entirely in keeping with the saying in vv. 11f.) in contrast to the Law and to the Rabbis, in Matthew the debate turns on the issue between the School of Hillel and Shammai as to the sufficient grounds for divorce (as Matthew actually introduces the words μὴ ἐπὶ πορνείᾳ into the appended saying in v. 9; cp. Matt. 5³² with Lk. 16¹⁸).[2] Matt. 17²⁴⁻²⁹ also properly belongs to the discussions of the schools; yet this passage is discussed below, since in its outward form it is a biographical apophthegm.

2. Biographical Apophthegms

Of the passages already discussed it is perhaps possible to add to this section Mk. 9³⁴⁻⁴⁰ and Lk. 9⁵¹⁻⁵⁶.

[1] B. H. Streeter, *The Four Gospels*, 1924, pp. 259ff. in considering the relation of Matthew to Mark draws the conclusion that Matthew must have had access to a parallel tradition for this passage. That is undoubtedly possible, but to my mind not certain. In Mark Jesus asks, in v. 3: τί ὑμῖν ἐνετείλατο M., and the Pharisees answer in v. 4: M. ἐπέτρεψεν. . . . In Matthew the Pharisees say in v. 7: τί οὖν M. ἐνετείλατο δοῦναι . . ., and Jesus answers in v. 8: ὅτι M. . . . ἐπέτρεψεν ὑμῖν ἀπολῦσαι. . . . Does not Mark's text have an echo in Matthew's ἐνετείλατο? But surely Matthew did have to say ἐπέτρεψεν on his own account as well (corresponding to εἰ ἔξεστιν in v. 3).

[2] Cp. the instructive treatment of the pericope in C. G. Montefiore, *The Synoptic Gospels*[2], I, pp. 225–36.

Mk. 1¹⁶⁻²⁰ par., 2¹⁴ par.: *Calling of Disciples*. The two passages are variations of the same motif. In the first of them there is a further doubling, for 1¹⁶⁻¹⁸ and vv. 19f. are themselves variants of the same theme. The motif is the sudden summons from business to 'following'. This does not involve any psychological interest in those who are called; the chief actor is not those who are called, but the Master who calls the disciples; cp. 1 Kings 19¹⁹. There is no need to argue that this is in no sense an historical record, but a description of an ideal scene.[1] The only question is whether this calling of fishermen has not been woven out of an already formulated metaphor of 'fishers of men'.[2] This need not imply that the metaphor ever circulated in some independent saying, for the story and the saying could well have been an unitary conception from the start. The analogies suggest that.

Lk. 9⁵⁷⁻⁶²; Matt. 8¹⁹⁻²²: *Following Jesus*. In the case of the first apophthegm preserved here (a tradition common to Matthew and Luke), it is plain that the dominical saying could have circulated without any framework. That must indeed have been the case if ὁ υἱὸς τοῦ ἀνθρώπου has been incorrectly substituted for 'man'.[3] And 'man' must have been in fact the original meaning; man, homeless in this world, is contrasted with the wild beasts. This is presumably an old proverb which tradition has turned into a saying of Jesus. This naturally means that the introduction in Luke v. 57 was primarily made for this saying. It also seems clear to me that the same is true about the last piece of the section, preserved by Luke alone: the pathos of the answer in v. 62 has no relationship whatever to v. 61. The only difference is that in this case the saying might well be a genuine saying of Jesus. The context sets it into an imaginary situation, for the introduction would immediately strike one as comic if one thought the situation were real. The position

---

[1] Cp. A. Schlatter (*Der Evangelist Matthaeus*, p. 303) who, writing on Mt. 9⁹, emphasizes the typical meaning of these anecdotes and appropriately indicates the meaning of the stories of the call of the disciples. They show 'an essential characteristic of discipleship'; this 'comes from the call of Jesus' which requires absolute surrender, and removes from all the old relationships. And in the telling of the story the behaviour of those who are called disappears 'before the exalted character of him who bestows the calling upon him'. Cp. also Schlatter, *Der Glaube im N.T.*⁴, p. 257.

[2] Cp. Klostermann on Mk. 1¹⁷ and Strack-B. I, 188 on the metaphor of catching and hunting.

[3] Cp. e.g. Fr. Schulthess, *Das Problem der Sprache Jesu*, pp. 55ff.: L. v. Sybel, *T.S.K.*, 100, 1927/8, p. 384: S. Luria, *Z.N.W.*, 25, 1926, pp. 282–6. I think it quite impossible that ὁ υἱὸς τ. ἀνθρ. in this context originally meant the divine envoy of Gnostic mythology—the *bar nasha* of Apocalyptic or the *Enoch* of the Mandaeans (Reitzenstein, *Das mand. Buch d. Herrn d. Gr.*, p. 58, *Z.N.W.*, 26, 1927, p. 59.2). Such a 'son of man' could have been contrasted with the blind men of this world (as in John.) but not with the beasts. Neither could the Greek text have meant it, understanding υἱὸς τ. ἀνθρ. as a self description of Jesus; for then nothing could have been said about 'following'.

is different in the second item of the material common to Matthew and Luke. It strikes me as improbable that ἄφες τοὺς νεκροὺς θάψαι τοὺς ἑαυτῶν νεκρούς could ever have been an independent saying: it seems a matter of course that it refers to some specific occasion, though it is impossible to say with any certainty what occasion it was.[1] But that the whole situation is imaginary is even more certain than this, for 'following' is clearly used in its figurative sense, since it was in common use by the Jews as a term for discipleship.[2] That the disciple 'followed his teacher' meant not only that he acquired knowledge from him, but also that he followed his example in practical affairs. Here a concrete situation brings to symbolic expression the truth that 'to follow' Jesus 'sets the disciple free from every duty, permits him no further obligation, but requires of him a surrender securing him wholly to Jesus alone'.[3]

Mk. 3[20f.], [31-35] par.: *The True Kinsmen*. It seems impossible to doubt that vv. 20f., and 31–35 belong together. It is true that if need be 31[31-35] can be conceived without vv. 20f., as Matthew and Luke show by omitting vv. 20f. But these two verses demand some continuation like vv. 31–35. It is just a characteristic variant of v. 21 in D for whom the continuation comes too late. So one has to suppose that vv. 20f. and vv. 31–35 were separated by vv. 22–30 (on these verses, *v.s.*). The editorial character of v. 20 is plain; ἀκούσαντες in v. 21 has no real reference back to it, and the chief problem is whether vv. 21, 31–35, are an unitary conception. Dibelius[4] considers that v. 34 is the original ending, with v. 35 a supplementary 'sermonic saying', i.e. it is not an originally independent saying, but a secondary construction which extracts a universal moral from the story. There is indeed some sort of discrepancy between the saying and the story, in so far as it does not follow without any more ado that the hearers to whom Jesus refers in v. 34 'do the will of God'. That is also why I believe that the association of vv. 31–34 and v. 35 is not original, but that v. 35 is, in view of the analogies original, and that vv. 31–34 (and vv. 20f. with them) are secondary. That is to say the discrepancy is accounted for with much greater

[1] It seems completely erroneous to me to trace this saying to an Egyptian fairy-tale, where the dead actually bury the dead (Gressmann, *Protestantenblatt*, 1916, p. 281). Neither is it at all clear that F. Perles has been successful in his attempt to show that the form of the saying is due to a mistranslation, and to read as the original saying 'leave the dead to their grave-digger' (*Z.N.W.*, 19, 1919/20, p. 20) or in his suggested modification in light of the objection in Strack-B. I, 489: 'leave the dead to the grave-digger, that he may accompany them'. There is indeed no reason to rob the saying of its paradox, particularly as Judaism also recognized the figurative use of 'the dead'.
[2] Cp. Strack-B. I, 187f., 528f.
[3] Schlatter, *Der Evangelist Matthaeus*, p. 288.
[4] *Formgeschichte*, pp. 29, 32.

probability by assuming that the situation described in vv. 31–34 is adapted to the saying in v. 35. The content of v. 35 should be set in the framework of some imaginary situation. But ποιεῖν τὸ θέλημα τοῦ θεοῦ is not something which can be put into a situation because it is not a single individual action. But it can be impressively symbolized if those who do God's will are depicted as an audience gathered around Jesus eager to learn from him. So again we have an imaginary situation. Admittedly the motif of v. 21 cannot be derived *simpliciter* from the saying in v. 35, but it manifestly rests upon good and ancient tradition. That such a tradition operated in the formulations of the Church I obviously have no doubts at all.

Lk. 11 27–28: *The Blessing of Mary.* The blessing in v. 27 is a widespread feature of Judaism. In Syr. Bar. 54.10 the seer who dreams the vision cries out:

> 'Blessing to my mother among those that give birth,
> And praised among women be she who bore me.'

And so Rachel is praised, who bore Joseph (Gen. R. 98 (62d)):
'Blessed be the breasts which have so given suck and the body which has thus brought forth' (Strack-B. II, 187). Jochanan b. Zakkai stirred by the oration of his pupils R. Eleazar b. Arach and Jehoshua b. Homeniah cries out: 'praise to thee, Abraham our father, that Eleazar b. Arach was brought forth from thy loins. Hail to thee, and hail to thy mother! Hail to mine eyes, which have seen such things!' (Hag. 14b in Strack-B. I, 663f.). When Messiah comes, Israel will say: 'Blessed is the hour when Messiah is created; blessed be the body from which he comes forth; blessed be the generation that sees him, blessed be the eye that is privileged to look on him' (Pesiq. 149a in Strack-B. I, 161). At the same time these examples (and there are more of them in Strack-B. I, 663f., II, 187f.) indicate that the sayings in Lk. 11 27 and 10 23f.//Matt. 13 16f. contain the same motif. In Lk. 10 23f. it is accepted without criticism. Here (in Lk. 11 27f.) it is rejected, and is subjected to correction in v. 28. This verse also contains a well-known motif, cp. Lk. 8 21; Jn. 13 17; also Lk. 6 46//Matt. 7 21; Lk. 6 47–49//Matt. 7 24–27; Rom. 2 13, and in addition to all this Strack-B. III, 84–88. But we are not obliged to assume that v. 28 circulated as an independent saying: it is more likely that Lk. 11 27f. was a section conceived as an unity, with its point in its opposition to the Jewish outlook of v. 27. So far as the relation to the previous passage (Mk. 3 20f., 31–35) is concerned, we can find the right attitude as early as D. Fr. Strauss's *Leben Jesu*, I (1835), 696, '. . . the unforgettable saying of Jesus when he puts

his spiritual kinsmen above his physical ones, appears in the story in two different versions or frames . . .' But nevertheless Mk. 3 ³⁵ and Lk. 11 ²⁸ must not be looked on as mere variants, for in Mark we have a transmutation of the idea of kinship, but not here. The agreement occurs only in the negatives, i.e. in asserting that physical kinship is of less importance *sub specie aeterni*, and in so far both apophthegms are related and are occasioned by identical motives. But I do not myself think there is any literary connection. Nor do I think it needs any argument to show that Lk. 11 ²⁷f· is also an imaginary situation.

Mk. 6 ¹⁻⁶ par.: *The Rejection in the Patris*. This seems to me to be a typical example of how an imaginary situation is built up out of an independent saying. I believe that Wendling's[1] view is right,[2] that the dominical saying preserved in Pap. Ox. I, 5, is more original than Mk. 6 ⁴f·:

οὐκ ἔστιν δεκτὸς προφήτης ἐν τῇ πατρίδι αὐτοῦ,
οὐδὲ ἰατρὸς ποιεῖ θεραπείας εἰς τοὺς γινώσκοντας αὐτόν.

It is hardly likely that the double proverb has grown out of Mk. 6 ¹⁻⁶, the reverse is on the other hand probable: the second half of the twin proverb is transposed in the story, and the γινώσκοντες αὐτόν becomes the συγγενεῖς of Mk. 6 ⁴. The conclusion in Mk. 6 ⁵ is limited, thus avoiding any report of a complete failure by Jesus, and that is why v. 5b (εἰ μὴ κτλ) contradicts v. 5a. The form does not derive in the first place from Mark, but was already before him, having its origin in the missionary experience of the Church.[3]

For the rest it is possible, since v. 2 sounds like a cry of genuine admiration, to understand v. 3 in the same way, down to the surprising addition: καὶ ἐσκανδαλίζοντο ἐν αὐτῷ . Was there originally an account of some successful appearance of Jesus? If so, the present text derives from two originals—the saying and the scene of this success, which then, in the light of later experience was turned into its opposite. The developments in Lk. 4 ¹⁶⁻³⁰ are quite charac-

---

[1] *Entstehung des Markus-Evangeliums*, p. 54. Similarly Preuschen, *Z.N.W.*, 17, 1916, pp. 33–48, 'Das Wort vom verachteten Propheten'.

[2] It is not surprising that this saying of popular wisdom should have numerous parallels; Wetstein gives some from Greek, Hellenistic, and Roman Literature in dealing with Matt. 13 ⁵⁷. There is a doubtful Jewish parallel in Strack-B. I, 678. Cp. further J. L. Burckhardt, *Arab. Sprichwoerter*, 1834, p. 129, No. 320: 'The piper has no friends (of his art) in his own town.'

[3] Cp. A. Fridrichsen, in S. Eitrem, *die Versuchung Christi*, 1924, p. 33: 'This fact (the οὐκ ἐδύνατο κτλ Mk. 6 ⁵) is commonly taken as a proof of the genuineness of the tradition: it certainly conflicts with the common idea of Jesus' sovereign miraculous power. But it is questionable whether it is not rather missionary psychology and Christian experience at work here: miracles are conditioned by receptive faith.' Cp. also Fridrichsen, *Le problème du miracle*, pp. 52f., where the meaning of οὐκ ἐδύνατο is properly explained: it is not a statement of Jesus' impotence, but is meant as a reproach to unbelief.

teristic: the course of thought in the speech in vv. 20–27 is by no means clear; obviously it leads directly to vv. 25–27—the opposition between Israel and the Gentiles, and from that follows the break with the Jews. Vv. 25–27 clearly came to Luke from the tradition (originally Aramaic? cp. Wellhausen). There is no proper connection between vv. 25–27 and what precedes; even if v. 24 is a gloss, there is no connection with v. 23, for that has as its point the contrast of Capernaum and Nazareth, and the πατρίς is not the Jewish people, but his native town. In order to fit vv. 25–27 in, Luke has, as I suppose, constructed a scene on the pattern of Mk. 6¹⁻⁶, and at the same time in v. 23 used the παραβολή which had been handed down in another context.[1]

Mk. 10¹³⁻¹⁶ par.: *Jesus blesses the children.* Here for the first time Dibelius' theory of 'sermonic sayings' finds some support, for the logion in v. 15 could well be a secondary piece inside vv. 13–16. But whether it can be taken as an edifying expansion of v. 14 is in my view nevertheless very doubtful. The point of v. 14 is quite different from that of v. 15: v. 14 simply states that children have a share in the Kingdom of God,[2] and the τῶν τοιούτων in v. 14 ought not to be interpreted, as has been customary ever since Origen, in the light of v. 15. That means treating v. 15 as an originally independent dominical saying, inserted into the situation of vv. 13–16.[3] It is certainly no use referring to Matt. 18³ for this verse is clearly not an independent tradition, but is the Matthean form of Mk. 10¹⁵ in another context. The other possibility is also improbable, that the setting in vv. 13–16 is made up on the basis of the saying in v. 15. For vv. 13–16 are a complete apophthegm without v. 15, and its point is stated in v. 14. The original unit, vv. 13, 14, 16 may well be an ideal construction, with its basis in the Jewish practice of blessing, and some sort of prototype in the story of Elisha and Gehazi (2 Kings 4²⁷) and an analogy in a Rabbinic story.[4] But if so, the insertion of v. 15 only makes the ideal character of the scene quite unambiguous: the truth of v. 15 finds symbolic expression in the setting of the story.

Mk. 12⁴¹⁻⁴⁴ par.: *The Widow's Mite.* This is an unitary com-

---

[1] It is not possible to separate vv. 22b, 24 as Marcan ingredients, and suppose that the basis of the scene is a Synagogue sermon not preached in Nazareth (K. L. Schmidt, *T.S.K.,* 1918, p. 284; *Rahmen der Geschichte Jesu,* pp. 40f.) since there is a Marcan element from Mk. 6² in v. 23. This verse includes the Nazareth-Capernaum issue, and the words ἐν τῇ πατρίδι σου, v. 23, are retained through the previous εἰς τὴν Καφαρναούμ. It is the fault of Luke as editor that v. 23 follows so awkwardly on v. 22. Preuschen (op. cit.) believes that he can prove that Luke also used the ancient twofold saying in his composition—cp. L. Brun, *Serta Rudbergiana,* 1931, pp. 7–17.

[2] The Rabbis held the same views. Cp. Strack-B. I, 786.

[3] Cp. A. Meyer, *Festg. f. A. Juelicher,* p. 45.   [4] Strack-B. I, 808.

position, and clearly an ideal construction, giving concrete expression to its fundamental theme. It had already been given like expression in Rabbinic literature, cp. Wetstein and Strack-B. ad loc. The relationship of Mk. 12⁴¹⁻⁴⁴ to a story in Buddhist tradition is particularly close, so much so that it is difficult to avoid concluding that there was some dependence on it. H. Haas assumes that originally there might have been an Indian story behind this one.[1] For the rest, the idea that the small sacrifices of the poor are more pleasing to the gods than the extravagance of the rich is also illustrated in Greek literature by a story which, in different versions, can be shown to have been in circulation from the sixth century B.C. to the first century A.D.[2]

Lk. 10³⁸⁻⁴²: *Mary and Martha.* An analysis of the section is made more difficult by the textual uncertainty in vv. 41f. Yet it is possible to say that even if a part of the context could be taken as original, the saying of Jesus could not be one which originally had an independent circulation. So the scene must be accepted as an unitary composition, and it is manifestly an ideal construction.

Lk. 17¹¹⁻¹⁹: *The healing of the ten lepers.* The point of the story, found in the saying of Jesus in vv. 17f., only makes sense inside the story. So, apart from an editorial introduction in v. 11 woven out of the story itself, this is an unitary composition. It is admittedly secondary, and Hellenistic in origin, depending on the miracle story in Mk. 1⁴⁰⁻⁴⁵. Sending the lepers to the priest originally had a different significance (cp. below), but it is necessary here because the point of the story requires that the healing should take place on the way to the priest—a touch which might show the influence of 2 Kings 5¹⁰ff. In itself it is quite unmotivated here, and in addition we may ask: What could a Samaritan want with Jewish priests? Moreover, Matt. 10⁵ᶠ. is much closer to the actual situation of the Palestinian Church. Thus Mk. 1⁴⁰⁻⁴⁵ has been transposed into an imaginary story, in which gratitude and ingratitude are depicted on one and the same dramatic canvas. For the rest, v. 19 is a schematic ending, perhaps first added by the editor.

Lk. 19¹⁻¹⁰: *Zaccheus.* This is not an unitary composition. Vv. 9f. follows on v. 7. This means that either vv. 7, 9f. must be regarded as secondary, or—much more probably—v. 8. In v. 9 πρὸς αὐτόν cannot mean 'with reference to him' but only 'to him'. If this is to be eliminated according to some MSS. then the difficulty

---

[1] H. Haas, *Das Scherflein der Witwe und seine Entsprechung in Tripitaka*, 1922. C. Clemen, *Religionsgeschichtliche Erklaerung des N.T.*², 1924, pp. 251ff., is sceptical of Haas' thesis. One of the texts is in J. Aufhauser, *Buddha u. Jesus* (Kl. Texte No. 157), 1926, pp. 13–16.
[2] R. Herzog in E. Horneffer, *Der junge Platon*, I, 1922, pp. 150–7.

arises that Jesus suddenly begins to talk about Zaccheus in the third person to those who are present, and this is much more possible if, with some texts, we read πρὸς αὐτούς. Further, Jesus does not establish his relationship to Zaccheus by appealing to his morality, as v. 8 seems to suppose, but on the simple fact that Zaccheus is as much a Jew as the rest. The detailed introduction is far better matched with v. 9 as its point than with v. 8, and so we may hold Luke himself responsible for this latter verse; and its moral suits him. Likewise we can ascribe the addition of v. 10 to him, a verse which is appended in different texts to 9^{56} and Matt. 18^{11} as well. What is left is a scene that is unitary in conception, though manifestly imaginary, an extended version of Mk. 2^{14} which, combined with vv. 15–17 gave rise to this story. That Zaccheus did not, like Levi, 'follow' Jesus, is hardly due to his being converted with his family, as Wellhausen mistakenly supposed from τῷ οἴκῳ τούτῳ in v. 9, but rather to the fact that the story had its origin much later, when 'following' could less easily be symbolized by the physical act.

Lk. 19^{39-40}, cp. Matt. 21^{15-16}: *The Praise of the Children.* This is a truncated section. It seems originally to have been told in connection with an act of homage paid to Jesus, which was combined with the story of the Entry into Jerusalem. The saying of Jesus in Lk. 19^{40} (Matthew gives a rabbinical transformation) could not have existed in isolation, the question is as to what the original unitary concept was. This could well have been of an imaginary character: Jesus recognized by the children (the παῖδες of Matthew is unconditionally preferable to Luke's μαθηταί; if this latter word is not just a variant of translation, Luke has inserted it in accordance with v. 37).

Matt. 17^{24-27}: *The Temple Tax.* This section, on account of its legendary character, could be classified as a legend. Nevertheless, the point lies in the brief dialogue of vv. 25f., which in the manner of its argumentation (a metaphor contained in a question and also the τί σοι δοκεῖ) gives an impression of age, so that one may suppose that vv. 25f. were originally connected with something quite different from the Temple Tax. As to what that was, it is no longer possible to guess. But it was given this supplementary use, to provide an answer to the question that was emerging in the Church as to the duty of paying the Temple Tax. The section cannot be concerned with the tax which the Jews had to pay to the Romans for Jupiter Capitolinus after the destruction of the temple instead of the Temple Tax, for this would not be suitable in a contrast with the βασιλεῖς τῆς γῆς. So the section must come from an earlier time.

whether from the discussions of the Palestinian Church about the Temple Tax,[1] or from Antioch or Damascus.[2] If it turns out that the members of the Church are the 'sons', that is but in keeping with the eschatological consciousness of the earliest days. The widespread legendary motif of v. 27 does not necessarily prove an Hellenistic origin to the section, for it is met also in Judaism.[3] It is typical that in v. 24 it is Peter and not first of all Jesus who is questioned. This is a problem of the Church, for which it seeks advice from Jesus, in this case perhaps by using a dominical saying handed down in the tradition. The section is well described as an imaginary scene; in its strict essentials it belongs to the scholastic dialogues, since it solves a community problem by using a saying of Jesus, instead of giving pictorial concretion to an universal truth.

Lk. 13 $^{31-33}$. *Jesus and Herod.* I have no explanation to offer of this singular item. I would hazard either one of two conjectures. Either on the one hand v. 33 is an unattached saying introduced *ad vocem*, σήμερον καὶ αὔριον, in which case the saying of Jesus finds its point and conclusion in v. 32. It would also be possible to take v. 32b as an unattached saying (ἰδοὺ ἐκβάλλω κτλ), though it would then be difficult to imagine how the situation in vv. 31, 32a could have been constructed. This would mean that vv. 31, 32 were an unitary item of the tradition. Or, on the other hand, v. 32b is secondary in the text, leaving only πλήν in v. 33 to be questioned as something due to the editor. V. 33 would then be the resigned reply: 'So I must set out on my journeying, and that is quite proper, since a prophet has to die in Jerusalem.' On this reading v. 32b is a secondary construction by the Church.[4] In any case there seems no ground for supposing that the scene is imaginary, but rather for thinking that we have here in the strict sense a piece of biographical material.[5]

[1] Matt. 17 $^{25f.}$ has no pertinent relationship to the Jewish parable Sukka 30a (Strack-B, I, 771) although it is formally parallel. Cp., however, J. Kreyenbuehl, *Z.N.W.*, 8, 1907, pp. 180f.
[2] Cp. B. H. Streeter, *The Four Gospels*, p. 504: only in Antioch and Damascus was the stater worth exactly two double-drachma.
[3] Gn.R. 11 (8b) in Strack-B. I, 613f.; Sabb. 119a, ibid., I, 675.
[4] Wellhausen seeks to bring coherence to the verses in another way. He reckons κα τῇ τρίτῃ τελειοῦμαι in v. 32 and σήμερον καὶ αὔριον καί in v. 33 to be additions. K. L. Schmidt (*Der Rahmen d. Gesch. Jesu*, pp. 265ff.) thinks that the old item of the tradition comprised vv. 31 and 32a (up to and including αὔριον); this was enlarged by the evangelist only with vv. 32b and 33 on the basis of a saying about the Passion and the Resurrection.
[5] The meaning of the metaphor of the fox is open to discussion. In Judaism 'fox' is mostly a pictorial description of an unimportant man, while an important man is a 'lion'! But the fox is also the picture of slyness, cp. Strack-B. II, 200f. In Arabic proverbs the fox is the figure of slyness, cp. G. W. Freytag, *Arabum Proverbia I*, 1838, p. 555, no. 97; p. 577, no. 199. Yet cp. L. Rademacher, *Beitr. z. Volkskunde aus dem Gebiet der Antike* (Kaiserl., Akad d. Wiss. in Wien, phil.-hist. Kl., 187 Bd., 3 Abh.), 1918.

Mk. 11$^{15-19}$ par.: *The Cleansing of the Temple*. The first sentence of v. 15 (καὶ ἔρχονται εἰς ᾽Ιεροσόλυμα) and vv. 18f. come from the editor. Is the rest of vv. 15–17 an unitary apophthegm? The striking introduction of the saying in v. 17: καὶ ἐδίδασκεν καὶ ἔλεγεν gives the impression that word and action did not originally belong together. As a matter of style the emphasis in an apophthegm must fall on the saying, but here it rests on the action, in relationship to which the saying is merely explanatory. For this reason vv. 15f. cannot be taken as an imaginary scene suggested by v. 17. It might be possible so to think of v. 15, but hardly v. 16. So perhaps v. 17 is a secondary interpretation—perhaps a 'sermonic saying'—of the scene in vv. 15f. that belonged to the original tradition, just as Jn. 2^{17} adds yet another such interpretation. But this means that the whole setting has become that of an imaginary scene, for the words ὑμεῖς δὲ πεποιήκατε κτλ can hardly be part of the address to the retailers, but much rather to the Jews at large. One may suppose that v. 17 has replaced an older saying of Jesus which has been preserved in Jn. 2^{16}. Yet even this can be an analogous secondary interpretation of the scene, like Mk. 11^{17}. Finally one may conjecture that in Mark's source the saying about authority (11$^{27-33}$) followed immediately on v. 16; though whether these sections originally formed a unit is very questionable indeed (cp. above, pp. 19f.).

Mk. 13$^{1-2}$ par.: *The Foretelling of the Destruction of the Temple*. Vv. 1, 2a may well be a scene constructed for a prophecy handed down in the Church, as it manifestly was in a variety of forms; cp. Mk. 14^{58}, 15^{29}; Jn. 2^{19}; also Acts 6^{14}.[1] If this be the case the form (v. 2b) would be determined by its context. This enables us to speak of an unitary literary conception on the basis of a traditional motif. There is little here to encourage us to think that this is the oldest form of the prophecy handed on to us complete with this setting; the address in v. 1 sounds far too much as if made for the specific purpose of evoking the prophecy. In any event this is no imaginary scene.

Lk. 19$^{41-44}$: *The Prophecy of the Destruction of Jerusalem*. The saying of Jesus in vv. 42–44 is a *vaticinium ex eventu*. Whether it was conceived together with the introductory scene in v. 41 it is impossible to say. But it is no imaginary scene.

Mk. 14$^{3-9}$ par.: *The Anointing in Bethany*. With Dibelius I think the point of the story lies in v. 7, to which we must also add v. 8, or at least the words ὃ ἔσχεν ἐποίησεν. Otherwise vv. 8f. are second-

---

[1] The prophecy itself is treated below.

ary material, which enables the section to be placed in the Passion narrative, a conclusion to which v. 7 also points.[1] Vv. 3–7 constitute an unitary composition, and certainly no imaginary scene, but one in the strictest sense biographical. For it is hard to imagine that the scene was originally simply a symbolic embodiment of the idea that in certain circumstances social duties must give place to religious ones, although the scruples expressed by the ἀγανακτοῦντες in vv. 4f. have their analogies in Judaism (Strack-B. I, 986). The tendency of the tradition is exemplified by the fact that the τινές who are said to be angry in v. 4, are in D and Matthew stated to be μαθηταί. Evidently the section did not originally belong to a setting in the life of Jesus in which Jesus is always conceived as accompanied by the (12) disciples. In John the story is even more successfully woven into a self-enclosed, intentionally historical scene.[2] Luke has made use of this material to fill a context in 7[41–43. 47] (see above, pp. 20f.).

Lk. 23[27–31]: *The Escort to the Cross.* The apophthegm is given its form in a most impressive fashion by placing a Christian prophecy in the mouth of Jesus on his way to the cross. The process of assimilation of scene and saying is illustrated by the variant readings which turn ἐροῦσιν and ἄρξονται into the second person. In such a case as this it is pointless to ask whether vv. 29–31 ever existed (as a saying of Jesus) in isolated form. The scene has been constructed from material supplied by primitive Christian apologetic. The form is old, because the saying in all probability goes back to an Aramaic form (see below) and because the scene has formal parallels in Jewish tradition.[3] The composition is not an imaginary, but in the strictest sense a biographical, scene. There is a noteworthy parallel in the Mandaean Ginza R., VI, Lidzb, pp. 211, 27ff., though it is mythological. It will not be possible to draw any inferences from it until the relationship of the Mandaean literature is made clear. Wetstein has already provided some relevant parallels: cp. now Klostermann.

---

[1] Cp. L. v. Sybel, *Z.N.W.*, 23, 1924, pp. 184f.
[2] Cp. Strauss, *Leben Jesu*, I, pp. 721f.
[3] Cp. G. Dalman, *Jesus-Jeschua*, 1922, p. 174: It was customary to weep for those who were led to their crucifixion. When R. Chanina b. Teradjon was led to execution his daughter wept for him, and he responded: 'If you weep for me and beat yourself it were better that an (earthly) fire that is kindled should consume me than the fire (of Hell) which is not kindled' (Sem. VIII). Cp. also the scene reported in Strack-B. II, 263f., Gn. R. 65 (42a) where the Rabbi who is taken out to his cross (and there is clearly mockery going on) says, 'If this (crucifixion) is what happens to those who do thy will, what will be the lot of those who offend against it?' These are admittedly not relevant parallels— G. Bertram, *Die Leidensgeschichte Jesu und der Christuskult*, 1922, p. 74, shows that the motif of the attitude of the populace is found in Christian and heathen martyrs.

ADDENDUM

Mk. 7²⁴⁻³¹ par.: *The Syro-Phoenician Woman.* The greater part of v. 24 and the whole of v. 31 must be recognized as editorial work which, in part, was known to Mark (see below). The remainder is an unitary composition, which does not however have the saying of Jesus for its point, but nevertheless belongs to the apophthegms. The miracle is not reported for its own sake, for the main point is the change in Jesus' behaviour as the dialogue goes on. Indeed this proves to be a controversy dialogue of a sort, though on this occasion Jesus proves not to be the victor, though in no sense is this a denigration. It is possible to ask whether Matthew used an older version of the story than lay before our Mark.[1] But the discussion with the disciples does not support that, for the heightening of the element of dialogue is normally a sign of a secondary form (see below). But the saying of Jesus in Matt. 15²⁴ certainly gives the impression of being old, and Matt. probably knew it as a logion in independent circulation[2] which he wove into the middle of Mark's dialogue at v. 23 (cp. Matt. 15¹²ᶠ). On the other hand, Mk. 7²⁷ seems to have been subject to later editing by the insertion of πρῶτον, which without any more ado makes a concession, and weakens the comparison on which the argument of Jesus is based. It is also possible that the whole sentence ἄφες πρῶτον χορτασθῆναι τὰ τέκνα is but a secondary addition to Mark's text.[3]

Matt. 8⁵⁻¹³//Lk. 7¹⁻¹⁰: *The Centurion from Capernaum.* Matthew has enlarged this story by the addition of the dominical saying in vv. 11f. which originally circulated independently (Lk. 13²⁸⁻³⁰). Thereby the accent has been shifted. The story is of the same type as the foregoing: A Gentile coming with a request is able, by a lucky meeting, to overcome Jesus' scruples. Indeed, I think the two stories are variants; both tell how a Gentile makes a claim on Jesus; in both his miraculous powers are sought for a child[4] by the father (or mother); and in both instances the miracle is worked from a distance (the only such miracles in the Synoptic tradition!). So it may well be assumed that the question asked by Jesus in Matt. 8⁷ is an indignant rejection of the woman's presumption. The cen-

---

[1] So B. H. Streeter, *The Four Gospels,* 1924, p. 260.

[2] According to v. Dobschuetz, *Z.N.W.,* 27, 1928, p. 339, Matthew fashioned the saying on the basis of 10⁶.

[3] This analysis seems to me a better explanation of the relationship of Mark and Matthew than Bussmann's supposition (*Synoptische Studien,* I, 1925, pp. 49ff.) that the whole pericope was lacking in Ur-Marcus and was only added to it by some redactor.

[4] Unquestionably παῖς in Matt. 8⁶ is to be understood as child: δοῦλος in Lk. 7² is an error in reproduction.

turion goes on in v. 8 to concede the rightness of this attitude: 'Certainly that would be too much to ask! But it is not necessary to do so——,' and then follows v. 9 with its apt saying which secures from Jesus the denied guarantee. This may have been even more clearly expressed in Q, from which the story would be taken. Yet it also seems that Luke had the story in a form in which it was plain that Jesus' scruples had to be overcome; though, since he no longer clearly understood the dialogue, he gave the persuasive role to the πρεσβύτεροι, who had to adduce other arguments, which to Luke seemed more illuminating. That means that he could only have understood the Centurion's saying in 7⁶ᵇ as a formula to express humility. So the idea that Jesus gave his aid to Gentiles found this twofold expression in the tradition. That is all the more reason for thinking that the scenes depicted are imaginary, and we must treat them as products of the Church. Further, hardly anybody will support the historicity of a telepathic healing.[1]

3. THE FORM AND HISTORY OF APOPHTHEGMS

(a) Controversy Dialogues

Scholastic and controversy dialogues are closely related, and we shall see that sometimes the one has passed into the other. Yet the two kinds, or subdivisions of one kind, remain two, and it is important to consider them separately.

The *starting-point* of a controversy dialogue lies in some action or attitude which is seized on by the opponent and used in an attack by accusation or by question. Clearly the typical character of a controversy dialogue is most marked when a single action like plucking corn or healing on the Sabbath constitutes the starting-point rather than when the opponent merely fastens on some general attitude of the person he criticizes. This fact also explains why an effort is made to describe some particular action, even when it is obvious that only a general attitude is under discussion; and when that is done the symbolic presentation in an imaginary scene is bound to appear artificial, as in Mk. 2¹⁵ᶠ·,¹⁸, 7¹ᶠ. Just as these latter situations are thus imaginary, i.e. not reports of historical occasions, but constructions giving lively expression to some idea in a concrete event—even so does the same judgement apply to those situations in which the reported action is in itself more likely, that is to say to the plucking of corn and the miracles of healing.[2] In other

---

[1] L. Koehler, in *Das formgeschichtliche Problem des NT*, 1927, p. 19, acknowledges the method of comparison in which the stories must be understood in terms of their constituent motifs. I am at a loss to understand why he resists the consequence of his views. .

[2] On the Sabbath healing, cp. Strauss, *Leben Jesu*, II, pp. 127f.

words, controversy dialogues are all of them imaginary scenes. Therefore, however, we must keep away at first from the question whether Jesus sometimes healed on the Sabbath day, or whether he used a certain expression which we find in a Controversy Dialogue in a discussion with his opponents. Of course it is quite possible that he did; indeed, very probable; but the first question to be asked, methodically speaking, must be about the literary form of the controversy dialogue, and its origin as a literary device. This is simply the question about the *Sitz im Leben*, which is not concerned with the origin of a particular report of a particular historical happening, but with the origin and affinity of a certain literary form in and with typical situations and attitudes of a community (see pp. 4f.).[1] Naturally the actual life of Jesus has been as it were precipitated in such literary forms and their individual examples; but the individual product can only be understood by us in terms of its literary kind. Hence it is methodologically false to start from some hypothetical 'original dialogue' and only afterwards to ask the question 'In what historical life do the stories of controversy dialogues have their proper place?'[2] It is much more important that this question should be put first, and, if so, the answer would be: 'In the apologetic and

---

[1] Thus the *Sitz im Leben* of Jesus' Controversy Dialogues is not to be looked for in the life of Jesus, as E. Fascher (*Die formgeschichtlichen Methode*, p. 221) supposes, but we must look for it in the Church. Opponents of Form Criticism sometimes ridicule the productivity of the Church which the Form critics ascribe to it. In reply we may say: 1. There can be no doubt about the Church's productivity, for it recognized itself to be the community of the Last Time, in which prophets were to appear; 2. We must remember that what was produced—at any rate so far as the apophthegms are concerned—shared in the traditional Rabbinic forms; 3. Form critics do not dispute the view that the Church had its origin in the works of Jesus, and has preserved many of his sayings in its literary creations.

[2] So M. Albertz, *Die synoptischen Streitgespraeche*, p. 100. In spite of many favourable reviews I cannot myself recognize this book as a real example of Form Criticism. The form-critical analysis is far too often burdened with psychological and general historical considerations. The uncertainty of the method reveals itself when what he gives with one hand in the section 'The Original Dialogue' (pp. 57–80) he has for the most part taken away with the other in the following section 'The Story' (pp. 80–101). In this section the Story is described as an 'abridgement of what is to be reported' (pp. 81, 83): the different persons or groups of persons who actually disputed with the historical Jesus were reduced in the dialogues as handed down to one party, and the various courses of the debates to one (p. 83). The final observations are often added in the process of writing down (p. 87), the expositions are literary creations (p. 87), the cause of questioning is now and then artificial (p. 89), the original answer has been now and again not only enriched, but even actually displaced (p. 95), there are also instances of interpolation and addition (p. 96). In short: 'It is not possible to determine in detail how far the form of the dominical sayings is due to the narrator' (p. 92). What then is left of 'original dialogue'? We only know that the Church portrayed the situation in which Jesus was attacked and defended himself in terms of its own situation. Whether the Church was right in so doing is a question that must probably be answered in the affirmative, but which can only be dealt with after the picture of the Church has itself been made clear. In any event this work of Albertz shows that the Controversy Dialogues as we have them are not reports of 'original dialogues' but creations of the Church. In addition he prejudices his enquiry by omitting to compare their style with that of Rabbinic dialogues.

polemic of the Palestinian Church.' In the form in which we have them the controversy dialogues are imaginary scenes illustrating in some concrete occasion a principle which the Church ascribed to Jesus.[1] But our further enquiry will make that more clear.

The *reply* to the attack follows more or less a set form, with special preference for the counter-question or the metaphor, or even both together. Nevertheless—like the attack—it can also consist of a scripture quotation. Answers in the form of a question can be found in Mk. 3[4], 2[19, 25f.], 11[30]; Lk. 13[15], 14[5]. Matt. 17[25] also belongs to this group, as does Mk. 12[16], which contains the answer *implicite*, even though it is subjected to further explanation. It is possible to observe in the rigidity of the style that Mk. 10[3] is a counter-question, although here its particular significance as such has been lost (see pp. 26f.), and further, that in the quite secondary controversy dialogue in Pap. Ox. 5, 840 (*Kleine Texte f. theol. u. phil. Vorl. u. Ueb. Nr.* 31) Jesus answers his opponent with a counter-question. A metaphor forms the answer in Mk. 2[17, 19]; 3[24f.]; Matt. 17[25]; Lk. 7[41f.]. But to this class also belong the replies given to the Phoenician woman and to the centurion, Mk. 7[28]; Matt. 8[9]. Scripture quotations, finally, serve as arguments in Mk. 2[25f.], 7[6], 10[6-8], 12[26]. In this same class we may likewise include the answers given in the scholastic dialogues, Mk. 10[19], 12[29f.].

To carry on disputes in this way is typically *Rabbinic*. So we have to look for the *Sitz im Leben* of the controversy dialogues in the discussions the Church had with its opponents, and as certainly within itself, on questions of law. It is quite inappropriate to call these passages paradigms, i.e. examples of preaching, as Dibelius does. A mere glance at Rabbinic sources shows that stylistic enquiries in that field would prove most valuable. However, so far as I can judge, the process of fixation was much more complicated in the Rabbinic tradition than in the history of the Synoptic tradition; and it seems to me that an enquiry into the Rabbinic history has as much to learn from a study of the Synoptics as the Synoptics from the Rabbinics.[2] In the Synoptic tradition the forms have been preserved more purely than in the Rabbinic, where the process was more self-conscious, the variations in motif artificial, and the items of the tradition were

---

[1] A. Schlatter (*Der Glaube im N.T.*[4], p. 105) has understood the meaning of the apophthegm better than many critics, who want to keep hold of some scene from the life of Jesus. The 'early Christian instruction does not set out to produce "contemporary scenes" from the life of Jesus, which the reader could easily impoverish by supposing that on those occasions Jesus did indeed so think, but on other occasions he thought differently; but, on the other hand it intends to keep before the Church what its Lord's will and promise was.'

[2] So also G. Kittel, *Die Probleme des palaest. Spaetjudentums u. das Urchristentum* 1926, p. 68.

subjected to metamorphosis.[1] Rabbinic controversy and scholastic dialogues (I treat them here together) find their starting-point, at any rate in part, in some particular occasion. Hillel was once asked by his pupils as he went to the bath how far he was fulfilling a commandment in doing so (Lev. R. 34[3] on Lev. 25[35]; Fiebig, *Erzaehlungsstil*, p. 64). Gamaliel was questioned on a similar occasion (Aboda Sara. 3, 4). Gamaliel was also questioned as he was reading the Shema on the first night of his marriage (Berach. 2, 5), or while he was bathing on the night after his wife died (Berach. 2, 6). Again, the sight of Jerusalem's ruins provided the occasion of an apophthegm (Aboth, R.N. 4; Strack-B. I, 500). When the guests at a wedding feast clapped their hands a Rabbi who was passing by took occasion to ask: 'Is that allowed on the Sabbath?' (cp. Beça, 5, 63a, 34; Strack-B. I, 622). Not infrequently a pagan philosopher or an emperor or even a proselyte would attack a Rabbi on account of some Jewish teaching or scripture and pose him some relevant question.[2]

The typical form for an answer is the *counter-question*, and often it appears in such a form as to be a metaphor in form, too. Sometimes instead of the metaphor the counter-question is a detailed *parable*, sometimes ending with a question, or at any rate interrogatory in character. I select a few examples from the abundant material:

1. When Hillel had taken leave of his disciples and had answered their question 'Where are you going?' with the answer 'To do a work of charity to this guest in my house,' they questioned him further: 'But do you have a guest every day?' He replied: 'And is not this burdened soul a guest in the body?' (Lev. R. 34[3] on Lev. 25[35]; Fiebig, *Erzaehlungsstil*, pp. 64f.).

2. A matron asked Rabbi Joseph ben Halaphtha: 'What is meant by the saying: "He gives wisdom to the wise and knowledge to the understanding" (Deut. 2[21])? Ought not the Scriptures to have said: "He gives wisdom to those who are not wise and knowledge to those without understanding?"' He replied, 'A parable. If two men

---

[1] Adequate enquiries into this field have not yet been made. There is some material in P. Fiebig, *Der Erzaehlungsstil der Evangelien*, 1925. There is abundant material easily accessible in the great commentary of Strack-Billerbeck; further in M. Gaster, *The Exempla of the Rabbis* (Asia Publ. Co., Orient. Ser. III.1) 1924—in the tradition of Islam there are also apophthegmatic items which would repay study. Cp. J. Goldziher, *Muhammedan Studien II*, 1890, p. 385.

[2] The Emperor as questioner: Sanh. 90b; 91a; Midr. Ecc. 8.17 (41a); Pesiq. R. 21 (99a); Chul. 59b; A.Z. 10a in Strack-B. I, 895, 581; II, 487, 252f.; III, 32; II, 474f., etc. A Heathen: Lev. R. 4 (107d); A.Z. 4.7; 65b in Strack-B. III, 104, 58.65; cp. also III, 102–4. A Philosopher: A.Z. 54b in Strack-B. III, 58, etc., cp . III, 102–4. A Sectarian: Sanh. 91a; Gen. R. 14(10c); Ex. R. 30 (89d) in Strack-B. I, 895f.; II, 462, etc., cp. III, 102–4. A Samaritan: Midr. Ecc. 5.10 (27b); Berach. 58a; Sanh. 90b in Strack-B. I, 39b, 176, 897, etc. A Proselyte, male or female: Hag. 9b; R.H. 17b in Strack-B. II, 210; I, 286, etc.

come to you to borrow money, and one of them is rich and the other poor, to which of them do you lend—the rich or the poor?' (Midr. Ecc. 1, 7; Strack-B. I, 661)

3. Rabbah b. Rab Huna visited the home of Rabbah b. Rab Nachman on a Sabbath day. He was offered cakes made from three seahs of flour. 'Did you know that I was coming?' he asked, and received the reply: 'Surely for us there is no-one greater than the Sabbath?' (Shabb. 119a; Strack-B. II, 202f.)

4. A certain sectarian raised an objection that despite the fourth commandment God himself worked on the Sabbath day. The Rabbis answered him, 'Surely on the Sabbath a man may carry something on his own farm?' 'Yes,' he said. 'The world above and the world below are God's farm!' (Exod. R. 30 [89d]; Strack.-B. II, 462.)

5. Gamaliel answered a question put by a philosopher as to why God was wroth not with idols but with the people who worshipped them. He said: 'What can serve as an illustration for that? Perhaps a real flesh and blood king, who had a son. This son got himself a dog to which he gave his father's name (i.e. he called the dog "Abba" = father). Thereafter whenever the took an oath he said "By the life of the dog Abba!" When the king heard of it, with whom would he be angry? Of course he would have been cross with his son.' The dispute went on, and the Rabbi again answered with a metaphor in question form; and finally on a third occasion he replied with a plain counter-question (A.Z. 54b; Strack-B. III, 58f.; cp. Mekh. Par. Jethro, 6; Fiebig, *Erzaehlungsstil*, p. 103).

6. The Emperor (Hadrian) objected to the doctrine of the resurrection of the dead, and asked: 'Is it possible for dust to live again?' This was met by the counter-question: 'In our city there are two potters. One makes his pots out of water and the other out of clay. Which deserves the greater praise?' To the answer 'The one who uses water' came the reply, 'If he (God) creates a man out of water (human semen), how much more can he do so out of clay (the dust in the tomb)?' (Sanh. 90b; Strack-B. I, 895).

7. The emperor's daughter asked R. Joshua b. Hananiah: 'Does wisdom seem praiseworthy to you when it is in a foul vessel?' The counter-question: 'In what sort of vessel does your father store his wine? Surely not in gold or silver ones?' 'No, in earthen ones . . .' (Taanit, 7a; Wuensche, *Neue Beitraege*, pp. 247f.).[1]

[1] Other examples of answer by counter-question: Sanh. 101a; Keth. 66b in Strack-B. I, 390; II, 415; cp. Fiebig, *Erzaehlungsstil*, pp. 78ff. The counter-question in form of a metaphor: Berach. 32b; Gen. R. 14(10c); Midr. Ecc. 5.10 (27b) in Strack-B. I, 278f. (cp. Fiebig, *Erzaehlungsstil*, pp. 95f.), 895, 396. The answer as parable without interrogatory form: Berach. 28b, 61b; Sanh. 91a; R.H. 17b; A.Z. 55a (two examples) in Strack-B. I, 581 (cp. Fiebig, *Erzaehlungsstil*, pp. 86f.); III, 131; I, 581, 286f.; III, 59.

In many cases the counter-question is not (only) a saying, but, as in Mk. 12[13-17] (the production of a coin) is made by a demonstration or a symbolic action.

8. An atheist said to Rabban Gamaliel: 'You say that where ten persons come together, there the Godhead (שכינא) descends; does that not mean there are many Gods?' When he heard this, R. Gamaliel called his questioner's servant and gave him a box on the ears, for letting the sun shine into his master's room. But the servant protested, 'The sun shines all over this world!' To which the Rabbi answered: 'If that be true of the sun, which is but one of the myriad servants of the Godhead, how much more must it apply to the brilliance of the Godhead itself' (Sanh. 39a; Wuensche, *Neue Beitr.*, p. 247).

9. A matron expressed doubts to R. Joseph b. Halaphtha about God's righteousness, because God chooses whom he will. The Rabbi answered, as he offered her a basket of figs from which she chose the best: 'You know how to choose the good figs from the bad ones: and you maintain that God doesn't know whom he has chosen as the best of his creation?' (Num. R. 3[2]; A. Marmorstein, *The Old Rabbinic Doctrine of God*, i, 1927, 182).

10. R. Jehoshua b. Hananiah explained to the Emperor Hadrian why the name of God was connected with only the first three commandments by pointing out that the portrait of the Emperor was placed everywhere in the city save in the lavatories (Pesiq. R. 21 (99a); Strack-B. II, 252f.). The same Rabbi (11) told the Emperor to look into the sun, when he objected to the invisibility of God (Chul. 59b; Strack-B. III, 32); and (12) when the Emperor reckoned himself more powerful than Moses, the Rabbi induced him to make a law that could not but be broken, in order thereby to disillusion him (Midr. Ecc. 8.17 (41a); Strack-B. II, 487). Antonius was taught by a Rabbi (13) using symbolic action (*A.Z.* 10a; Strack-B. II, 474f.). Another Rabbi (14) reminded a pagan of the disunity in his family as a means of refuting him (Lev. R. 4 (107d); Strack-B. III, 104). A Samaritan (15) asked the Rabbi Meir whether God, who fills heaven and earth, could possibly have spoken with Moses between the two carrying poles of the ark. The Rabbi answered: 'Fetch me a large glass (i.e. a magnifying glass)' and then said to him 'Look at yourself in it' and he saw a large image. Then R. Meir said, 'Fetch me a little glass (i.e. a condenser)!' He fetched the little glass and the Rabbi said, 'Look at yourself in this!' He saw a small image. Then the Rabbi said: 'If you, who are but flesh and blood can change to whatever size you want, how

much more can he, who spake, and the world was . . .?' (Gen. R. 4 (4a); Strack-B. III, 452).

One has only to review such examples as these to see clearly that the same kind of argument is found here as there, among the Rabbis as in the Synoptic controversy dialogues. In turn that provides us with the criterion for eliminating the additions that destroy the force of the argument, as in Mk. 2^{18-22}, 11^{27-33}.

To illustrate the spirit of this sort of argument I quote the well-known saying of R. Joshua ben Hananiah (Berachot, 8b): 'They asked him: "If the salt is bad, how shall it be salted?" And he answered, "With the afterbirth of a mule!" "But does a mule have an afterbirth?" "Very well, can salt become unsalted?" ' Here the counter-question itself is attributed to the opponent by the Rabbi's answer. Yet the basic form is quite clear: an argument by means of a counter-question leading the opponent *ad absurdum*. Lastly we may compare the type of dialogue in 2 Esdras, e.g., $4^{39f.}$: 'And for our sakes peradventure it is that the threshing time of the righteous is kept back, because of the sins of them that dwell upon the earth!' And the answer: 'Go thy way to a woman with child, and ask of her when she hath fulfilled her nine months, if her womb may keep the birth any longer within her.' Further, see 5^{46}, 7^{52}.

It stands to reason that *scriptural quotation* played its part in Rabbinical discussion. To cite examples: Sanhedrin, 91b (Wuensche, p. 537): 'Antonius once asked R. Jehuda, at what time does the evil inclination begin to exercise its dominion in men's lives, at the moment of conception or the hour of birth? The Rabbi answered, "The hour of birth, for it is written (Gen. 4^7) 'sin coucheth at the door'"' (Git.7a, Strack-B. I, 370); Mar Uqba sent the following question to R. Elazar: 'People are risen up against me, whom it is in my power to hand over to the government. What shall I do?' The Rabbi drew lines on a piece of paper and wrote to him (Ps. 39^2): 'I will take to heed my ways, that I sin not with my tongue . . .' And the same thing a second time.—Yoma 56b (Strack-B. III, 103): A sectary attacked R. Haninan with Lam. 1^9 and the Rabbi replied by quoting Lev. 16^{16}.—Tanch. B., בראשית § 20 (8a) (Strack-B. III, 846): A matron who thought she could prove from scripture that Israel could only last as long as the heavens and the earth continued, was answered by R. Joseph with Isa. 66^{22}. There is a long discussion with scripture quotations in Sanh. 43a (Strack-B. II, 417).[1]

---

[1] Of course scripture quotations and parables can be combined, as e.g. Shabb. 153a in Fiebig, *Erzaehlungsstil*, pp. 40f.

For the rest, it is possible that an enquiry that dealt more accurately with the history of Rabbinic discussion, would show that its literary style has grown out of the form of question and answer. This was already in use in the ancient wisdom, and remained as the primitive form alongside the development of dialogue proper. It is a question whether it is not in the end an accident that the following passage is not given dialogue form: Mischna Rosh Hashana II, 7 (Wuensche, p. 271): 'Why is it that the seventy elders, who went with Moses, etc., up into Mount Sinai, are not mentioned by name? (Exod. 24 9). To teach you that every court composed of three judges must be respected in the same way as that established by Moses himself.' Shabb. f. 114a (Wuensche, p. 272): 'R. Johanan said: Who is the scholar whose work it is the duty of his fellow townsmen to perform? The one who abandons his own interests and occupies himself with heavenly things.' Tamid, f. 28a (Wuensche, p. 292). 'Rabbi says: What way shall a man choose for himself? Let him keep to honesty above all . . .'

But the origin of this Rabbinic style is to be found not only in the discussions of the schools. It is also manifestly influenced by the oriental way of talking and discussing and by the primitive art forms such as the fairy-tale has preserved and developed. The sultan in a fairy story was at a loss and asked his vizier: 'Vizier, give me your advice,' and he answered: 'Can any possession give advice to its owner?'[1] It is a favourite trick of fairy-tales and jokes to ask a foolish question or make a foolish statement leading on *ad absurdum* and to cap it with an even more foolish question or statement. These are to be found in the widely circulated story of 'The Mouse who fed on Iron' (e.g. *Indian Fairy Stories*, edited by J. Hertel in Maerchen der Weltliteratur, pp. 60f.) and in the tale of 'The Clever Peasant Girl'.[2] There is an example in *New Fairy Tales of Greece*, edited by P. Kretschmer in Maerchen der Weltliteratur, p. 105. The king asked 'Is food ever cooked in sea foam?' (as the girl had maintained to reduce the king's assertion *ad absurdum*). The clever maiden replied: 'But then, Sire, does a woman ever marry and in three days bear a child?' Cp. the end of Fairy Tale No. 7 in *Turkish Fairy Stories* (edited by F. Giese in Maerchen der Weltliteratur, p. 74). Constructed on this same motif are also the short story in H. Schmidt and P. Kahle, *Volkerzaehlungen aus Palaestina*, II, 1930, No. 72, pp. 14ff., and also story No. 117, p. 161.

This individual analysis of the Synoptic controversy dialogues

---

[1] H. Schmidt u. P. Kahle, *Volkserzaehlungen aus Palaestina*, I, 1918, p. 177.
[2] Cp. the notes by Bolte-Polivka on no. 94 of the Children's and Household Fairy Tales of the Brothers Grimm (Kinder- und Hausmaerchen), II pp. 370–2.

has further shown that we must always raise the question whether we are dealing with an unitary composition, or whether the scene is a secondary construction for a saying originally in independent circulation.[1] If the saying is comprehensible only in terms of its contextual situation, then it clearly has been conceived together with it. But that is commonly not the case either in the controversy or scholastic dialogues. Instances such as Mk. 2[15-17], 7[1-23], 10[2-12], where the artificiality of the composition is clear as day; or such as Mk. 2[1-12]; Lk. 7[41-43], where the insertion into an alien narrative is quite plain; or such as Matt. 12[11f.] and Lk. 14[5], which are proverbs given different places in the tradition—all these show that the arguments were in many cases already there before the narratives themselves. I add an example from apocryphal tradition. Clem. Hom. 8, 7, contains Lk. 6[46] as an apophthegm: ὁ Ἰησοῦς ἡμῶν πρός τινα πυκνότερον κύριον αὐτὸν λέγοντα, μηδὲν δὲ ποιοῦντα ὧν αὐτὸς προσέταξεν, ἔφη· τί με λέγεις· κύριε, κύριε, καὶ οὐ ποιεῖς ἃ λέγω; οὐ γὰρ ὠφελήσει τινὰ τὸ λέγειν, ἀλλὰ τὸ ποιεῖν.

One can make the same estimate of other passages like Mk. 2 [18-22], [23-28], etc. As a counter-consideration we may ask whether it is not a pure accident that dominical sayings like Mk. 4[21]; Matt. 5[13], 7[3f., 9f., 16]; Lk. 6[39] have remained independent and not been framed in some concrete scene. But I admit that I have not prescribed a recipe for dealing with all the controversy and scholastic dialogues: rather does each one require special treatment. Naturally enough, our judgement will not be made in terms of objective criteria, but will depend on taste and discrimination. The individual analyses have shown that I regard a whole series of controversy and scholastic dialogues as unitary in conception. And that is enough to have established a tendency of the Tradition: dominical sayings, or arguments from the discussions of the Church were given vividness by being set in a concrete scene,[2] as was the fashion of the Rabbis. In any case—and this must be emphasized once more—the sayings have commonly generated the situation, not vice-versa.[3] A clear example of this is the story of the feet-

[1] The distinction between unitarily conceived apophthegms and secondary constructions in which the primary element is a saying from the tradition is naturally not the same as that between imaginary scenes and historico-biographical reports. An imaginary scene can as easily be an unitarily conceived apophthegm as a secondary construction. An imaginary scene can be described as one whose origin is not in historical events but in some idea which it is meant to illustrate pictorially.

[2] We must of course keep this question of the unity of the conception quite distinct from that of a secondary expansion by the addition of other sayings. That will be discussed later on.

[3] This naturally applies, so far as it concerns sayings, to those which contain a real point and are not merely incidental illustrations of the situation, as e.g., Matt. 26[2]. For such cases, see below. For the rule thus enunciated see, e.g., E. Norden, *Agnostos Theos*, 1913, p. 307, 1 and the example in Lidzbarski, *Das Johannesbuch der Mandaeer*, II, p. 96.3.

washing in John 13[4f., 12-15]. The evangelist has made use of this
story in constructing Chapter 13, which derives from Lk. 22[27] (or
some similar saying), though admittedly it no longer has the primitive style of the old apophthegm.

This means, in my view, that we can firmly conclude that the formation of the material in the tradition took place in the *Palestinian
Church*—and that holds for those with unitary conceptions as well
as for other passages. This is shown by the parallelism with Rabbinic
stories, as well as by the intellectual content of problems and arguments where we can only seldom find any trace of Hellenistic influence, as, e.g., in Lk. 6[5] D, or the late addition in Mk. 7[20-23].[1]
For this reason I think the question how far such formulations took
place in an oral or written stage of tradition to be relatively unimportant. Both stages of the tradition need to be taken into account.
It is clear that Mk. 2[1-12, 15-17], 7[1-23], 10[2-12], were given their
present form in the written tradition. On the other hand passages
like Mk. 3[1-5], 10[17-30], 12[13-17], could well have been shaped
orally. There are many passages which could be either. That it
was the Church that gave form to these stories, and—even in cases
of unitary conception—did not without further ado reproduce historical events, is shown very clearly by the fact that the conduct of
the disciples is defended.[2] They pluck corn on the Sabbath, they
do not fast as John's disciples do, they eat with unwashed hands—
but was Jesus himself so correctly behaved in all these things that he
was not attacked? And how can we explain the free behaviour of
the disciples if he were so conservative? Or did no-one dare to
launch a direct attack on him? But if that were so, why should they
venture to do so when he healed on the Sabbath? No! It is the
disciples who are attacked, i.e. it is the Church, which defends
itself by appealing to its Master. It is the healings on the Sabbath
that make it necessary for the attack to be directed against Jesus
himself, for the healings are at the same time miracles meant to
glorify him. It is in the highest degree characteristic that the controversy dialogue in Pap. Ox. v. 840, which is a late Hellenistic
production, has the opponent's accusation laid against Jesus and the

---

[1] I need but to point to Strack-B. in regard to the parallelism of problems and arguments; cp. on the same point also M. Albertz, *Die synopt. Streitgespr.*, pp. 59f.

[2] L. Koehler, *Das formgeschichtliche Problem des N.T.*, p. 31, in tracing such stories solely
to the memory that individual disciples had of things that happened in the life of Jesus,
fails to consider that these stories nevertheless exhibit a specific literary form, in particular
that of Rabbinic stories. This compels us to speak of a literary 'genus', to explain its
origin and to understand individual stories in terms of it. That in no way calls in question
the belief that memories of Jesus, his words and deeds played their part in the literary
productions of the early Church.

disciples; for this dialogue does not grow out of the situation of the Church, and it is inevitable that a later age should think it self-evident that it was Jesus himself who would be first and foremost subjected to attack. It is further characteristic that Mk. 2[15f.]; Matt. 17[24], raise a question about the conduct of Jesus, though the question is not put direct to him, but to the disciples: the Church is the means by which man's relation to Jesus is mediated to those outside.[1]

If any part of these controversy dialogues does go back to Jesus himself, it is, apart from their general spiritual tenor, the decisive saying. And since it is quite probable that such sayings of Jesus were preserved in the Church, we can find confirmation here that the primary element in the controversy dialogues is the dominical saying. Yet we must also freely recognize that we may find Church formulations even among the arguments themselves. That would particularly be so when the arguments consist of quotations from scripture for it is surely obvious that many an argument in the Church's debates would use proof texts, and that a collection of such polemico-apologetic material would be made, and used to good effect in the controversy dialogues. This is confirmed, e.g. when sometimes new scriptural proofs penetrate into such dialogues as secondary material, as in Matt. 9[13a], 12[5f.,][7]. In cases like Mk. 7[9-13], 10[6-9], 12[18-27], it is otherwise an idle question whether before it was framed in a concrete scene such a saying was already in circulation as a dominical utterance; it was quite simply available as one item in the polemical equipment of the Church about which, in reflecting on it, the consciousness grew that it had been received from the Master, naturally with a certain inward historical truth. But that clearly does not exclude the possibility that now and again there was also outer historical truth, i.e. that this or that scripture which the Church used, was also used by Jesus in his struggle; only that is something it is no longer possible to establish. It is, e.g., probable that the way in which Mk. 10[2-9] sets one quotation of

---

[1] A. Fridrichsen has shown the probability that the Controversy Dialogue in Mk. 3[22-26] or Matt. 12[22-26]//Lk. 11[14f.,][17f.] has the stamp of being formed by the Church. It is in fact hardly thinkable that a mere exorcism of a demon would give rise to an accusation of being in league with the Devil. It is more likely that the opponents 'derived the δυνάμεις of Jesus as a whole from a league with the Devil. The apologists then adapted this general assertion by making it specific: exorcisms of demons certainly belong to the δυνάμεις, and if they are set in the forefront for consideration it is quite easy to show that the opponents have got themselves entangled in fulminating self-contradiction. This means that in its present form the accusation has been adapted to the defence.' (Fridrichsen in S. Eitrem, *Die Versuchung Christi*, 1924, p. 33: to the contrary O. Bauernfeind, *Die Worte der Daemonen in Markus-Evang.*, 1927, p. 79 (78.1)). In *Le Problème du Miracle*, 1925, pp. 71-73, Fridrichsen admittedly thinks that behind the Church's formulation there lay an historical scene with an ironic saying of Jesus.

scripture against the other actually goes back to Jesus. For, so far as I know, this was unheard of among the Rabbis. They often enough constructed an aporia out of two apparently contradictory texts of scripture, but only in order to pass on to its solution.[1]

So in the end the question can very well be put, whether the Tradition has not repressed the prophetic-apocalyptic character of the mission of Jesus in favour of his activity as a Rabbi (cp. the question, whether Jesus ever baptized, p. 20, n.1). Yet in face of the entire content of the Tradition it can hardly be doubted that Jesus did teach as a Rabbi, gather disciples and engage in disputations. The individual controversy dialogues may not be historical reports of particular incidents in the life of Jesus, but the general character of his life is rightly portrayed in them, on the basis of historical recollection. And just as such recollections were preserved in connection with certain places (see below) without the localization of a particular dialogue being necessarily historical, so is the Tradition also capable of using recollections that are otherwise historical, e.g. in the statement about the attitude of his relatives to Jesus in Mk. 3[31] (see above, pp. 29f.), or about his intercourse with the tax-gatherers.

Of course the same remarks apply to the Rabbinic stories. In terms of their significance for the discussion they are in no sense meant to be historical reports, but illustrations of a proposition. But in the same way they may contain historical elements, not only in their correct representation of the historic sphere of actual discussion, but also in their preserving recollections of actual historical occasions. That they cannot possibly be taken as historical reports is shown in the first place by the variants of certain stories,[2] and then by the historical impossibility of particular discussions, e.g. discussions between a Rabbi and the Emperor. There are also reports of disputations with the prophet Elijah[3] and of controversy between God and the angelic prince of the ocean.[4] There is an instructive

---

[1] The Rabbinic view that 'the Prophetic Writings and Hagiographa were added to the Torah solely because of Israel's sin' (Strack-B. I, 246) is naturally no relevant analogy to πρὸς τὴν σκληροκαρδίαν ὑμῶν Mk. 10[5]. There may be some sort of analogy occasionally when particular prophetic texts are set against texts from the Torah; yet the meaning of this procedure is not clear. Cp. A. Marmorstein, 'The Background of the Haggadah', *Hebrew Union College Annual*, VI, 1926, pp. 187f. (separately, pp. 47f.).

[2] The two stories about Hillel in Lev. R. 34[3] on Lev. 25[35] (Fiebig, *Erzaehlungsstil*, pp. 64f.) are manifestly variants. Another example in Fiebig, op. cit., pp. 78–86 (cp. Strack-B. II, 414f.) clearly shows the uninhibited control exercised by the Tradition, precisely because historical recollections are obviously being used at this point. Conversation with the Emperor in Hul. 59b has its variants in Joseph's talk with Potiphar in Tanch. B. אשׁנ, § 34 (22b), Strack-B. III, 32. Other variants, or references to them are to be found in Strack-B. II, 462, 476f.; III, 109f., 281, 361.

[3] Strack-B. I, 499, 663 (Seder Elij. R. 18 and 16).

[4] Strack B. III, 411 (on 1 Cor. 10[9]). Disputations of the Fathers with God, cp. A. Marmorstein, *The Background* (see n. 1 above), pp. 188f.

story ending in miraculous punishment,[1] and equally so the story of the matron, who to refute God's government of the world, had her thousand servants and thousand handmaidens married[2] in a particular order in one single night.

There is also a general analogy for the formation of such a tradition in Greek literature, in so far as it deals with the tradition of scholars and teachers who did not themselves engage in literary activities and were significant less for science than for their personal way of life, like Socrates or Diogenes. But much the same sort of thing applies to the tradition of the Delphic oracle.[3]

Upon a survey of all this material, it becomes possible to talk of a *productive power of the controversy dialogue*, of the increasing tendency of the Church to clothe its dominical sayings, its views and its fundamental beliefs in the form of the controversy dialogue. The tendency[4] is shown when the type of the controversy dialogue now and again colours other passages. Thus the question about which is the greater commandment in Mk. 12^{28-34}, is a pure scholastic dialogue in Mark, and it ends with the questioner being praised. But Matthew and Luke make a controversy dialogue out of it, by deleting the conclusion and imputing to the questioner the motive of 'tempting' Jesus. And Luke has further conformed to the style of the controversy dialogue by giving Jesus' answer (Lk. 10^{26}) in the form of a counter-question. Further Mk. 12^{35-37} (the question about who is David's son) is a passage that does not appear in Mark in the form of a debate, but in Matt. 22^{41-46}, it becomes a controversy dialogue, in which, on this occasion, Jesus himself launches the attack. In the same way it is to be noted that Matt. $19^{16ff.}$ omits Mk. 10^{21a}, and that in the Nazarene edition of Matthew the rich young ruler has become a real villain. It is quite impossible any longer to suppose that Jesus used to engage in harmless debates. Finally there is a fine example of how this type of argument had its influence on Hellenistic soil in the fragment Pap. Ox. V, 840 (*Kl. Textef. theol. u. phil. Vorl. u. Ueb. Nr.* 31): the discussion of purity by means of specifically Hellenistic arguments is here given in the form of a quite impossible debate between Jesus and Levi the 'Pharisee and High Priest'.

[1] *A.Z.* 65b in Strack-B. III, 65.
[2] Pesiq. 11b in Strack-B. I, 803.
[3] Cp. P. Wendland, *Die hellenistisch-roemische Kultur*[2], 1912, p. 77, for the Diogenes tradition. For the stories of Delphi, cp. R. Herzog in E. Horneffer, *Der junge Platon*, I, 1922, pp. 149–70. There are numerous examples of the spread and variation of apophthegms, not confined to ancient literature, in W. Gemoll, *Das Apophthegma*, 1924.
[4] Naturally in this connection we do not understand by 'tendency' a conscious intention based on dogmatic motives, but rather the somewhat elastic 'law' governing the propagation of the tradition.

There is a further observation of importance for the history of controversy dialogues in the Tradition. In Mk. 3[1-5] the opponents of Jesus are not described either as Scribes or Pharisees, but are unspecified. It is only in the secondary v. 6 that they are identified as Pharisees. Luke on the other hand has already at the beginning (6[7]) described the opponents as Scribes and Pharisees. The demand for a sign was obviously made in Q by unnamed persons (Lk. 11[16]); in Matthew (12[38]) these are replaced by Scribes and Pharisees, while in Mk. 8[11f.] the secondary character of this identification is even more clear, for the author has Jesus in another territory and must in consequence bring the Pharisees out to him so as to create the opportunity for the words to be spoken. It is the same situation when the accusation of being in league with the Devil is brought by τινές in Q (Lk. 11[15]), but in Matt. 12[24] and in Mk. 3[22] by Pharisees and Scribes respectively.[1] There is an active tendency seeking always *to present the opponents of Jesus as Scribes and Pharisees.* Even their appearance in Mk. 2[16f.] is inappropriate; they are always present when the editor needs them (as in Mk. 2[6]) as typical participants in debate. In Mk. 2[18] they are secondary to John's disciples,[2] and in Mk. 10[2] possibly rightly omitted from D; in Mk. 7[1] the γραμματεῖς were summoned from Jerusalem! These same opponents are forced into other passages, too: in Mk. 9[14] the γραμματεῖς are pressed in only as a belated addition; they have no business there at all, and are in neither Matthew nor Luke. The same applies to the Pharisees in Lk. 19[39]—they are not in Syr[sin]; Matthew inserts into his parallel ἀρχιερεῖς καὶ γραμματεῖς (21[15]). The saying about the blind leading the blind is conceived in quite general terms by Luke (6[39]), but Matt. 15[14] addresses it to the Pharisees. In the same way Matthew adapts the saying about the good and the bad tree (Matt. 12[33-35]) to the polemic against the Pharisees (though Lk. 6[43-45] addresses it to no-one in particular, and Matthew himself gives it another special application in 7[16-20]). In Matt. 12[27]//Lk. 11[19] we can see from the οἱ υἱοὶ ὑμῶν that the saying was originally directed against the Jews, though here both Matthew and Luke turn it against the Pharisees; the phrase 'sons of the Pharisees' is a quite impossible one. In the saying about following Jesus in Lk. 9[57] we are given, doubtless from Q a τις. Matthew (8[19]) has turned that into a γραμματεύς, obviously

---

[1] Cp. M. Albertz: *Die synoptischen Streitgespraeche*, p. 111: 'The typical dialogue with Scribes and Pharisees is completely lacking in this source.'

[2] Or even secondary with them. It is possible that Lk. 5[33] understood Mark as having no specified subject.

because he supposes that the man is unable to decide to follow Jesus.[1] In Matt. 22 [41] the Pharisees appear as the debaters with Jesus on the question about David's son, in distinction from Mk. 12 [35]. In Lk. 17 [20] the Pharisees come forward as the questioners, although they had no particular interest in eschatological matters. It is the same sort of tendency, when the Sadducees are introduced from time to time, as in Matt. 16 [1] in contrast with Mk. 8 [11]; or Matt. 16 [6], where Matt. seems to think they fit the Pharisees better than does Herod in Mk. 8 [15] (cp. Matt. 16 [11f.]). In the same way the Baptist in Matt. 3 [7] does not address his call for repentance to the ὄχλοι as Luke does in 3 [7] (Q), but to the Pharisees and Sadducees. It should be clear that in all this the specific statements are the secondary ones. That means we are compelled to speak of a specific tendency of the Tradition. This again has light thrown on it by the fragment Pap. Ox. V, 840 (see above), where the debater is described as Φαρισαῖός τις ἀρχιερεύς; and with that we may compare how often in John the Φαρισαῖοι καὶ ἀρχιερεῖς appear in league together against Jesus. If we reflect upon these examples we see clearly that this is not a process confined to Palestine, but one which has affected the Hellenistic world, too, and there the historical relationships were no longer known, but Pharisees, Scribes, Sadducees and High Priests were all of them conceived as typical opponents of Jesus. That is why it is almost always said that *the* Pharisees, etc. (with the definite article) appear. But it is important to make that unambiguously clear. It will not do to think of the Scribes and Pharisees as an exclusive opposition to Jesus and the Early Church. They are only seen in this light as a result of the gospel Tradition. The distinction between those who did and those who did not believe on the Messiah in the Palestinian Church must be seen as something quite different from that between Pharisee and non-Pharisee. There were differences amongst the Pharisees themselves, and there were some Pharisees inside the Church. In many cases it is rather the great mass of the people who must be thought of as the opponent of the Church, as for example in the demand for a sign or the controversy about Beelzebub. It is also quite possible that many controversy dialogues originated in debates within the Church, e.g. those about fasting, purity, divorce. Naturally I do not mean to banish Scribes and Pharisees from all controversy dialogues; I only want to indicate a tendency of the Tradition, and

---

[1] Even modern exegesis arbitrarily follows this tendency. Cp. Klostermann on μὴ κρίνετε in Matt. 7 [1]: 'Those addressed are to avoid doing what the Pharisees do and assume the position of judge over others', though this has no real basis in the text.

to issue a warning about the schematic understanding so characteristic of the gospels.[1]

(b) *Scholastic Dialogues*

In view of the close relationship between the scholastic and the controversy dialogues, little needs to be said about the construction of the former. The essential difference between them is that in the scholastic dialogues it is not necessary to have some particular action as the starting-point but for the most part the Master is simply questioned by someone seeking knowledge. That leads to an answer which is sometimes itself in question form, as in Lk. 12[13-14], 13[1-5], but not with a view to taking the questioner *ad absurdum*. It is understandable that sometimes a request (Mk. 10[35]; Lk. 12[13]) or a simple communication (Mk. 9[38]; Lk. 13[1]) can provide the starting-point instead of a question—Rabbinic stories offer parallels here, too, as we have already seen.

Here, as before, we must ask how far the *conception is unitary*. Analysis has shown that it is so in most instances. Only in Mk. 11[20-25]; Matt. 11[2-19]; Lk. 17[20-21], are there compelling grounds for supposing that an originally independent dominical saying was subsequently provided with a setting. And there is also the particularly clear instance of a miracle story being used as the setting of an apophthegm (Mk. 11[20-25]). Clearly we must distinguish that from the other widespread category of additional dominical sayings being added to a scene already extant. It is probably not so easy to decide about the *imaginary character of the scholastic dialogues*, as it was in the case of the controversy dialogues. In general it has to be asserted here as there: even where there was no dominical saying in the Tradition we find that the outlook of the early Church could be clothed in the form of a scholastic dialogue as easily as in the form of a controversy dialogue. Mk. 10[17-31], 12[28-34] must be so understood, in my opinion. It is in itself highly probable that Jesus was asked questions about the way to life, or about the greatest commandment, but it is quite another thing to ask whether the scenes which relate those questions to us are historical reports or not. They are such only in the sense that the Church formulated such scenes entirely in the spirit of Jesus. Passages like Matt. 11[2-19], par.; Mk. 9[38-40], 11[20-25]; Lk. 9[51-56], 17[20-21], can on quite other grounds be seen probably or surely to be formulations of the Church. This can perhaps be shown in the case of Lk. 13[1-5], where

[1] Cp. G. Hoelscher, *Urgemeinde u. Spaetjudentum*, 1928, pp. 5f.; C. Montefiore, *The Synoptic Gospels*, I, p. cxxv.

reference is made to what is reported in Jos. Ant. XVIII, 4, 1. Admittedly it could also refer to some earlier rising of the Zealots, for the Zealots seem to have been called 'Galileans' occasionally (Justin, *Dial.* 80; Hegesippus in *Eus. H.E.*, IV, 22, 7)—though that does not of itself prove that the apophthegm is historical.

On the other hand we must admit that such a dialogue could easily contain an historical reminiscence, and the less the specific interests of the Church were expressed, the more likely that would be. But whether on that basis it would be possible to plead for the historicity of a passage like Lk. 12[13-14], is to me very questionable. If such an anecdote were related of some other historical figure one would scarcely think of it as historical save in the sense that it gave fitting expression to his spiritual attitude. And the same would have to be said of Mk. 10[17-31], 12[28-34]; Lk. 13[1-5], if there were not other reasons for the judgement.

But we must raise the question whether the *Palestinian or the Hellenistic Church* was responsible for formulating the scholastic dialogues. Their form and their relationship with both the controversy dialogues, and the Rabbinic scholastic dialogues, show that the former was the case. But Lk. 17[20f.], 6[5]D; 2 Clem. 12[2], show that in the Hellenistic Church they were fashioned anew on the analogy of the scholastic dialogues. That leads us to ask whether an Hellenistic origin must not be assumed for passages like Lk. 12[13f.], 9[51-56]. On the question of their formulation in oral or written tradition what is said on p. 52 about controversy dialogues applies.

The passages Lk. 17[20f.], 6[5]D; 2 Clem. 12[2], show that we can speak of a *productive power of scholastic dialogues*. The custom of clothing a traditional saying of the Lord in dialogue form continued (Lk. 17[20f.]; 2 Clem. 12[2]) as did the habit of expressing in a dialogue a quite independent account of the attitude of Jesus to some question of interest (Lk. 6[5]D). Mk. 11[20-25] also belongs here, a miracle story being used to give the dominical saying a dialogue form. But the propagative power of the scholastic dialogue is shown most of all in the tendency to provide a frame for dominical sayings unattached to specific situations by introducing them with a question from a disciple. But that is to be treated in detail in the context of studying the technique of the evangelists.

(c) *Biographical Apophthegms*

The formal construction of biographical apophthegms is naturally more varied than others. In general, Jesus' saying, which is the point of the apophthegm, comes at the end. The only exceptions are Mk. 6^{1-6} (where the conclusion appears in the course of the report, by the transposition of a part of the basic saying); 10^{13-16}; Matt. 17^{24-27}. The decisive word that Jesus speaks is called forth by a request or a question (Mk. $3^{20f.,\ 31-35}$, 13^{1-2}, Matt. 17^{24-27} Lk. 9^{57-62}, 13^{31-33}, 19^{39-40}), by conduct (Mk. 6^{1-6}, 10^{13-16}, 11^{15-19}, 12^{41-43}, 14^{3-9}, Lk. 10^{38-42}, 11^{27-28}, 17^{11-19}, 19^{1-10}, 23^{27-31}) and less frequently by Jesus' own initiative (Mk. 1^{16-20}, 2^{14}).

The analysis has shown that not even the biographical apophthegms are all *unitary compositions*. They are the less so, the less their purpose is to characterize the person of Jesus or to throw light on a particular situation, or the more they contain a general statement which is meaningful apart from its situation, as, e.g. Lk. $9^{57f.,\ 61f.}$; Mk. 6^{1-6}, 3^{31-35}. They are on the other hand the more unitary the more the saying and the scene express the point together, the more the saying is intelligible only in relation to the situation, as e.g. Mk. 12^{41-44}, 14^{3-9}; Lk. 10^{38-42}, 19^{1-10}.

The *ideal character* of almost all these biographical apophthegms is clearly manifest. The only exceptions are Lk. 13^{31-33} and Mk. 14^{3-9}, where the meaning is really restricted to the quite unique situation, and we can therefore speak of biographical character in the strict sense. There are also Mk. 13^{1-2}, Lk. 19^{41-44}, 23^{27-31}, which are not in the same category, but yet are not just symbolic or imaginary, but use some moment of the life of Jesus simply as a fitting place to introduce a prophecy.[1] Mk. 11^{15-19} tells of an action (the cleansing of the Temple) which is probably historical, but which, by the addition of a saying, has been turned to an ideal scene.

I call the remaining apophthegms 'ideal' because they embody a truth in some metaphorical sort of situation which, by reason of its wider reference, gives the apophthegms their symbolic character. They differ, however, according as to whether it is the person of the Master or the Church (its code of conduct, its destiny) etc. that is in the foreground. The Master calls his disciples (Mk. 1^{16-20}, 2^{14}), his native town rejects him (Mk. 6^{1-6}), the children cheer him (Lk. 19^{39-40}, par.). The saying about the true kinsman applies to the Church (Mk. 3^{31-35}); scenes like Lk. 10^{38-42}, 11^{27-28}, and the saying about discipleship in Lk. 9^{57-62}, speak of the one worthwhile

[1] The difference between Mk. 13^{1-2} and an imaginary situation is clear, just because it reminds us of a type of story whose point is the contrast between present glory and threatened destruction. Cp. in addition to the example on the next page, Git. 68b (Strack-B. I, 879): The prince of demons Ashmedai 'saw a wedding ceremony where there was much merrymaking. He wept . . . and he was asked: 'Why did you weep when you saw the wedding ceremony?' He answered, 'The husband will be dead within thirty days. . . .' (Cp. also Berach. 5b, Strack-B. II, 3.) But Mk. $13^{1f.}$ has no general meaning of that kind, but is conceived of as a specific prophecy.

endeavour; Mk. 10$^{13-16}$ praises child-like understanding; Lk. 17$^{11-19}$ is a reminder of gratitude; Mk. 12$^{41-44}$ provides the proper standard for judging a sacrifice; Lk. 19$^{1-10}$ gives consolation to the sinner who needs it.

As a rule the ideal or symbolic character of the situation derives from the incongruity between the occasion and the pathos of the saying, e.g. Lk. 9$^{57-62}$; Mk. 3$^{31-35}$, 10$^{13-16}$. Sometimes it is quite plain how little the occasion could really have evoked the saying: how could Jesus see what individuals contributed, and how could he have known that the widow had given her all? How did Jesus know (Lk. 19^{7,9}) that the people murmured about his visit to Zaccheus, and in what situation and to whom were the words of v. 9 really spoken? Or again, did the hierarchy actually ask Jesus to forbid the praises of the children (Lk. 19$^{39f.}$ par.)? There is no need to say anything about apophthegms containing a miracle story (Mk. 11$^{20-25}$; Lk. 17$^{11-19}$). Hardly anyone will doubt that Mk. 1$^{16-20}$, 2^{14} condensed into one symbolic moment what was actually a process, and finally we may say quite generally: a biographical apophthegm from its very nature is not an historical report—and that applies to Jesus as much as to any other historical personality.

In considering the origin of biographical apophthegms we must again turn in the first place to *Rabbinic stories*. They offer parallels in profusion. And their ideal character is also generally clear; i.e. they are not intended to be actual historical reports, but rather metaphorical presentations of a life.[1] Such is the story of Abba Tachna (Midr. Ecc. 9.7 (41b); Strack-B. I, 134f.), who broke the Sabbath to help a leper, or of R. Jirmeja (Yom. 87a; Strack-B. I, 287), who humbled himself in front of R. Abba's house seeking reconciliation, or of R. Simon b. Eleazar (Taan. 20a; Strack-B. I, 285f.) who was put to shame for his pride. Frequently, as here, the teaching meant to be gained is placed first as the basis of the story;[2] or it is introduced by some such phrase as 'from this we have learnt' (T. Pes. 1.27f. (157); Strack-B. I, 528 f.). Of course historical reminiscence can be retained in such stories, but in any case the report is stylized and frequently it is quite evident that the story as a whole is a construct. This is the case in the story of R. Joseph b. Kisma (*circa* 120 A.D., P.A. app., 9), who was offered 1,000 gold denarii with pearls and precious stones if he would move to another city, and who refused them all

---

[1] So also Nidda 61a; Shab. 127a; Strack-B. I, 230, 441f. Other characteristic examples of Rabbinic biographical stories are p. B.M. 2.8c.18; Lev. R. 28 (126b); Yom. 35b (Strack-B. I, 240, 515; II, 419f.); Berach. 28b; Shab. 31a; (Fiebig, *Erzaehlungsstil*, pp. 86ff., 99ff.).

[2] Since the teaching is often directly stated, the distinction from the scholastic dialogues is not always sharp. Among the examples cited above, pp. 42–45, it is possible to reckon nos. 1 and 3 as biographical apophthegms.

C

because he wanted to live in a city of the Torah, because 'in the hour of death neither silver nor gold nor precious stones nor pearls, but only good works and the Torah could accompany a man'. The story itself shows that it is fictitious. The same thing is apparent in the stories which are parallels to Mk. 12⁴¹⁻⁴⁴ (cp. Strack-B., ad loc., II, 46, and see above, pp. 33f.).

Similarly the story in Sanh. 105b (Strack-B. I, 370) about R. Joshua b. Levi who wanted to rid himself of an undesirable neighbour by some spell, but who slept away the time for the spell, and so concluded that cursing was unseemly. In other stories it is the miracles which show their fictitious character, as in Midr. Ecc. 9.7 (41b) (Strack-B. I, 134f.), where God caused the sun to shine again after it had set and a Bath-Qol has to testify that Abba Tachna had acted rightly; or in the story told in Gen. R. 11 (8b) (Strack-B. I, 613f.), where the pious man who bought the costly fish in honour of the Day of Atonement was rewarded by finding a pearl inside it. The following stories are also characteristic: When the disciples of R. Eliezer wept round his sick-bed, R. Akiba laughed at the sight of his teacher's pain, because he knew thereby that he had not yet received all his reward (Sanh. 101a; Strack-B. I, 390). When R. Johanan b. Zakkai fell ill he was visited by his disciples. He wept, and they asked him why. He replied with a parable, and then continued: 'There are two ways before me, one leading to the (heavenly) Gan Eden, and the other to Gehinnom, and I do not know by which I shall be taken.' (Ber. 28b; Strack-B. I, 581; Fiebig, *Erzaehlungsstil*, pp. 86f.). Also Mak. *f*. 24ab (Wuensche, p. 299): R. Akiba visited the ruins of Jerusalem with three companions. His friends wept, but Akiba laughed. Both parties gave the same answer—that what they saw proved that divine promises were fulfilled. Of course the stories are historical in the same degree as the anecdote about Xerxes (in Herod., VII, 45f.), who on seeing his mighty army at first happily praised himself but then wept and afterwards explained his tears with a saying about the brevity of human life.[1] Finally two very characteristic anecdotes are told about Hillel in Lev. R. 34³, (Fiebig, *Gleichnisreden Jesu*, pp. 7f.), which both give a basis for caring for the life of the body, yet are variants of the same theme. It is plain that the situations are constructed. Besides, the fact that the

---

[1] Cp. the story of weeping Ashmedai, p. 56, n. 1. The closeness of laughing and weeping is a popular theme. Thus it is in the one story of Ber. 18b (Strack-B. II, 229f.). More frequently in fairy-tales: In *A Thousand and One Nights* Haroun el Raschid began to weep and to laugh as he read a book. Buddhist fairy stories (Maerchen der Weltlit.), pp. 334f.; *Kaukasische Maerchen* (ibid.), pp. 100, 108. Baumgartner refers me to Bloomfield, *Journ. Am. Or. Soc.*, 36, 1916, p. 68; Chauvin, *Bibl. d'ouvrages arabes*, II, p. 172; Tawney-Penzer, *The Ocean of Story*, I, p. 47 note; VII, pp. 38, 221, 254, 260, 261.

same dispute is ascribed to two different authorities in two different parts of the tradition also proves the ideal character of the scene, e.g. Abodah Zarah, II, 7, reports a conversation with Jewish elders in Rome which is ascribed to Gamaliel in Mechilta Par. Jethro, Par. 6 (Fiebig, *Gleichnisreden Jesu*, p. 56).[1]

Similarly the question as to whether the *conception is itself unitary* has also to be answered in the same way for Rabbinic stories as for the Synoptic passages. There is an unitary conception in Pirqe Aboth, 2, 6, where the anecdote is told of Hillel when he saw a skull floating on the water and said: 'Because thou drownedst thou hast been drowned, and in the end they that drowned thee shall be drowned.' There is also an unitarily conceived apophthegm which metaphorically presents the teaching about retaliation. The parallel to the Widow's Mite is also an unitary conception. There was a woman once who brought a handful of flour (as an offering). The priest despised it and said: 'Look what you bring! How much of that can be eaten (remain as the priest's share)? and how much can be used for sacrifice?'. Then the priest saw in a dream, 'Do not despise her; for she is as one who has offered her life (נפשה, her very self)' (Lev. R. 3 (107a); Strack-B. II, 46). In some of the other instances that are quoted the sentence containing the point is the primary, and I give a very characteristic example, the traditional story of R. Hanina b. Dosa (Fiebig, *Juedische Wundergeschichten*, p. 25), from Ber. 33a: He put his heel over a lizard's hole, and when it bit him, it died, not he. Then he said: 'It is not the lizard that kills, but rather sin.' And then is added: 'In that hour they said: "Woe to the man whom a lizard meets, but woe to the lizard that R. Hanina b. Dosa meets." ' There can be no question that the miracle story is secondary. Presumably it was constructed out of the last quoted proverb, or possibly from the first sentence. In either case it would be a secondary expansion of the passage. In Rabbinic stories it often happens that the primary element from which the situation is constructed is not a component sentence but a text of scripture which is meant thus to be given a metaphorical illustration, e.g. the anecdote in Mak. 24ab, and Lev. R. 34[3], which has already been mentioned.

The story about R. Hanina b. Dosa that I have just quoted shows that Rabbinic stories did occasionally undergo *supplementary expansion*. I have still to make this point in regard to the Synoptic apophthegms, but at this point I want to make it in regard to Rabbinic

---

[1] There are many examples of differences in authors' names: e.g. in Strack-B. I, 705; II, 5, 318, 353, 362; III, 575.

stories of every kind. A clear example in addition to those already referred to is found in the comparison of Aboda Zarah, IV, 7 and Mechilta Par. Jethro, Par. 6 (Fiebig, *Gleichnisreden Jesu*, p. 56). The argument in the first passage as to why God does not destroy the heathen deities is subordinated in the second to a comprehensive discussion about God's relationship to idolatry, and in addition is enlarged by an added quotation of scripture. This last part shows that in other cases too we have to treat the text attached to a story as a secondary addition, as e.g. at any rate in part the three texts attached to the story of R. Jose b. Kisma in Pirqe Aboth, 6, 9.

After all this there can be no doubt that *biographical apophthegms*, like the others, have their parallels in Rabbinic tradition. Admittedly they have parallels also in the classical tradition and it will need a closer stylistic enquiry into the biographical apophthegms of classical antiquity to yield a confident judgement about their origin on the basis of their form alone. Meanwhile there are also objective criteria which yield the sure conclusion that at least the greater part of the doubtful passages were formed in the *Palestinian Church*. The concept of 'following' and an Old Testament parallel like 1 Kings 19$^{19ff.}$, support that in respect of the stories about the calling of the disciples and the apophthegms about discipleship. The concept of God's will or his word confirm it for Mk. 3$^{31-35}$; Lk. 11$^{27-28}$, quite apart from any other arguments. Similarly it is possible to argue for Mk. 6$^{1-6}$, 10$^{13-16}$, 12$^{41-44}$ (partly from the form, partly from the content of the saying of Jesus, but also from the context). In other cases it may be just the saying that belongs to the Palestinian tradition and the framework may be of Hellenistic origin, e.g. Mk. 13$^{1-2}$. Finally we can conjecture or assume an Hellenistic origin for a whole passage—Mk. 14$^{3-9}$; Lk. 10$^{38-42}$, 17$^{11-19}$. It is impossible to attain certainty in every case. The accumulation and analysis of parallels is the way to clarity.

But along with the question about origin goes the conjecture about where to look for the place in the life of the Church to which we owe the origin and fostering of biographical apophthegms. This is the point where, in my view, Dibelius' theory of sermon paradigms has its greatest validity. To say that preaching is the starting-point of all the spiritual products of early Christianity, that it was preaching that begat the tradition,[1] seems to my mind a gross overstatement that endangers the understanding of numerous items of the tradition,

---

[1] Cp. M. Dibelius, 'Die alttestamentlichen Motive des Petrus- und Johannes-Evangeliums', im 33. Beiheft *Z.A.W.* (*Festgabe f. Baudissin*), 1918, p. 125. Ibid., p. 146: 'In the beginning was the sermon!'

as can be seen in the case of the Scholastic and Controversy Dialogues. Apologetics and polemics, as well as edification and discipline must equally be taken into account, as must scribal activity. But the biographical apophthegms are best thought of as edifying paradigms ror sermons. They help to present the Master as a living contemporary, and to comfort and admonish the Church in her hope. And like the Scholastic and Controversy Dialogues they have received their form in the oral (e.g. Mk. 1^{16-20}, 2^{14}; Lk. 9^{57-62}, 11^{27}, etc.), as well as in the written tradition (e.g. Lk. 17^{11-19}, 23^{27-31}).

(d) *The Form and History of the Apophthegm in General*

Analysis has already shown that apophthegms developed in the tradition when independent sayings were joined[1] to an already existing situation, whether this were unitarily conceived or compounded of elements. I need only recall how Mk. 7^{1-8} is expanded down to v. 23; 10^{1-9} down to v. 12; 10^{17-22} down to v. 31, or how Lk. has used a preceding apophthegm as a frame for the parables or exemplary stories in 10^{30-37}, 12^{16-21}, 13^{6-9}, or how Matthew has added sayings to completed scenes in $8^{11f.}$, $12^{11f.}$, $15^{13, 14}$, 19^{28}, or how some element peculiar to one evangelist, occasionally receives an addition, as in Lk. 19^8. The most peculiar case, though it still illustrates the same laws, is where Mark separates an apophthegm from its original situation and introduces it into another so as to make double use of one situation (3^{22-30}). We may also compare how Matt. $17^{19f.}$, by using a disciple's saying, adds a saying to a miracle story (the healing of the possessed boy) and so makes something very like an apophthegm. Methodically it is interesting to see how such tendencies betray themselves in the manuscript tradition, e.g. Lk. 9^{56}; Mk. 11^{26} (even Mk. 11^{25} did not form a part of the original text of Mark, I suppose).

Further, it is possible to speak of a *generating power of apophthegms*, even apart from what has been said already in particular instances. In the passages already discussed the situation has frequently been composed out of the dominical saying; and frequently, in like manner, on the analogy of the apophthegm, a situation has been provided for a dominical saying though we cannot call the product a true apophthegm, since it is not a situation of a symbolic kind. There is a clear example in Mk. 9^{36}, where Mark has taken over the motif of Jesus taking a child in his arms from the tradition in Mk. 10^{16} in order somewhat awkwardly to provide an introduction to a

---

[1] Cp. Yom. f. 20b (Wuensche 335) where an additional saying is added to an apophthegm by means of the phrase 'Some say: Thus did he reply . . .'.

complex of sayings. In a similar way Mark has made use of the motif of calling the disciples so as to give the list of the apostles in the form of an actual situation. The motif of the disciples' questioning Jesus is very frequently utilized, and Luke has very deliberately fashioned all sorts of situations, sometimes on the analogy of those in the tradition, sometimes developing them out of the Lord's sayings. All this will be discussed as we consider the technique of each evangelist.

There is another way in which we may see the generating power of the apophthegm—in the *variation of motif*. We have three variants of Sabbath healing: Mk. 3^{1-6}; Lk. 13^{10-17}, 14^{1-6}, three variants of the call of the disciples: Mk. $1^{16-18, \ 19-20}$, 2^{14}. The theme of 'following' is found in threefold variation: Lk. $9^{57f., \ 59f., \ 61f.}$. The stories of the Phoenician woman and the centurion in Capernaum are variants. The theme of a visit to a tax-gatherer is made use of in Mk. 2^{15-17} and Lk. 19^{1-10}. The motif of kinship has been given different treatment in Mk. 3^{31-35} and Lk. 11^{27-28}.

There is also something more to be said about the construction of apophthegms. Dibelius has said all that is necessary about their 'finish' and their compactness (*Formgeschichte*, pp. 22f.), i.e. about their character as originally individual elements. This is perhaps seen to best advantage by seeing how these primary originally isolated items of the tradition which for the most part Mark (and Matthew) leave in unconnected succession, are often taken from their isolatedness by Luke and interwoven with each other. Mk. 2^{18-22} follows 2^{15-17} without any sort of connection, but Lk. 5^{33-39} occurs in the same situation as 5^{29-32}, after Luke has tried in v. 29 to bridge the gap that Mark leaves between 2^{14} and 2^{15-17}. In Q the section on the Beelzebub controversy (Matt. 12^{22-30}//Lk. 11 $^{14-23}$) and the demand for a sign (Matt. 12^{38-42}//Lk. 11^{29-32}) are neighbouring items without connection, but Luke has prefaced an introduction to both passages in $11^{15f.}$.

On the other hand all the evangelists are sensitive to the unity of an apophthegm's situation; and if they supplement the original apophthegm they sometimes re-emphasize the unity by a connecting or concluding phrase. Thus Mark motivates the saying about the blasphemy against the Holy Spirit, $3^{28f.}$, with the phrase, v. 30, ὅτι ἔλεγον· πνεῦμα ἀκάθαρτον ἔχει. And Matt. 15^{20} closes the section about purity with the remark: τὸ δὲ ἀνίπτοις χερσὶν φαγεῖν οὐ κοινοῖ τὸν ἄνθρωπον.

The interest of the apophthegms is entirely confined to the *sayings of Jesus*. The saying is given in as concise a form as possible, and this is proper to the apophthegmatic style. How different is the prolixity of the apocryphal fragment in Pap. Ox. V, 840, and how ceremonious are Jesus' words in the Nazarene adaptation of Matt. 19$^{16ff.}$ (Orig. in Matt. Tom. XV, 14, in Latin text). Jesus' saying comes in correct style at the end of the apophthegm; it is only infrequently that anything comes after it, as in the passages where the consummation of some miracle is reported, e.g. Mk. 2$^{11f.}$, 3^5, 7$^{29f.}$; Matt. 8^{13}, par., and quite unique, Mk. 12$^{32-34}$. Sometimes the saying is followed by a report of the impression made by Jesus' saying: Mk. 10^{22}, 12^{17b}; Lk. 14^6, and this is stylistically correct, as Mk. 3^{4b} shows, earlier in the apophthegm, where a similar effect of a saying is reported. But more often the evangelists have themselves added a sentence about the impression created by the saying: Mk. 3^6, 11^{18}, 12^{34b} (καὶ οὐδεὶς κτλ.); Lk. 13^{17b}, 20^{39}; Matt. 22$^{33, 46}$, and in doing this they were acting on the analogy of the tradition. But on the other hand there is no need to talk of a 'choral ending' (Dibelius, op. cit., 29) in the apophthegms. The instances are the secondary construction Lk. 13^{17b}, and apart from that only Mk. 2^{12}, i.e. at the end of what is really a miracle story, though here it is made secondary to an apophthegm. So such an ending really belongs to the discussion of miracle stories, and has nothing at all to do with edifying or sermonic stylization.

We can see very clearly from the three apophthegms about 'following' how the interest is concentrated throughout on the saying of Jesus. Nothing is said as to how those conversing with Jesus received his word, though in the stories of calling the disciples their following him must of course be reported. The Tradition has no further interest in the sick who were being healed on the Sabbath, or in the sinner who anointed Jesus' feet. What did the sons of Zebedee say to Jesus' statement (Mk. 10$^{35ff.}$)? What the questioner on the disputed inheritance (Lk. 12$^{13f.}$)? What impression did the refusal of a sign make? There is just as little interest in these questions. The apocryphal apophthegm in John 7^{53}–8^{11} is typical. Here, in proper fashion, Jesus is first of all asked for a judgement, to which he replies with a saying that has been conceived of as an unity with the situation itself. But the initial silence of Jesus is unusual and can be classed as novelistic; if so, the circumstantial ending, introducing the conversation with the woman, is more than anything else novel-like and secondary.

The economy in the *description of the situations*[1] is a feature corresponding to all this. The apophthegms are not tied up to a

---

[1] Cp. Dibelius, *Formgeschichte*, p. 24.

particular place and time, or at most only accidentally so, as it were. The stories about calling the disciples in Mk. 1^{16-20} have to be placed at the seaside, yet the details about the situation perhaps derive from the metaphor about 'fishers of men'; in any case such details have no historical value, no more than the information in Mk. 2^{14} that Levi was called from the customs. At this point the tradition is only interested to report that a tax-gatherer had been summoned from his occupation to discipleship; where Levi practised his tax-gathering, we do not know for certain. That Jesus was rejected in Nazareth is a conclusion from the saying on which the scene was built. The saying about the destruction of the temple finds its natural setting in the temple. The prophecy in Lk. 23^{29-31} is most impressively placed on the road to the crucifixion. We can put it that all these particulars belong to the symbolism of the situation. Indirect indications form a still higher grade of fortuitousness, such as Mk. 2^{23-28} which has to take place in springtime and it is childish to make capital out of this for the chronology of the life of Jesus.[1] The same can be said of the indirect indications of place which ensue from localizing the apophthegms in Mk. 11 and 12 in Jerusalem. It is no part of the tradition that Lk. 13^{1-5} took place in Jerusalem, but a conjecture, as is the admittedly better grounded localization of Lk. 13^{31-33} in Galilee.

On the other hand there are a few apophthegms that contain *specific references to place*. The location of Lk. 9^{51-56} at a Samaritan village is not one of these, because, like Mk. 1^{16-20}, it is part of the very stuff of the story. It is otherwise with passages like Mk. 2^{1-12} and Matt. 8^{5-13} par., which give Capernaum as the location; like Mk. 7^{24-31} which gives the district of Tyre; or like Matt. 14^{3-9} or Lk. 19^{1-10}, which name Bethany and Jericho respectively. Since precise indications of place are obviously unsuited to the apophthegmatic style, we cannot avoid the question whether they are all secondary additions. But they are not all in the same plane. At the outset Mk. 7^{24} must be reckoned as an editorial trimming (which admittedly may well have been in Mark's source material). The statement is evidently, like Lk. 17^{11}, a conclusion, this time from the fact that the story is about a Συροφοινίκισσα and the statement at the end in v. 31 tallies with that; for Jesus has to be brought back into the familiar environment from this pointless excursion. And this opinion is the more certain if, as we have shown, Mk. 7^{24-31} must be recognized as a variant of Matt. 8^{5-13} par. Finally the judgement is confirmed by the analogy of the miracle story in Mk. 8^{22-27a}.

[1] Cp. K. L. Schmidt, *Der Rahmen der Geschichte Jesu*, pp. 90f.

Here too we find geographical indications at the beginning and end of the story, the first of which, Bethsaida, is at once shown to be editorial by the fact that the incident happens, according to v. 23, outside a κώμη, that is, not outside Bethsaida. So we must take Jesus' journey north as a phantasy, and eliminate it from history.

Elsewhere we cannot with confidence distinguish the place location as editorial; and even if it is not in keeping with the style, it is still not impossible for the early tradition itself to have passed on this or the other apophthegm complete with localization. The situation is the same in respect of the Rabbinic stories. Most of them as a matter of style contain no particular localization,[1] and in the rest they have been added, although the additions have no significance for the stories themselves.[2] It is thus possible e.g. that the story in Mk. 2 1–12 had already been localized in the tradition before Mark, although it has to be admitted that there is Marcan editorial work in the connecting verses, vv. 1f. It is evident that in Q the story of the centurion was localized at Capernaum (Matt. 8 5//Lk. 7 1). It was known in the Church that Capernaum was a centre of Jesus' Ministry; it is fixed in the saying of Matt. 11 23//Lk. 10 15.[3] In other places the indication clearly derives from the editor, as in Mk. 1 21, 9 33. Thus Matthew makes Capernaum Jesus' home (4 13); some manuscripts of Lk. 7 11 use it instead of Nain. Lk. 4 23 also shows how natural it was to suppose that it was Jesus' home. It could well have been that the tradition named it as such in Matt. 17 14 for some locality is very likely in this context, since the temple tax was usually paid in one's home town.[4] The localization in Mk. 14 3–9 will be as old as the fragment itself. As to the story of Zaccheus in Lk. 19 1–10, Wellhansen has said that the first part must have taken place *outside* some town, since Zaccheus climbs a tree and not a roof. That means that the first sentence localizing the story in Jericho (καὶ εἰσελθὼν διήρχετο τὴν Ἱερειχώ.) is from the editor's pen. But Dalman (*Orte and Wege Jesu*[3], 1924, 15) objects: 'When Luke tells us (19 1) that Jesus "passed through Jericho" after he entered

---

[1] Of the examples on pp. 43–46 only no. 4 contains a definite localization and this (Rome) is something inferred from the context (polemic against heathen derision of the Sabbath). Among the stories which Fiebig has collected in *Erzaehlungsstil*, pp. 77–107 in nos. 1–10, only no. 1 (and even then differently in each of the four variants) and no. 4 have specific localizations.

[2] Cp. the exceptions cited in the previous note; also G. Dalman, *Orte u. Wege Jesu*[2], p. 14, though he only remarks on suchlike exceptions.

[3] Cp. K. L. Schmidt, *R.G.G.*, III[2], Col. 125, Col. 113. Schmidt is right in thinking that historical reminiscence can be tucked away in such localizations, even where they belong to the hand of an editor.

[4] Strack-B. I, 763ff.; Schlatter, *Der Evangelist Matthaeus*, p. 538.

it, he would be thinking of the outskirts of the town; that is to say, not of the small ancient site on the hill with the spring, but of the greater Jericho of Herodian times within whose boundaries sycamores grew along the street.' (Cp. also pp. 243f.) Thus it is impossible in this instance also to reach decisive proof one way or the other.

It is characteristic of the primitive apophthegm that it makes the occasion of a dominical saying something that happens to Jesus (with the exception of the stories of the call of the disciples). It is a sign of a secondary formation if Jesus himself provides the initiative. In this respect we may compare Mk. 9^{33} with 10^{35} or 9^{36} with 10^{13}; in the same way 7^{14} with 7^5 and correspondingly 10^{23} with 10^{17}. It is also characteristic that in the apocryphal fragment Luke 6^5D Jesus should begin to speak without having been questioned. From this point of view it is clear—quite apart from other reasons (see below)—that Mk. 12^{35-37} is a secondary form, and a characteristic light is thrown on Mk. 8^{27}, of which we shall speak later. To make it quite clear what is typical in these instances we may compare Mk. 8^1 with 6^{35}.[1] The secondary style of John is quite clear, where all that Jesus does springs from his own initiative (5^6, 9^6) and premature requests are put aside ($2^{3f.}$, $7^{3ff.}$, $11^{3f.}$).

As far as *action* is concerned it is enough for men to come to Jesus and question him, or that some characteristic behaviour is briefly described, which evokes either the accusation of the opponent or the saying of Jesus; the disciples pluck corn; women bring their children to Jesus and the disciples try to stop them; his relatives seek him and he is told so; Martha busies herself with διακονία and Mary sits at his feet. Corresponding to this there is in the case of some miracles a conciseness of story as in Mk. 3^5, $7^{29f.}$; Matt. 8^{13}, par. But this must not be criticized as 'edifying stylization'.[2] In these instances the healings are not written in the style of a miracle story, but in that of an apophthegm and it is characteristic that when the healing is reported in the style of a miracle story (Mk. 2^{1-10}) an originally independent miracle story has actually been made use of.

One particular *awkwardness* in the construction of apophthegms is seen in the fact that the appearance of the characters is sometimes unmotivated or unfitting. They are necessary and so have to be in their place. It is particularly striking that there are often uninvited guests at meals: Mk. $2^{15f.}$, 14^3; Lk. 7^{37}, 14^2. Yet these instances are mostly in secondary forms. It is a sign of a more developed style, when Lk. $5^{17f.}$ prepares for the intervention of the Pharisees.

---

[1] Cp. Wendling, *Entstehung des Marcus-Evangeliums*, p. 103.
[2] Dibelius, *Formgeschichte*, pp. 26f.

Personal characteristics are at the most given indirectly, as, e.g., in the case of the rich young ruler (Mk. 10$^{17-22}$), of the scribe who asked which was the greatest commandment (Mk. 12$^{28-34}$), of Mary and Martha (Lk. 10$^{38-42}$), and of the woman who anointed him (Mk. 14$^{3-9}$; Lk. 7$^{36-50}$). For the most part those who figure in the stories are types, Scribes, Pharisees, disciples, publicans, inhabitants of Nazareth, etc. Dibelius is right when he speaks of collective treatment. But even the individual persons who are indirectly characterized are in essence types. It would be false even here to speak of edifying stylization, or to suppose there were any motif from the life of the Church. It is much more likely that we are simply faced with the characteristics of folk-tales, just as they appear in folk-song, folk anecdote and simple fairy-tales.[1]

This is where the development begins. As soon as the apophthegm is affected by an interest in history or developed story telling we meet with more precise statements. This is shown in the first place by a specific description of the questioner. In the controversy dialogues we can see that originally the questioners were for the most part unspecified persons, but that as the tradition developed they were characterized as opponents, Pharisees or Scribes (pp. 52f.). But where harmless or commendable questions are discussed, it is possible for the disciples to appear instead. There are such secondary questions by the disciples in Mk. 4^{10}, 7^{17}, 9$^{11,\ 28}$, 10$^{10,\ 28}$, 13^{3}. Indeed it is significant that it is nearly always the whole band of disciples (οἱ μαθηταί) who put the question. Once only (10^{28}) Peter asks a question, as he starts a conversation in 11^{21}; and once also the four intimate disciples question Jesus (13^{3}). Originally perhaps μαθηταί does not mean the particular group of the Twelve, but an unspecified number of followers. That seems to be behind the expression in Mk. 4^{10}, where Mark finds in his source ἠρώτουν αὐτόν οἱ περὶ αὐτόν, and added the words σὺν τοῖς δώδεκα, while later copyists, for whom the equation οἱ μαθηταί with the Twelve is self-evident, have instead simply written οἱ μαθηταὶ αὐτοῦ. This same identification is also self-evident for Matthew, and it explains why in 24^{1} he makes the whole band of the μαθηταί question Jesus instead of εἷς τῶν μαθητῶν αὐτοῦ (Mk. 13^{1}). It is understandable that, with his interest in the Twelve, he should make all the disciples ask the question instead of Peter in 21^{20} (Mk. 11^{21}), and instead of the four in 24^{3} (Mk. 13^{3}). Other instances, where he makes Peter appear as the questioner, correspond more to the general tendency

---

[1] The occasional appearance of Christian terms only proves their origins in the Christian community, not in preaching as such.

of the development: 15[15], where he speaks instead of the μαθηταί of Mk. 7[17]; and 18[21], which has no parallel. In the same way Peter is the interrogator in Lk. 12[41] and 2. Clem. 5[2f.]; and in the Nazarene version of Matt. 19[16ff.], v. 24 is addressed especially to Peter (Orig. in Matt. Tom. XV, 14, Latin text). This tendency grew to such an extent in the later tradition that more and more disciples who were mere supernumeraries in the Synoptics are given speaking parts, such as Andrew, Philip, etc., in John and as, e.g., Salome in the Gospel according to the Egyptians,[1] Judas in the tradition preserved in Iren. V, 33, 3f., and Hippol. in Dan. Comm., 4, 60, and as the mother of the sons of Zebedee, who in Matt. 20[20] comes to make a request.

But such considerations give rise to the question whether we must not regard in the same light those instances in the Synoptic apophthegms where specific persons are named, and ask whether the whole pericope is not thereby shown to be a relatively late form or, alternatively, whether at least the provision of a name is not secondary. Were the sons of Zebedee the original questioners in Mk. 10[35ff.], or was it some anonymous pair of followers, or even an unspecified number of disciples? And is it the case that the sons of Zebedee were first introduced into the narrative when the vaticinium in vv. 38f. was inserted into the apophthegm? We may ask similar questions about the stories of Martha and Mary and Zaccheus specifically in relation to their early origin, and the same applies to John's enquiry in Mk. 9[38-40] and the question of James and John in Lk. 9[51-56]. The apophthegm in Mk. 14[3-9] is a clear example of the tendency of the tradition. In Mk. the murmurers are just τινές, in Matt. 26[8] they have become the μαθηταί and in Jn. 12[4] they finally turn into Judas. Besides this in John the woman who anoints Jesus is named Mary, and Martha is said to have waited at the meal at which Lazarus was host. Finally in the apocryphal fragment Pap. Ox. V, 840, one of the questioning opponents is named—the Pharisee and High Priest Levi. This incursion of novel-like tendencies can be observed again later in other types of literary forms.

Yet I want now to draw attention to the way in which the characteristics of the Novelle come out in apophthegms. The Rich Man of Mk. 10[17] becomes a νεανίσκος in Matt. 19[20], and an ἄρχων in Lk. 18[18]. In the Gospel according to the Hebrews (loc. cit.) two rich men are spoken of, and one of them scratched his head *et non placuit ei*. The same tendency is apparent when Lk. 7[4f.] provides a detailed description of the centurion, and when once more in the

---

[1] Cp. W. Bauer, *Das Leben Jesu im Zeitalter der neutestamentlichen Apokryphen*, p. 449.

Gospel according to the Hebrews (Jerome. Comm. in Matt. on 12[13]), the man with the withered hand is a mason, who prays, 'I was a mason seeking a livelihood with my hands: I pray thee, Jesu, to restore me mine health, that I need not beg meanly for my food.'

B

Dominical Sayings

This is not an enquiry into all the sayings of Jesus in the Synoptics, but into those only which have, or could have been independent elements of the tradition; that is, we are not concerned with sayings which constitute an essential part of the story as direct speech, like Lk. 22[48]: Ἰούδα, φιλήματι τὸν υἱὸν τοῦ ἀνθρώπου παραδίδως; further, Mk. 1[38], 4[11f.] 9[16ff.] 14[48]; Matt. 8[10, 13]; Lk. 5[4], etc., but also passages like Mk. 10[38f.], etc.

The dominical sayings can be divided into three main groups, according to their actual content, though formal differences are involved as well: 1, Sayings, or Logia in the narrower sense, Wisdom-sayings; 2, Prophetic and Apocalyptic sayings; 3, Laws and community regulations.[1] In each of these three groups I list the 'I-sayings' and at the end add an independent treatment of the parables and related material, which demand it by reason of their form, even if by reason of their content they belong also to the first three groups.

1. Logia (Jesus as the Teacher of Wisdom)

(a) The form of the Logia in general

Previous attempts to classify the logia by their form, like that of J. Weiss (*R.G.G.*, III[1], 2176–8), seem to me inadequate, in spite of many sound observations. Even W. Baumgartner's (*Z.A.W.*, XXXIV, 1914, 165–9) attempt to analyse the forms of proverbial wisdom in Sira, though it goes much farther, seems to me not to reach its goal, since he too confuses different points of view. I mean

---

[1] This classification corresponds to the species indicated in Jer. 18[18]: 'Counsel', (עֵצָה) is expected from the wise, a 'Word' (דָּבָר) from the prophet, and 'Law' (תּוֹרָה) from the priest; cp. Baumgartner, *Z.A.W.*, 34, 1914, p. 191.

that it is necessary to distinguish between *constitutive and ornamental motifs*. To the latter class belong such forms as simile, metaphor, paradox, hyperbole, parallelism, antithesis and the like, motifs which can be applied, individually or in combination to different basic forms, though they can also be entirely lacking. I consider a motif constitutive when it constitutes the form of a saying; and indeed a saying has to appear necessarily in a form conditioned by it. It is given along with the logical form of the sentence, and I distinguish three basic forms, whose subdivisions can afterwards make themselves manifest. The basic forms are:

1. Principles (Declaratory form).
2. Exhortations (Imperative form).
3. Questions.

It hardly needs any proof to show that the sayings in the Synoptics exhibit the same forms—even if they are in part somewhat modified —as the proverbial wisdom of the Old Testament and of Jewish literature. Indeed, so far as I can see, the proverbial literature of all peoples exhibit more or less the same forms.

Before dealing with the Synoptic material I give, for the sake of clarity, a survey of the most important forms by citing some proverbs and sayings from the Old Testament. In doing so I indicate the ornamental motifs only incidentally.

1. PRINCIPLES

(a) *Material formulation (i.e. some material thing is the subject)*

1 Sam. 24[14]: Out of the wicked cometh forth wickedness.
Prov. 14[4]: Where no oxen are, the crib is clean.
   (Figurative: cp. 2 Sam. 5[8]; Jer. 31[29]. In Prov. 14[4] there is at the same time the form of relative circumstance—where . . . there; cp. Did. 4[1]; Herm. Mand. IV, 1.3; X, 1.6; see Klostermann on Matt. 6[21].)
Prov. 15[30]: The light of the eyes rejoiceth the heart:
   and good tidings make the bones fat.
   (Synonymous parallelism.)
Prov. 20[17]: Bread of falsehood is sweet to a man:
   But afterwards his mouth shall be filled with gravel.
   (Synthetic parallelism with change of figure.)
Sir. 3[9]: For the blessing of the father establisheth the houses of children;
   But the curse of the mother rooteth out the foundations.
   (Antithetic parallelism with change of figure: cp. Prov. 10[4, 6], 4[18f.])
Prov. 17[3]: The fining pot is for silver, and the furnace for gold:
   But the Lord trieth the hearts.
   (Figure and material in antithesis.)

Sir. 28[17]: The stroke of a whip maketh a mark in the flesh;
But the stroke of a tongue will break bones.
(The same, but with change of metaphor and hyperbole.)
Prov. 15[16]: Better is little with the fear of the Lord,
Than great treasure and trouble therewith.
Prov. 15[17]: Better is a dinner of herbs where love is,
Than a stalled ox and hatred therewith.
(Form of comparative relationship, which is frequent in the Proverbs of
Amen(em)ope: Chaps. 6 and 13: Altorient. Texte zum AT[2], pp. 40,
42.)
B.B. 16b (Strack-B. III, 334): 'As the day advances, illness lightens.'
Ber. 48a (Strack-B. I, 467): 'Every pumpkin can be told from its sap.'
B.Q. 92a (Strack-B. I, 661): 'Poverty follows the poor.'
Ber. 51b (Strack-B. I, 882): 'Gossip comes from pedlars and vermin from
rags.'
(Material and figure in synthetic parallelism.)[1]

(b) *Personal Formulae*

Ez. 16[44]: As is the mother, so is her daughter.
Sir. 13[1]: He that toucheth pitch shall be defiled. (Figurative.)
Sir. 6[15]: There is nothing that can be taken in exchange for a faithful
friend;
And his excellency is beyond price.
(Synonymous parallelism.)
Prov. 25[15] : By long forbearing is a ruler persuaded,
And a soft tongue breaketh the bone.
Prov. 11[22]: As a jewel of gold in a swine's snout,
So is a fair woman which is without discretion.
(Material in synthetic parallelism: cf. Prov. 25[13].)
Prov. 11[17]: The merciful man doeth good to his own soul:
But he that is cruel troubleth his own flesh.
(Antithetic parallelism, cp. Prov. 12[4]—with figure; 10[5].)
Er. 13b (Strack-B. II, 402): Him who humbles himself the Holy One,
blessed be He, raises up, and him who exalts himself the Holy One,
blessed be He, humbles;
from him who seeks greatness, greatness flees but him who flees from
greatness, greatness follows;
he who forces time (masters his fate) is forced back by time, but he who
yields to time finds time helping him.

---

[1] In my view the Rabbis offer relatively few such proverbs. The 'indicative propositions
with proof' which Fiebig quotes in *Erzaehlungsstil*, p. 22, belong, as the 'proof' itself indicates, more to law than to wisdom. Cp. Suk. 49b: 'The reward of charity depends
entirely upon the extent of kindness in it, for it is said . . .' (Hos. 10[12]). P.A. 1[18]. 'On
three things the world stands; on Judgement, and on Truth, and on Peace.' The first
proverb shows clearly the language of law, the second can be described as a catechetical
proverb; yet this is also related to law. Yet the Rabbis also made use of genuine wisdom
proverbs; in addition to the above examples cp. esp. P.A. and Strack-B. I, 445f. (on
Matt. 7[2] B no. 3).

(Antithetic parallelism with metaphor.)

Shab. 127a (Strack-B. I, 441): He who judges his neighbour in the scale of
merit is himself judged (by God) favourably.
(Synthetic parallelism.)

(c) *Blessings*[1]

Prov. 3[13f.]: Happy is the man that findeth wisdom,
And the man that getteth understanding.
For the merchandise of it is better than the merchandise of silver
And the gain thereof than fine gold.
(Blessing with subsequent reason, and double use of synonymous
parallelism, both in the form of a comparison; cp. Prov. 8[34f.])

(d) *Arguments* a maiore ad minus

Prov. 15[11]: Sheol and the abyss are open before Yahweh,
How much more then the hearts of men.
(Cp. Prov. 11[31], 17[7], 19[9]; Sir. 17[31].)

2. EXHORTATIONS[2]

Prov. 1[8f.]: My son, hear the instruction of thy father,
And forsake not the law of thy mother:
(Exhortation with reason and double use of synonymous parallelism and
metaphor.)
Prov. 3[11f.]: My son, despise not the chastening of the Lord;
Neither be weary of his reproof:
(With reason and double use of synonymous parallelism.)
Sir. 6[2]: Exalt not thyself in the counsel of thy soul;
That thy soul be not torn in pieces as a bull:
(With final clause and use of simile or metaphor.)
B.Q. 92b (Strack-B. I, 341): If thy neighbour calls thee an ass put a saddle
on thy back.
(Exhortation with metaphor.)
Pes. 112a (Strack-B. II, 402): Strive to be on good terms with the man on
whom the hour smiles.[3]

3. QUESTIONS[4]

Prov. 6[27-29]: Can a man take fire in his bosom,
And his clothes not be burned?

---

[1] Rabbinic examples in Strack-B. I, 189 (on Matt. 5[3]), 663f. (on Matt. 13[16]); Fiebig,
Erzaehlungsstil, p. 29; *Jesu Bergpredigt*, 1924, p. 1.
[2] This is the dominant form in the Proverbs of Amen(em)ope, and almost always in
negative form 'Don't do this or that!' for the most part some reason is given afterwards.
Altorient. Texte zum. A.T., pp. 38ff.
[3] Other examples in Fiebig: *Erzaehlungsstil*, pp. 15-19.
[4] Rabbinic examples in Fiebig: *Erzaehlungsstil*, pp. 26f.

Or can one walk upon hot coals,
And his feet not be scorched?
So he that goeth in to his neighbour's wife;
Whosoever toucheth her shall not be unpunished.
(Rhetorical questions in synonymous parallelism and in figurative language, with synthetic parallelism between them.)

Prov. 23²⁹ᶠ·: Who hath woe? Who hath sorrow? Who hath contentions?
Who hath complaining? Who hath wounds without cause?
Who hath redness of eyes?
(Catechetical questions and answers using synonymous parallelism.)

It is tempting to give an analysis of many more instances and further comparable material, but it would not shed much light on our particular problem, so I refrain.

(b) The Synoptic Material

The following selection is meant to be as complete as possible. Yet one can have doubts about the inclusion of a particular saying. Only very seldom have I offered a critical justification for quoting a particular saying which does not include at the same time a judgement on the literary relationships of the tradition. The approach must commend itself as a whole, and the summarizing notes that follow will fully justify it. I have refrained from indicating the ornamental motifs, since, in my view, the review just made should be sufficient guide.

1. Principles

(a) Material Formulations

Matt. 12³⁴ᵇ (Lk. 6⁴⁵ᵇ): ἐκ (γὰρ) τοῦ περισσεύματος τῆς καρδίας τὸ στόμα λαλεῖ.

Matt. 6³⁴ᵇ: ἀρκετὸν τῇ ἡμέρᾳ ἡ κακία αὐτῆς.

Lk. 16¹⁵ᵇ: τὸ ἐν ἀνθρώποις ὑψηλὸν βδέλυγμα ἐνώπιον τοῦ θεοῦ.

Matt. 5¹⁴ᵇ: οὐ δύναται πόλις κρυβῆναι ἐπάνω ὄρους κειμένη
(Matthew inserts this into the saying about light.)

Mk. 9⁴⁹: πᾶσα (γὰρ) θυσία ἁλὶ ἁλισθήσεται
(Text and meaning uncertain.)

Matt. 24²⁸ (Lk. 17³⁷): ὅπου ἐὰν ᾖ τὸ πτῶμα, ἐκεῖ συναχθήσονται οἱ ἀετοί
(For the form see above, Prov. 14⁴ and cp. Matt. 6²¹; 18²⁰.)

Mk. 4²² (Par. also Matt. 10²⁶//Lk. 12²): οὐ (γὰρ) ἐστιν τὶ κρυπτόν,
ἐὰν μὴ ἵνα φανερωθῇ.
οὐδὲ ἐγένετο ἀπόκρυφον,
ἀλλ' ἵνα ἔλθῃ εἰς φανερόν.

Lk. 12³ (Matt. 10²⁶): ἀνθ' ὧν ὅσα ἐν τῇ σκοτίᾳ εἴπατε, ἐν τῷ φωτὶ ἀκουσθήσεται, καὶ ὅ πρὸς τὸ οὖς ἐλαλήσατε ἐν τοῖς ταμείοις, κηρυχθήσεται ἐπὶ τῶν δωμάτων.

Mk. 7¹⁵ par.: οὐδέν ἐστιν ἔξωθεν τοῦ ἀνθρώπου εἰσπορευόμενον εἰς αὐτόν,
    ὃ δύναται κοινῶσαι αὐτόν·
    ἀλλὰ τὰ ἐκ τοῦ ἀνθρώπου ἐκπορευόμενά ἐστιν
    τὰ κοινοῦντα αὐτόν.

Mk. 3²⁴⁻²⁶ (Matt. 12²⁵ᶠ·; Lk. 11¹⁷ᶠ·): (καὶ) ἐὰν βασιλεία ἐφ' ἑαυτὴν μερισθῇ,
    οὐ δύναται σταθῆναι ἡ βασιλεία ἐκείνη·
    καὶ ἐὰν οἰκία ἐφ' ἑαυτὴν μερισθῇ
    οὐ δυνήσεται ἡ οἰκία ἐκείνη σταθῆναι.
    καὶ εἰ ὁ σατανᾶς ἀνέστη ἐφ' ἑαυτόν (better, with Matt: τὸν σατανᾶν
                                                                [ἐκβάλλει)
    ἐμερίσθη καὶ οὐ δύναται στῆναι, ἀλλὰ τέλος ἔχει.

Matt. 6²²ᶠ· (Lk. 11³⁴⁻³⁶): ὁ λύχνος τοῦ σώματός ἐστιν ὁ ὀφθαλμός.
    ἐὰν ᾖ ὁ ὀφθαλμός σου ἁπλοῦς, ὅλον τὸ σῶμά σου φωτεινὸν ἔσται,
    ἐὰν δὲ ὁ ὀφθαλμός σου πονηρὸς ᾖ, ὅλον τὸ σῶμά σου σκοτεινὸν ἔσται.
    εἰ οὖν τὸ φῶς τὸ ἐν σοὶ σκότος ἐστίν, τὸ σκότος πόσον.

Lk. 6⁴³ᶠ· (Matt. 7¹⁶⁻²⁰, 12³³):
    οὐ (γὰρ) ἐστιν δένδρον καλὸν ποιοῦν καρπὸν σαπρόν.
    οὐδὲ πάλιν δένδρον σαπρὸν ποιοῦν καρπὸν καλόν.

    ἕκαστον γὰρ δένδρον ἐκ τοῦ ἰδίου καρποῦ γινώσκεται.
    οὐ γὰρ ἐξ ἀκανθῶν συλλέγουσιν σῦκα,
    οὐδὲ ἐκ βάτου σταφυλὴν τρυγῶσιν.

Like Luke, Matthew has altered his source (Q), most notably by his inserting it in c. 7, which explains why v. 16a is reformulated and why v. 20 comes outside the form, and also why v. 19 has been inserted. But v. 17 is a Matthean formulation, too. On the other hand, Luke's formulation of 44b and his late placing of it are secondary features compared with Matthew's interrogatory form in 7¹⁶ᵇ and its place at the beginning.[1]

(b) *Personal Formulations*

Lk. 10⁷ᵇ (Matt. 10¹⁰ᵇ): ἄξιος (γὰρ) ὁ ἐργάτης τοῦ μισθοῦ αὐτοῦ.
Matt. 22¹⁴: πολλοὶ γάρ εἰσιν κλητοί, ὀλίγοι δὲ ἐκλεκτοί.
Mk. 10³¹ (Matt. 20¹⁶; Lk. 13³⁰): πολλοὶ (δὲ) ἔσονται πρῶτοι ἔσχατοι καὶ οἱ ἔσχατοι πρῶτοι.
Mk. 2¹⁷ par.: οὐ χρείαν ἔχουσιν οἱ ἰσχύοντες ἰατροῦ ἀλλ' οἱ κακῶς ἔχοντες.
Lk. 5³⁹: οὐδεὶς πιὼν παλαιὸν θέλει νέον· λέγει γάρ· ὁ παλαιὸς χρηστός ἐστιν.
Mk. 10⁹ par.: ὃ (οὖν) ὁ θεὸς συνέζευξεν, ἄνθρωπος μὴ χωριζέτω.
Lk. 9⁶²: οὐδεὶς ἐπιβαλὼν τὴν χεῖρα αὐτοῦ ἐπ' ἄροτρον καὶ βλέπων εἰς τὰ ὀπίσω εὔθετός ἐστιν τῇ βασιλείᾳ τοῦ θεοῦ.

---

[1] Mk. 4²⁴ and Matt. 6²¹ are quoted below. Mention might also be made of Matt. 15¹³ πᾶσα φυτεία ἣν οὐκ ἐφύτευσεν ὁ πατήρ μοῦ ὁ οὐράνιος ἐκριζωθήσεται.

Mk. 10¹⁵ par.: ὃς ἂν μὴ δέξηται τὴν βασιλείαν τοῦ θεοῦ ὡς παιδίον οὐ μὴ εἰσέλθῃ εἰς αὐτήν.

Mk. 10²³ᵇ par.: πῶς δυσκόλως οἱ τὰ χρήματα ἔχοντες εἰς τὴν βασιλείαν τοῦ θεοῦ εἰσελεύσονται.

Mk. 10²⁵ par.: εὐκοπώτερόν ἐστιν κάμηλον διὰ τῆς τρυμαλιᾶς τῆς ῥαφίδος διελθεῖν, ἢ πλούσιον εἰς τὴν βασιλείαν τοῦ θεοῦ εἰσελθεῖν.

Matt. 17²⁰ (Lk. 17⁶ cp Mk. 11²³ par.): ἐὰν ἔχητε πίστιν ὡς κόκκον σινάπεως, ἐρεῖτε τῷ ὄρει τούτῳ· μετάβα ἔνθεν ἐκεῖ, καὶ μεταβήσεται. The following words καὶ οὐδὲν ἀδυνατήσει ὑμῖν are an addition by Matthew. Otherwise Matthew's form is probably original by comparison with Luke. Matthew's ὄρος is confirmed by Mark and 1 Cor. 13² over against Luke's συκάμινος. On Mark's form see below.

Mk. 3²⁷ par.: (ἀλλ᾽) οὐ δύναται οὐδεὶς εἰς τὴν οἰκίαν τοῦ ἰσχυροῦ εἰσελθὼν τὰ σκεύη αὐτοῦ διαρπάσαι, ἐὰν μὴ πρῶτον τὸν ἰσχυρὸν δήσῃ, καὶ τότε τὴν οἰκίαν αὐτοῦ διαρπάσει.

Mk. 9⁴⁰ par.: ὃς (γὰρ) οὐκ ἔστιν καθ᾽ ἡμῶν, ὑπὲρ ἡμῶν ἐστιν.

Matt. 12³⁰//Lk. 11²³: ὁ μὴ ὢν μετ᾽ ἐμοῦ κατ᾽ ἐμοῦ ἐστιν,
καὶ ὁ μὴ συνάγων μετ᾽ ἐμοῦ σκορπίζει.

Mk. 6⁴ par. (cp Lk. 4²⁴): I give it in the form which is in my view original (see above).

Pap. Ox. I, 5: οὐκ ἔστιν δεκτός προφήτης ἐν τῇ πατρίδι αὐτοῦ,
οὐδὲ ἰατρὸς ποιεῖ θεραπείας εἰς τοὺς γινώσκοντας αὐτόν.

Matt. 13⁵²: (διὰ τοῦτο πᾶς γραμματεὺς μαθητευθεὶς τῇ βασιλείᾳ τοῦ θεοῦ ὅμοιός ἐστιν ἀνθρώπῳ οἰκοδεσπότῃ, ὅστις ἐκβάλλει ἐκ τοῦ θησαυροῦ αὐτοῦ καινὰ καὶ παλαιά).
This may well rest upon a twofold proverb:
As a father brings out of his treasure things new and old,
So is a Scribe, who is wise unto heaven.

Mk. 4²⁵ par. (Matt. 25²⁹//Lk. 19²⁶): ὃς (γὰρ) ἔχει δοθήσεται αὐτῷ,
καὶ ὃς οὐκ ἔχει, καὶ ὃ ἔχει ἀρθήσεται ἀπ᾽ αὐτοῦ.

Lk. 14¹¹ (Lk. 18¹⁴; Matt. 23¹²):
(ὅτι) πᾶς ὁ ὑψῶν ἑαυτὸν ταπεινωθήσεται,
καὶ ὁ ταπεινῶν ἑαυτόν ὑψωθήσεται.

Matt. 12³⁵//Lk. 6⁴⁵ᵃ: ὁ ἀγαθὸς ἄνθρωπος ἐκ τοῦ ἀγαθοῦ θησαυροῦ ἐκβάλλει τὰ ἀγαθά, καὶ ὁ πονηρὸς ἄνθρωπος ἐκ τοῦ πονηροῦ θησαυροῦ ἐκβάλλει τὰ πονηρά.

Mk. 8³⁵ par. (or Matt. 10³⁹//Lk. 17³³; Jn. 12²⁵):
ὃς (γὰρ) ἐὰν θέλῃ τὴν ψυχὴν αὐτοῦ σῶσαι, ἀπολέσει αὐτήν.
ὃς δ᾽ ἂν ἀπολέσει τὴν ψυχὴν αὐτοῦ (—), σώσει αὐτήν.

Mk. 2²⁷: τὸ σάββατον διὰ τὸν ἄνθρωπον ἐγένετο
καὶ οὐχ ὁ ἄνθρωπος διὰ τὸ σάββατον.

Matt. 6²⁴//Lk. 16¹³: οὐδεὶς δύναται δυσὶ κυρίοις δουλεύειν·
ἢ γὰρ τὸν ἕνα μισήσει καὶ τὸν ἕτερον ἀγαπήσει,
ἢ ἑνὸς ἀνθέξεται καὶ τοῦ ἑτέρου καταφρονήσει.
οὐ δύνασθε θεῷ δουλεύειν καὶ μαμωνᾷ.

Matt. 10²⁴ᶠ·//Lk. 6⁴⁰: οὐκ ἔστιν μαθητὴς ὑπὲρ τὸν διδάσκαλον
    οὐδὲ δοῦλος ὑπὲρ τὸν κύριον αὐτοῦ.
    ἀρκετὸν τῷ μαθητῇ ἵνα γένηται ὡς ὁ διδάσκαλος αὐτοῦ,
    καὶ ὁ δοῦλος ὡς ὁ κύριος αὐτοῦ.
Matt. 8²⁰//Lk. 9⁵⁸: αἱ ἀλώπεκες φωλεοὺς ἔχουσιν
    καὶ τὰ πετεινὰ τοῦ οὐρανοῦ κατασκηνώσεις,
    ὁ δὲ υἱὸς τοῦ ἀνθρώπου οὐκ ἔχει ποῦ τὴν κεφαλὴν κλίνῃ.
Lk. 16¹⁰⁻¹²: ὁ πιστὸς ἐν ἐλαχίστῳ καὶ ἐν πολλῷ πιστός ἐστιν,
    καὶ ὁ ἐν ἐλαχίστῳ ἄδικος καὶ ἐν πολλῷ ἄδικός ἐστιν.
    εἰ οὖν ἐν τῷ ἀδίκῳ μαμωνᾷ πιστοὶ οὐκ ἐγένεσθε,
      τὸ ἀληθινὸν τίς ὑμῖν πιστεύσει;
    καὶ εἰ ἐν τῷ ἀλλοτρίῳ πιστοὶ οὐκ ἐγένεσθε,
      τὸ ὑμέτερον τίς δώσει ὑμῖν;
Lk. 12⁴⁷ᶠ·: ἐκεῖνος (δὲ) ὁ δοῦλος ὁ γνοὺς τὸ θέλημα τοῦ κυρίου αὐτοῦ
    καὶ μὴ ἑτοιμάσας ἢ ποιήσας πρὸς τὸ θέλημα αὐτοῦ
      δαρήσεται πολλάς·
    ὁ δὲ μὴ γνούς,
      ποιήσας δὲ ἄξια πληγῶν,
      δαρήσεται ὀλίγας.
    παντὶ δὲ ᾧ ἐδόθη πολύ, πολὺ ζητηθήσεται παρ' αὐτοῦ,
    καὶ ᾧ παρέθεντο πολύ, περισσότερον αἰτήσουσιν αὐτόν.
Mk. 2²¹ᶠ· par.:
    οὐδεὶς ἐπίβλημα ῥάκους ἀγνάφου ἐπιράπτει ἐπὶ ἱμάτιον παλαιόν·
    εἰ δὲ μή, αἴρει τὸ πλήρωμα ἀπ' αὐτοῦ (—), καὶ χεῖρον σχίσμα γίνεται,
    καὶ οὐδεὶς βάλλει οἶνον νέον εἰς ἀσκοὺς παλαιούς,
    εἰ δὲ μή, ῥήξει ὁ οἶνος τοὺς ἀσκούς, καὶ ὁ οἶνος ἀπόλλυται καὶ οἱ ἀσκοί.
Mk. 10⁴²⁻⁴⁴ par. (or Lk. 22²⁵ᶠ·: οἴδατε ὅτι)
    οἱ δοκοῦντες ἄρχειν τῶν ἐθνῶν κατακυριεύουσιν αὐτῶν
    καὶ οἱ μεγάλοι αὐτῶν κατεξουσιάζουσιν αὐτῶν.
    οὐχ οὕτως δέ ἐστιν ἐν ὑμῖν·
    ἀλλ' ὃς ἂν θέλῃ μέγας γενέσθαι ἐν ὑμῖν, ἔσται ὑμῶν διάκονος,
    καὶ ὃς ἂν θέλῃ ὑμῶν γενέσθαι πρῶτος, ἔσται πάντων δοῦλος.
Matt. 19¹²: εἰσὶν (γὰρ) εὐνοῦχοι οἵτινες ἐκ κοιλίας μητρὸς ἐγεννήθησαν
                                          [οὕτως,
    καὶ εἰσὶν εὐνοῦχοι οἵτινες εὐνουχίσθησαν ὑπὸ τῶν ἀνθρώπων,
    καὶ εἰσὶν εὐνοῦχοι οἵτινες εὐνούχισαν ἑαυτοὺς διὰ τὴν βασιλείαν τ. θ.

(c) *Blessings*

These are discussed among the 'Prophet Sayings'. I need cite only
Lk. 11²⁸:
    (μενοῦν) μακάριοι οἱ ἀκούοντες τὸν λόγον τοῦ θεοῦ καὶ φυλάσσοντες.

(d) *Arguments* a maiore ad minus

Matt. 6²³ appears above. Matt. 6²⁶, ³⁰, 7¹¹ are included in a longer passage. Here it is necessary simply to consider Matt. 10²⁹ᶠ·//Lk. 12⁶⁻⁷ᵃ, which, however, has a question as its first component:

οὐχὶ δύο στρουθία ἀσσαρίου πωλεῖται;
καὶ ἓν ἐξ αὐτῶν οὐ πεσεῖται ἐπὶ τὴν γῆν ἄνευ τοῦ πατρὸς ὑμῶν.
ὑμῶν δὲ καὶ αἱ τρίχες τῆς κεφαλῆς πᾶσαι ἠριθμημέναι εἰσίν.

2. EXHORTATIONS[1]

Lk. 4²³: ἰατρέ, θεράπευσον ἑαυτόν.

Matt. 8²²ᵇ//Lk. 9⁶⁰: ἄφες τοὺς νεκροὺς θάψαι τοὺς ἑαυτῶν νεκρούς.

Lk. 6³¹//Matt. 7¹²ᵃ: (καὶ) καθὼς θέλετε ἵνα ποιῶσιν ὑμῖν οἱ ἄνθρωποι,
         καὶ ὑμεῖς ποιεῖτε αὐτοῖς ὁμοίως.

Matt. 10¹⁶ᵇ: γίνεσθε (οὖν) φρόνιμοι ὡς οἱ ὄφεις
         καὶ ἀκέραιοι ὡς αἱ περιστεραί.

Mk. 11²⁴ par.: πάντα ὅσα προσεύχεσθε καὶ αἰτεῖσθε, πιστεύετε ὅτι
         ἐλάβετε, καὶ ἔσται ὑμῖν.

Lk. 16⁹: ἑαυτοῖς ποιήσατε φίλους ἐκ τοῦ μαμωνᾶ τῆς ἀδικίας,
         ἵνα ὅταν ἐκλίπῃ, δέξωνται ὑμᾶς εἰς τὰς αἰωνίους σκηνάς.

Matt. 7⁶: μὴ δῶτε τὸ ἅγιον τοῖς κυσίν,
         μηδὲ βάλητε τοὺς μαργαρίτας ἔμπροσθεν τῶν χοίρων,
         μήποτε καταπατήσουσιν αὐτοὺς ἐν τοῖς ποσὶν αὐτῶν
             καὶ στραφέντες ῥήξωσιν ὑμᾶς.

Matt. 6³⁴: μὴ (οὖν) μεριμνήσητε εἰς τὴν αὔριον·
         ἡ γὰρ αὔριον μεριμνήσει ἑαυτῆς.

Matt. 10²⁸//Lk. 12⁴ᶠ·:

(καὶ) μὴ φοβεῖσθε ἀπὸ τῶν ἀποκτεννόντων τὸ σῶμα,
         τὴν δὲ ψυχὴν μὴ δυναμένων ἀποκτεῖναι.
φοβεῖσθε δὲ μᾶλλον τὸν δυνάμενον καὶ ψυχὴν καὶ σῶμα ἀπολέσαι
                                                    [ἐν γεέννῃ.

Matt. 6¹⁹⁻²¹//Lk. 12³³ᶠ·:

μὴ θησαυρίζετε ὑμῖν θησαυροὺς ἐπὶ τῆς γῆς,
         ὅπου σὴς καὶ βρῶσις ἀφανίζει,
         καὶ ὅπου κλέπται διορύσσουσιν καὶ κλέπτουσιν.
θησαυρίζετε δὲ ὑμῖν θησαυροὺς ἐν οὐρανῷ,
         ὅπου οὔτε σὴς οὔτε βρῶσις ἀφανίζει,
         καὶ ὅπου κλέπται οὐ διορύσσουσιν οὐδὲ κλέπτουσιν.
ὅπου γάρ ἐστιν ὁ θησαυρός σου, ἐκεῖ ἔσται καὶ ἡ καρδία σου.

Matt. 7¹³ᶠ· (cp Lk. 13²⁴): εἰσέλθατε διὰ τῆς στενῆς πύλης,
ὅτι πλατεῖα καὶ εὐρύχωρος ἡ ὁδὸς ἡ ἀπάγουσα εἰς ἀπώλειαν.
         καὶ πολλοί εἰσιν οἱ εἰσερχόμενοι δι᾽ αὐτῆς.
ὅτι στενὴ καὶ τεθλιμμένη ἡ ὁδὸς ἡ ἀπάγουσα εἰς τὴν ζωήν.
         καὶ ὀλίγοι εἰσὶν οἱ εὑρίσκοντες αὐτήν.

[1] I pass over the unintelligible saying in Mk. 9⁵⁰ᵇ: ἔχετε ἐν ἑαυτοῖς ἅλα καὶ εἰρηνεύετε ἐν ἀλλήλοις. Matt. 5³⁹⁻⁴², ⁴⁴⁻⁴⁸, 6²⁵ᶠᶠ·, 7¹, ⁷ᶠ· follow below. Other imperative sayings like Matt. 5²³ᶠ·, 6²ᶠᶠ· are not in place here, but are really legal sayings or community regulations.

Mk. 9⁴³⁻⁴⁷ par. (or Matt. 5²⁹ᶠ·):

(καὶ) ἐὰν σκανδαλίση σε ἡ χείρ σου, ἀπόκοψον αὐτήν·
   καλόν ἐστίν σε κυλλὸν εἰσελθεῖν εἰς τὴν ζωήν,
ἢ τὰς δύο χεῖρας ἔχοντα ἀπελθεῖν εἰς τὴν γέενναν (εἰς τὸ πῦρ τὸ
καὶ ἐὰν ὁ πούς σου σκανδαλίζῃ σε, ἀπόκοψον αὐτόν·   [ἄσβεστον).
   καλόν ἐστίν σε εἰσελθεῖν εἰς τὴν ζωὴν χωλόν,
ἢ τοὺς δύο πόδας ἔχοντα βληθῆναι εἰς τὴν γέενναν.
καὶ ἐὰν ὁ ὀφθαλμός σου σκανδαλίζῃ σε, ἔκβαλε αὐτόν·
   καλόν σέ ἐστιν μονόφθαλμον εἰσελθεῖν εἰς τὴν βασιλείαν τοῦ θεοῦ,
ἢ δύο ὀφθαλμοὺς ἔχοντα βληθῆναι εἰς τὴν γέενναν.

Lk. 17³ᶠ· (or Matt. 18¹⁵, ²²): ἐὰν ἁμάρτη ὁ ἀδελφός σου, ἐπιτίμησον
   καὶ ἐὰν μετανοήσῃ, ἄφες αὐτῷ.   [αὐτῷ,
   καὶ ἐὰν ἑπτάκις τῆς ἡμέρας ἁμαρτήσῃ εἰς σὲ
   καὶ ἑπτάκις ἐπιστρέψῃ πρός σε λέγων· μετανοῶ, ἄφες αὐτῷ.

Lk. 14⁸⁻¹⁰: ὅταν κληθῇς ὑπό τινος εἰς γάμους, μὴ κατακλιθῇς εἰς τὴν
                                                [πρωτοκλισίαν,
   μήποτε ἐντιμότερός σου ἦ κεκλημένος ὑπ' αὐτοῦ,
   καὶ ἐλθὼν ὁ σὲ καὶ αὐτὸν καλέσας ἐρεῖ σοι· δὸς τούτῳ τόπον,
   καὶ τότε ἄρξῃ μετὰ αἰσχύνης τὸν ἔσχατον τόπον κατέχειν,
   ἀλλ' ὅταν κληθῇς, πορευθεὶς ἀνάπεσε εἰς τὸν ἔσχατον τόπον,
   ἵνα ὅταν ἔλθῃ ὁ κεκληκώς σε ἐρεῖ σοι· φίλε, προσανάβηθι
                                                [ἀνώτερον·
   τότε ἔσται σοι δόξα ἐνώπιον πάντων τῶν συνανακειμένων σοι.

Lk. 14¹²⁻¹⁴: ὅταν ποιῇς ἄριστον ἢ δεῖπνον,
μὴ φώνει τοὺς φίλους σου μηδὲ τοὺς ἀδελφούς σου μηδὲ τοὺς συγγενεῖς
                                                [σου μηδὲ γείτονας πλουσίους,
   μήποτε καὶ αὐτοὶ ἀντικαλέσωσίν σε καὶ γένηται ἀνταπόδομά σοι·
   ἀλλ' ὅταν ποιῇς δοχήν,
   κάλει πτωχοὺς ἀναπήρους χωλοὺς τυφλούς,
   καὶ μακάριος ἔσῃ, ὅτι οὐκ ἔχουσιν ἀνταποδοῦναί σοι.
   ἀνταποδοθήσεται δέ σοι ἐν τῇ ἀναστάσει τῶν δικαίων.

3. QUESTIONS[1]

Matt. 6²⁷//Lk. 12²⁵: τίς (δὲ) ἐξ ὑμῶν μεριμνῶν δύναται προσθεῖναι ἐπὶ
   τὴν ἡλικίαν αὐτοῦ πῆχυν ἕνα;
Mk. 2¹⁹ par.: μὴ δύνανται οἱ υἱοὶ τοῦ νυμφῶνος, ἐν ᾧ ὁ νυμφίος μετ'
   αὐτῶν ἐστιν, νηστεύειν;
Lk. 6³⁹//Matt. 15¹⁴: μήτι δύναται τυφλὸς τυφλὸν ὁδηγῆσαι;
                        οὐχὶ ἀμφότεροι εἰς βόθυνον ἐμπεσοῦνται;
Mk. 9⁵⁰ (cp Matt. 5¹³; Lk. 14³⁴ᶠ·): καλὸν τὸ ἅλα· ἐὰν δὲ τὸ ἅλα ἄναλον
   γένηται, ἐν τίνι αὐτὸ ἀρτύσετε;

---

[1] Lk. 16¹¹ᶠ· is quoted above; Matt. 5⁴⁶ᶠ·, 6²⁶, ²⁷, 7³ᶠ· ⁹ᶠ· follow below. Here perhaps I
should mention Matt. 7¹⁶: μήτι συλλέγουσιν ἀπὸ ἀκανθῶν σταφυλάς; ἢ ἀπὸ τριβόλων σῦκα;
which is mentioned above under Lk. 6⁴³ᶠ· Rabbinic examples are contained in numerous
apophthegms. Cp. besides e.g. in Kid. 4¹⁴: 'Have you ever in your life seen a wild beast or
bird carrying on a trade?' etc. Strack-B. I, 436, etc.

Even if the Marcan form ought to be abbreviated, its interrogative character on which the reconstructed Q version in Matthew and Luke is based is manifestly original.

Mk. 4²¹ par. (or Matt. 5¹⁵//Lk. 11³³): μήτι ἔρχεται ὁ λύχνος ἵνα ὑπὸ τὸν μόδιον τεθῇ ἤ ὑπὸ τὴν κλίνην; οὐχ ἵνα ἐπὶ τὴν λυχνίαν τεθῇ; Even if the Marcan version ought to be abbreviated, the interrogative form is in any case original.

Mk. 8³⁶ᶠ· par.: τί (γὰρ) ὠφελεῖ ἄνθρωπον κερδῆσαι τὸν κόσμον ὅλον
[καὶ ζημιωθῆναι τὴν ψυχὴν αὐτοῦ;
τί γὰρ δοῖ ἄνθρωπος ἀντάλλαγμα τῆς ψυχῆς αὐτοῦ;

4. Longer Passages

Matt. 5³⁹ᵇ⁻⁴²//Lk. 6²⁹ᶠ·:
(ἀλλ') ὅστις σε ῥαπίζει εἰς τὴν δεξιὰν σιαγόνα, στρέψον αὐτῷ καὶ
[τὴν ἄλλην.
καὶ τῷ θέλοντί σοι κριθῆναι καὶ τὸν χιτῶνά σου λαβεῖν, ἄφες αὐτῷ
[καὶ τὸ ἱμάτιον.
καὶ ὅστις σε ἀγγαρεύσει μίλιον ἕν, ὕπαγε μετ' αὐτοῦ δύο.
τῷ αἰτοῦντί σε δός,
καὶ τὸν θέλοντα ἀπὸ σοῦ δανίσασθαι μὴ ἀποστραφῇς.
Matt. 5⁴⁴⁻⁴⁸//Lk. 6²⁷ᶠ·, ³²⁻³⁶:
ἀγαπᾶτε τοὺς ἐχθροὺς ὑμῶν,
καλῶς ποιεῖτε τοῖς μισοῦσιν ὑμᾶς,
εὐλογεῖτε τοὺς καταρωμένους ὑμᾶς,
προσεύχεσθε περὶ τῶν ἐπηρεαζόντων ὑμᾶς.

ὅπως γένησθε υἱοὶ τοῦ πατρὸς ὑμῶν τοῦ ἐν οὐρανοῖς,
ὅτι τὸν ἥλιον αὐτοῦ ἀνατέλλει ἐπὶ πονηροὺς καὶ ἀγαθούς,
καὶ βρέχει ἐπὶ δικαίους καὶ ἀδίκους.
ἐὰν γὰρ ἀγαπήσητε τοὺς ἀγαπῶντας ὑμᾶς, τίνα μισθὸν ἔχετε;
οὐχὶ καὶ οἱ τελῶναι τὸ αὐτὸ ποιοῦσιν;
καὶ ἐὰν ἀσπάσησθε τοὺς ἀδελφοὺς ὑμῶν μόνον, τί περισσὸν ποιεῖτε;
οὐχὶ καὶ οἱ ἐθνικοὶ τὸ αὐτὸ ποιοῦσιν;
ἔσεσθε οὖν ὑμεῖς τέλειοι ὡς ὁ πατὴρ ὑμῶν ὁ οὐράνιος τέλειός ἐστιν.

I give the first imperative section in Luke's version. His is more likely to be the original form, since he gives otherwise parallel elements in abridged form. Matthew puts the second section on the final motive into imperative form for considered stylistic reasons. Because he uses this section at the end of the whole complex, Luke has to insert before it some new-formed imperatives. In this and in the third passage Matthew also has the more original form in respect of detail. Whether the last imperative is to be taken as the end of the complex, or whether, as in Luke (and then in Luke's form) it is the beginning of what follows, is, in my view, uncertain.

Matt. 7¹⁻⁵//Lk. 6³⁷ᶠ·, ⁴¹ᶠ· Neither Matthew nor Luke seems to have preserved the original form at the beginning. Since it is sure that Luke has added vv. 39f., perhaps vv. 37b, 38 more or less derive from him too. With some reserve I have inserted into the text of Matthew what seems to me original in Luke. Perhaps Luke's καὶ μὴ καταδικάζετε is an alternative translation in which the saying was also handed down, and which Luke has simply inserted at this point. To it belongs the stylistically cited motive ᾧ γὰρ μέτρῳ κτλ and this by association secured the introduction of the quite different saying δίδοτε κτλ. With the end of Luke, v. 38, cp. Mk. 4²⁴.

μὴ κρίνετε, ἵνα μὴ κριθῆτε·
   ἐν ᾧ γὰρ κρίματι κρίνετε, κριθήσεσθε.
καὶ μὴ καταδικάζετε, καὶ οὐ μὴ καταδικασθῆτε.
ἀπολύετε, καὶ ἀπολυθήσεσθε·
   ᾧ γὰρ μέτρῳ μετρεῖτε, ἀντιμετρηθήσεται ὑμῖν.
τί δὲ βλέπεις τὸ κάρφος τὸ ἐν τῷ ὀφθαλμῷ τοῦ ἀδελφοῦ σου,
   τὴν δὲ ἐν τῷ σῷ ὀφθαλμῷ δοκὸν οὐ κατανοεῖς;
ἢ πῶς ἐρεῖς τῷ ἀδελφῷ σου· ἄφες ἐκβάλω τὸ κάρφος ἐκ τοῦ
                             [ὀφθαλμοῦ σου,
   καὶ ἰδοὺ ἡ δοκὸς ἐν τῷ ὀφθαλμῷ σου.
ὑποκριτά, ἔκβαλε πρῶτον ἐκ τοῦ ὀφθαλμοῦ σου τὴν δοκόν,
καὶ τότε διαβλέψεις ἐκβαλεῖν τὸ κάρφος ἐκ τοῦ ὀφθαλμοῦ τοῦ
                             [ἀδελφοῦ σου.

Matt. 7⁷⁻¹¹//Lk. 11⁹⁻¹³: αἰτεῖτε, καὶ δοθήσεται ὑμῖν,
          ζητεῖτε, καὶ εὑρήσετε,
          κρούετε, καὶ ἀνοιγήσεται ὑμῖν.
     πᾶς γὰρ ὁ αἰτῶν λαμβάνει,
     καὶ ὁ ζητῶν εὑρίσκει,
     καὶ τῷ κρούοντι ἀνοιγήσεται.
ἢ τίς ἐστιν ἐξ ὑμῶν ἄνθρωπος, ὃν αἰτήσει ὁ υἱὸς αὐτοῦ ἄρτον,
   μὴ λίθον ἐπιδώσει αὐτῷ;
ἢ καὶ ἰχθὺν αἰτήσει,
   μὴ ὄφιν ἐπιδώσει αὐτῷ;
εἰ οὖν ὑμεῖς πονηροὶ ὄντες οἴδατε δόματα ἀγαθὰ διδόναι τοῖς
                         [τέκνοις ὑμῶν,
πόσῳ μᾶλλον ὁ πατὴρ ὑμῶν ὁ ἐν τοῖς οὐρανοῖς δώσει ἀγαθὰ
                         [τοῖς αἰτοῦσιν αὐτόν.

Matt. 6²⁵ᶠ·, ²⁸ᵇ⁻³³//Lk. 12²²⁻²⁴, ²⁷⁻³¹:
  (—) μὴ μεριμνᾶτε τῇ ψυχῇ ὑμῶν τί φάγητε,
   μηδὲ τῷ σώματι ὑμῶν τί ἐνδύσησθε.
οὐχὶ ἡ ψυχὴ πλεῖόν ἐστιν τῆς τροφῆς,
   καὶ τὸ σῶμα τοῦ ἐνδύματος;
ἐμβλέψατε εἰς τὰ πετεινὰ τοῦ οὐρανοῦ,
   ὅτι οὐ σπείρουσιν οὐδὲ θερίζουσιν οὐδὲ συνάγουσιν εἰς ἀποθήκας.
καὶ ὁ πατὴρ ὑμῶν ὁ οὐράνιος τρέφει αὐτά.
οὐχὶ ὑμεῖς μᾶλλον διαφέρετε αὐτῶν;
καταμάθετε τὰ κρίνα τοῦ ἀγροῦ πῶς αὐξάνουσιν·
   οὐ κοπιῶσιν οὐδὲ νήθουσιν.

λέγω δὲ ὑμῖν ὅτι οὐδὲ Σολομὼν ἐν πάσῃ τῇ δόξῃ αὐτοῦ περιεβάλετο
[ὡς ἓν τούτων.
εἰ δὲ τὸν χόρτον τοῦ ἀγροῦ σήμερον ὄντα καὶ αὔριον εἰς κλίβανον
[βαλλόμενον ὁ θεὸς οὕτως ἀμφιέννυσιν,
οὐ πολλῷ μᾶλλον ὑμᾶς, ὀλιγόπιστοι;
μὴ οὖν μεριμνήσητε λέγοντες· τί φάγωμεν ἢ τί πίωμεν ἢ τί περι-
πάντα γὰρ ταῦτα τὰ ἔθνη ἐπιζητοῦσιν.   [βαλώμεθα;
οἶδεν γὰρ ὁ πατὴρ ὑμῶν ὁ οὐράνιος ὅτι χρῄζετε τούτων ἁπάντων.
ζητεῖτε δὲ (πρῶτον) τὴν βασιλείαν (—) αὐτοῦ.
καὶ ταῦτα πάντα προστεθήσεται ὑμῖν.

Matt. 6²⁷//Lk. 12²⁵ stands out clearly as an intrusive insertion, and
because of it there follows the new formulation of Matt. 6²⁸ᵃ//Lk. 12²⁶, in
order to link on with the context (Matthew) or alternatively to render the
insertion fruitful in the context (Luke).

(c) Form and History of the Logia[1]

We can clearly recognize the basic forms of the Old Testament
and Jewish mashal in these sayings. Exceptions can be made of
sayings like Lk. 9⁶²; Mk. 10¹⁵, ²³ᵇ, 11²⁴; Matt. 17²⁰, 19¹², sayings
which in their express religious character are too far from a proverb
alike in their type of piety and in their form. Otherwise there is a
whole series of sayings which in their form are completely single-
stranded meshalim: Mk. 2¹⁷ᵃ ¹⁹ᵃ, 9⁴⁰, ⁴⁹, 10⁹, ³¹; Mat.t. 5¹⁴ᵇ,.
6²⁷, ³⁴ᵇ, 8²²ᵇ, 12³⁴ᵇ, 22¹⁴, 24²⁸; Lk. 4²³, 5³⁹, 6³¹, 10⁷ᵇt, 16¹⁵ᵇ
There are further sayings with the form of a double-stranded
mashal: Mk. 2²⁷, 3²⁷?, 4²¹,²²,²⁵, 7¹⁵, 8³⁵, ³⁶ᶠ., 9⁵⁰ᵇ?, 10²⁵; Matt.
6³⁴ᵃ, 10¹⁶ᵇ, 12³⁰, ³⁵, 13⁵²?; Lk. 6³⁹, 12³, 14¹¹, 16⁹; Pap. Ox.
I, 5.
It is but a slight development of the two-stranded mashal when
one part is divided into two synonymous halves. This happens in
Matt. 8²⁰, where the first part, an antithetic parallelism, is double-
stranded and yet constitutes one part of a synonymous parallelism.
In a similar way the imperative in Matt. 7⁶ is given in synonymous
parallelism, with the motive for it (hardly conceivable as two-
stranded) following as a third line. Of the two imperatives in Matt.
10²⁸, the first makes reference to its object in a double way. Such
development is quite natural, and it can be traced in the Old
Testament mashal.[2]
Another sort of development takes place when the brief mashal
is enlarged with an illustration, as often happens in the wisdom

[1] On C. F. Burney, *The Poetry of Our Lord*, cp. J. Hempel, *Th.L.Z.*, 51, 1926, col. 435f.,
and M. Dibelius, *Th.R.*, N.F. 1, 1929, p. 212.
[2] Evidence for this is given below in treating of individual examples.

literature of the Old Testament, e.g. instead of Prov. 4[18f.] being in the form of a double-stranded mashal:

> 'The way of the wicked is as darkness,
> But the path of the righteous is as the shining light.'

we actually have:

> 'The way of the wicked is as darkness;
> They know not at what they stumble.
> But the path of the righteous is as the shining light,
> That shineth more and more unto the perfect day.'

Or a description of the nature of the wicked man, Prov. 4[16f.] is attached to the warning against him, 4[14f.], just as 4[12] describes the good way to which 4[11] is an exhortation. Such illustrations can become relatively detailed moral pictures, where the mocker, the drunkard, the harlot are described; cp. Prov. 1[11-14], 5[3-6], 7[6-23], 23[31-35], etc.[1] Not infrequently, we find direct speech interwoven in such illustrations, cp. Prov. 1[11-14], 5[9-14]; Sir. 29[24-28]. Among the Synoptic sayings Lk. 14[8-10, 12-14]; Matt. 6[19-21, 25-33], 7[13f.], belong to this class, and perhaps Matt. 5[44-48], as well. Prov. 6[6-8], demands special comparison with Matt. 6[25-33]. In certain circumstances such illustrations can obviously be an enlargement of an original mashal, where some Wisdom poet has given spiritual amplification to some popular proverb. The question whether the same can be said of Synoptic sayings leads us to consider the history of the logia.

First we may note a distinct tendency in the tradition to combine different but similar sayings. In Mk. 8[34-37] at least three sayings are joined together, which originally were certain to have been separate.

(34) εἴ τις θέλει ὀπίσω μου ἐλθεῖν,
    ἀπαρνησάσθω ἑαυτὸν καὶ ἀράτω τὸν σταυρὸν αὐτοῦ
    καὶ ἀκολουθείτω μοι.

(35) ὃς γὰρ ἐὰν θέλῃ τὴν ψυχὴν αὐτοῦ σῶσαι,
    ἀπολέσει αὐτήν.
    ὃς δ' ἂν ἀπολέσει τὴν ψυχὴν αὐτοῦ [—],
    σώσει αὐτήν.

(36) τί γὰρ ὠφελεῖ ἄνθρωπον
    κερδῆσαι τὸν κόσμον ὅλον
    καὶ ζημιωθῆναι τὴν ψυχὴν αὐτοῦ;

(37) τί γὰρ δοῖ ἄνθρωπος ἀντάλλαγμα τῆς ψυχῆς αὐτοῦ;

We find the first two sayings also in Matt. 10[38f.] (apart from the

---

[1] Such illustrations are also found in the Proverbs of Amen(em)ope, e.g. Chs. 9 and 11; *Altorient. Texte zum A.T.*, pp. 41f.

parallels to Mk. 8³⁴⁻³⁷), though without the last, and also in Lk. 14²⁷, 17³³. This means that we must regard the conjunction of Mk. 8³⁴ᶠ· with 8³⁶ᶠ· as secondary, as we must that of Mk. 8³⁴ with 8³⁵ (and Matt. 10³⁸ with 10³⁹)—and this quite apart from arguments which could be based upon the contents of the sayings. It is also evident that possibly Mk. 8³⁶ᶠ· is in the same way composed of two originally independent sayings. Indeed, that it is so is highly probable, for if we examine the points of v. 36 and v. 37 accurately, they are quite different. Both sayings are clearly proverbial, and v. 36 expresses the same idea as Lk. 12¹⁶⁻²⁰: riches are of no avail at death, whereas v. 37 states: Life is the highest good.[1] Thus Mk. 8³⁴⁻³⁷ is a secondary combination, conditioned by slight associations.

Similarly two originally independent logia have been joined in Q, Lk. 12²ᶠ·//Matt. 10²⁶ᶠ·

> (2) οὐδὲν (δὲ) συγκεκαλυμμένον ἐστὶν
>   ὃ οὐκ ἀποκαλυφθήσεται,
> καὶ κρυπτὸν
>   ὃ οὐκ γνωσθήσεται.
> (3) ἀνθ' ὧν ὅσα ἐν τῇ σκοτίᾳ εἴπατε,
>   ἐν τῷ φωτὶ ἀκουσθήσεται,
> καὶ ὃ πρὸς τὸ οὖς ἐλαλήσατε ἐν τοῖς ταμείοις,
>   κηρυχθήσεται ἐπὶ τῶν δωμάτων.

We find the first of these logia as an isolated saying in Mk. 4²². On the other hand some similar sort of combination lies behind Mk. 4²¹ᶠ·, since v. 22 is clearly secondary, being used as an explanation of v. 21, which, in turn, was originally also an isolated logion, appearing in another context in Lk. 11³³ and Matt. 5¹⁵.

We must clearly think of Matt. 5³⁹ᵇ⁻⁴²//Lk. 6²⁹ᶠ· in the same way: already in Q the injunction not to lend was joined (Matt. v. 42, Lk. v. 30) with one to give to those who asked. This in turn makes possible to conjecture that in Lk. 6⁴³ᶠ· the sentence ἕκαστον (γὰρ) δένδρον ἐκ τοῦ ἰδίου καρποῦ γινώσκεται was originally an unattached maxim[2] which has been attached to v. 43 (if it is not supposed that v. 43 has been composed out of the maxim itself, see below); but the conclusion (which in its interrogative version in Matt. 7¹⁶ᵇ is more original) seems without doubt to have been originally an unattached saying:

---

[1] This makes it understandable that Luke should pass over Mark's v. 37. If it were really not in his text of Mark, v. 37 would be a secondary accretion in Mark (W. Bussmann, *Synoptische Studien*, I, p. 24), and what has been argued above would be completely confirmed.

[2] Cp. the proverb in Ber. 48a (Strack-B. I, 467): 'Every pumpkin can be told from its sap.'

μήτι συλλέγουσιν ἀπὸ ἀκανθῶν σταφυλάς;
ἢ ἀπὸ τριβόλων σῦκα;

But in any case the junction of Lk. 6⁴⁵ with vv. 43f. which was already made in Q is secondary; for in vv. 43f. it is not only words that are thought of as among the fruits, but deeds especially, whereas v. 45 speaks only of words. Finally it is possible that in v. 45 too we have a combination of two originally independent sayings. Matthew gives them in reverse order in 12³⁴ᵇ, ³⁵.[1]

It is possible in the same way that the last sentence of Matt. 6¹⁹⁻²¹//Lk. 12³³ᶠ. ὅπου (γάρ) ἐστιν ὁ θησαυρός σου, ἐκεῖ ἔσται καὶ ἡ καρδία σου could have been originally an independent maxim. And perhaps one may think of Lk. 12⁴⁸ᵇ παντὶ (δὲ) ᾧ ἐδόθη πολὺ κτλ as another originally independent saying out of which the similitude-like sentence vv. 47, 48a has been compiled. Whether we have to think of Mk. 2²⁷ᶠ. in the same way seems to me doubtful (see pp. 16f.); v. 28, that man is lord of the Sabbath, could only have existed as a conclusion from v. 27—that the Sabbath was made for man. By contrast v. 27 could have existed as a saying in its own right, as in fact a Rabbinic saying was also handed down: 'The Sabbath was given to you, not you to the Sabbath' (Strack-B. II, 5). In the same way Rabbinic tradition confirms the view that in Matt. 6³⁴ two originally independent sayings have been added on to vv. 25-33.

With v. 34a compare San. 100b: 'Fret not over tomorrow's trouble, for thou knowest not what the day may bring forth.' And with v. 34b compare the oft-quoted saying: 'Sufficient is the evil in the time thereof' (Strack-B. I, 441). The verse is not found in Luke.

In a whole series of these instances we are admittedly dealing simply with probabilities, or even bare possibilities. But it is a necessity of right method that we should be concerned with such possibilities, because the sure instances make the tendency of the tradition clear, and we still have to reckon with the tendency even when the sources do not permit of an unambiguous judgement. But it would be wrong even here to talk about a law that had no exceptions, for I should be far from denying that occasionally a saying has been abridged, perhaps because it would not have fitted the context of the evangelist. In this way we may reckon e.g. Mk. 10⁴³ᶠ. (ὃς ἂν θέλῃ κτλ) as original compared with Mk. 9³⁵ (εἴ τις θέλει κτλ), or Matt. 10²⁴ compared with Lk. 6⁴⁰ (see below). And it is always possible that Lk. 12²ᶠ. is original in comparison with Mk. 4²², though I think that the converse is more likely.

---

[1] Again this seems to have confirmation in the Rabbinic tradition in which the saying circulated: 'That which is in the heart, is also in the mouth'; cp. Strack-B. I, 639.

Another tendency of the tradition can be seen (even in the oral stage, which I have not intended to exclude from what I have already said) when to a saying already in circulation a new formulation (analogous formulation) is fitted and occasioned by it. It is plain that not only in ancient Israel (as its proverbial wisdom shows)[1] but also among the Rabbis ingenuity contrived to present a truth (or the meaning of an author) in the greatest possible multiformity, whether by forming a double saying or a double similitude or by inventing a new saying or similitude to add to the one in circulation. There is an example in B.B. 12b:

> 'If a man is in disfavour (with Heaven)
> he does not readily come into favour,
> And if a man is in favour
> he does not readily fall into disfavour.'

The first half of this double saying did circulate alone (Strack-B. I, 661) and it would have existed alone in the first place. The same is true of the three parallel sayings in 'Er. 13b (see above, p. 71), of which at least the second is an analogous formulation to the first.[2] That this is true also of the Christian tradition can be shown in the first place by some extra-canonical examples. When Pseudo-Ign. writes in Ad Magn. 9[3], that in the λόγια it says:

> ὁ μὴ ἐργαζόμενος (γὰρ) μὴ ἐσθιέτω,
> ἐν ἱδρῶτι (γὰρ) τοῦ προσώπου σου φάγῃ τὸν ἄρτον σου,

it is quite plain that the proverb quoted in 2 Th. 3[10] has been enlarged by a new formulation in the manner of Gen. 3[19]. Even clearer is 1 Clem. 13[2].

> ἐλεᾶτε, ἵνα ἐλεηθῆτε,
> ἀφίετε, ἵνα ἀφεθῇ ὑμῖν·
> ὡς ποιεῖτε, οὕτως ποιηθήσεται ὑμῖν·
> ὡς δίδοτε, οὕτως δοθήσεται ὑμῖν·
> ὡς κρίνετε, οὕτως κριθήσεσθε·
> ὡς χρηστεύεσθε, οὕτως χρηστευθήσεται ὑμῖν·
> ᾧ μέτρῳ μετρεῖτε, ἐν αὐτῷ μετρηθήσεται ὑμῖν.

No-one can doubt that this series of proverbs has come into being in regard to both form and content, by analogous formulation, no

---

[1] We may suggest that Prov. 6[27f.]; 15[16f.] and especially perhaps Sir. 10[1–5] are to be understood thus.

[2] The first and the last sayings also circulated alone (Strack-B. I, 921). For similitudes, see examples below. For proverbs, I quote an example from Alb. Socin, *Arabische Sprichwoerter und Redensarten* (Tuebinger Universitaetsschr. 1878), no. 397: 'Not everything which is round is a nut.' The saying is also found with addition: 'And not everything that is long is a banana (or an almond).'

matter which parts one may identify as earlier or later.[1] Similarly Did. 1[3-5] is composite, made up of material from Matt. 5[39-48] (or Lk. 6[27-36]) and some new formulations. Lastly I cite Clem. Alex. Strom., IV, 6, 41:

... μακάριοι (φησίν) οἱ δεδιωγμένοι ὑπὲρ τῆς δικαιοσύνης,
ὅτι αὐτοὶ ἔσονται τέλειοι.
καὶ μακάριοι οἱ δεδιωγμένοι ἕνεκα ἐμοῦ,
ὅτι ξουσι τόπον ὅπου οὐ διωχθήσονται ...

So it seems almost too much of a good thing in Mk. 9[43-47] when one after another hand and foot and eye are called seducers, particularly in the case of the foot, which could play the role of seduction, though it is not very obvious. Actually in Matt. 5[29] only hand and eye are mentioned, and the saying about the foot can be shown as a secondary analogous formulation to the saying about the hand. The situation is the same, in my view, in regard to Lk. 16[10-12]; vv. 11f. is an explanatory development of v. 10.[2] So it is possible at least to ask the question whether Mk. 2[22] is an analogous formulation to 2[21], while admitting that Matt. 7[9f.]; Mk. 3[24f.] (or Matt. 12[25]; Lk. 11[17]) give the impression of being unitary compositions. But it is possible that to Matt. 10[24]:

οὐκ ἔστιν μαθητὴς ὑπὲρ τὸν διδάσκαλον,
οὐδὲ δοῦλος ὑπὲρ τὸν κύριον αὐτοῦ.

the saying in v. 25a was added later:

ἀρκετὸν τῷ μαθητῇ ἵνα γένηται ὡς ὁ διδάσκαλος αὐτοῦ,
καὶ ὁ δοῦλος ὡς ὁ κύριος αὐτοῦ (on v. 25b see below).

In the same way, it is possible that Lk. 17[4] (καὶ ἐὰν ἑπτάκις τῆς ἡμέρας ἁμαρτήσῃ κτλ) is a later expansion of v. 3 (ἐὰν ἁμάρτῃ ὁ ἀδελφός σου κτλ).

Matt. 7[1-5] (on Judging) is more complicated. Possibly vv. 3-5 (The Mote and the Beam) did not originally belong to the exhortation in vv. 1f., whether 3-5 were originally independent, or whether they were formulated as an addition to 1f. A comparison with Lk. 6[37] · and 1 Clem. 13[2] shows how easily new formulations do accumulate in the tradition. Very likely both sorts can be found in the Lucan

---

[1] Cp. R. Knopf, ad loc. in *Ergaenzungsband zum Handbuch zum N.T.*
[2] Juelicher, *Gleichnisreden*, II, p. 513, thinks that v. 10 sounds like an originally secular 'maxim', while v. 11f. introduces a religious meaning, and perhaps never existed in Aramaic at all. I do not believe this latter assumption to be necessary. The dominical saying, found in 2 Clem. 8[5]; Iren., II, 34[3] and Hilarius, *Epistula seu lib.*, Ch. 1, and whose Greek form K. Koehler gives (*T.S.K.*, 1922, pp. 173-8) as: εἰ ἐν τῷ μικρῷ πιστοὶ οὐκ ἐγένεσθε, τὸ μέγα τίς δώσει ὑμῖν I would not think of, as Koehler does, as the original form, originally in Luke alone, but rather as a secondary formulation based on Lk. 16[10-12].

text: secondary formulation in v. 37 and insertion of a different saying in 38a. Similarly Matt. 7⁷⁻¹¹ is a passage that has had several stages of development, or has been enlarged by the addition of originally independent sayings, though naturally judgement on which has taken place is bound to be subjective.¹ Further, in all these instances, it is immaterial whether the oral or the literary tradition has been operative: there is no difference in principle.

We must also raise the question about *secondary expansion* even when there is no series of complete sayings, each one comprehensible in itself; but it must also be asked where a complete saying is followed by a sentence only intelligible in the light of what it follows.² The question in that case is this: Do we have an unitary conception, or a later addition? So we can conjecture with some probability that the saying about salt is retained in its original form in Mk. 9⁵⁰: (καλὸν τὸ ἅλα) ἐὰν (δὲ) τὸ ἅλα ἄναλον γένηται, ἐν τίνι αὐτὸ ἀρτύσετε; What follows in Q (εἰς οὐδὲν ἰσχύει ἔτι κτλ Matt. 5¹³) looks like secondary expansion. But the reverse possibility must always be kept open. The same has to be said of the relation of Mk. 4²¹ to the Q form in Matt. 5¹⁵; Lk. 11³³ (Light).

One may also conjecture that in Matt. 6²⁴ the saying οὐδεὶς δύναται δυσὶν κυρίοις δουλεύειν is independent, and that it has been expanded by the next two sentences ἢ γὰρ τὸν ἕνα μισήσει κτλ. The concluding sentence in particular,³ with its application in the second person, gives the impression of being an edifying addition. Then we may suppose that in Matt. 6²²ᶠ· the first sentence: ὁ λύχνος τοῦ σώματός ἐστιν ὁ ὀφθαλμός is the original kernel, and that it has been explained in the two following lines. But maybe the sentence is too weak in content, so that it is better regarded as a secondary introduction to the original double saying (ἐὰν ᾖ ὁ ὀφθαλμός σου ἁπλοῦς . . . ἐὰν δὲ . . .) (Klostermann). But the conclusion is certainly secondary expansion (εἰ οὖν τὸ φῶς τὸ ἐν σοί . . .) and it is still further expanded in Luke. Lk. 11³⁴⁻³⁶ shows that the saying really demanded explanatory expansion. In a somewhat different way Mk. 10⁴³ᵇ, ⁴⁴ (ὃς ἂν θέλῃ μέγας γενέσθαι ἐν ὑμῖν κτλ) may be deemed an originally independent saying, the foil for it having been

---

¹ In the Mandaean Ginza R., I, Lidzb., p. 18.8, among other exhortations reminiscent of Matt. 25³¹ᶠᶠ· there is the saying: 'For everyone who gives, receives, and everyone who lends, receives payment.' The saying about seeking and finding is frequently and variously cited in Ginza R.; cp. in Lidzb., p. 285.9: 'What ye seek, ye shall find: what ye ask, ye shall be given.' Cp. pp. 190.11f.; 271.8.

² Thus the continuation of the saying in Sanh. 100b, quoted on p. 84 is: 'Peradventure tomorrow he is no more: thus he shall be found grieving over a world that is not his.' This is manifestly a secondary formulation.

³ οὐ δύνασθε θεῷ δουλεύειν καὶ μαμωνᾷ.

added later in vv. 42, 43a (οἱ δοκοῦντες ἄρχειν κτλ.), when perhaps the second person was used in the saying for the first time. We may support this conclusion by appealing to Mk. 9[35] which, even if it be in like manner an abbreviation of what was originally a double saying, is still in a form that does not contain the second person.

On Matt. 5[44-48] I simply point to the possibility that vv. 46f. may very well be secondary in relation to vv. 44f.: and further, that it is by no means certain that v. 48 was originally connected with vv. 44–47, as the divergent tradition in Luke itself shows.[1] We have already rejected v. 27 from Matt. 6[25-34] as a secondary insertion, and v. 34 as a duplicate supplement. It is hardly possible to determine how far the rest of the composition is an unity. It is conceivable that v. 25 is an independent logion; vv. 26, 28–30 could also have been originally independent, and thereafter joined with v. 25, though they could also be a further continuation of v. 25. We may more confidently regard vv. 31–33 as a secondary construction. How far, in all these examples the oral tradition has been at work, or how far the written, is a question which neither can be decided, nor is of chief importance.

Again the essential problem concerns *possibilities*. In such matters we ought not too quickly to raise the question of 'genuineness'. Just as a saying with an unitary conception cannot without more ado be reckoned as a genuine saying of Jesus, no more is a secondary composition of necessity not genuine. For the tradition could have combined[2] genuine sayings of Jesus and Jesus could have taken a saying already in circulation, and himself enriched it. Neither may we argue from the aesthetic value of the sayings, e.g. in Matt. 6[25-34]: for what is artistic in these sayings is not due to their individual, personal way of seeing things and speaking, but rests entirely on their popular character, which is their inheritance in the care that society takes of the whole genus of proverbial sayings. Similar proverbs appear—naturally alongside inferior ones—in the wisdom of the Old Testament, as in popular proverbial literature in general. But in the end individual cases must not be treated on their own. The issue is not what judgement is made upon one particular instance, but only whether we have to reckon with a tendency of the tradition to enlarge upon older sayings. And that does seem to me to be the case. E.g. this is how we must account for the collection of Ben Sira: the author took over an ancient popular collection of sayings, combined and enlarged

---

[1] The parallel in Mandaean Ginza R., VII, Lidzb., pp. 216, 7f.: 'The merciful who feels pity is like the sun which shines on good and evil' permits no provisional conclusion to one side or the other.

[2] I recall again the procedure in Did. 1[3-5]; 1 Clem. 13[2]; cp. also perhaps Justin, Apol., I. 15.

it, and in all probability also collected combinations and enlargements of other 'sages' which he had before him. Some doubtful instances of such a kind at once come under discussion from a particular point of view. I will here quote two examples, 'possibilities' for all I care, but which, in my view, have the greater support of the evidence.

Sir. 29[1-6], first, combines some sayings, which were manifestly independent originally:

> 'He that sheweth mercy will lend unto his neighbour;
> And he that strengtheneth him with his hand keepeth the commandments.'

Further:

> 'Lend to thy neighbour in time of his need;
> And pay thou thy neighbour again in due season.'

Possibly v. 3 has to be reckoned as a form of secondary development:

> 'Confirm thy word, and keep faith with him;
> And at all seasons thou shalt find what thou needest.'

However this can also be an independent saying. The same applies to v. 4:

> 'Many have reckoned a loan as a windfall,
> And have given trouble to those that helped them.'

But the detailed description of the slow-paying debtor and the cheated believer which occupies four lines in vv. 5 and 6, is no longer a proverb, but a secondary construction of the teacher of Wisdom.

In the same way 11[18] is obviously a proverb.

> 'There is that waxeth rich by his wariness and pinching,
> And this is the portion of his reward.'

But in v. 19 there is added an explanatory enlargement:

> 'When he saith, I have found rest,
>   And now I will eat of my goods;
> Yet he knoweth not what time shall pass,
>   And he shall leave them to others, and die.'

But these possibilities appear in a new light, if we keep other instances in mind, in which we may with certainty detect on the part of the sources an *expansion of an original saying by addition*. Indeed this is a case of expansion in the written tradition, whereas in the cases previously examined it might have been either oral or written. When at the end of the saying in Matt. 17[20] about the power of faith we read: καὶ οὐδὲν ἀδυνατήσει ὑμῖν, we can, by comparison with Lk. 17[6] and with the Marcan variant (Mk. 11[23]) show that this pedantic observation is an addition. An addition is attached to the

D

Golden Rule in Matt. 7¹²: οὗτος γάρ ἐστιν ὁ νόμος καὶ οἱ προφῆται. This corresponds to the addition made in Matt. 22⁴⁰ in the greatest commandment: ἐν ταύταις ταῖς δυσὶν ἐντολαῖς ὅλος ὁ νόμος κρέμαται καὶ οἱ προφῆται. The addition made in Matt. 15²⁰ᵇ to the last saying about purity has been discussed already; it is more important in the present context to note that for the saying about the tree and the fruit an application is provided: ἄραγε ἀπὸ τῶν καρπῶν αὐτῶν ἐπιγνώσεσθε αὐτούς. There is a similar addition to the saying about the disciple and the master in Matt. 10²⁵ᵇ: εἰ τὸν οἰκοδεσπότην βεελζεβοὺλ ἐπεκάλεσαν, πόσῳ μᾶλλον τοὺς οἰκιακοὺς αὐτοῦ, though that may well not be a sentence coined by Matthew, but one in which he has made use of an independent saying. So too the μὴ οὖν φοβεῖσθε κτλ Matt. 10³¹//Lk. 12⁷ᵇ may be an editorial ending already suggested by Q, in joining vv. 29f. to v. 28. Matt. 12³⁶ may possibly be regarded in the same way.

Luke has augmented the saying in 9⁶⁰ ἄφες τοὺς νεκροὺς κτλ by adding σὺ δὲ ἀπελθὼν διάγγελλε τὴν βασιλείαν τοῦ θεοῦ, and that this is an addition can be seen by a comparison with Matt. 8²², just as additions may be detected by comparing Lk. 4⁴³, 9², ¹¹, 16¹⁶, 18²⁹, 21³¹ with Mk. 1³⁸, 6⁷,³⁴; Matt. 11¹²; Mk. 10²⁹, 13²⁹. The addition to the saying about the kingdom divided against itself Lk. 11¹⁸ᵇ is more clumsy: ὅτι λέγετε ἐν βεελζεβοὺλ ἐκβάλλειν με τὰ δαιμόνια. We can also see how in the Nazarean version of Matt. 18²² the saying of Jesus is expanded by an explanatory motive: καὶ γὰρ ἐν τοῖς προφήταις μετὰ τὸ χρισθῆναι αὐτοὺς ἐν πνεύματι ἁγίῳ εὑρίσκετο ἐν αὐτοῖς λόγος ἁμαρτίας.[1] From the history of the text I cite the great insertion of, e.g., Codex D in Matt. 20²⁸ where, by means of the transitional ὑμεῖς δὲ ζητεῖτε ἐκ μικροῦ αὐξῆσαι καὶ ἐκ μείζονος ἔλαττον εἶναι a variant from Lk. 14⁸⁻¹⁰ has been introduced. There is a very instructive example from the apocryphal tradition in 2 Clem. 5²⁻⁴: after a quotation of a variant of Matt. 10¹⁶//Lk. 10³, there follows, after a question by Peter, an explanatory dominical saying: μὴ φοβείσθωσαν τὰ ἀρνία τοὺς λύκους μετὰ τὸ ἀποθανεῖν αὐτά. Akin to this is the version of Matt. 19¹⁶ꜰꜰ. found in the Nazarean version, where Jesus comments on the demand to keep the commandments which he had made in reply to the rich young man's question: *Quomodo dicis, legem feci et prophetas? Quoniam scriptum est in lege: diliges proximum tuum sicut te ipsum; et ecce multi fratres tui filii Abrahae amicti sunt stercore, morientes prae fame, et domus tua plena est multis bonis, et non egreditur omnino aliquid ex ea ad eos.*

[1] A. Schmidtke, *Neue Fragmente und Untersuchungen zu den judenchristlichen Evangelien*, p. 23. Cp. Jerome, c. Pelag., III. 2.

Naturally such additions are not found exclusively at the end of a saying. We may cite the form which Matt. 10[26] has found in Pap. Ox. 654[5]:

[πᾶν τὸ μὴ ἔμπροσ]θεν τῆς ὄψεως σου καὶ [τὸ κεκρυμμένον] ἀπὸ σοῦ
ἀποκαλυφθήσετ[αι σοι
οὐ γάρ ἐσ]τιν κρυπτὸν ὃ οὐ φανε[ρὸν γενήσεται]
καὶ τεθαμμένον ὃ ο[ὐκ ἐγερθήσεται].

As a rule the *expansion which any saying undergoes at its beginning* derives from the context in which it is found. A primitive example is the way in which the saying in Mk. 4[24] is introduced by βλέπετε τί ἀκούετε. Similarly ἔχετε πίστιν θεοῦ in Mk. 11[22] constitutes the introduction for the saying in v. 23. In the same way we may regard ἐγὼ δὲ λέγω ὑμῖν μὴ ἀντιστῆναι τῷ πονηρῷ in Matt. 5[39] as an introduction by Matthew to insert the following saying in the context of interpreting the law. Correspondingly, ἐγὼ δὲ λέγω ὑμῖν μὴ ὀμόσαι ὅλως in Matt. 5[34] may very well be a formulation by Matthew in place of an originally simpler form such as 'Swear not!', unless indeed, Matthew has himself formulated the whole section vv. 34–37 on the basis of some copy, to which Matt. 23[16-22] may correspond. Doubtless ἀπὸ τῶν καρπῶν αὐτῶν ἐπιγνώσεσθε αὐτούς in Matt. 7[16a] is a transition formulation by Matthew. The same may be judged of Matt. 12[34a]: γεννήματα ἐχιδνῶν, πῶς δύνασθε ἀγαθὰ λαλεῖν πονηροὶ ὄντες, which does not accord with anything in Luke. Matthew wanted to make the connection of the following saying with the context even stronger by this insertion—and so turned them both round. Another connecting piece by Matthew is 10[26a]: μὴ οὖν φοβηθῆτε αὐτούς. And likewise the famous saying in Lk. 12[57]: τί δὲ καὶ ἀφ' ἑαυτῶν οὐ κρίνετε τὸ δίκαιον is nothing else than a connecting piece by Luke intended to join vv. 58f. to vv. 54–56. A simpler connecting piece is that in Lk. 6[27a]: ἀλλὰ ὑμῖν λέγω τοῖς ἀκούουσιν. The following are perhaps introductory formulations: καλὸν τὸ ἅλας (Mk. 9[50]) and ὁ λύχνος τοῦ σώματός ἐστιν ὁ ὀφθαλμός Matt. 6[22] (see above, p. 87).

Metaphorical sayings in particular invite such introductory or concluding sentences. Of the additions already quoted possibly Matt. 10[25b] and certainly Lk. 11[18b] are of this kind. Matt. 7[16a, 20] may also be classed here, formulations by which Matthew adapts the saying about fruits to the false prophets. Similarly the saying in Matt. 6[24c] οὐ δύνασθε θεῷ δουλεύειν καὶ μαμωνᾷ, which we have already supposed to be an addition, may be correspondingly classified here. Similar explanations manifestly apply to the introductions to the sayings about salt and light in Matt. 5[13] and [14]: ὑμεῖς ἐστε τὸ ἅλα τῆς γῆς or τὸ φῶς τοῦ κόσμου by which Matthew ascribes to the disciples sayings which in Mark and Luke alike have been handed on without interpretation; similarly with Matt. 5¹⁶ where the application is given by οὕτως λαμψάτω τὸ φῶς ὑμῶν κτλ. The same must be said of the phrase with which Matthew introduces the saying about the blind leaders of the blind in Matt. 15¹⁴: ὁδηγοί εἰσιν τυφλοὶ τυφλῶν. We have already shown (p. 17) that Mk. 7¹⁵ must be regarded as an enigma to which a commentary is provided in 7¹⁸ᶠ· and which is joined to v. 15 with vv. 16f., and that there is a still later expansion in vv. 20–23. Further, Mk. 2¹⁹ᵇ, ²⁰, which on other grounds has for a long time been considered secondary, is a dubious usage of the original saying in 19a, which has the typical form of a question and as such is used stylistically as a counter-question (see above, p. 41). But the second half of Mk. 2¹⁷ οὐκ ἦλθον καλέσαι δικαίους ἀλλὰ ἁμαρτωλούς, to which Lk. 5³² adds εἰς μετάνοιαν¹ is also a secondary explanation of the saying about the physician; however, in Justin, Apol., I, 15 it appears with the addition: θέλει γὰρ ὁ πατὴρ ὁ οὐράνιος τὴν μετάνοιαν τοῦ ἁμαρτωλοῦ ἢ τὴν κόλασιν αὐτοῦ. It does not seem so probable to me that Mk. 3²⁶, or alternatively Matt. 12²⁶; Lk. 11¹⁸, is a secondary explanation of the saying about the house and the kingdom divided against itself. How easy it was for an explanation of a dominical saying to be itself regarded as a component part of it is shown in 2 Clem. 8⁵ᶠ· where after the quotation of a variant of Lk. 16¹⁰ᶠ· we read: ἄρα οὖν τοῦτο λέγει (what is referred to is what follows) τηρήσατε τὴν σάρκα ἁγνὴν καὶ τὴν σφραγίδα ἄσπιλον, ἵνα τὴν ζωὴν ἀπολάβωμεν.² W. Luetgert proffered a modern example of this procedure at the Theological Conference in Frankfurt-on-Main on 12 October 1928 when he quoted Jn. 15⁵ᵇ in the form:

> 'Without me ye can do nothing,
> With me ye can do everything.'

Finally the history of the text illustrates the procedure we have described, e.g. Lk. 11³⁴⁻³⁶. This pericope is hardly analysable any more; only this much is plain—that there are various attempts in vv. 35 and 36 to explain the obscure saying.

Manifestly we are here dealing with phenomena that are univer-

---

¹ The saying appears with this addition in Justin, Apol., I, 15.8; Ps. Justin, De Resurr., 7, p. 593B. It is minus the addition in 2 Clem. 2⁴; while in Barn. 5⁹ the manuscripts vary.

² Cp. also 2 Clem., Hom. 3⁵: οὐκ ἔξεστιν τὰ ἡτοιμασμένα τοῖς υἱοῖς τῆς βασιλείας ἀγαθὰ τοῖς διὰ τὸ ἀδιάκριτον ἀλόγοις ζῴοις παρεικασθεῖσιν παρασχεῖν. On this occasion the commentary has displaced the saying (Mk. 7²⁷); and in the process Mk. 7⁶ has had its effect. The tradition of the Lord's sayings at the Last Supper shows the same sort of thing, where in various ways 1 Cor. 11²⁶ has been co-ordinated with the dominical sayings in the words of institution. Cp. G. P. Wetter, Altchristliche Liturgien, I, 1921, pp. 62f.

sally applicable, and not just with peculiarities of one or other Evangelist. It is possible to differ about the precise limits, but in my opinion it is impossible to deny the *general tendency of the tradition*. It is also clear that we cannot confine our observations simply to those occasions where we can make a comparison with a source, but that we must push our considerations back even behind our earliest sources, Q and Mark, and in this way gain a glimpse into the growth of the tradition before it was fixed in the sources to which we have access.

It is further characteristic of the tradition of the sayings that, alongside expansions of a different kind, we may detect transformations, in part associated with them, for which various motives come into play. The most superficial motive is linguistic, and this is particularly operative in Luke. He avoids Semitisms and not infrequently recasts parallelisms, a procedure which has been noticed for a very long time now. This enables me to make but a brief reference to Lk. 6[40], 11[17], 12[33f.], 13[23f.] as convenient examples.[1] It is moreover characteristic of such transformations for the question in Mk. 4[21] (saying about the light) to become a (negative) statement in Matt. 5[15]//Lk. 11[33]: there is a similar relationship between Matt. 7[16b] (about fruits) and Lk. 6[44b] and between Lk. 6[39] (about the blind leaders of the blind) and Matt. 15[14b]. Generally speaking the interrogative form may well be more original, since it better matches the argumentative character of the mashal. But it is not possible to affirm that as a universal law without qualification, for Mk. 3[27] (on the spoiling of the strong man) appears as a question in Matt. 12[29].

The *dogmatic motive* which we saw at work in Mk. 2[17b, 19b, 20] also operates in Mk. 8[35], where ἀπολέσαι τὴν ψυχήν is given a christological expansion by the addition of the words ἕνεκεν ἐμοῦ καὶ τοῦ εὐαγγελίου (this last noun is not read by either Matthew or Luke), in the same way as Matthew has inserted the words (10[39]) ἕνεκεν ἐμοῦ in the supposed Q version, which lacks the inserted words in Lk. 17[33], as they were also lacking in John's copy for Jn. 12[25]. A well-known dogmatic transformation can be seen in Mk. 10[45], the original form of which may well be found in Lk. 22[27] (see below). By dogmatic motive I naturally do not mean a conscious introduction of particular dogmas, but something which is for the most part an unconscious tincture of Christian ideas. In this way we can understand the relationship of Mk. 11[22f.] to Matt. 17[20], or Lk. 17[6]. The original saying about the faith that removes mountains is formally just as much a paradox as the saying about the camel and the

---

[1] Cp. also P. Wendland, *Die urchristlichen Literaturformen* (Handbuch zum N.T., I, 3), p. 285; E. Norden, *Agnostos Theos*, pp. 357ff.

needle's eye in Mk. 10²⁵ par., though it does not refer to faith that works miracles, but rather applies to the ὀλιγόπιστοι in general (cp. Matt. 6³⁰ par.). Matthew gave it its relationship to miracle-working faith by inserting it into the context of a healing story. Mark related it specifically to the prayer of faith as the addition of v. 24 shows, and so he inserts: καὶ (ὃς ἂν) μὴ διακριθῇ κτλ; in this way he has recoined the saying for discussions of the kind that appear in Jas. 1⁶ᶠ·; Herm. Mand., IX.[1]

There is no lack of parallels in the extra-canonical literature. The version of Matt. 7²³ in the Nazarean version runs: ἐὰν ἦτε ἐν τῷ κόλπῳ μου καὶ τὸ θέλημα τοῦ πατρός μου τοῦ ἐν οὐρανοῖς μὴ ποιῆτε, ἐκ τοῦ κόλπου μου ἀπορρίψω ὑμᾶς.[2] And we may compare with this 2 Clem. 4⁵: εἶπεν ὁ κύριος· ἐὰν ἦτε μετ' ἐμοῦ συνηγμένοι ἐν τῷ κόλπῳ μου καὶ μὴ ποιῆτε τὰς ἐντολάς μου, ἀποβαλῶ ὑμᾶς καὶ ἐρῶ ὑμῖν· ὑπάγετε ἀπ' ἐμοῦ, οὐκ οἶδα ὑμας, πόθεν ἐστέ, ἐργάται ἀνομίας. From this it can be seen very clearly how very liable dominical sayings were to such changes. Or we may recall the indirect reproduction of Matt. 28¹⁹ in Ap. Const., V, 7³⁰: μαθητεῦσαι πάντα τὰ ἔθνη καὶ βαπτίσαι εἰς τὸν θάνατον αὐτοῦ. How easily such variations could be regarded as the actual form of a dominical saying. It makes no difference to the principle that we are here concerned not with actual logia, but with other dominical sayings. As an example of change in an actual logion we may cite, perhaps, 2 Clem. 8⁵: εἰ τὸ μικρὸν οὐκ ἐτηρήσατε, τὸ μέγα τίς ὑμῖν δώσει; λέγω γὰρ ὑμῖν ὅτι ὁ πιστὸς ἐν ἐλαχίστῳ καὶ ἐν πολλῷ πιστός ἐστιν (cp. Lk. 16¹⁰; see above, p. 86 n. 1), the continuation of which is quoted above. Further, the form which has been given to the saying about the city set on a hill, Matt. 5¹⁴, Pap. Ox. 1⁶: πόλις οἰκοδομουμένη ἐπ' ἄκρον (ὄ)ρους ὑψηλοῦς καὶ ἐστηριγμένη οὔτε πε[σ]εῖν δύναται οὔτε κρυ[β]ῆναι. Finally the continuation of Matt. 7⁷ᵃ in Orig. De Orat. 14¹:

αἰτεῖτε τὰ μεγάλα καὶ τὰ μικρὰ ὑμῖν προστεθήσεται,
καὶ αἰτεῖτε τὰ ἐπουράνια καὶ τὰ ἐπίγεια ὑμῖν προστεθήσεται.

Also the addition which has been made to the end of Matt. 10²⁶ in Pap. Ox. 654⁵ (see above, p. 91), has to be described as dogmatically motivated; for the words (οὐ) τεθαμμένον ὃ οὐκ ἐγερθήσεται are obviously an expression of the doctrine of the resurrection.[3]

Other alterations are due to an insertion into a context; and, indeed, that can also produce specifically 'Christian' changes in that

[1] Cp. A. Fridrichsen, *Le Problème du Miracle*, pp. 54–56.
[2] Schmidtke, op. cit., pp. 297ff. In general it is the Nazarean version that is thought of.
[3] Cp. Reitzenstein, *Goett. gel. Anz.*, 1921, p. 172.

the introduction of a logion into the Christian tradition in certain circumstances determines its form, and puts the saying in quite a new light.

The outlook of the context has given form to the composition in Matt. 7¹⁶⁻²⁰. As we have already seen, v. 16a ἀπὸ τῶν καρπῶν αὐτῶν ἐπιγνώσεσθε αὐτούς is a transitional formula, which establishes a connection with the warning against false prophets in v. 15. The words μήτι συλλέγουσιν κτλ in v. 16b are a saying from the tradition, but v. 17 (οὕτως πᾶν δένδρον ἀγαθὸν καρποὺς καλοὺς ποιεῖ κτλ) is a new and pedantic formulation, corresponding to nothing in Luke, and disturbs the connection between v. 16b and v. 18 (οὐ δύναται δένδρον ἀγαθὸν κτλ) in Q. The words πᾶν δένδρον μὴ ποιοῦν καρπὸν καλὸν κτλ in v. 19 are a formulation by association of ideas which 3¹⁰ follows: and to be able to connect the saying Matthew has inserted the word καλόν, which, rightly, is missing from 3¹⁰. Finally we have already shown that v. 20 (ἄραγε — ἐπιγνώσεσθε αὐτούς) is a summarizing end-formulation.

Similarly Matthew has provided a connection in 10²⁶⁻³¹. The introductory words μὴ οὖν φοβηθῆτε αὐτούς and v. 31 (μὴ οὖν φοβεῖσθε) are, as we have already shown, editorial constructions. Whereas for the most part Matthew clearly takes the logia in the order they have already received in Q and gives them in what is essentially their original form, he has, for the sake of making his connection, introduced in v. 27 a modification that has been generally misinterpreted. He has modified the original mashal by introducing the first person into a saying about the relationship of the mission of the disciples to the preaching of Jesus. That is to say, Luke is not secondary because he distinguished two periods of the Christian mission (how could the first period have been described as an εἰπεῖν ἐν τῇ σκοτίᾳ and a λαλεῖν πρὸς τὸ οὖς ἐν τοῖς ταμείοις!), but Matthew has made the modification: originally the proverb was not in any way a 'comfortable word', a fact which the unaffected conception of Matt. 10²⁶//Lk. 12² (or Mk. 4²²) should have made clear. It was rather a warning from folk-lore to tell someone a secret, and just as profane, for example, as the German saying, 'The sun will bring it to light'.[1] The saying in Q (as in Mark) has already been interpreted as a promise, for only so was it serviceable to the

---

[1] So also v. Sybel, T.S.K., 1927/8, p. 386. For a parallel cp. Ecc. 10²⁰: 'Curse not the king, no, not in thy thought; and curse not the rich in thy bedchamber: for a bird of the air shall carry the voice, and that which hath wings shall tell the matter.' Further the Arabian proverb (L. Bauer, Volksleben im Lande der Bibel, 1903, p. 235): 'One word, exchanged between two persons will be spread among two thousand.' There are Rabbinic examples in Strack-B. I, 578f.

Christian tradition. In the changes he makes, Matthew carries straight on with this particular process.

Corresponding to this, as we have in part mentioned already, are the facts about Matt. 5¹³⁻¹⁶: The audience is addressed as ὑμεῖς ἐστε κτλ. Vv. 13 and 14 are formulae by Matthew, to join the sayings on to the context of the discourse to the disciples; v. 16 is his closing formulation which provides the application, while the saying about the city set on a hill is inserted into v. 14 from some other tradition, and its meaning is now determined by its context.

We can see the same processes at work in Luke in spite of the fact that in general he is more conservative in the way he orders the logia. Thus he has tried in 6²⁷⁻³⁵ to make one unitary section on the theme of loving one's neighbour out of the pericopes on retaliation and loving one's neighbour. First the words ἀλλὰ ὑμῖν λέγω τοῖς ἀκούουσιν form a Lucan introduction (see above). Then it is very hard to say whether in vv. 27f. Luke has added to the text of Q or had it in a form different from that of Matthew; in just the same way as, in my view, it is hard to say whether in v. 29b he is more original than Matthew. But in any case it is he who has introduced vv. 29f. and indeed v. 31 at this point, as a comparison with Matthew shows. I think that v. 34 is a formulation peculiar to Luke who wants here to make use of the motif of δανίσασθαι (Matt. 6⁴²) that has been overlooked in v. 30. In the same way v. 35a (πλὴν ἀγαπᾶτε τοὺς ἐχθροὺς ὑμῶν κτλ) is Luke's formulation: here he has to repeat the imperative from v. 27 in order to be able to introduce the promise in v. 35b (in Matt. v. 45 it directly follows the imperative with which the verse begins), because he omitted it earlier so as to bring the imperative of the other pericope in v. 29 (retaliation) after v. 28. We have already discussed Lk. 6³⁶ = Matt. 5⁴⁸: one of the two has made alterations; either Matthew to use the saying as the conclusion of what has preceded it, or Luke to make it the introduction to what follows.

The remarkable section Matt. 5²⁵ᶠ·//Lk. 12⁵⁸ᶠ· has undergone a complete change in consequence of its introduction into an alien context. In Matthew the words are simply an exhortation to reconciliation, understood in part metaphorically, in that the judge points to God. Originally it appears to have been a similitude: just as in civil society we do everything at the proper time so as not to be brought before the judge, we must do the same in the sight of God. That means, we must do penance at the right time! (The imperative form is striking; yet Matt. 7⁶ is likewise a metaphor in the same form.) It is not entirely clear how Luke understood the pericope; he seems to have retained it in better state than Matthew.

As some of the examples quoted have shown, and most strikingly Matt. 10²⁶ᶠ·//Lk. 12²ᶠ· (or Mk. 4²²), we are not simply concerned with editorial changes to which the traditional material was subjected, but we also find that without any such change some new light was often thrown upon material by its incorporation into the Church's tradition. A typical example of how a mashal with the profane wisdom of folk-lore as its content was given a religious, indeed a specifically 'Christian' meaning by its absorption into the tradition of the Church, is supplied by the two sayings that have been joined together in Mk. 8³⁶, ³⁷. Jewish wisdom literature offers many parallels to the first of them, the meaning of which, as we have seen above (pp. 82f.), is constitutive for the story of the rich fool (Lk. 12¹⁶⁻²⁰). We may cite as an example Sir. 11¹⁸ᶠ·:

> 'There is that waxeth rich by his wariness and pinching,
> And this is the portion of his reward.
> When he saith, I have found rest
> And now will I eat of my goods;
> Yet he knoweth not what time shall pass,
> And he shall leave them to others, and die.[1]

Were Mk. 8³⁶ to be by some chance among the proverbs or in the Book of Sira, no-one would misinterpret its meaning. Mk. 8³⁷, which is linked to it by association of ideas (see above), is a proverb that gives expression, exactly as folk-lore does, to the idea that life is itself the highest good; and oriental literature offers parallels to that. This is the theme of the passage in *A Thousand and One Nights*:

> 'Thou canst easily exchange thine estate for another,
> But for thy life thou canst find no substitute.'

Further (ibid.):

> 'When a slave has plunged thee into misfortune,
> With what willst thou then redeem thy life?
> Bondservants indeed willst thou find in plenty
> But for thy life thou canst find no substitute.'[2]

---

[1] Cp. further Strack-B. II, 190f. and Ps. Phokyl., 116f. (J. Bernays, *Ges. Abh*, I, p. 258).

οὐδεὶς γινώσκει τί μεταύριον ἢ τί μεθ' ὥραν·
ἄσκοπός ἐστι βροτῶν κάματος, τὸ δὲ μέλλον ἄδηλον.

Otherwise this idea is only a constitutive presupposition for Lk. 12¹⁶⁻²⁰. The specific point lies in the warning against provoking God by too great assurance and confidence of prosperity. It rests upon a faith in God which is effective in the widespread fear of being 'called home'. Cp. the proverb: 'The birds, which sing at dawn, are devoured by the cats', and others in Pfister, *Blaetter zur bayr. Volkskunde*, 10, 1925, pp. 13f.

[2] Cp. also G. W. Freytag, *Arabum Proverbia*, I, 1838, p. 97, no. 284: *Quum mortis tempus adest, amplus campus angustus est*; ibid., II, 1839, p. 577, no. 591: *Non est obiurgatio post mortem*. Pantschatranta (German tr. by R. Schmidt, p. 134), I, p. 443: 'On the loss of a

The same kind of remarks apply to Matt. 8²⁰//Lk. 9⁵⁸, a saying which is completely full of the pessimism of folk-lore, as it has found its artistic expression in Ecc. and Job, and which was applied to the person of Jesus for the first time, perhaps, in the Greek Church (see p. 28).[1]

We must think of this process as particularly active in the metaphorical sayings. Were the sayings about salt and light in Matt. 5¹³, ¹⁴ᶠ·; Lk. 14³⁴ᶠ·, 11³³ or Mk. 9⁵⁰, 4²¹ in their origin proverbs of a secular 'wisdom'? It is plain that neither the evangelists' explanations nor the place that the sayings have in their context give us any information as to their original meaning. No more does the position of Mk. 2²¹ (new cloth and new wine) provide any sort of guarantee for its original meaning. Were these originally quite secular meshalim? Certainly the contrast of old and new seems to constitute the point of the saying and not to be used just fortuitously as an example of irreconcilable opposites. But does it favour the old or the new? The situation seems clearer in Mk. 3²⁷. The saying could originally have meant that the victory of Jesus over the demon had demonstrated that God had already overthrown the devil's reign. Yet here too it is possible that some 'proverbial saying' (Klostermann) is being used; cp. Isa. 49²⁴ᶠ·

> 'Shall the prey be taken from the mighty,
> Or the lawful captures be delivered? . . .'

Ps. Sol. 5⁴ᶠ·:

> οὐ γὰρ λήψεται σκῦλα παρὰ ἀνδρὸς δυνατοῦ.
> καὶ τίς λήψεται ἀπὸ πάντων ὧν ἐποίησας, ἐὰν μὴ σὺ δῷς;

What was manifestly in its origin a secular proverb ὁ μὴ ὢν μετ' ἐμοῦ κτλ is applied as early as Q (Matt. 12³⁰//Lk. 11²³) to the person of Jesus. The saying about the harvest and the labourers (Matt. 9³⁷ᶠ·// Lk. 10²) is applied to the Christian mission; what is its original meaning (and its original form) likely to have been? Matt. 15¹³ (πᾶσα φυτεία κτλ) refers in its context to the Pharisees; as does

---

good piece of land or of a good slave we may say: In the loss of a slave the Prince of death also strikes; lost land is easily recovered, but not a lost slave.' Wetstein, who says on the verse (as parallel to Matt. 16²⁶): *sententia est proverbialis, quam Christus a vita temporali ad alteram et aeternam transfert*, brings a whole series of parallels from classical literature to mind; cp. esp. Hom., *Il.*, 9, 401f.: οὐ γὰρ ἐμοὶ ψυχῆς ἀντάξιον οὐδ' ὅσα φασὶν "Ἴλιον ἐκτῆσθαι, εὖ ναιόμενον πτολίεθρον.

[1] The parallel mentioned by Wetstein from Plutarch Tib. Gracch. 9, p. 828c which has already been cited has a much more particular meaning, but it illustrates the folk-lore character of the language. ὡς τὰ μὲν θηρία τὰ τὴν Ἰταλίαν νεμόμενα καὶ φωλεὸν ἔχει καὶ κοιταῖόν ἐστιν αὐτῶν ἑκάστῳ καὶ καταδύσεις, τοῖς δὲ ὑπὲρ τῆς Ἰταλίας μαχομένοις καὶ ἀποθνήσκουσιν ἀέρος καὶ φωτός, ἄλλου δὲ οὐδενὸς μέτεστιν, ἀλλ' ἄδικοι καὶ ἀνίδρυτοι μετὰ τέκνων πλανῶνται καὶ γυναικῶν. The use of the parallel in Luria, *Z.N.W.*, 25, 1926, pp. 282–6 is fantastic.

Matt. 15¹⁴ (blind leaders of the blind) which Matthew has adapted for the purpose by applying the first sentence directly to the Pharisees: τυφλοί εἰσιν ὁδηγοί τυφλῶν. We can no longer recover its original meaning. Luke has it, without this particular reference in 6³⁹, obviously because he meant it to be understood in the light of vv. 37f. He has inserted it between sayings about judgement so that it comes to mean: how canst thou set thyself up for a judge, who art thyself blind! Luke follows this with a saying about the disciple and his master (6⁴⁰) from which he has omitted that half of the parallelism which is not suitable in the context; but the remainder derives its meaning from the context: there is only one true judicial authority, Jesus. By contrast Matt. 10²⁴ reports the saying: the disciple can expect no better fate than that of his master! So one can have no confidence even if a metaphorical saying is already woven into its context in Q, e.g. the eschatological interpretation of Matt. 24²⁸// Lk. 17³⁷ᵇ (the carcase and the eagles). The situation in Matt. 5²⁵f.// Lk. 12⁵⁸f· is different to this extent: that it is possible to go beyond the tradition and infer the original meaning of the saying as a call to repentance (see above); but in this case we are not dealing with a proper logion. And for the great majority of metaphorical sayings we have to confess that we can no longer determine their original meaning, if it was anything more than general proverbial teaching (the same applies, as we shall show later to the similitudes proper). So we have to reckon on a certain amount of the stuff of the tradition having been secular in its origin.

Before I pursue the consequences any further I would like to mention a parallel phenomenon. I have already remarked that the book of Ben Sira is in some ways analogous to the collection and editing of the spoken material in the Synoptics. That is true even to the extent that very often secular wisdom has been set in the light of legal piety by the author's editing of his material.[1] The basic principle of this editing becomes clear if Sir. 4¹⁴ is compared with Prov. 8¹⁷.

Prov. 8¹⁷: 'I (Wisdom) love them that love me
    And those that seek me diligently shall find me.'

Sir. 4¹⁴: 'They that do her (Wisdom) service shall serve the Holy One
    And them that love her the Lord doth love.'

The name of God appears here in the place of Wisdom. As for the mode of editing we may first quote Sir. 37¹⁰⁻¹⁵ as an example:

10. Take not counsel with one that looketh askance at thee;
    And hide thy counsel from such as are jealous of thee.

[1] In another way this applies, as is well known, to the Book of Ecclesiastes.

11. Take not counsel with a woman about her rival;
    Neither with a coward about war;
    Nor with a merchant about exchange;
    Nor with a buyer about selling;
    Nor with an envious man about kindliness;
    Nor with a sluggard about any kind of work;
    Nor with a hireling in thy house about any kind of work;
    Nor with an idle servant about much business:
    Give not heed to these in any matter of counsel.
12. (But rather be continually with a godly man,
    Whom thou shalt have known to be a keeper of the command-
        ments,
    Who in his soul is as thine own soul,
    And who will grieve with thee, if thou shalt miscarry.)
13. And make the counsel of thy heart to stand;
    For there is none more faithful unto thee than it.
14. For a man's soul is sometime wont to bring him tidings,
    More than seven watchmen that sit on high on a watch tower
15. (And above all this intreat the Most High,
    That he may direct thy way in truth.)

It is at once apparent that v. 15 is a supplement; but the same is true
of v. 12. The more it embodies pedantic logic the more it is opposed
to the spirit of popular wisdom. The author has edited a passage of
old time 'wisdom' which had for its theme 'The Best Counsellor',
and which in the resigned and humorous scepticism of the proverb
said: 'In the end there is only one counsellor a man can rely on—his
own heart.'[1] Naturally the pious editor has to reckon that his law-
abiding contemporaries are no less good a counsellor, and can only
say as much of his own heart if it is directed by God. In Sir. 9[15f.] the
editor has split up an older double saying and constructed for each
half a parallel member of his own, to connect the piety of the Law
with the old secular wisdom:

15. Let thy converse be with men of understanding;
    (And let thy discourse be in the law of the Most High).

16. Let just men be the companions of thy board;
    And let thy glorying be in the fear of the Lord.

[1] Cp. with this the Egyptian saying: 'A heart that is strong in the abode of evil is a good
companion for its lord.' (A. Erman, *Die Literatur der Aegypter*, 1923, p. 150); further the
Arabian proverb in *Alb. Socin, Arabische Sprichwoerter und Redensarten* (Tuebing. Universitaetsschr., 1878), no. 299: 'Thy true friend is thine own bosom.' In the same way in Pindar,
Pyth. 3, pp. 28f. the νοῦς of Loxias is his 'most honoured confidant' who will not touch a lie,
and whom neither God nor man can deceive.

In Sir. 11[10-13] the editor has used a passage from ancient wisdom (perhaps a combination of passages) in which it is described how a man's success is not dependent upon his activity, how busy care often remains in vain, and how God often brings the slothful to honour. Perhaps v. 14 is also an ancient proverb:

> Good things and evil, life and death,
> Poverty and riches, are from the Lord.

But we can be sure that in v. 15 the editor gives expression to his own new piety:

> The gift of the Lord remaineth with the godly,
> And his good pleasure shall prosper for ever.

Similarly the popular wisdom of 11 [18-19] (or [20]) is corrected by the spirit of vv. 21, 22. In the same way Ch. 24 has vv. 1–22 from traditional wisdom and v. 25 is related to the Torah.[1]

In this discussion I have in the first place postponed any question as to the *genuineness of the logia*. But in regard to it there are a number of possibilities. It is quite possible that Jesus sometimes took a popular proverb and altered it, and he could certainly sometimes have coined a secular proverb himself. But it is also possible for secular proverbs to have been turned into sayings of Jesus by the Church when it set them into the context of its tradition. Are there any criteria by which we can make decisions in particular instances? In general it may be said that the tradition would hardly have preserved the occasional use of a popular proverb by Jesus; and it is also difficult to believe that the changes and revaluation of such meshalim as are to be found in the tradition have in fact retained some reminiscence of such changes and revaluations by Jesus. For these are most closely conditioned by their contexts (cp. Lk. 12[2f.]; Mk. 8[36f.]; Matt. 5[13, 14f.]) and they in turn are certainly secondary. It is much more likely that we have among the logia many sayings coined by Jesus, and the more so as their individual content is greater or the more they show Jesus as the preacher of repentance and the coming kingdom, as the one demanding truthfulness. Actually many logia have been derived from the traditional wisdom and first taken into the Christian tradition by the Church, and treated as a saying of Jesus.[2] It is of course quite possible that there was no original

---

[1] Cp. G. Klein, *Der aelteste christl. Katechismus und die jued. Propaganda-literatur*, 1909, pp. 32f.; cp. there pp. 30–33 generally on the struggle between the Torah and Hochmah; also A. Schlatter, *Die Sprache und Heimat des vierten Evangelisten*, 1902, pp. 14f.

[2] A parallel to this can be seen when later sayings from the Christian tradition were put into the mouth of Mohamed: cp. J. Goldziher, *Muhammedanische Studien*, II, 1890, pp. 384–393.

intention to turn these sayings into dominical utterances by taking them into the Christian tradition, but that they were first of all accepted as useful paranetic material, just as may be the case with eschatological prophecies. *Was Q originally a collection of dominical sayings and nothing else?* Did it not perhaps contain alongside a few apophthegms and some sayings of Jesus, some late Jewish proverbs, laws and prophecies which were taken over by the Church, or originated in it —and indeed with full awareness of the fact? In any case we can understand how easily sayings which were handed down in the Church for edification and warning could be treated as dominical. We need only to remember what was said above (pp. 91f.) about secondary explanations to see how quickly sayings of another origin could be quoted as dominical sayings in later literature. In this way ἀγάπη καλύπτει πλῆθος ἁμαρτιῶν (1 Pet. 4⁸, cp. Jas. 5²⁰) is given as a dominical saying in Did. lat. II, 2³, and so is a formulation made out of Eph. 4³⁰; 1 Thess. 5¹⁹ in Ps. Cyprian De Aleator., 3. Eph. 4²⁶ appears repeatedly as a saying of the Lord (cp. Klostermann, *Kleine Texte*, no. 11, p. 10); 1 Cor. 7³¹ is quoted as εὐαγγελικὸν ῥῆμα, etc.[1]

When we pass from general considerations to examine the logia concretely, it is frequently impossible to do more than pass a subjective judgement. It seems to me that the following belong to the secular meshalim which have been made into dominical sayings in the tradition:

Lk. 12²ᶠ·//Matt. 10²⁶ᶠ·or Mk. 4²² (on what is hidden), see pp. 95f., 97.

Mk. 8³⁶ par. (Of what use is it at Death to have gained the world?), see pp. 82f., 97.

Mk. 8³⁷ par. (Life is the highest good), see p. 97.

Matt. 8²⁰//Lk. 9⁵⁸ (Man's homelessness), see pp. 28, 98.

Mk. 6⁴ (A prophet in his own country), see pp. 31f.

Mk. 9⁵⁰ or Matt. 5¹³//Lk. 14³⁴ᶠ· (Salt), see p. 98.

Mk. 4²¹ par. or Matt. 5¹⁵//Lk. 11³³ (Light), see p. 89.

Mk. 2²¹ᶠ· par. (New patches and new wine), see pp. 97f.[2]

Matt. 12³⁰//Lk. 11²³ (ὁ μὴ ὢν μετ' ἐμοῦ κτλ), see p. 99.

Matt. 15¹⁴//Lk. 6³⁹ (Blind leaders of the blind), see p. 99.

---

[1] I think it a rewarding task to seek out the logion-like sayings of the N.T. Epistles, and of the early Christian literature outside the gospels in general. How far is it taken from primitive Christian proverbial literature, how far further developed and how far newly coined? The Synoptic tradition is only one, though admittedly the most important section of this field.

[2] Even in the case of Mk. 2¹⁹ᵃ we could ask whether we are not concerned with a proverb (μὴ δύνανται οἱ υἱοὶ τοῦ νυμφῶνος ἐν ᾧ ὁ νυμφίος μετ' αὐτ ὧν ἐστιν νηστεύειν); cp. the Indian proverb: 'Who eats gruel on a Divali day (i.e. on a feast day)?' J. Hertel, *Katharatnakara*, I, 1920, p. 97.3.

Matt. 10²⁴//Lk. 6⁴⁰ (Disciples and Master), see p. 99.

Matt. 24²⁸//Lk. 17³⁷ᵇ (The carcase and the eagles), see p. 99.

Lk. 5³⁹ (The virtues of old wine). It is hardly likely that the genuine-ness of this saying will be defended since it is already under sus-picion through comparison among the Synoptics.¹

Matt. 6²⁷//Lk. 12²⁵ (Adding to one's stature), a saying which could just as fittingly come between two Old Testament proverbs as it is ill-fitted to be between Matt. 6²⁶ and ²⁸.

Matt. 5¹⁴(The city set on a hill), a saying which is just as badly placed.

Matt. 5⁴²//Lk. 6³⁰ (τῷ αἰτοῦντί σε δός κτλ). In the proverbial wisdom of the Old Testament the saying would have been accepted as wholly congruous: it is scarcely in place between sayings about revenge and love of enemies.

Matt. 7⁶ (Pearls before swine).²

Lk. 10⁷ᵇ//Matt. 10¹⁰ᵇ (The Labourer and his hire), evidently a proverb which has been turned to use by the Church for the instructional material it produced.

Matt. 10¹⁶ᵇ (Wise as serpents), a proverb which has been introduced into the instructional material in the same way.

Matt. 7¹²//Lk. 6³¹ (The golden rule). It is a piece of self-deception to suppose that the positive form of the rule is characteristic for Jesus, in distinction from the attested negative form among the Rabbis. The positive form is purely accidental, for whether it be given positive or negative formulation the saying, as an individual utterance, gives moral expression to a naif egoism.³

Lk. 14¹¹ or Lk. 18¹⁴: Matt. 23¹² (πᾶς ὁ ὑψῶν ἑαυτὸν κτλ), clearly a familiar saying, attached here and there to the tradition.⁴

Mk. 4²⁵ or Matt. 25²⁹; Lk. 19²⁶ (Having and not Having) in which the same remarks apply.

Lk. 16¹⁰ (Faithful in Little Things), see p. 86.

Matt. 13⁵² (The Householder). Matthew was evidently the first to make this into a dominical saying since it suited the end of the similitude speech.

Lk. 14¹²⁻¹⁴ (The Proper Guests). This saying is much more akin to the grudging spirit of the last chapter of Eth. Enoch than to the preaching of Jesus.

¹ Cp. the parallels in Wetstein and Klostermann.
² Cp. Mand. Ginza R., VII, Lidzb., 218.30: 'The words of the wise to the foolish are as pearls to a sow.'
³ Besides the parallels in Strack-B. I, 459 and in Wetstein and Klostermann, cp. also Mand. Ginza R., I, Lidzb., pp. 22, 42f.: 'Do nothing to your neighbour which you yourself dislike.'
⁴ Cp. the parallels in Strack-B. I, 774 (on Matt. 18⁴) and 921 (on Matt. 23¹²) and in Dalman, Jesus-Jeschua, p. 204. See above, p. 71.

Lk. 14$^{8-10}$ (Warning against ambition at table). This is so typical of Wisdom, and so secular a rule of prudence, that we cannot help wondering how it ever came to be included among the sayings of Jesus (cp. Prov. 25$^{6f.}$; Sir. 3$^{17f.}$; Ps. Arist., 263; Lev. R. 1 (105c) in Strack-B. II, 204; stylized as a story in Bin Gorion, *Der Born Judas*, IV, p. 263).

These sayings are hardly if at all characteristic of a new and individual piety that sprang up in Judaism, but are observations on life, rules of prudence and popular morality, sometimes a product of humour or scepticism, full now of sober, popular morality, and now of naif egoism. Quite apart from that, most of these sayings, especially the metaphorical ones, do not have a specific meaning until they appear in a concrete situation. If the Church was really moved to take up these sayings because Jesus had occasionally used or coined one of them, then it failed in so doing to preserve anything characteristic of him. But this judgement must be taken a good deal further than that. The saying (or sayings) about fruit-bearing (Lk. 6$^{43f.}$// Matt. 7$^{16-20}$ or 12^{33}) can hardly be called characteristic. As the connection of Lk. 6$^{43f.}$ with 45 shows (or of Matt. 12^{33} with $^{34f.}$) the proverb, even in Q, ought to go on to the words of men as its fruit. Matthew makes the opposite use of it 7$^{16-20}$, in using it of deeds as opposed to words. Both Matthew and Luke seem to have contradicted the original meaning of the saying which is manifestly concerned with the fruits of human sentiment whether in words or deeds. No one wants to maintain that the saying rises above the standards and outlook of secular wisdom.

But there are sayings which cannot be described as secular wisdom, but have to be reckoned as the expression of a particular piety. But the situation is not really different even with them, in so far as the spirit of such a piety is that of the popular belief in God, which—alongside a recognition of God's sovereign sway—sees a retributive righteousness in world events, much in the way that Lk. 14^{11} (πᾶς ὁ ὑψῶν ἑαυτὸν κτλ) can be interpreted; which trusts God's providence, as Matthew 6$^{25-33}$ expresses it (why is there, e.g., here no characteristically eschatological motivation?); and which reckons on the hearing of prayer, as Matt. 7$^{7-11}$ teaches. Finally not even the sayings about laying up treasure in Matt. 6$^{19-21}$ have anything characteristic; they likewise have no eschatological frame.

It is even more precarious to try to indicate which of the logia Jesus could have taken from secular wisdom and made his own. In itself it is obviously by no means impossible that he should have taken the widespread figure of the doctor who tends the sick and not the healthy (Mk. 2[17]), and used it to defend his own way of going to work. It is equally possible that in a time of resignation he should have applied to himself the proverb about the prophet who is without honour in his native place (Pap. Ox. 1[5]). Or why could he not have used the saying about serving two masters (Matt. 6[24]) in his Sermon if he knew it already as a proverb? Why could he not have expressed his eschatological consciousness and justified his behaviour by the proverb about the senselessness of fasting at a wedding feast (Mk. 2[19])? One can go on asking questions like this about one saying after another, without getting any further. It is necessary to see that the tradition has taken many logia from popular wisdom and piety into itself, and to reckon with the fact that it has done so now and then because Jesus has made use of or coined such a saying.[1] But it must also be seen that many a saying owes its reception into the tradition only to its suitability for a specific sphere of the Church's interests. It will only be in very few cases that one of the logia can be ascribed to Jesus with any measure of confidence: such sayings as arise from the exaltation of an eschatological mood, like Mk. 3[27] (Satan is already overcome) or like the saying about the kingdom divided against itself (Mk. 3[24-26]) if the interpretation in terms of Satan is reliable; further sayings which are the product of an energetic summons to repentance, like Mk. 8[35] (losing life and finding it);[2] Lk. 9[62] (The hand on the plough); Mk. 10[23b, 25] (The Rich and the Kingdom of God); Lk. 9[60a] (ἄφες τοὺς νεκροὺς κτλ); Matt. 7[13f.] (The Narrow Gate). To these we may add the sayings about the first and the last (Mk. 10[31]) and about the many called and the few chosen (Matt. 22[14]), if this last be not a traditional saying of Jewish apocalyptic.[3] And finally we may include sayings which demand a new disposition of mind, like the sayings about purity (Mk. 7[15]), children (Mk. 10[15]), exultation and humility (Lk. 14[11] and 16[15]), revenge (Matt. 5[39b-41]), loving enemies (Matt. 5[44-48]). All these sayings, which admittedly are in part no longer specific examples of logia, contain something characteristic, new, reaching out beyond popular wisdom and piety and yet are in no sense scribal or rabbinic nor yet Jewish apocalyptic. So here if anywhere we can find what is characteristic of the preaching of Jesus.

[1] This is the position of Dalman (*Jesus-Jeschua*, 1922, pp. 200f.) in regard to proverbs and sentences, which are found among the logia of Jesus. But this does not affect the problem of the tradition. In the first example that he deals with in detail (Matt. 7[2]) he ignores the fact that logion appears in the twofold tradition in the Synoptics (Matt. 7[2]; Mk. 4[24]).

[2] To Mk. 8[35] there is a Rabbinic parallel in Dalman, *Jesus-Jeschua*, p. 206; cp. Strack-B. I, 588.

[3] Cp. on Mk. 10[31] and Matt. 22[14] the Rabbinic parallels in Dalman, *Jesus-Jeschua*, p. 205.

These considerations need to be expanded somewhat in a direction where I can at least give some hints.   If the formal and critical analysis permit the conjecture that many Synoptic logia are proverbs from traditional Jewish Wisdom, that conjecture is confirmed by the *many parallels to be found in Jewish and oriental literature generally*.   It is not my task to collect these parallels or to assemble all that others have collected; yet my enquiry would be incomplete were I not to give some samples and so support what I have said, and fill out the impression left by previous presentations.   After Wetstein and Wuensche had made their collection of such parallels the material is amply available in Billerbeck's commentary.   Some particular enquiries also need to be mentioned: Heinrici has brought some to our notice in his enquiry into the history of the ideas of the Sermon on the Mount; there is a fuller collection of such material in regard to the Sermon on the Mount made by E. Bischoff, even if his judgement is sometimes wrong, and P. Fiebig has done the same.[1]   In *Jesus-Jeschua* Dalman has compared the logia of Jesus with Rabbinic parallels (p. 200–209).   This material is made useful for the exegete in the Synoptic commentaries of E. Klostermann's Handbook to the N.T.

With Matt. 5^{42} compare the numerous similar admonitions in Prov. 28^{27}; Sir. $4^{4f.}$, $29^{1f.}$; Tob. 4^{7}; further Bousset, *Religion des Judentums*[3], p. 141 and Stade-Bertholet, *Theologie des A.T.*, II, pp. 91, 186f., 196, 430, 433f.

With Matt. 6^{21}: Baba bathra 11a: 'My fathers stored in a place which can be tampered with, but I have stored in a place which cannot be tampered with.'[2] Cp. Prov. 10^{2}, $11^{4, 28}$.

With Matt. 6^{26}: Kid. 82b (Strack-B. I, 43.6): 'In my whole lifetime I have not seen a deer engaged in gathering fruits, a lion carrying burdens, or a fox as a shopkeeper, yet they are sustained without trouble, though they were created only to serve me, whereas I was created to serve my Maker.   Now, if these, who were created only to serve me are sustained without trouble, how much more should I be sustained without trouble, I who was created to serve my Maker!'[3]

With Matt. 6^{34}: Sanh. 100b: 'Fret not over tomorrow's trouble, for

---

[1] E. Bischoff, *Jesus und die Rabbinen* (Schriften des Instit. Judaic. in Berlin 33), 1905; P. Fiebig, *Jesu Bergpredigt*, 1924. Some of this is quoted above. For Mk. 2^{19a}, p. 102 n. 2; Mk. 8^{37}, pp. 97f. Matt. 12^{34}, p. 84 n. 1. Lk. 6^{44} or Matt. 7^{20}, p. 70 1; Lk. 12^{3} or Matt. 10^{27}, pp. 95f.; Lk. 12^{16-20}, p. 97; Lk. 14^{11}, p. 71.

[2] This saying appears in the tradition in a variety of forms: cp. Strack-B. I, 430.

[3] There are variants to this saying too. Cp. Strack-B. I, 436f. and further Ps. Sol. 5^{9-11}. There is a Mandaean parallel in Ginza R., II, 4, Lidzb., pp. 61, 20ff.: 'Go up to the sea shore, and see the fish in the sea: They swim away into the sea in pairs and do not perish. And regard the birds in the heavens: they fly away in pairs and do not perish. And now behold, why wilt thou perish?'

thou knowest not what a day may bring forth, and peradventure tomorrow he is no more: thus he shall be found grieving over a world that is not his.' (This last sentence occurs frequently in the Rabbinic tradition, see above, p. 84; cp. too A. Erman, *Die Literatur der Aegypter*, p. 167: 'Do not prepare for the morrow before it comes; for no-one knows what evil it brings'; further Alb. Socin, *Arabische Sprichwoerter und Redensarten*, Tuebing. Universitaetsschr., 1878, no. 513: 'The god of the morrow will care for the morrow'; no. 514: 'Every day brings its own sufficiency with it.' *Tuerkische Maerchen* (Maerchen der Weltlit.), p. 220: 'Be ready to regard today as a prize and enjoy it gladly. God will take care of the morrow.').

With Matt. 7[1f.]: Rosch hasch. 16b (second century): 'He who calls down (Divine) judgement on his neighbour is himself punished first.' Pirqe Aboth, I. 6: 'Judge every man by his good side.' II. 4: 'Judge not thy friend until thou comest into his place.' Shab. 127b: 'Our Rabbis taught: He who judges his neighbour in the scale of merit is himself judged favourably.' (This is evidently a traditional proverb, which in its context has a meaning corresponding but little to its original one, cp. Bischoff, op. cit., 89; Dalman, *Jesus-Jeschua*, pp. 201f.).

With Matt. 7[7]: Pesikta 176a: 'When he knocks, the door is opened for him.' (So R. Bannajah, A.D. 200, in reference to the study of the Mishnah using what is probably a traditional saying. Further material in Strack-B. ad loc.)

With Matt. 10[16]: Juda b. Simon in the Midrash in Cant. 2[14] (101a): 'God says of the Israelites: To me they are upright as doves, but to the nations they are wise as serpents.'

With Matt. 10[24f.], and especially with the sentence: ἀρκετὸν τῷ μαθητῇ ἵνα γένηται ὡς ὁ διδάσκαλος αὐτοῦ a whole series of parallels in Billerb. I, 578; Dalman, *Jesus-Jeschua*, p. 207.

With Matt. 10[29]: The rabbinic proverb is frequent in the tradition: 'Not a bird falls to the ground without heaven (= God), so how much less does a man?' Strack-B. I, 582f.

With Matt. 24[28]: Job 39[30]: 'Where the slain are, there is she' (the eagle).

With Lk. 4[23]: Gen. R. 23 (15c): 'Physician, rise and heal thine own lameness.'[1]

With Lk. 6[43f.]: Examples of the image of fruit can be found at choice in Wuensche, pp. 105f.

[1] Cp. J. L. Burckhardt, *Arab. Sprichw.*, p. 162, no. 404: 'A physician who heals others but is sick himself', p. 300, no. 679: 'A wonderful thing is a man with diseased eyes who proposes to be an oculist.'

With Lk. 14 [7-11]: Prov. 25 [6f.]:
  'Put not thyself forward in the presence of the king,
    And stand not in the place of great men:
    For better is it that it be said unto thee, Come up hither;
    Than that thou shouldest be put lower in the presence of the
        prince.'
With Mk. 2 [27]: The rabbinic saying is found frequently: 'The Sab-
bath is given over to you, not you to the Sabbath.' (Strack-B. II, 5.)
With Mk. 4 [21]: Mek. 60a: 'Is a light of any sort of use save in a dark
place?'
With Mk. 4 [25]: 4 Ezra 7 [25]. 'For the empty are empty things, and for
the full are the full things.' ('Emptiness for the empty and fullness
for the full.') Similar proverbs in Strack-B. I, 66of. on Matt.
13 [12]; Dalman, *Jesus-Jeschua,* p. 205. Further the Arabian proverb:
'He who has milk keeps milk and he who has water keeps water.'
(A. Socin, *Arab. Sprichwoerter u. Redensarten,* Tueb. Universitaetsschr., 1928, p. 5, no. 70.)
  Naturally these examples can never in any instance indicate the
source of a particular logion. It is perhaps possible in some cases to
trace the history of an individual saying. But the most important
thing is that these examples of parallel subject-matter show the
Synoptic sayings can be understood in relationship with Jewish
'Wisdom' and that we must therefore consider the possibility that
they may in part derive therefrom. [1]

2. Prophetic and Apocalyptic Sayings

  While it is necessary in the ancient prophetic preaching to distinguish visions (and auditions) put into the form of a story from prophetic foretelling, threats and exhortations, etc., there is no occasion
for such a distinction in the Synoptic sayings of Jesus. There is but
one saying which could be classed as a report of a vision. Lk. 10 [18]:

ἐθεώρουν τὸν σατανᾶν ὡς ἀστραπὴν ἐκ τοῦ οὐρανοῦ πεσόντα. [2]

[1] Our frequent citing of Arabic proverbs has indicated that the oriental proverbial
literature in general contains a deal of comparative material. I quote for Matt. 12 [34]b par.
from the Arabic collection 'Pearls that are cast' (in M. H. L. Fleischer, *Ali's hundert
Sprueche 1837*), no. 199: 'A man's speech makes known what is in his heart.' Further to
Mk. 9 [40] from the same collection, no. 252: 'Thy friend is he who is not thy foe.' From
G. W. Freytag, *Arabum Proverbia,* I, 1838, p. 629, n. 82: *celeriter quaere, celeriter invenies;*
ibid. II, 1839, p. 41, n. 46: *quaere, invenies;* similarly p. 703, n. 387: cp. Mk. 4 [24] par.
Admittedly we must allow for the possibility, among others, that a Synoptic proverb is the
source of the saying; so evidently for Freytag, II, p. 335, n. 115: *Quomodo festucam in fratris
tui oculo vides et signum transversum in oculo tuo non vides?* Other examples under 'Similitudes'.
[2] Though it is possible that the saying merely puts into metaphor the eschatological
intuition, 'that the end of the devil's power was now being experienced' (Klostermann),
thus making it a substantive parallel to Mk. 3 [27].

Perhaps this is due to the tradition, which, in conformity with its conception of Jesus, could have suppressed other passages reporting visions or auditions. Yet that could not have been done on any large scale; for in late Judaism visions and auditions were features of the apocalyptist, and Jesus was not an apocalyptist in the strict sense. But the justification of other distinctions will arise in what follows.

(a) *Preaching of Salvation*

Lk. 14[15]: μακάριος ὅστις φάγεται ἄρτον ἐν τῇ βασιλείᾳ τοῦ θεοῦ. This saying has to be quoted here; it can only be an accident that it is not put in the mouth of Jesus.[1] In any event, Luke has borrowed it from the tradition and used it for his editorial construction of the story of the supper.

Lk. 10[23f.]//Matt. 13[16f.]: *Blessedness of the Eye-witnesses.* However much Luke may have shortened the parallelism here, and however much we may discuss the relationship of βασιλεῖς in Luke to δίκαιοι in Matthew, Luke is more original at least in this, that the hearers are not congratulated just on their seeing and hearing, but because of what they see and hear, i.e. what they experience.[2] And that can be none other than the Messianic age, for it has been this that the pious of the past have longed to see.[3] Matthew has made up for the reproof of the disciples in Mk. 4[13] by putting the saying in an artificial context so that the disciples are congratulated just because they hear and so that the βλέπειν of the ὀφθαλμοί has no correlative object any more. The saying did not originally refer to Jesus in this connection, though the evangelist might well have thought so.

Lk. 6[20-23]//Matt. 5[3-12]: *The Beatitudes.* Their number in Luke is the more original. They fall into two groups:

1. Lk. 6[20f.]//Matt. 5[3-9]: Blessedness of those who yearn for the Messianic salvation. Luke in general is probably more original; I simply think that the change from the third person in Matthew to the second in Luke is Luke's work.[4] Clearly by this change Luke wanted

---

[1] The picture of a Messianic Feast is ancient; cp. Isa. 25[6]; EE 60[7f.], 62[14]; 4 Ezra 6[52]; Syr. Bar. 29[4]; Rev. 3[20], 19[9]; Matt. 8[11]; Lk. 22[29f.]; cp. Strack-B. I, 180f.

[2] Cp. Klostermann. In Matthew the βλέπειν of the ὀφθαλμοί no longer retains its specific meaning, but must be interpreted quite generally as 'understand'. According to Burney, *The Aramaic Origin of the Fourth Gospel*, 1922, p. 77, ὅτι in Matthew is admittedly a mistranslation of the relative pronoun. The meaning would then be the same as in Luke.

[3] On 'seeing' the Messianic age, cp. Lk. 2[30]; Jn. 8[56]; Heb. 11[13] and esp. Ps. Sol. 17[50]: μακάριοι οἱ γενόμενοι ἐν ταῖς ἡμέραις ἐκείναις, ἰδεῖν τὰ ἀγαθὰ Ἰσραήλ... Pesikta, § 12b, p. 149ab, ed. Buber: '. . . Salvation to that generation, whose (eyes) behold him (i.e. the Messiah)!'

[4] 'Beatitudes' are usually formulated in the third person. Cp. Lk. 10[23], 11[28], 14[15]; Jn. 20[29]; Jas. 1[12]; Rev. 14[13], 16[15], 19[9], 20[6], 22[14]. Naturally we cannot take into account Matt. 16[17]; Lk. 1[45], 14[14].

to introduce a comparison with vv. 22f., where the second person was in the traditional form. Whether Luke added the two-fold νῦν in v. 21 is a matter which, like other deviations from Matthew, can be left out of account for our purposes.

2. Lk. 6²²ᶠ·//Matt. 5¹⁰⁻¹²: Blessedness of those persecuted for the sake of the Son of Man.[1] Matt. 5¹⁰ is a Matthean formulation, intended to bring the number of beatitudes in vv. 3–9 (v. 5 is secondary in Matthew) up to seven. See below on ἕνεκεν ἐμοῦ in Matthew instead of ἕνεκα τοῦ υἱοῦ τ. ἀνθ. in Luke. In general differences are not important for our purposes. But it is essential to see that Lk. 6²² or Matt. 5¹¹ᶠ· is a new element of the tradition which is clearly distinguished from the older element Lk. 6²⁰ᶠ· or Matt. 5³⁻⁸ in form (second person and detailed grounds of blessedness) and content, arising *ex eventu* and for that reason created by the Church. It is in this second set that we first have a direct reference to the person of Jesus.

Matt. 11⁵⁻⁶//Lk. 7²²⁻²³: *The Time of Salvation.* The description is applied to the present, and that could also be the sense of the originally isolated saying (see p. 23), if v. 6 originally went along with v. 5. But that is probable, since the description in v. 5 has no real point on its own. So the saying has a primary reference to Jesus; the only question is whether it is a direct reference to his person or to his preaching; on this see below.

Mk. 10²⁹⁻³⁰ par. *The hundredfold Reward* (see pp. 22f.). This saying has been changed about as can be seen by comparing Mark with Matthew and Luke with the textual tradition. Yet we can no longer be certain at what stage all this took place. It is essential to note that originally the saying only went as far as ἑκατονπλασίονα.[2] What follows is a distinction between rewards in this life and in the life to come, in which the latter (admittedly quite secondary) is still further specified. Without doubt the hundredfold reward originally applied to the life to come, i.e. it was the reward in the Messianic Kingdom.

Whether the saying originally read ἕνεκεν ἐμοῦ καὶ ἕνεκεν τοῦ εὐαγγελίου is extremely doubtful, in face of the differences among the three Synoptists. At the least it is uncertain what came after ἕνεκεν. The logic of the saying supports Luke's εἵνεκεν τῆς βασιλείας τ. θ.: whoever abandons earthly possessions for the sake of the King-

---

[1] I think it improbable that we have a mistranslation in Mt. 5¹⁰ (Burney, in Montefiore, *The Synoptic Gospels*, II², p. 39) and that the original meaning was: 'Blessed are those who pursue righteousness.'

[2] M. Goguel, *R.H.Ph.R*, 8, 1928, pp. 264–77 thinks that only v. 30c is a Marcan addition: καὶ ἐν τῷ αἰῶνι τ. ἐρχ. ζωὴν αἰών. He believes the previous promise is an ironic answer to Peter's foolish question in v. 28: the special meaning of v. 30 is its promise of διωγμοί. This seems impossible to me.

dom, he will receive a hundredfold reward—in the Kingdom. Further the words ἕνεκεν ἐμοῦ καὶ τοῦ εὐαγγελίου in Mk. 8³⁵ are also certainly secondary (see p. 93). Finally it is not so easy to account for Luke's text on the basis of Mark's as the other way round. So the saying could originally have been a parallel to Mk. 8³⁵: Whoever abandons his earthly possessions will receive a hundredfold reward in their place. So originally the saying had no reference to the Person of Jesus.

After what has been said we may reckon Mk. 8³⁵ (*Losing and Finding Life*) among the prophetic sayings, and its paradoxical form is well suited there. In the same way we may add Mk. 10³¹ par. to the prophetic sayings for it too is clearly a minatory saying. As distinctive salvation sayings we may nevertheless cite Lk. 10²⁰ (... χαίρετε δὲ ὅτι τὰ ὀνόματα ὑμῶν ἐγγέγραπται ἐν τοῖς οὐρανοῖς) and Lk. 12³² (The Little Flock), which are both quite secondary community formulations, in which the ascended Lord speaks.

Finally, the *Messianic preaching* of John the Baptist in Mk. 1⁷⁻⁸ or Matt. 3¹¹⁻¹²; Lk. 3¹⁶⁻¹⁷ is a salvation prophecy. For our purpose it must be noted that this section has been given, within the Christian tradition, a secondary reference to the Person of Jesus, partly for the simple reason of its being inserted into the report of Jesus' own deeds, and partly by the changing of baptism by fire into baptism by the Spirit (Mark) or the combining of both (Matthew and Luke, Q?).[1] Perhaps, too, the aorist ἐβάπτισα Mk. 1⁸, which Matthew and Luke turn into the present, is the result of Christian editing, though it can admittedly be understood as a Semitism (Wellhausen, *Einleitung*², p. 18).

(b) Minatory Sayings

Lk. 6²⁴⁻²⁶: *Woes on the Rich*. Apart from v. 26, which is formally in antithesis to vv. 22f., I do not think these woes are a Lucan formulation, even if they seem not to have appeared at this point in Q; for

---

[1] Like Wellhausen I believe that the original text was only: 'he will baptize you with fire,' meaning by that the fire of judgement. It is hardly possible to tell whether the baptism by fire was already joined with the (Christian) baptism by the Spirit in Q (thus Wellhausen) or whether the combination came about by Matthew and Luke joining Q and Mark. I think it quite impossible that baptism by fire and baptism by the Spirit meant the same thing (so H. Leisegang, *Pneuma Hagion*, 1922, pp. 72–80, on the basis of the Greek idea of a fiery spirit) and that the whole prophecy finds its motif in Hellenistic mysticism. The fire of judgement is an idea such as we find in Matt. 3¹² and also in Mal. 3²ᶠ·, and we find baptism as a symbol of annihilation in Mk. 10³⁸ᶠ·; Lk. 12⁵⁰— Sanh. 39a (Strack-B. I, 121f.) on the basis of Num. 31²³, speaks of baptism by fire as one of the means of purification that were superior to baptism by water. According to Reitzenstein (*Z.N.W.*, 26, 1927, p. 63) the connection of πῦρ with πνεῦμα derives from the Mandaean idea of water being at once both splendour and heat.

v. 27a is manifestly a transition, which again leads us back to a source (Q) passage (see p. 91). Vv. 24f. may be ancient tradition. For a juxtaposition of Blessings and Woes see SEn 52; EEn 5[7]; Sukka 56b; Yoma 87a (Strack-B. I, 664 on Matt. 13[16]); John of the Mandaeans ed Lidzb., II, 160.170ff., 178ff.[1] Woes in prophetic denunciations are found in Isa. 5[8ff.], 10[1], 33[1]; Hab. 2[6ff.]; EEn 94–103; Mk. 13[17], (14[21]); Matt. 11[21] par., 18[7] par., 23[13ff.] par.; Jud. 11; Rev. 8[13], (9[12]), (11[14]), 12[12], 18[10ff.]. There is no relation to the Person of Jesus.

Matt. 10[32f.]//Lk. 12[8f.] or Mk. 8[38] par.: *Confessing the sayings of Jesus.* This saying contains both a promise of salvation and a threat of damnation. But the emphasis is on the latter, which alone is given by Mark, who abbreviates the saying because of the context. If that seems uncertain, it appears certain to me that the distinction between Jesus and the Son of Man is primary. On this point Mark and the original Q form agree. By ignoring this distinction Matthew has introduced the Christian reference of the saying to the Person of Jesus, a thing which in Mark and Q is given by the context only. It is hardly possible to decide whether the original subject was the Person of Jesus or his sayings; in any event the significance would be the same. I think it impossible that one should be bound to conclude from Lk. 12[9] that the Son of Man is secondary in the saying. Luke would, as elsewhere, have ruined the parallelism.

Matt. 11[21–24]//Lk. 10[13–15]: *Woes on the cities of Galilee.* Matthew's form is in all probability more original than Luke's. In any case we have here a community formulation, since the sayings look back on Jesus' activity as something already completed, and presuppose the failure of the Christian preaching in Capernaum. Moreover it would have been difficult for Jesus to imagine that Capernaum could be exalted to heaven by his activity (Wellhausen). So the saying comes from the same situation as Matt. 10[15]//Lk. 10[12].

Lk. 11[31–32]//Matt. 12[41–42]: *This Generation and the Queen of the South and the Ninevites.* Matthew has effected a transposition; for in a saying which is obviously an originally independent one, the historical order is natural. By his transposition Matthew has strengthened the standard association he found in Q for joining his saying to the preceding one on the sign of Jonah. It is only by its being joined with the preceding saying that this one gains any reference to the Person of Jesus; originally it was a minatory saying

---

[1] H. Leisegang, who (*Pneuma Hagion*, pp. 137f.) thinks that such juxtaposition 'stands in crass opposition to Jewish forms', maintains that the Woes of Luke are a secondary formulation, behind which lurks the figure of the wandering Cynic philosophers!

directed against this generation (i.e. the Jews), which failed to recognize the decisive hour. If one regards the saying for itself, there is no need to take it as a community formulation. Yet it has a striking parallelism with the passage just considered, Matt. 11 21–24// Lk. 10 13–15.[1] In both cases Gentiles are contrasted with unrepentant Israel, which has refused to have faith in the κήρυγμα or the δυνάμεις of Jesus. The structure of the two passages is the same, in that each accusing contrast has two parallel members, and after each of them there is a refrain-like repetition of the reproach: Matt. 12 41, 42: καὶ ἰδοὺ πλεῖον .. . ὧδε, Matt. 11 22, 24: πλὴν λέγω ὑμῖν . . . ἀνεκτότερον ἔσται. . . . In this way the impression is given that both passages have been constructed according to 'a scheme of early Christian polemic' (Fridrichsen).

Lk. 11 43, 46, 52, 42, (39, 44, 47//Matt. 23 (4, 6), 13, 23, 25, 27, 29 or Mk. 12 38–40: *Woes on the Scribes and Pharisees*. It would seem that the seven woes quoted here formed one oracle in Q, and that Matthew and Luke, each in his own way, have joined them into a larger combination. Matthew has done this by adding them to Mk. 12 38–40, by uniting them with material from his special source (vv. 2f. 5. 8–10?, 11, 12, 15, 16–22, 24) and some unimportant formulations of his own (vv. 8–10?, 28, 33). Luke has done it by giving it a setting in a particular scene, by interrupting a piece of dialogue (vv. 37–39a, 45) and by adding a closing section (vv. 53f.). The individual differences are not of particular importance for our purposes, though I would mention the addition in Matt. 23 34b, which is a community *vaticinium ex eventu*. The fact that the Woes were originally directed against the models of piety, the Pharisees and the Scribes (mentioned by Luke in v. 53 only; but νομικοί in vv. 45, 46, 52 has the same meaning), prescribes their content. For our purposes it is important to note: (1) Matthew has clearly turned sayings which were not handed down in the tradition as Woes, into such, viz., vv. 16–22, a tradition which he has also used in 5 33–37. It is possible that the form of the Woe in v. 15 also goes back to it. (2) The parallels in Mark have no Woes in them. (3) What was in 'Q' was already a literary form, i.e. a composition, which as such is secondary, a fact which follows from its sevenfold form. This means that Matt. 23 34–36//Lk. 11 49–51 were already joined to the Woes in Q. These three considerations mean that no certainty can be reached as to whether there is primary material in all seven sections. It is possible that individual Woes are original, and that others are secondary, and that possibly some sayings not originally Woes have

[1] This has rightly been recognized by A. Fridrichsen, *Le Problème du Miracle*, p. 49.

been used in formulating the latter. Yet we must not without more ado conclude that because Mark is more concise than Q, Q is later than the Mark tradition. Mark can give a selection, as he evidently does in 6[8-11]. But it is essential that we keep alert to the possibility of a growth of the tradition. It is not characteristic of the Woes that they relate to the Person of Jesus. They only came to do so, and that as early as Q, by association with the following section, in so far as there the Pharisees are presented as the persecutors of Jesus.

Lk. 11[49-51]//Matt. 23[34-36]: *A Threat to this Generation.* In Q this saying was a quotation from some lost writing, which Matthew has put straight into the mouth of Jesus.[1] As Luke shows in v. 49 it was originally the divine Wisdom that spoke. V. 36 in Matthew and v. 51b in Luke states that the saying applies to the γενεὰ αὕτη, and is thus in Q conceived of as an illustration of the saying by Jesus. In addition to this Matthew seems to have enlarged it in v. 34 from the experiences of the time of persecution (cp. Matt. 10[17, 23]); the remaining differences may well derive from this. It is characteristic that a Jewish prophetic saying should be adapted by the Christian tradition. I do not think it certain that the saying must have arisen after A.D. 70 (Wellhausen and Reitzenstein). If it did not, then it is possible that Jesus made the quotation, though equally possible that it was ascribed to him by the tradition. In any event the tendency of the tradition to allow the maximal amount to appear as sayings of Jesus comes clearly to view when Matthew omits the introductory formula: see the same.

Matt. 23[37-39]//Lk. 13[34-35]: *Threat to Jerusalem.* This saying is also originally a Jewish prophecy, whether Jesus himself quoted it or whether the Church ascribed it to him. This follows from the consideration that Jesus could not himself have said that he would often have gathered his children, not even if he had been often and for long active in the city, as is probable from the Synoptics. For the one making this statement must be a supra-historical entity, namely Wisdom, which has just spoken in Matt. 23[24-36] par.[2] It is actually

---

[1] Proof that the saying is a quotation is found pre-eminently in Luke's introductory formula: διὰ τοῦτο καὶ ἡ σοφία τοῦ θεοῦ εἶπεν, in which the aorist εἶπεν is noteworthy. Likewise the enumeration of the envoys in Matthew as: προφήτας καὶ σοφοὺς καὶ γραμματεῖς could be original in a Jewish writing only, which Luke then altered to προφήτας καὶ ἀποστόλους. Cp. especially A. Merx, *Das Evang. Matth.*, 1902, pp. 336ff; A. Harnack, *Sprueche und Reden Jesu*, 1907, p. 72; R. Reitzenstein, *Das mandaeische Buch des Herrn der Groesse* (Heid. Ak. d. W., phil.-hist. KL. 1919), pp. 41ff. More recently Reitzenstein has admittedly expressed the view that Matthew's introduction to the section is original (*Z.N.W.*, 26, 1927, p. 55.1).

[2] The information such as was given by K. Holl (S.B. pr. Ak. d. W., 1921, p. 933.1) that the children of Jerusalem meant not only the inhabitants of the city, but all Jews, does not affect this statement. Klostermann rightly points out that the O.T. image of a bird also signifies God. Cp. J. Hempel, *Gott und Mensch im A.T.*, pp. 140f. The same is true of Judaism, cp. Strack-B., I, 943.

highly probable that Matthew has here preserved the order of sections in Q, while Luke has introduced the threat to Jerusalem 13 ³⁴ᶠ.
ad vocem Ἱερουσαλήμ. And it would seem that Matt. 23 ³⁷⁻³⁹ is the
original continuation of the quotation in vv. 34–35.[1] It is a matter
for consideration whether the not easily understood v. 39 is a Christian addition foretelling the death and parousia of Jesus (Klostermann), or whether only the words from λέγω ὑμῖν to ἀπ' ἄρτι (in Luke
from λέγω ὑμῖν to ἴδητέ με) demand deletion as a Christian expansion (the position adopted in the first edition of this work). But the
whole verse has to be understood in the light of the myth of divine
Wisdom, in which, after Wisdom dwells on the earth and calls men to
follow her in vain, leaves the world, and man now searches for her
in vain. Wisdom foretells that she will remain hidden until the
coming of Messiah; for only he can be meant by the one ἐρχόμενος
ἐν ὀνόματι κυρίου.[2] Admittedly the fragments of Jewish Wisdom
speculation that have survived for us do not say that Wisdom, on her
departure, referred to her (or her representatives) coming to judgement, but it is quite intelligible in the context of the myth. Another
myth, parallel to that of Wisdom, namely the myth of the Archetypal
Man, confirms the view that a reference to coming in judgement
belonged to the original myth.[3] The very description of the world as
a 'house' in any event confirms the view that the saying derives from
the myth.[4] If ἔρημος is an explanatory addition made by Matthew
(in the manner of Jer. 22[5]) then ἀφίεται is just a bad rendering of a
verb meaning: 'will be abandoned' (cp. Matt. 24 ⁴⁰ᶠ.).

Lk. 23 ²⁸⁻³¹: *Woe to the Daughters of Jerusalem.* On the composition of the whole scene, see p. 37; it was there stated that
vv. 29–31 is a Christian prophecy put into the mouth of Jesus, and

---

[1] So too Merx, Wellhausen, Harnack, Loisy and Reitzenstein. M. Plath, *T.S.K.*, 78,
1905, pp. 455–60 differs. She takes Matt. 23 ³⁷⁻³⁹ par. not as an utterance of Wisdom, but
of some prophet, such as Jeremiah. But she has not really reckoned with the myth of
Wisdom.

[2] In this case it does not matter whether the text of Matthew or that of Luke is original.
The latter can be understood to mean: 'till the time come, that you will say . . .' or (with
Wellhausen: ὅτε = *is cui*): till he comes, to whom. . . .

[3] On the Wisdom Myth cp. my treatment in Εὐχαριστήριον (presented to H. Gunkel), II,
1923, pp. 6–11; on the Myth of Archetypal Man see my essay in *Z.N.W.*, 24, 1925,
pp. 100–50. While the other scholars mentioned in note 1 conceive of Matt. 23 ³⁷⁻³⁹ as
a whole, or up to v. 39 as a quotation thus making it a saying of 'Wisdom', R. Reitzenstein (*Das. mand. Buch d. Herrn d. Groesse*, pp. 41–59) interprets the section as consistent
with the Myth of Wisdom or of Archetypal Man and seeks more precisely to determine the
source. This would, namely, be more intelligibly preserved in the Mandaean Apocalypse,
which is properly set out in Ginza R. I and II.1 (Lidzb., pp. 29f. and 47f.). It seems probable to me that the same tradition lies behind this; but I do not think that any literary
dependence can be proved. Cp. further H. H. Schaeder, in Reitzenstein-Schaeder, *Studien
zum antiken Synkretismus*, pp. 332–6.

[4] In the Mandaean texts 'House' is a typical description of the 'world'. Cp. Lidzbarski's index to the Ginza.

that v. 28 belongs to it as its introduction. V. 31 is then seen to be making use of a proverbial saying.[1] Certain stylistic and linguistic peculiarities (v. 29: ἰδοὺ ἔρχονται ἡμέραι ἐν αἷς ἐροῦσιν, the use of direct speech; v. 30: τότε ἄρξονται λέγειν; v. 31: ἐν corresponding to ⊐) give grounds for surmising that the saying derives from an Aramaic original; whether the tradition itself handed it down as a saying of Jesus in Aramaic we can, of course, no longer determine.

Lk. 12[54-56]: *The Signs of the Times* (in Matt. 16[2f.] a later addition). The saying enjoins the menacing seriousness of the hour of decision, but has no reference to the Person of Jesus.

Matt. 8[11-12]//Lk. 13[28-29]: *The Gentiles and the Kingdom.* This is a warning which has no reference to the Person of Jesus.

Lk. 4[25-27]: *Jews and Gentiles.* This is an independent piece of the tradition, which Luke has used in constructing Jesus' sermon in the Synagogue, see pp. 31f. It may well be a secondary community construction, introduced into the anti-Jewish polemic of the Gentile Christian Church.

Lk. 6[46]//Matt. 7[21]: *Those who say 'Lord, Lord'.* Luke's form of the saying could well be original.[2] Like Matt. 11[6]//Lk. 7[23] it has a reference to the Person of Jesus, or to his preaching. Matthew has made the reference more emphatic by his formulation: τὸ θέλημα τοῦ πατρός μου. Clearly this reference was emphasized already in Q by its association with the saying that followed, which Luke has obviously taken from its context in Q and placed in a new artificial one (13[26f.]). That Matthew's is that of the tradition seems to me to follow from 2 Cl. 4[5]: ἐὰν ἦτε μετ' ἐμοῦ συνηγμένοι ἐν τῷ κόλπῳ μου καὶ μὴ ποιῆτε τὰς ἐντολάς μου, ἀποβαλῶ ὑμᾶς καὶ ἐρῶ ὑμῖν· ὑπάγετε ἀπ' ἐμοῦ, οὐκ οἶδα ὑμᾶς πόθεν ἐστέ, ἐργάται ἀνομίας. This dominical saying (see p. 94) seems to have come about by the amalgamation and transformation of Matt. 7[21] (or Lk. 6[46]) with 7[22] (or 13[26f.]); and it does not go back to Matthew's form, but to that preserved in Luke, as is proved by the words καὶ μὴ ποιῆτε τὰς ἐντολάς μου.[3] By contrast we can compare the variants of the Matthew text

---

[1] Cp. Merx ad loc. and Strack-B. I, 263, esp. Seder Elij. R. 14 (65): 'when the fire takes hold of the green wood, what will happen to the dry?'

[2] Cp. W. Bousset, *Kyrios-Chr.*[2], p. 51. It is not necessary to suppose, with Bousset, that Matthew had in mind the calling on 'Lord, Lord' in the cultus, with the Christian Liturgy thus providing the form of the saying. Yet the word κύριε certainly had a religious connotation for Matthew, though in Luke the address is only to the teacher. In A. Fridrichsen's view, *Le Problème du Miracle*, p. 106, Luke refers to a cultic address, while κύριε, κύριε in Matthew is addressed to the Judge at the Last Judgement.

[3] It is difficult to argue 2 Cl's dependence on Matthew from the fact that 2 Cl. 4[5] has ἐργάται ἀνομίας, while Luke has ἐργάται ἀδικίας and Matthew οἱ ἐργαζόμενοι τὴν ἀνομιαν. It is much more likely that Luke has changed an original ἀνομίας into ἀδικίας, since he always avoids the use of ἀνομία.

in the Nazarean version (see p. 94), where Matthew's words θέλημα τοῦ πατρός μου again find their rightful place. In addition this is additional proof of the secondary character of Matt. 7²¹ when compared with Lk. 6⁴⁶.

Matt. 7²²⁻²³//Lk. 13²⁶⁻²⁷: *Rejection of False Disciples*. In Luke the saying is linked to the preceding section by v. 25 (using a parable-fragment) and it is clearly a rejection of the unbelieving Jews; in Matthew, it is the false Christian teacher who is rejected; and this is of course secondary. But in any case this rests on a secondary community formulation, one that looks back to Jesus' completed ministry and depicts him as proclaiming himself judge of the world.

Matt. 24³⁷⁻⁴¹//Lk. 17²⁶⁻²⁷, (²⁸⁻³⁰), ³⁴⁻³⁵: *Warning of the Parousia*. Luke has in any event expanded the source by vv. 31–33, which he took in part from another tradition (vv. 31, 33) and in part formulated himself (v. 32). He may have found vv. 28–30, which are parallel to vv. 26f. (=Matt. 24³⁷⁻³⁹), at this point in Q; and if that be so it is then hardly possible that the verses were omitted by Matthew, much rather is it likely that they are a new formulation occasioned by vv. 26f. (see pp. 87f.). Luke's additions rest on the proper perception that there are two different sayings joined together in Q: vv. 26–27 (or 26–30) = Matt. 24³⁷⁻³⁹ and vv. 34f. = Matt. 24⁴⁰ᶠ. The first saying warns of the surprising suddenness of the Parousia, the second of the division that will ensue (Matthew appears to have misunderstood this and consequently made the labourers ἐν τῷ ἀγρῷ out of the two ἐπὶ κλίνης μιᾶς). And there are two warnings which have no reference to the Person of Jesus.

Matt. 3⁷⁻¹⁰//Lk. 3⁷⁻⁹: *The Warning of the Baptist*. That these sayings are ascribed to the Baptist in Q does not, of course, prove that he actually spoke them. The supposition is hardly likely to be wrong that the sayings were in circulation in the Christian tradition, and were ascribed to the Baptist out of a desire to have some record of his preaching for repentance. It would have been possible e.g. to have have attributed Lk. 6²⁴ᶠ·, 11³¹ᶠ·, 13²⁸ᶠ· to him as well. So we must reckon it as quite accidental that Jesus is not said to have uttered these warnings.

We have dealt with some passages as Logia which could be classed as Minatory Sayings, e.g. Matt. 10³¹, Lk. 13³⁰ (The First and the Last); Mk. 10²³, ²⁵ (Saying against the Rich); Matt. 22¹⁴ (Many called, few chosen). But finally, we can include Mk. 8¹² or Matt. 12³⁹ᶠ·//Lk. 11²⁹ᶠ· (Refusal of a Sign). But we cannot be sure whether the form in Q, which refers the present generation to the sign of Jonah, is a secondary expansion.[1] But it seems clear to me that the interpretation of the sign of Jonah in terms of the death and resurrection of Jesus is a quite secondary formulation of the Church. The meaning of the saying (in the Luke version) seems to me to be: Just as Jonah came to the Ninevites from a distant country, so will the Son of Man come to this generation from heaven; i.e. the sign asked for the preaching of Jesus is the Son of Man himself, when he comes to judgement.[2]

(c) *Admonitions*

Mk. 1[15] par.: *The Theme of Jesus' Preaching*. This is a quite secondary formulation made under the influence of a specifically Christian terminology (πιστεύετε ἐν τῷ εὐαγγελίῳ) which might very well derive from Mark himself. Reference to the Person of Jesus is involved in the fact that Jesus is himself part of the gospel.

Lk. 12[35-38]: *The Returning Householder*. This pericope is a secondary composition. We cannot determine whether it already stood in Q as a whole or in part, and Matthew replaced it by 25[1-13].

V. 35 is a metaphorical admonition to be watchful, which could well have been originally independent, and used by Luke as an introduction to what follows. V. 36 is a similar admonition in the form of a comparison (not a parable), which is developed allegorically in vv. 37f. It is hardly likely that an original parable lies behind it. One gets the impression that what confronts us here are some gathered fragments of the tradition which in their form and content are secondary and show themselves to be community formulations from the time when the delay in the Parousia began to be recognized. But v. 35 can be made an exception to this judgement. The reference to the Person of Jesus does not need to be expressly mentioned here, because the word κύριος has just that meaning without any more ado.

---

[1] According to v. Dobschuetz, *Vom Auslegen des N.T.*, 1927, p. 39, it is clear that Jonah has been introduced into the refusal of a sign from the double saying about the Queen of Sheba and the Ninevites (Matt. 12[41f.] or Lk. 11[31f.]) which had already been joined in Q with Matt. 12[39] or Lk. 11[29f.]. But is not the opposite possible—that Jonah's appearance in both passages occasioned their combination in Q. And Mark could very easily have omitted the (to him) incomprehensible saying about the sign of Jonah! Admittedly there are others, e.g. Bousset, *Kyrios Christos*[2], p. 7, who think similarly to v. Dobschuetz.

[2] Cp. Matt. 24[30] where the σημεῖον τοῦ υἱοῦ τ. ἀνθρ. is referred to, and in the same way the eschatological σημεῖα in Did. 16[6]. The saying would have to be interpreted differently if J. H. Michael were right (*J.T.S.*, XXI, 1920, pp. 146–59) who follows others in supposing that originally 'the sign of John' was meant, instead of the sign of Jonah. Then the sign would be ambiguous; the τελῶναι and πόρναι had understood it (Matt. 21[32]; Lk. 7[29f.]). If so, perhaps Matt. 12[41-42] or Lk. 11[31-32] also referred to the Baptist? (But even then I could not accept the genuineness of Matt. 12[40] = Lk. 11[30] which Michael intends to establish.)

Mk. 13³³⁻³⁷: *The Returning Householder.* This is similarly not an organized composition. The arrival of the Master by night is un-motivated, because here, unlike Lk. 12³⁶ where he returns from a feast, he comes home from a journey, and this makes the demand of the servants' watchfulness quite pointless. While this motif is a variant of Lk. 12³⁶, the other motif—that of the journeying Master who leaves his house in the care of his servants—is a variant of Matt. 24⁴⁵⁻⁵¹. The porter matches Matt. 24⁴³ᶠ. See below on the Parables.

Matt. 24⁴³⁻⁴⁴//Lk. 12³⁹⁻⁴⁰: *Parable of the Thief.*

Matt. 24⁴⁵⁻⁵¹//Lk. 12⁴²⁻⁴⁶: *Parable of the true and untrue servants.*

Both these passages are unitary in composition and reveal no secondary characteristics. In my view the second cannot be thought of as a special warning to office bearers in the Christian Church, but only as coming from a later period when the delay in the Parousia was taken for granted. Nevertheless it is quite possible that Jesus should himself depict the conviction of his contemporaries with the words χρονίζει μου ὁ κύριος. There was no need to introduce a reference to the Person of Jesus into the Church tradition, because it was self-evident that υἱὸς τ. ἀνθρ. or κύριος meant Jesus.

Matt. 25¹⁻¹³: *Parable of the Ten Virgins.* This is a Church formula-tion completely overgrown by allegory, and having a strongly emphasized reference to the Person of Jesus. Elements of older traditions could very well be related to this.

Lk. 12⁴⁷⁻⁴⁸: *Punishment according to Responsibility.* The proverb in v. 48b may perhaps have been originally independent (see p. 84) and given rise to the parable-like amplification in vv. 47, 48a. In any case vv. 47, 48a are secondary formulations, concerning the Christian teacher and layman.

Lk. 21³⁴⁻³⁶: *Injunction to Watch.* This is a quite late Hellenistic formulation with a terminology so characteristic and akin to Paul's that one could hazard a guess that Luke was here using a fragment from some lost epistle written by Paul or one of his disciples.

Not all these monitory sayings are characteristically prophetic; they can all be reduced to the injunction to be watchful and are more akin to the apocalyptist than the prophet. For contrast one can compare with them such real prophetic warnings as Am. 5⁴⁻⁶, ¹⁴ᶠ·; Isa. 1¹¹⁻¹⁷; Jer. 7¹⁻⁷, etc. It is easier to describe a number of warnings included among the Logia as characteristically prophetic, e.g. Matt. 8²²; Lk. 9⁶²; Matt. 10²⁸, 5³⁹ᶠ·, 7¹³ᶠ·

(d) *Apocalyptic Predictions*

Mk. 13² par: βλέπεις ταύτας τὰς μεγάλας οἰκοδομάς;
οὐ μὴ ἀφεθῇ λίθος ἐπὶ λίθον, ὃς οὐ μὴ καταλυθῇ.

Mk. 14⁵⁸: ἐγὼ καταλύσω τὸν ναὸν τοῦτον τὸν χειροποίητον
καὶ διὰ τριῶν ἡμερῶν ἄλλον ἀχειροποίητον οἰκοδομήσω.

Matt. 26⁶¹: δύναμαι καταλῦσαι τὸν ναὸν τοῦ θεοῦ
καὶ διὰ τριῶν ἡμερῶν αὐτὸν οἰκοδομῆσαι.

(Cp. Mk. 15²⁹: οὐὰ ὁ καταλύων τὸν ναὸν καὶ οἰκοδομῶν (ἐν) τρισὶν
ἡμέραις.

Jn. 2¹⁹: λύσατε τὸν ναὸν τοῦτον, καὶ ἐν τρισὶν ἡμέραις ἐγερῶ αὐτόν.

Acts 6¹⁴: . . . ὅτι Ἰησοῦς ὁ Ναζωραῖος οὗτος καταλύσει τὸν τόπον
τοῦτον.)

In all these examples it seems that the same tradition has left its mark without making it possible for us to determine which is the original form. In Mk. 13² the tradition has found its features in a concrete scene, and the saying is formulated in the light of it. As to the relationship of Mk. 14⁵⁸ and Matt. 26⁶¹, Mark is secondary in respect of the adjectives χειροποίητος and ἀχειροποίητος which he adds to ναός, in contrast to Matthew who in his reflecting amendment keeps the particular assertion to the realm of the possible. I do not venture to say what the historical occasion of the saying was. At least it does not follow from Mk. 14⁵⁸ that it played some part in the trial of Jesus, since Mk. 14⁵⁷⁻⁵⁹ is an insertion into the story of the sitting of the Sanhedrin. See below.

The prophecy of the destruction of the temple demands fuller investigation. I think there are a number of possibilities in regard to its origin and meaning: (1) Long before the destruction of Herod's temple in A.D. 70 the hope was current that a new and more glorious temple would arise in the Messianic Age (Bousset, *Die Religion d. Judentums*³, p. 239; Strack-B. I, 1003); and it is even suggested on occasion that the 'old building' would first have to be done away (EEn, 90²⁸ᶠ·).[1] Mk. 13² need not imply anything more than this; and if this were so, it could rest on an actual dominical saying. But it would then hardly be comprehensible why it gave such offence as Jesus spoke it, and how the Church was able by its aid to explain why Jesus was condemned (see below). But could such a saying be the basis for ascribing another one with a different meaning to him, making him say that he himself would destroy the Temple and build a new one (Mk. 14⁵⁸ and variants)? (2) Reitzenstein has pointed to the parallels in the Mandæan Book of John, ch. 76 (Lidzb., II, p. 242)

---

[1] The Rabbinic tradition also recognized a future destruction of the temple: b. Yom. 39b (Fiebig, *Jued. Wundergesch.*, p. 27): j. Yom. 43c (Strack-B. I, 1045); Jos., *Bell*, VI, 5³ § 295): cp. O. Weinrich, *Genethliakon Wilh. Schmid*, 1929, p. 274.

and the Manichaean Turfan fragment T11 D18 (Das mand. Buch d. Herrn d. Gr. 65–70). The Manichaean fragment differs from these since it is manifestly dependent on the Christian tradition. Nevertheless in my opinion the Mandaean text could very well have given expression to the eschatological myth of Primeval Man, independently of the Christian tradition. And this myth could in fact be the basis of the dominical saying. The prophecy of a cosmic catastrophe was perhaps already associated with the prediction of the destruction of the temple in Jewish heretical circles.[1] In that case Jesus' foretelling of the destruction of the Temple goes closely with the prophecies in Matt. 23[34–36, 37–39] (pp. 114ff.). And that makes it possible for Jesus to have taken this prophecy up, as he did others, which spoke of the Son of Man. All this of course is nothing more than a possibility. For my own part I find the hypothesis of a mythological origin the more probable because of the 'three-days' in Matt. 14[58] and its variants.[2]

Mk. 9[1] par.: εἰσίν τινες ὧδε τῶν ἑστηκότων κτλ. This is an isolated saying joined to its context by the formula καὶ ἔλεγεν. It is a community formula of consolation in view of the delay of the Parousia: at any rate some will still live to see it. It is significant for the history of the tradition that in Matt. 16[28] instead of the βασιλεία τ. θ. we have the Son of Man coming in his βασιλεία. For Matthew this is naturally Jesus. It is further significant that even in Mark's source the saying provided the occasion for a discussion, which is found in vv. 11–13: see below.

Lk. 17[20f.]: *The Refusal of a Sign.* The content of this saying gives the impression of being in the primitive tradition. The saying must not be 'modernized' and ἐντὸς ὑμῶν be understood as applying spiritually or meaning the actual presence of Jesus and his disciples. That would deny not ἔρχεσθαι but μετὰ παρατηρήσεως. So the meaning is: when the Kingdom comes, no-one will ask and search for it any more, but it will be there on a sudden in the midst of the foolish ones who will still

---

[1] Cp. H. Odeberg, Uppsala Univ-Årsskrift 1930. *Theol*, 2, pp. 18f.

[2] Gressmann's guess I think entirely mistaken (*Z.K.G.*, N.F., III, 1922, p. 189): a saying of the Zealot 'Messiah' Menahem (on whom see Jos., *Bell.*, II, 17[8f.] = §§ 443–8) has been ascribed to Jesus, to the effect that the temple would be destroyed 'for his sake' or 'immediately after him' (?) and then rebuilt. The text p. Ber. 2[4] (5a, 10ff. in Strack-B. I, 83) comes from the fourth century A.D. Even later is the variant in Midr. Echa Rabbati (tr. by A. Wuensche, 1881, p. 88). Whether some memory of the Zealot Messiah is at work here is very doubtful (cp. e.g. J. Klausner, *Die messian. Vorstellung d. jued. Volkes im Zeitalter d. Tannaiten*, 1903 pp. 68f.; G. F. Moore, *Judaism*, II, 1927, p. 348). What is most certain is that the prophecy is not reported as one of Menahem; but when his mother cursed him (while he was still a child) because the temple was destroyed on the day he was born, she was consoled by the assurance 'Our confidence is unshakeable, that it was destroyed on his account, and that it will also be rebuilt for his sake.' Cp. further M. Goguel, *Jean-Baptiste*, pp. 132–5.

E

want to calculate its arrival; cp. the next saying. The saying lacks any reference to the Person of Jesus.

Lk. 17$^{23-24}$//Matt. 24$^{26-27}$: *The Sudden Coming of the Son of Man.* This is a variant of the previous saying. The only essential difference is that here it is the coming of the Son of Man and not of the Kingdom that is spoken of. Both sayings could well have been the same originally. Lk. 17$^{23f.}$ refers to the Person of Jesus only in the intention of the Evangelist; but since he did not create the saying it can hardly in this form have been a prophecy originally. Moreover there is no ground for thinking that Jesus could not have spoken it—though only about the Son of Man, not about his own Person. Luke has added v. 25 in keeping with the Christian gospel: the Parousia of the Son of Man presupposes his Passion.[1]

Mk. 13$^{5-27}$ par.: *The Synoptic Apocalypse.* Mk. 13$^{7f.,\ 12,\ 14-22,}$ $^{24-27}$ are Jewish apocalyptic sayings, which comprised a context that had been preserved intact before it was worked into Mark. Vv. 5f., 9–11, 13a, 23 are Christian additions. Significant are (1) the fact that a Jewish apocalypse was taken over and used as a saying of Jesus, so that the Messiah (21f.) or the Son of Man (26f.) was simply identified with Jesus; (2) the way it is treated: (*a*) The Person of Jesus is introduced (5f, 9, 13a, 23); (*b*) *vaticinia* from the Church's mission and persecution are introduced (9–11, 13a); (*c*) a *vaticinium* of historical events is introduced (5f.).

It is moreover of significance for the history of the tradition, that Matthew has worked the prophecy of Mk. 13$^{9-13}$ into another context (Matt. 10$^{17-22}$). As a substitute, in chapter 24, he has added vv. 10–12 to his reproduction of Mark, and this consists in parts of variants, thus: v. 10 is a variant to 10^{21} = Mk. 13^{12}; v. 11 to 10^{24} = Mk. 13^{22}. We cannot determine whether Matthew composed these verses himself or took them from some Jewish or Christian tradition. Neither can we say whether v. 12, which has no parallel in the other contexts, was originally a Jewish (cp. 4 Ezr. 5^{2}; E. En. 91^{7}) prophecy or a Christian. By contrast Matt. 10^{23} which Matthew has used to enlarge the corresponding section in the charge to the Disciples, is clearly a Christian *vaticinium* deriving from the missionary activity of the Church.

Apart from some small details, Luke has added to the tradition in

---

[1] M. Goguel, *Critique et histoire à propos de la vie de Jésus*, 1928, p. 30, thinks he can establish the genuineness of Lk. 17^{25} (as of Mk. 14^{62}) in that the verse has no reference to the Resurrection on the third day. But Luke could well owe his formulation to the 'Urmensch' tradition, where the Resurrection played no part at all. But comparison with Matthew shows that the verse is a Christian addition to Luke's text: the sentence is not in circulation for Q.

much the same way, in vv. 21b, 22, 25b, 26a, 28 (verses which could well be Luke's own) and the section already reviewed 21 ³⁴⁻³⁶. But Luke's corrections are just as important, while Matthew's are of less significance for our purposes. Luke has added πρὸ δὲ τούτων πάντων in 21 ¹² in order to postpone the events prophesied in 21 ¹⁰f. Similarly he has omitted Mk. 13 ²¹⁻²³ and the words ἐν ἐκείναις ταῖς ἡμέραις in Mk. 13 ²⁴, because he wants to postdate the Parousia (21 ²⁵ff.) and separate it from vv. 12–14 by a long interval. He has altered Mark's text in vv. 20–24 *ex eventu*, i.e. after the Jewish war.

Mk. 13 ²⁸⁻²⁹ par.: *Parable of the Fig Tree.* I can see no valid objection to the originality of this section which Mark has placed, along with other material, at the end of the eschatological discourse. The saying is not really about a particular tree; the definite article is proper to parabolic style which Luke (21 ²⁹) spoils. There is no reference to the Person of Jesus in the parable. But that admittedly does not determine the question whether it was spoken by Jesus, or was derived from Jewish or Christian tradition.

Mk. 13 ³⁰ par.: *The Imminence of the Parousia.* It is hardly likely that the saying was always independent in this particular form. It could be a variant of 9 ¹, adapted for this context. In any event it seems not to have belonged to vv. 28f. originally. On the other hand it would be possible for it to be the original conclusion of the Jewish apocalypse (with v. 32? see below). It would go well after v. 7.

Mk. 13 ³¹ par.: *The certainty of Jesus' prophecy.* This saying too could hardly have belonged to the end of a Jewish apocalypse (the speaker would in that case be God): it is much more likely to be a Christian formulation.

Mk. 13 ³² par.: *God alone knows the Time.* This is perhaps a Jewish saying up to its Christian ending (οὐδὲ ὁ υἱός, εἰ μὴ ὁ πατήρ)[1]; with v. 30 this could have been the ending of the Jewish apocalypse. For dogmatic reasons Luke passed over this saying.

Lk. 19 ⁴²⁻⁴⁴: *Prophecy of the Destruction of Jerusalem.* This is a Christian construction *ex eventu*, and perhaps it is fairly old (with an Aramaic origin? Cp. Wellhausen).

Matt. 25 ³¹⁻⁴⁶: *The Last Judgement.* Perhaps the specifically Christian content of this passage is that the good works or their omission are seen as related to the Son of Man. For even if the Son of Man had occasionally played the role of judge in Judaism, the reference of human action or inaction to him is readily conceivable only if he be conceived as much more than an individual personality, i.e. if he be identified with Jesus. On the other hand it is man as such who stands

[1] *Vide* Dalman, *The Sayings of Jesus*, I, p. 159.

before the judge, which means that the story was conceived at a time when the antithesis of Christian and non-Christian was no longer important. Accordingly the moral of this section is not specifically Christian; cp. Isa. 58[7]; Test. Jos. 1[5f.]; Slav. En 9, 42[8], 63; Sot. f. 14a: 'In reference to Deut. 13[5] it is asked: How can a man walk after God? . . . But the meaning is that you acquire his properties (Middoth). Just as God clothes the naked (Gen. 3[21]), so must you clothe the naked; as God visits the sick (Gen. 18[1]) so do you; as God comforts the mourners (Gen. 25[11]) so must you; as God buries the dead (Deut. 34[6]) you must do likewise'.[1] Cp. further the Mandaean text in R. Ginza, I and II, 1, pp. 18.5ff.; 36.13ff Lidzb. There are Egyptian and Persian parallels also available, which explain how these ethical demands played such a special part in Jewish eschatology. Cp. the Egyptian Book of the Dead, chapter 125 (Gressmann, *Altorientalische Texte und Bilder zum A.T.*[2], I, p. 12; *Textbuch zur Religionsgesch.*[2], p. 274; G. Roeder, *Urkunden zur Religion des alten Aegypten*, pp. 277f.), and for Parseeism: Huebschmann, 'Die parsische Lehre vom Jenseits und juengsten Gericht', *Jahrbuecher fuer prot. Theologie*, 1879, pp. 223, 229; Boecklen, *Die Verwandtschaft der juedisch-christlichen mit der parsischen Eschatologie*, pp. 19, 43; C. Clemen, *Religionsgeschichtl. Erklaerung des NT*[2], p. 254. Thus it is impossible to avoid thinking that Matt. 25[31-46] derives from Jewish tradition. Perhaps, when it was taken up by the Christian Church the name of God was replaced by the title Son of Man, see below, pp. 142f. on Mk. 9[37, 41]//Matt. 10[40, 42].

Matt. 7[15]: *Warning about False Prophets*. We can hardly trace this saying, for it is apparently quite a secondary formulation of Matthew himself, which he was constrained to make on the one hand by the dangers threatening the Church and on the other by the logion he used in 7[16-20].

Mk. 9[12-13] par.: *The Coming of Elijah*. This section in its present context serves at least to verify the fulfilment of an apocalyptic prophecy. The saying, together with the question asked by the disciples in v. 11 which originally went along with it, in Mark's source followed straight on from v. 1, and Mark separated them by inserting the story of the Transfiguration vv. 2–10 (see below). That it originated in the Church's theological discussion should be clear enough. The old saying in v.1, which contradicts the Jewish theory of a forerunner to the Kingdom of God, can be reconciled

---

[1] From G. Klein, *Der aelteste christliche Katechismus und die juedische Propaganda-Literatur*, 1909, p. 49.1. The text is now available in greater detail in Strack-B. I, 561. In general cp. the excursus *die altjuedischen Liebeswerke* in Strack-B. IV, i, 559–610.

with it, since it states that the forerunner has already appeared. No doubt Mark thought that the Baptist was he, and Matt. 17[13] adds that express statement. In addition to this Matthew has further supported the Christian interpretation of the Jewish expectation of a forerunner by making it in 17[12b] analogous to the Christian treatment of the concept of the Messiah. That is why there is an interpolation in Mark's text; for I cannot think of the intrusive and unconnected saying about the Son of Man in Mk. 9[12b] as anything else than an interpolation.[1]

(e) *The History of the Tradition*

The first basic observation is to the effect that Jewish material has been taken over by the Christian tradition and ascribed to Jesus. Clear proof of that is seen in Mk. 13[5-27], which is a Jewish Apocalypse with a Christian editing.[2] The prophecies against this generation and against Jerusalem are quotations from a Jewish Wisdom scripture, and in regard to the prophecy of the destruction of the temple in Mk. 13[2] there is at least the possibility that it was first ascribed to Jesus by the Church.

This means that we are obliged to ask to what extent the rest of the traditional material must be similarly judged. For our purposes passages like Lk. 14[15]; Mk. 10[29f.] are relatively unimportant; they are not sufficiently characteristic to support a judgement. By contrast it is easy to suppose that Matt. 25[31-46] was Jewish in origin and received a Christian editing. As we saw in the case of Mk. 13[5-27] some verses perhaps need treating separately from the rest. Perhaps vv. 30 and 32 are the end of the Jewish Apocalypse, and vv. 28f. could similarly derive from Jewish tradition. The situation is different in regard to sayings like Lk. 17[21, 23f.]; with their dispensing with apocalyptic calculations they form a contrast to the typical prophecies and warnings about the end, and therefore it is not very likely that they had a Jewish origin.

But we have to ask this question not only about apocalyptic sayings, where we find it easy to understand why they were taken

---

[1] Because Mk. 9[12b] does not expressly mention the death of the Son of Man, M. Goguel (*Jean-Baptiste*, p. 59) is able to see in this verse (as in Lk. 17[25]; see p. 122 n. 1) an authentic dominical saying, which I think impossible. For this reason he understands v. 12 in the traditional way as the formulation of an aporia which in turn gives rise to the rejection of the expectation of the Forerunner. But that would involve a quite different formulation for v. 12a, to make it a conditional clause or a question. (Cod. D certainly makes this revision); cp. Klostermann. Goguel is then inclined to regard v. 13 as an addition by the Evangelist. But if one accepts the original connection of v. 11 with v. 1 (cp. Klostermann) there can be no doubt, in my view, that v. 13 is the proper continuation of v. 12a.

[2] There is an analogy to this in the way that the Didache takes over Jewish prophecy, Did. 16[3-7].

over from Judaism, but also about other, more prophetic sayings. Admittedly we may not be able to reach more than possibilities, but for all that we must consider them. The following are the passages where it is most likely that there was a Jewish origin: Matt. 24$^{37-41}$ par., $^{43-44}$ par., $^{45-51}$ par. We are bound to make the same conjecture about Matt. 24$^{10-12}$ and Lk. 6$^{24-26}$. The prophecies of salvation in Lk. 6$^{20-21}$ par. could just as easily have come somewhere in the last chapters of E. En., as could the Woes of Lk. 6$^{24-26}$. And certainly they contain nothing that is specifically characteristic of the preaching of Jesus.[1] Nevertheless in the Christian tradition they are not thought of just as general prophecies of future salvation, but as referring to the present. The longed-for age is breaking in *now*; so we can say: blessed are the saints who long for it! And in so far as this eschatological consciousness is something new in distinction from Judaism, so far are these beatitudes in any case unJewish. Similarly the immediacy of eschatological consciousness is given such emphatic expression in Lk. 10$^{23f.}$//Matt. 13$^{16f.}$ and Matt. 11$^{5f.}$//Lk. 7$^{22f.}$ that it is impossible for any Jewish tradition to provide an origin. To the same group of sayings belong Lk. 11$^{31f.}$//Matt. 12$^{41f.}$ and Lk. 12$^{54-56}$, which announce the critical character of the hour of decision.

On the other hand we cannot without more ado be sure that passages whose Jewish origin is improbable are genuine sayings of Jesus. For our second basic observation is that we find a whole series of Christian formulations, i.e. Church formulations, among the passages we have reviewed. In the first place we may notice *Christian revisions of elements from older traditions*. We have already identified the motives underlying the Christian revision of Jewish apocalypses; but they can be detected elsewhere as well. The picture of the Last Judgement in Matt. 25$^{31-46}$ and the interpretation of the Sign of Jonah in Matt. 12^{40} have been connected with the Person of Jesus. Matt. 17^{12} and Lk. 17^{25} have introduced the identification of the Son of Man's sufferings with those of Jesus, while Matt. 16^{28} (Mk. 9^1) identifies the Son of Man as Jesus. By ignoring the introductory formula Matthew in 23^{34} has identified Jesus with the divine Wisdom. In 10$^{32f.}$ he has edited the saying about confessing to the sayings of Jesus in the light of the Christian identification of Jesus with the Son of Man, just as he gives it even more forceful formulation in 7^{21}. The understanding of the Person of Jesus is also the reason for Luke's omission of the saying in Mk. 13^{32}, where it has already

[1] Sayings of this kind express the spiritual attitude of the circles that have been called 'the poor' (Anawim) by M. Dibelius (*Der Brief des Jakobus*, in Meyers Kommentar, 1921, pp. 37–44) and W. Sattler (*Festgabe fuer A. Juelicher*, 1927, pp. 1–15).

received a Christian interpretation (in the closing words οὐδὲ ὁ υἱός, εἰ μὴ ὁ πατήρ)—it contradicts his own understanding of Jesus' divine character.

In chapter 21 Luke has attempted several corrections of apocalyptic prophecies in Mk. 13 (see p. 123), partly under the influence of historical events (21 [20-24]). Pap. Ox. 654.1 provides a correction of Mk. 9[1]: [πᾶς ὅστις] ἂν τῶν λόγων τούτ[ων ἀκούσῃ, θανάτου] οὐ μὴ γεύσηται. The Church's destiny mirrors Matthew's addition to the sayings about the Pharisees in 23 [34], the appearance of false Christian teachers in Matt. 7 [15] and the formulation in Matt. 7 [22f.]. In addition the Baptist's Messianic preaching is amended by the reference to Christian Spirit baptism (Mk. 1 [7f.] par.), the promise of an hundredfold reward (Mk. 10 [29f.]) is expanded, and the Beatitudes are edited and added to in Matt. 5 [3-9].

The addition to the old Beatitudes of some new ones in which the persecuted disciples are blessed Lk. 6 [22-23] par. is itself part of a *specifically Christian tendency*. And just as the passage cited gives expression to the Christian conception of the Person of Jesus, so too does the Parable of the Ten Virgins in Matt. 25 [1-13]. And the apocalyptic expectation which is the theme of this parable, is the theme also of the Christian passages Mk. 9[1], 13[31, 33-37]; Lk. 12[32, 35-38, 47f.], 21[34-36]. The destiny of the Church and its mission finds its expression in passages like Lk. 6 [22-23] par., and Matt. 11 [21-24], and the destruction of Jerusalem in Lk. 19[42-44], 23[28-31]. Christian interests are displayed in Mk. 9[12f.] and Lk. 4[25-27]. Mk. 1[15] is a summary of the Christian message of salvation, and finally we have a Christian formulation also in the warning of John the Baptist in Matt. 3 [7-10] par. We can see with complete clarity what the process of reformulation of such dominical sayings was like in sayings like Rev. 16[15]: ἰδοὺ ἔρχομαι ὡς κλέπτης· μακάριος ὁ γρηγορῶν καὶ τηρῶν τὰ ἱμάτια αὐτοῦ κτλ or like Rev. 3[20]: ἰδοὺ ἕστηκα ἐπὶ τὴν θύραν καὶ κρούω κτλ. To such instances we may add the saying quoted in Justin, Dial. 47 and elsewhere: ἐν οἷς ἂν ὑμᾶς καταλάβω, ἐν τούτοις καὶ κρινῶ. Here, as above (p. 102), it is possible to ask whether it was originally intended to ascribe such prophetic sayings to Jesus. They could very easily have gained currency at first as utterances of the Spirit in the Church. Sometimes the ascended Christ would assuredly have spoken in them—as in Rev. 16[15]—and it would only be gradually that such sayings would come to be regarded as prophecies by the Jesus of history.[1] The Church drew no distinction between

---

[1] Cp. H. Gunkel, *Reden u. Aufsaetze*, 1913, p. 173: 'One can suppose that not a few sayings, which have come down to us in the N.T. as utterances of Jesus, were originally

such utterances by Christian prophets and the sayings of Jesus in the tradition, for the reason that even the dominical sayings in the tradition were not the pronouncements of a past authority, but sayings of the risen Lord, who is always a contemporary[1] for the Church.

Accordingly we cannot avoid raising the question of a possible Christian origin even for those passages where it seems intrinsically unlikely. Such an origin is the more questionable, the less we can discern any relation to the Person of Jesus or to the lot and interests of the Church, and the more, on the other hand we can trace a characteristically individual spirit. This applies to the passages already mentioned, which express the acute eschatological consciousness with its combined gladness and gravity in the face of decision, i.e. Lk. 6[20f.] par., 10[23f.] par.; Matt. 11[5f.] par. as also Lk. 11[31f.] par., 12[54-56]. If Matt. 11[5f.] par. does refer to Jesus, it is not necessarily in his messianic role, but much more probably to his preaching, and so it would actually be Jesus' self-consciousness coming to expression in the same way as in Lk. 12[8] par., where the Son of Man will judge a man in the light of his attitude to the teaching of Jesus. The same may be said of Lk. 6[46] (Matt. 7[21]). A similar conclusion would apply to the refusal to give a sign (Mk. 8[12] or Matt. 12[39f.] par.) and the rejection of signs (Lk. 17[21]). In its original form the discourse about the Pharisees, Matt. 23//Lk. 11[39ff.] is to be traced back to Jesus, and perhaps the saying about the Temple (in the form of Mk. 13[2](?)) can be ascribed to him even if with some reserve. I do not think we can reach any firm conclusion about Matt. 8[11f.] par., 24[43-44] par., [45-51] par. The discourse about the Pharisees shows that we must be cautious in every case, for it has been subjected to a certain amount of editing in Q, and the Beatitudes in Matt. 5[3-9] show the same need for caution, for we can see in them very clearly how new sayings can grow on to old ones.

Finally the apocryphal tradition at this point shows how new dominical sayings arise, which can be more or less taken from the Jewish tradition. In this category we must include the apocalyptic passage in 1 Th. 4[15-17] which appears as a word of the Lord. We must also include the passage preserved in Iren. V, 33[3f.] which speaks of the miraculous fertility of the Kingdom of God, the

---

spoken by such inspired men (like the Singer in the Od. Sol. 42) in the name of Christ. H. v. Soden had already made the same point, *Das Interesse des apostol. Zeitalters an der evg. Geschichte*, 1892, p. 153. He refers to the circular letters of Rev. And Rev in general provides like the Od. Sol., quite clear examples of this phenomenon. Od. Sol. 42[6] gives clear expression to it:

> 'For I have risen and stand by them
> And speak through their mouth.'

[1] Cp. J. Schniewind, *Th.R.*, N.F. 2, 1930, pp. 140, 142, 159f.

prophecy appearing in Justin, Dial. 35 and Didasc. Syr. 6⁵ ἔσονται σχίσματα καὶ αἱρέσεις,[1] and further the promise quoted in Clem. Alex. Strom., II, 9.45 and V, 14.96 from the Gospel to the Hebrews, which appears in a very similar form in Pap. Ox. 654.2: μὴ παυσάσθω ὁ ζητῶν ἕως ἂν εὕρῃ καὶ ὅταν εὕρῃ θαμβηθήσεται καὶ θαμβηθεὶς βασιλεύσει καὶ βασιλεύσας ἐπαναπαήσεται. Many other sayings could be added. How one such proverb can be fashioned on the basis of an older one can be illustrated by Hom. Clem. 12.29: τὰ ἀγαθὰ ἐλθεῖν δεῖ, μακάριος δέ, φησί, δι' οὗ ἔρχεται· ὁμοίως καὶ τὰ κακὰ ἀνάγκη ἐλθεῖν, οὐαὶ δὲ δι' οὗ ἔρχεται.

The history of the material also includes the fact that by being woven into the Gospel tradition the sayings have in part been seen in a new light. It is of less importance that the blessing of the participants in the feast of the Kingdom of Heaven is put into the mouth of one of the guests (Lk. 14¹⁵), and more remarkable that a section of a minatory sermon in Matt. 3⁷⁻¹⁰//Lk. 3⁷⁻⁹ is ascribed to the Baptist. Above all it is significant that often by means of such devices the original meaning of a saying is changed.

The report in Matt. 11⁵ᶠ· par. was originally intended as a Beatitude: the day of salvation will come now, and forthwith will be experienced all the wonders of salvation of which the ancient promises spoke. Indeed one can see—e.g. in Jesus' exorcizing of demons—the New Age already breaking in. Like Q, the Evangelists have narrowed the meaning: the report is now concerned with the acts of Jesus, his miracles, which establish his identity as Messiah. In particular Luke has made the point by adding 7²¹. The reference of Lk. 11³¹ᶠ· par. (this generation in comparison with the Queen of the South and the Ninevites) to the Person of Jesus had been made in Q too: after the demanding of a sign (i.e. of something to establish Jesus as Messiah) the words πλεῖον ὧδε can no longer refer to the message, but only to the Person of Jesus: since this generation fails to recognize Jesus as Messiah, the Queen of the South and the Ninevites will shame it. The same applies to the saying in Matt. 8¹¹ᶠ· par. where the context in Matthew as in Luke produces the reference to the Person of Jesus: the Gentiles exhibit the faith which recognizes his Person. Similarly with Matt. 13¹⁶ᶠ· par.: The Blessing of the eyes that see is no longer—as would correspond to the original meaning of the saying—based on the experience of the dawn of the time of salvation, but on the fact that Jesus is recognized as Messiah, as e.g. by the aged Simeon in Lk. 2²⁵ᶠᶠ· Moreover, both evangelists limit the blessing to the disciples; this is a treatment suffered also by the

---

[1] Modelled on 1 Cor. 11¹⁹? Or is Paul himself quoting an apocryphal saying?

saying in Mk. 10²⁹f· (hundredfold reward), which was indubitably originally thought of as universal in its application but which has been restricted especially to the disciples by Mark's introduction (Peter's statement: ἰδοὺ ἡμεῖς ἀφήκαμεν πάντα κτλ). It goes without saying that the tradition relates all the passages to Jesus where the υἱὸς τοῦ ἀνθρώπου or (in parables) the κύριος is mentioned.

Just as the logia have given the evangelists occasion for the addition of *formal introductory or transitional passages*—apart from any editing of contents—so have the prophetic and apocalyptic sayings. That is the meaning of ὑμεῖς δε βλέπετε· προείρηκα ὑμῖν πάντα in Mk. 13²³; similar formulations are to be found in Mk. 13³³: βλέπετε, ἀγρυπνεῖτε κτλ, and Mk. 13³⁷: ὃ δὲ ὑμῖν λέγω, πᾶσιν λέγω, γρηγορεῖτε. In this way Matthew has linked the condemnation of the generation that kills the prophets with the discourse on the Pharisees by the phrase: ὄφεις, γεννήματα ἐχιδνῶν, πῶς φύγητε ἀπὸ τῆς κρίσεως τῆς γεέννης (23³³), in which he has made use of the motif of 3⁷. Similarly Matt. 24⁴² (γρηγορεῖτε οὖν κτλ) uses a motif from Mk. 13³³⁻³⁷ to link together different traditional passages (24³⁷⁻⁴¹ and 24⁴³⁻⁴⁴) and at the end of 24⁵¹ᵇ he has added the well-known ἐκεῖ ἔσται ὁ κλαυθμὸς καὶ ὁ βρυγμὸς τῶν ὀδόντων. Luke who composes his eschatological discourse 13²²⁻³⁰ from all sorts of pieces, has linked this saying about the narrow door v. 24 with the rejection of Jesus' contemporaries by formulating the connecting verse 25 for which he has borrowed the motif from a parable similar to that in Matt. 25¹⁻¹³. This is extremely clumsy, for the door in v. 25 is quite different from that in v. 24 where the πολλοί certainly do not seek this door. It is possible that Lk. 17²²: ἐλεύσονται ἡμέραι ὅτε ἐπιθυμήσετε μίαν τῶν ἡμερῶν τοῦ υἱοῦ τ. ἀνθρ. ἰδεῖν καὶ οὐκ ὄψεσθε is similarly a formulation by Luke (or some earlier editor), meant to serve as an introduction to the following eschatological discourse. On any view Lk. 21²⁸ is a Lucan concluding formula (ἀρχομένων δὲ τούτων γίνεσθαι . . . διότι ἐγγίζει ἡ ἀπολύτρωσις ὑμῶν).

3. LEGAL SAYINGS AND CHURCH RULES

(a) *Survey and Analysis*

Here I first cite the sayings that have been treated of already to some extent among the logia and which also indicate a position in regard to the Law or Jewish piety.

Mk. 7¹⁵ par.: οὐδέν ἐστιν ἔξωθεν τοῦ ἀνθρώπου . . . κοινῶσαι αὐτόν

Mk. 3⁴ par.: ἔξεστιν τοῖς σάββασιν ἀγαθὸν ποιῆσαι κτλ.

Mk. 2²⁷: τὸ σάββατον διὰ τὸν ἄνθρωπον ἐγένετο κτλ.

Matt. 12¹¹ᶠ·//Lk. 14⁵: . . . ὃς ἕξει πρόβατον ἕν, καὶ ἐὰν ἐμπέσῃ τοῦτο τοῖς σάββασιν εἰς βόθυνον κτλ. Matthew's v. 12, which is without parallel in Luke, is one of Matthew's well-known explanatory additions.

Mk. 3²⁸ᶠ· or Matt. 12³¹ᶠ·; Lk. 12¹⁰: *The Sin against the Spirit*. Mark has the relatively most original form: every sin can be forgiven the sons of men (originally the son of man, i.e. men) save blasphemy against the Spirit. I agree with Wellhausen about the form in Q which Matthew has joined to Mark. It arose from a misunderstanding: any word spoken against the Son of Man (i.e. against Jesus) can be forgiven, but blasphemy against the Spirit cannot.[1]

Mk. 2¹⁰ par.: ἐξουσίαν ἔχει ὁ υἱὸς τ. ἀνθρ. ἐπὶ τῆς γῆς ἀφιέναι ἁμαρτίας. I cite this saying here with some reserve, though the accepted meaning is probable (p. 12f.).

Possibly Mk. 2¹⁹ᵃ par. (no fasting in the time of rejoicing) should also be included here, if it does not in fact have a less normative character. Possibly Mk. 8¹⁵ too (Warning against the leaven of the Pharisees), a saying whose original form, like its original meaning, is almost beyond recovery.

Further we must add two sayings from the discourse on the Pharisees in Q:

Matt. 23²³⁻²⁴//Lk. 11⁴²: . . . ἀποδεκατοῦτε τὸ ἡδύοσμον κτλ. Matt. 23²⁴, which has no counterpart in Luke could well be an addition adapting it to proverbial form. The end of Matt. 23²³: ταῦτα ἔδει ποιῆσαι κἀκεῖνα μὴ ἀφεῖναι, were missing from the original text of Luke, but were probably in Q (as a secondary expansion?)

Matt. 23²⁵⁻²⁶//Lk. 11³⁹⁻⁴¹: *The Pharisees seek outward purity only.* Luke's form is original in the first verse. Matthew's in the second, cp. Wellhausen. But this saying has also been subject to secondary expansion in Q. Matt. 23²⁶ = Lk. 11⁴¹ seems to be such an addition. The controversy saying originally ended with the

---

[1] A. Fridrichsen, *R.H.Ph.R.*, III, 1923, pp. 367–72, believes that the Q form is original and explains the saying by reference to the Jewish Mission of the infant Church: the Jews can indeed be forgiven the sins they have committed against Jesus, but not their disobedience to the spirit operating in the apostolic preaching. In its Lucan context the saying begets a new meaning, by being addressed to Christians undergoing persecution. The saying is 'une règle de la discipline ecclésiastique définissant les différantes catégories de *lapsi*'. By contrast the Marcan form identifies the spirit with Jesus and protests against the Gentile charge that Jesus was a magician. M. Goguel, in *Jean-Baptiste*, also thinks the Q form original, in accordance with his belief that all Synoptic references to Jesus as the bearer of the Spirit, p. 194, are secondary. H. Leisegang (*Pneuma Hagion*, pp. 96–112) reconstructs in terms of the older version, which he finds in the text common to Mark and Matthew, an original form of the saying based on the (actually secondary!) context where the unforgivable sin is parallel to blasphemy against the divine name (. . . ὃς δ' ἂν βλασφημήσῃ εἰς τὸ ὄνομα τὸ ἅγιον. . .); it was under Hellenistic influence that ὄνομα was first replaced by πνεῦμα!

rhetorical question (cp. Matt. 23[17, 19]) which is retained in Lk. 11[40] only, being deleted by Matthew who failed to understand it.

To these 'legal sayings' belongs also a group of sayings which are formulated in legal style, i.e. they are sentences whose first clause contains a condition (ἐάν, ὅταν, ὃς ἄν, ὅστις, etc., or instead a participle) and whose second part is an imperative or an assertion (sometimes in the future), and which has the sense of a legal prescription. Naturally, sayings are also included in which this form is not followed all through, but has had a general effect.[1]

Mk. 10[11f.] par., or Lk. 16[18]//Matt. 5[32]: ὃς ἂν ἀπολύσῃ τὴν γυναῖκα αὐτοῦ . . . μοιχᾶται ἐπ' αὐτήν. καὶ ἐὰν γυνὴ κτλ (according to D, etc.) or according to Lk. (Q): καὶ ὁ . . . γαμῶν . . . μοιχᾶται.

In 19[9] Matthew has abbreviated his Mark copy and inserted the concessionary addition μὴ ἐπὶ πορνείᾳ. We can see that the saying was subject to change in the tradition from the relationship of Mark and Q, as from the tradition of the Mark text. The original text of Mark forbids a man to divorce his wife, and his wife to marry again; while Q (Lk. 16[18] and Matt. 5[32]) forbids a man to divorce his wife or to marry a divorced woman. I believe the latter form to be original, and account for the form in Mark by supposing that a legal ruling was wanted not only for the man, but for the woman too. The later version in Mark (ℵ, B, etc.) adapts this ruling to other legal relationships. But Matthew has also made alterations in the first part of 5[32]. For to say that the guilt of a man who divorces his wife consists in the fact that he is thereby the cause of her second marriage is obviously artificial. Originally it would be that the man was guilty if he divorced his wife in order to marry another woman.

Mk. 11[25] or Matt. 6[14f.]: *Reconciliation the condition for the answering of prayer.* The sayings are variants, and one may suppose that Matt. 6[14f.] has been fashioned from the version in Mark to serve as a commentary on the petition in the Lord's Prayer for the forgiveness of sins. Mk. 11[25] is itself legal in style: ὅταν στήκετε προσευχόμενοι, ἀφίετε κτλ.

Matt. 5[23-24]: ἐὰν (οὖν) προσφέρῃς τὸ δῶρόν σου . . . ἄφες ἐκεῖ . . . Matthew puts the saying into an alien setting. It is in any case a variant to Mk. 11[25], and indeed most probably a more original form, which presupposes the existence of the sacrificial system in Jerusalem.

---

[1] Examples for such a legal style (distinguished from the 'Thou shalt' of the Torah):' if (anyone) . . . so (must) . . .' or 'whoever . . . he (must) . . .': Exod. 21[12ff.]; Deut. 13[2ff.], 17[2ff.], 22[1ff.], etc. There are Rabbinic examples in P. Fiebig, *Der Erzaehlungsstil der Evangelien*, pp. 4ff., 20. Of the sayings cited on p. 131 we may include Matt. 12[11f.] par. and Mk. 3[28] or Matt. 12[31f.] par. Cp. further Mk. 10[15]; Lk. 14[11].

Matt. 6$^{2-4}$: ὅταν (οὖν) ποιῇς ἐλεημοσύνην, μὴ σαλπίσῃς . . .
σοῦ δὲ ποιοῦντος ἐλεημοσύνην μὴ γνώτω . . .

Matt. 6$^{5-6}$: (καὶ) ὅταν προσεύχησθε, οὐκ ἔσεσθε ὡς . . .
σὺ δὲ ὅταν προσεύχῃ, εἴσελθε . . .

Matt. 6$^{7-13}$: προσευχόμενοι (δὲ) μὴ βατταλογήσητε ὥσπερ . . .
οὕτως οὖν προσεύχεσθε ὑμεῖς . . .

Matt. 6$^{16-18}$: ὅταν (δὲ) νηστεύητε, μὴ γίνετε ὡς . . .
σὺ δὲ νηστεύων ἄλειψαι . . .

The four sections, which are in Matt. 6^1 preceded by a special
introduction (by Matthew?), are alike in exhibiting the antithetic
scheme of opposing the right line of conduct to the wrong. In addition, with one exception, the imperative is always followed by a
promise (καὶ ὁ πατήρ σου κτλ). But Matt. 6$^{7-13}$, where the promise
is missing, has a special character for other reasons: the Lord's Prayer
spoils the conciseness of an antithesis. It can hardly be doubted that
its appearance here is secondary, and confirmation of that can be
found in the different tradition of Lk. 11$^{2-4}$. Nevertheless we may
ask whether the Lord's Prayer in Matt. 6$^{7-13}$ is put in place of some
previous antithesis, which had to be removed to make place for it, or
whether it is not more likely that Matt. 6$^{7f.}$ is a formulation (by
Matthew?) analogous to the other sections fashioned specially to
bring the Lord's Prayer into this particular context. I think this
latter the more likely, for in that case the complex would have consisted originally of one saying each about almsgiving, prayer and
fasting; the duplication of instruction about prayer must be secondary. In any case we may suppose that the need for catechetical formulations, constructed like each other, and easy to remember, had led to
the assimilation of alien material into such forms.[1]

Related to these passages is Matt. 23$^{16-22}$, first the antagonistic
theses of vv. 16 and 18 (. . . ὃς ἂν ὀμόσῃ . . . οὐδέν ἐστιν or ὀφείλει)
and their repetition in vv. 17 and 19; then the special theses in
vv. 20–22 (ὁ οὖν ὀμόσας . . . ὀμνύει). Here the theses of vv. 20–22
only appear to have a legal style, for the indicative actually entails no
regulation, declares no 'ought', but simply announces a fact. In

---

[1] I think that what M. Albertz says (*Die synopt. Streitgespraeche*, pp. 150f.) about
Matt. 6$^{1-6, 16-18}$, which he describes as a 'didactic poem' is fantastic. Here, where only
the disciples are addressed, and not (as in controversy sayings, antitheses and woes)
opponents, there is 'the last possible phase of conflict'. 'The whole piety of the opponents
is done away.' But this cannot be maintained, because this is nothing whatever to do with
the keeping of the law, but about specially worthy exercises of piety, about which there is a
great deal said in Judaism akin to Matt. 6; cp. the parallels in Strack-B. and in Fiebig,
Jesu Bergpredigt. The composition is much more like a Church catechism in character, and
as to its individual sections deriving from Jesus (see below), we cannot see why he should
not have been able to have spoken them during his ministry. It is possible to put Albertz'
train of thought into precise reverse.

addition, the highly rhetorical questions of vv. 17 and 19 contain all that has to be said, and they form a more potent rejection of the Jewish customs in swearing oaths than the somewhat pedantic explanations of vv. 20–22. Finally, v. 22 comes out of the context: up till now there has been no mention of swearing by heaven. For these reasons I hold vv. 20–22 to be a secondary construction. The polemical sayings in vv. 16–19 are original, for they are born out of anger with a foolish casuistry. Vv. 20–22 are an addition which uses that polemic as the motivation for the special treatment of oath-swearing: i.e. vv. 20–22 is a community product.

Matt. 5²¹⁻⁴⁸:

1. Matt. 5²¹⁻²²: (a) the opposing standpoint: ἠκούσατε ὅτι ἐρρέθη . . . οὐ φονεύσεις· ὃς δ᾽ ἂν φονεύσῃ, ἔνοχος ἔσται τῇ κρίσει.
    (b) the new standpoint: ἐγὼ δὲ λέγω ὑμῖν ὅτι πᾶς ὁ ὀργιζόμενος . . . ἔνοχος ἔσται . . . ὃς δ᾽ ἂν εἴπῃ . . . ἔνοχος ἔσται.

It is self-evident that εἰκῇ, which has crept into some manuscripts here, and which e.g. the Nazarean editor of Matthew did not read, is a secondary addition, clearly illustrating the tendency to depress enthusiastic demands to the level of a bourgeois morality. But perhaps v. 22b (ὃς δ᾽ ἂν εἴπῃ κτλ) is also a secondary addition. The passage is not only without any analogy in parallel sayings, but it diminishes the hitting power of the antithesis. Further, if v. 22b be original, κρίσις must be understood differently in v. 22a from v. 21 (v. 21 generally, judgement, v. 22a: the local court) so as to contrive a climax: κρίσις, συνέδριον, γέεννα. But in fact the Sanhedrin was not an example of something higher than a local court. Neither can one see why a term of abuse should be more harshly punished than anger, especially in a passage where the concern is to reject the application of external standards! So we have to reckon v. 22b as one of the additional formulations of a juridical kind.[1]

2. Matt. 5²⁷⁻²⁸: (a) . . . οὐ μοιχεύσεις.
    (b) . . . πᾶς ὁ βλέπων . . . ἤδη ἐμοίχευσεν.
3. Matt. 5³¹⁻³²: (a) . . . ὃς ἂν ἀπολύσῃ . . . δότω . . .
    (b) . . . πᾶς ὁ ἀπολύων . . . ποιεῖ αὐτὴν μοιχευθῆναι.
    . . . καὶ ὃς ἐὰν . . . γαμήσῃ, μοιχᾶται.
4. Matt. 5³³⁻³⁷: (a) . . . οὐκ ἐπιορκήσεις, ἀποδώσεις δὲ . . .
    (b) . . . μὴ ὀμόσαι ὅλως, μήτε . . .
    ἔστω δὲ ὁ λόγος ὑμῶν . . .

We may ask whether the succession of four examples of culpable

[1] Cp. J. Weiss, ad loc., in the *Schriften des N.T.* Whether the addition is to be understood as persiflage of a scribal characteristic or as homiletic expansion in view of the widespread vice of insult is a matter for question.

oath-taking is original. The first three examples, swearing by heaven, by the earth, and by Jerusalem, reject such oaths for being encroachments upon the sphere of God's majesty. The last examples, swearing by one's own head, makes the oath ridiculous: the man who makes it cannot in any sense so dispose himself. Are the first three examples, with their scripture quotations, secondary?[1]

5. Matt. 5$^{38-41}$: (a) . . . ὀφθαλμὸν ἀντὶ ὀφθαλμοῦ . . .
   (b) . . . μὴ ἀντιστῆναι τῷ πονηρῷ.
      ἀλλ' ὅστις σε ῥαπίζει . . . στρέψον . . .
      καὶ τῷ θέλοντι (or ὁ θέλων) . . . ἄφες . . .
      καὶ ὅστις σε ἀγγαρεύσει . . . ὕπαγε . . .

We have already seen (p. 83) that here an originally alien saying has been attached with v. 42.

6. Matt. 5$^{43-48}$: (a) . . . ἀγαπήσεις . . . καὶ μισήσεις . . .
   (b) . . . ἀγαπᾶτε . . .

Once more a complex of similarly constructed sayings lay before Matt. 5$^{21-48}$, to which v. 20 is Matthew's own introduction. Here again we find on closer inspection that the particular items are not all homogeneous.

In Matt. 5$^{31f.}$ the saying about divorce appears as an antithesis to the legal saying in Deut. 24^{1}, while in Lk. 16^{18} (Q) and Mk. 10$^{11f.}$ it does not appear in antithesis, and this is doubtless the original version. The same conclusion follows from a comparison of Matt. 5$^{38-41}$ and $^{43-48}$ with Lk. 6$^{27-35}$. In Luke the sayings about revenge and loving one's enemy show no trace of antithetical adjustment. And if one is tempted to put that down to the editorial activity of Luke, which is otherwise certainly to be reckoned with in these passages (cp. p. 96), then the parable form and the breadth of the execution which goes beyond the needs of an antithesis to a legal saying support the view that these sayings originally were not clothed in an antithetical setting.

There is still one more point. The introductory forms in vv. 31, 32a, 38, 39a, 43, 44a, are obviously moulded on the pattern of the antithetical forms in vv. 21f., 27f., 33-37, and in these passages the antithesis was plainly never an isolated saying, for it is only intelligible in relation to the thesis, and does not have the form of a mashal. Finally, in distinction from the three secondary formulations, these three passages are alike in putting the thesis in the form of a prohibition (οὐ φονεύσεις, οὐ μοιχεύσεις, οὐκ ἐπιορκήσεις), and this prohibition is not abolished, but surpassed. In the three other formu-

---

[1] Cp. C. G. Montefiore, *The Synoptic Gospels*, II^{2}, pp. 68f.

lations there is no prohibition, but an instruction (or a concession 5³¹) which is not surpassed, but overthrown.[1]

Thus the older formulation 5²¹ᶠ·, ²⁷ᶠ·, ³³⁻³⁷ has given rise to analogous formulations, in which unattached dominical sayings have found a home.[2] The motive for the formulation is clear: the antithetical form commends itself by its catechetical character.

Further, I reckon among the legal sayings those which, by means of a proverb or by an appeal to scripture, justify or base the new outlook over against the old.

Mk. 2²⁵⁻²⁶ par.: *Scripture proof for breaking the Sabbath* from 1 Sam. 21¹⁻⁶ (David's actions); augmented in Matt. 12⁵⁻⁶ by a proof from the official actions of the priests, 12⁷ and citing Hos. 6⁶, which Matthew also uses in 9¹³ (cp. p. 16).

Mk. 7⁶⁻⁸ par.: Attack on lip-service, using Isa. 29¹³ in connection with the answer to the question about washing hands (cp. pp. 17f.).

Mk. 10³⁻⁹ par.: *Debate on divorce*, making use of Deut. 24¹; Gen. 1²⁷, 2²⁴ (cp. pp. 26f.).

Mk. 12²³⁻²⁵ par.: *Debate on the resurrection of the dead*, using Deut. 25⁵ᶠ· (cp. p. 26).

Mk. 12²⁶⁻²⁷ par.: *Proof of the resurrection of the dead* from Exod. 3⁶ (cp. p. 26).

Mk. 12²⁹⁻³³ par.: *The Question about the greatest commandment*, answered with Deut. 6⁴ᵇ, ⁵; Lev. 19¹⁸ᵇ; 1 Sam. 15²² (cp. pp. 22f.).

Mk. 12³⁵⁻³⁷ par.: '*David's Son*' or, the problem of Ps. 110¹.

In all these passages, except the last, we have already shown that there was traditional polemical or theological material in them, that has been used in the construction of the apophthegms. But we have shown on p. 66 that even in the last case, Mk. 12³⁵⁻³⁷ we are dealing with a community product. This receives confirmation by reflecting that the proof that Messiah could not be David's Son could hardly have had any meaning for Jesus. If he really knew himself to be Messiah, I can see but two possibilities: (1) He knew he was David's Son; in that case we may suppose that his affirmation was attacked by criticism of his descent. But the tradition preserves no trace of that anywhere else, and so Mk. 12³⁵⁻³⁷ cannot be an answer to such criticism. (2) He knew he was the 'Son of Man'. But he could only know this in the way that Reitzenstein has understood: Jesus knew that he was the divinely sent one, who was to go in lowliness on

---

[1] I cannot think E. v. Dobschuetz right in his view (*Z.N.W.*, 27, 1928, p. 342) that only Matt. 5²¹ᶠ· and ²⁷ᶠ· are original formulations and that all four passages are analogy formulations.

[2] Cf. H. Weinel, *Bibl. Theologie des N.T.*⁴, p. 79; M. Albertz, *Die synopt. Streitgespraeche*, pp. 146f.

earth, to lead the erring back to God by his life and his teaching, and wait for his exaltation.[1] For it seems too fantastic to me to suppose that Jesus believed that he would one day become the 'Son of Man'.[2] But Reitzenstein's conception seems to me to come to grief in having to ascribe to Jesus some consciousness of pre-existence (of which the Synoptic tradition knows nothing) and in supposing that the Synoptic Jesus never spoke of his exaltation. Reitzenstein interprets the self-consciousness of Jesus in terms of the Fourth Gospel. For all that it is quite possible that the contrast to 'David's Son' in Mk. 12^{35-37} is in fact the 'Son of Man'; that would imply that the hope of a political Messiah was countered with the expectation of a heavenly Messiah.[3] That being so it would, of course, not be impossible for Jesus to have spoken the words (though, admittedly, not with reference to himself). But since his reference to the coming Son of Man never turns on that opposition, and since the proof offered in Mk. 12^{35-37} has the air of a scribal sophistry about it, and since, lastly, the dogma of Jesus being the Son of David would hardly have become dominant so early in the life of the Church (Paul himself presupposed it) if Jesus had contested the idea of Messiah being the Son of David, the more probable conclusion is that Mk. 12^{35-37} is a community product, and one that admittedly expresses the point of view of a limited circle only. Indeed there are two possibilities. *Either* the saying comes from a section of the primitive Church, in which case it is intended to represent that tension between faith in the Son of Man and hope in the Son of David (if, that is, it were not meant simply to refute the accusation that Jesus' Davidic descent could not be established). *Or* it comes from the Hellenistic Church, in which case it would be meant to prove that Jesus was more than the Son of David, viz. the Son of God.[4]

[1] Cp. R. Reitzenstein, *Das mand. Buch d. Herrn. d. Gr.*, p. 45; *Das iran. Erloesungsmyst.*, pp. 117–31; *Z.N.W.*, 20, 1921, pp. 1–23.

[2] If we so suppose, Mk. 12^{35-37} has to be interpreted with A. Schweitzer, *The Quest of the Historical Jesus*, p. 393, *The Mysticism of Paul the Apostle*, 1930, p. 83: 'The solution of the problem (of Ps. 109^1) is this: that the Messiah, who, quite unknown by the Scribes, was present in the person of Jesus first as a man of David's seed living in humility among men, afterwards being transformed into the transcendent Messiah, as which, although a son of David, he would be David's Lord. . . .' Such fantasies and their consequences seem to me wholly unjustified by the tradition we have of the Lord's sayings.

[3] Cp. G. Hoelscher, *Urgemeinde u. Spaetjudentum*, 1928, p. 9.

[4] This last position is that adopted by W. Wrede, *Jesus als Davidssohn, Vortraege u. Studien*, 1907, pp. 147–77. In this interpretation the quotation from the Ps. is related also to Barn 12^{10}, and we can easily imagine that Mk. 12^{35-37} came from the same Scribal, Jewish-Christian section of the Hellenistic world as the *Epistle of Barnabas*. In this case the 'Lord' of the Psalm would have been understood in terms of the cultic title although, if the saying really came from the primitive Church, it would have the secular meaning of 'Lord' (in contrast to 'slave'). Cp. W. Bousset, *Kyrios Christos*[2], p. 78.7; *Jesus der Herr*, pp. 15f. Otherwise it is probable that Mark who would have understood by κύριος the Lord worshipped in the cult, had no specific interpretation of the saying, but included it

Matt. 5$^{17-19}$ (cp. Lk. 16^{17}): *Jesus' attitude to the Law*. While the section we have just considered comes from the debates that the Church had with its Jewish opponents, Matt. 5$^{17-19}$ derives from the discussions between the more conservative (Palestinian) communities and those that were free from the law (Hellenistic). The words μὴ νομίσητε show that v. 17 comes from debates, and ἦλθον reflects the actual ministry of Jesus. It was already customary to think of his ministry in terms of his teaching, for πληρῶσαι and καταλῦσαι do not refer to what he does, as indeed v. 19 makes quite clear. In its formulation of principle and its contradiction to the primitive tradition, v. 18 cannot but be a community product; while v. 19 cannot be any sort of polemic against Jewish, but only against Hellenistic teachers of the law. (V. 20 does not really belong to this complex, but is most probably a heading or introduction by Matthew to 5$^{21-48}$.) Matt. 5$^{17-19}$ thus records the attitude of the conservative Palestinian community in contrast to that of the Hellenists. Luke has used but a fragment of this section, whose tone was not to his liking. Matthew took it from Q.

There is also a group of sayings of a somewhat different kind, which do not express an attitude to the law of the O.T. but give prescriptions for the Christian community. Nevertheless they belong to the previous sayings about the law, because they were also in some measure prescriptions for the new community appearing as antitheses to the old law.

Matt. 16$^{18-19}$: *Peter as the authority in the new community*. This whole section to which these words are a conclusion will be considered at a later stage. Here we may note the following points; the Church preserved a tradition of a saying by Jesus in which Peter is promised authority in matters of doctrine, or discipline; for I do not think that λῦσαι and δῆσαι can have any other meaning.[1] By the same token

among the controversy sayings as an example of how Jesus refuted the Scribes. See Strack-B. IV, i, 452–65 for Ps. 110 in Rabbinic Literature. The problem posed by Mk. 12$^{35-37}$ was apparently not discussed by the Rabbis. The Messianic interpretation of the psalm can be traced among them no earlier than the second half of the third century A.D. Then there is occasional discussion of the relationship of Abraham to the Messiah (Strack-B. IV, i, 457), which has its basis in the fact that the psalm was for by far the most part given an interpretation in reference to Abraham.

[1] Δέειν and λύειν can admittedly be technical terms of magic and as such mean 'bind by magic' and 'set the magic-bound free'. But we cannot interpret Matt. 16^{19} thus as A. Dell, *Z.N.W.*, 15, 1914, pp. 38–46, following others seeks to do. For if we try to think of the authority of λύειν in terms of Mk. 7^{35}; Lk. 13^{16} as the ἐξουσία τῶν πνευμάτων τῶν ἀκαθάρτων (Mk. 6^7), how shall we interpret δέειν? The context in Matt. 18^{18} shows quite plainly that Matthew did not so understand them. But the context of 16^{19} also shows that they must be concerned with specific functions of Church officials; and finally the formulation of the promise (ἐπὶ τῆς γῆς – ἐν τοῖς οὐρανοῖς) indicates that a judicial function is in mind. The verbs אֲסַר and שְׁרָא (Heb. אָסַר and הִתִּיר) which undoubtedly lie behind δέειν and λύειν can be used to describe either doctrinal authority (declaring something to be for-

the saying is shown to come from the Palestinian Church, even if we cannot suppose, as J. Kreyenbuehl did ($Z.N.W.$, 8, 1907, pp. 81–109, 163–89) that it is the reply of the Early Church to Paul's attack in Galatians. Apart from the concepts λῦσαι and δῆσαι, we cannot entertain a later origin for the saying because the play on words in Πέτρος — πέτρα could not be conceived in Greek, because of the awkward change of gender.[1] A Semitic origin is also indicated by πύλαι ᾅδου, as does the whole thought of v. 18; in the end, when the powers of the underworld overcome mankind, the Church will be saved.[2] Here the Palestinian Church expresses its eschatological

bidden or permitted) or disciplinary powers (banished, i.e. excommunication, or the lifting of the same; this is the usage of Jos., *Bell.*, I, p. 5.2 = § 111 δεσμεῖν var. δέειν and λύειν. Related to this is the use of שְׁרָא for a declaration of innocence). Examples of the usage are in Dalman, *Worte Jesu* 1, pp. 175–8; Strack-B. I, 738–41. Schlatter, *Der Evangelis Matthaeus*, pp. 510f. It is not feasible to make too sharp a line of demarcation between doctrinal and disciplinary authority; both were in the hands of one individual in Judaism. It is also a Jewish idea that God (ἐν τοῖς οὐρανοῖς) recognizes the decisions of lawfully constituted authority in the Church on earth (ἐπὶ τῆς γῆς); cp. Dalman, op. cit.; Strack-B. I, 743–7; J. Jeremias, *Golgatha*, 1926, p. 72. Finally the metaphor of the power of the keys, which Dell (op. cit., pp. 33–38); Bousset (*Kyrios Christos*[2], p. 30.3) etc. seek to explain in terms of magical terminology, is also found in Rabbinic writings and stands for doctrinal authority; cp. Dalman, op. cit., pp. 176f.; Strack-B. I, 737, 741; J. Jeremias, op. cit., p. 72, and cp. Matt. 23[13]. It is clearly not right for Jeremias to claim that ἐκκλησία and βασιλεία τ. οὐρ. are identical as descriptions of the Church. The distinction between ἐπὶ τῆς γῆς and ἐν τ. οὐρ. shows clearly that the earthly and heavenly kingdoms are still separate, but that the Church (as the community of the end) has a close relationship to heaven. It is the entrance to (or the beginning of) the βασιλεία τ. οὐρ. Cp. H. Windisch, $Z.N.W.$, 27, 1928, p. 186.

[1] Cp. my essay $Z.N.W.$, 19, 1919/20, pp. 165–74, esp. pp. 170f. The attempt to avoid the difficulty in Strack-B. I, 732 is absurd: Retranslation into Aramaic makes it impossible to interpret: 'I say to you, thou art Peter . . .' but we must understand, 'I tell you, yes, you, Peter (I tell you because you were first to confess my Messiahship and my divine Sonship): On this rock (on the reality of my Messiahship and divine Sonship) I will build my Church.'

[2] The πύλαι ᾅδου are also a Greek picture for death (Homer, *Il.*, V, 646 and cp. Wetstein) but are characteristically semitic (שַׁעֲרֵי שְׁאוֹל Isa. 38[10], LXX: πύλαι ᾅδου etc.; cp. Klostermann, ad loc.). The promise καὶ πύλαι ᾅδου οὐ κατισχύσουσιν αὐτῆς is interpreted by Dell ($Z.N.W.$, 15, 1914, pp. 27–33), Bousset (*Kyrios Chr.*[2], p. 30), etc. (cp. Clemen, *Rel. Gesch. Erk. des N.T.*[2], pp. 90 and 241 and O. Weinreich, Genethliakon W. Schmid, 1929, pp. 436–45) in line with their understanding of δέειν and λύειν and of the metaphor of the keys, that Christ, who has burst the gates of Hell by his descent into Hades, promises the Church protection from the demonic powers. But apart from the fact that the descent into Hades is nowhere hinted at in the text, it is not possible to see any connection between the bursting of the gates of Hades by Christ's descent into hell, and the phrase οὐ κατισχύσουσιν: the Church had not been imprisoned in Hades! indeed is not so much as on the way there (οἰκοδομήσω fut.)! Victory over death and its power is promised. If we do not interpret in this way (on this see further C. A. Bernoulli, *Joh. d. Taeufer u. die Urgemeinde*, 1918, pp. 279–86), then Schlatter's explanation is possible (*Der Evglist. Matth.*, pp. 509f.): the Church, i.e. its individual members are promised not deathlessness but resurrection. J. Jeremias (*Golgatha*, pp. 68–77) wants to relate αὐτῆς in v. 18 not to ἐκκλησία but to πέτρα— a point ostensibly demonstrated by the structure of these verses). But that leaves the security of the Church still in question; a rock is discovered for her, which guarantees security to her. But this wrecks Jeremias' interpretation of the πέτρα as the cosmic rock, namely the keystone of Sheol. According to Jeremias the promise means 'that in case of death Peter would not be lost to the dead world of the godless' (p. 71). But what connection has this promise with the conception of Peter as the πέτρα for the ἐκκλησία? Now

consciousness of being the eschatological community of the Just. So the content of the verses no less than the language of v. 17 that goes along with vv. 18–19 shows the Semitic origin of the saying.[1] On the other hand I freely admit that it seems to me quite impossible to take Matt. 16[18-19] as a genuine saying of Jesus, as K. L. Schmidt (see note 1) wishes to do, finding in this saying the foundation of a special community (a כְּנִישְׁתָּא). The price that has to be paid for this information is that the ἐκκλησία is deprived of its radically eschato-logical character.[2]

Jeremias sees the point precisely in this, that the idea of a rock contains a peculiar contradiction: 'on the one hand a rock must support the sacred edifice and constitute an entrance into the Kingdom of God, and yet at the same time it must repel the powers of the underworld' (p. 73); the 'cosmic rock' is just like this. In my view Jeremias with his 'cosmic' rock, about which, it seems to me, the Rabbinic parallels (following note) know nothing, only complicates the simple thought of the text. R. Reitzenstein (*Das iran. Erloesungsmyst.*, p. xii) seeks to interpret the office given to Peter as Aion's office of door-keeper, standing as Christ's servant (the great Aion) on the borders of this earth and the kingdom of light and keeping watch over the faithful (especially over right doctrine). If Matt. 16[18f.] were really incomprehensible otherwise (as R. believes), we should have to accept this interpretation; actually it seems to me a long way from the truth. A. v. Harnack's interpretation is based on a reconstruction of an older text (οὐ κατισχύσουσίν σου with omission of καὶ ἐπὶ τ. τ. πέτρα up to τ. ἐκκλησίαν), and in that Peter is promised that he will not die (*Sitzungsber. d. Berl. Ak.*, 1918, pp. 637–54; cp. H. Windisch, *Z.N.W.*, 27, 1928, pp. 186f.), I think this impossible; cp. J. Sickenberger, *Theol. Revue*, 19, 1920, pp. 1–8; E. Meyer, *Urspr. u. Anf. d. Christent.*, I, 1921, p. 112.1; S. Euringer, 'Beitr. z. Gesch. d. christl. Altert. u. d. byz. Lit.' (*Festg. f. Ehrhard*), 1922, pp. 141–79.

[1] In addition to the points noted we may add to the linguistic indications the following matters of content: The metaphor of the building which is the Church is frequent in Judaism; cp. Strack-B. I, 732f.; Schlatter, *Der Evglist. Matth.*, pp. 506f. So it is entirely unnecessary to make a conjecture that ἐκκλησία is a forced translation for 'house' (T. Hermann, *Theol. Bl.*, 5, 1926, cols. 203–7). It is quite indifferent for Matt.· 16[18f.] whether ἐκκλησία stands for קָהָל or עֵדָה or כְּנִישְׁתָּא; cp. Strack-B. I, 733–6; K. L. Schmidt, *Festg. f. A. Deissmann*, 1927, pp. 258–319, *Theol. Bl.*, 6, 1927, pp. 293–302. K. L. Schmidt and W. Michaelis in *Taeufer, Jesus, Urgemeinde*, pp. 106–10 have rightly realized that in any case Matt. 16[18] treats of the eschatological community. The metaphor of the rock, which is the support of the Church, and even referred to a particular individual (esp. Abraham), is not infrequent in later Rabbinic literature; cp. Strack-B. I, 733; K. G. Goetz, *Z.N.W.*, 20, 1921, pp. 165–9; J. Jeremias, *Golgatha*, pp. 73f. Characteristic of v. 17 is Peter being called Σίμων Βαριωνᾶ (otherwise Jn. 1[42], 21[15ff.]); further the beatitude in the second person, is found very seldom in Greek examples (cp. H. L. Dirichlet, 'De veterum macarismis', *Religionsgesch., Vers. u. Vorarb.*, XIV, 4, 1914; E. Norden, *Agnostos Theos*, 1913, p. 100.1) but is frequent in semitic languages; finally σάρξ καὶ αἷμα are the recognized semitic description of man over against God. On the whole subject see further K. G. Goetz, *Petrus*, 1927, esp. pp. 30–44.

[2] Such a special community would be a συναγωγή, a 'School' (cp. 1 Macc. 2[42], 7[12]; Acts 6[9]). That such a community should maintain that it represented the קְהַל יְהֹוָה is hardly credible. The Synagogue takes its place alongside the temple, and is not primarily a cultic assembly as the קָהָל was; it was constituted by its participants, who came together to it, and not by God as the קָהָל was. Admittedly such a special community could say of itself that it had the true doctrine, and its members could regard themselves as people waiting for the appearance of the eschatological קָהָל, and as predestined for it (cp. e.g. Eth. En. 38[1], 62[8]; Did. 9[4], 10[5]). The linguistic usage is characteristic: Ps. Sol. 10[7] puts into synonymous parallelism with the singular ἐκκλησία λαοῦ and Ἰσραήλ the plural συναγωγαί

Matt. 18¹⁸: . . . ὅσα ἐὰν δήσητε ἐπὶ τῆς γῆς. . . . The saying is a variant, and surely a later one, of Matt. 16¹⁹.¹ The right to make laws is here promised to the Church, i.e. practically to its representatives, if indeed those were not the original recipients. So it will have come from the time of the primitive Church, when an institutional authority of Church leaders had taken the place of the personal authority of Peter, which by conjecture could be the period after Agrippa's persecution, in which James, and very likely John too, the sons of Zebedee, were victims, and in which Peter was driven from Jerusalem. This expulsion was probably the last; the Apostolic Council must have taken place before Agrippa's persecution, and by the time of Paul's last visit to Jerusalem Peter is no longer in Jerusalem. By putting the saying in its context (after vv. 15–17) Matthew has related it specially to the Church's (or its authorities') given right to allow or withhold forgiveness of sins.

Matt. 18¹⁵⁻¹⁷, ²¹⁻²², or Lk. 17³⁻⁴: *Rules for Church discipline.* This title admittedly applies only to Matt. 18¹⁵⁻¹⁷ and here it is indeed particularly clear how an ancient dominical saying could be reformulated into a disciplinary Church regulation. Luke had the older version which enjoined the forgiveness of personal injuries in front of him; in Matt. 18¹⁵⁻¹⁷ this has been edited, though the conclusion, which is not easily adapted to such editing, has been attached to a supplementary transitional question vv. 21f. We can offer no conjecture as to the origin of the older version in Lk. 17³ᶠ. The expanded version comes from the Palestinian Church, as the language and the terminology show (μεταξὺ σοῦ καὶ αὐτοῦ μόνου v. 15, ἐθνικός and τελώνης, v. 17).²

'Ισραήλ, and 17⁸ describes the pious as those ἀγαπῶντες συναγωγὰς (plural!) ὁσίων. Because the saying in Matt. 16¹⁸ᶠ· means the eschatological ἐκκλησία (the קָהָל irrespective of whether this concept or some other were used), we have the future of promise: οἰκοδομήσω, and the μου added to ἐκκλησίαν characterizes the Church as messianic, and not as the special synagogue of some individual. In actual fact the primitive Church, in so far as it still hopes for the coming of the βασιλεία, thought of itself as the true Israel (cp. the institution of the Twelve!) for whose appearance the apocalyptics still waited (cp. also my essay, 'Kirche u. Lehre im N.T.', Zw. d. Zeiten, 7, 1929, pp. 18ff.). Finally, the mere fact that the primitive Church was driven by necessity to become a special Synagogue, and that the tradition makes Jesus a participant in the Sabbath worship of any local Synagogue (K. G. Goetz, *Petrus*, pp. 24), clearly shows that Matt. 16¹⁸ cannot be thought of in terms of a special Synagogue, but only of an eschatological Church of God. Cp. further H. Windisch, Z.N.W., 27, 1928, pp. 186f.

¹ Wellhausen takes the opposite view, that Matt. 18¹⁸ is perhaps older than 16¹⁹; similarly, and yet more convincingly, E. Meyer, *Urspr. u. Anf. d. Christent.*, I, p. 112.1.

² According to Strack-B., I, 787–90 the (limited) duty of bringing an erring brother to the right way by reproof (ἐλέγχειν = הוֹכִיחַ) was known to the Synagogue, though no such definite instructions had been developed as Matt. 18¹⁵⁻¹⁷. The parallel in Mandaean R.G., I, pp. 24.8ff., Lidzb. shows how natural it was for a young community forced into opposition to formulate such regulations. It is possible that the Q form was available to

Matt. 18¹⁹⁻²⁰: *The Hearing of Prayer*. This section is a promise about prayer to the Christian Church, and indeed v. 20 is a Christian version of a Jewish saying, quoted e.g. in P.A. III, 2: 'When two sit and there are between them words of Torah, the Shekinah rests between them.' Further instances are in Strack-B. I, 794f. But v. 19 is also an older saying in Christian form, whether originally a dominical saying or a Jewish proverb can hardly be determined. But we must not suppose, just because a Rabbinic proverb is made use of, that this section has a Palestinian origin, in spite of the role given to the ὄνομα of Jesus. There is a variant to Matt. 18²⁰ in Hellenistic literature, cp. Pap. Ox., I, 4: ὅπου ἐὰν ὦσιν [β', οὐκ] ε[ἰσὶ]ν ἄθεοι, καὶ [ὅ]που ε[ἷς] ἐστιν μόνος, λέγω· ἐγώ εἰμι μετ' αὐτοῦ κτλ.

Mk. 9³⁷, ⁴¹//Matt. 18⁵; Lk. 9⁴⁸ᵃ, or Matt. 10⁴⁰⁻⁴²; Lk. 10¹⁶: *Kindness to children*. The tradition of this saying is complicated and can hardly be unravelled with any certainty. The relationship of Mk. 9³⁷⁻⁴¹ and Matt. 10⁴⁰⁻⁴² seems to me to indicate that Mk. 9³⁷, ⁴¹ and Matt. 10⁴⁰, ⁴² belong together.[1] Mk. 9³⁸⁻⁴⁰ is an alien insertion, and in the same way Matt. 10⁴¹ is an insertion due to an association of ideas, being perhaps an old Jewish proverb. If then we look at Mk. 9³⁷, ⁴¹ and Matt. 10⁴⁰, ⁴² one after the other, it becomes plain that παιδία or μικροί which in Mark are in the earlier and in Matthew in the latter part, are part of the original saying and were also originally in both parts, while ὑμεῖς which Matthew puts at the beginning and Mark at the end is a secondary correction, making it possible for the saying to be applied to the Christian Church.[2] For the παιδία or μικροί were doubtless originally meant: the reception and refreshment of a little child was reckoned as equivalent to the greatest service that could be rendered. Later by a transference of ideas the παιδία or μικροί were understood to mean (unimportant) Christians. It was perhaps in connection with this change and the partial replacement of the saying that it came to be enlarged, namely by the addition (according to Mark) of: καὶ ὃς ἂν ἐμὲ δέχηται, οὐκ ἐμὲ δέχεται ἀλλὰ τὸν ἀποστείλαντά με, which in the second half (Mk. 9⁴¹) has no parallel. Instead Mark's original ἐν ὀνόματί μου has been interpreted by the addition of ὅτι Χριστοῦ ἔστε and, to the

---

Matthew (Streeter, *The Four Gospels*, pp. 257f. traces the section to the special source M) and that he introduced the connexion of v. 16b with Lev. 19¹⁷; for after v. 16a and v. 17 the point cannot be the increase in the number of witnesses, but only the widening of the authority of the admonitor.

[1] So also Klostermann.

[2] Since Matt. 10⁴² has obviously been added after the catchword παιδία or μικροί, clearly in Mark or in Mark's original there was one of these words instead of the ὑμᾶς of v. 41.

same effect Matthew has changed it to εἰς ὄνομα μαθητοῦ.[1] So it is possible that the original form of the saying had no reference to the person of Jesus, but that it was a Jewish saying, which said that kindness to the least of men was reckoned by God as done to him. So in the source and in the revision there is a precise parallel to Matt. 25³¹⁻⁴⁶, p. 124.[2] If the judgement lack certainty, this at least is sure, that here we have an older saying so edited by the Christian tradition that it can serve as a rule of the exalted Christ—for he speaks here—for the behaviour of his people, and for his people in their mutual relationships;[3] cp. on Mk. 9⁴² the parallels below. The relationship of Lk. 10¹⁶ to the Mark-Matthew saying seems to me to be this: Matthew and Luke found the saying at the end of the missionary commission. Luke reproduced it, while Matthew replaced it with a passage from another tradition in vv. 40, 42, and so the version of v. 40 was influenced by the Q saying (Lk. 10¹⁶). So Lk. 10¹⁶ is not a special variant of Matt. 10⁴⁰, Mk. 9³⁷, but an independent construction, related to the other only in this, that here again it is the risen Lord who speaks, and that treatment of his followers affects him. Naturally Lk. 10¹⁶ is also a product of the Church, and here too we surely have a Jewish saying as the basis, for 'a proposition often quoted (by the Rabbis) runs: A man's envoy (i.e. his representative or plenipotentiary) is the same as himself'.[4] There is an independent variation in Jn. 13²⁰.

Mk. 3³⁵ par.: *The true Kinsmen*. If the judgement on pp. 29f. were right and this be a saying that once had an independent existence, we have to adduce it here as a product of the Church. This makes much the same point as the previous saying in saying that so far as it is possible for them Christ's people are to have a relation to him that has to be reckoned as personal.

Mk. 10⁴²⁻⁴⁵//Matt. 20²⁵⁻²⁸; Lk. 22²⁵⁻²⁷ or Mk. 9³⁵; Lk. 9⁴⁸ᵇ: *Greatness in Service*. The manifestly original tradition of Mk. 9³⁵ and Lk. 9⁴⁸ᵇ as isolated units makes it probable that Mk. 10⁴³ᶠ· par., was also originally handed down without its setting.[5] The same con-

---

[1] So too Dalman, *The Sayings of Jesus*, I, pp. 250ff. Bousset in *Kyrios Chr.*², p. 5.1 holds εἰς ὄνομα μαθητοῦ as original, but on p. 42 as 'at least relatively more original'.

[2] There are similar Rabbinic sayings about the reward of hospitality especially to fellow members of the Rabbinic school (which were reckoned equal to the worshipping of the Shekinah!) in Strack-B. I, 589f. So we may wonder whether 'disciple' was not intended in the original saying. But Strack-B. has shown that the term 'little one' (and the same is true of 'child') was not used alone as a description of 'disciple'. This throws us back to the Rabbinic parallels cited in Strack-B. I, 774, which deal with the reward of kindnesses to orphan children.

[3] Cp. L. v. Sybel, *T.S.K.*, 100, 1927/8, pp. 398ff.

[4] Strack-B. IV, 590; cp. II, 167.

[5] A trace of this old proverb may also exist in Matt. 23¹¹, where it is appended to the rule of humility 23⁸⁻¹⁰ along with the saying about the lowly and the exalted 23¹².

clusion is reached by an analysis of Mk. 10⁴²⁻⁴⁵: the section is made out of an older saying in v. 43f. And indeed Mk. 10⁴³ᶠ· may well be more original than 9³⁵ in this, that it is a double saying; for in the double antithesis to πρῶτος in 9³⁵: πάντων ἔσχατος and πάντων διάκονος there is surely an echo of 9³⁵ having come from a double saying. On the other hand the absence of ἐν ὑμῖν or ὑμῶν in 9³⁵ could be more original than 10⁴³. In this discussion we need not consider whether Mk. 9³⁵ was originally alien to Mark's text (cp. D, etc.), though on other grounds I do not think it likely.

This judgement will also mean that a saying which originally referred generally to the greatness of service, was applied especially to the Christian Church in the Christian tradition. To that end it was provided with a foil in Mk. 10⁴² par. and at the end a reference to the example of Jesus was added. Indeed at the end Lk. 22²⁷ is doubtless original over against Mk. 10⁴⁵, which has formed its conception of Jesus from the redemption theories of Hellenistic Christianity.[1]

Matt. 23⁸⁻¹⁰: ὑμεῖς δὲ μὴ κληθῆτε ῥαββεί κτλ. This has been inserted by Matthew because of an association of ideas, and therefore is not a section constructed by himself. In the piece as we have it vv. 8–10 are a community rule, but it is not unitary: v. 10 seems to be a development of what was originally a double saying, declaring God to be the one Teacher and Father.[2] We can hardly tell where vv. 8f. came from. It could be a genuine dominical saying, but it could also be a product of the Church, and it could also have been taken over from Jewish tradition; for that here, on the basis of a simple piety, there is incidental polemic against the Rabbinic titles, is wholly credible, and the parallels give support.[3]

Mk. 9⁴² or Matt. 18⁶⁻⁷; Lk. 17¹⁻²: *Woe to the Seducer*. Matthew who follows the Marcan context, has first reproduced Mark's text in v. 6 and then brings the surplus text of Q into v. 7, while Luke uses only the Q text. Here too we seem to have a case of the Christian Church taking over an old proverb, whose origin can no longer be recovered,[4] and indeed in Q, it seems without Christian alterations, though in Mark it is christianized by the addition of τῶν πιστευόντων (Matthew adds here εἰς ἐμέ) to what was originally really intended:

---

[1] Cp. W. Bousset, *Kyr. Chr.*[2], pp. 7f.

[2] Cp. W. Bousset, *Kyr. Chr.*[2], p. 5.1. Also Dalman, *Worte Jesu*, I, p. 251, thinks that v. 10 is an editorial doublet of v. 8.

[3] Strack-B. I, 917–19.

[4] Cp. Strack-B. I, 779, esp. Sanh. 55a: 'R. Shesheth said, We have learnt it: if in the case of trees, which neither eat nor drink nor smell, the Torah decreed that they should be burnt and destroyed (cp. Deut. 12²ᶠ·) because they had proved a stumbling block (an occasion of sin—tr.): how much more so [must then destroy him] who seduces his neighbour from the path of life to that of death.'

τῶν μικρῶν τούτων. So there was a parallel precedent to Mk· 9³⁷, ⁴¹ par. (pp. 142f.).

Matt. 18¹⁰: *Despising the Children*. The same process can be discerned here. A saying, originally warning against despising children, has been christianized, by putting it in a context where the μικροί is applied to the Christian Church. Here too it is impossible to say where the saying came from.

Lk. 3¹⁰⁻¹⁴: *The Baptist's Preaching*. This is a catechism-like section, naïvely put into the Baptist's mouth, as though soldiers had gone on a pilgrimage to John. There is one thing that makes it improbable that we are here dealing with a product of the primitive Christian Church—that the profession of a soldier is taken for granted. Neither does the passage appear to be Jewish. It is perhaps a relatively late Hellenistic product, developed (by Luke himself) out of the saying from the tradition in v. 11 (ὁ ἔχων δύο χιτῶνας κτλ).

Mk. 6⁸⁻¹¹ par. or Matt. 10⁵⁻¹⁶; Lk. 10²⁻¹²: *The Missionary Charge*. This section must also in the end be included among the regulations of the Church. It has been more completely preserved in Q: Mark seems to give but an excerpt. As an Hellenistic evangelist he well knew that these instructions no longer applied to the mission in the oikumene, and so made of them a charge for the mission of the Twelve during the ministry of Jesus, and Matthew and Luke followed him in that.[1] But originally it was the risen (or ascended) Lord who spoke (cp. Matt. 28¹⁹ᶠ·; Lk. 24⁴⁷ᶠᶠ·), i.e. we have a Church product here. We can hardly tell now to what extent Jewish material was taken over; perhaps in δωρεὰν ἐλάβετε, δωρεὰν δότε Matt. 10⁸,[2] though this could equally well be an addition by Matthew to Q. We have already discussed the sayings in Matt. 10¹⁰ par. (ἄξιος γὰρ ὁ ἐργάτης κτλ) and 10¹⁶ (serpents and doves), (pp. 74f.; 103).

(b) *The History of the Material*

The history of the tradition of the dominical sayings can be seen with desirable clarity in the material we have been examining. The tradition gathered dominical sayings, gave them a new form, enlarged them by additions and developed them further: it collected other (Jewish) sayings, and fitted them by adaptation for reception into the treasury of Christian instruction, and produced new sayings

---

[1] I cannot see how any conclusion can be drawn for the historicity of the instruction during the life of Jesus from the difference in the missionary charge ascribed to the risen Lord (Lk. 24⁴⁸ᶠᶠ·; Matt. 28¹⁹ᶠ·). (E. Fascher, *Z.N.W.*, 26, 1927, pp. 7f.) In any case the evangelists had no intention of depicting a development (from Matt. 10⁵ to 28¹⁹). But the variety of the texts shows the development of the primitive Christian idea of Mission.

[2] Cp. Strack-B. I, 561–563.

from its consciousness of a new possession, sayings which they in-
genuously put into the mouth of Jesus. It is clear that the community
regulations are the earliest of those we have handled. In them the
risen Lord speaks, the exalted Lord addresses his Church. In part
these are sayings created independently by the Church, like Matt.
16[18-19], 18[15-17, 18] and the missionary charge; in part they are older
sayings edited in appropriate fashion, like Mk. 10[42-45]; Matt. 23[8-10],
etc. Sayings formulated in legal style are mostly also older, having
received their form essentially in the Church, but with whose content
the Church and the brotherhood within the Church had nothing to
do, like Matt. 6[2-18], 5[23f.], 23[16-22]; Mk. 11[25]; Lk. 17[3f.] I want to
call these *Rules of Piety*. In them the Church was conscious, not of its
churchly duties but of its characteristic piety in distinction from that of
Judaism.[1] From the apocryphal tradition there is a typical example of
such a rule of piety which is also formulated in legal style, *Pap. Ox.*, I,:[2]

ἐὰν μὴ νηστεύσηται τὸν κόσμον, οὐ μὴ εὕρηται τὴν βασιλείαν τ. θ.,
καὶ ἐὰν μὴ σαββατίσητε τὸ σάββατον, οὐκ ὄψεσθε τὸν πατέρα.

Further, the saying quoted in Clem. Alex. *Strom*. III, 15.97:

ὁ γήμας μὴ ἐκβαλλέτω καὶ ὁ μὴ γαμήσας μὴ γαμείτω.

Finally the apocryphal saying (Lagarde *Rell. Jur. eccl.*, ὅρος κανονικὸς
τῶν ἁγίων ἀποστόλων 3, p. 36): εἴ τις μεταλάβῃ τὸ σῶμα τοῦ κυρίου
καὶ λούσεται, ἐπικατάρατος ἔστω. But cp. also Jn. 3[(3),5]. Next to
these come the passages I would like to call debating sayings, which
serve polemic and apologetic purposes—substantially with Jewish
opponents. Here belongs the material used in the conflict—and
academic dialogues, which use scripture in their argument, like
Mk. 2[25f.], 7[6-8], 10[3-9], 12[23-25, 26f., 29-33,35-37]. Also here we may
reckon the passages gathered in Matt. 5[21-48]; for it is not a matter of
great moment whether the opposing idea is put in dialogue form into
the mouth of an opponent, or whether Jesus is made to give voice to
it himself.[2] There is no essential difference between (ἠκούσατε ὅτι)
ἐρρέθη in Matt. 5 on the one hand and ὑμεῖς λέγετε Mk. 7[11] or πῶς
λέγουσιν οἱ γραμματεῖς Mk. 12[35] or οἱ δὲ εἶπαν Mk. 10[4] or, finally
the opponent's words in Mk. 2[24], 7[5]. Nor is it of any consequence
whether in any particular place we have a controversy dialogue or a
scholastic dialogue. As we have seen already the material used in the
dialogues goes back substantially to the debates of the Church. In
the same way the passage Matt. 5[17-19] which derives from the debate
with the Hellenistic Church is a community product, and we have

---

[1] This naturally applies even when these rules of piety have their Jewish parallels.
[2] The Rabbinic style also knew how to oppose its own point of view to that of its
opponents with 'But I say ...'. Cp. G. Dalman, *Jesus-Jeschua*, 1922, p. 68.

seen that three of the passages collected in Matt. 5 [21-48] are in their present form analogy formulations using older material. It cannot be determined whether Matt. 5 [21f.] (murder), [27f.] (adultery), [33-37] (false witness) are Church constructions or not. In my opinion the words 'I say unto you' can here be historical; but this naturally does not take us beyond a possibility, and we must be content to affirm a 'genuineness' only in the sense that the Church's new possession, from which these sayings derive, goes back to the preaching of Jesus. But the oldest material is clearly in the brief conflict sayings which express in a parable-like form the attitude of Jesus to Jewish piety, e.g. Mk. 7 [15], 3 [4]; Matt. 23 [16-19, 23f., 25f.]. In my view this is the first time that we have the right to talk of sayings of Jesus, both as to form and content. Nevertheless Mk. 2 [27], which is perhaps a Jewish saying taken over by the Church (see p. 108), shows how careful we must be. Here too the extra-canonical literature affords good illustration. Schmidtke (*Neue Fragmente und Untersuchungen,* pp. 193f.), has explained the development of the saying ostensibly belonging to the Gospel of the Hebrews: ἦλθον καταλῦσαι τὰς θυσίας· καὶ ἐὰν μὴ παύσησθε τοῦ θύειν, οὐ παύσεται ἀφ' ὑμῶν ἡ ὀργή. The regrettably much mutilated fragment *Pap. Ox.* 654.6 shows what need the Church had of dominical sayings which prescribed the proper attitude to fasting, praying and almsgiving. Passages like the fragments of the Egyptian Gospel in Clem. Alex. *Strom.* III, 9.63; 13.92, and the sayings in ibid. III, 15.97; Pap. Ox. 655.1b; 2 Clem. 8.5f., etc. give instruction about the attitude to marriage, etc.[1]

Closer consideration gives the following picture. There was a stock of dominical sayings, the number of which cannot any longer be established with certainty, and to which, above all, the conflict sayings belong. The stock was enlarged by other valuable sayings. From *Jewish tradition* presumably come Mk. 9 [37, 41] par. (Kindness to Children); Matt. 10 [41] (Reward of Kindness), 18 [20] (οὗ γάρ εἰσιν δύο ἢ τρεῖς συνηγμένοι κτλ); Lk. 10 [16] (ὁ ἀκούων ὑμῶν κτλ). Of uncertain origin, though possibly Jewish are Mk. 10 [43f.] par., or Mk. 9 [35] (Greatness in Service); Mk. 9 [42] or Lk. 17 [1f.] (Woe to the Seducer); Matt. 18 [10] (Despising Children), 19 (Hearing Prayer), 23 [8f.] (ὑμεῖς δὲ μὴ κληθῆτε ῥαββεί). Besides Matt. 5 [17-19], 16 [18-19], 18 [18] and the missionary charge in full, Christian constructions are perhaps Matt. 5 [23] or Mk. 11 [25]; Matt. 6 [14] (Reconciliation as the Condition of Offering or Prayer); Lk. 17 [3f.] (The Duty of Forgiving one's Brother), 3 [10-14] (Preaching of the Baptist).

[1] The texts cited in Klostermann's collection: *Kleine Texte fuer theol. und phil. Vorlesungen und Uebungen,* edited by H. Lietzmann, no. 3, 8, 11.

But now above all we must consider Christian activity in the *editing of the material*, a process which belongs substantially, but not exclusively, to the written period.[1] In part it was enough simply to put the borrowed material in the tradition to make them appear in a new light, as Matt. 10⁴¹ (Reward of Kindness to Prophets and the Righteous), 18¹⁰ (Despising Children). But mostly this is accomplished by making certain alterations as well; for the μικροί or παιδία of Mk. 9³⁷, ⁴¹ par., or Matt. 10⁴⁰, ⁴² we find ὑμεῖς, so as to make it speak to the members of the Church, a thing which Mk. 9⁴¹ makes quite clear by adding ὅτι Χριστοῦ ἐστέ. Mark adds τῶν πιστευόντων (Matthew εἰς ἐμέ) to τῶν μικρῶν τούτων 9⁴². The saying about the Greatness of Service in Mk. 10⁴³ᶠ· is related to the Christian Church by the addition of ἐν ὑμῖν or ὑμῶν and the reference to the example of Jesus in Mk. 10⁴⁵ is reformulated in terms of the developed faith of the Church. In Matt. 18²⁰ the ὄνομα of Jesus appears instead of the Torah, and he himself instead of the Shekinah. The necessity for reconciliation before making an offering (Matt. 5²³ᶠ·) is universalized and referred to prayer (Mk. 11²⁵), and Matthew edits the saying to use it as a commentary on one of the petitions in the Lord's Prayer (Matt. 6¹⁴ᶠ·). The saying on divorce (Mk. 10¹¹ᶠ· par.; Lk. 16¹⁸) undergoes various editings;[2] in Matt. 5³¹ᶠ· it is made into a law in the form of an antithesis. Similarly other dominical sayings and the Lord's Prayer Matt. 5³⁸⁻⁴¹, ⁴²⁻⁴⁸, 6⁷⁻¹³ are given antithetical form in the editorial process. Examples of smaller commentatory additions are found in παρεκτὸς λόγου πορνείας and μὴ ἐπὶ πορνείᾳ Matt. 5³², 19⁹ and in εἰκῆ in Matt. 5²²D, etc.

To such alterations we can add *additions, and expansions*, such as are in evidence in Matt. 23²⁰⁻²² (on oaths), and Matt. 23²⁴ and ²⁶ (ὁδηγοὶ τυφλοί, οἱ διϋλίζοντες κτλ. and Φαρισαῖε τυφλέ, καθάρισον πρῶτον κτλ.). In Lk. 3¹⁰⁻¹⁴ an older saying, exhorting the man of possessions to charity is perhaps expanded. The exhortation to forgiveness in Matt. 18¹⁵ is transformed in 18¹⁶ᶠ· into a disciplinary regulation. The saying about the Greatness of Service in Mk. 10⁴³ᶠ· or Lk. 22²⁶ has been given a contrasting introduction in v. 42 (or 25) and in v. 45 (or 27) a conclusion which points to Jesus as the exemplar. The polemic against high-sounding titles in Matt. 23⁸ᶠ· has been given a specifically Christian ending in v. 10.

It has been said already many times that in many of these sayings

---

[1] Cp. L. v. Sybel, 'Vom Wachsen der Christologie in den synopt. Evangelien,' *Th.S.K.*. 100, 1927/8, pp. 362–401.

[2] To these also belongs the saying from Clem. Alex. quoted above p. 146.

it is particularly the risen Lord who speaks, above all in Church rules like Matt. 16$^{18-19}$, 18$^{18,\ 19f.}$; in the missionary charge, and further in Mk. 9$^{37,\ 41}$ par., 10$^{42-45}$ par.; but also in Matt. 5$^{17-19,\ 21-48}$, 6$^{2-18}$ the exalted Jesus is thought of as speaking (see pp. 127f.). Apart from these, *references to Jesus* have also been introduced into many sayings. Indeed it is only a misunderstanding that the Son of Man in Mk. 2^{10}; Matt. 12$^{31f.}$ par. has been interpreted of him. He appears in God's place as the recipient of kindnesses in Mk. 9$^{37,\ 41}$ par., as the teacher of the Church alongside God in Matt. 23^{10}; and as the one who stays with his own he has replaced the Shekinah Matt. 18^{20}. He has given the great example of service in Lk. 22^{27} or Mk. 10^{45}. He himself proves by scripture that the title Son of David does not apply to the Messiah, Mk. 12$^{35-37}$.

As the last stage of the development we are following we must consider the collections of sayings, in which legal sayings and Church rules were gathered together into a catechism. By this means passages which were originally much more polemic than legal in character were also turned into rules, like Matt. 5$^{21f.,\ 27f.,\ 33-37}$, passages which now appear as 'rules', by which the 'better righteousness' of the Church must judge itself. In the same way, between and alongside such passages there have been introduced logia which originally had no connection at all with the Church. The exhortation to be reconciled in Matt. 5$^{23f.}$ is followed by a passage in $^{25f.}$ which is part of a parable of the Parousia turned into a rule for piety. To the saying about adultery has been added in Matt. 5$^{29f.}$ the saying about 'stumbling'. Logia such as those about revenge and loving one's enemies are in this way given a form analogous to that of the preceding saying, Matt. 5$^{38-41,\ 42-48}$. Naturally the result is that we have such collections in various stages of development. What Matthew and Luke found in Q and Mark has been further transformed, particularly by Matthew. Examples can be found on a large scale in the Sermon on the Mount, and on a smaller scale in the collection in Matt. 23$^{8-12}$. Mk. 9$^{33-50}$, or Matt. 18$^{1-35}$ is another typical example. Clearly Mark's source was already a sort of catechism which, by providing the introduction in vv. 33f. Mark has turned into a scene in the life of Jesus. In v. 36 he has also given a most unsuitable introduction to v. 37 for which he has borrowed the motif from 10$^{13-16}$.[1] In the source vv. 38–40 were inserted (by a later hand?) *ad vocem* ἐπὶ (ἐν) τῷ ὀνόματι. V. 42 in the source followed vv. 37, 41 after the cue παιδίας

---

[1] In saying this I presuppose that v. 35 belongs in its entirety to the original text of Mark. If it were a later insertion, nothing is altered in respect of the principles I am considering.

or μικροί, and then vv. 43–48 after the cue-word σκανδαλίζεσθαι, and because their content was thought appropriate to the Church's catechism. Then vv. 49 and 50 are arranged after their cue words (πῦρ and ἅλας); then ἔχετε ἐν ἑαυτοῖς ἅλα καὶ εἰρηνεύετε ἐν ἀλλήλοις could well serve as the end of the catechism. Matthew still further strengthened the character of a Church ordinance by introducing the parable of the Lost Sheep 18[12–14], which in Matthew (in distinction from Lk. 15[4–7]) is referred to erring members of the Church. In vv. 15–22 he has arranged what was perhaps before him as a collection of Church rules, and then added the parable of the Unforgiving Servant, which now appears in this particular light (18[23–35]). Besides this he has at the beginning completed (v. 7) and polished Mark's source, by replacing here (v. 3) Mk. 10[15] for Mk. 9[35], and by inserting his own formulation in v. 4, which gives a connection between the occasion of the teaching (v. 1) and v. 3. Editorial formulations such as this last are naturally found elsewhere, as in the heading in Matt. 5[20], 6[1].

4. 'I'-Sayings

Our previous enquiry has shown that a reference to the person of Jesus is frequently a secondary introduction into the sayings. It is often done without changes or new formulations, and quite simply when a saying is put into a particular *context*. This applies to the blessing of the eyewitnesses in Matt. 13[16f.] par. (p. 109), for the sayings about the Queen of the South and the Ninevites Lk. 11[31] par. (pp. 112f.), the Gentiles in the kingdom Matt. 8[11f.] par. (p. 116), the hundredfold reward Mk. 10[29] (pp. 110f.), disciple and master Lk. 6[40] par. (p. 99). As the 'I' in the proverb in Matt. 12[30] (ὁ μὴ ὢν μετ' ἐμοῦ κτλ) is interpreted of Jesus, so is the Son of Man in the sayings about discipleship, blasphemy against the Spirit, forgiveness, and the Lordship over the Sabbath Matt. 8[20] par., 12[31f.] par.; Mk. 2[10, 28] and everywhere where apocalyptic sayings refer to the Son of Man, or parables to the householder.

Elsewhere the reference to the person of Jesus is effected by small alterations or additions. We can detect such alterations in the sayings about what is hidden Matt. 10[27] (p. 95), confessing the words of Jesus Matt. 10[32f.] (p. 112), the reward of kindness to children Mk. 9[37, 41] par. (p. 142), and being gathered in the name of Jesus Matt. 18[20] (pp. 141f.). Jesus is introduced under the title 'Son of Man' into the saying about the coming of the Kingdom Matt. 16[28] (p. 121) and also, surely, in the description of the Last Judgement Matt.

25³¹⁻⁴⁶ (pp. 123f.). By addition the person of Jesus is referred to in the saying about losing and gaining life Mk. 8³⁵ (p. 93). Similar additions are found in the Beatitudes in Lk. 6²²ᶠ·; Matt. 5¹⁰⁻¹² (p. 110), in the saying about greatness in service Lk. 22²⁷ (p. 144), the warning against high sounding titles Matt. 23¹⁰ (pp. 144f.), and the saying about the time of the Parousia Mk. 13³² (p. 123).

Additions which refer to the passion, death or resurrection of Jesus are to be found in the sayings about fasting Mk. 2¹⁹ᵇ, ²⁰ (p. 92), the Sign of Jonah Matt. 12⁴⁰ (p. 118), the return of Elijah Matt. 17¹² (pp. 124f.); while Lk. 17²⁵ (p. 121) inserts one in the eschatological discourse; to this corresponds the alteration which Mk. 10⁴⁵ (p. 144) has taken from his source (Lk. 22²⁷).

It is distinctive how Matt. 23³⁴⁻³⁵ (pp. 113f.) has made a Wisdom saying into one of Jesus' 'I' sayings by omitting the introductory formula. In this connection we have *specifically Christian formulations*, of which Mk. 13²³, ³⁷ is relatively harmless (ὑμεῖς δὲ βλέπετε· προείρηκα ὑμῖν πάντα and ὃ δὲ ὑμῖν λέγω, πᾶσιν λέγω, γρηγορεῖτε). More important are the sayings about the certainty of Jesus' sayings Mk. 13³¹ (p. 123), and the rejection of false disciples Matt. 7²²ᶠ· par (p. 117). Here too we must mention the woes over the Galilean cities Matt. 11²¹⁻²⁴ par. (pp. 117f.) with its indirect reference to the person of Jesus, and further the allegory of the Ten Virgins Matt. 25¹⁻¹³ (p. 119) and the question about the Son of David Mk. 12³⁵⁻³⁷ (pp. 136f.). Finally we must remember that in numerous legal sayings and Church rules the risen Lord is conceived of as the speaker.

This review shows that in all these secondary formulations Jesus appears not only as the prophet sent by God at the decisive hour, but he is the *Messiah and Judge* of the world. References to his death and its effect and to the resurrection are also beginning to appear. His ὄνομα has a religious meaning (Mk. 9³⁷, ⁴¹; Matt. 7²², 18²⁰), as in the sayings which are put into the mouth of the risen Lord Matt. 28¹⁹;[1] Lk. 24⁴⁷. In distinction from these the sayings Matt. 11⁵ par. (. . . μακάριός ἐστιν ὃς ἐὰν μὴ σκανδαλισθῇ ἐν ἐμοί); Mk. 8³⁸ cp. Lk. 12⁸ᶠ· (confession of the sayings of Jesus) and also the rejection of those who say 'Lord, Lord' Lk. 6⁴⁶ par. in all probability belong to the primary tradition. In them the prophetic self-consciousness of Jesus speaks, and they have no specifically Christian ring at all. Here again we must emphasize that some sayings about the Son of Man

---

[1] Did εἰς τὸ ὄνομά μου stand alone in the original text of Matthew? According to Loisy and others the whole passage from βαπτίζοντες to πνεύματος is an ancient interpolation. Cp. Klostermann, ad loc.

are manifestly not Christian formulations at all, but belong to the primary tradition, such as the saying just mentioned Mk. 8³⁸ or Lk. 12⁸ᶠ· and further Lk. 17²³ᶠ· par. These sayings could come from Jesus. Much the same applies to Matt. 24³⁷⁻³⁹ par., ⁴³ᶠ· par.; yet these sayings could also have been taken from Jewish tradition, as we can certainly suppose Mk. 13²⁴⁻²⁷ was. If one could ascribe other sayings of this kind to Jesus, if one could hold, say, that Jesus himself quoted the Wisdom Saying (Lk. 11⁴⁹⁻⁵¹ and 13³⁴ᶠ·, p. 119), in no circumstances could one follow the evangelist's idea, which holds that the identity of Jesus and the Son of Man is self-evident, but one must first prove the point.

After such considerations we may pass on to the sayings as yet unexamined, where the person of Jesus plays a substantial part, and these I call I-sayings *a parte potiori*. Nevertheless I shall not spend much time on the predictions of the passion and resurrection, which have long been recognized as secondary constructions of the Church: Mk. 8³¹, 9³¹, 10³³ᶠ· par. and their deposits Mk. 9⁹ ⁽¹²ᵇ⁾, 14²¹, ⁴¹; Matt. 17¹², 26²; Lk. 17²⁵, 24⁷.[1]

The first sayings to come into question are those in which Jesus speaks of his coming.

Mk. 2¹⁷: . . . οὐκ ἦλθον καλέσαι δικαίους ἀλλὰ ἁμαρτωλούς.

Lk. 19¹⁰ (in some MSS. also Lk. 9⁵⁶ and Matt. 18¹¹): ἦλθεν γὰρ ὁ υἱὸς τοῦ ἀνθρώπου ζητῆσαι καὶ σῶσαι τὸ ἀπολωλός.

Lk. 12⁴⁹⁻⁵⁰: πῦρ ἦλθον βαλεῖν ἐπὶ τὴν γῆν, καὶ τί θέλω εἰ ἤδη ἀνήφθη, βάπτισμα δὲ ἔχω βαπτισθῆναι, καὶ πῶς συνέχομαι ἕως ὅτου τελεσθῇ.

Matt. 10³⁴⁻³⁶: μὴ νομίσητε ὅτι   Lk. 12⁵¹⁻⁵³: δοκεῖτε ὅτι εἰρήνην
ἦλθον βαλεῖν εἰρήνην ἐπὶ τὴν   παρεγενόμην δοῦναι ἐν τῇ γῇ;
γῆν·   οὐχὶ λέγω ὑμῖν ἀλλ᾽ ἢ διαμερισμόν.

[1] What W. Wrede advanced about these predictions of the passion and resurrection in *Das Messiasgeheimnis*, pp. 82–92, still holds: they are an expression of the faith of the early Christians. But one may very well ask how far the (gnostic) myth of the Son of Man has affected the development of this faith or its formulation to which Reitzenstein has ascribed a normative influence (see p. 137, n. 1). The question merits further enquiry. I cannot meanwhile persuade myself that the Synoptic sayings about the Son of Man come direct from the gnostic myth, but think that they have been mediated through Jewish apocalyptic (which has taken over parts only of the myth), and that it is in line with it that Christian faith has identified Jesus with the Son of Man, modifying it *ex eventu*. In Q there are no sayings at all which speak of the Son of Man as the divine envoy walking in humility on earth. When Jesus is referred to as the Son of Man in Q, we are dealing with a misunderstanding (on Matt. 8²⁰ par., cp. pp. 28 and 97f; on Matt. 11¹⁹ par. see below; on Matt. 12³² par., cp. p. 131; and the same for Mk. 2¹⁰, ²⁸). For the rest Q speaks of the coming of the Son of Man as does Jewish apocalyptic (Matt. 24²⁷, ³⁷, ⁴⁴ par.; further the sayings which can with all probability be ascribed to Q Lk. 11³⁰, 12⁸ᶠ·, 17³⁰; Matt. 10²³, 19²⁸). Mk. 8³⁸, 13²⁶, 14⁶² also share this meaning. Next we have the passages in Mark on the suffering, dying Son of Man 8³¹, 9⁹ ⁽¹²⁾, ³¹, 10³³ᶠ·, ⁴⁵, 14²¹, ⁴¹ (all the component items are not used in each of these passages!), to which we must add Matt. 17¹², 26²; Lk. 17²⁵, 24⁷. But these sayings lack the following motifs characteristic of the myth: (1) The pre-

οὐκ ἦλθον βαλεῖν εἰρήνην ἀλλὰ
μάχαιραν.

          ἔσονται γὰρ ἀπὸ τοῦ νῦν πέντε ἐν
          ἑνὶ οἴκῳ διαμεμερισμένοι.

ἦλθον γὰρ διχάσαι   τρεῖς ἐπὶ δυσὶν καὶ δύο ἐπὶ τρισὶν
ἄνθρωπον κατὰ τοῦ πατρὸς αὐτοῦ διαμερισθήσονται,
καὶ θυγατέρα κατὰ τῆς μητρὸς πατὴρ ἐπὶ υἱῷ καὶ υἱὸς ἐπὶ πατρί,
  αὐτῆς   μήτηρ ἐπὶ θυγατέρα καὶ θυγάτηρ
καὶ νύμφην κατὰ τῆς πενθερᾶς ἐπὶ μητέρα,
  αὐτῆς,   πενθερὰ ἐπὶ τὴν νύμφην καὶ νύμφη
καὶ ἐχθροὶ τοῦ ἀνθρώπου οἱ   ἐπὶ τὴν πενθεράν.
  οἰκιακοὶ αὐτοῦ.

Matt. 5¹⁷: μὴ νομίσητε ὅτι ἦλθον καταλῦσαι . . .
    οὐκ ἦλθον καταλῦσαι ἀλλὰ πληρῶσαι.

Mk. 10⁴⁵: καὶ γὰρ ὁ υἱὸς τοῦ ἀνθρώπου οὐκ ἦλθεν διακονηθῆναι,
    ἀλλὰ διακονῆσαι καὶ δοῦναι τὴν ψυχὴν αὐτοῦ λύτρον ἀντὶ
                                 πολλῶν.

Matt. 11¹⁸⁻¹⁹//Lk. 7³³⁻³⁴: ἦλθεν γὰρ Ἰωάννης . . .
    ἦλθεν ὁ υἱὸς τοῦ ἀνθρώπου ἐσθίων καὶ πίνων . . .

Mk. 1³⁸ par.: ἄγωμεν ἀλλαχοῦ . . . ἵνα κἀκεῖ κηρύξω· εἰς τοῦτο γὰρ
    ἐξῆλθον.

Matt. 15²⁴: οὐκ ἀπεστάλην εἰ μὴ εἰς τὰ πρόβατα τὰ ἀπολωλότα οἴκου
    Ἰσραήλ.

Lk. 10¹⁶: ὁ ἀκούων ὑμῶν ἐμοῦ ἀκούει, καὶ ὁ ἀθετῶν ὑμᾶς ἐμὲ ἀθετεῖ·
    ὁ δὲ ἐμὲ ἀθετῶν ἀθετεῖ τὸν ἀποστείλαντά με.

Mk. 9³⁷: . . . καὶ ὃς ἂν ἐμὲ δέχηται, οὐκ ἐμὲ δέχεται ἀλλὰ τὸν
    ἀποστείλαντά με.

Matt. 10⁴⁰: ὁ δεχόμενος ὑμᾶς ἐμὲ δέχεται, καὶ ὁ ἐμὲ δεχόμενος δέχεται
    τὸν ἀποστείλαντά με.

    There are no possible grounds for objecting to the idea that Jesus
could have spoken in the first person about himself and his coming;
that need be no more than what befits his prophetic self-consciousness.
Yet as individual sayings they rouse a number of suspicions. If we
want to understand Lk. 12⁴⁹ᶠ· as simply a natural expression of
Jesus' consciousness of his vocation—can we understand the 'baptism' as anything else than his martyrdom, as in Mk. 10³⁸? and if
that be so, must we not take the sayings as a *vaticinium ex eventu*, like
Mk. 10³⁸ and other vaticinia? Nevertheless it is possible to look on
v. 50 as a secondary development of v. 49; for these sentences in

existence of the Son of Man (contrariwise Jn. 3¹³, 6⁶²); (2) his exaltation (contrariwise
Jn. 3¹⁴, 8²⁸, 12³⁴); (3) his judicial office (contrariwise Jn. 5²⁷); (4) the connection of his
destiny with that of the redeemed (contrariwise Jn. 12³²).

F

parallel do not really match each other properly, since v. 49 is clearly referring to the aims of Jesus' ministry, while v. 50 speaks of 'a passing personal experience'[1] (Wellhausen).

So perhaps we can take v. 49 as a genuine saying of Jesus. But what would it mean, if so? The suggestion is that πῦρ in v. 49 is not to be interpreted as the purification and preparation for the coming of the Kingdom through repentance, but much rather as a final state; only so does τί θέλω κτλ have its right and proper sense. Neither can the reference be to the fire of judgement. So can the fire be anything else than the Christian Church or the spirit which works in it? If so, v. 49 is a construction of the Church. There would be a completely different picture if we could interpret Lk. 12⁴⁹ᶠ· in terms of the gnostic myth of salvation. The baptism would then be the consecration by the spirit which the 'envoy' receives on his ascent into the heavenly world, as is depicted in Od Sol 24¹ (applied to the redeemed soul in 28¹ᶠ· and 35¹). The fire would be the judgement in which the earth perishes, as is foretold in Od Sol 24²ᶠᶠ· though, admittedly, without using the metaphor of fire. And then too, τί θέλω κτλ can be made to refer to the judgement; moreover vv. 49 and 50 have an intelligible parallelism; cosmic catastrophe corresponds to the saviour's ascension. In this case πῶς συνέχομαι refers to the frequently depicted anxiety of the one who has been sent, which he feels because he is a stranger in this world (cp. Jn. 12²⁷ and *Z.N.W.* 24, 1925, pp. 123–6). If this interpretation could be adopted there would be no genuine dominical saying as the source of Lk. 12⁴⁹ᶠ·, but a section (a quotation?) of the myth would have been transferred to his lips

We are also faced with difficulties in considering Lk. 12⁵¹⁻⁵³; Matt. 10³⁴⁻³⁶. The prophecy in Lk. 12⁵²ᶠ· par. is the well-known prediction of the troubles of the end from Mic. 7⁶, which is also the source behind Mk. 13¹². Cp. E. En 100²; Sanh. f. 97a: 'In that age, when the son of David comes . . . the daughter will rise against her mother and the daughter-in-law against her mother-in-law.'[2] That this prophecy now appears in Matt. 10³⁵ in the form ἦλθον γὰρ διχάσαι κτλ is obviously a secondary transposition. The Church, putting Jesus in God's place as the ruler of history, has made him proclaim that he will bring the time of terror, and had obviously

---

[1] J. Weiss (*Arch. f. Rel. Wiss.*, 16, 1913, p. 441) thinks that the genuineness of the saying in Lk. 12⁴⁹ and 12⁵⁰ is hidden because 'here the death of Jesus appears as a consequence of an immense discord and conflict which he must inflame', and this does not lead us to think of trial and crucifixion, but of something like fighting in the streets. I cannot read this out of the saying. J. Weiss: (1) interprets v. 49 in terms of vv. 51–53 and (2) he constructs a connection between v. 49 and v. 50 which is not even hinted at.

[2] Cp. Strack-B. I, 585f.

experienced the fulfilment of the prophecy in its own life. But then it is clear, that the previous saying Matt. 10³⁴ = Lk. 12⁵¹ has the same meaning: in the experience of the Church can be seen the fulfilment of that eschatological prophecy, and in it all the Church knows, to its comfort in suffering, that Jesus himself has both willed it and brought it to pass. There is express defence against doubting his person and work in μὴ νομίσητε (or the questioning δοκεῖτε), which also introduces the saying in Matt. 5¹⁷ which comes from the debates of the Church.

Formal considerations have already been seen to cast doubts on Mk. 2¹⁷ᵇ (p. 92). This is now matched by the suspicion underlying all sayings about the coming of Jesus. The variant in Lk. 19¹⁰ is certainly a late formulation which by turning the apocalyptic title Son of Man on to the earthly Jesus shows that it is an Hellenistic product. This applies also to Matt. 11¹⁸ᶠ.//Lk. 7³³ᶠ., though here some older saying might have provided the source, in which the Son of Man was not an apocalyptic figure, but like Mk. 2¹⁰, ²⁸; Matt. 8²⁰ par., simply meant 'man'.

Matt. 5¹⁷ and Mk. 10⁴⁵ have already been shown (pp. 138f., 144 on other grounds to be secondary formulations of a later stage. The same can be said of Mk. 9³⁷ and Lk. 10¹⁶ and the saying they have both influenced (pp. 192f.). If Matt. 15²⁴ be originally an independent logion (see p. 38), it would most probably, in view of its formulation of a principle, have derived from the missionary debates of the Palestinian Church, like Matt. 10⁵ᶠ· Finally Mk. 1³⁸ manifestly does not belong to any old piece of tradition, but to an editorial section Mk. 1³⁵⁻³⁹, a passage which in contrast to the character of the old tradition gives us no particular scene and no particular saying, but describes a transition, or the motive and general character, of Jesus' ministry.

Since such serious considerations arise against so many of these sayings, one can have but little confidence even in regard to those which do not come under positive suspicion, such as Lk. 12⁴⁹; Mk. 2¹⁷ᵇ; Matt. 15²⁴. We must now add that all these sayings which speak of the ἐλθεῖν (or ἀποσταλῆναι cp. esp. Lk. 4⁴³ with Mk. 1³⁸) of Jesus, are also under suspicion of being Church products because this terminology seems to be the means of its looking back to the historical appearance of Jesus as a whole. This is certainly the case in looking back on the Baptist—ἦλθεν in Matt. 11¹⁸ (ἐλήλυθεν Lk. 7³³) and Matt. 21³²; the same applies to the Baptist as Elijah—ἐλήλυθεν Mk. 9¹³ and ἦλθεν Matt. 17¹². Later developments confirm this impression. The Fourth Gospel shows how ἐλθεῖν and ἀποσταλῆναι (or πεμφθῆναι) are typical of the terminology of a later time (cp. esp. Jn. 18³⁷, 8⁴², 16²⁸, 3¹⁹). 1 Tim. 1¹⁵ says: πιστὸς ὁ λόγος καὶ πάσης ἀποδοχῆς ἄξιος, ὅτι Χριστὸς Ἰησοῦς ἦλθεν εἰς τὸν κόσμον ἁμαρτωλοὺς σῶσαι. The history of the Text and the apocryphal tradition provide further evidence: At Lk. 9⁵⁵ᶠ·, F etc., read: ... ὁ υἱὸς τοῦ ἀνθρώπου οὐκ ἦλθεν ψυχὰς (ἀνθρώπων) ἀπολέσαι ἀλλὰ σῶσαι. In Lk. 22²⁷D reads: ἐγὼ γὰρ ἐν μέσῳ ὑμῶν ἦλθον (instead of εἰμί!) οὐχ ὡς ὁ ἀνακείμενος ἀλλ' ὡς ὁ διακονῶν. In *Strom.* III, 9.63 Clem. Alex. quotes the Gospel of the Egyptians: ἦλθον καταλῦσαι τὰ ἔργα τῆς θηλείας. Jerome constructed a dominical saying: ἦλθον καταλῦσαι τὰς θυσίας (see p. 147).

The situation would not be altered if one had to suppose that in the supposed Aramaic source ἦλθον were to be represented by 'I come' or 'I am there'.[1] For even if that be true of Matt. 5¹⁷ as a saying in all probability deriving from the primitive Church (see pp. 138f.) and of other not necessarily Hellenistic-Christian sayings, a phrase such as 'I come' or 'I am there' only serves to gather up the significance of the appearance of Jesus as a whole. Naturally it is always possible to ask whether such a phrase were possible to Jesus himself. And little as I am against that *a priori*, I am yet doubtful about proceeding by taking other sayings out of the complex of ἦλθον-sayings, where there are certainly community products and making genuine sayings of Jesus out of them, even though they may well be appropriate expressions for his consciousness of his calling.[2] My scepticism is reinforced by considering that on the one hand Jesus was reckoned by the earliest faith to be the 'Coming One', i.e. 'the future one' (ὁ ἐρχόμενος) in the eschatological sense, and that on the other hand the O.T. nowhere speaks of a prophet's coming or having come. My conjecture is that the assertion of Jesus having come derives from a quite different sphere.[3]

Next comes a series of other sayings in which Jesus speaks of his

---

[1] So C. G. Montefiore, *The Synoptic Gospels*, II², p. 47 on Matt. 5¹⁷.

[2] It is the inadmissible isolation of these sayings, both in their general and individual examination that is, in my view, Harnack's error ('ich bin gekommen', *Z.Th.K.*, 22, 1912, pp. 1–30). A. Froevig has no appreciation of the problem at all, *Das Selbstbewusstsein Jesu*, 1918, pp. 115–18. W. Wrede, *Das Messiasgeheimnis*, p. 222. 2 rightly puts the Synoptic and Johannine ἦλθον-sayings together and asks: 'Does this constitute a looking back on the life of Jesus?' W. Bousset, *Kyrios Chr.*², p. 6 establishes 'that especially the frequently recurring formula ἦλθεν ὁ υἱὸς τοῦ ἀνθρώπου gives the impression from the first that it is a specifically hieratic stylization'. L. v. Sybel, *T.S.K.*, 100, 1927/8, pp. 382f. attempts to treat them as 'I-sayings'.

[3] The O.T. never speaks of the prophets coming or having come in the technical sense, much less does any prophet say, 'I am come'. The O.T. frequently speaks of God's coming, and this is partly in reference to a theophany Gen. 33²; Exod. 19⁹; Hab. 3³. Mostly the eschatological coming of God is meant, both for salvation (Isa. 40¹⁰, 59¹⁹ᶠ·; Zech. 14⁵, cp. Isa. 60¹, 62¹¹) and for judgement (Isa. 13⁹?; Mal. 3¹ᶠ·; Ps. 96¹³); and this is also true of the N.T. Heb. 10³⁷; Jud. 14. Parallel to this the N.T. speaks of the eschato-

person. It is useful, before considering them, to quote some 'I-sayings' that have no independent character but are woven into a narrative. They are to be found in part in the apophthegms already considered and in part in other narrative sources.

Mk. 1¹⁷: . . . ποιήσω ὑμᾶς γενέσθαι ἀλεεῖς ἀνθρώπων.

Matt. 8¹⁰//Lk. 7⁹: ἀμὴν λέγω ὑμῖν, οὐδὲ ἐν τῷ Ἰσραὴλ τοσαύτην πίστιν εὗρον. To these sayings, to which Matt. 15²⁴ cited above may be added, we may say the same as we did about the character of the corresponding apophthegms (pp. 27f., 38).

Mk. 9¹⁹ par.: . . . ὦ γενεὰ ἄπιστος, ἕως πότε πρὸς ὑμᾶς ἔσομαι; ἕως πότε ἀνέξομαι ὑμῶν; We shall deal later on with the legendary character of Mk. 9¹⁴⁻²⁹, but here it is already apparent, that it is a God of an epiphany who is speaking, 'who appears in human form only for a time, and will soon return to heaven'.[1]

Lk. 22³²: ἐγὼ δὲ ἐδεήθην περὶ σοῦ, ἵνα μὴ ἐκλίπη ἡ πίστις σου.

Lk. 23⁴³: ἀμήν σοι λέγω, σήμερον μετ' ἐμοῦ ἔση ἐν τῷ παραδείσῳ. The legendary character of both passages, in which the sayings occur, is beyond question (see below).

Finally, I add the sayings in which the *risen Lord speaks of his person*, though they could in part have been ante-dated by the evangelists into the lifetime of Jesus.

Matt. 28¹⁸⁻²⁰: . . . ἐδόθη μοι πᾶσα ἐξουσία ἐν οὐρανῷ καὶ ἐπὶ γῆς. πορευθέντες μαθητεύσατε πάντα τὰ ἔθνη . . . καὶ ἰδοὺ ἐγὼ μεθ' ὑμῶν εἰμι πάσας τὰς ἡμέρας ἕως τῆς συντελείας τοῦ αἰῶνος.

Lk. 24⁴⁹ (after the missionary command has been previously given in direct speech) κἀγὼ ἐξαποστέλλω τὴν ἐπαγγελίαν τοῦ πατρός μου ἐφ' ὑμᾶς.

Matt. 16¹⁸ᶠ: κἀγὼ δέ σοι λέγω ὅτι σὺ εἶ Πέτρος, καὶ ἐπὶ ταύτη τῆ πέτρα οἰκοδομήσω μου τὴν ἐκκλησίαν . . . δώσω σοι τὰς κλεῖδας τῆς βασιλείας τῶν οὐρανῶν. . . .

logical coming of Christ 2 Thess. 1¹⁰; Rev. 1⁷, 2⁵, ²⁵, 22¹⁷, ²⁰. Ὁ ἐρχόμενος in Matt. 11³//Lk. 7¹⁹ had evidently become a secret Messianic title in Judaism on the basis of O.T. passages; cp. Klostermann on Matt. 11³. (The title is also found among the Mandaeans: GR, V, 4, p. 193.10 Lidzb; Lit. p. 131.1 Lidzb.) We meet the phrase 'I am come' in Egypt when the God addresses Thutmosis III at the beginning of each of the ten verses in which the God promises the king his support (Erman, *Die Literatur der alten Aegypter*, pp. 320–2; Gressmann, *Altoriental. Texte zum AT²*, pp. 18f.). Among the Mandaeans the divine envoy uses the phrase, Joh-Buch 57, 14; 94, 23ff.; 132, 11; 165,31; cp. further *Z.N.W.*, 24, 1925, pp. 106f. In Orig. *Contra Celsum* the Hellenistic prophet also says ἥκω, VII, 9, pp. 161, 6ff. Solon, p. 1 rests on the tradition of the prophetic style:

αὐτὸς κήρυξ ἦλθον ἀφ' ἱμερτῆς Σαλαμῖνος,
κόσμον ἐπέων ᾠδὴν ἀντ' ἀγορῆς θέμενος.

The pleonastic use of 'coming' has nothing whatever to do with this usage examined here, though P. Fiebig (*Jesu Bergpredigt*, p. 27, nos. 74–77) on Matt. 5¹⁷ gives pointless examples. Cp. Jn. 1³⁹, ⁴⁶.

[1] Dibelius, *Formgeschichte*, p. 87; also Windisch, *T.T.*, LII, 1918, pp. 214–16.

Matt. 18²⁰: οὗ γάρ εἰσιν δύο ἢ τρεῖς συνηγμένοι εἰς τὸ ἐμὸν ὄνομα, ἐκεῖ εἰμι ἐν μέσῳ αὐτῶν.

Without more ado I add to such sayings the following:

Matt. 10¹⁶ª//Lk. 10³: ἰδοὺ ἐγὼ ἀποστέλλω ὑμᾶς ὡς πρόβατα ἐν μέσῳ λύκων. Here too the risen Lord is giving the missionary command; and besides the passages named we may further compare Matt. 23³⁴, where by omitting the introductory formula a quotation is made into a dominical saying, to read: ἰδοὺ ἐγὼ ἀποστέλλω πρὸς ὑμᾶς . . .

Lk. 10¹⁹⁻²⁰: ἰδοὺ δέδωκα ὑμῖν τὴν ἐξουσίαν τοῦ πατεῖν ἐπάνω ὄφεων καὶ σκορπίων κτλ.[1] Clearly v. 19 did not originally go with v. 18; and even the original conjunction of vv. 19 and 20 is not certain. It is possible that v. 19 was originally an isolated promise of the exalted Lord (for he speaks here no less than in the apocryphal ending to Mk. 16¹⁷ᶠ·) to the missionary, or to the Church at large, much as in Lk. 12³²: μὴ φοβοῦ, τὸ μικρὸν ποιμνίον· ὅτι εὐδόκησεν ὁ πατὴρ ὑμῶν δοῦναι ὑμῖν τὴν βασιλείαν. V. 20 could also have circulated originally as a detached saying, as the apocryphal saying of Jesus in Makarius Eg. Hom. XII, p. 17 shows: τί θαυμάζετε τὰ σημεῖα; κληρονομίαν μεγάλην δίδωμι ὑμῖν, ἣν οὐκ ἔχει ὁ κόσμος ὅλος. Actually the joining of v. 19 and v. 20 with πλήν makes a characteristically Lucan impression. The exalted Lord also speaks in v. 20, and the saying comes from a time when the Church was in danger of overrating miracle.[2]

Lk. 22²⁸⁻³⁰//Matt. 19²⁸: ὑμεῖς δέ ἐστε οἱ διαμεμενηκότες μετ᾽ ἐμοῦ . . . κἀγὼ διατίθεμαι ὑμῖν, καθὼς διέθετό μοι ὁ πατήρ μου βασιλείαν, ἵνα ἔσθητε καὶ πίνητε . . . καὶ καθήσεσθε ἐπὶ θρόνων τὰς δώδεκα φυλὰς κρίνοντες τοῦ Ἰσραήλ. Here too it is unquestionably the risen Lord who speaks. V. 28 is a connecting verse supplied by Lk. to put the saying into this particular setting, but the original beginning of the saying was incorporated into it, for οἱ διαμεμενηκότες is parallel to οἱ ἀκολουθήσαντες in Matt. 19²⁸. Otherwise it is not

---

[1] The reading δέδωκα is original; for Luke has purposely placed the saying after the mission and has used v. 17, which he made himself, and v. 18, which he took from the tradition, to introduce it. So the saying is intended to explain the success which the disciples have enjoyed: δέδωκα fits that. The reading δίδωμι (Dsyrr, etc.) is however highly characteristic, for it gives expression to the special character of the verse as a promise to the Christian missionary. There is no need to think of the influence of Hellenistic motifs (as Frz. Boll, *Aus der Offenbarung Johannes*, 1914, pp. 116f.). Ps. 91¹³ and Jewish linguistic usage (cp. Strack-B. II, 168f.) account for the construction of the saying.

[2] Cp. A. Fridrichsen, *Le Problème du Miracle*, pp. 94–96. Fridrichsen thinks vv. 19, 20 come from the Church; the relationship of the clauses in v. 20, formally a contradiction (not this . . . but that), is conceived in Semitic fashion as a comparative (less this . . . than that). That does not sound convincing to me, any more than the reproof of 'joy', which was also a characteristic of ancient Hellenistic Christianity.

easy to reconstruct the original form of the saying.[1] The analogies suggest that Luke's 'I-form' is secondary, and perhaps Luke uses διατίθεμαι because it makes the saying into a testamentary disposition, which makes it fit the context extremely well. The analogies also suggest that the distinction between the Son of Man and the Jesus who was speaking was primary in Matthew,[2] though such a distinction in a saying of the risen Lord cannot be seriously meant. Matt. 16[13] shows that for Matthew the identity of Jesus and the Son of Man goes without question, so that he can substitute the pronoun 'I' for the title. He could have done this here.[3] He means to say: 'When I as the Son of Man . . .'. In any event we are dealing with a formulation deriving from the early Church, for it was there that the Twelve were first held to be the judges of Israel in the time of the end.[4]

Matt. 11[25-30]//Lk. 10[21-22]. ἐξομολογοῦμαί σοι πάτερ . . . ὅτι ἔκρυψας ταῦτα . . . πάντα μοι παρεδόθη ὑπὸ τοῦ πατρός μου καὶ οὐδεὶς ἐπιγινώσκει τὸν πατέρα εἰ μὴ ὁ υἱὸς καὶ ᾧ ἐὰν βούληται ὁ υἱὸς ἀποκαλύψαι. δεῦτε πρός με πάντες οἱ κοπιῶντες κτλ.[5] I am convinced that the three 'strophes' of this saying did not originally belong together. That the last (δεῦτε κτλ) did not go with the first two is shown, in my view, by its absence from Luke, but above all for its quite different character from Matt. v. 27 (πάντα μοι παρεδόθη κτλ). While v. 27 promises revelation, in vv. 28–30 the teacher makes his appeal and promises a reward for obeying his commands. While v. 27 sounds like a Hellenistic revelation saying, vv. 28–30 throughout resembles Wisdom literature, and Sir. 51[23ff.], 24[19ff.]; Prov. 1[20ff.], 8[1ff.] are the corresponding parallels, and not Corp-Herm. I, 27f., VII, 1f.; Philo, De Sacrif. Ab et Caini 70; Od. Sol 33.[6] For in vv. 28–30 the sinner is not called from the path of destruction to repentance, but the man who cares and strives in vain is shown a more profitable way. The dualism, which is presupposed in the cited Hellenistic parallels is completely lacking. It seems to me that

[1] Loisy thinks that Matt. 19[28] was the original answer to the disciples' question in Mk. 10[28], which Mark replaced with vv. 29f. for anti-Judaistic reasons (see p. 22).
[2] Cp. Mk. 10[32f.] with Lk. 12[8f.]; Matt. 16[21] with Mk. 8[31] and Matt. 5[11] with Lk. 6[22]. The 'I' in Matt. 26[24] Syr^{sin} is also an emendation.
[3] Cp. Matt. 26[2].
[4] W. Bousset (in his Commentary on Rev.) thinks it possible that Rev. 3[21] is a more original form of this saying: ὁ νικῶν, δώσω αὐτῷ καθίσαι μετ' ἐμοῦ ἐν τῷ θρόνῳ μου, ὡς κἀγὼ ἐνίκησα καὶ ἐκάθισα μετὰ τοῦ πατρός. W. Hadorn agrees, while E. Lohmeyer simply asks whether Rev. 3[21] used another form of the dominical saying as its source. The connection of Rev. 3[21] with 3[20] makes it highly probable that it belongs to the same tradition. But I am inclined to think that Rev. 3[21] is the universalizing of a saying which applied originally only to the Twelve.
[5] I refrain from going into the basis for the above version of v. 27 here.
[6] Dibelius, Formgeschichte, p. 90. It seems probable to me that the Od. Sol was in its turn influenced by the style of Wisdom literature.

Matt. 11²⁸⁻³⁰ is a quotation from Jewish Wisdom literature put into the mouth of Jesus. By contrast v. 27 is specifically an Hellenistic Revelation saying, as Dibelius has rightly characterized it.[1] The similarity of the beginning with Matt. 28¹⁸ makes it easy to suppose that in the tradition Matt. 11²⁷ was originally handed down as a saying of the risen Lord. Matt. 11²⁵ᶠ·//Lk. 10²¹ is further, in my opinion, a saying originally Aramaic.[2] I also think it possible that it comes from a lost Jewish writing; it seems to be torn out of some context (to what does ταῦτα refer?). It is different from the sayings of Jesus; yet, on the other hand, I see no compelling reason for denying it to him.

It is more difficult to reach a conclusion in the following instance: Lk. 14²⁶//Matt. 10³⁷: εἴ τις ἔρχεται πρός με καὶ οὐ μισεῖ τὸν πατέρα αὐτοῦ . . . οὐ δύναται εἶναί μου μαθητής. We can be certain that οὐ μισεῖ in Luke is more original than Matthew's φιλῶν . . . ὑπὲρ ἐμέ; for the former could hardly have developed from the latter. Moreover the reference to the Person of Jesus is strengthened by the phrase ὑπὲρ ἐμέ, and the analogies show that to be secondary. Finally Luke's εἶναι μαθητής is more primary than Matthew's ἄξιός μου; it is somewhat more concrete than 'being worthy of Jesus', which cannot very well be other than christian terminology.[3] This receives confirmation, as I believe, when Luke uses the same expression in making his application of the parable in v. 33; but this application, which narrows the parable's meaning, is his own, and it is therefore probable that he had some example in front of him, namely v. 26 (and 27); in the same way, in the form in which Luke gives them, v. 26 (and 27) are in the precise form to make them more easily understandable as an introduction to the parables in vv. 28–32. In addition Luke has altered the list of relatives by doing away with the parallelism and by some pedantic additions.

Lk. 14²⁷//Matt. 10³⁸ or Mk. 8³⁴ᵇ par.: *Discipleship in bearing the Cross.* Once more Luke seems to have retained the Q form better than Matthew. Moreover the negative version of Q seems more original

---

[1] Cp. further W. Bousset, *Kyrios Chr.*², pp. 45–50. Among the parallels from Hellenistic mysticism should also be included the ancient parallel from Akhnaton's Hymn to the Sun:

'No other knows thee save thy Son Akhnaton.
Thou hast initiated him into thy plans and thy power.'

(Gressmann, *Altorient. Texte zum AT*², p. 18; cp. A. Erman, *Die Literatur der Aegypter*, p. 361; G. Loeder, *Urkunden zur Religion des alten Aegyptens*, p. 65). I believe that a close examination of the concept of revelation and knowledge (of God), which J. Schniewind (*Th.R.*, N.F.², 1930, pp. 169f.) rightly desires, would confirm this judgement.

[2] Cp. Strack-B. I, 606f.; Klostermann, ad loc.; Schlatter, *Der Evangelist Matthaeus*. pp. 380–3; also P. Fiebig, *Der Erzaehlungsstil der Evangelien*, pp. 137f.

[3] Cp. G. Kittel, *Die Probleme des palaest. Spaetjudentums*, 1926, pp. 54f.

than Mark, where 'discipleship' is no longer a condition required but has already attained a lustre of its own.

The question has now to be asked, whether these two sayings are to be taken as Church formulations. They do not seem to me to come under suspicion in the way that 'I-sayings' usually do, for it is not necessary to think that they were spoken originally by the risen Lord. That would be the case, of course, if the figure of cross-bearing in Lk. 14²⁷ were to presuppose the martyr death of Jesus. But that is not proven in my opinion. If σταυρός had already become a Christian symbol of martyrdom, would we not expect to find simply τὸν σταυρόν (without ἑαυτοῦ)? If so, then could not σταυρός have been at an earlier stage a traditional figure for suffering and sacrifice?[1] If that may be assumed, it seems clear to me that 14²⁷ no more than 14²⁶ really refers to anything beyond a sense of vocation, as do sayings like Matt. 11⁵ᶠ·; Lk. 6⁴⁶, 12⁸ᶠ· But a confident judgement as to whether they are genuine sayings of our Lord is prevented by the fact that they are obviously variants.

Mk. 3³⁵ par.: *The True Kinsmen.* This saying must be mentioned here once again. We have already seen, on p. 143, that it is probably a Church formulation.

Lk. 10¹⁸: ἐθεώρουν τὸν σατανᾶν ὡς ἀστραπὴν ἐκ τοῦ οὐρανοῦ πεσόντα. Almost nothing can be said about the originality of this saying, since its meaning is almost lost to us. It gives a strong impression of being a fragment.[2]

---

[1] It is of no significance for this present use of the word 'cross' that Ps. 22¹⁷(?) and Plato. Rep., 362a refer to the crucifixion of the righteous (though both instances fail to use the actual words σταυρός or σταυρωθῆναι). According to Strack-B. I, 587 the older Rabbinic literature did not know the phrase 'to take up one's cross', but used the phrase 'take up one's sufferings' (קַבֵּל יִסּוּרִין) instead. Yet Strack-B. cites GenR., 56 (36c), on which A. Meyer had already said (*Jesu Muttersprache*, 1896, p. 78): 'Abraham took the wood for the burnt offering and laid it on his son Isaac (Gen. 22⁶). Just as one does who carries his cross on his shoulder.' Schlatter (*Der Evangelist Matthaeus*, pp. 350f.) who also quotes this passage, thinks it possible that the idiom grew up among the Zealots, whose followers would have to reckon with the cross, and from them passed on to the disciples of Jesus. Also, the expression ἔρχεσθαι (Luke; ἀκολουθεῖν, Matthew) ὀπίσω is Semitic; the form ἀπαρνεῖσθαι ἑαυτόν, which is foreign to Semitic usage, is first introduced into Mark's version. Cp. Schlatter, *Der Evangelist Matthaeus*, p. 519; G. Dalman, *Jesus Jeschua*, 1922, pp. 172f. When Dalman says that the expression 'follow' in metaphorical usage is not paralleled in Rabbinic literature that can only be sustained if following means taking on the same fate; for the Rabbis not only talk of the following of disciples in the sense that they actually follow the Rabbis as they walk, but also use the derived meaning of learning from and imitating their mode of life (Strack-B. I, 187f., 528f.), and this meaning is adequate for Lk. 14²⁷.

[2] Conjectures are easy enough. First, naturally, that the saying refers to a vision of Jesus. Hence H. Windisch, e.g. 'Jesus und der Geist', *Studies in Early Christianity*, 1928, p. 235) is inclined to suppose that Jesus' 'apocalyptic announcements were fertilized in greater degree by ecstatic experiences, than the canonical tradition hints'—which is by no means impossible; cp. pp. 108f. We can be sure of this only: that the saying foretells the end of the Kingdom of Satan, even if it does not carry with it the special form of that idea which we have in Rev. 12⁸ᶠ·

Matt. 12²⁷//Lk. 11¹⁹: (καὶ) εἰ ἐγὼ ἐν Βεελζεβοὺλ ἐκβάλλω τὰ δαιμόνια, οἱ υἱοὶ ὑμῶν ἐν τίνι ἐκβάλλουσιν; κτλ.

Matt. 12²⁸//Lk. 11²⁰: εἰ (δὲ) ἐν δακτύλῳ θεοῦ ἐγὼ ἐκβάλλω τὰ δαιμόνια, ἄρα ἔφθασεν ἐφ᾽ ὑμᾶς ἡ βασιλεία τοῦ θεοῦ.

The two sayings placed together in Q have nothing to do with each other originally (cp. p. 14). The former looks very much like Church polemic, though without supplying the basis for anything to be said confidently about it. But the latter can, in my view, claim the highest degree of authenticity which we can make for any saying of Jesus: it is full of that feeling of eschatological power which must have characterized the activity of Jesus.[1]

Confidence in the antiquity of the 'I-sayings' is in the last resort considerably lessened by observing how such sayings multiply more and more in later tradition. Among such are sayings which look back on the work of Jesus as Orig. *Comm. Matth. tom* 13[2]: διὰ τοὺς ἀσθενοῦντας ἠσθένουν καὶ διὰ τοὺς πεινῶντας ἐπείνων καὶ διὰ τοὺς διψῶντας ἐδίψων (cp. already pp. 155f.). Further the saying of the risen Lord in the Freer Logion (*kl. Texte*, 31, p. 31): . . . καὶ ὑπὲρ ὧν ἐγὼ ἁμαρτησάντων παρεδόθην εἰς θάνατον, ἵνα . . . κληρονομήσωσιν. Finally the saying which comes from Hellenistic piety, *Pap. Ox.*, I, 3 (*kl. Texte*, 8, p. 16): ἔστην ἐν μέσῳ τοῦ κόσμου καὶ ἐν σαρκὶ ὤφθην καὶ εὗρον πάντας μεθύοντας καὶ οὐδένα εὗρον διψῶντα ἐν αὐτοῖς. καὶ πονεῖ ἡ ψυχή μου ἐπὶ τοῖς υἱοῖς τῶν ἄνων ὅτι τυφλοί εἰσιν τῇ καρδίᾳ αὐτῶν. . . .

The heavenly judge uses different language, as in Matt. 7²²ᶠ·, or the variant of this saying in 2 Clem. 4⁵, which is very like the version found in the Nazarean edition of Matthew: ἐὰν ἦτε μετ᾽ ἐμοῦ συνηγμένοι ἐν τῷ κόλπῳ μου καὶ μὴ ποιῆτε τὰς ἐντολάς μου, ἀποβαλῶ ὑμᾶς καὶ ἐρῶ ὑμῖν· ὑπάγετε ἀπ᾽ ἐμοῦ, οὐκ οἶδα ὑμᾶς πόθεν ἐστέ, ἐργάται ἀνομίας. In addition there is Rev. 3²⁰, 16¹⁵ and the logion cited on p. 127, which was quoted by Justin and others, ἐν οἷς ἂν ὑμᾶς καταλάβω, ἐν τούτοις καὶ κρινῶ (*kl. Texte*, 11, p. 1). Related to this is the saying in the Nazarean edition of Matthew, which rests on the idea of Matt. 25³¹⁻⁴⁶: 'I choose for myself those good ones whom my heavenly Father has given me.' Further we may add the saying quoted by Orig. in Jer. Hom. Lat. 3³ and Didym. in Ps. 80⁸: ὁ ἐγγύς μου ἐγγὺς τοῦ πυρός . ὁ δὲ μακρὰν ἀπ᾽ ἐμοῦ μακρὰν ἀπὸ τῆς βασιλείας and the saying in Barn. 7¹¹: οὕτως (φησὶν) οἱ θέλοντές με ἰδεῖν καὶ ἅψασθαί μου τῆς βασιλείας ὀφείλουσιν θλιβέντες καὶ παθόντες λαβεῖν με.

[1] On the question whether ἐν πνεύματι (Matthew) or ἐν δακτύλῳ (Luke) is original see e.g. Windisch, op. cit., pp. 217f. I think Leisegang's assumption unfounded (cp. p. 131 n. 1) that the original wording was ἐν ὀνόματι θεοῦ.

The motif of continual presence from Matt. 18²⁰, 28²⁰ is rendered variously in other terms, as in Pap. Ox., I, 4: ὅπου ἐὰν ὦσιν β' οὐκ εἰσὶν ἄθεοι, καὶ ὅπου εἷς ἐστιν μόνος, λέγω· ἐγώ εἰμι μετ' αὐτοῦ. ἔγειρον τὸν λίθον κἀκεῖ εὑρήσεις με· σχίσον τὸ ξύλον, κἀγὼ ἐκεῖ εἰμι (Supplementations as in *kl. Texte*, 8, p. 16). Ephraem. Syr. *conc. exp* 165 (ed. Moesinger): *ubi unus est, ibi et ego sum, et ubi duo sunt, ibi et ego ero.* The saying quoted by Clem. Alex. *Strom.* V, 10.63 is, finally, unique: μυστήριον ἐμὸν ἐμοὶ καὶ τοῖς υἱοῖς τοῦ οἴκου μου. To conclude we may mention various sayings in the so-called Odes of Solomon, in which the exalted Lord speaks, or the Gospel according to St. John, where the sayings about his own self (particularly those which contain the form ἐγώ εἰμι) are in principle on the same level as those which are ascribed to the historical Jesus.

The 'I-sayings' were predominantly the work of the *Hellenistic Churches*, though a beginning had already been made in the *Palestinian Church*. Here too Christian prophets filled by the Spirit spoke in the name of the ascended Lord sayings like Rev. 16¹⁵. The following Synoptic I-sayings can be considered as coming from the Palestinian Church. Matt. 5¹⁷ points directly to the legal debates of the early Church, and Matt. 15²⁴ to discussions about the Gentile mission. Matt. 10¹⁶ᵃ (ἰδοὺ ἐγώ ἀποστέλλω ὑμᾶς ὡς πρόβατα κτλ), Lk. 10¹⁶ (ὁ ἀκούων ὑμῶν κτλ) and perhaps Lk. 10¹⁹⁻²⁰ (ἰδοὺ δέδωκα ὑμῖν τὴν ἐξουσίαν κτλ) also comes from the mission of the early Church. Matt. 12²⁷ (εἰ ἐγώ ἐν Βεελζεβοὺλ ἐκβάλλω κτλ) has come from the conflict with the Jews. Matt. 11²⁵ᶠ·, ²⁸⁻³⁰ (ἐξομολογοῦμαί σοι . . . δεῦτε πρός με πάντες κτλ) perhaps circulated as a dominical saying in the early Church, and then came to give expression to the antithesis to the legal piety of the scribes, and Mk. 2¹⁷ᵇ (οὐκ ἦλθον καλέσαι κτλ) is in all probability to be understood in the same way. In addition Mk. 3³⁵ (The true kinsman), Lk. 14²⁶ (εἴ τις ἔρχεται πρός με) and perhaps Lk. 14²⁷ (discipleship in Cross-bearing) could well have come from the primitive Church. Lk. 22²⁸⁻³⁰ or Matt. 19²⁸ (The Twelve on twelve thrones) is related to the inner life of the early Church; as are Lk. 22²⁷ (. . . ἐγώ δὲ ἐν μέσῳ ὑμῶν κτλ), Mk. 9³⁷, ⁴¹ or Matt. 10⁴⁰, ⁴² (reward of kindness to children), and Matt. 18²⁰ (οὗ γάρ εἰσιν δύο ἢ τρεῖς κτλ). Matt. 10³⁴⁻³⁶ or Lk. 12⁵¹⁻⁵³ (μὴ νομίσητε ὅτι ἦλθον βαλεῖν εἰρήνην κτλ) have come out of the bitter experiences of the primitive Church. It is less certain that Lk. 10¹⁸ (fall of Satan) and Lk. 12⁴⁹ᶠ· (πῦρ ἦλθον βαλεῖν κτλ) derived therefrom. For all the rest, especially for the sayings about the coming of the Son of Man, we have to assume an Hellenistic origin.

SUPPLEMENT

Two passages of a special character have not been discussed in what has gone before. I treat them now as an addition:

Matt. 12⁴³⁻⁴⁵//Lk. 11²⁴⁻²⁶: *The Return of the Exorcized Demons.* This section is different from the other sayings of Jesus in both form and content. In style it is more closely related to a parable, and may actually have originated as such, Matthew perhaps having preserved its application in his οὕτως ἔσται καὶ τῇ γενεᾷ ταύτῃ τῇ πονηρᾷ. But its original meaning is hardly discernible, though it seems to me to be the same as in certain Arabic proverbs. Cp. Alb. Socin, *Arabische Sprichwoerter und Redensarten* (Tuebinger Universitaetsschr., 1878), no. 73: 'He went away; and then he returned bringing Mahmud and Gillo with him as well.' No. 94: 'He died like a dog, and set us free from his service; but he left behind a young dog that was worse than his father.' On no. 73 Socin refers to J. L. Burckhardt, *Arabische Sprichwoerter oder die Sitten und Gebraeuche der neueren Aegypter,* 1875, no. 5. Matt. 12⁴³⁻⁴⁵ par. does not seem to be a community construction, as it entirely lacks any Christian features; perhaps it is taken from some Jewish writing. Its appearance in the Christian tradition is due to the demonological material. It is not intended to function as a criticism of exorcism, but rather to warn the person who is healed to be wary of demonic powers.[1]

Matt. 11⁷⁻¹⁹//Lk. 7²⁴⁻³⁵; Matt. 21³²//Lk. 16¹⁶: *Sayings about the Baptist.* Matt. 11⁷⁻¹⁹ par. which had already achieved essentially the same unity in Q, is made up of various units.[2] The Christian attitude to John the Baptist is a divided one: while some passages make the Baptist appear as a confederate in Christian affairs, others emphasize his inferiority to Jesus. Understandably, for both points of view were occasioned by the anti-Baptist polemic. Matt. 11⁷⁻¹¹ᵃ, ¹⁶⁻¹⁹, 21³² give expression to the solidarity of Jesus with John the Baptist. Mk. 11i²⁷⁻³⁰ is a piece of the same kind.[3] The rivalry between the Christian and the Baptist communities is exemplified in their each having their own prayer (Lk. 11¹ᵇ, most probably from Q; v. 1a a construction by Luke) and an independent practice in regard to fasting (Mk. 2²⁰). The relegation of the Baptist is seen most clearly in the Christian addition in Matt. 11¹¹ᵇ par. (ὁ δὲ μικρότερος κτλ), and in Matt. 11¹²ᶠ· par., which is no longer patent of confident interpretation, but which at least seems to be saying that the Baptist

---

[1] Cp. Jn. 5¹⁴; Act. Thom. 46. Klostermann refers to Dio Chrys., V, 32.
[2] On this and the following cp. M. Dibelius, *Die urchristliche Ueberlieferung von Johannes dem Taeufer* (Forschungen 15), 1911; M. Goguel, *Jean-Baptiste,* 1928.
[3] Do passages like Matt. 12³⁸ᶠ·, ⁴¹ᶠ· also belong here? Cp. p. 118 n. 2.

belongs to a bygone age.[1] Correspondingly the Christian tradition has applied the saying about the mightier one in Mk. 1 [7], or Matt. 3 [11b]; Lk. 3 [16b]; Acts 13 [25] to Jesus, and in this way depicted the Baptist as unworthy to perform for Jesus even the lowliest duties of a slave. Thus it carried on its polemic against the view that the Baptist was the Messiah (Lk. 3 [15]), and subordinated his water baptism to Christian baptism—Mk. 1 [8], or Matt. 3 [11a, c]; Lk. 3 [16a, c]; Acts 1 [5], 11 [16], 19 [1ff.]. It is something of a compromise when the Baptist is given the role of the Forerunner: Jesus makes his appearance in connection with John's baptism, Mk. 1 [9ff.] par.; Acts 1 [22], 10 [37]; the Baptist (whose Messianic preaching was reinterpreted thus) pointed to Jesus as the coming Messiah Mk. 1 [7f.] or Matt. 3 [11f.]; Lk. 3 [16f.]; Acts 13 [24f.], 19 [4]. This theory of John as the Forerunner was eventually to be given expression in his being identified as Elijah, the one to prepare the way of the Lord, Mk. 9 [12f.] par.; Matt. 11 [14].

Nevertheless part of the material in the Synoptic tradition concerning this matter derives from the early Palestinian Church. Perhaps a genuine saying of Jesus is preserved in it at Matt. 11 [7–11a]. The qualifying addition in Matt. 11 [11b] was already in Q and could well have come from the early Church too, but it is in any event Christian, as is the intrusive verse 11 [10] par. If Matt. 11 [16f.] is also an ancient parable by Jesus, then the appended interpretation Matt. 11 [18f.] is also in any case a community product, which owes its form (ἦλθεν ὁ υἱὸς τ. ἀνθρ. !) to the Hellenistic Church. Clearly Mk. 11 [27–30] (cp. pp. 20f.) and possibly also the other passages concerned with prayer and fasting (Mk. 2 [19b, 20]; Lk. 11 [1b]) are products of the Palestinian Church. Similarly Matt. 11 [12] par., which is as early as Q, will also have come from the primitive Church. The same must be said of Lk. 7 [29f.] (the form in Matt. 21 [32] is secondary), which can hardly be claimed as a genuine saying of Jesus; it is retrospective, and reads as though there were already a Christian baptism established (Well-hausen). Finally it is manifest that in the early Church the Baptist's messianic preaching was applied to Jesus and the saying about the mightier one correspondingly interpreted.

But the rivalry between the community of Jesus and that of the Baptist also persisted, as Acts and John show, in certain circles of the Hellenistic Church, and this means that we have to reckon with the possibility of this or that questionable saying having an Hellenistic origin. In this category may well belong the Elijah theory, which Matt. 11 [14] has even introduced into the text of Q. Perhaps also we may include the opposition of the Johannine water baptism to the

---

[1] Cp. M. Goguel, op. cit., pp. 65–69; H. Windisch, Z.N.W., 1928, pp. 168f.

Christian Spirit baptism; and in addition, everything, of course, which has to be taken as the special editorial work of the evangelists, as also the corresponding passages in Acts.

5. SIMILITUDES AND SIMILAR FORMS

(a) Survey and Analysis

The whole of the material we have discussed under the heading of dominical sayings is, in respect of its formal character, uniform throughout, and shows that the chief elements of these did not originate in an Hellenistic, but in an Aramaic environment. Actually there are but three considerable passages which are not covered by this judgement and which seem at first sight to be Hellenistic formulations: Mk. 7[20-23] (the second supplement to the saying about purity); Matt. 11[27]//Lk. 10[22] (πάντα μοι παρεδόθη κτλ) and Lk. 21[34-36] (exhortation at the end of the eschatological discourse). There is of course no lack of lesser expansions, new- and analogy-formulations, which attached themselves to the original material when it reached an Hellenistic environment. Sometimes even a proverb could have come from an Hellenistic background, even though it bears no marks of doing so, as perhaps Matt. 24[28]//Lk. 17[37] (ὅπου ἐὰν ᾖ τὸ πτῶμα, ἐκεῖ συναχθήσονται οἱ ἀετοί), since certain proverbial forms are the same all over the world. But we have only to compare our material with what we know of the hortatory and edificatory literature of Hellenistic Judaism, or with the letters of Paul and other Christian Hellenists, to realize most clearly how un-Hellenistic, seen as a whole, is the Synoptic tradition of the sayings of Jesus.

The *artistic form of the language* is also uniform.[1] We have already discussed the basic forms of the *Mashal*; as they correspond to a stage for a popular, unliterary artistic tradition, so does the great *plastic art of language*. Ideas and conditions, characters and commands are all given expression in immense concreteness, and we can enumerate certain typical items. In Matt. 5[39ff.] an injunction not to retaliate for evil is rendered into concrete particular demands; in Matt. 5[44] the command to love one's enemies is expanded into particular requirements. In Matt. 5[45] the goodness of God is pictured by saying that he makes his sun to shine on the evil and the good, and sends his rain on the just and the unjust. Anxious folk are depicted in Matt. 6[25, 31] by their own questions: 'What shall we eat? What shall we

---

[1] I can only point to the following literature, without having worked over it: H. Hoertnagel, *Bausteine zur einer Grammatik der Bildersprache*, 1922. J. Breitenstein, 'Les paraboles de Jésus', *R.Th.Ph.*, 1921, pp. 97-113.

drink? and Wherewithal shall we be clothed?' Direct speech is also used in other places: Matt. 7[4] to characterize the critic who has a beam in his eye. Cp. further Matt. 17[20]; Lk. 5[39], 14[8-10], 17[3f.]. The commandment to absolute forgiveness is put in the form that forgiveness must be given until seventy times seven (per diem) Matt. 18[22] (or Lk. 17[4]). The son's request to the father in Matt. 7[9f.] is concretely expressed as asking for fish or bread. The separation consequent upon the parousia is made crystal clear (Lk. 17[34f.]) by two illustrations: two men on a bed, two women grinding corn—they will be separated. The most menial task is pictured in Mk. 1[7] as loosing the shoe latchet. Concrete pictures describe the hypocrite at his almsgiving, his prayers and his fasting, in Matt. 6[2-18], etc.

The concrete can be raised to *hyperbole*. Evil desire must be exterminated, even to plucking out the eye or cutting off the hand (Matt. 5[29f.]). The right hand must not know what the left hand does (Matt. 6[3]). In order to keep fasting secret, a man must anoint his head and wash his face (Matt. 6[17]). There must be no retaliation! But 'whosoever smiteth thee on the one cheek, turn to him the other also', and him who would 'take away thy coat, let him have thy cloke also' (Matt. 5[39f.]). God's providence is so far reaching that 'the very hairs of your head are all numbered' (Matt. 10[30]). God is 'able of these stones to raise up children to Abraham' (Matt. 3[9]). The law must remain so firm, that 'one jot or one tittle shall in no wise pass away' from it (Matt. 5[18]), etc.

Paradox is related to hyperbole: the man who seeks his life shall lose it; and he who loses it shall find it (Matt. 10[39]). The man who has, shall receive; and the man who has not shall suffer deprivation (Mk. 4[25]). Whoever wants to be first must be the slave of all (Mk. 10[44]). The dead must be left to bury their own dead (Matt. 8[22]). A camel goes more easily through a needle's eye, than a rich man enters the kingdom of God (Mk. 10[25]). The Pharisees strain at gnats and swallow camels (Matt. 23[24]). The self-righteous man sees the splinter in his neighbour's eye but fails to notice the beam in his own (Matt. 7[3ff.]), etc.[1]

The use of comparisons and images in every form is particularly characteristic. Even in the meshalim of the Old Testament the form which I call 'a figure' occurs with extraordinary frequency with image and thing juxtaposed without any connecting particle, e.g. Sir. 3[25]:

---

[1] W. Baumgartner refers me to R. Petsch, *Das deutsche Volksraetsel*, 1917, p. 17.1 and to the appearance of the impossible in popular song; cp. O. Boeckel, *Psychologie der Volksdichtung*[2], 1913.

Where there is no apple of the eye, light is lacking,
And where there is no knowledge wisdom is wanting.[1]

Ber. 51b:

'Gossip comes from pedlars
and vermin from rags.' (Strack-B. I, 882.)

It also happens that the metaphorical part of the saying is handed down by itself and circulates as a popular proverb. In that case either the meaning is apparent from the metaphor itself, or the saying derives a concrete meaning by being used in a particular situation. There is a whole series of such sayings in the Synoptic gospels.

Matt. 5[14]: The city on the hill.   Mk. 2[17]: The physician and the sick.

Matt. 3[10]: The barren tree is cast into the fire.   Mk. 2[19]: Fasting at the Wedding-feast.

Mk. 24[28]: The carcase and the eagle.

Lk. 5[39]: Old Wine.   Lk. 4[23]: Physician, heal thyself.

Such metaphorical sayings are now and then made out of two parts, joined by καί (Mk. 2[22]; Matt. 12[30]), οὐδέ (Lk. 6[44]; Matt. 9[17], 10[24]; Pap. Ox. I, 5) or ἤ (Matt. 7[9, 16]).

Pap Ox. I, 5: The prophet in his own country, the physician and his relations.

Lk. 6[44b]: Figs from thistles and grapes from thorn bushes.

Matt. 10[24]: Disciples and Teacher, slaves and Lord.

Mk. 2[21f.]: New patches and new wine.

Mk. 3[24f.]: Divided kingdom and divided house.

Matt. 7[9f.]: Son's request for bread and fish.

Matt. 12[30]: For and against, gathering and scattering.[2]

Metaphors may also be expanded in other ways:

Lk. 6[39]: Blind leaders of the blind.   Mk. 3[27]: Spoiling the strong.

Lk. 6[43]: Tree and fruit.   Mk. 4[21]: The light.

Lk. 14[34]: Salt.

The following passages provide instances of this expansion together with the use of antithetic parallelism:

Matt. 6[24]: Serving two masters.

Lk. 12[47]: Punishment and responsibility.

The application of some of these metaphors is stylized: namely Mk. 2[17] (asyndeton); 3[24-26] (with καί); Matt. 6[24] (asyndeton); –7[911] (οὖν); Lk. 12[47f.] (δέ). No objection against the originality of

---

[1] Cp. W. Baumgartner, Z.A.W., XXXIV, 1914, p. 166.

[2] Old Testament examples of such duplex metaphorical sayings are found in Am. 6[12]; Isa. 28[27]; Jer. 12[5]; Prov. 6[27f.], etc.

this connection can be made on stylistic grounds; though they do not completely validate it (cp. pp. 91f.). The rest, if they are not simply placed by their catchword like Lk. 5 [39]; Mk. 9 [50], are given their place through the context, to which they have been firmly attached by editorial formulations, cp. Matt. 5 [13-16], 7 [15-20] (cp. pp. 95f.); 10 [25b] (cp. p. 90). But since the introduction of a saying into a context is almost always secondary, we can determine, in the case of almost all the metaphors only the most general significance, not the concrete meaning which it had in the mind of Jesus (or the Church). Indeed because of the different insertions of the different evangelists it is clear in regard to the sayings about salt and light that we can no longer determine with what reference they were originally used. At the most we may suppose that they were used for moral exhortation. The same has to be said of Matt. 3 [10]; Lk. 6 [43f.], and, it would seem, of Matt. 6 [24] apart from the interpretation probably added later. It is questionable whether Lk. 6 [39] was originally used against the scribes. Mk. 3 [27] seems to be in its proper context: because the demons are overcome, the devil's dominion is overthrown (by God); just as the use of Mk. 3 [26] rightly gives the meaning of Mk. 3 [24, 25]. Matt. 12 [30] could easily have referred originally to the reception given to the preaching of Jesus, and have been intended to rouse the indifferent. One is also inclined to suppose that the connection of Mk. 2 [19a] with fasting is original, though it must be made clear that if the saying were originally an isolated one (cp. p. 87), there is no support for such an interpretation. Instead we might interpret: just as fasting is impossible at a marriage, so in the joyful era now dawning any foolish conduct corresponding to fasting, such as mourning or fear, is equally impossible. But who will say whether the meaning could not be different again: just as anyone who fasts at a wedding is foolish, so is anyone who gathers earthly treasure when the Kingdom of God is breaking in? It is absolutely impossible now to determine what was the original meaning of Matt. 10 [24, 25a], 24 [28]; and the same applies to Mk. 2 [21f.]

The editorial additions, introductions and explanations with which the metaphors were furnished in the tradition have already been dealt with on pp. 91f.

Metaphors are related to 'figures', being shortened comparisons lacking the comparative word. Not infrequently particular elements in figures are used by the evangelists as metaphors in their editorial formulations, as in Matt. 5 [13, 14, 16], 7 [16, 20]. But originally metaphors were used in other places. The saying about the mote and the beam (Matt. 7 [3-5]) can be counted as such. Matt. 7 [6] (casting pearls before swine) hovers between being a 'figure' and a warning in metaphor. The saying about the narrow way and the narrow gate (Matt. 7¹³ᶠ·), good and bad treasure in the heart (Matt. 12³⁵), the labourers and the harvest (Matt. 9³⁷), putting one's hand to the plough (Lk. 9⁶²), the plants not planted by God (Matt. 15¹³) are also metaphorical; as is the warning to keep the loins girded and the lamps burning (Lk. 12³⁵). The saying of John the Baptist about sifting the corn is a further example (Matt. 3¹²).

We have already discussed the history of all these sayings. Here I will simply refer to Lk. 6⁴⁵ as a typical example, where Luke has added to the metaphor of θησαυρός the explanatory τῆς καρδίας (cp. Matt. 12³⁵).

We seldom find the simple form of correct comparison 'as (-so)'. It occurs, e.g. in Matt. 10¹⁶: 'Behold, I send you forth as sheep in the midst of wolves: be ye therefore wise as serpents, and harmless as doves.' Further, in Lk. 11⁴⁴: οὐαὶ ὑμῖν ὅτι ἐστὲ ὡς τὰ μνημεῖα τὰ ἄδηλα κτλ (Matt. 23²⁷ with its παρομοιάζετε τάφοις . . . is equivalent); Lk. 12³⁶: καὶ ὑμεῖς ὅμοιοι ἀνθρώποις προσδεχομένοις τὸν κύριον ἑαυτῶν.

Matt. 24.²⁷ is even clearer: ὥσπερ γὰρ ἡ ἀστραπὴ ἐξέρχεται . . . οὕτως ἔσται ἡ παρουσία τοῦ υἱοῦ τ. ἀνθρ. So is the somewhat extended comparison of the suddenness of the parousia with the days of Noah and Lot (Lk. 17²⁶ᶠ·, ²⁸⁻³⁰) and the interpretation of the sign of Jonah (Matt. 12⁴⁰). And so is Matt. 13⁵²: διὰ τοῦτο πᾶς γραμματεὺς μαθητευθεὶς τῇ βασιλείᾳ τοῦ οὐρανοῦ ὅμοιός ἐστιν ἀνθρώπῳ οἰκοδεσπότῃ, ὅστις ἐκβάλλει κτλ.

Next I would cite as pure *similitudes*[1] such formulations as are distinguished from comparisons or figures only by the detail in which the picture is painted, and indeed a similitude can be formed from a figure or a comparison indifferently. If Matt. 7⁹ᶠ· has to be classed as a figure, Lk. 17⁷⁻¹⁰ must be classed as a similitude: *Master and Servant*, that is formulated in just this way, namely, with no conjunction of comparison and as a rhetorical question, as in Mk. 2¹⁹ᵃ, 4²¹; Matt. 7⁹ᶠ·; Lk. 6³⁹. After the figurative part, follow the words οὕτως καὶ ὑμεῖς which are used to make the application. The question as to the originality of the application hardly arises here, for—at least if ἀχρεῖοι be regarded as a gloss—it precisely repeats the meaning of the similitude: a slave cannot boast of any merit.

The same may be said of Lk. 14²⁸⁻³³: *The Tower and the War*. There is no conjunction of comparison. Both similitudes begin with a rhetorical question. The application in v. 33 follows with the phrase οὕτως οὖν καὶ πᾶς ἐξ ὑμῶν. Here the application is manifestly

---

[1] Besides Juelicher's basic work, *Die Gleichnisreden Jesu*, I³, II², 1910, we must mention H. Weinel, *Die Gleichnisse Jesu* (Aus Natur und Geisteswelt 46), 1929.

secondary, for it completely fails to express the point of the parable: self-examination before any undertaking; while on the other hand vv. 28–32 contain nothing of the idea of sacrifice of possessions which is found in v. 33.

Lk. 15⁴⁻¹⁰ or Matt. 18¹²⁻¹⁴: *The Lost Sheep and the Lost Coin.* In Luke both similitudes begin without a conjunction and as a rhetorical question, and both have an application: v. 7: λέγω ὑμῖν ὅτι οὕτως χαρά . . . ἔσται; v. 10: οὕτως, λέγω ὑμῖν, γίνεται χαρά. In relationship to Lk. 15⁴⁻⁷, Matt. 18¹²⁻¹⁴ is essentially more original. Matthew's opening question τί ὑμῖν δοκεῖ, also found in Matt. 17²⁵, 21²⁸, is original. Luke's fuller form seems secondary to me, and the force of the parable gains nothing by the filling out. But then one is driven to the conclusion that the application in Lk. 15⁷ is also a secondary formulation, echoing the original ending (Matt. 18¹³ᵇ). But admittedly the application in Matt. 18¹⁴ is also secondary, for it narrows down the original meaning in saying that no member of the *Christian* community will be lost, and gives no expression to the joy over finding the lost, which is nevertheless the essential feature of the similitude. But have we to think of the second of the two similitudes as an old element of the tradition that has been lost in Matthew, or as a newer additional formulation? The fact that Lk. 15⁴⁻⁷ itself closes with its own application suggests the latter alternative. For if both similitudes had a common origin we should expect the application to come after both had been told, as is actually the case in Lk. 14²⁸⁻³³. But the question of double similitudes is discussed below.

Lk. 12³⁹⁻⁴⁰//Matt. 24⁴³⁻⁴⁴: *The Thief.* This has no comparative conjunction in the form the assertion is given; the application follows on with (διὰ τοῦτο Matthew) καὶ ὑμεῖς γίνεσθε ἕτοιμοι; it is imperative, like Lk. 16⁹; Mk. 13³⁵; Matt. 24⁴⁴, 25¹³, and no suspicion has been advanced as to its originality. The introduction that was found already in Q τοῦτο δὲ (or ἐκεῖνο δὲ Matthew) γινώσκετε ὅτι seems a secondary connecting link.

Lk. 12⁴²⁻⁴⁶//Matt. 24⁴⁵⁻⁵¹: *The Faithful Servant.* This has neither comparative conjunction nor application. The interrogative form has a significance here different from the other examples; it does not demand an affirmation of the point of the similitude, but asks who will identify himself with the subject. It is thus given to allegory. Lk. 12⁴⁶ = Matt. 24⁵¹ does not suit the picture at all (a fact which is but emphasized by Matthew's addition), and this shows that the similitude is not an organic unity, but mixed with allegory.[1]

---

[1] I find no evidence that Luke has edited the parable, as K. G. Goetz supposes (Petrus, 1927, pp. 12f.), in the light of Peter's leading position in the Church.

Lk. 12⁵⁴⁻⁵⁶: *Signs of the Times* (cp. p. 116). There is no comparative conjunction, and the similitude is in the form of a statement in the second person. The application follows *e contrario* as a rhetorical question and seems thoroughly original.

Lk. 12⁵⁷⁻⁵⁹//Matt. 5²⁵⁻²⁶: *Timely Agreement* (cp. p. 96). This is a typical example of a similitude made out of a 'figure'. Since both comparative conjunction and application are missing, the similitude ceased to be so considered in the tradition, but was taken as a warning to be reconciled with a legal opponent in this world, whereas the original meaning in all probability was: As in your civil life at times you place the greatest emphasis on not having to appear before the judge, so you should take care that you need fear no accuser before the heavenly judge. Lk. 12⁵⁷ is a Lucan transitional formulation, see p. 91.

If we may regard all these similitudes as developments of 'figures', others are developed out of comparisons.

Matt. 11¹⁶⁻¹⁹//Lk. 7³¹⁻³⁵: *Children at Play*. This similitude is introduced by a question, indeed, in Luke by a double question, which is very likely original (τίνι οὖν ὁμοιώσω . . . καὶ τίνι εἰσὶν ὅμοιοι; cp. Lk. 13¹⁸ or Mk. 4³⁰). Then, beginning with the words ὅμοιοί εἰσιν, follows the figure itself, in turn followed by the application, connected by γάρ (which gives the reason for ὅμοιοί εἰσιν). This application of the similitude to Jesus and the Baptist, at any rate in its present form, cannot belong to the oldest tradition (pp. 155f.), though the form shows that the similitude itself is an ancient piece of the tradition.

Mk. 4³⁰⁻³² or Matt. 13³¹⁻³²; Lk. 13¹⁸⁻¹⁹: *The Mustard Seed*. Luke substantially reproduces the similitude from Q, while Matthew combines Q's text with Mark. Both Mark and Q preface it with a double question, the parable then following with ὡς (or, in Luke, ὁμοία ἐστίν). There is no application.

Matt. 13³³//Lk. 13²⁰⁻²¹: *The Leaven*. Luke introduces the similitude with a question, which is probably original. The similitude proper starts, in both Matthew and Luke, with ὁμοία ἐστίν. There is no application here either. The sharp break would seem to indicate that the similitude of the leaven is a secondary accretion to that of the mustard seed, even if Luke's shorter form (καὶ πάλιν εἶπεν) is the original Q form. We should expect ἤ alone if it were a more original form; cp. Lk. 14³¹; Matt. 7⁹, ¹⁶.

Mk. 4²⁶⁻²⁹: *The Seed Growing of Itself*.¹ The formulation is the same

¹ I do not think it credible that this parable was originally fused into one parable along with that of the mustard seed and that it had been omitted from the Mark manuscript used by Matthew and Luke by homioteleuton (B. H. Streeter, *The Four Gospels*, pp. 171, 190).

as in the preceding example, save that there is no introductory question. Instead we have: οὕτως ἐστὶν ἡ βασιλεία τ. θ. ὡς ἄνθρωπος βάλῃ. . . . It is questionable whether this is original, for (1) it is not easy to relate this similitude to the Kingdom of God, and (2) it gives the impression of being one of the introductory formulae that are frequently added. Possibly the similitude originally circulated in the tradition beginning with ὡς ἄνθρωπος βάλῃ; cp. 13³⁴; Matt. 25¹⁴ and Jewish similitudes; see below. There is no application.

Matt. 13⁴⁴: *The Treasure in the Field*, introduced by ὁμοία ἐστίν ἡ βασιλεία τ. οὐρ., without any subsequent application.

Matt. 13⁴⁵⁻⁴⁶: *The Pearl of Great Price*, similarly without application, and attached to the previous similitude with the phrase πάλιν ὁμοία ἐστὶν ἡ βασιλεία τ. οὐρ. which means that it is unlikely that the two similitudes originally belonged together, since Matthew uses the same formula to conclude the following quite different parable of the fish net. It is questionable in all these three cases whether ὁμοία ἐστὶν ἡ βασιλεία τ. οὐρ. is original.

Matt. 13⁴⁷⁻⁵⁰: *The Fish Net*. Here, with the words οὕτως ἔσται an application is added about whose originality to the similitude there is, in my view, no need to entertain doubts.

Matt. 7²⁴⁻²⁷//Lk. 6⁴⁷⁻⁴⁹: *The House Builder*. Luke's circumstantial introduction could very well be the form in which the similitude began in Q: πᾶς ὁ ἐρχόμενος πρός με . . . ὑποδείξω ὑμῖν τίνι ἐστὶν ὅμοιος. But that does not settle the question whether the introduction is really original, i.e. whether the similitude really fits the sayings of Jesus in the context, though it probably does, as the parallels cited in Strack-B. show. The similitude itself properly begins with the comparison formula: ὅμοιός ἐστιν ἀνθρώπῳ. There is no application.

Mk. 13²⁸⁻²⁹ par.: *The Fig Tree*. This pericope falls due for consideration here, for the fact that it does not begin with ὡς is not significant (nothing is altered even if one imagines it prefixed), as it is replaced in this case by the introduction: ἀπὸ τῆς συκῆς μάθετε τὴν παραβολήν. And this is likely to be original, for such introductory phrases are entirely coherent with the style. It is the more removed from suspicion in being irrelevant to the application. The application begins with: οὕτως καὶ ὑμεῖς, and it is a striking fact that the truth which the similitude illustrates is not to be seen in the ὑμεῖς, but that the ὑμεῖς are to draw the concluding application (cp. by contrast Lk. 17¹⁰). But apart from this the application seems secondary too, in providing a needful connection with the context to which the similitude certainly did not originally belong.

Mk. 13³⁴⁻³⁷: *The Returning Householder*. This is an unorganic

composition, see p. 119. Doubtless v. 33 is a Marcan editorial formulation. Perhaps v. 34 is an element from the ancient tradition (cp.
Matt. 24$^{45-51}$) and appropriately begins with an unrelated ὡς
(see below). Down to πότε ὁ κύριος τῆς οἰκίας ἔρχεται it could be
original, though what follows then is an allegorical expansion, for it
is ill-suited to v. 34, that all slaves should keep watch at night. But it
is possible that the whole of v. 35 is secondary formulation, for
γρηγορεῖτε οὖν is concerned only with the doorkeeper and ignores the
other servants.

Juelicher rightly distinguishes the Similitude from the *Parable*, which
does not bring two sets of facts together, but transposes the facts which
serve for a similitude into a story, or, to put it in different terms,
gives as its picture not a typical condition or a typical, recurrent
event, but some interesting particular situation. But if the distinction
in principle is clear, particularly if the second formulation be adopted,
the boundaries fluctuate. Even the figure in certain circumstances
approaches the narrative, cp. Matt. 7$^{9f.}$ (The Son's Request) or Mk.
3^{27} (The Spoiling of the Strong). It is also possible to be uncertain
whether Lk. 15$^{4-10}$ (The Lost Sheep and The Lost Coin) ought not
rather to be counted as Parables. In part these two are in narrative
form, though it is a story of typical events, whereas Lk. 15$^{11-32}$ (The
Prodigal Son) is clearly a story of a particular incident. In addition
the rhetorical question can be closely related to the figure, as is
shown in Lk. 15$^{4-10}$. But this is also the form of Lk. 11$^{5-8}$ (The
Importunate Friend) where the typical so gives place to the particular that we have to reckon the passage as a parable. In the same
way doubts may be entertained about the similitudes of the Treasure
in the Field and the Pearl of Great Price, though here it seems to me
that the similitude is so strongly marked and the narrative form so
little dominant that I have to reckon them among the similitudes.
They can also be understood as representations of typical events.
They recount what a crafty farmer, or a merchant will always do!
This is what always happens if one is cautious—or incautious—over
building! Mk. 4$^{26-29}$ (The Seed Growing Secretly) has also been
influenced by the story form, as have Matt. 13$^{47-50}$ (The Fish Net)
and the Q form of the Similitude of the Leaven (Lk. 13^{19}: ὃν λαβὼν
ἄνθρωπος ἔβαλεν . . . v. 21: ἣν λαβοῦσα γυνὴ ἔκρυψεν . . .). All the
same these similitudes describe typical events, so that they do not
amount to parables. The same could also be said about the Similitude of the Sower, though here the story form is too strongly marked.
Thus, conceptual differentiation is necessary for understanding the
motive which determines the form; but no intelligent person would

expect any particular instance to give pure expression to any particular form. This means that there is no point in much debate over any particular example.

Lk. 11⁵⁻⁸: *The Importunate Friend.* This begins as a rhetorical question: τίς ἐξ ὑμῶν ἕξει φίλον καὶ . . . No application.

Lk. 18¹⁻⁸: *The Unjust Judge.* Formulated wholly as narrative. The application in vv. 6–8 is certainly secondary (cp. Juelicher); it is marked off by εἶπεν δὲ ὁ κύριος and is not found in the parallel 11⁵⁻⁸. In v. 8b it is augmented by a secondary supplement.

Mk. 4³⁻⁹ par.: *The Sower.* Entirely in narrative form, without an application. Introduced by ἀκούετε only, and finished by ὃς ἔχει ὦτα ἀκούειν ἀκουέτω.

Lk. 13⁶⁻⁹: *The Barren Fig Tree.* Entirely in narrative form, without an application.

Lk. 14¹⁶⁻²⁴//Matt. 22²⁻¹⁴: *The Supper.* Matthew's ὡμοιώθη ἡ βασιλεία τ. οὐρ. . . . is probably secondary as over against Luke's thorough-going narrative form. Moreover it is probably a secondary factor that in Matthew it is a King who gives a wedding feast for his son instead of the simple ἄνθρωπος of Luke; not that a king in a parable is to be suspected as such, but that the marriage of a son looks very much like an allegory. Similarly Matthew has manifestly made an alteration in the double invitation in vv. 3f. Similarly the numbers of servants probably goes back to Matthew, since it would seem to be more appropriate that a king should have more than one δοῦλος. In Luke the slave can only be traced back to allegory if he did not also convey the final invitation (v. 23) which can refer to nothing other than the Gentile mission. But in Matthew, vv. 6 and 7 are certainly secondary allegory. On the other hand in Luke the double invitation to new guests and their characterization in v. 21 are secondary. Further, in the emphatic conclusion in v. 24 of Luke we have what seems to be some interplay of allegory, and v. 10 of Matthew must be therefore esteemed as the more original. Admittedly Matthew then develops the parable in vv. 11–13 further in an allegorical supplement on the moral merits of a Christian Church member, and then added a dominical saying in v. 14, which, in his view, expresses the point of the whole passage. The original parable has no application.

Lk. 15¹¹⁻³²: *The Prodigal Son.* In form entirely narrative with no application. On whether vv. 25–32 with its new point is a later addition, see below.

Lk. 16¹⁻⁸: *The Unjust Steward.* Entirely narrative in form. The application in v. 8 (marked off by καὶ ἐπῄνεσεν ὁ κύριος; cp. Lk. 18⁶) is secondary.[1] Luke conceived of it as nevertheless belonging to the similitude, as a saying of the Lord of the οἰκονόμος, for introduced by καὶ ἐγὼ ὑμῖν λέγω, he adds other proverbs to vv. 9–13, which are meant to provide an application. There is a saying from the (Jewish?) tradition in v. 9; on vv. 10–12 see p. 86.

Matt. 25 14–30//Lk. 19 12–27: *The Talents.* In Luke the narrative form is dominant throughout. By contrast it is possible to reckon the anacolouthic introduction in Matthew ὥσπερ γὰρ ἄνθρωπος ἀποδημῶν ἐκάλεσεν as the original, if one could avoid the suspicion that it is a Matthew product of the motif in Mk. 13 34; for the motif of a journeying householder does not in essentials harmonize with the dividing up of his capital. Similarly we may detect in v. 19 a like allegorical addition by Matthew, referring to the parousia. Other traces of allegory in Matthew are the distribution of bliss and damnation in vv. 21, 23, 30, which turns the Lord of the parable into Christ the Judge of the World. The certainty of such considerations is somewhat weakened by reflecting that Luke has edited the parable even more markedly, namely by joining it with the story of a king who punished rebels (hardly an original similitude, but a quite secondary allegory). Even in the basic version of Matthew and Luke there stood, at the end of the Parable, a dominical saying Matt. v. 29 = Lk. v. 26, which does not quite fit the sense of the Parable, as it is not simply dependent upon having, but upon keeping. But the position of the verse is nevertheless an emphatic confirmation of the view that Matt. v. 30 and Lk. v. 27 did not originally belong to the parable.

Matt. 25 1–13: *The Ten Virgins.* The introductory formula: τότε ὁμοιωθήσεται ἡ βασιλεία τ. οὐρ. can be regarded as Matthean trimming. For the rest the narrative form is predominant, though the course of events is not clear, and the story is an allegory[2] constructed from the application. It is no longer possible to decide whether an original Similitude underlies it. Its content—the delay of the Parousia—also reveals that it is a secondary formulation. The application in v. 13 which is given as a warning: γρηγορεῖτε οὖν κτλ could well be drafted along with the allegory; but is, in all probability, like 24 42, a conclusion or transition fashioned by Matthew on the basis of Mk. 13 35.

---

[1] The terminology of the ὅτι clause in v. 8 is in all probability syncretistic. Rabbinic language recognized the expression 'Son of the World to come' (and one would expect to find this expression used in contrast here) but not 'Son' or 'Child' of 'this world' (children of the world means simply 'men'). Nor is the term 'Children of Light' (Strack-B. II, 219) to be expected with any more likelihood; this latter we find in 1 Thess. 5 5; Eph. 5 8; Jn. 12 36; E. En 108.11 (who belong to the generation of Light) also in a syncretistic context.
[2] The marriage custom which obviously serves as the basis of the fable is misinterpreted. Cp. A. Musil, *Arabia Petraea*, III, pp. 194f., L. Bauer, *Volksleben im Lande der Bibel*, 1903, p. 94.

Matt. 13²⁴⁻³⁰: *The Wheat and the Tares.* The parable is again introduced by the Matthew formula ὡμοιώθη ἡ βασιλεία τ. οὐρ. Otherwise the form is purely narrative. There is no application. I think this is a pure parable, and not, as Juelicher supposes, an allegory.

Matt. 18²³⁻³⁵: *The Unmerciful Servant.* To this parable, begun again with (διὰ τοῦτο) ὡμοιώθη ἡ βασιλεία τ. οὐρ., and continuing thenceforward entirely in narrative form, an application is added by the phrase οὕτως καὶ ὁ πατὴρ . . . ποιήσει ὑμῖν, which rightly expresses its meaning, though admittedly this does not establish its original character.

Matt. 20¹⁻¹⁶: *The Labourers in the Vineyard.* The introductory formula is: ὁμοία (γάρ) ἐστιν ἡ βασιλεία τ. οὐρ. otherwise it is wholly in narrative form. By the words οὕτως ἔσονται an unattached saying is introduced as an application (cp. Mk. 10³¹; Lk. 13³⁰). But this does not fit the meaning of the parable, for it expresses the reversal of earthly relationships, and nothing about the undifferentiated rewards of the Kingdom of God.

Mk. 12¹⁻⁹ par.: *The Vineyard and the Wicked Husbandmen.* This has no introductory formula, and is in pure narrative form. Admittedly this is not a parable but an allegory, for the course of events is intelligible only on that basis. The contents also show that the passage is a community product. At the close the author has used a typical parable ending, and he finishes with a question which demands a response from the hearer. In this case the answer is given by the narrator himself. In vv. 10f. Mark has inserted yet another polemical quotation.

Lk. 7⁴¹⁻⁴³: *The Two Debtors.* This parable has no introductory formula and is in pure narrative form. It ends with a question which makes the hearer answer and so give his own judgement.

Matt. 21²⁸⁻³¹: *The Two Sons.* This parable is introduced by τί ὑμῖν δοκεῖ; (in all probability this was original, cp. Matt. 17²⁵, 18¹²) and otherwise is constructed as the preceding one. There is but this to say with regard to the text tradition, that the hierarchy has to give the right answer (thus, ὁ πρῶτος, as the son who says 'No' comes first) for this corresponds to the style, that it should express their judgement (see below). With the words ἀμὴν λέγω ὑμῖν in 31b is added an application whose originality need not be doubted. On the other hand the concrete reference to the attitude of the hierarchy to the Baptist in v. 32 is an addition which Matthew has in all probability constructed on the basis of the tradition in Lk. 7²⁹f.

Exemplary stories have a striking formal relationship to parables, and must therefore be discussed here, even if they have no figurative element at all.[1]

Lk. 10³⁰⁻³⁷: *The Good Samaritan.* This passage composed throughout in narrative form has been artificially blended into its context by Luke. For whereas the point of the story lies in the contrast of the unloving Jews and the loving Samaritan, there is an artificial reference back in vv. 36f. to the introduction vv. 25–29, and its question is answered: Who is my neighbour? For the rest, I believe that originally the passage ended with a question and answer, like Lk. 7⁴¹⁻⁴³; Matt. 21²⁸⁻³¹. For it is clear that the question begun in v. 36: τίς τούτων τῶν τριῶν and the answer in v. 37: ὁ ποιήσας τὸ ἔλεος μετ' αὐτοῦ, were given to Luke, and the question in v. 36 to some degree has been artificially prepared for it. Luke was obliged, in terms of his introduction, so to construct his question and answer as to make the attacked man the neighbour. Finally an imperative is appended.

Lk. 12¹⁶⁻²¹: *The Rich Fool.* The insertion of this purely narrative pericope is naturally the work of the editor. The application, beginning with οὕτως is also secondary, and is typical of secondary interpretation of similitude and parable. Possibly it did not occur in the original text of Luke. D, etc., do not give it.

Lk. 16¹⁹⁻³¹: *The Rich Man and Lazarus.* Pure narrative without introduction or application. The story has two points: (1) vv. 19–26: The balancing of earthly destinies in the world to come. (2) vv. 27–31: The uselessness of the return of a dead person to produce belief in the will of God among the obdurate rich. It is clear that these two points vie with each other. For the purpose of the first part (vv. 9–15: The vanity of Riches) could not originally have been to prepare for the second (vv. 16–18: the validity of the law). In any event the story already lay before Luke in this form; for his introduction prepares in an unique way for both points: v. 14 (editorial construction) and v. 15 for the first, vv. 16–18 for the second: see below.

Lk. 18¹⁰⁻¹⁴: *Pharisee and Publican.* After the editorial preparation in v. 9[2] the passage begins as pure narrative; the point is formulated in v. 14, marked out by λέγω ὑμῖν, and an unattached saying is joined on to this by ὅτι (cp. Lk. 14¹¹; Matt. 23¹²) and this latter is

---

[1] The synoptic exemplary stories are distinguished from the paradigms of ancient rhetoric (cp. K. Alewell, *Ueber das rhetor.* παράδειγμα, Diss. Kiel, 1913, and E. Fascher, *Die formgeschichtl. Methode,* pp. 191–5) not only by their compass but by their content, in so far as no historical *exempla* belong to them (as cp. Lk.13³¹.; Acts 5³⁴⁻³⁷), but also conceptually. Paradigms are *exempla* illustrating some theme, making it concrete; the exemplary stories offer examples = models of right behaviour. M. Dibelius uses the word paradigm in its ancient meaning. Naturally in particular instances a story can be a 'paradigm' in that one sense as in the other.

[2] V. 9 clearly does not derive in the first place from Luke himself, for he would most certainly have directed it to the Pharisees.

certainly secondary, especially in so far as it does not fit the story, as the Publican had not really humbled himself.

As a similitude can be the first part of a parable, so the two following passages can be the first part of an exemplary story:

Lk. 14⁷⁻¹¹: *The Wedding Guest*, and 14¹²⁻¹⁴: *The Proper Guests*. Luke reckons both as παραβολαί, as he expressly states in v. 7 of the former. Admittedly their stylistic relationship to similitudes and parables is faint; actually they are but somewhat expanded warnings (see pp. 103f.). The logion in 18¹⁴, already dealt with, is added to the first passage.

(b) *Form and History of the Material*

Just as the figurative saying begins *without any special introduction* so does the similitude which is a development of it, e.g., Lk. 17⁷⁻¹⁰, 14²⁸⁻³³, 15⁴⁻¹⁰, 12³⁹⁻⁴⁰ par., 12⁴²⁻⁴⁶ par., 12⁵⁴⁻⁵⁶, ⁵⁷⁻⁵⁹. Naturally it would be wrong to suppose in every case that this primitive form were the original of a similitude. Contrariwise the introductory question in Matt. 18¹² can very well serve as the antecedent of Lk. 15⁴. That is to say that the antecedent stylistic form is very often an introductory question, and this is true also of Jewish similitudes. We meet it in Matt. 18¹², 21²⁸ in the form τί ὑμῖν δοκεῖ; and in one instance a figurative saying is used, viz. in Matt. 17²⁵. The argumentative character of the similitude comes out very well in this case. There is a corresponding example in Mk. 3²³: πῶς δύναται σατανᾶς σατανᾶν ἐκβάλλειν; but the question in Lk. 13²⁰ is more characteristic: τίνι ὁμοιώσω τὴν βασιλείαν τ. θ. (avoided in Matt. 13³³), and more especially the similarly formulated double question in Mk. 4³⁰ or Lk. 13¹⁸ and Lk. 7³¹ (avoided in Matt. 13³¹ and 11¹⁶ by the substitution of one simple question). In Jewish similitudes the formula is: לְמָה הַדָּבָר דּוֹמֶה, cp. P.A. III, 18: 'The man whose wisdom is greater than his deeds, what is he like? He is like a tree. . . . But the man whose deeds are greater than his wisdom, what is he like? He is like ink. . . .' IV, 20: 'And the man who learns when he is old, what is he like? He is like ink. . . .' The double question is found as early as Isa. 40¹⁸: 'To whom will ye liken God? or what likeness will ye compare unto him?' though here it is admittedly with the implication that such a comparison is impossible.[1]

---

[1] Examples of this and other introductory formulae are in Strack-B. I, 653 and especially II, 7-9. Cp. also P. Fiebig, *Der Erzaehlungsstil der Evangelien*, pp. 36f. and particular examples in P. Fiebig, *Altjuedische Gleichnisse u. die Gleichnisse Jesu*, 1904, pp. 17, 23, 24, 25. (I refer to this book in what follows as Fiebig I, and in contrast I refer to P. Fiebig, *Die Gleichnisreden Jesu*, 1912, as Fiebig II.) Philo also inclines to such formulae. Cp. *De Ebriet.* 155: τίνι οὖν ἀπεικάσωμεν τῶν ἐν τῷ σώματι τὸ ἐν ψυχῇ πάθος ὃ κέκληται ἄγνοια ἢ τῇ τῶν αἰσθητηρίων πηρώσει;

The similitudes which have grown out of a comparison, those intro-duced by some comparison formula, begin with or without such introductory questions. The simple form ὡς or ὥσπερ is itself enough: Matt. 25 [14]; Mk. 4 [31], 13 [34]; perhaps also originally Mk. 4 [26]. In Jewish similitudes the corresponding form is the introductory לְ (with or without a preceding מָשָׁל, e.g. Fiebig, I, pp. 36, 41, 42, 43, 50, 78; II, pp. 92, 93, etc.). For the most part we find instead ὅμοιός ἐστιν or ὁμοία ἐστίν: Matt. 11 [16] = Lk. 7 [32]; Matt. 13 [31] = Lk. 13 [19] (Mk. 4 [31] has the simple ὡς; the version in Matthew and Luke may well derive from Q); Matt. 13 [33] = Lk. 13 [20]; Matt. 13 [44, 45, 47], 20 [1]. Here also belongs Lk. 6 [47]: πᾶς ὁ ἐρχόμενος πρός με . . . ὑποδείξω ὑμῖν, τίνι ἐστὶν ὅμοιος. ὅμοιός ἐστιν ἀνθρώπῳ (Matt. 7 [24] reads otherwise and is in all probability secondary, see ad loc.). On this cp. perhaps Fiebig, I, p. 17: אֶמְשֹׁל לְךָ מָשָׁל, etc. The subject of the comparison, apart from Matt. 11 [16] par.; and Lk. 6 [47] is always ἡ βασιλεία τ. οὐρ., and the significance of that, as Matt. 20 [1] especially shows, is not necessarily that the object of comparison and the King-dom of God can be treated exactly alike, but generally stated, that it is with the βασιλεία as the following story relates. That is also true of the formula that is peculiar to Matthew: ὁμοιωθήσεται: 7 [24] (on Lk. 6 [47], see above); 25 [1] (subject: ἡ βασιλεία τ. οὐρ.) or ὡμοιώθη (ἡ βασ. τ. οὐρ.) 13 [24], 18 [23], 22 [2]. (Lk. 14 [16] without an introductory for-mula.) This imprecise version of the introductory formula is also found in Jewish similitudes, e.g. Fiebig, II, p. 73: '(The situation is like) a King who . . .' The more precise form in which two distinct realities are compared, is found, e.g., Fiebig, I, p. 59: 'In that hour the Israelites were like a dove, flying from the sparrow-hawk.'[1]

The differences in such formulae to be found in parallel passages is enough to show that we must reckon with changes taking place in the course of the tradition. In particular we may conjecture that the stereotyped phrases in Matthew are due to the evangelist himself.

The construction of the similitude is naturally something which can vary. It often begins as a *question*, and thereby reveals its likeness to the mashal as well as its argumentative character: the hearer is required to make an answer. While figurative sayings like Mk. 2 [19a], 4 [21]; Matt. 7 [9f.]; Lk. 6 [39] are all formulated as pure questions, it is quite understandable that in an extended similitude the question should turn into a story: Lk. 11 [5-8], 14 [28-30, 31-32], 15 [4-6, 8-9]. In this same way the figurative saying about salt in Q (Lk. 14 [34f.]; Matt.

---

[1] Mark precedes the parable of the Sower with ἀκούετε (cp. Mk. 7 [14] = Matt. 15 [10], 21 [33]) but this is not an introductory formula characteristic of similitudes, though naturally enough it can be found in them. Cp. Fiebig II, p. 60. Herm. *Mand.*, XI, 18; *Sim.*, V, 2.1.

5^{13}) which also starts off as a question, is continued as an affirmative statement. On the other hand Lk. 17^{7-9} is formulated entirely as a question. (The interrogatory form in Matt. 24^{45}//Lk. 12^{42} must be differently understood, see p. 171.) For a Jewish parallel, see Fiebig, I, p. 53: 'Is a lamp of any use save in a dark place? And have the sun and the moon any need for a lamp?'[1] 4 Ezra 4^{40}, 5^{46}, 7^{52}. As early as Jer. 2^{32}: 'Can a maid forget her ornaments, or a bride her attire?' Further Jer. 8^4, 15^{12}, 18^{14}.[2] The similitudes in Herm., *Sim* IX, 12.5; 32.3 are throughout constructed as questions.

The form of statement can for its part be quite varied. If the similitude is introduced with an expression like ὡς or ὅμοιός ἐστιν, there is often a *relative clause* following the noun of comparison (which is in the dative), e.g. Mk. 4^{31}; Matt. 7^{24}, 11^{16} par., 13^{33} par., 13^{44}, 18^{23}, 22^1, 25^1. The same is true of Jewish similitudes, e.g. Fiebig, I, p. 45 (twice); II, ppy. 57, 58, 73, 74. Equivalent to the relative clause is the participle that sometimes replaces it: Mk. 13^{34}; Matt. 13^{24}, 25^{45} also Lk. 6^{48}, where Matt. 7^{24} has the relative clause. Characteristic of the similitude in the narrower sense is a *conditional clause*, which can equally provide the start, as in Mk. 3^{24} (instead of which Matt. 12^{25}// Lk. 11^{17} has the participle). It follows an introductory clause in Mk. 9^{50}//Lk. 14^{34}; Mk. 13^{28}; and it is inserted into the relative clause in Mk. 4^{31}. In such cases the conditional means: whenever the situation is like this, then it happens that . . . (It is otherwise with Lk. 12^{39}, where a misleading conditional clause introduces the similitude.) Jewish similitudes also contain these conditional clauses: Fiebig, I, pp. 16, 45, 69 ('if a worker works for the master of the house, then he must plough for him'); II, p. 84.

In those similitudes which begin with a rhetorical question the *tense* is often a gnomic future: Lk. 11^5, 14^{31}, $17^{7f.}$; yet sometimes it is the present: Lk. 14^{28}, $15^{4, 8}$. For the rest, similitudes in the narrower sense are in the present tense, cp. Matt. $11^{16f.}$//Lk. 7^{32}; Mk. $4^{26, 31f.}$, 13^{28}; and Herm. *Sim* V, 2. Contrariwise the tense suited to the style of the parable and its narrative character is the preterite, cp. Lk. $7^{41f.}$, 13^{6-9}, 14^{16-24} par., 15^{11-32}, etc. (the same naturally applies to exemplary stories). But it is characteristic that the narrative form is imposed upon some real similitudes, which makes them akin to parables. Thus for example while Mk. 4^{31} (Mustard

---

[1] Rabbinic similitudes in interrogatory form, further Midr. Qoh. 5^{10} (b); ExR 27 (88a); DtR 7 (204a) (Strack-B. I, 396, 865, 866).

[2] Cp. Baumgartner, *Die Klagegedichte des Jeremia*, 1917, pp. 57, 61f. In Arabic proverbs there are many instances of figurative sayings in rhetorical questions, cp. Alb. Socin., *Arabische Sprichwoerter und Redensarten* (Tuebing. Universitaetsschr. 1878), no. 34: 'Does one fig ripen before another?' No. 39: 'Can you harness two stallions with one halter?' Nos. 66, 73, 149, 181.

Seed) is in the present tense, Matt. 13[31]//Lk. 13[19] is in the past. Cp. further Matt. 13[44, 45, 47], 7[24-27] par. and particularly Mk. 4[3-9]. Cp. Fiebig, II, pp. 57 and 59 where the same similitude is in one instance constructed entirely in the present, and in the other begins with the historic past tense.

Inside the similitude the *point* (not the application!) is marked out by (ἀμὴν) λέγω ὑμῖν: Lk. 14[24]; Matt. 18[13]; Matt. 5[26]//Lk. 12[59]; Lk. 12[44]//Matt. 24[47]; Lk. 12[37]; also in the exemplary story Lk. 18[14]. Apart from Lk. 14[24] the narrator in these instances interrupts the story to make the point, and this is psychologically quite intelligible, since the phrase so marked out constitutes the *tertium comparationis* (cp. also Matt. 25[12, 40, 45]). This brings us naturally to the idea of the application, though without its thereby becoming an allegorization. Next there are instances where the application is introduced by the same formula: Lk. 15[7, 10], 16[8]D; Mk. 13[30]; Matt. 21[31]. This gives rise to the conjecture that these are secondary accretions for which the original form has supplied the pattern. This is what may be thought of the relationship of Matt. 18[13] to Lk. 15[7]. Secondary additions have manifestly been made to Lk. 16[8]; Mk. 13[30]. This hypothesis is not necessary, in my view, to explain Matt. 21[31].

Finally, as in the case of figurative sayings Matt. 7[6]; Lk. 4[23], in one instance the *imperative* is used in a similitude: Lk. 12[58]//Matt. 5[25]. It may well be asked whether the imperative is not in this instance itself an amendment, so that the similitude should no longer be understood as such, but as an exhortation to reconciliation. Contrariwise it is quite possible that the imperative form itself has been the basis of misunderstanding.[1]

The *ending of a similitude* is likewise varied in its construction. The following end *without any application* whatever: Mk. 4[3-9, 26-29]; Matt. 13[24-30] par., 13[44, 45, 46], 7[24-27] par.; Lk. 11[5-8], 13[6-9], 14[16-24] par., 15[11-32]. Cp. Fiebig, I, pp. 17, 23.

Some parables end with a *question* directed to the hearer: Lk. 7[41-43]; Matt. 21[28-31]; Mk. 12[1-9]; and in the same group Lk. 10[29-37]. This expresses the argumentative character of the similitude much more emphatically than the question found at the beginning of many similitudes, or the introductory τί ὑμῖν δοκεῖ. Of course this presupposes that the hearer will give the right answer, whether that is only presupposed or whether it is given actual expression. But it is questionable on occasions when the similitude is given in a frame-

---

[1] Similitudes constructed with imperatives, Herm. *Mand.*, XI, 18 (λάβε λίθον καὶ βάλε εἰς τὸν οὐρανόν, ἴδε, εἰ δύνασαι ἅψασθαι αὐτοῦ· ἢ πάλιν λάβε σίφωνα ὕδατος καὶ σιφώνισον εἰς τὸν ρανόν, ἴδε νόει δύνασαι τρυπῆσαι τὸν οὐρανόν) and 20.

work by the answer being provided in the text, whether the framework is as original as the similitude itself. Here the editorial work of the evangelists has to be taken account of, as is perfectly clear from Lk. 10³⁶ᶠ· For Jewish similitudes cp. Fiebig, I, p. 16 (without an answer; the same similitude is in Aboda Zara f. 54b, 55a; here the question is answered, Fiebig, *Erzaehlungsstil*, 60); p. 17 (with an answer by the interlocutor); II, p. 86 (with no answer); p. 92 (no answer); quite like the first half of a similitude, II, p. 93 (the narrator himself provides the answer; likewise Fiebig, *Erzaehlungsstil*, 62). Like these is 4 Ezra 7⁵, ⁹ (answer by the interlocutor). The form of the question in 4 Ezra 4¹⁸ after the preceding similitude is very characteristic: 'If now you were a judge, to whom would you give justice and to whom injustice?' (Answer by the interlocutor.) A very ancient popular form lies behind Isa. 5¹⁻³: 'Judge . . . between me and my vineyard!' Similarly in Nathan's parable in 2 Sam. 12¹ᶠᶠ· where David himself pronounces judgement and then has to hear its application: 'Thou art the man!' For the rest we may compare 1 Kings 20⁴⁰ and Jonah 4¹⁰ᶠ· In Midr. Eccles. 1⁷ R. Joshua b. Halaphta (*c.* 150) answers a matron who has objected to the saying 'He gives wisdom to the wise, and knowledge to the men of understanding' (Dan. 2²¹): 'A parable: If two men come to you to borrow money, and one were rich and the other poor, to whom would you lend your money, to the rich man or the poor man?' She said, 'To the rich man.' He asked, 'Why?' And she replied: 'If the rich man were to lose my money he would have something from which to repay me, whereas if the poor man were to lose it, how could he pay me back?' He then said to her: 'And can't you hear what your own lips are saying? If God were to give wisdom to fools, they would sit and talk about it in water closets, theatres and public baths; God has given wisdom to the wise only, and they sit and talk of it in the synagogues and schools.' (Strack-B. I, 661. Like this, and with the formula 'Can't you hear what your own lips are saying?' in Midr. Ecc. 5¹⁰, Strack-B. I, 396 and Strack-B. 896; cp. further Strack-B. I, 886 with Matt. 21³¹; and 880 with Matt. 22³.) This form is also found in fairy-tales, e.g. in different variations among the Low German fairy-tales edited by W. Wisser (Jena, 1914 in the collection Die Maerchen der Weltliteratur), p. 229: There they undertake all sorts of enterprises and pose riddles to each other and the one knows this and the other that. Then the princess asks them whether she should not set them a poser too. Yes, say the others. Well, she then says, she had a box, and she had lost the key to it, and so she had a new one made for it. But afterwards she had found the old. And now should she choose the old one or the new? To this they all reply 'the old one'. Well, she then says, I had a husband, and I had lost him, and so I got myself a new one; and now the old one has come back. So now I want to take him back again too. And then she took Hans back again and the other had to go away. Further pp. 176, 273f. and *Deutsche Maerchen seit Grimm I* (ibid., 1912), *Tuerkische Maerchen* (ibid., 1925), p. 74.[1]

It is quite common for a similitude to have an *application linked to it by* οὕτως:

Lk. 17¹⁰: οὕτως καὶ ὑμεῖς . . .	Matt. 13⁴⁹: οὕτως ἔσται καὶ ἐν τῇ συντελείᾳ τοῦ αἰῶνος . . .
Lk. 14³³: οὕτως οὖν καὶ πᾶς ἐξ ὑμῶν . . .	Mk. 13²⁹: οὕτως καὶ ὑμεῖς . . .
Lk. 15⁷: λέγω ὑμῖν ὅτι οὕτως χαρὰ . . . ἔσται . . .	Matt. 18³⁵: οὕτως καὶ ὁ πατὴρ . . . ποιήσει . . .
Lk. 15¹⁰: οὕτως, λέγω ὑμῖν, γίνεται χαρὰ . . .	Matt. 20¹⁶: οὕτως ἔσονται . . .
Lk. 12²¹: οὕτως ὁ θησαυρίζων αὐτῷ . . .	Matt. 18¹⁴: οὕτως οὐκ ἔστιν θέλημα . . .

There are Jewish examples of this to be found in Fiebig, I, pp. 24f., 26, 59, 73; II, pp. 55f., 86, 88, etc. Roughly equivalent to this is the linking on of the application with γάρ in Matt. 11¹⁸ par. (ἦλθεν γάρ Ἰωάννης), 21³² (the same), 22¹⁴ (πολλοὶ γάρ εἰσιν κλητοί . . .). In Mk. 3²⁶ or Matt. 12²⁶//Lk. 11¹⁸ (καὶ εἰ ὁ σατανᾶς ἀνέστη . . .) the application is joined without οὕτως but with a similar meaning. Finally, mention must be made here of the applications, already referred to, which are introduced by λέγω ὑμῖν. Though little can be said against such an application on stylistic grounds (for even a figurative proverb can contain one) yet it is very clear that the applications we find in the gospels are very often secondary. We have shown that already in the case of those that are joined to the similitude by οὕτως, Lk. 14³³, 15⁷, ¹⁰, 12²¹ (lacking here in D, etc.); Mk. 13²⁹; Matt. 18¹⁴, 20¹⁶; and the same applies to the clauses linked on with λέγω ὑμῖν in Mk. 13³⁰; Lk. 16⁸. In this way Matthew has added an application to the proverb about the Light in 5¹⁶: οὕτως λαμψάτω τὸ φῶς ὑμῶν . . . On the other hand the application in Lk. 17¹⁰: Matt. 13⁴⁹ᶠ·, 18³⁵, 21³¹ could very well be original; caution in making such a judgement can only be enjoined by noticing the tendency of the tradition to add such applications.

In some of the passages cited οὕτως is followed by an *imperative*:

[1] Cp. Bolte-Polivka, *Anm. zu K.H.M.*, II, p. 59; III, p. 40. For African fairy-tales: Westermann, *Orientalist. Lit.-Zeitung*, 28, 1925, Col. 331.

Lk. 17¹⁰; Mk. 13²⁹ (?). An imperative can also lead to the application in other ways: Lk. 12⁴⁰ par.: καὶ ὑμεῖς γίνεσθε ἕτοιμοι . . .

Mk. 13³⁵: γρηγορεῖτε οὖν . . .   Lk. 16⁹: . . . ἑαυτοῖς ποιήσατε
                                                        φίλους . . .

Matt. 25¹³: γρηγορεῖτε οὖν . . .   Lk. 10³⁷ᵇ: πορεύου καὶ σὺ ποίει
                                                        ὁμοίως.

These applications, apart from Lk. 12⁴⁰; Mk. 13³⁵, are just as secondary as that attached to the saying about light in Matt. 5¹⁶.

The conclusion *a maiore ad minus* which is not infrequent in Jewish similitudes[1] (e.g. Fiebig, I, pp. 110f.; II, pp. 84f.; *Erzaehlungsstil*, pp. 64f.; Strack-B. I, 279, 655, 896) is found in the Synoptics only in the saying in Matt. 7¹¹ par. Lk. 11⁵⁻⁸ is in fact based on this kind of conclusion, though it is not actually expressed, and Lk. 18⁶ᶠ· is a correspondingly secondary application.

That an application can be made *e contrario* can be seen in the O.T., e.g. Isa. 1³.

> 'The ox knoweth his owner,
> And the ass his master's crib:
> But Israel doth not know
> My people doth not consider.'

Further Jer. 2³², 8⁷; and in Jewish similitudes (4 Ezra 9³⁴⁻³⁶; Fiebig, I, pp. 19, 41, 43, 64–73; some examples in Strack-B. I, 731; also 664). Lk. 12⁴⁰ is an example in the Synoptics, where after a description of the burglary the text continues: καὶ ὑμεῖς γίνεσθε ἕτοιμοι, viz., so that nothing like that happens to you. Lk. 12⁵⁶ must be taken here: ὑποκριταί, τὸ πρόσωπον τῆς γῆς καὶ τοῦ οὐρανοῦ οἴδατε δοκιμάζειν, τὸν δὲ καιρὸν τοῦτον πῶς οὐ δοκιμάζετε;

Among the passages already considered there have been some in which the *application is given in a logion*: Matt. 20¹⁶ (The First and the Last); 22¹⁴ (Called and Chosen); Lk. 18¹⁴ (πᾶς ὁ ὑψῶν ἑαυτόν. . .). There are also Matt. 25²⁹//Lk. 19²⁶ (τῷ γὰρ ἔχοντι παντὶ δοθήσεται . . .), where the logion was already in the form known to the evangelist: Lk. 14¹¹ (as 18¹⁴), 16⁹⁻¹³ (sayings on Mammon). It is possible also to include the addition of a quotation from Scripture, Mk. 12¹⁰ᶠ· In all these instances the added sayings were not conceived along with the similitudes but were taken up by themselves and added to them. Lk. 14¹¹ and 18¹⁴ᵇ are especially good illustrations of this point. It is impossible to say how far back in the tradition such additions went, but supposedly it is universally secondary. The tendency of the tradition also comes out in the history of the text:

---

[1] For the O.T. cp. W. Baumgartner, *Die Klagegedichte des Jeremia*, p. 57.

G

Matt. 20[16] in D, etc., has a second logion (Called and Chosen attached to the first. A comparison can be made at this point with Rabbinic similitudes where scriptural quotations were also added as interpretations, e.g. P.A. III, p. 18; Fiebig, I, pp. 29f., 47; II, pp. 86, 95.[1] I do not venture to say how far we are here dealing with later additions. But it is clear that in R. Johanan b. Zakkai's similitude quoted in Fiebig, II, pp. 17f., there is a later expansion in a quotation by R. Meir. It is characteristic that this addition then grew together with the similitude and was expanded again by a new quotation (ibid., pp. 19f.). But a still better analogy to the appended logion is found in the sentences that are so readily added in popular poetry to legends, fairy-tales, ballads and other songs, so as to give expression to their point in a way that can be easily remembered. A Jewish legend tells how the angel of death spared a certain man because he had given alms to a blind person. The story closes: 'If the life of a man who gives alms to the blind is prolonged, how much more will that of a man who practises righteousness every day, every hour.'[2] In the same way is added to the Ballad of Tannhaeuser:

> 'Wherefore no sinner shall be damned
>   By Cardinal or Pope
>   However great the sinner be,
>   God's grace remains his hope.'

Or at the end of the song of the maiden who was seduced by the Knight (Bluebeard), we read:

> 'Hearth and home stay by for ever,
>   A wand'ring Knight shall you trust never.'

Occasionally here we find itinerant lines which are found in various songs.[3] Thus at the end of the song 'I have not seen my darling for so long', we find:

> 'Ah! had the fire not burnt so very bright,
>   Then had my love not then been set alight.
>   The fire it burnt so sore
>   But love burnt even more.
>   The fire I'll make to die,
>   But love will live for aye,
>   For ever, ever more.

Likewise in the song 'The sun doth shine no more' is the refrain:

---

[1] Occasionally in Jewish similitudes also a sentence is (prefixed or) appended: cp. Fiebig, *Erzaehlungsstil*, pp. 68f.

[2] Bin Gorion, *Der Born Judas*, II, p. 176; M. Gaster, Exempla No. 387.

[3] Cp. J. W. Bruinier, *Das deutsche Volkslied*[6], 1921, pp. 32f.

'The fire I'll make to die,
But love will live for aye.
The fire, it burns so sore
But love burns even more.'

In the same way a sentence is sometimes added at the end of a
fairy-tale. Thus a Russian fairy story ends with the proverb: 'To
whom the Lord gives an office, to him he gives understanding.' Or
another: 'The one who talks biggest does best.' ('Russian Fairy Tales,'
ed. by Loewis of Menar in Die Maerchen der Weltliteratur, 1921,
pp. 71 and 156; cp. pp. 74, 221; and cp. R. Petsch, *Formelhafte Schluesse
im Volksmaerchen*, 1900, pp. 53-55.)

Finally two similitudes in the Synoptic tradition have been given a
detailed interpretation: the Similitude of the Sower, Mk. 4^{3-9} in 4^{13-20}
and that of the Tares in Matt. 13^{24-30} in 13^{36-43}. These interpretations are without doubt secondary, but not because the interpretation
turns them into allegories.[1] Nor yet because the mere addition of an
interpretation is in itself unusual, for that happens often enough in
the Rabbinic tradition.[2] But even such scribal interpretations re-
semble those in Mk. 4^{13-20}; Matt. 13^{36-43}, and that these are
less like the style of ancient dominical sayings than the concise
applications, is quite clear. But most particularly the Christian
terminology of Mk. 4^{13-20} (the absolute use of ὁ λόγος, etc.), and
the looseness of the interpretation of particular features shows that
it is secondary; and in Matt. 13^{36-43} most of all it is the absence
from the interpretation of a specific point, viz., the exhortation to
patience.[3]

Before I trace any further the history of the tradition, which my previous observations have already to some degree brought to light, I

[1] This apparent reason only arises because the interpretation states the correspondences
between figure and reality in simple assertions of identity and uses metaphors. Rabbinic
interpretation does the same without being liable to a charge, which Fiebig tries to make,
of passing to allegory. Neither is there allegory in the example given in Fiebig, *Erzaehlungsstil*, p. 53, though the similitude is in conundrum form; cp. Prov. 25^{14-18}, $30^{15, 24-28}$.
[2] Cp. Strack-B. I, 137 (after: 'This King is Adam, the woman Eve, the elder who asked
for vinegar, is the serpent,' etc.), 664f. 665, 671; Fiebig, *Erzaehlungsstil*, p. 53.
[3] Not because the βασιλεία is no longer thought of eschatologically, but as the Church.
The phrase συλλέξουσιν ἐκ τῆς βασιλείας αὐτοῦ in v. 41 means: out of the kingdom which
will appear *then*. Nor is ὁ δὲ ἀγρός ἐστιν ὁ κόσμος in v. 38 'universalistic', cp. the interpretation of the similitude in Strack-B. I, 655: 'The garden is the world.' Perhaps the secondary
character of Matt. 13^{36-43} is also shown by the sowing of tares being regarded as the false
prophets in the Church. Cp. A. Fridrichsen, *Le Problème du Miracle*, pp. 108f. Examples of
secondary interpretation of parables are the explanation of the similitude of the fig tree
which in the Ethiopian Tractate translation *Z.N.W.*, 14, 1913, pp. 66ff. is put into the
mouth of Jesus, and the allegorical interpretations which are attached in the Herm. *Sim.*,
V, 4-7 to the parabolic interpretation (V, 3) of the parable of the Loyal Slave (V, 2),
though the parable is already expanded by certain allegorical features. Cp. M. Dibelius,
'Exkurs. zu Herm. *Sim.* V, 2' in *Ergaenzungsband zum Handbuch zum N.T.*

must deal[1] with the *technique of telling a similitude*, in order to complete the analysis of style. The *conciseness* of the narrative is characteristic. Only the necessary *persons* appear. Thus in the story of the Prodigal Son there is no mother, or in the parable of the Importunate Friend no wife of the disturbed sleeper. There are never more than three chief characters, and for the most part only two: slave and master (Lk. 17[7ff.]), the judge and the widow (Lk. 18[1ff.]), the importunate man and his friend (Lk. 11[5ff.]), the father and the prodigal son (Lk. 15[11-24]), the Pharisee and the publican (Lk. 18[9ff.]), etc.

But often there are three: the lender and his two debtors (Lk. 7[41f.]), the king and his two debtors (Matt. 18[23ff.]), the father and the two sons (Matt. 21[28ff.]), etc. If there are not two (or three) persons, there are two (or three) parties or groups: the wicked husbandmen and the master (Mk. 12[1ff.]), the host and guests (Lk. 14[16ff.]), the master of the vineyard and the labourers (Matt. 20[1ff.]), the master and his servants (Matt. 25[14ff.]), etc. *Groups* of people are treated as a single person (the wicked husbandmen Mk. 12[1ff.], the σύνδουλοι Matt. 18[31], 24[49], etc.) and only differentiated in so far as it is necessary (the guests who make excuses Lk. 14[18ff.], the labourers hired at different times Matt. 20[1ff.], the debtors Lk. 16[5ff.], the priest and the Levite Lk. 10[29ff.], etc.). The law of stage duality is operative, i.e. only two persons speaking or acting come on at a time. If others are present, they remain in the background. If more than two have to speak or act, they have to do it in separate successive scenes. The steward deals with his master's debtors one by one (Lk. 16[5-7]); the father asks his sons one at a time to go into his vineyard (Matt. 21[28-30]); the servants come with their talents one after another to their master, and he does not receive a report from all three before he distributes rewards and punishment, but everyone receives his reward immediately he has given an account of himself (Matt. 25[19ff.]).

There is also the *law of the single perspective*, i.e. one is not asked to watch two different series of events happening at the same time. In the parable of the prodigal son the whole story is told from the point of view of the prodigal. How the father took his son's departure, and what he thought while he was absent is never stated. The parable of the unforgiving servant is similarly told. Admittedly the King and his servant come in turns to the forefront, but even so the scenes are so arranged that they never overlap. What the visitor thought or did in Lk. 11[5-8] while his friend went to his neighbour is also unrecorded.

[1] Cp. Axel Olrik, 'Gesetze der Volksdichtung', *Ztschr. f. deutsches Altertum* 51, 1909, 1–12; cp. E. Fascher, *Die formgeschichtl. Methode*, p. 40.

The only time when it is otherwise is in Luke's version of the parable of the talents, but that is due to secondary editing. In Matthew the story flows from a single perspective, and where the master was between his first and second appearance we are not told.

Only seldom are the *characters* portrayed by some attribute, like the judge who 'feared not God and regarded not man' (Lk. 18²) or the ten virgins of whom five were wise and five foolish (Matt. 25²). For the most part people are characterized by what they say or do, or how they behave, like the prodigal son and his loving father, or the magnanimous King and the merciless debtor, or the two so different sons, etc. Or it may be that in the story itself some characterizing judgement is made of one of the actors: the king calls his merciless servant δοῦλε πονηρέ; the first two servants who bring their talents back with interest are praised as δοῦλε ἀγαθὲ καὶ πιστέ, while the third is rebuked as πονηρὲ δοῦλε καὶ ὀκνηρέ; and God calls the rich man who is concerned only about his worldly prosperity ἄφρων.

Feelings and motives are mentioned only when they are essential for the action or the point. Thus in the parable of the unforgiving servant, as the servant fell down before the king and entreated him we read: σπλαγχνισθεὶς δὲ ὁ κύριος . . . ἀπέλυσεν αὐτόν; when the servant then mercilessly threw his fellow-servant into prison: ἰδόντες οὖν οἱ σύνδουλοι αὐτοῦ . . . ἐλυπήθησαν σφόδρα; and finally when the king heard what had happened: ὀργισθεὶς . . . παρέδωκεν αὐτὸν . . . It is said of the Good Samaritan, ἐσπλαγχνίσθη, as it is of the father when he saw his lost son returning home; and the shepherd who finds his sheep puts it on his shoulder χαίρων. But for the most part feelings are only portrayed indirectly or left to the hearer's own imagination. The feelings of the prodigal are indicated at best simply by εἰς ἑαυτὸν δὲ ἐλθών, and for the rest are conveyed by the account of what he said and did. In the same way the feelings of the Pharisee and the publican are presented only in their prayers and gestures. And there is, e.g. no description of feelings at all in the parables of the importunate friend, the importunate widow, or the ten virgins.

Other participants are described only in so far as it is necessary. In Lk. 10³⁰⁻³⁵ there is no description of either the man who went down to Jericho or the innkeeper. The widow who importuned the judge is not characterized save for her persistency (Lk. 18¹ff·); nothing turns on her motives and their justification. In the differentiation of these 'extras' the similitudes are governed by the wise economy of popular story telling: two debtors suffice in the story of the unjust steward, and they are presented quite like each other, though with slight variation of their debt and the fraudulent dealing. Three types of guests are brought into the similitude of the supper; in this case two would be too scanty, more than three superfluous. In the parable of the Labourers in the Vineyard there are five groups of labourers; the story turns only on the first and last groups, but the emphatic contrast of the extremes has to be mitigated by some sort of intermediates; otherwise the story would sound all too improbable.

Above everything else, there is complete lack of *motivation* in the exposition, for the simple reason that it is irrelevant to the point. Thus the request of the younger son for his share of the inheritance (Lk. 15[12f.]) and his journey into a far country is quite unmotivated. Similarly we are not told why the employer in Matt. 20[1ff.] needed so many labourers for his vineyard as to go out every three hours to take on more hands. For what reason the various travellers in Lk. 10[29ff.] made their journey is not disclosed. Likewise the reason for the different answers and the different behaviour of the two sons in Matt. 21[28ff.] remains outside the story.

In the same way some passages, looked at objectively, *do not have a conclusion*, if, that is, it is self-evident or not relevant. We are not told that the rich fool actually died the same night, any more than we learn what success the steward's deceit had. What happened to the barren fig tree? Did it bear fruit that year? It really doesn't matter. Did the man the Good Samaritan helped recover quickly, or did he have to spend more money on him? We do not need to know.

There is similar economy governing the *description of events and actions*. Anything unnecessary is omitted; e.g. we are not told how the steward dissipated his master's wealth. There is no description of how the widow importuned the judge, but just a very brief indication that she did, etc. In understandable antithesis to this whatever is reported is described in very concrete terms. The debts of the two debtors in Lk. 7[41f.] amount to 500 and 50 denarii, in Matt. 18[23ff.] to 10,000 talents and 100 denarii; Lk. 16[5ff.] gives 100 measures of oil and 100 measures of wheat. The prodigal son becomes a swineherd; when he comes home the father clothes him with the best robe, adorns him with a ring, and kills the fatted calf for him. The luxury of the rich man and the lamentable state of poor Lazarus are vividly portrayed. The wage of the workers in the vineyard is concretely stated as one denarius. The owner of the unfruitful fig tree has come already for three years to find no fruit, etc. In all this there is a correspondence with the art of popular story telling.

There is another point of correspondence in the use of *direct speech and soliloquy.*[1] Similitudes are found in the Lost Sheep and the Lost Coin, the Master and Servant, the Children playing in the Market Place or in the parables of the Barren Fig Tree (for this reason the ἀμπελουργός has to appear next to the owner), of Labourers in the Vineyard (for the same reason there has to be an ἐπίτροπος), of the Sowing of Tares, of the Great Supper, etc. (cp. Herm, *Sim* V, 2.2, 7; IX, 32.3). Soliloquies can be found in the parables, etc., of the Prodigal Son, the Unjust Steward, the Unjust Judge, the Rich Fool, the Unfaithful Servant (Lk. 12⁴⁵), the Wicked Husbandmen (Lk. 20¹³ expanded). Under this category we must also include the prayers of the Pharisee and the publican (cp. Herm. *Sim* V, 2.4).

We can find other elements of style typical of popular story telling, like the *law of repetition*: the phrase μακροθύμησον ἐπ' ἐμοί, καὶ πάντα ἀποδώσω σοι appears twice in the parable of the Unmerciful Servant. The confession of the prodigal son comes twice. The servants in Matt. 25²⁰ᶠᶠ· present their accounts and receive their reward in words that are repeated; similarly, with variations, are recorded the excuses of the invited guests Lk. 14¹⁸ᶠᶠ·, and the dealings of the steward with the debtors Lk. 16⁵ᶠᶠ. A threefold repetition can be found in the parable of the Great Supper: three types of guests make their excuses; also Matt. 25¹⁴ᶠᶠ·: three sorts of servants who are entrusted with money; Lk. 10²⁹ᶠᶠ·: Priest, Levite and Samaritan go down the Jericho road; also Lk. 13⁷, the owner of the fig tree has already looked for fruit on it in vain for three years. There is also the law of *End-stress*, i.e. the most important thing is left to the end. The clearest example is Mk. 4³ᶠᶠ·: the fruitful seed is mentioned last of all. Further, Lk. 16¹⁹ᶠᶠ·: the rich man is portrayed before the poor man; for manifestly the story is not intended to preach renunciation to the rich, but contentment with their lot to the poor. Lk. 18⁹ᶠᶠ·: the publican is introduced after the Pharisee. Matt. 25¹⁴ᶠᶠ·: the servant who has not used the money entrusted to him is presented last, so as to accord with the hortatory nature of the story. On this issue we have to consider the point of textual criticism in the parable of the two sons Matt. 21²⁸⁻³¹. Did the first one say yes or no? An answer is admittedly difficult, because the two sons can be considered equally important. But my view is that the one who said no is the more interesting or paradoxical character and must therefore be deemed the second.

Finally it is important to notice how and why the *hearers' judgement*

---

[1] Both frequent in Jewish similitudes. E.g. direct speech Rh. 17b (Strack-B. I, 286f.); NuR 16 (180d) Midr. Ecc. 5¹⁰ (28b) (both Strack-B. I, 665); soliloquy GnR 46 (29a); Tanh. B. לך — לך - §'23 (40a) (both Strack-B, I, 386); LvR 20 (120a) (Strack-B. II, 355f.).

is precipitated. The *moral* quality of the man who found the treasure or the one who bought the pearl is not the subject of judgement; naturally, too, there is no verdict on the institution of slavery (Lk. 17[7ff.]) or upon imprisonment for debt (Matt. 18[23ff.]). It is plain that the steward is fraudulent and the judge unscrupulous, but not in order that they should be judged on those grounds, but that we should realize that it is possible to learn something even from such rascals as these. In other instances we are required to pass a moral verdict on some action, not only in exemplary stories (with the exception of Lk. 16[19ff.]) but also in the parable of the prodigal son, of the talents, of the unforgiving servant, of the two sons, where the point of the parable is directed just to this verdict. Naturally some judgement is in general required by all similitudes, and their argumentative character is often expressed in their form, as has been shown. Such a purpose is also often served by the *antithesis of two types*: the two debtors (Lk. 7[41f.]), the two sons, the wise and foolish virgins, the two servants (Lk. 12[42ff.]), the rich man and the poor, the Pharisee and the publican, the Priest and Levite and the Samaritan.[1] Often the contrasting types are introduced one after the other in two independent descriptions, producing a sort of double similitude; thus the similitude of the house building (Matt. 7[24-27] par.), of the two servants (Lk. 12[42-46]) and the formally related passages of the great feast (Lk. 14[7-11, 12-14]) give a positive and negative example in the two halves of the story.[2]

Our considerations have already shown that in the tradition similitudes have had a history, as their form has been changed here and there, and applications have been added to them. But to that history we must add that the similitudes have been *introduced into a context*, and that they have often on that account been *provided with an introduction*, which does not strictly belong to the similitude as such. The most obvious example is the story of the Good Samaritan, for which Luke has used the question about the greatest commandment as an introduction. Another clear case is in Lk. 19[11] where Luke has constructed an introduction to the parable of the talents by depicting a situation in terms of which, in his view, the parable can be understood, but which he has in fact created in terms of his interpretation. Moreover it cannot be doubted that he has used the apophthegm on

---

[1] Naturally we find antithesis of contrasting types in Rabbinic similitudes, e.g. ExR 27 (88a); 30 (90b); DtR 7 (204a); Sab. 153a; Midr. Ecc. 9.8 (42a) (in Strack-B. I, 865, 462, 866, 878). It stands to reason that this means of ethical or religious instruction is frequently used in popular literature, cp. e.g. Buddhist fairy stories in Die Maerchen der Weltlit., ed. E. Lueders, 1921, pp. 26ff., 34ff.

[2] Jewish examples. P.A., 3.18, 4.20; Wuensche, p. 110; Fiebig II, pp. 81f.; *Erzaehlungsstil*, pp. 48, 92; Strack-B. 518 (on Matt. 9[17]).

dividing the inheritance in 12 $^{13f.}$ as an introduction to the story of the rich fool; and has formed v. 15 to serve as a transition from the one to the other. The introduction in 18^1 (the unjust judge) and 18^9 (Pharisee and Publican) will also derive from him. Nor need we be surprised that 12^{15} and 18^9 are adapted to what follows, since they are pure exemplary stories. On the other hand the introduction in 18^1 (ἔλεγεν δὲ παραβολὴν αὐτοῖς πρὸς τὸ δεῖν πάντοτε προσεύχεσθαι αὐτοὺς καὶ μὴ ἐγκακεῖν) is admittedly far too generalizing; the application added in vv. 6–8a is obviously much more appropriate: the parable is specifically concerned with prayer for the coming of God's kingdom. For his introduction to the similitude of the Great Supper Luke has not undiscerningly used the beatitude in 14^{15}, and thus shown that his understanding of the parable was allegorical. He has provided a suitable introduction to the similitudes of the lost in 15$^{1f.}$ In a similar way Mark has formulated an introduction for the parable of the returning householder in 13^{34} which is quite appropriate; and Matthew has used the same saying as an introduction to the similitude of the robber 24^{42}. Luke has formulated a question by Peter in 12^{41} and used it as an introduction to the similitude of the two servants, and has thereby intended to apply it to the officials of the Christian Church—quite against its original meaning, it would seem.

But the evangelists' interpretation is often found not in some formulation of their own, but is given simply by the *introduction of a similitude into a particular context*. Thus Matthew has cleverly attached the parable of the unforgiving servant to the saying about forgiveness (18$^{21f.}$), where Luke evidently did not read it. Similarly Luke has used the apophthegm on repentance in 13$^{1-5}$ as the peg on which to hang the parable of the barren fig tree (on Lk. 12$^{13f.}$ as introduction for vv. 16–21, see above p. 23). Even in Q the similitude on building a house was the end of a collection of sayings and had gained its meaning thereby. Naturally we cannot be certain whether such an interpretation is right, i.e. whether the similitude originally went with sayings of Jesus. It could e.g. have also been attached to the Word of God. There is no doubt that the similitude of the lost sheep has been given a new meaning by its introduction in Matthew (18$^{12-14}$), one which Matthew makes explicit in the appended interpretation in 18^{14}, see above, p. 171. It is questionable whether the similitudes of building the tower and going to war in Lk. 14$^{28-32}$ originally belonged to a section on Discipleship, as Luke asserts both by the context he gives them and the interpretation he provides in v. 33. So we must always raise the question whether the evangelists have given the similitudes their right setting. Elsewhere the evangelists have not shown themselves completely masters of their material, as many similitudes are not inserted into a context at all, but are simply joined together for purely formal reasons. This is true of ch. 4 in Mark, and even more of Matt. 13, and also of Lk. 14, etc. In the way in which a similitude in a tradition can be adapted to a particular context—and that needs no further explanation—we may compare how in Fiebig, II, pp. 73–75 the same similitude is related both to the exegesis of Lev. 4[2] and to a disputation with Antonius.

But in the history of the tradition the similitudes have undergone even more radical expansions and transformations. The so-called *double similitudes* are a good example of this. But in this connection I am not thinking of the instances cited on p. 192, where two similitudes provide an example and a counter example, but instances where a new similitude is put alongside another quite complete and independent in itself, providing a parallel structure in which the same proposition is clothed in new material. Thus

Lk. 14[28–32]: The Building of   Matt. 13[31–33] par.: Mustard
the Tower and Going to War.   Seed and Leaven.

Mk. 3[24–25]: Divided Kingdom   Matt. 13[44–46]: The Treasure and
and Divided House.   the Pearl.

Lk.[4] 15[–11]: The Lost Sheep and the Lost Coin.

This doubling is the same as was found in the figurative sayings (e.g. Mk. 2[21f.]; Matt. 7[9f.]), and as then, we may ask whether the doubling be original or whether the second portion is a secondary accretion. It is the former alternative that is in principle the more likely; for such a doubling is a very old and widespread instrument of the story teller's art.[1] Cp. e.g. Isa. 1[22], 17[5f.]; Jer. 2[32], 8[4], 18[14]; Amos 7[1–6]; 4 Ezra 4[13–18], [47–50], 7[3–9]; Herm. *Mand.* XI, 18–21 Fiebig, I, pp. 23, 24f.; II, pp. 81f.; *Erzaehlungsstil*, p. 58; and it is scarcely necessary to add any further parallels from Buddhism. But some particular examples demand special consideration. Thus the two similitudes in Fiebig, II, pp. 81f. (each one with both positive and negative) come from one Rabbi. On the other hand we can see two instances in Fiebig, I, pp. 23, 24f. where a later Rabbi has added a new parallel to the similitude of an earlier teacher. In the same way a figurative saying parallel in meaning has been added to the similitude of another Rabbi in Sabb. f. 31b (Wuensche, pp. 195f.). A double similitude of Rab Nahman has been added in Exod. 21b. (Strack-B. I, 653f.), and to it have been attached three parallel similitudes by three other Rabbis. Indeed it might be said that there

---

[1] Cp. W. Baumgartner, *Die Klagegedichte des Jeremia*, p. 57.

was a certain attraction about adding a new similitude to some other thought suitable, even perhaps to surpass it. Now in the Synoptic tradition there are two places where in one version of the tradition there is a double similitude and in the other only one of them, Matt. 13 31-33 par. by comparison with Mk. 4 30-32; and Lk. 15 4-11 by comparison with Matt. 18 12-14. Further we must notice that in both cases the second member of the double similitude is sharply separated from the first; in the former case by ἄλλην παραβολὴν ἐλάλησεν αὐτοῖς (Matthew) or καὶ πάλιν εἶπεν (Luke); in the latter through the former similitude being given an interpretation before the second is stated. We must then ask whether it is just an accident that in both cases the more concise tradition contains the first member of the double similitude. If the brevity had come about by a process of mutilation one would then perhaps have expected to find that some second member of a double similitude would have been part of the shorter tradition. If we must at least reckon with the possibility that Matt. 13 33 par. and Lk. 15 8-10 are later additions, so are we obliged to raise the same questions in regard to the other double similitudes. Matt. 13 45 is also strongly marked off from 13 44 by πάλιν ὁμοία ἐστὶν ἡ βασιλεία τ. οὐρ., so that the possibility of a later addition must be reckoned with here too. It is also noticeable that the theme of a similitude can appear in varied form without the variations being brought together into a double similitude. Thus 1 Cl. 23 4 is a variant of Mk. 4 26-29, and I think the same is true of Lk. 11 5-8 (the Importunate Friend) and 18 1-8 (The Unjust Judge), of Matt. 13 24-30 (Tares) and 13 47-50 (The Net). The idea that has sometimes been considered, that these were originally double similitudes is thus to be rejected. On the other hand there is no basis, in my view, for doubting any original connection between Mk. 3 24 and 3 25 (which are joined by καί as Mk. 2 22), or between Lk. 14 28-30 and 14 31-32 (joined by ἤ as is Matt. 7 9). But naturally one's judgement in all these cases is made with cautious reserve.

There are further *expansions and combinations* of another kind in the tradition. One simple instance is in Lk. 12 42-48, where a narrower meaning is given to the similitude of the loyal and the unloyal servants vv. 42-46 by combining it with the figurative saying in vv. 47f. (punishment in proportion to responsibility). Similarly the parable of the Great Supper in Matt 22 1-10 is enlarged by an allegorical appendix in vv. 11-14 (scarcely an independent similitude) which can be seen to be secondary by a mere comparison with the Lucan parallel. Similarly a comparison with Matt. 25 14-30 shows that Lk. 19 12-27 is a secondary combination of the parable of the Talents with an allegory of the departure and return of Jesus. An example from outside the canon of scripture occurs in the parable of the loyal slave in Herm. *Sim.*, V, 2; the original parable 2 $^{1-8}$ has been enlarged by an addition in 2 $^{9-11}$ in the interests of an allegorical interpretation (see p. 187, n. 3). On these grounds we may ask whether in the parable of the Prodigal Son the second part Lk. 15 $^{25-32}$ is not a secondary expansion of the first vv. 11–24. Surely the narrator's purpose, to make plain the fatherly goodness of God, which unconditionally forgives self-condemning remorse, is already attained in v. 24? And is not the point of the parable shifted when God's forgiveness is defended against the charge of injustice? Yet vv. 25–32 are not an allegorical fabrication, but remain completely within the parable so far as formal features are concerned. But neither does this second half of the parable really differ in context from the first, but rather makes plain by contrast the paradoxical character of divine forgiveness. This parable then belongs to those in which two types are contrasted with each other (p. 192), and so has its parallel as far as meaning is concerned, in Matt. 21 $^{28-31}$ (the Two Sons), and it would be proper to call Lk. 15 $^{11-32}$ the parable of the Lost Son. One can only wonder whether originally the first part was told more briefly. The situation is quite different, in my opinion, in regard to the parable of Dives and Lazarus in Lk. 16 $^{19-31}$. This has two points (p. 178): whereas vv. 19–26 is meant to console the poor, or alternatively warn the rich by pointing to the equalization in the world to come, vv. 27–31 says that Moses and the prophets have made God's will sufficiently plain, so that there is no need to ask for a miracle of the resurrection of a dead person in order to induce belief. H. Gressmann wanted to trace the first part back to an Egyptian fairy-tale, which also circulated amongst the Jews, and then to understand the second part as a development by Jesus himself.[1] But the real point of that fairy story is quite different: the proof of divine justice by the assimilation of destinies in the world to come (see below).

---

[1] H. Gressmann, *Vom reichen Mann und armen Lazarus*, Abh. d. Kgl. Pr. Akad. d. W., 1918, Phil.-hist. Kl., no. 7, Berlin, 1918. Cp. Klostermann; Bin Gorion, *Der Born Judas*, II, pp. 140–7. Gr. has misconceived the meaning of Lk. 16 $^{27-31}$. It answers the question, whether God will have to confirm the revelation of his will in the Law and the prophets by a miracle; thus it is wholly Jewish with no inner connection with 16 $^{19-26}$ which simply teaches the levelling of earthly relationships. This section is also wholly Jewish, and Gressmann's proposition that Jesus could not have said such things, and so vv. 10–26 could not have existed by itself is a *petitio principii*. H. Windisch defends the genuineness and unity of the parable (*N.T.T.*, 1925, pp. 343–60) by seeing the whole parable in terms of the meaning of the first part which he quite rightly characterizes by referring to Lk. 6 $^{21-26}$ and Ja. 2 ^{13}. He is right in thinking that the secondary character of these verses will not be demonstrated by their Christian character since they are better described as 'pre-Christian'. But the distinctive motif of vv. 27–31, which really establishes their secondary character in relationship to vv. 19–26, is not really brought out by Windisch.

On the other hand there is another Jewish legend,[1] which tells (in a very fairy-story, fantasy manner) of a rich and godless married couple. The woman goes to Hell; a boy who offers to journey to Hell, a thing for which the husband has no heart, in order to see the woman, comes back after having seen her in the torture of the fire, and along with her ring brings the message: 'Tell my husband to turn over a new leaf, for the power of repentance is great.' Deeply moved, the husband repents. In the form in which we find it, this story is relatively old: it is hard to imagine that it derives from the gospel story. That gives rise to the alternative suggestion that a Jewish story lies behind Lk. 16[19-31] (likewise of a man called Lazarus?); its conclusion which originally told of a message from the underworld,[2] undergoes a polemical change[3] and was thus provided with a point completely destroying the original unity of the story. Mk. 13[33-37] is also a secondary composition, cp. the analysis, pp. 173f., as is Lk. 12[35-38], cp. pp. 118f.

What has been said applies also in part to a special class of transformations, viz. the *allegorical expansions*. To this class belong Matt. 22[11-14] and Luke's addition in 19[12-27]. There is a more instructive instance, and one because of the parallel in Matthew and Luke much more clearly recognizable, viz. the Parable of the Marriage Feast. By using the features so inappropriate to the story as the killing of the commissioned servants and the retaliatory action of the king Matthew has clearly introduced into the story both the hostile attitude of the Jews to Jesus and his disciples, and the destruction of Jerusalem. Luke, by the double invitation to new guests, has introduced a picture of the Gentile mission. The possibility of other allegorical elements is worth considering, see p. 175.

If the view that the different style of allegorical additions demonstrate their secondary character be contested, or if it be held that Juelicher's method of dismissing everything allegorical is only a violation of the material for a more abstract idea, then this has to be said:

1. The secondary character of the allegorical sections is without doubt demonstrated in a whole series of instances by comparison with the parallel tradition.

2. A further criterion is provided by the test of subject-matter

---

[1] In Bin Gorion, *Der Born Judas*, VI, pp. 75ff., from 'Un recueil de contes juifs inédits', § XI, *R.E.J.*, pp. 35, 76-81.

[2] Cp. R. Basset, *1001 Contes*, I, 1924, p. 64. One who died as a punishment for his wantonness appears to his friends as a warning. Rabbinic literature also recounts some appearances of the dead: Strack-B. II, 233 on Lk. 16[30].

[3] There is a parallel in the Mandaean literature Ginza R., XI, 253, 20ff., Lidzb.

which shows many allegorical elements to be later community products.

3. Most of all we must ask of Juelicher's critics a clarity of concept, and whether this be understood in Aristotelian or other terms is not a matter of fundamental significance. In my view the difference between the nature of similitudes and parables on the one hand and allegory on the other is most clearly formulated by saying that the former involve the transference of a judgement (derived from some neutral field) from one sphere to another, which is under discussion. But allegory does not involve such a transference of judgement, but is concerned with disguising some situation in secret or fantastic forms, so as to serve prophetic and other purposes. So what Fiebig, e.g. adduces as allegorical features in Rabbinic similitudes are really nothing of the kind; they are rather examples of quite customary metaphors for God (as king) for man (as slave), etc., in the similitudes; or it may simply be that the correspondence between the image and the reality has been expressed in the primitive form of an identification. I have not found[1] any instance in Fiebig of allegory in Jewish similitudes, corresponding to the frequent features in the Synoptic similitudes. For the rest it would always be a debatable point, if any such instance were found, whether Fiebig's conclusions about the Synoptic similitudes were right, and we could always ask whether the somewhat allegorical features of Rabbinic similitudes were not secondary too. Methodically speaking, Juelicher is entirely right as over against Fiebig. It is another question whether Juelicher is always right in particular instances when he detects allegorical features. For example, when a king appears in Mt. 18[23], that is but the appearance of a well-known metaphor, of a king for God. We can no more talk of allegory here than we can speak of a dash of allegory in Lk. 17[7-10] which uses the common description of man as the slave of God. When some specific relationship between two things a and b is illustrated by a similitude, there must naturally be two complementary things a' and b' in the similitude;[2] but that is not allegory, especially when the comparisons are provided under the influence of popular metaphors, and if an application should then run: 'The field is the world', that does not mean 'The field is an allegorical representation of the world', but that the significance

---

[1] There is a striking instance of the absurdity of Fiebig's views in Fiebig I, p. 28, n. 2. Cp. also II, pp. 35ff., and his assertion of 'multiple climax in Rabbinic similitude', II, pp. 17ff. His judgements are more accurate in *Erzaehlungsstil*, p. 52; though it has to be admitted that the examples he quotes on pp. 53–55 are not allegories. In the material found in Strack-B. I have discovered allegory only in the interpretation of the O.T.; cp. I, 449. The interpretation of Lev. 11[4-7] in LvR 13 (114c).

[2] What W. Foerster has to say in correction of Juelicher's interpretation of the similitudes in *Herr ist Jesus*, 1924, pp. 268–72 does not basically differ from this.

given to the field in the story of the Sower is that which the world has in the history of the proclamation of the Word. So, e.g., there is no allegory in either Lk. $7^{41f.}$ (The two debtors) or Matt. 13^{47-50} (The Fishing Net). But it is in all probability allegory when a saying about Christian fasting is attached to the figure in Mk. 2^{19a}, or when in the Parable of the Talents the saying about the departure and return of Jesus forces its way into the text. Here, indeed, as we saw in the other instances already noted, something is reported or affirmed in the similitude which has nothing whatever to do with the point of the similitude and its application, but is simply an intrusion. In particular instances we may be uncertain. Thus it can remain undecided whether or not the birds that come and nest in the branches of the mustard tree are an allegorical representation of the Gentiles who are converted, etc. Most important is the methodological insight into the tradition's tendency to expand similitudes and parables with allegorical elements, and even to conceive them completely as allegories. Proof of this is provided by the two interpretations of similitudes in Mk. 4^{14-20}; Matt. 13^{36-43}, and by the quite secondary verses in Mk. 4^{10-12}, where the similitudes are expressly treated as esoteric utterances. On this basis we may finally regard as late community products the almost entirely allegorical passages Mk. 12^{1-12}; Matt. 25^{1-13}, which in any event have been entirely overgrown by allegory.

What has so far been said occasionally, must be emphasized once more in this summary: *The original meaning of many similitudes has become irrecoverable* in the course of the tradition. Admittedly there is no doubt that the similitudes of the fig tree in Mk. $13^{28f.}$ and the faithful steward in Lk. 12^{42-46} are rightly interpreted in the tradition as similitudes of the Parousia. In other instances the general meaning is clear enough, but not the special point, because the occasion which prompted the similitude is not known. Matt. $11^{16f.}$ could very well be a picture of a capricious people, though whether the reference to Jesus and the Baptist is original remains doubtful. Lk. 11^{5-8}, 18^{1-8} were originally an exhortation to prayer: but to some specific petition? to prayer for the coming of God's reign? Matt. 20^{1-16} obviously teaches God's impartial goodness to all his servants; but against whom was the parable directed originally? Were the parables about the lost in Lk. 15^{4-10} originally meant as comfort and invitation, or as pure polemic? And to what kind of self-examination were the parables of the Building of the Tower and of Setting out to War in Lk. 14^{28-32} originally meant to lead? The Parable of the Unjust Steward in Lk. 16^{1-9} is obviously meant to say that one can learn even from the slyness of a deceiver; but in what way?[1] And as for the Parable of the Sower in Mk. 4[3-9]!—is it a consolation for every man when his labour does not all bear fruit? Is it in this sense a monologue by Jesus, half of resignation, half of thankfulness? Is it an exhortation to the hearers of the divine Word? Of Jesus' preaching? or of the message of the Church? or was there originally no meditation at all on the Word, and have we to understand it as akin to 4 Ezra 8[41]: 'For just as the husbandman sows much seed upon the ground and plants a multitude of plants, and yet not all which were sown shall be saved in due season, nor shall all that were planted take root; so also they that are sown in the world shall not all be saved.'[2] The original point of the similitudes of the mustard seed and the leaven Matt. 13[31-33] is quite irrecoverable now. The introductory formula merely asserts—apart from any question as to its originality—that it is concerned with some truth pertaining to the Kingdom of God. Since, in my view, the Kingdom of God was not thought of, either by Jesus or the early Church, as an human community, there can be no talk of its 'growth': and that is even more true of the results of the preaching of Jesus or the Church.[3] Or has it to be interpreted in relation to the individual?: do not despair if there seems to be little result from your labour (or from your striving after righteousness)? But no-one is able to say whether the meaning is just the reverse, viz. a warning against the evil that poisons the heart or the fellowship.[4] Much the same has to be said of the Similitude of the Seed Growing Secretly (Mk. 4[26-29]). No doubt the point lies in the words *growing by itself*: but what does 'by itself' mean? that the Kingdom of God comes without your agency with the same certainty as the seed grows and produces fruit? In any case the formally related similitude in 1 Clem. 23[4] is meant to illustrate the same certainty with which the divine judgement comes.[5] But alongside that inter-

---

[1] A peculiar Jewish story has a certain relationship to this, and it appears in three variations in Bin Gorion, *Der Born Judas*, IV, pp. 36–38, 229–34 (The King of the Year); the point is that the man is happy who, when his time is shortened, makes wise provision for the future.

[2] Cp. also C. G. Montefiore, *The Synoptic Gospels*, I[2], pp. 99f.

[3] C. R. Bowen, *Am.J.Th.*, XXII, 1918, pp. 562–9: the Similitude of the Mustard Seed is not one about the Kingdom of God, but an illustration of the work of Jesus. (Cp. Windisch, *Z.N.W.*, 20, 1921, p. 84.)

[4] This is the sense of the formally related similitudes of Wormwood in Herm. *Mand.* V, 1, 5 and of Hailstone in *Mand.*, XI, 20. Cp. the proverbs 'If you give the devil your finger, he'll snatch your whole hand'; 'Just one rotten egg will spoil all the broth'; '*Morbide factum pecus totum corrumpit ovile*'. Somewhat different is the Koran, p. 31: 'God will bring both good and evil to light, even if they are no bigger than a mustard seed'.

[5] 1 Clem. 23[4]: ὦ ἀνόητοι, συμβάλετε ἑαυτοὺς ξύλῳ, λάβετε ἄμπελον. πρῶτον μὲν φυλλοροεῖ, εἶτα βλαστὸς γίνεται, εἶτα φύλλον, εἶτα ἄνθος, καὶ μετὰ ταῦτα ὄμφαξ, εἶτα σταφυλὴ παρεστηκυῖα. ὁρᾶτε ὅτι ἐν καιρῷ ὀλίγῳ εἰς πέπειρον καταντᾷ ὁ καρπὸς τοῦ ξύλου. 5 . ἐπ' ἀληθείας ταχὺ καὶ ἐξαίφνης τελειωθήσεται τὸ βούλημα αὐτοῦ συμμαρτυρούσης καὶ τῆς γραφῆς, ὅτι ταχὺ ἥξει καὶ οὐ

pretation there are all the other possibilities that have been considered for the similitudes of the Mustard Seed and the Leaven.

The *material* used in the figures, similitudes, parables, etc., extends over a wide area: a house and its inhabitants, especially father and son; its everyday things, like salt and food and kneading dough, the patching of clothes and the bottling of wine; lighting lamps at evening, and looking for a lost coin. Then there is the playing of children and the doings of grown-ups; seedtime and harvest, cattle breeding and fishing, work and holiday, enterprises, lawsuits, wars. We find rich and poor, creditors and debtors, masters and slaves, kings and merchants, judges and clients, Pharisees and Tax Gatherers, Jews and Samaritans. There are figures from nature: the growth of seed, the fruit-bearing of a fig tree, the waving reed, dogs and foxes, doves and serpents, lightning flashing across the sky, and finally heaven and hell.

The *conservation of the tradition* comes out in this brief review: it can further be seen by comparing it with *Jewish parallels*, especially in Fiebig's collection, and as they can be found in the pages of Strack-B. I cannot here attempt to be exhaustive, but for the sake of conveying an impression of the material, and of the results issuing from it, I quote a short selection:

Lk. 17$^{7-10}$: cp. P.A., I, 3: 'Be not as slaves that minister to the Lord with a view to receive recompense; but be as slaves that minister to the lord without a view to receive recompense.'

Matt. 20$^{1-16}$: cp. Ber., II, 5c (Klostermann ad loc. and Fiebig, II, pp. 87f.; Strack-B. IV, 493). The material is the same: the same reward for different hours of work; but the Jewish similitude is motivated by the consideration that one worker has done more in two hours than the others have achieved in the whole day. But other similitudes using the same material in varying Rabbinic similitudes, are more akin to the gospel similitude, esp. Tanch. כי תצא 19b; Dt R. 6 (203a); Tanch. כי אשו 110a (Strack-B. IV, 493, 498f.).

Matt. 21$^{28-31}$: cp. ExR 27 (88a) in Strack-B. I, 865: Various peasants refuse the king's commission; the last one accepts it, but does not carry it out. With whom will the king be most angry?

Matt. 22$^{1-10}$: cp. the similitude which appears in different versions, cited by Klostermann ad loc., Fiebig, II, pp. 17ff. and Strack-B. I, 878f.: the unworthy guests who are not ready for the

χρονιεῖ καὶ ἐξαίφνης ἥξει ὁ κύριος (the same similitude is in 2 Clem. 11$^{2f.}$). In any event it is clear that the idea of natural development is of no use in the exposition of Mk. 4$^{26-29}$. W. Michaelis, *Taeufer, Jesus, Urgemeinde*, pp. 7of., holds that the similitude emphasizes the independence of the appearance of the Kingdom from the work of the preacher of repentance.

royal feast at the right time, have to look on and go hungry; the wise ones, who are ready, enjoy the happiness of the feast. This is also comparable with Matt. 22 $^{11-14}$ and 25 $^{1-13}$; in addition for 25 $^{1-13}$ there is Sab. 152b (Klostermann ad loc.): the wise take care of their festival garments which the king distributes, while the foolish ones wear them for work.

Matt. 7 $^{24-27}$: cp. P.A., III. 27: 'Whosesoever wisdom is in excess of his works, to what is he like? To a tree whose branches are abundant, and its roots scanty; and the wind comes and uproots it, and over-turns it. And whosesoever works are in excess of his wisdom, to what is he like? To a tree whose branches are scanty, and its roots abundant; though all the winds come upon it, they stir it not from its place.' Cp. with this the very analogous similitude in the Aboth of R. Nathan—ch. 24 in Fiebig, II, pp. 81f.

Matt. 13 ^{44}: cp. Mek. 26b/27a (Fiebig, I, pp. 24f.): in the field sold by the proprietor the purchaser finds treasures of silver and gold.

Lk. 15 $^{4-7}$//Matt. 18 $^{12-16}$: cp. GnR 86 (55b) in Strack-B. I, 785: a cattle drover, one of whose twelve beasts has run away, leaves the eleven behind and goes after the one that is lost.

Mk. 4 $^{3-9}$: cp. 4 Ezra 8 ^{41}: 'For just as the husbandman sows much seed upon the ground and plants a multitude of plants, and yet not all which were sown shall be saved in due season, nor shall all that were planted take root; so also they that are sown in the world shall not all be saved.'[1]

What we have observed of this relationship between the synoptic

---

[1] Since the interpretation of Matt. 11 ^{16} is open to contradiction, I would instance the Arabic proverb quoted in A. Socin, *Arab. Sprichwoerter und Redensarten* (Tueb. Universitaetsschrift, 1878), no. 22: 'If he claps you, then you are to cheer him.' In earlier discussion reference has been made from time to time to Arabic proverbs; it would certainly be possible to interpret some figures and proverbs in terms of oriental literature. Cp. E. Nestle, *Marginalien und Materialien*, 1893, pp. 6off. From Socin, op. cit., I quote no. 112: 'At the same time water carrier and policeman', i.e. No-one can pursue two incompatible occupations, cp. Matt. 6 ^{24} (Socin refers to J. L. Burckhardt, *Arab. Sprichwoerter*, 1875, no. 230: 'At the same time baker and weights inspector'). Further, no. 178: 'Don't play a drum that is covered with carpet'; cp. Mk. 4 ^{21}; also there is the proverb from the Pantshatantra, § 400 (tr. R. Schmidt, 1901, p. 119): 'What can learning accomplish, if it is given to injustice? It is like a lamp put into a covered pot.' From G. W. Freytag, *Arabum Proverbia*, I, 1838 (Meidani), p. 79, n. 210: *tu ex rubis uvas non colliges*; II, 1839, p. 516, n. 358: *non decerpuntur a spinis uvae*; similarly p. 699, n. 367; cp. Matt. 7 ^{16}. I, p. 252, n. 137: *sub pelle ovilla lupinum cor est*; p. 516, n. 71: *lupus, qui ovis haberi vult*; cp. Matt. 7 ^{15}. I, p. 581, n. 222: *saepe angustia ad locum amplum et fatigatio ad quietem ducit*; cp. Matt. 7 $^{13f.}$ Admittedly here the Synoptic proverb could sometimes be the source. For the rest we could refer to the Arabic proverb quoted in L. Bauer: *Volksleben im Lande der Bibel*, 1903, p. 226 in connection with Matt. 6 ^{24}: 'No-one can carry two melons in one hand.' Cp. further E. Klotz, *Im Banne der Furcht. Sitten und Gebraeuche der Wapare in Ostafrika*, 1922, p. 225: 'You don't pull two beehives up into the tree with one tendril of a creeper.' And on p. 234 (cp. Matt. 25 $^{14-30}$ par.): 'Hoarding yields no profit, but lending does save.' And at p. 236 (cp. Matt. 7 $^{3-5}$): 'The monkey laughs at its neighbour's hump because it cannot see its own.'

and Jewish similitudes in respect of their material, and as many of the examples show, in respect of their general tendency, can also be seen in regard to their form which has already been considered. And this fact leads to the further question as to the *origin of the synoptic similitudes*. The relationship to Jewish similitudes by itself may mean no more than that Jesus, to whom the synoptic similitudes are ascribed, was himself in the Jewish tradition and, in common with his conporary fellow countrymen, created similitudes. But particularly in view of the fact that in other places it is possible to suppose or to maintain that Jewish material has been introduced into the synoptic tradition, we cannot but raise the question whether some of the synoptic similitudes have not been taken from the Jewish tradition by the Church and put into Jesus' mouth. In my opinion we can point to one example of very great probability, Lk. 16^{19-31}. We have already shown on pp. 178, 196 that the point of the passage is this: It is not right to ask God for a miracle as a confirmation of his will: we have all that is necessary in Moses and the prophets. But such a thought is specifically Jewish, and this version of it can hardly derive from Jesus or the Christian Church; it illustrates the O.T. passage Deut. $30^{11.14}$. But the same is true of the first part, Lk. 16^{19-26}, which can hardly come from Jesus or the Church, for it breathes the rancorousness of Judaism as it pervades the last chapter of Eth. Enoch, and treats sinners and rich men, the pious and the poor alike. And we must add to this that the material of the similitudes also points to the tradition of Jewish legend (pp. 196f.).

Of the remaining material we need to take special note of the specifically Jewish sections Lk. $14^{7-11, 12-14}$. Matt. 22^{11-13} looks like a fragment of a Jewish similitude. Apart from these it is not possible then to think in quite general terms of the possibility of borrowing from Jewish tradition. Similitudes about the Parousia, like that of the Thief (Lk. $12^{39f.}$) of the Fig Tree (Mk. $13^{28f.}$), of the Two Servants (Lk. 12^{42-46}) have nothing in them that is characteristic of the preaching of Jesus. But similarly the similitude of the Tares and the Net (Matt. $13^{24-30, 47-50}$) and that of Building a House (Matt. 7^{24-27}) could be Jewish in origin. And the same can be said of the similitude of the Seed Growing Secretly if the similitude in 1 Clem 23^4 = 2 Clem 11^3 be originally Jewish, as E. Nestle ($Z.N.W.$, I, 1900, p. 180) believes.[1] But we have to reckon with these possibilities. Perhaps in order that by occasionally quoting specific Jewish parallels, we may turn a possibility into a probability.

[1] We must not quote Philo *de op. mundi* 41. At this point Philo draws on the tradition of the diatribe; cp. Antiphon Fr. 60 in Diels *Frgm. d. Vorsokr.* II, 302; Epikt. *Diss.*, I, 14.3, 15.7; IV, 8.36; Ps. Plut. *De lib. educ.*, 4; Cic. *Tusc.*, II, 13.

But perhaps the example of Lk. 16[19-26] shows that the material of the similitudes can have an even longer history. That is, if Gressmann makes his case out that the story of the Rich Man and Lazarus is a variant of a story often found in the Jewish tradition, and which finally derives from an Egyptian fairy story (see p. 196). This seems to me to be just about as uncertain as it appears that there is little to be said in principle against it (and this in spite of E. Norden, *Die Geburt des Kindes*, 1924, pp. 84f.), and for two reasons: (1) Because the points are different, in that the Egyptian and Jewish stories defend the divine justice and show that reward and punishment are meted out in proportion to piety and sin,[1] whereas Lk. 16[19-26] simply teaches the reversal of earthly fortune in the world to come as a warning to the rich and a consolation for the poor. (2) Because Luke does not have the characteristic form of the problem: the different burial of the rich and the poor.[2] Moreover, it is possible that the story in Lk. 16[19-26] derives from another Jewish legend (see p. 197).

In addition mention must be made of the parallel to Lk. 12[16-21] which Bousset[3] has produced from the Thousand and One Nights, and which according to Perles reached there from a collection of Jewish legends:[4] A certain king, who had collected rich treasures, was summoned by the angel of death at the very moment when he was sitting at a luxurious table, and saying to himself: 'Soul, you have amassed for yourself all the good things of the world, and now you can enjoy them in a long life and good fortune.' Von Hertel, e.g. has brought some parallels to the Parable of the Talents from Indian tradition.[5] The motif of Matt. 24[48-51] is found in the Ahikar story.[6] Kastner[7] and Orth[8] have drawn attention to the parallelism of Lk. 10[30-37] (The Good Samaritan) and 2 Chron. 28[5-15], to which Orth has added the well-known fairy-story motif of the three brothers, who, one after the other, meet some old man or woman; while the two first pass by, the third willingly gives money or food. There is a parallel to the Parable of the Fig Tree (Lk. 13[6-9]) in Ahikar's Parables (Syrian) 8[35] (Charles, *The Pseudepigrapha*, II, p. 775).[9] The

---

[1] This is also the case in a Chinese parallel in R. Wilhelm, *Chinesische Volksmaerchen*, 1917, pp. 116ff.

[2] This leads to the supposition that the story, especially in v. 22 has suffered considerable mutilation. Understandably in the Christian version the fact that in the Jewish tradition the rich man was a tax-collector has to be omitted.

[3] *Nachr. d. Ges. d. Wiss. zu Goettingen*, Phil.-Hist. Kl., 1916, 484.

[4] *M.G.W.J.*, XXII (which I have not been able to consult).

[5] *Geist des Ostens*, I, 1913/4, pp. 247ff.; cp. Van den Bergh van Eysinga, *Indische Einfluesse auf evangelische Erzaehlungen*[2], 1909, p. 62; R. Garbe, *Indien und das Christentum*, 1914, pp. 42ff.

[6] F. C. Conybeare, J. Rendel Harris, A. Smith Lewis, *The Story of Ahikar*[2], 1913, pp. lxii–lxvi.   [7] *Bibl. Zeitschr.*, 1914, pp. 29ff.   [8] *Protestant. Monatshefte*, 1914, pp. 406ff.

[9] We do not need to deal with the parallel to the Parable of the Prodigal Son suggested by Van den Bergh van Eysinga (*Indische Einfluesse auf evang. Erzaehlungen*, pp. 57–59) any

ways by which such material could have entered into the Synoptic tradition may naturally be very diverse. And Jesus could himself have borrowed from some out-of-the-way tradition.

But here, finally, we must ask, in regard to the material that remains, whether it does not also contain some *community formulations*. An affirmative answer on that question has to be given in respect of Mk. 12$^{1-12}$ (The Wicked Husbandmen) and Matt. 25$^{1-13}$ (The Wise and Foolish Virgins), at least in the form in which they appear in the gospels. The same applies to the secondary composition Mk. 13$^{33-37}$ and Lk. 12$^{35-38}$; and for the similitudes of the Lost Coin and of the Leaven, if we have rightly seen them as analogous-formulations to those of the Lost Sheep and the Mustard Seed. For the rest, the possibility remains even when no proof can be provided in particular cases. We can only count on possessing a genuine similitude of Jesus where, on the one hand, expression is given to the contrast between Jewish morality and piety and the distinctive eschatological temper which characterized the preaching of Jesus; and where on the other hand we find no specifically Christian features.

more than the fairy story in J. G. v. Hahn, *Griech. und Albanes. Maerchen*, I, 1864, pp. 140ff. which makes similar use of the motif of the contrasted brothers only in the introduction. Neither is there any more need to reckon with a parallel to Mk. 4$^{3ff.}$ in Garbe, *Indien und das Christentum*, pp. 41f. On Hellenistic parallels to the Parable of the Sower and of the Wheat and the Tares, cp. Windisch, *T.T.*, III, 1918, pp. 227f.

II. The Tradition of the Narrative Material

A. Miracle Stories

1. MIRACLES OF HEALING

EVEN among the apophthegms we found individual passages where a healing miracle was reported: The Healing on the Sabbath Mk. 3^{1-6} par.; Lk. 13^{10-17}, 14^{1-6}; The Exorcism of Demons Matt. 12^{22-36} par.; The Healing of the Ten Lepers Lk. 17^{11-19} and the Stories of the Syro-Phoenician Woman and the Centurion from Capernaum Mk. 7^{24-31}; Matt. 8^{5-13} par. These passages are not told in the style of miracle stories, for the miracle has been completely subordinated to the point of the apophthegm. Accordingly we shall mention them but incidentally here. By contrast in Mk. 2^{1-12} (The Healing of the Paralytic) there is a miracle story proper, which is a secondary continuation of an apophthegm (see pp. 12ff.).

Mk. 1^{21-28} par.: *The Healing in the Synagogue.* Mark introduces this story in the context of 1^{16-39}, which is plainly meant to give a paradigmatic illustration of the ministry of Jesus. The beginning in v. 21, καὶ εἰσπορεύονται εἰς Καφ. could well be a Marcan formulation—as could the conclusion in v. 28. Besides this v. 22 derives from him, and from v. 27 the words διδαχὴ καινὴ κατ' ἐξουσίαν·καὶ, passages which conflict with the point (the motif from $6^{2f.}$).[1] The passage so emended[2] exhibits the typical characteristics of a miracle

[1] It is possible to suppose (cp. 1st edition) that in v. 24 οἶδά σε τίς εἶ, ὁ ἅγιος τοῦ θεοῦ has been added by Mark, since it fits his theory of the demonic recognition of the Messiah. But since the first edition O. Bauernfeind, *Die Worte der Daemonen im Mk.-Evg.*, 1927, pp. 3–18 (cp. also pp. 29–34 and 68f.) has convinced me that those words must nevertheless be understood in the traditional demonological sense, viz., as 'protective words' which anyone threatened by a demon says to him; his 'recognition' of the demon gives power over him. Bauernfeind's attempt to understand these words as 'protective' rather than as a confession of Messiahship—and we know such sayings in other traditions (cp. Bauernfeind, p. 8.2) seems to me to have been successful at Mk. 1^{24}. But nevertheless we have to call special attention to the unusual situation that the demon appears in the role of the threatened man, who utters his 'protective' words, while Jesus takes on the role of the demon! (cp. Mk. 5^7). There is no analogy to Mk. 1^{24} with its self-identification of the human being who speaks with the spirit dwelling in him, as with the Samaritan prophets (Bauernfeind, pp. 1f., 10–12). For apart from the fact that such an identification is a technical device for the purposes of magic, or of receiving a revelation, it is impossible for the one who utters the protective saying to identify himself with the demon who is threatening him! It is naturally a special question how Mark understood this story from the tradition. Unquestionably he took οἶδά σε τίς εἶ κτλ as a Messianic confession by the demon, and Jesus' word φιμώθητι as a demand for silence in line with his theory of the Messianic secret (cp. $3^{11f.}$). Cp. A. Fridrichsen, *Le Problème du Miracle*, pp. 78f.

[2] L. v. Sybel, *T.S.K.*, 100, 1927/8, p. 374, also recognizes that the two motifs of teaching and healing are in Mk. 1^{21-28}, but wrongly believes that the latter is secondary in this story.

story, and especially of an exorcism: (1) the demon recognizes the exorcist and puts up a struggle; (2) a threat and a command by the exorcist; (3) the demon comes out, making a demonstration; (4) an impression is made on the spectators (parallels below). In Luke's reproduction of the story μηδὲν βλάψαν αὐτόν in 4³⁵ is interesting, as it shows that Luke no longer understands the motif, but instead emphasizes the healing itself as much as possible.

Mk. 5¹⁻²¹ par.: *The Gerasene Demoniac.*[1] In all probability this story was known to Mark as part of a complex already in the tradition (4³⁷–5⁴³). Apart from the transition and v. 8 it is hardly possible to establish what is editorial work. Clearly the story is essentially intact in its original form.[2] It also exhibits the typical feature of exorcism of demons, and in their characteristic order: (1) meeting with the demons; (2) description of the dangerous character of such sickness; (3) the demon recognizes the exorcist; (4) the exorcism; (5) demonstrative departure of the demon; (6) the impression on the spectator. In this instance the shaping of (4) and (5) has been particularly influenced by the motif of the devil being deceived. It has been recognized for a long time[3] that it is in this sense that we must understand the permission for the demons to enter the swine, as well as the outcome that the devils were defrauded of their lodgings (Wellhausen). Must we not understand the question and answer in the same way? Or why does the demon willingly state his name which puts him in the power of the exorcist? He seems indeed to boast: λεγιὼν ὄνομά μοι, ὅτι πολλοί ἐσμεν without thinking that by so doing he is betraying himself. Or must it be supposed that the story has been obscured by omitting the compulsion which the exorcist used to discover the name, when the story was applied to Jesus.[4] For there is no doubt that this is a popular jest applied to Jesus.[5] On the demon's request for a concession, and on the manner

[1] I pass over the questions of textual criticism here, as they do not affect our particular concerns.

[2] Cp. O. Bauernfeind, op. cit., pp. 34–56. Bauernfeind prefers to get over the difficulty of v. 8 by assuming that originally it preceded v. 7 (perhaps in place of v. 6). That seems to me (with the complicated suggestions of Bauernfeind, pp. 48–54) too ingenious.

[3] Cp. H. Gunkel, *Das Maerchen im Alten Testament*, 1917, p. 87; cp. A. Wuensche, *Der Sagenkreis vom geprellten Teufel*, 1905. In my view Bauernfeind has rightly shown (op. cit., pp. 38–40) that the demons were not sent into the swine so as to perish with them (to depart into the abyss Lk. 8³¹). But I cannot accept his view that it was not the demons who were deceived, but on the contrary that they deceived Jesus, by making him responsible for the destruction of the herd so that he had to leave the territory; though admittedly they could not prevent the spreading abroad of his miracle in the district (pp. 42–45).

[4] According to Bauernfeind (op. cit., pp. 16f.) the demon tells his name because Jesus' question itself was a compulsion. The Christian narrator in all probability thought so; but that could hardly have been the implication of the story in the first place.

[5] Bauernfeind is right in thinking that for the Christian narrator the demon played the role of the enemy of Messiah, and that in this sense this story, like the preceding one

of the demonstration see below. There is no need for special comment on Luke's reproduction of the story, which fills the picture out at points and adds to the details. Matthew abbreviates, as he so often does. Why he has two possessed persons in his version will be discussed in the section on the technique of story telling.

Mk. 9¹⁴⁻²⁷ par.: *The Epileptic Boy.* In any event vv. 28f. is an editorial addition. At the beginning the editorial hand has confined itself to the introduction of the intrusive γραμματεῖς, while in the textual tradition the original ἐλθών — εἶδεν (D syr^sin codd it) has been changed into the plural and in this way the connection with the immediately preceding story has been strengthened. In all probability v. 15 is also an editorial insertion. For the rest, two miracle stories are combined in this section (in its pre-Marcan form), and they were presumably brought together because of the similarity of the illness and the healing.[1] The first story has as its point the contrast of the Master and the magician's disciples, whose inability to heal provided the foil for the master's power (see below). Hence it was originally presupposed that the Master (naturally, alone) had parted from his disciples and now joined them again. And on this basis the story in some way was suitable for joining on to what preceded. The second story is more of an apophthegm, and describes the paradox of unbelieving faith. Evidence: (1) The disciples have a part to play in vv. 14–19 only, and thereafter pass from the scene, whereas in vv. 21ff. the father takes the chief role though he has only a minor one in vv. 17–19. (2) The illness is described twice in vv. 18 and 21f. (3) The crowd is already present in v. 14, yet, according to v. 25, comes on the scene for the first time. It is no longer possible to make absolutely clear decisions, but it appears that the first story occupies roughly vv. 14–20 and the second vv. 21–27. The conclusion of the first story has been broken off, unless it has been put in v. 25, and so too has the end of the second which has been replaced (in Mark) by vv. 28f. It is easy to explain the facts by means of synoptic comparisons, but that, in my view, accomplishes nothing. Once more there are typical descriptions of the illness, which are both given to the father, as in Philostr., *Vit. Apoll.*, III, 38 they are given to the mother. The distinctive character of the first of these descriptions in Mark lies in the disciples' inability to effect a cure, while the second is distinguished by its typical

(Mk. 1²¹⁻²⁸) presupposes the Messiahship of Jesus. It is noteworthy that once again, here as there (cp. p. 209, n. 1) Jesus appears as the demon who is addressed in the aversion-formula of v. 7.

[1] Cp. O. Proksch, *Petrus u. Johannes bei Matth. u. Mark.*, 1920, pp. 47f. and Bauernfeind, op. cit., p. 74.1.

ἐκ παιδιόθεν. Further the reaction of the demon is found in vv. 20 and 26.

Matt. 9³²⁻³⁴: *The Dumb Demon.* This is a variant of the story considered on pp. 13ff. from Matt. 12²²⁻²⁴ par., just as the passage preceding it (9²⁷⁻³¹) is a secondary variant of 20²⁹⁻³⁴ (following Mk. 10⁴⁶⁻⁵²)—see below. Both passages are probably Matthew's own formulations made from traditional motifs, by which Matthew provided illustrations of the healing of τυφλοί and κωφοί 11⁵. The formulation 9³²ᶠ· (v. 34 is a later insertion from 12²⁴ and is rightly not found in D. syrˢⁱⁿ codd it) is wholly literary and tells us nothing about the style of miracle stories.[1]

Mk. 1²⁹⁻³¹ par.: *Peter's Mother-in-law.* This passage is woven into its context by the introductory formula. It is very simply told: the healing gesture (κρατήσας τῆς χειρός) and the demonstration of the consequent healing (διηκόνει αὐτοῖς) are stylistic elements. Luke adds, for explanatory purposes, ἐπετίμησεν τῷ πυρετῷ. It is a noteworthy fact that Matthew and Luke refer simply to the οἰκία Πέτρου or Σίμωνος and do not reproduce either καὶ Ἀνδρέου or μετὰ Ἰακώβου καὶ Ἰωάννου from our Mark text. Actually our Mark text seems to have been edited under the influence of 1¹⁶⁻²⁰.

Mk. 1⁴⁰⁻⁴⁵ par.: *The Leper.* Additions by Mark are to be found in the words καὶ ἐμβριμησάμενος αὐτῷ εὐθὺς ἐξέβαλεν αὐτόν in v. 43, and ὅρα μηδενὶ μηδὲν εἴπῃς ἀλλά in v. 44 and in v. 45.[2] For the rest the healing gesture (ἐκτείνας τὴν χεῖρα αὐτοῦ ἥψατο) and the command σεαυτὸν δεῖξον τῷ ἱερεῖ κτλ as a demonstration of the consequent healing are stylistic in character (as Dibelius also has rightly seen).

Mk. 2¹⁻¹² par.: *The Paralytic.* As has been shown on pp. 14f., vv. 5b–10a must be disregarded. In addition there must be some sort of editorial link at the beginning, which for our purposes we do not need precisely to define. In any case the story demands some report of Jesus staying in a house. The rest is told according to style. The great faith which is manifested in the overcoming of material difficulties is naturally meant to direct attention to the miracle worker who merits such trust. Any psychological interest in the sick man and his friends is as far removed as it is in the story of the woman

---

[1] One can hardly assume, as Klostermann conjectures on Matt. 12²²⁻²⁴ (though otherwise on 9²⁷⁻³⁴), that the source of the story told in Matt. 12²²⁻²⁴ par. has been preserved in Matt. 9³²⁻³⁴.

[2] A. Fridrichsen, *Le Problème du Miracle*, pp. 8of. believes that the command to be silent in Mk. 1⁴⁴ does not derive (in contrast to 5⁴³, 7³⁶) from the editing of Mark, but was already attached to the story as he adopted it. He believed that it had an apologetic purpose (cp. Matt. 12¹⁵⁻²⁰), meaning: Jesus made no advertisement of his miracles as magicians did. I think this improbable.

with an issue of blood (see below). The miracle working word, Jesus' command and its execution which demonstrates its effectiveness are typical characteristics, as is the impression made upon the onlookers.

Mk. 7³²⁻³⁷: *The Deaf and Dumb.* V. 31 is an editorial conclusion to the story which precedes. The command to silence, which breaks into the context, is a formulation by Mark. Stylistic elements in this story are found in the manipulation, the magic word as a ῥῆσις βαρβαρική (see below) and the impression made by the miracle in v. 37. There is also the taking aside of the sufferer (see below). Matthew makes the story into a collective report of all kinds of healing.

Mk. 8²²⁻²⁷ᵃ: *The Blind Man.* The first phrase in v. 22: καὶ ἔρχονται εἰς Βηθσαιδάν is part of the editorial matter, which puts individual stories into a geographical and chronological context (see below); for originally the story took place in or near a κώμη (v. 23) which Bethsaida certainly is not. V. 27a is also an editorial conclusion.[1] The original conclusion is evidently in the words: καὶ ἀπέστειλεν αὐτὸν εἰς τὸν οἶκον αὐτοῦ v. 26, which correspond to ὕπαγε εἰς τὸν οἶκόν σου in 2¹¹, 5¹⁹. Mark uses λέγων κτλ in v. 26 to add his command to silence. For the rest the story is of the same type as the foregoing; it exhibits almost the same characteristics and is in all probability to be taken as a variant. But it is unusual that there is no magic word, and that the healing is by degrees. On this see below.

Mk. 10⁴⁶⁻⁵² par.: *Blind Bartimeus.* This story shows its secondary character in giving the name of the blind man (see below), and it is the only name in any miracle story in the Synoptics, apart from Mk. 5²² (see below). Yet it is possible that it was put into Mark at a later date, as it does not occur in Matthew or Luke. But the close interlacing of the story into its context also seems to show that in the form in which we have it it is a late formulation. Is it put hereabouts because it was originally associated with Jericho? It is further an exception to have Jesus addressed as the Son of David (Matt. 9²⁷, 15²² are secondary) which seems to clash with ῥαββουνεί in v. 51. It is hardly possible to believe that there is an original, conventionally narrated miracle story at the basis of this passage. In Matthew the healing gesture has been added in 20³⁴. Luke's reproduction makes no significant contribution for our purposes. Why one blind man should have become two in Matthew, see below.

---

[1] For the rest it follows that in v. 22 Bethsaida is surely the correct reading; for only Bethsaida can be reckoned as neighbouring on Caesarea Philippi.

Matt. 9²⁷⁻³¹: *Two Blind Men.* Like Matt. 9³²⁻³⁴ this is secondary editorial matter from Matthew (see above), for which he has adopted a typical Mark motif. Once more we are struck by the number of those healed being two, as in 20²⁹ff., 8²⁸ff. See below.

Mk. 5²¹⁻⁴³ par.: *The Woman with an Issue of Blood and Jairus' Daughter.* The weaving together of two miracle stories, which seem to have been already available to Mark,[1] is unique. Similarly it would seem that the editorial link with the preceding passage in v. 21 did not originate with Mark. Very probably, too, v. 37 is also editorial, since it anticipates the awkward v. 40 and brings the story into closer relationship to the 'life of Jesus'. To be sure I think v. 37 does not come from Mark, since I ascribe most passages where individual disciples are mentioned by name to an earlier stage of the tradition (see below). On the other hand the command to silence in v. 43a, which does not fit its context, does derive from Mark.

I have no doubt that we are here dealing with what was originally two miracle stories, and the motive for joining them seems quite clear to me: the interval between the father's statement ἐσχάτως ἔχει in v. 23 and the crowd's news in v. 35 'ἀπέθανεν' should be taken as a more or less considerable space of time. For the rest v. 21b was in all probability the original introduction to the story of the woman with the issue of blood: (καὶ) συνήχθη ὄχλος πολὺς ἐπ' αὐτόν. καὶ (v. 25) γυνὴ οὖσα ἐν ῥύσει αἵματος . . . For it is only this story that demands the presence of a crowd, not that of the raising from the dead.

Both miracle stories contain typical characteristics of style (parallels, see below): The record of the time the sickness had lasted in v. 25 is typical, as is the emphasis on the fruitless treatment by the doctors in v. 26, which are meant to call attention to the seriousness of the complaint and, consequently the greatness of the miracle. Typical too, is the specially developed motif of physical contact vv. 27–32, and the instantaneousness of the cure in v. 29. In the story of the raising of Jairus' daughter there is the peculiar device of heightening the tension by having Jesus summoned to a fatal illness only to come in the end to someone who had died. This provides an example of the typical motif of heightening the effect by emphasizing the greatness of the task (cp. esp. v. 35) as does also the laughter of the mourning crowd vv. 38–40a. Further typical features are the dismissal of the crowd v. 40, the healing gesture and the magic word v. 41, the instantaneousness of the miracle v. 42 and the statement of the girl's age which is here given in an impressive place along with

---

[1] Otherwise A. Meyer, *Festg. f. Juelicher*, p. 40.

the report of the effect the miracle had. There is a final typical feature in the request that the restored girl should be given something to eat v. 43, which here serves the motif of demonstration. This is particularly clear in this instance, for if the request is interpreted as a medical prescription, it results in a grotesque combination of the rational and the miraculous.[1] Rather is the reality of the resuscitation demonstrated in that ghosts (*revenants*) do not themselves eat human food.[2]

In the usual Mark text the name of the girl's father is given as Jairus. Since the name is not to be found in D and is lacking in Matthew it must be regarded as in analogous instances (see below) as secondary. It has been introduced from Luke.

Lk. 7[11-17]: *The Widow's Son at Nain.* V. 17 is an editorial formulation by Luke, after v. 16 has provided the proper stylistic conclusion. Luke also provides ἐγένετο ἐν τῷ ἑξῆς at the beginning, and perhaps also the name Nain, though it must have belonged to the original story that Jesus came to a town. The story belongs to the Hellenistic type of miraculous resuscitations: see below for parallels of the miracle worker meeting the coffin. Typical too is the ὄχλος ἱκανός which escorted it, and provided the witnesses. We may also take it as a typical feature that the mother of the young man is a widow; cp. 1 Kings 17[7ff.]. Finally there is a typical material in the impression made by the miracle in v. 16 and this is formulated in the terminology of the *LXX*. These different moments we have named make it probable that there was an Hellenistic Jewish-Christian origin for this formulation which certainly seems to be rather secondary.

2. NATURE MIRACLES

Mk. 4[37-41] par.: *The Stilling of the Storm.* In vv. 35f. there is some of Mark's editorial work which can no longer be accurately separated out. Since the sleeping of Jesus in v. 38 belongs to the essential basis of the story (see below) the mention of the late hour would have been an original part of the introduction. On the other hand ἐν ἐκείνῃ τῇ ἡμέρᾳ is editorial, as is ὡς ἦν (ἐν τῷ πλοίῳ) which is bound up with vv. 1ff., while the mention of the ἄλλα πλοῖα is old, and has been ren-

---

[1] Cp. also the paraphrase in K. Bornhaeuser, *Das Wirken des Christus*, 1921, p. 56: 'She walked and takes some food. She is really and truly alive.' Catena 321 had already rightly so interpreted: εἰς ἀπόδειξιν τοῦ ἀληθῶς αὐτὴν ἐγηγέρθαι (Klostermann). Since the eating does not actually document the recovery, the passage quoted in Strack-B. I, 10 and Klostermann from Ber. 5.9d.21 is not a true parallel.

[2] Thus the risen Lord in Lk. 24[41-43] shows that he is no 'πνεῦμα' by his eating food. Cp. *Deutsche Maerchen seit Grimm*, I (Maerchen d. Weltlit.), p. 194; *Zigeuner-Maerchen* (ibid.), p. 117; *Des Knaben Wunderhorn*, I, 1819, p. 69 (end of 'Die Eile der Zeit in Gott').

dered unintelligible by the editing.[1] Typical features are to be found in the saying of v. 39 which indicates the menace of the elements, and the impression created by the miracle in v. 41 (the question in v. 41 naturally does not belong to the same level of the tradition as the disciples' questions in Mark). It is noteworthy that in Matthew's version (8²⁷) it is the ἄνθρωποι who marvel. If this is not the appearance of a more ancient Mark-text, then in all probability it can only be an expression of an instinctive feeling that this was basically a miracle story with no context of its own.

Mk. 6⁴⁵⁻⁵² par.: *Walking on the Water*. It is possible to try to regard this story as a variant of the one just discussed. If so, the stilling of the storm would be the original motif (for it has a part to play in this story (vv. 48, 51)) but one that was displaced when the walking on the water was added and made the main theme. This theme was further elaborated in Matt. 14²⁸⁻³¹, until finally in Jn. 6¹⁶⁻²⁶ the stilling of the storm was entirely dropped and the walking on the water and the miraculous coming to land were emphasized. These last two observations are indeed right; but the original motif for this story is really the walking on the water, and the storm motif has been added to it (from 4³⁷⁻⁴¹) as a secondary feature. This is clear from the way in which its introduction has made the manifestly original ἤθελεν παρελθεῖν αὐτούς in v. 48 unintelligible. Along with that there is the supplementary motivation in v. 50: πάντες γὰρ αὐτὸν εἶδον καὶ ἐταράχθησαν, which conflicts with v. 49 (οἱ δὲ ἰδόντες αὐτὸν . . . ἔδοξαν ὅτι φάντασμά ἐστιν καὶ ἀνέκραξαν). Whether this mixture of sources was already before Mark we are not able to determine, though in any event v. 52 (the failure of the disciples to understand) derives from him. The expansion in Matt. 14²⁸⁻³¹ which we have already mentioned is a variant of the familiar motif of the disciple in subjection to the master, if its purpose be not doctrinal and symbolic. Matthew has christologized the conclusion (v. 33). At the beginning of the story there is an editorial link from Mark in vv. 45f.: the separation of Jesus from the disciples is given a double origin: (1) Jesus wants to get away from the crowd, and (2) he wants to be alone and pray. The first reason stated is editorial, intended to link 6⁴⁷⁻⁵² with ³⁴⁻⁴⁴; further, it is not possible to see why the disciples themselves should be a hindrance if the crowd was to be dismissed.

---

[1] I fail to understand K. L. Schmidt's sceptical attitude to such an analysis. He posed a remarkable question when he confronted Wellhausen and J. Weiss (*Der Rahmen der Geschichte Jesu*, p. 137.1): 'What can be said, e.g. to the following schedule of opinions?' But it is easily answered: Wellhausen's methodical analysis is consistently right as over against Weiss' impressionist review.

Mk. 6³⁴⁻⁴⁴ par.: *The Feeding of the Five Thousand.* Mark's editorial activity has affected the beginning of this story. As in 8¹ᶠ·, Jesus' σπλαγχνίζεσθαι would have referred originally to the hunger of the multitude, and his teaching would have been a secondary motif, by which Mark was able to introduce the traditional saying about the sheep without a shepherd. The construction of the story is according to form: the dialogue between Jesus and the disciples increases the tension; the miracle itself is illustrated only by its success in the distribution, the eating and the satisfaction of those fed. A final effect is that more was left at the finish than was available at the beginning, and the number of the participants is kept impressively to the end. It is characteristic that in the versions of Matthew and Luke we find alterations contrary to the form precisely at the points where Mark's editorial work shows itself. Thus both of them emphasize Jesus' teaching more than his healing and in addition Luke records, as his custom is, the content of the teaching (περὶ τῆς βασιλείας τ. θ. 9¹¹ cp. 4⁴³, 21³¹). For the rest, it is worth mentioning that in Matthew (14²¹) we can trace a tendency to enhance a story in his χωρὶς γυναικῶν καὶ παιδίων.

Mk. 8¹⁻⁹ par.: *The Feeding of the Four Thousand.* This is a variant of the above story, in contrast to which it is more original in having almost no editorial additions at its opening; further, because it has no reflection of the κύκλῳ ἀγροὺς καὶ κώμας in v. 3; and also perhaps because there is no mention of fishes—if the addition of ἰχθύδια in v. 6 is an addition to the text supplied from 6³⁴⁻⁴⁴. But for the rest this variant is secondary: for (1) The action begins with the initiative of Jesus himself (vv. 1f., see pp. 65f.); (2) the ἐσπλαγχνίσθη of 6³⁵ has become direct speech in 8²: σπλαγχνίζομαι; (3) the request of the disciples in 6³⁶ has become a reflection of Jesus in 8³. For the rest the two stories are constructed exactly alike. Here too Matthew has introduced the same heightening effect at the end as in the previous story.

Lk. 5¹⁻¹¹: *The Miraculous Draught of Fishes.* This story, which by its meaning is really a legend (see below) is considered here because of the miracle reported in it. The miracle could have been developed out of the saying about 'fishers of men' (v. 10) just as could the stories of the calling of the disciples, this being its symbolic actualization. It is probably doubtful whether some fairy-story motif has intermixed with it.[1] The composition is secondary: the exposition in vv. 1–3 is constructed on the lines of Mk. 1¹⁶⁻²⁰, 4¹ᶠ·, and Jesus himself takes the initiative (see pp. 65f.). The variant in Jn. 21¹⁻¹⁴

[1] Cp. Klostermann on Lk. 5¹⁻¹¹.

H

seems to me a later version, which in some way derives from Luke.[1]

Mk. 11[12-14, 20] par.: *The Accursed Fig Tree.* We must suppose that originally the cursing of the Fig Tree and its results were reported together and that their separation by vv. 15–19 is due to editorial activity which broke up the admittedly unoriginal connection of 11[15-19] with 11[27-33], though that connection did arise in some earlier stage of the tradition (see pp. 20f.). This editorial activity is to be ascribed to the evangelist Mark, and in that case we may also have to assume that he has edited the story of the cursing of the fig tree itself. The present story ends in an apophthegm (vv. 21–26) that is certainly secondary (p. 25); the withered fig tree is actually a 'special proof of faith' (Wellhausen). The end of the first section (καὶ ἤκουον οἱ μαθηταὶ αὐτοῦ v. 14) and the beginning of the second (καὶ παραπορευόμενοι πρωὶ εἶδον τὴν συκῆν ἐξηραμμένην ἐκ ριζῶν v. 20) could be original, and perhaps the story originally ended with v. 20. There is editorial work in the beginning at v. 12, which links the section with its context, though its extent cannot be determined with certainty. I believe that Matthew had the story before him in the same form in which we have it in Mark. He has done away with the interval and, following a familiar motif, asserted the instantaneousness of the miracle.

Matt. 17[24-27]: *The Shekel in the Fish's Mouth.* This story is already outside the real class of miracle stories; for the miracle is a secondary consideration, and the doctrinal purpose the main thing.[2] The apophthegmatic side of the section and the possibility of its origin have already been discussed on pp. 34f.

3. THE FORM AND HISTORY OF MIRACLE STORIES[3]

Jn. 20[30f.] shows clearly, as Dibelius (*Formgeschichte*, p. 18.2) quite rightly points out, that it is of the very essence of the gospel to con-

---

[1] Cp. the analysis of Jn. 21[1-14] in L. Brun, *Die Auferstehung Christi in der urchristl. Ueberlieferung*, 1925, p. 58.

[2] This miracle belongs to the category of 'miraculous self-aids' (M. Dibelius, *Th.R.*, N.F., I, 1929, p. 206; also *Evangelium u. Welt*, 1929, p. 51), a motif which is very frequent in the legends of the saints.

[3] A. Fridrichsen, in *Le Problème du Miracle*, 1925, discusses the question what meaning the miracle and the miracle story had for early Christianity, especially for its missionary work. It is from this point of view that he interprets the N.T. (especially the Synoptic) miracle stories and sayings about miracles. In Fridrichsen, p. 114, is a very full note of the literature on miracle stories and the whole question of miracle as such. H. Rust, *Die Wunder der Bibel* (I, Die Visionen des N.T.; II, Das Zungenreden; III, Die Weissagungen; in: *Die Okkulte Welt*, nos. 67/70, 103, 129, no date) seeks to establish criteria for distinguishing real happenings from products of fantasy or combination on the basis of investigation into occult phenomena.

tain miracle stories. The meaning and form of the miracle stories in the Synoptics bear this out entirely. They are not told just as remarkable occurrences, but as miracles of Jesus. This is partly why healings preponderate and nature miracles are relatively few. Yet their purpose is hardly biographical in the strict sense. The miraculous deeds are not proofs of his character but of his messianic authority, or his divine power. For this reason it is not usually said that pity, or the intention to quicken faith is a motive of Jesus.[1] It is for this reason that the Evangelists are not conscious of the problem of the relationship of his miraculous actions to his refusal of a sign. The miracles are, as it were, something apart from his individual will, an automatic functioning.[2] This is particularly clear in the story of the woman with an issue of blood: Jesus feels, when the woman touches him, that a δύναμις has gone out of him. It is for this reason that the exorcisms of demons are in the first place the chief demonstrations of the Messiahship of Jesus. It is consistent with this to observe that what is as good as no notice at all is taken of the inner disposition of the person healed. Admittedly it goes without saying that it is a condition of healing the sick that those who ask for the cure should have πίστις. But this πίστις is not a believing attitude to Jesus' preaching or to his Person in the modern sense of the word, but is a trust in the miracle worker which is his proper due.[3] The inhabitants of Nazareth are said to have ἀπιστία, when Jesus fails to perform any miracle among them (Mk. 6⁶, see p. 32, n. 1). How little πίστις is mentioned as a matter of psychological interest, or as a psychical condition of the possibility of healing is shown by that fact that the basis for Jesus to effect a cure need not be the πίστις of the sick person, but can quite well be the πίστις of those who seek a healing on his behalf (Mk. 2⁵, 9²⁴; Matt. 8¹⁰, 15²⁸). Since πίστις involves the acknowledgement of Jesus, all the light falls on him who deserves such acknowledgement, instead of on the sick person. So e.g. no consideration is given to the spiritual condition of the man sick of the palsy in Mk. 2¹⁻¹²; he comes into view simply as an object of the miraculous cure. For the same reason the interest in him ceases once

---

[1] Pity is only mentioned, infrequently: perhaps Mk. 1⁴¹, though here it could well be that ὀργισθείς was original, not σπλαγχνισθείς; 8² (otherwise Mk. 10⁵²); Lk. 7¹³. Also A. Froevig, *Das Selbstbewusstsein Jesu als Lehrer und Wundertaeter*, 1918 sees, pp. 256ff., that pity is not thought of as the distinctive motive of Jesus.

[2] Cp. J. Wellhausen, *Einleitung in die drei ersten Evangelien*, 1911, p. 157: 'His miracles are but involuntary eruptions of his true nature.' The same is stated by E. Bickermann, *Z.N.W.*, 22, 1923, p. 134.

[3] '*La foi, c'est le tribut dû au grand prophète*'—Fridrichsen, *Probl. d. Mir.*, p. 51. Cp. the section pp. 51–56 in Fridrichsen in its entirety and the notes, pp. 120f. On ἀπιστεῖν as an affront to the God of our Salvation; cp. O. Weinreich, *Antike Heilungswunder*, 1909, pp. 87f.

the miracle has been reported. In Mk. 9¹⁴⁻²⁷ neither the grateful joy of the paralytic nor that of his father is mentioned at all. It is only in Mk. 5¹⁹, in an editorial supplement that the healed person is said to have asked ἵνα μετ' αὐτοῦ ᾖ, though that in turn was probably intended but to serve as the occasion for the injunction to spread the fame of Jesus in the Decapolis.¹ (There is a special case in Lk. 17¹¹⁻¹⁹ where the miracle story has been given an apophthegmatic character, leaving the point in a contrast between gratitude and ingratitude.) The same applies to the other miracle stories; they lack, as it were, a conclusion. Thus the feeding stories have no indication of the impression the miracle made, as the secondary addition in Jn. 6¹⁴ᶠ· makes plain. In the same way a conclusion is lacking to the story of walking on the water, where once more John exposes the need of an apocryphal addition (6²²ᶠ·). And if Mark reports the impression made by the stilling of the storm (Mk. 4⁴¹) he does it manifestly without any psychological interest in the disciples themselves, but rather for the sole purpose of focusing attention on the magnitude of the miracle. The style of the miracle story is related to that of the apophthegm (pp. 63f.) to this extent—the 'absence of portraiture' (Dibelius loc. cit.) and all that it involves is characteristic of both. Here as there nothing but the point matters—there a saying of Jesus, here a miracle. Not until John is there any interest in the consequences of a miracle in its setting in the story of Jesus. He uses the miracle in chap. 5 to give rise to the situation for his discussion with the Jews, and finally makes Jesus' miracles the cause of the last catastrophe (11⁴⁵ᶠᶠ·, 12⁹ᶠ·).²

From this standpoint we must examine the *style of the miracle* stories individually. Contributions to the phenomenology of miracle stories can be found in many places, especially in O. Weinreich, *Antike Heilungswunder*.³ What follows is only a brief review, in so far as it is necessary for the understanding of the Synoptic miracle stories.⁴

¹ I do not think we can interpret Mk. 5¹⁹ᶠ· as a 'command to silence', i.e. the healed man may recite Jesus' deeds only in his own home, the place of secrecy; though he actually exceeded his instructions (Wrede, *Messiasgeh.*, pp. 140f.). Even if Mark so understood the passage it cannot possibly be the original meaning of the verse (as it obviously came to Mark). O. Bauernfeind is here quite right (op. cit., pp. 44f., 69f.); I just cannot believe that vv. 19f. is thought of as Jesus' final victory over the demons (see above, p. 210 n. 3.). Fridrichsen, op. cit., p. 82, is right: '*Ces paroles de Jésus après la guérison sont la voix du mission-aire, qui se sert du miracle pour propager la foi. Il en était du christianisme primitif comme de toute autre oeuvre missionaire, la propagande se faisait en grande partie par la famille.*'
² There is some sort of beginning of this point of view in Mk. 3⁶; though here it is the breaking of the Sabbath rather than the miracle itself which is the essential thing.
³ *Religionsgeschichtliche Versuche und Vorarbeiten*, VIII, 1, Giessen, 1909.
⁴ I cannot see why just because Dibelius somewhat broadly distinguishes miracle stories from apophthegms and discovers similar motifs outside early Christianity, he has to classify them as 'profane', 'worldly', or 'secular'. (M. Dibelius, *Formgeschichte*, pp. 41f.; *Geschichte der urchristl. Lit.*, I, 1926, p. 28; *Evangelium u. Welt*, pp. 51f.)

There are characteristic features for the *exposition* of the miracle stories which depict the gravity of the complaint so as to bring the act of the healer into its proper light.

The length of the sickness: Mk. 5²⁵ᶠ· (12 years), 9²¹ (ἐκ παιδιόθεν); Lk. 13¹¹; Acts 3², 4²², 9³³, 14⁸; Jn. 9¹; Philostr. *Vit. Apoll.*, III, 38; Ditt. *Syll.*, II, 802, 95; 805.5; *Neugriech. Maerchen*, hrsg. v. P. Kretschmer (in Die Maerchen der Weltliteratur), 1917, p. 237.

(Here too must be placed details of the age of the sick person or of the dead: Mk. 5⁴²; *Vit. Apoll.*, III, 38, 39.)

The dreadful or dangerous character of the disease: Mk. 5³⁻⁵, 9¹⁸, ²²; *Act. Thom.*, 64, p. 81, 6ss; Lucian, *Philops.*, 11, 16 (καταπίπτοντας πρὸς τὴν σελήνην καὶ τὼ ὀφθαλμὼ διαστρέφοντας καὶ ἀφροῦ πιμπλαμένους τὸ στόμα); *Vit. Apoll.*, IV, 20.

The ineffective treatment of physicians: Mk. 5²⁶; Tob. 2¹⁰; Parallels in Weinreich, op. cit., pp. 195–7; also *Neugriech. Maerchen*, p. 237.

Doubt and contemptuous treatment of the healer: Mk. 5⁴⁰ (κατεγέλων αὐτοῦ); 2 Kings 5¹¹; IG, IV, 951, pp. 23f. (ἀπίστει τοῖς ἰάμασιν καὶ ὑποδιέσυρε τὰ ἐπιγράμματα). 35f. (τῶν ἰαμάτων τινὰ διεγέλα). 74f. (ἔψεγον δή τινες . . . τὰν εὐηθίαν αὐτοῦ τὸ νομίζειν βλεψεῖσθαι . . .). 84f.; *Vit. Apoll.*, IV, 45; cp. Weinreich, op. cit., pp. 87f.

Here too we may place the motif of the *contrast of the master and the disciples*: Mk. 9¹⁴ᶠᶠ·; Matt. 14²¹⁻³¹?; 2 Kings 4³¹; Lucian *Philops.*, 36; Aelian, *De Nat. An.*, IX, 33. Cp. Weinreich, op. cit., pp. 81ff. and Bolte-Polivka, *Anm. zu den K.H.M.*, II, p. 162 on no. 81.

It is a traditional feature of revivifying the dead for the *healer to meet the funeral procession*: Lk. 7¹¹ᶠᶠ·; *Vit. Apoll.*, IV, 45; Apul., *Florida*, 19; cp. Weinreich, pp. 171–3. IG, IV, 952, pp. 27ff.—the God meets a sick person carried on a stretcher.

It is characteristic of the *miracle itself* that the actual miraculous event is almost never described, such as the actual multiplication of the bread by the miracle worker, but only the accompanying circumstances.

Further under the standpoint which determines the exposition we must include cases where the *difficulty of the healing* is emphasized, as in Tac., *Hist.*, IV, 81. In the miracle stories of the N.T. that is only the case when occasionally some special manipulation is reported: Mk. 7³³, 8²³.¹ But it is characteristic that it should occur so in-

---

¹ On the use of spittle cp. O. Weinreich, op. cit., pp. 97f.; Klostermann on Mk. 7³³ beside those mentioned there: Doughty, *Travels in Arabia Deserta*, I, 1888, p. 527; S. Seligmann, *Der boese Blick*, I, 1910, pp. 293–8; J. J. Hess, *Z.A.W.*, 35, 1915, pp. 130f. (Spittle mixed with water for healing blindness, with earth for healing skin diseases); K. Sittl, *Die Gebaerden der Griechen u. Roemer*, 1890, p. 120; J. Doelger, *Der Exorcismus im altchristl. Taufritual*, 1909, pp. 118ff., 130ff. Frequent in fairy stories; cp. from the Maerchen der Weltlit., *Ind. Maerchen*, pp. 227, 233; *Afrikan. M.*, p. 257; *Suedsee M.*, pp. 224f.; *Turkestan M.*, p. 115. Cp. also Bin Gorion, *Der Born Judas*, II, pp. 33f.

frequently there, and yet be a frequent feature in Hellenistic miracle stories,[1] e.g. Jos., *Ant.*, VIII, 2.5 where the Jewish exorcist Eleazar draws the demon out of the nose of the possessed person by means of a ring in which there is a root as prescribed by Solomon; further, Lucian, *Philops.*, 11, where a piece of a virgin's tombstone is placed on the invalid's foot; cp. the manipulations and, as they may be called, operative interventions in IG, IV, 951, pp. 27f., 40f., 77, 99f., 120f., etc.; cp. Weinreich, 173.3. H. Jahnow has shown the probability[2] (*Z.N.W.*, 24, 1925, pp. 155–8) that the removal of the roof in Mk. 2[4] goes back to an exorcist custom (the proper way into the house must be kept hidden from the demon). But the Christian tradition either forgot or transformed the meaning of this motif, in ascribing the crowd surrounding the house as the reason for the stripping of the roof. Matthew completely omits it.

Besides this it is sometimes reported that the *healer comes to the invalid* (or to his dwelling place): Lk. 4[39] (ἐπιστάς); IG, IV, 951, pp. 37, 69; Lucian, *Philops.*, 16 (ἐπειδὰν γὰρ ἐπιστῇ κειμένοις); Diod. Sic., I, 25; Suidas under Θεόπομπος, cp. Weinreich, 1ff.; G. Dehn, *Arch. Jahrb.*, 1913, pp. 399ff.: Sarapis went to the sick bed to heal.

Very often the miracle working *gesture is a touch* (by the hand), and it is difficult to tell whether the primitive idea of it as a transference of power is still active. *Touching or grasping with the hand:* Mk. 1[31, 41], 5[41], 7[33], 8[22]; Matt. 9[29], 20[34]; Lk. 7[14], 13[13], 14[4]; Acts 3[7] (9[41] no longer understood here and reported at the wrong place), 28[8]; Ber. 5b; P. Kil. 9[32b], 23[35] (Strack-B. II, 2f.; IV, 771); *Act. Thom.*, 53, p. 169, 14f.; *Vit. Apoll.*, III, 39; IV, 45; Weinreich, 1–75; J. Behm, *Die Handauflegung im Urchristentum* (1911), pp. 102–16.[3] *The touching of garments:* Mk. 5[27–29], 6[56]; Matt. 14[36]; Acts (5[15]), 19[12].

The miracle working word: Mk. 1[41], 2[11], 3[5], 10[52]; Lk. 8[54], 13[12], 17[14]; Jos., *Ant.*, VIII, 2.5; Lucian, *Philops.*, 7f., 10, 11, 12, 16 (ἐξάδοντες), etc.

The miracle working word is frequently given in strange, incomprehensible sounds, or alternatively handed down in some foreign language: Mk. 5[41], 7[34]; Jos., *Ant.*, VIII, 2.5; Lucian, *Philops.*, 9 (ῥῆσις βαρβαρική); 31 (προχειρισάμενος τὴν φρικωδεστάτην ἐπίρρησιν αἰγυπτιάζων τῇ φωνῇ); *Vit. Apoll.*, IV, 45 (καί τι ἀφανῶς ἐπειπών); cp. Orig., *Contra Celsum*, I, 24; V, 45; A. Dieterich,

---

[1] Ecclesiastical authors consequently emphasize this distinction too. Cp. Fridrichsen, *Probl. du Mir.*, p. 61.

[2] The objections raised by S. Krauss, *Z.N.W.*, 25, 1926, pp. 307–10 are not convincing.

[3] Cp. also J. Goldziher, *Muhammedanische Studien*, II, 1890, p. 383; M. Dibelius on Herm. *Vis.*, I, 4.2 (*Ergaenz. Band zum Handb. zum N.T.*).

Mithrasliturgie[2], pp. 39f., 221; H. Leisegang, *Pneuma Hagion*, p. 102.1; E. Underhill, *Mysticism*, 1928, pp. 208f.

Healing by the use of a *miracle working name* is not reported of Jesus himself, but cp. Mk. 9[38]; Acts 3[6ff.], 9[34], 16[18], 19[13]; Tos. Hullin, II, 21–23 (Fiebig, *Jued. Wundergeschichten*, pp. 35f.); Jos., *Ant.*, VIII, 2.5 (the name of Solomon); Lucian, *Philops.*, 10 (ὑπὸ ἱερῶν ὀνομάτων), 12 (ἐπειπὼν ἱερατικά τινα ἐκ βίβλου παλαῖας ὀνόματα ἑπτά), etc.

The original idea is that the demon who has caused the sickness is threatened by the miracle working word; hence more frequently ἐπιτιμᾶν and ἐπιδιατάσσειν are used, and, naturally, particularly where there is an expulsion of demons in the narrower sense: Mk. 1[25, 27], 9[25]; Lk. 4[41]; Lucian, *Philops.*, 16 (ὅρκους ἐπάγων . . . καὶ ἀπειλῶν); *Vit. Apoll.*, III, 38; IV, 20.

But this same style is employed for miracles where it is impossible to say whether the old idea of threatening the demon is still alive or not: Mk. 4[39] (threatening the wind); Lk. 4[39] (threatening a fever). In Lk. 13[11] the πνεῦμα ἀσθενείας is specifically mentioned, but there is no mention of a threat; the expression is probably purely formal. Cp. Reitzenstein, Poimandres, 18.8; an amulet in which are mentioned the ἄγγελος τοῦ ῥιγοπυρετοῦ and the ἄγγελος who has ἐξουσία over the ἀσθενοῦντες and the ὀδυνώμενοι.[1]

Demon healings[2] are distinguished by special peculiarities: *the demon senses his master*,[3] he knows the exorcist's power: Mk. 1[24], 5[7], 9[20]; Acts 16[17], 19[15]; *Altoriental. Texte*[2], edited by Gressmann, 78f. (the evil spirit addresses the Egyptian God who has been brought to the sick man, and says: 'Thou, great God, comest in peace; thou to whom the evil spirits bow down,' etc.), Pes. f. 112b/113a (Fiebig, *Jued. Wundergeschichten*, pp. 25f.); Lucian, *Abdicat*, 6. In some circumstances the demon can defend himself too: Acts 19[16]; cp. Bauernfeind, op. cit., pp. 33f.

[1] The stilling of the storm in B.B. 73a is also thought of as a threat to the demons (Strack-B. I, 490): the wave was struck with a stick which had a sacred formula engraved on it.

[2] The material collected by A. Titius (*Theol. Festschr. fuer G. N. Bonwetsch*, 1918, pp. 34–36) from recent psychiatric literature can only be used for the development of the miracle story style in general, and not, as the author thinks, for particular N.T. stories. Since his work, there has appeared on the psychological question: T. K. Oesterreich, *Die Besessenheit*, 1921; E. R. Micklem, *Miracles and the New Psychology*, 1922; B. Grabinski, *Wunder, Stigmatisation u. Besessenheit in der Gegenwart*, 1923; Herb. Seng, *Die Heilungen Jesu in medizin. Beleuchtung*[2], 1926. On the history of religion or the ethnological side cp. J. Tamborino, *De antiquorum daemonismo* (Religionsgesch. Vers. u. Vorarb., VII, 3), 1909; R. Wuensch, 'Zuer Geisterbannung im Altert.', *Festschr. z. Jahrh. feier der Univ. Breslau*, 1911, pp. 9–32; J. Manninen, Die daemonischen Krankheiten im finnischen Volksglauben (*F.F.C.* 45), 1922; J. A. Janssen, *Naplouse et son district*, 1927 (here pp. 229ff. on possession, exorcism of demons and questioning of demons); T. Canaan, *Daemonenglaube im Lande der Bibel*, 1929. Cp. also Klostermann on Mk. 1[23].

[3] It is a common notion that the demon himself speaks through the invalid: cp. Klostermann on Mk. 1[24].

The demon asks a favour: Mk. 5⁷; *Act. Thom.*, 76, p. 190, 18ff.; *Vit. Apoll.*, IV, 20, or at least the *concession of some right*; *Altoriental. Texte*², pp. 78f. (the spirit asks that a sacrifice be given him before he departs); Pes. loc. cit. ('Let me have a little more time to play yet!') and he was given Sabbath nights and Wednesday nights.¹ In addition to these we occasionally find a dialogue between the exorcist and the demons Mk. 5⁹; Lucian, *Philops.*, 16 (ἐπειδὰν γὰρ... ἔρηται ὅθεν εἰσεληλύθασιν εἰς τὸ σῶμα, ὁ μὲν νοσῶν αὐτὸς σιωπᾷ, ὁ δαίμων δὲ ἀποκρίνεται ἑλληνίζων ἢ βαρβαρίζων ἢ ὅθεν ἂν αὐτὸς ᾖ, ὅπως τε καὶ ὅθεν ἐπῆλθεν ἐς τὸν ἄνθρωπον); *Act. Thom.*, 31–33, 45f., 75–77. Then it is characteristic to have a command for the demon to be silent: Mk. 1²⁵ (4³⁹); cp. E. Rohde, Psyche, II⁵, 424; Pap. Osl. Fasc., I, 1925, no. 1, 7, 164.²

It is a special feature if the *public is withdrawn* when the miracle is performed: Mk. 5⁴⁰, 7³³, 8²³; Acts 9⁴⁰; 1 Kings 17¹⁹; 2 Kings 4⁴, ³³, 9⁵ᶠ·; Ta'an 23b (cp. Bickermann, *Z.N.W.*, 22, 1923, p. 133.2); Life of St. Ephraem the Syrian (c. Brockelmann, *Syr. Grammatik*², *Chrestomathie*), 37.19ff. This has nothing to do with the Messianic secret, as Dibelius has rightly discerned (*Formgeschichte*, pp. 51f.); yet he misconceives the motive in thinking that it prevents Jesus from appearing like a magician on the look-out for propaganda. The original meaning is much more likely that the miracle was unobserved because it was not fitting to see the Godhead at his work. For the same reason a divine saying is received in secret, Jg. 3¹⁹ᶠ·; and the Godhead works by night (Gunkel on Gen. 19¹⁴⁻¹⁶); Lot and his family are not permitted to see God's judgement, and Lot's wife, who looked on it, was changed to a pillar of salt (Gen. 19²⁶). The motif was then admittedly misunderstood and further developed and became a conventional feature.³

Traditional features are also used to describe the *successful accomplishment of a miracle*. The success seldom comes by degrees: Mk. 8²⁴ᶠ·; *Neugriech. Maerchen*, p. 237 ('. . . thus the blind man . . . could

---

¹ Cp. K. Muellenhoff, *Sagen, Maerchen u. Lieder der Herzogtuemer Schleswig-Holstein u. Lauenberg*, 1845, p. 195: 'He (the banned spirit) had only one more request, that he might take his place under the drawbridge'; p. 259: 'The evil spirit was also ready to yield, he only asked that he might be exiled on dry land and not to the waters in the bay.

² It is somewhat different when Jesus commands the demons to be silent Mk. 1³⁴, 3¹¹ᶠ·, so that they should not reveal him as the Messiah. These passages are literary compositions by Mark on the basis of his theory of a messianic secret. Bauernfeind's explanations of Mk. 3¹¹ᶠ· (op. cit., pp. 56–67) appear to me to be quite impossible.

³ In folk-tales and fairy story the motif is very frequent: cp. B. Gutmann, *Volksbuch der Wadschagga*, 1914, p. 77 (while the dog practises magic, the master must shut his eyes); p. 106 (Dangerous to see the spirits' dance). From the Maerchen der Weltlit.: *Afrikan. M.*, pp. 105f. (Magic disturbed is ineffective); *Indianerm. aus Suedamerika*, pp. 270f.; *Indianerm. aus Nordamerika*, pp. 21, 25; *Finn. u. estn. M.*, pp. 121, 179f.; *Zigeuner M.*, p. 138; *Nord. M.*, I, pp. 116f., etc. Cp. Wundt, *Voelkerpsych.*, IV², pp. 93f.; V², p. 174.

... see a little the fourth time, and the youth had to rub in the ointment six times before he could see properly'); the same occurs in a healing of the blind in *Franzoes. Maerchen*, II, p. 24. The motif has been correctly interpreted by Strauss, *Leben Jesu*, II pp. 72–75: the successive stages are meant to serve as illustration: what happens instantaneously cannot be seen. Perhaps some sort of rationalization was also at work, as e.g. in primitive creation stories where the process of creation sometimes takes place by degrees; cp. B. N. Soederblom, *Das Werden des Gottesglaubens*, 1916, pp. 129ff.; A. Lang, *Myth, Ritual and Religion*, I, 1887, pp. 191, 198; W. Schmidt, *Rel. u. Myth. der austrones. Voelker* (*Sz. B. d. Wiener Ak.*, 1916), pp. 6, 7f. In the majority of cases the instantaneousness of the miracle is emphasized: Mk. $5^{29, 42}$, 10^{52}; Matt. 21^{19}; Lk. 4^{39}, 5^{25}, 8^{47}, 13^{13}; Acts 3^7, 5^{10}, 12^{23}, 13^{11}, 16^{26}; Jn. 5^9. There are parallels in Weinreich, pp. 197f.[1]

Particularly miraculous are *healings at a distance*: Mk. 7^{29}; Matt. 8^{13}; Jn. 4^{50}; Ber. f. 34b (Fiebig, *Jued. Wundergeschichten*, pp. 19f.). In all these cases it is stated that the miracle took place at the very time that the miracle working word was spoken.

On one occasion stress is laid on the παράδοξον of a miracle: Lk. 5^{26} (indirectly in Lk. $5^{5f.}$); this is according to style, cp. Weinreich, pp. 198f.; E. Peterson, Εἷς θεός, 1926, pp. 184, 190.

A *demonstration* of the cure is meant to serve as a conviction of its reality: Mk. $1^{31, 44}$, $2^{11f.}$, 5^{43} (see p. 214); Jn. 5^8; Lucian, *Philops.*, 11, 'The lame man who was healed carried his stretcher out); IG, IV, 951, pp. 105ff. (the person cured carried an enormous stone).

Here too we must consider the cases where the exorcized demon creates some *disturbance as he departs*: Mk. 5^{13}; Jos., *Ant.*, VIII, 2.5 (Turning a vessel of water upside down); *Vit. Apoll.*, IV, 20 (Knocking down a statue). Parallels of demons going into animals can be found in Wohlstein, *Ztschr. f. Assyriologie*, IX, 1894, p. 31; cp. *Z.N.W.*, XV, 1914, p. 45; and in the *Autobiography of Barth. Sastrow* (ob. 1603) in *Das Unerkannte*, edited by E. Nielsen, 1922, p. 101.

But sometimes all that is said is that the *healed person is dismissed* (ὕπαγε and such words); Mk. $5^{19, 34}$, 7^{29}, 10^{52}; Matt. 8^{13}; Lucian, *Philops.*, 16 (ἀποπέμπει ἀρτίους); Diog. Laert, VIII, 67 (ἀποστείλας τὴν νεκρὰν ἄνθρωπον, i.e. Empedocles dismissed the resuscitated woman).

Finally, it accords with the style of miracle stories that the *impression the miracle creates upon the crowd* that sees it is reported; by this means the παράδοξον of the miracle is stressed at the same time as belief in the miracle is demanded. The public is frequently described

---

[1] The word characteristic of certain miracle stories ἐξαίφνης (E. Peterson, Εἷς θεός, p. 184.1) is not found in N.T. stories of healing, though it is used in the epiphanies of Lk. 2^{13}; Acts 9^3, 22^6 and is used in Lk. 9^{39} of an attack by a demon.

as πάντες (ἄπαντες): Mk. 1²⁷, 2¹²; Lk. 4³⁶, 5²⁶, 7¹⁶; Acts 9³⁵; or as ὁ ὄχλος (οἱ ὄχλοι): Matt. 9⁸, ³³, 12²⁵, 15³¹; Lk. 11¹⁴, 13¹⁷; or as ὁ λαός Lk. 18⁴²; Acts 3⁹. In describing the effect of the miracle characteristic words are: θαυμάζειν Matt. 8²⁷, 9³³, 15³¹, 21²⁰; Lk. 8²⁵, 11¹⁸; Acts 2⁷; φοβεῖσθαι Mk. 4⁴¹, 5¹⁵ (cp. 9⁶); Matt. 9⁸, 17⁶; φόβος Mk. 4⁴¹; Lk. 7¹⁶; Acts 5¹¹ (cp. 19¹⁷); θαμβεῖσθαι Mk. 1²⁷; θάμβος Lk. 4³⁶, 5⁹; Acts 3¹⁰; ἐξίστασθαι Mk. 2¹², 5⁴², 6⁵¹; Matt. 12²³; Acts 2⁷, 8¹³ (cp. 8⁹, ¹¹, 10⁴⁵); ἔκστασις Mk. 5⁴² (cp. 16⁸); Lk. 5²⁶; Acts 3¹⁰; ἐκπλήττεσθαι Mk. 7³⁷; Lk. 9⁴³ (cp. Acts 13¹²). While these expressions have their parallels in Hellenistic miracle stories (cp. E. Peterson, Εἷς θεός, pp. 193–5), the following words which are associated with them or replace them, clearly derive from a Jewish-Christian background: δοξάζειν (τ. θεόν) Mk. 2¹² par.; Matt. 15³¹; Lk. 18⁴³; διδόναι αἶνον (τ. θεῷ) Lk. 18⁴³ (cp. Acts 3⁹); χαίρειν Lk. 13¹⁷ (cp. Acts 8⁹). Peterson draws attention to the fact that the frequent acclamation (μέγας ὁ θεός and the like) which often come at the end of a miracle story in later Christian and pagan miracle stories is not found in the N.T. stories. That can hardly be explained by the secret character of the life of Jesus in the Gospels (op. cit., 319), for the acclamation is absent from Acts as well. So the reason is in all probability to be found in literary history: the acclamation formula was first introduced into miracle stories in later times from Egypt (op. cit., 195). On the significance of the public witness to the miracles cp. P. Wendland, *De Fabellis*, pp. 7f.; H. Werner, Zum Λούκιος ἢ ὄνος, *Hermes*, 53, 1918, p. 242.

Even if one confines one's attention to the N.T. material it can be seen that *miracle stories have their own history in the tradition*. The motifs change, variations develop and themes are worked up.

The stories of the *exorcism of demons* were of especial significance to the Church as proofs that Jesus was Messiah. They were frequently emphasized in the summaries: Mk. 1³²⁻³⁴, ³⁹, 3¹¹, 6⁷; Matt. 4²⁴, 10⁸; Lk. 7²¹; Acts 5¹⁶, 10³⁸. It is thus understandable that when the motif of exorcism was embodied in different particular stories, they were not all traceable, in terms of literary criticism, to one story. Mark reports four (or five) healings of demon-possessed persons: 1²¹⁻²⁸ (3²²), 5¹⁻²⁰, 9¹⁴⁻²⁷ (a combination of two cases). In addition in Q we find Matt. 12²²⁻²⁴ par., which is a more distinct variant of Mk. 3²² and Matt. 9³²⁻³⁴, which is a secondary editing of the motif.

In *other healings*[1] it is not so important to know what disease Jesus

---

[1] Whether originally all Jesus' healings were exorcisms is a fair question, cp. J. Weiss, *R.E.*³, IV, p. 413; H. Jahnow, *Z.N.W.*, 24, 1925, p. 158. It is not probable that they were, though it is noteworthy that the healings in Mk. 7³³, 8²³ are also thought of as exorcisms as can be seen from the use of spittle.

healed, as to recognize the miracle as such. This is the case in the healing of the deaf mute Mk. 7³¹⁻³⁷ and its clear variant, the healing of the blind man Mk. 8²²⁻²⁶. The healing of two blind men and of the dumb man possessed of a devil Matt. 9²⁷⁻³¹ and Matt. ³²⁻³⁴ are only variants of Markan miracles.[1] And Mk. 3¹⁻⁵; Lk. 13¹⁰⁻¹⁷, 14¹⁻⁶ are likewise but variations on the theme of Sabbath healing. The miracle of healing the ten lepers in Lk. 17¹¹⁻¹⁹ is a heightened version of Mk. 1⁴⁰⁻⁴⁵, as the command in Lk. 17¹⁴ particularly shows: ἐπιδείξατε ἑαυτοὺς τοῖς ἱερεῦσιν. The distant healings in Mk. 7²⁴⁻³⁰ and Matt. 8⁵⁻¹³ par. are variants (see pp. 38f.). Accordingly it is not safe to say that Matt. 8⁵⁻¹³ par. and the raising of Jairus' daughter Mk. 5²¹⁻³⁴ are variants (K. L. Schmidt, *Rahmen der Geschichte Jesu*, p. 73); but it is quite likely that the raising of the widow's son at Nain Lk. 7¹¹⁻¹⁷ is a counterpart to the raising of Jairus' daughter in the Synoptic tradition.

The course of the development and change of motifs becomes particularly clear if the Johannine healings are included. In Jn. 5⁸ᶠᶠ· the motif of the lame man who has to carry his bed is combined with that of Sabbath healing. The manipulation at the healing of the man born blind in Jn. 9¹ᶠᶠ· derives from Mk. 8²³, and again the motif of Sabbath breaking provides a secondary element in combination. With this we may compare how the miracle of the bird made out of soil is combined, in the Nativity Gospel of St. Thomas 2²ᶠᶠ· with the motif of Sabbath breaking. Jn. 4⁴⁶⁻⁵⁴ is a heightened version of the story of the Centurion from Capernaum: the healing is at an even greater distance; its occurrence at the precise moment is expressly established by witnesses.[2]

The same sort of considerations apply to the *nature miracles*. The two feeding miracles are clearly variants Mk. 6³⁴⁻⁴⁴, 8¹⁻⁹, and even indeed in their formulation they agree fully in structure and in part even verbally. The motif is used also in Jn. 6¹ᶠᶠ·, though here σπλαγχνίζεσθαι has dropped out at the beginning and the question asked by Jesus serves only to put the disciples to the test, αὐτὸς γὰρ ἤδει τί ἔμελλεν ποιεῖν. The stories of stilling the storm and walking on the water in Mk. 4³⁷⁻⁴¹, 6⁴⁵⁻⁵² are admittedly not properly variants, but the motif of the first is used in the second (see above). And how another motif can be added to a miracle story is seen in the expansion of Matt. 14²²⁻³³ by vv. 28–31. On the other hand in Jn. 6¹⁶⁻²⁶ the motif of stilling the storm has been left out of the story

---

[1] Cod. Δ adds to τυφλόν at Mk. 8²² the word δαιμονιζόμενον (W. Bauer, *Das Leben Jesu im Zeitalter der neutest. Apokr.*, 1909, p. 367.

[2] A further variant of the story is to be found in the *Historia Societatis Jesu* (Koeln 1685) transferred to Francis Xavier (*Das Unerkannte*, edited by E. Nielsen, 1922, p. 98).

of walking on the water and the miraculous coming to land has been added instead.

An *increase of the miraculous element* is also frequently to be found in particular features. Apart from the fact that Matthew and Luke relate some new miracles over and above Mark and Q, this appears in the editorial passages where summaries of Jesus' miracles are given: Mk. 1³²⁻³⁴, 3⁷⁻¹², 6⁵³⁻⁵⁶; further Matt. 4²³⁻²⁵, 9³⁵ᶠ·, 15²⁹⁻³¹. In addition Matt. 14¹⁴, 19², 21¹⁴ add healings to the text of Mark. Finally, he adds some small individual features to his Markan copy. After the feeding stories he remarks in 14²¹, 15³⁸ that the number given must be taken as excluding women and children.[1] Whereas in Mk. 1³²ᶠ· (cp. 3¹⁰) it states that all the sick were brought and many were healed, Matt. 8¹⁶ (cp. 12¹⁵) states the reverse—that many were brought and all were healed. The statement in Mk. 6⁵: καὶ οὐκ ἐδύνατο ἐκεῖ ποιῆσαι οὐδεμίαν δύναμιν, εἰ μὴ ὀλίγοις ἀρρώστοις ἐπιθεὶς τὰς χεῖρας ἐθεράπευσεν is weakened in Matt. 13⁵⁸ to: καὶ οὐκ ἐποίησεν ἐκεῖ δυνάμεις πολλάς. There is a similar relationship of Lk. 4⁴⁰ᶠ· (all the sick were brought and all were healed) to Mk. 1³²⁻³⁴. And instead of Mk. 3¹⁰: πολλοὺς γὰρ ἐθεράπευσεν Luke writes in 6¹⁹ (influenced by Mk. 6⁵⁶): καὶ πᾶς ὁ ὄχλος ἐζήτουν ἅπτεσθαι αὐτοῦ, ὅτι δύναμις παρ' αὐτοῦ ἐξήρχετο καὶ ἰᾶτο πάντας. The same tendency is also visible in John, especially in comparing the story of Lazarus with the Synoptic raisings of the dead. Jn. 20³⁰, 21³⁵ hints in traditional terms at the many miracle stories in circulation: the miracles are so many that it is impossible to tell them all (cp. Weinreich, pp. 199f.; Dibelius, *Formgeschichte*, 18.2; W. Bauer, *Leben Jesu im Zeitalter d. neutest. Apokr.*, 364).

Yet it would not be right to consider the gospel miracle stories in the bounds of the N.T. only. The less the miracle stories as such are truly historical reports the more we need to ask *how they have found their way into the Gospel tradition*. And even if some historical events underlie some miracles of healing, it is still true that their narrative form has been the work of the Tradition. And even if the motifs have grown up spontaneously in the early Church, there would be both central and peripheral motifs taken over from popular and even perhaps literary miracle stories. That is clear, as far as the peripheral motifs are concerned, from the parallels to the Synoptic miracle stories quoted above. The process of transferring some available miracle story to a hero (or healer or even a god) is frequently to be found in the history of literature and religion. Ovid, *Metam.*, VI, 313ff. may be cited as an example where the motif of changing a peasant

[1] Cp. *Franzoes. Maerchen* (Maerchen d. Weltlit.), I, p. 212.

into a frog is transferred to Latona; it was originally a folk-tale about an old witch, as can be seen from Apul., *Metam.*, I, 9 (p. 8.24f. Helm).[1] In The Thousand and One Nights Harun al Rashid has been made the hero or participant in countless fairy stories. In Caucasian and Swiss stories alike all sorts of jests are attributed to King Solomon.[2] In German anecdotes and fairy-tales, 'Old Fritz'[3] has been made a hero, while in Austria it has been Joseph II.[4] The fairy story of the fortunate fellow with his death warrant is attached to Henry III in the German Saga.[5] The story of the Master Thief is told in Russia about Peter I.[6] In the Armenian and Georgian languages it is Alexander the Great who is given the part of fairy hero, as he once was in the Alexander Romance.[7] For the rest, reference can be made to R. Reitzenstein, *Hellenistiche Wundererzaehlungen*, 1906; and *Historia Monachorum und Historia Lausiaca*, 1916, e.g. pp. 14, 40ff., 76.3, 115.2, 163.3: K. Lehrs, *Populaere Aufsaetze²*, 1875, pp. 385–408; W. Hertz, *Ges. Abhandl.*, 1905, p. 323, and H. Gunkel, *Das Maerchen im AT*, 1917, p. 167.[8]

The O.T. used to be thought of very highly as a *source of the gospel miracle stories*. The Rabbinic thesis of Moses as the type of the Messiah (Midr. Qoh. f. 73.3 כְּגוֹאֵל רִאשׁוֹן כֵּן גּוֹאֵל אַחֲרוֹן; cp. Schoettgen, *Horae*, II, pp. 251f.; Strauss, *Leben Jesu*, I, 1835, p. 72 note 31; II, 1836, p. 1 note 1) would have led the Church to deck out the story of Jesus with miraculous features from the story of Moses. There is actually little evidence of that; there is something of the sort in the story of the Transfiguration, but that is hardly a miracle story in the strict sense. It is highly improbable that the feeding stories have arisen out of the story of the Manna in Exod. 16. But the expectation that the Messiah would work miracles (Isa. 61[1], 35[5f.], 29[18f.]; 4 Ezr. 7[27f.], 13[50]: 'And then shall he show them very many wonders'; Test. Zeb. 9[8]; Sim. 6[6]) has certainly contributed to the practice already in the Palestinian Church of telling stories about the miracles of Jesus. And in details the O.T. has made its own contribution. Yet the resus-

---

[1] Cp. H. Werner, On Λούκιος ἢ ὄνος *Hermes*, LIII, 1918, pp. 225–61.

[2] *Kaukas. Maerchen* (Maerchen der Weltlit.), pp. 254–8; *Schweizer Maerchen*, edited by H. Baechtold, 1916, pp. 40–44.

[3] *Deutsche Maerchen seit Grimm* (Maerchen d. Weltlit.), II, pp. 268–73; *Plattdeutsche Volksmaerchen* (ibid.), I, pp. 100ff., 146ff., 248ff.; II, pp. 203ff., 247ff.

[4] *Donau-Maerchen* (Maerchen d. Weltlit.), pp. 201–5.

[5] Grimm, *Deutsche Sagen*, no. 486.

[6] *Russ. Maerchen* (Maerchen d. Weltlit.), pp. 286ff.

[7] *Kauk. Maerchen*, pp. 259f.

[8] An instance of ascribing an alien story to Jesus is found in the apocryphal passage in Jn. 7[53]–8[11]. There is a parallel to this in *Neugriechischen Maerchen* edited by Kretschmer, 1917, pp. 153f. (The Two Fig Thieves), where the obviously original humorous character is plainly in evidence.

citations of the dead accomplished by Elijah and Elisha have not had any effect, though analogous resuscitations were expected from the Messiah in Tanchuma f. 54[4] (Schoettgen, *horae* II 74); the raisings from the dead which are reported of Jesus have no similarity at all with them. The only possible motif deriving from that source is that the young man at Nain was a widow's son. The story of Jesus walking on the water can hardly have derived from the hyperbole in which God is said to walk on the waves of the sea (Job 9[8], 38[16]; Sir 24[6]), any more than the story of the stilling of the storm has come from Ps. 105[9], 106[23-31], 88[10]. Nor is 2 Kings 5[1-27] (Naaman's leprosy) a type of Mk. 1[40-45]. On the other hand it is possible that 2 Kings 4[42-44] (Feeding of a hundred men from twenty barley loaves) is *one* source of the Feeding stories: the stories of the cruse of oil 1 Kings 17[10-16]; 2 Kings 4[1-7] do not, however, have any relevance.

But the less probable it is that we can take the transference of miracle stories to Jesus to be literary process, the less the O.T. can occupy our attention as a source. It is possible to ask about certain miracle stories whether they have originated in the Christian Church itself, either as Easter stories carried back into the ministry of Jesus, or as forms fashioned out of dominical sayings. Just as sayings of the exalted Jesus can obviously become sayings of the earthly Jesus (see pp. 127f., 149), and the stories of Peter's confession and of the Transfiguration are Easter stories brought back into the life of Jesus (see below), so the same things would be possible with miracle stories. That is particularly true in the case of the Miraculous Draught of Fishes, especially if the version in Jn. 21[1-14] be considered more original than that in Lk. 5[1-11]. For the other water miracles in Mk. 4[37-41] (Stilling of the Storm) and 6[45-52] (Walking on the Water) the same position has often been adopted, and it has even been asked about the Feeding stories whether they have not arisen 'out of the early Christian celebration of the Eucharist, perhaps by some sort of vision'.[1] But in none of these instances is certainty obtainable.

It is possible to observe elsewhere the process by which a miracle story can be developed out of a saying.[2] I think it likely that the story of the miraculous draught of fishes in Lk. 5[1-11] had its origin in the saying of Jesus about 'Fishers of Men' (p. 217), in the same way that this saying may also have led to the stories of the calling of the disciples in Mk. 1[16-20] (see pp. 27f.). It has frequently been supposed that the cursing of the fig tree in Mk. 11[12-14, 20] has

---

[1] H. Rust, *Wunder der Bibel*, I, pp. 53f.; on the whole question cp. G. Bertram in the *Festgabe fuer A. Deissmann*, 1927, pp. 188–91.

[2] Cp. M. Wundt, Apollonius von Tyana, *Z.W.T.*, 49, 1906, pp. 309–66; Tor Andrae, *Mohammed in Lehre u. Glauben*, 1918, pp. 154f.

grown out of a parable (cp. Hos. 9[10, 16]; Mi. 7[1]). Such an origin is hardly possible with any other miracle stories.

It is more probable that folk stories of miracles and miracle motifs have come into the oral tradition, a process which is quite plain in Mk. 5[1-21]. In particular instances this can be confirmed by adducing parallels. In general the stylistic characteristics of the Synoptic miracle stories we have considered show that these stories have grown up in the same atmosphere as the Jewish and Hellenistic miracle stories. There is still much for research to do at this point. What I now give in what follows is in essentials a review of material already collected.[1]

(a) Exorcisms of Demons

From Jewish literature we can include the following demon exorcisms: Pes. 112b/113a (Fiebig, Jued. Wundergeschichten, pp. 25f.): Hanina b. Dosa exorcized 'Agrath, a female demon that appeared each night, though she gained a concession from him that she could operate on the nights of Sabbaths and Wednesdays. Other Rabbinic stories are in Strack-B. IV, 534f.

From Hellenistic literature: Jos., Ant., VIII, 2.5: The Jewish exorcist Eleazar banned a demon before Vespasian, which overturned a basin of water as it departed.

Philostr., Vit. Apoll., III, 38: An Indian sage was consulted by a woman on behalf of her son who was possessed by a demon. She described the course of his sickness and the sage gave her a letter for the demon with ξὺν ἀπειλῇ καὶ ἐκπλήξει.

Philostr., Vit. Apoll., IV, 20: Apollonius expelled a demon from a young man which smashed a statue as it came out.

Lucian, Philops., 31: A ghost is banished that had made a house unsafe.

How widespread such stories were is shown by Lucian, Philops., 16: 'I would greatly like to ask you what you think of all those who free demoniacs from the spirits that trouble them and so manifestly exorcize spectres. I do not need to go into details about them. Everyone knows about the Syrian from Palestine who understood such matters thoroughly. Whoever he came to, the moonstruck,

---

[1] Cp. apart from the Commentaries and O. Weinreich, Antike Heilungswunder; P. Wendland, De Fabellis antiquis earumque ad Christianos Propagatione, Progr., Goettingen, 1911; W. Gemoll, Das Apophthegma, 1924, pp. 78–82, 128; P. Fiebig, Juedische Wundergeschichten des N.T. Zeitalters, 1911, and Antike Wundergeschichten (Kleine Texte 79), 1911. That the miracle in Jewish stories is frequently the fulfilment of a prayer is no hindrance to bringing them into our own context, even if it means that this has to be stressed as characteristic, as it is for Jewish stories. The connection between miracle and prayer is very close; cp. how in Mk. 11[20] the saying about the power of prayer (vv. 21–25) follows immediately on the miracle of cursing the fig tree. Cp. also Jn. 11[41ff.]

those that rolled their eyes or foamed at the mouth, he really put right and dismissed them cured for a high fee, after he had freed them from their affliction. For when he came up to some prostrated person and asked whence the affliction had come into the body, the sick person himself kept silent, but the demon answered in Greek or some foreign tongue or in that of its own country and told how and whence it had come into the man. But the Syrian then used his exorcisms, and if the demon failed to respond, he would cast him out with threats. I have myself seen one come out, black and dark in colour.'

Formulae for casting out demons are given in Strack-B. IV, 352f. and in A. Dieterich, *Abraxas*, 189, pp. 11ff.; cp. also Jerome, *Vit. Hil.*, 42; Reitzenstein, *Hellenist. Wundererzaehlungen*, p. 124; Wiedemann, 'Magie und Zauberei im alten Aegypten' in *Der alte Orient*, VI, 4, p. 22; Maspero, *Contes Populaires*[3], p. 159.

The idea behind Mk. 5^{1-21}, that to know the name of the demon gives power over it is a well-known and widespread motif. It will suffice in this regard to refer to Bolte-Polivka, *Anmerkungen zu den Kinder- und Haus-maerchen der Brueder Grimm* (I, 1913, pp. 490ff. to no. 55).

(b) *Other Healings*[1]

Jewish Miracles of Healing: Ber. 34b (Fiebig, *Jued. Wundergesch.*, pp. 19f.): Hanina b. Dosa healed the son of R. Gamaliel II and of Johanan b. Zakkai by prayer. Both are healings at a distance in so far as the sick person is not at the place where the healer offers his prayer. It would be erroneous not to consider these as proper miracle stories just because they are concerned with healing by prayer. The express statement that the healing took place at the very time the prayer was offered is quite in the style of the miracle story (see also p. 231, n. 1). Hag. 3a (Strack-B. I, 526) tells the story of two dumb men; other examples can be found in Strack-B. II, 2f., 10 (on Mk. 1^{31}, 5^{43}); IV, 771.

Hellenistic Miracles of Healing: These are fairly brief reports of the healing of lame persons in Sueton, *Vesp.*, 7 and Philostr., *Vit. Apoll.*, III, 39. They are also recounted in IG, IV, 951, pp. 107ff., 110ff., 113ff.; 952, pp. 86ff., 110ff., 132f. It is a frequent element in the stories that the lame person is brought on a stretcher and after

[1] The Serpent miracle characteristic of Jewish stories (e.g. Strack-B. II, 169, 545, 772; cp. Acts 28^{3-6}) and the miracle of punishment (e.g. Strack-B. II, 78f., 709, 772; 1 Macc. 6; 2 Macc. 9; Jos., *Ant.*, XII, 9.1 = § 357; XVII, 6.5 = § 168f.; XIX, 8.2 = § 343ff.; frequent in the Hellenistic tradition since Herod., IV, 205; cp. Acts 12^{20-25} and the Commentaries thereon; also Acts 5^{1-11}, 13^{11}; frequent in Apocryphal Acts but absent from the Synoptic tradition.

being healed is able to go home alone (Weinreich, p. 174): this is also the case in the detailed story in Lucian, *Philops.*, 11, where Midas is brought on a bed having been bitten by a serpent, but after being healed carries his bed away himself.

The healing of a paralysed hand by Vespasian in Alexandria before many witnesses is reported by Tacitus, *Hist.*, IV, 81, and by Cassius Dio, *Hist. Rom.*, LXVI, 81. There is a very brief mention of such a healing by an Indian sage in Philostr., *Vit. Apoll.*, III, 39. There are healings of paralysed hands also in the ἰάματα of Epidauros: IG, IV, 951, pp. 22ff.; 955, pp. 23ff.

There are likewise accounts of the healing of the blind by Vespasian in Tac., *Hist.*, IV, 81 and Cass. Dio, *Hist. Rom.*, LXVI, 8, and similarly in Philostr., *Vit. Apoll.*, III, 39 of an Indian Sage. And as spittle is used on this occasion as the healing medium, so it is in other parallels, see p. 221, n. 1. From the ἰάματα of Epidauros, cp. *IG*, IV, 951, pp. 33ff. (χωλοὺς καὶ τυφλοὺς ὑγιεῖς γίνεσθαι ἐνύπνιον ἰδόντας μόνον), 72ff., 90ff., 121ff., 126f.; 952, pp. 8ff., 64ff., 120ff. According to an etymologizing legend Asclepius healed the blind Phinides (Weinreich, p. 383).

(c) *Raisings from the Dead*

Fiebig (*Jued. Wundergesch.*, pp. 36f.) advances a text from the Mekilta which gives expression to the belief that a Rabbi could also quicken the dead; some examples are noted in Strack-B. I, 557, 560, though they are for the most part highly artificial stories.[1] There are much closer parallels in the Hellenistic tradition. According to Weinreich, p. 172, raising of the dead was an element in the legends of the Philosophers. Herakleides Pontikus tells of a raising of a dead person by Empedocles (*Diog. Laert.*, VIII, 67): Ἡρακλείδης μὲν γὰρ τὰ περὶ τὴν ἄπνουν διηγησάμενος ὡς ἐδοξάσθη Ἐμπεδοκλῆς ἀποστείλας τὴν νεκρὰν ἄνθρωπον. (Weinreich, p. 172.1). Dieterich, *Abraxas*, pp. 167ff. gives a formula for raising the dead (Kleine Texte, 79, p. 27; Reitzenstein, *Hellenistische Wundererz.*, 41, 3). In Lucian, *Philops.*, 26, the physician Antigonos asks the question: τί θαυμαστόν; . . . ἐγὼ γὰρ οἶδά τινα μετὰ εἰκοστὴν ἡμέραν ἢ ᾗ ἐτάφη ἀναστάντα, θεραπεύσας καὶ πρὸ τοῦ θανάτου καὶ ἐπειδὴ ἀνέστη τὸν ἄνθρωπον. And Alexander of Abonuteichos advertises the fact that he ἐνίους δὲ καὶ ἤδη ἀποθανόντας ἀναστήσειε Lucian, *Alex.*, 24).

Philostr., *Vit. Apoll.*, tells a detailed story: Apollonius meets the stretcher of a bride who has died, followed by the bridegroom and

---

[1] Cp. also J. Bergmann, *Die Legenden der Juden*, 1919, pp. 35, 40.

others, mourning: Apollonius raises the dead bride προσαψάμενος αὐτῆς καί τι ἀφανῶς ἐπειπών. Pliny tells of the raising of a (seemingly) dead person in *Hist. Nat.*, VII, 124 (XXXVII); XXVI (III, 7) and a more coloured version of the same story appears in Apuleius, *Florida*, 19 (Kl. Texte, 79, pp. 18–20).

(d) *Nature Miracles*

From Jewish Tradition: There are all sorts of stories telling how a Rabbi's prayer produced rain in Fiebig, *Jued. Wunderg.*, pp. 14–18, and Strack-B. I, 558, 864; II, 413f. But they are hardly describable as miracle stories, being more in the nature of Jewish prayers of faith. Ta'an 24a (Strack-B. IV, 539 tells how the grain store of the beneficent Eleazar was miraculously filled when it had only a little wheat left in it, and Ta'an 24b/25a (Fiebig, *Jued. Wunderg.*, pp. 22f.) tells the story of R. Hanina b. Dosa's wife who, every evening before the Sabbath although she had nothing to cook, used to heat up her oven, so as to hide her poverty. One day, when some curious neighbour came to investigate, the oven was miraculously full of bread and the trough with dough. Such stories are obviously a contribution to our knowledge of Jewish belief in miracle but they are not true parallels to the N.T. *feeding stories*; nor are the Rabbinic legends of the inexhaustible supply of oil for anointing during the wandering in the wilderness or of the oil for the Sabbath lamp (cp. Strack-B. I, 688; II, 539f.). One would sooner refer to the fact that according to Yom. 39a (Strack-B. I, 687f.) there was a blessing on the Shewbread in the days of Simon the Just by which every priest who ate even a piece the size of an olive from it was satisfied and always left some more. It is recounted in Ta'an 24a that a fig tree produced miraculous fruit so that the workers had no need to be hungry (Strack-B. II, 26). A carob tree and a spring of water were miraculously provided to nourish R. Simon b. Jochai and his son when they fled from the Romans (Shab 33b in Strack-B. IV, 228).

The story told in B.M. 59b, how a storm rose during a sea voyage taken by R. Gamaliel when he confessed a wrong he had done to R. Eliezer,[1] is no parallel to the *stilling of the storm* in Mk. 4$^{35-41}$, but the story repeated in Fiebig (op. cit., p. 61) from the Jer. Ber., II, 1 of R. Tanchuma (about A.D. 350) is probably one: A Jewish child went on a voyage in a heathen ship. When a storm brought the ship into danger, all the heathen called on their gods and when that proved useless, finally urged the Jewish child to call on his God. When the child

---

[1] In Fiebig, *Jued. Wunderg.*, p. 33 and Strack-B. I, 489f.

prayed, the storm ceased and the heathen paid respectful admiration.[1] This is evidently an old story which first comes to view in Jon. 1 and is there interwoven with the story of Jonah and the whale. Here we find, admittedly not intact, yet clearly recognizable in v. 3b (apart from the last words 'from the presence of the Lord'), 4a α, 5a α, b, 6, 8 (apart from the words 'for whose cause this evil is come upon us)— 10a α, 15b, 16 the story of a Jew asleep in a heathen ship during a storm, who then brings the storm to an end by calling on his God.[2] Now Mk. 4[35-41] is manifestly the stage between the story and the previously noted Rabbinic legend. The agreement of the Synoptic and O.T. variants is particularly remarkable in the small detail of the place where 'Jonah' or Jesus was asleep. For the rest the contrast of the heathen crew and the Jewish passenger becomes, in the Christian tradition the contrast between Jesus and his disciples. I cannot myself doubt that in this instance an alien miracle story has been transferred to Jesus.

It ... ible to cite as a distant parallel to the miracle of the c... *tree* in Mk. 11[12-14, 20] the story told in B.M. 59b about ..., *Jued. Wunderg.*, pp. 31f.): To prove the correctness ... the law he caused a carob tree to be uprooted ... ry at least shows what sort of ideas in this field ... environment. And that is illustrated even ... mples of the efficacy of a curse quoted in

[1] ... II, 851; IV, 778; another story in Strack-B. IV, 555f. Cp. J. Bergma... *...er Juden*, p. 33; M. Gaster, *Exempla*, no. 400; Bin Gorion, *Der Born Judas*, II, pp. 94f.; ..., pp. 142ff.

[2] For the source analysis see on the one hand H. Schmidt, 'Die Komposition des Buches Jona', *Z.A.W.*, XXV, 1905, pp. 285–310 and in 'Die Schriften des ATs', II, 2, ad loc. Though I am in essential agreement, I differ in some details; especially I have to take vv. 15b, 16 as part of the story of the stilling of the storm: the heathen give honour to Yahweh; in the other story of the casting of lots that does not make sense. On the other hand see W. Baumgartner, *Eucharisterion f. H. Gunkel*, I, 1923, p. 147.5 with whom I agree when he gives the original order of the verses as: 4a α, 5a α, b, 6 . . . 15b, 10a α, 8, 9, 16. But how was this story originally closed? By Jonah being swallowed by the fish? Evidently; for this was a story given to the author of Jonah and he adapted it for the prophetic legend. But that implies that the meaning of the story was originally different; the swallowing and vomiting of Jonah must originally have had point quite apart from the prophetic legend. But that could only be so if the original story was that the ship sank and Jonah as the man whose guilt had been established by casting lots was the only one to be saved. This same point—that the discovery of the apparent cause of evil by casting lots saved the one who was in fact innocent from the disaster which encompassed all the others —is found in a Chinese fairy story (R. Wilhelm, *Chinesische Volksmaerchen*[2] in Die Maerchen der Weltliteratur, 1917, p. 10). The motif of casting lots for the one who brings disaster at sea is widespread, cp. Athenaios, *Deipnosoph.*, II, 5 (after the Sicilian historian Timaios of Tauromenion 352–6): H. Lambel, *Erzaehlungen und Schwaenke* (Deutsche Klassiker des Mittelalters 12), 1872, p. 211 (Der Wiener Mervart); *Vlaemische Sagen* (Deutscher Sagenschatz, edited by P. Zaunert), 1917, p. 128; Buddhist. *Maerchen*, p. 50; *Finn. und Estn. Maerchen*, p. 285; *Tuerk. Maerchen*, p. 52; *Franzoes. Maerchen*, I, p. 159; Wiel and, *Oberon.*, 7. Gesang.

From Hellenistic and other Traditions. There are stories of miraculous feedings in Hellenism too. Thus Celsus maintained (Orig. *C.C.*, I, 68) that heathen magicians could also accomplish feeding miracles. The motif reappears in the Christian tradition: Ac. J. 93 Bonnet; Pionius, *Vit. Polyc.*, 4.5 Lightf.; Palladius, *Hist. Laus.*, 51 Butler. There are Indian, and indeed extraordinarily close, parallels in R. Garbe, *Indien und das Christentum*, 1914, pp. 59f.; in Haas, *Zeitschr. fuer Missionskunde*, 1914, pp. 148ff.; *Das Scherflein der Witwe*, 1922, pp. 36–38; and in J. Aufhauser, *Buddha und Jesus* (Kl. Texte, no. 157), 1926, pp. 20f. From the fairy story world Gunkel (*Das Maerchen im AT*, pp. 58f.) cites a Finnish fairy story of a maid who prepared food for a whole army out of three barley corns. In the *Plattdeutschen Maerchen* (I, 1914) there is one of a miraculous loaf which fed a whole army (p. 159). The pitcher which never runs dry is also to be found in *Chinesischen Volksmaerchen* (ed. R. Wilhelm, 1917), p. 80. Cp. also *Indianermaerchen aus Nordamerika*, p. 87; *Zigeunermaerchen*, p. 101; Hahn, *Griech. und alban. Maerchen*, 1864, II, p. 157. When we read in Pomponius Mela, III, 87 (Klostermann on Mk. 6³⁴ff.): *est locus adparatis epulis semper refertus, et quia ut libet vesci volentibus licet, Heliu trapezan adpellant, et quae passim adposita sunt, adfirmant innasci subinde divinitus*, we are not dealing with a real feeding miracle, but with the motif of 'Table, set yourself', with which we may compare Bolte-Polivka, op. cit., I, pp. 349ff. on no. 36.[1]

There must also have been stories of *walking on water* in Hellenism. Admittedly it is hyperbole when Dio Chrys. speaks of the power of Xerxes, that when he so wishes he is able πεζεύεσθαι μὲν τὴν θάλατταν, πλεῖσθαι δὲ τὰ ὄρη. But the capacity to do so is often attributed to demons. P. Berol., I, 120 thus describes the power of the δαίμων πάρεδρος: πήξει δὲ ποταμοὺς καὶ θάλασσα[ν συντ]όμως(?) καὶ ὅπως ἐνδιατρέχῃς (Reitzenstein, *Hellenist. Wundererzaehlungen*, p. 125). Also A. Dieterich, *Abraxas*, p. 190, 13: ἐγώ εἰμι ὁ ἐν οὐρανῷ σχολὴν ἔχων φοιτώμενός τε ἐν ὕδατι, and on another tablet (Rhein. Mus., 55, 261, cp. 264): *qui solus per mare transis*. But according to Lucian, *Philops.*, 13 the same things are reported of human wonder workers:

---

[1] There are feeding miracles also in the Islamic Hadîth. But how far biblical and other traditions have influenced it is still a matter for enquiry. Cp. J. Goldziher, *Muhammedanische Studien*, II, 1890, 383. P. Saintyves, in his *Essais de Folklore Biblique*, 1923, pp. 231–306 has collected a wealth of material of stories of miraculous feedings, and multiplication of bread from all over the world, showing how very widely the motif has been spread. If he be right in supposing that such stories have originally derived from the cultus (viz. out of vegetation rites) such an origin does not immediately arise for the Synoptic stories, even if Saintyves assumes so from the dating of the Feeding of the Five Thousand at Passover time in Jn. 6⁴. Bousset also assumes that the cultus lies behind the Synoptic stories, when he remarks in *Kyr. Chr.*, p. 62.2: 'Perhaps matters could be taken further if one asked the question where else in the cult of a God bread and fish have been used as sacred food. . . .'

εἶδες . . . τὸν Ὑπερβόρεον ἄνδρα πετόμενον ἢ ἐπὶ τοῦ ὕδατος βεβηκότα. Further material may be found in A. Gercke, *Jahrb. f. Philol. Suppl.* XXII, 1895, pp. 205ff.; A. Abt, 'Die Apologie des Apuleius von Madaura und die antike Zauberei', *Religionsgesch. Vers. u. Vorarb.*, IV, 2, 1908, pp. 129, 2. We may add from the Christian tradition: *Hist. Aegypti monachorum XI*, 18, p. 58; cp. XX, 16, p. 75, Preuschen; *Ps. Cypr., Confess.*, 12.[1] Indian parallels also come up for consideration in this regard, and there are stories of walking or flying over the water, which could even have influenced Hellenistic literature: cp. R. Garbe, *Indien und das Christentum*, 1914, pp. 57f. Most notable is a Buddhist parallel to Matt. 14[28-31] (the text is in J. Aufhauser, *Jesus und Buddha*, Kl. Texte, no. 157, p. 12). It tells of a disciple 'who wanted to visit Buddha one evening and on his way found that the ferry boat was missing from the bank of the river Aciravati. In faithful trust in Buddha he stepped on to the water and went as if on dry land to the very middle of the stream. Then he came out of his contented meditation on Buddha in which he had lost himself, and saw the waves and was frightened, and his feet began to sink. But he forced himself to become wrapt in his meditation again and by its power he reached the far bank safely and reached his master.' (Garbe, pp. 56f. and *Buddhist. Maerchen*, pp. 46f.) Garbe thinks that the gospel story was borrowed from the Buddhist tradition.[2]

It has been customary, in regard to the *miracle of stilling the storm*, to cite the well-known anecdote about Caesar who exhorted his faint-hearted coxswain in a storm by saying: δέδιθι μηδέν· Καίσαρα φέρεις καὶ τὴν Καίσαρος τύχην συμπλέουσαν (so Plut., *Caes.*, 38, p. 726c; it occurs in a different form in Cassius Dio, XLI, 46). But that is only a distant parallel, as is that in Calpurnius, *Bucol.*, IV, 97ff. Stories tell how Asclepios or the Dioscuri save from perils at sea (Weinreich, 14). Aristides, II, 337 (Kl. Texte, no. 79, p. 22) tells the story of Asclepios: ἤδη τοίνυν τινῶν ἤκουσα λεγόντων ὡς αὐτοῖς πλέουσι καὶ θορυβουμένοις φανεὶς ὁ θεὸς χεῖρα ὤρεξεν. The same

---

[1] In the language of Christian edification this miracle motif may have attained a symbolic significance and the walking on the water become the treading of the mythical waters of death, which Christ and his mystic followers achieve. Cp. Dibelius (*Formgeschichte*, p. 86) who adduces Od. Sol. 39: 'He walked and went over them on foot, and his footprints stayed on the water and were not obliterated. . . . And a path was prepared for those who followed him.' What the relation of Mand. Ginza R., II, 1, pp. 499f. Lidzb. is to this (Christ the seducer says, 'I walk over the water. Come with me; you shall not drown') can well be left undecided here.

[2] Cp. W. N. Brown, *The Indian and Christian Miracles of Walking on the Water*, 1928. Saint-yves, who again traces these stories to cultic narratives (initiation rites), amasses a wealth of material, op. cit., pp. 307-63. Cp. also *Indianermaerchen aus Nordamerika*, p. 31; *Turkestan. Maerchen*, p. 69; Muellenhoff, *Sagen*, etc., p. 351.

Aristides tells the story most impressively (II, 362) of the rescue by Serapis from danger at sea. And the writer of the letter BGU, II, 423, pp. 6ff. (Deissmann, *Light from the Ancient East*, 167ff.) refers to Serapis in the same terms. Theocritus praises the Dioscuri as rescuers from the perils of the sea, XXII, 1, 17–22. Two epigrams about Cypris honour her as protectress on sea voyages (*Anth. Pal.*, IX, 143, 144). Apuleius, *Metam.*, VI, 9 says: *Iam iam sursum respicit et deam spirat mulier, quae . . . ventis ipsis imperat* (Wendland, *De Fabellis*, 28; *die hellenist.-roem. Kultur*, 218, 4). I do not know of any miracle story where the stilling of a storm has been ascribed to a θεῖος ἄνθρωπος, a saviour. But Porphyry., *Vit. Pyth.*, 29 states: προρρήσεις τε γὰρ ἀπαράβατοι σεισμῶν διαμνημονεύονται αὐτοῦ καὶ λοιμῶν ἀποτροπαὶ σὺν τάχει καὶ ἀνέμων βιαίων χαλαζῶν τ' ἐκχύσεως καταστολαὶ καὶ κυμάτων ποταμίων τε καὶ θαλαττίων ἀπευδιασμοὶ πρὸς εὐμαρῆ τῶν ἑταίρων διάβασιν (similarly Iamblichus, *Vit. Pyth.*, 135).[1]

The story of the *shekel in the fish's mouth* Matt. 17[27] contains the widespread motif of Polykrates' ring (Herod., III, 42), to which there are also variants in the Rabbinic tradition (Shab. 119a in Fiebig, *Jued. Wunderg.*, pp. 62f.; Strack-B. I, 675 and GnR 11 (8b) in Strack-B. I, 614); the motif is first found in the Christian tradition in Aug., *Civ. Dei*, XXII, 8. On further parallels cp. R. Koehler, *Kleinere Schriften*, II, 209; P. Saintyves, *Essais sur folklore biblique*, pp. 364–404; H. Guenther, *Die christl. Legende des Abendlandes*, 1910, pp. 83f.

How later on Hellenistic miracle stories found their way into the Christian tradition can be illustrated at least by one example: *The turning of water into wine at Cana* in Jn. 2[1-12] is an application to Jesus of a miracle of the epiphany of Dionysos. On the festival day of Dionysos the temple springs at Andros and Teos were supposed every year to yield wine instead of water. In Elis on the eve of the Feast three empty pitchers were put into the temple and in the morning they were full of wine. The date of the Dionysos feast is the night of 5–6 January, i.e. the date of the early Christian Feast of the Baptism = the Epiphany of Christ; apart from that the 6th January has from very early times been reckoned as the day of the wedding in Cana. Cp. Bousset, *Kyrios Christos*[2], p. 62; J. Grill, *Untersuchungen ueber die Entstehung des 4. Evang.*, II, 1923, pp. 107–19; P. Saintyves, *Essais sur Folklore Biblique*, pp. 205–29; W. Bauer on Jn. 2[12] (in *Handbuch zum N.T.*). Also K. Holl, *Der Ursprung des Epiphanienfestes* (S. B. d. Berl. Akad., 1917, XXIX).

It is clear that the material cited cannot be reckoned as the source

---

[1] On Jn. 6[21] cp. also the Homeric hymn to Pythian Apoll., 394ff., where, once the God goes on board, the ship reaches its destination with miraculous speed.

for the miracle stories in the Synoptics, or only in the rarest cases. But it illustrates the atmosphere, shows motifs and forms, and so helps us to understand how miracle stories came into the Synoptic tradition. In this regard it is further of importance to ask at what stage the Tradition was enriched by the addition of miracle stories, and to a less degree whether it took place in the oral or written stage. No doubt both have to be accepted, but here as elsewhere this distinction is in my view relatively unimportant for the gospel Tradition, since the fixing of the tradition in writing was in the first place a quite unliterary process. Much more important is the *distinction between the Palestinian and Hellenistic stages of the Tradition.*

Miracles were certainly ascribed to Jesus in the *Palestinian Church.* Proof of this is to be found in the saying in Matt. 12 $^{27, 28}$ par. (from Q) where Jesus puts his own exorcisms of demons alongside those of the Jewish exorcists, and concludes from his success that the Kingdom of God has come. Further proof lies in the apophthegms which have a probable origin in Palestine, including a miracle such as Matt. 12 $^{22ff.}$ par. or Mk. 3 $^{12ff.}$ (expulsion of a demon); and further Mk. 3 $^{1-5}$ (Sabbath Healing); 7 $^{24-30}$ (Syro-Phoenician Woman); Matt. 8 $^{5-13}$ (The Centurion from Capernaum). Naturally it is not necessary that all these apophthegms of miracle stories should have been formed in the Palestinian Tradition: the variants of the Sabbath Healing could very well have been fashioned in an Hellenistic setting, once the type was provided. Further, the differentiation of the stories of the Centurion from Capernaum and the Syro-Phoenician woman could have quite easily been accomplished in the Hellenistic stage. The story of the grateful Samaritan in Lk. 17 $^{11-19}$ is very probably Hellenistic in origin; but we can hardly tell whether the miracle of the shekel in the fish's mouth first came into the Hellenistic Tradition as an appendix to the dialogue about the Temple dues.

In the case of *miracle stories not included in apophthegms* judgement seems to me to be even more uncertain. It is made the more difficult by the fact that there are very few real miracle stories in the Rabbinic Tradition; they are for the most part so interwoven into the Rabbinic debates that they have retained their apophthegmatic character.[1] Assuredly miracle stories proper were told among the people, but we

---

[1] Cp. E. Peterson, Εἰς θεός, 1926, p. 216: 'The Rabbis' miracle stories seem to show Hellenistic influence only in small degree. On the other hand it seems many passages have been retained which even in the form given to them, cannot entirely hide such influences. In particular we have the Daniel stories and those about Abraham to consider.' Unfortunately Peterson gives no examples. So far as I know no enquiry has yet been made on this point. G. Kittel (*Die Probleme des palaest. Spaetjudent.*, 1926, pp. 169–94) has shown that the Rabbinic legends of Joseph's grave in the Nile are dependent on the Osiris myth. But this is not really concerned with a miracle story proper.

are unable to say how far in the exchange of cultures such story telling was subject to Hellenistic influences in motif and form. But in any case the Hellenistic miracle stories offer such a wealth of parallels to the Synoptic, particularly in style, as to create a prejudice in favour of supposing that the Synoptic miracle stories grew up on Hellenistic ground.

Enquiry into the *linguistic form* hardly takes us any further. Phrases like ἐν πνεύματι ἀκαθάρτῳ (Mk. 1²³, 5²), φωνῇ μεγάλῃ (Mk. 1²⁶, 5⁷); ἐφοβήθησαν φόβον μέγαν (Mk. 4⁴¹); εἷς instead of τις (Mk. 5²²), ἔρχονται ἀπὸ τοῦ ἀρχισυναγώγου *scil.* τινές (Mk. 5³⁵), the distributive συμπόσια συμπόσια and πρασιαὶ πρασιαί (Mk. 6³⁹ᶠ·), the detached nominative ἡμέραι τρεῖς (Mk. 8²), etc., can in themselves be Semitisms, but such phrases and others similar could also have found their way into the koine Greek, and it is possible at least in part to show that they did. In addition the Hellenistic-Christian linguistic usages were influenced by the LXX, which would the more readily occur in the literary stage of the Tradition; and this explains a good many other Semitisms, e.g. Lk. 7¹⁶. Naturally words which come under the classification of ῥῆσις βαρβαρική (see p. 222) prove nothing, words like ταλιθὰ κούμ (or however Mk. 5⁴¹ is to be read) and ἐφφαθά (Mk. 7³⁴). More readily we may infer a Palestinian origin for υἱὲ Δαυείδ and ῥαββουνεί (Mk. 10⁴⁷, ⁵¹). Only seldom is there a Semitism of demonstrable force, as e.g. ψυχὴν σῶσαι ἢ ἀποκτεῖναι (Mk. 3⁴), where judgement as to the Palestinian origin of the story already follows from its apophthegmatic character. In the same way we can be sure of the Palestinian origin of the miracle story in Mk. 2¹⁻¹², if we may reckon, with Wellhausen, that ἀπεστέγασαν τὴν στέγην is a mistranslation. Perhaps we may also count the expressions ἡ πηγὴ τοῦ αἵματος αὐτῆς (Mk. 5²⁹, cp. Strack-B. on this) and ὕπαγε εἰς εἰρήνην (Mk. 5³⁴) as true Semitisms.

Judging Mk. 4³⁵⁻⁴¹ (Stilling of the Storm) by its content, a *Palestinian* origin seems probable if the Jewish parallels are taken into consideration. The same holds for Mk. 6³⁴⁻⁴⁴ or 8¹⁻⁹ (Feeding Stories). The healing of the leper (Mk. 1⁴⁰⁻⁴⁵) will also have come from the Palestinian Church; σεαυτὸν δεῖξον τῷ ἱερεῖ κτλ could hardly be formulated in an Hellenistic environment. The same does not hold of Lk. 17¹⁴, for it is fashioned on the pattern of Mk. 1⁴⁴.

For the rest, the *Hellenistic* origin of the miracle stories is overwhelmingly the more probable. The difference between Mark and Q is characteristic. If miracle stories are almost entirely absent from Q we must not explain that by saying that Q contains no narrative of events; for the edifying, paraenetic and polemico-apologetic purposes of Q could have introduced miracle stories very easily. The deeper reason for their absence is the different lght in which Jesus appears. In Q he is above everything else the eschatological preacher of repentance and salvation, the teacher of wisdom and the law. In Mark he is a θεῖος ἄνθρωπος, indeed more: he is the very Son of God walking the earth. This mythological light in which Jesus is set by Mark (cp. Dibelius, *Formgeschichte*, p. 87) is there for the most part on the author's own account but also in part on account of his material, and especially of the miracle stories. But this distinction between Mark and Q means that in Q the picture of Jesus is made essentially from the material of the Palestinian tradition, while in Mark and most of all in his miracle stories Hellenism has made a vital contribution. So naturally we can rightly assume in the first place an Hellenistic origin for the miracle stories which Matthew and Luke have over and above those found in Q and Mark.

We have already said that *within the Christian Tradition* miracle stories have their own history, and indeed it is there that the interest lies in the telling of the story as such. But here once more we must raise the question of the history of the Christian tradition of Miracle Stories, in so far as miracle stories belong to narrative material in general. And here there are a few observations analogous to those in the above history of apophthegms which must be made and set alongside the others, just as for their part they can only find their completion in the concluding consideration of the technique of Gospel narratives.

At some point in the course of time there arose a *novelistic interest* in the persons of the miracle stories. Thus the woman with the issue of blood was given the name Veronica (e.g. Gosp. Nicod., 7) and in Macar. Magn. I, 6 she has become a princess of Edessa. The Phoenician woman and her daughter are called Justa and Bernice in Clem., *Hom.*, 2, 19; 3, 73, etc. We may also remember that whereas in the story of Lazarus in Jn. 11 the man raised from the dead and his sisters all have names, the young man at Nain and his mother have none. We can see this novelistic interest already at work in the Synoptists, when the ruler of the Synagogue in Lk. 8[41] is called Jairus, a name which has crept into most manuscripts of Mk. 5[22] (see above, p. 215). In face of such facts we are bound to be sceptical of the name Bartimaeus in Mk. 10[46]. And we may also recall in this connection that in the Nazarean edition of Matthew the man with the withered hand (Matt. 12[10] = Mk. 3[1]) has been made a bricklayer (see above, pp. 68f.).

But more important is what has to be said on the indications of *circumstance and place* of the miracle stories which is analogous to what has already been said about the apophthegms. They are scanty for the miracle stories too. They are absent from Mk. 1⁴⁰, 5²², ²⁵, 7³², 9¹⁴. Elsewhere they are made quite general: Mk. 1²¹ the Synagogue, 1²⁹ Peter's house, 2¹ a house, 4³⁷ the sea journey, 5²ᶠ· the tombs, 6³⁴ and indirectly 8¹ the ἔρημος τόπος, 6⁴⁵ᶠᶠ· the sea, 8²³ the village, 11¹²ᶠ· (indirect) the way. All these indications are incidental or almost accidental, being of importance only for the understanding of the story. They do not have the character of definite geographical statements.

The tradition was unable to rest content with that. The evangelists have expounded or added to these statements because they had to make *editorial links* to connect up the individual stories. Such editorial statements are also in part quite general. Thus Mark makes the first feeding miracle take place near the sea 6³²ᶠ·; and similarly the whole complex of incidents in Mk. 4³⁵–5⁴³ had already been grouped together as near the sea at the pre-Marcan stage of editing, and as a consequence a statement about place is given e.g. in 5²¹ just before the beginning of the story at 5²² which has no indication of place at all. In a large number of connecting phrases there are general place indications as in Mk. 1²⁹: καὶ εὐθὺς ἐκ τῆς συναγωγῆς ἐξελθόντες or in Matt. 9²⁷: καὶ παράγοντι ἐκεῖθεν, 9³²: αὐτῶν δὲ ἐξερχομένων.

But there are some quite specific *geographical references*, and it is clear that, at any rate in part, they belong to the editorial stage. That has been shown to be true already of Mk. 7²⁴, ³¹, 8²², ²⁷ᵃ on pp. 64f.; and we have also said that Capernaum in Mk. 1²¹, 2¹; Matt. 17²⁴ must be reckoned as due to the editor. Matt. 6⁴⁵ is recognized in the analysis as editorial; Mk. 8¹⁰ and Mk. 6⁵³ belong to the same stage. In Mk. 11¹² there is also some editorial linking, and following analogous examples we may suppose that the mention of Bethany is part of it. From Mark there remain only Gerasa (or however the text should be read) in 5² and Jericho in 10⁴⁶, which evidently belong to at any rate an earlier stage of editing than Mark. But that admittedly does not settle the question whether they are original, which can hardly be finally determined; yet the apocryphal, or secondary nature of the stories is manifest, and with these two we may couple Lk. 7¹¹⁻¹⁶ with its mention of Nain. In any event we have to say on the whole that specific geographical statements are as foreign to miracle stories as to apophthegms.[1]

---

[1] This judgement is on the grounds of critical analysis, and not on grounds of a general idea of miracle stories. (We might in fact expect on the basis of general anticipations that

The elements of the Tradition very seldom contain *dates and times*. Yet ὀψίας γενομένης in Mk. 4³⁵ must certainly belong to the original story, since for one thing it is the reason for Jesus going to sleep and for another it is inconsistent with the way in which Mark continues the story, with the sun apparently not having set. In the same way the reference to night time in Mk. 6⁴⁷ᶠ· must belong to an ancient tradition, as perhaps do the words ὥρα πολλή in Mk. 6³⁵, even though they are lacking in the variant at 8¹. On the other hand the indications of time in Mk. 1³², ³⁵ belong to the editorial stage. For the rest all such statements are quite general in character. Apart from the Sabbath, feasts are not mentioned (cp. John!); nor are intervals of time, apart from the three days during which the multitude was with Jesus (Mk. 8²). The μετὰ ἡμέρας ἕξ in Mk. 9² is part of a legendary story. We shall consider later on the dates and times in the Jerusalem stories and particularly in the passion narrative itself.

Finally there is one more thing to add to the formal characteristics of these particular stories as we consider the apophthegms and miracle stories together, and it is a matter of importance in recognizing the editorial work of the evangelist. It is, namely, to show quite briefly what the indications of place which we dealt with above mean for the *exposition* of the stories, and to observe how primitive is the way in which this exposition is given. Certain stories begin with the ancient formula καὶ ἐγένετο (or γίνεται): Mk. 2¹⁵, ²³; as does the section coming under another classification Mk. 1⁹. It is a matter of indifference whether καί belonged to the story as it circulated in the oral tradition or was first added to it when the stories were put into a larger context.[1] For the rest this formula is used by Matthew and Luke for their editorial introductions, about which we shall have something to say later on. Otherwise the passages begin with a brief recital of the appearance of the chief character (Jesus) or the opponents (or opponent) and where necessary, the place is indicated. We may quote some examples from Mark.

geographical statements would be characteristic of miracle stories in order to quicken trust in the reliability of the miracle!) Hence G. Dalman's polemic counts for nothing (*Orte und Wege Jesu*³, p. 14) when he also refers correctly to the fact that there are geographical statements in many Rabbinic miracle stories. In others they are missing, and often precisely in those places where they might be expected (e.g. Strack-B. II, 26, 169, 413; IV, 228, 771); elsewhere they are quite general, like Synagogue, house, market place (Strack-B. I, 558; II, 2f.; IV, 539). Among the miracle stories I have collected from Strack-B. there is but one unmotivated definite indication of place in I, 490, 526. Such cases, where the place signifies something for the event (e.g. II, 78f.; IV, 534f.), are naturally exceptions.

[1] Mk. 1⁴, where K. L. Schmidt, *Rahmen der Geschichte Jesu*, pp. 18f., postulates a καί as the original opening, is somewhat different, for in this case ἐγένετο does not mean 'it happened that', but 'he appeared', and the Baptist is the subject of the verb.

1¹⁶: καὶ παράγων παρὰ τὴν θάλασσαν ... εἶδεν ...

1²¹: καὶ [. . .] εἰσελθὼν (perhaps to be omitted) εἰς τὴν συναγωγὴν ἐδίδασκεν [. . .] καὶ ... ἄνθρωπος ...

1⁴⁰: καὶ ἔρχεται πρὸς αὐτὸν λεπρός ...

2¹⁴: καὶ παράγων εἶδεν ...

3¹: καὶ εἰσῆλθεν ... εἰς συναγωγήν, καὶ ἦν ἐκεῖ ἄνθρωπος ...

5²²: καὶ ἔρχεται εἷς τῶν ἀρχισυναγώγων ...

6¹: καὶ ἔρχεται εἰς τὴν πατρίδα ...

7¹: καὶ συνάγονται πρὸς αὐτὸν (οἱ Φαρισαῖοι) ...

7²⁵: (ἀλλ’) ἀκούσασα γυνὴ περὶ αὐτοῦ ... ἐλθοῦσα προσέπεσεν ...

7³²: καὶ φέρουσιν αὐτῷ κωφὸν καὶ μογιλάλον ...

8²²: καὶ φέρουσιν αὐτῷ τυφλόν ... etc.

Sometimes the story itself demands a more detailed reference to its place:

Mk. 2²³: καὶ ἐγένετο αὐτὸν ἐν τοῖς σάββασιν παραπορεύεσθαι διὰ τῶν σπορίμων καὶ οἱ μαθηταὶ αὐτοῦ ἤρξαντο ὁδὸν ποιεῖν τίλλοντες τοὺς στάχυας.

Mk. 5²¹ᵇ: καὶ [. . .] συνήχθη ὄχλος πολὺς ἐπ’ αὐτόν (then follows v. 25, p. 214).

A similar reference must have preceded the introduction to the Feeding story in Mk. 6³⁴, though it has now disappeared into the editorial section 6³⁰⁻³³. By contrast such a reference is much clearer in 8¹, which is furnished with but a brief editorial link: [ἐν ἐκείναις ταῖς ἡμέραις πάλιν] πολλοῦ ὄχλου ὄντος κτλ.

Mk. 9¹⁴: καὶ ἐλθὼν πρὸς τοὺς μαθητὰς εἶδεν ὄχλον πολύν ...

A similar introduction must always have preceded the healing of the sick of the palsy in Mk. 2¹ff·, though it cannot now be accurately differentiated. Similarly the story of the demoniac in Gerasa required a detailed indication of place, Mk. 5¹ff·; though, again, it can no longer be precisely differentiated from the editorial links.

How the evangelists edited their Traditional material on the basis of these presuppositions will be described in context below.

B. Historical Stories and Legends

To *define terms* I would say that I would describe legends as those parts of the tradition which are not miracle stories in the proper sense, but instead of being historical in character are religious and edifying.[1]

---

[1] In positive definition of concepts I agree with what M. Dibelius has said in *Th.R.*, N.F., I, 1929, pp. 203–9. If at the same time I naturally do not deny that historical

For the most part they include something miraculous but not necessarily so, as e.g. the cult legends of the Last Supper do not exhibit anything distinctively miraculous. They are distinguishable from miracle stories chiefly by not being, as they are, unities, but gain their point only when set into their context. This context can be the life of some religious hero: that yields a biographical legend. Or the context may be the faith and the cult of community; that yields a faith—or cult—legend.[1] Naturally the various kinds of legends are closely related to each other and to miracle stories; nor is the boundary with biographical apophthegms always easy to draw. All the same, the conceptual distinction is necessary, for it corresponds to different motives which play upon the telling of religious stories.[2]

Further it is quite natural for legends and historical stories to run into each other in ancient, and especially popular stories of religious interest, even though here too the difference is quite clear conceptually. It would certainly have been possible to give special treatment to the presentation of the miracle stories in the Synoptics; yet even so I do not think it is possible to separate historical stories from legends, for although there are admittedly some passages of a purely legendary character, the historical stories are so much dominated by the legends that they can only be treated along with them.

1. ANALYSIS OF THE MATERIAL

(a) From the Baptism to the Triumphal Entry

Mk. 1 [1-8] or Matt. 3 [1-12]; Lk. 3 [1-18]: *The Ministry of John the Baptist.* The actual beginning of the pericope concerning the Baptist starts in Mark with v. 4,[3] v. 1 being part of the evangelist's editorial work. It is immaterial for our purposes whether v. 2f. derives from Mark him-

happenings may underlie legends, I mean that 'unhistorical' applies to the idea of legend negatively in the sense that legends not only 'have no special interest in history' (Dibelius) but that they are not, in the modern scientific sense, historical accounts at all.

[1] This distinction is the same as Dibelius' between 'aetiological cult legends' and 'personal legends'.

[2] For this reason Fascher (*Die formgeschichtl. Methode*, p. 202) misses the mark with his question 'What precisely is this?' about Matt. 17 [24-29] (a passage which in my view could equally well be classed as a biographical apophthegm, as a scholastic dialogue, or a legend). It is in fact characteristic that the three motives operate here together. The same applies to Lk. 5 [1-11] (Fascher, p. 202). It is not the aim of Form Criticism neatly to classify particular elements of the Tradition, but to exhibit the motives which led to their formulation. The fact that in some cases some section of the tradition belongs to different classification is an objection neither to the method nor to the terminology adopted by the scholars. These considerations apply also to the treatment by B. S. Easton in *The Gospel before the Gospels*, pp. 61ff. (see above, pp. 4f.).

[3] Cp. K. L. Schmidt, *Der Rahmen der Geschichte Jesu*, pp. 18ff.

self or came into the text of Mark later from Matthew. K. L. Schmidt has an illuminating analysis which holds ἐν τῇ ἐρήμῳ in v. 4 and the whole of v. 6 as secondary because these two passages turn the Jordan Baptist into a wilderness preacher. Since they are not editorial in character, it is a question of secondary importance whether they come from the evangelist or were found by him in the tradition. The main thing is to recognize a growth of the tradition. And these are no doubt specifically Christian accretions; for the idea that the Baptist was a wilderness preacher in all probability rests upon the Christian view which saw in him the forerunner of Jesus, in fulfilment of Isa. 40³. But the question also arises whether the Christian treatment does not go further.¹ Actually it is Christianizing editing when Mark fails to mention the fire of judgement in the Baptist's messianic preaching, though Q has preserved it, and it fits the preaching of μετάνοια. But when instead he has the coming Messiah proclaimed as the bearer of the Spirit, and contrasts John's baptism with the Christian rite, that is the same as the idea of the Church which is also verbally expressed in Acts 1⁵, 11¹⁶. Q has preserved the original saying in his prophecy of the baptist of fire (Matt. 3¹¹; Lk. 3¹⁶). We may leave unresolved the question whether the Spirit was already joined with the fire in Q, or whether this is effected in Matthew and Luke under the influence of Mark. If the prophecy of baptism with the Spirit refers to Christian baptism which bestows the spirit (see above), the latter must be the case. In any event it is the prophecy of the Messiah as he who comes with the fire of judgement that is original.² And probably the saying about the mightier one, which in Mark precedes, but in Q (Matt. 3¹¹ᵇ; Lk. 3¹⁶ᵇ) is right in the middle of the saying about baptism, is also a Christian addition reflecting the rivalry between the Christian Church and the disciples

---

¹ Cp. M. Dibelius, *Die urchristl. Ueberlieferung von Johannes dem Taeufer*, 1911, pp. 46–59; M. Goguel, *Jean-Baptiste*, 1928, pp. 34–43.

² H. Leisegang, *Pneuma Hagion*, 1922, pp. 72–80 pays no regard to sources and in holding the baptism by fire and by the Spirit to be synonymous, believes the idea is alien to the original gospel, coming from a Greek mystical motif. But in the surrounding verses in Q (Matt. 3¹⁰ and 3¹² par.) the fire is specifically meant to be the fire of judgement. The idea of a fire of judgement is old (Isa. 66¹⁴ᶠ·; Mal. 3²ᶠ·) and it is indeed manifestly meant to convey that in so far as it destroys what is unclean, it purifies the community; so that it cannot be right absolutely to oppose the purifying to the judgement fire (Klostermann). We can clearly no more think of the cosmic fire of a world conflagration in connection with the words ὑμᾶς βαπτίσει than we can suppose a reference to the spiritual fire of Greek mysticism, which is concerned with the individual, not with the community. That elsewhere baptism is not associated with the judgement of fire does not seem to me a difficulty. On the one hand Sanh. 39a (Strack-B. I, 121f.) interprets ritual purification by fire as fire baptism, and on the other baptism appears elsewhere (Matt. 10³⁸ᶠ·, Lk. 12⁵⁰) as a figure of destruction, cp. M. Goguel, *Jean-Baptiste*, pp. 40f., 43.1. A. Schweitzer's belief (*Die Mystik des Apostels Paulus*, 1930, pp. 161f.) that by the baptizer who was to come was meant Elijah and not the Messiah I take to be erroneous.

of John (see pp. 164ff.). In any event it is clear that the tradition has undergone Christian editing; and indeed the fact that the passage had found acceptance in Q, and the language indicate that the Palestinian Church had already made this piece of the tradition its own. If the prophecy of the baptism by the Spirit stood in Q, it could have been intended to have the meaning given to it in the Jewish hope, where an outpouring of the spirit was expected in the messianic age (Isa. 44³; Joel 3¹ᶠ·; Test. Levi 18; cp. Strack-B. Reg.). Mark of course applies the prophecy to Christian Baptism as the sacrament of the gift of the Spirit.[1] The report in Q is more embracing than that in Mark. The preaching of repentance (Matt. 3⁷⁻¹⁰; Lk. 3⁷⁻⁹) is a Christian formulation (see p. 117). In any case the public of the Pharisees and Sadducees is reckoned with in Matthew (Matt. 3⁷, see pp. 52f.), while Luke has enlarged the passage by a further addition (Lk. 3¹⁰⁻¹⁴, see p. 145). The introduction which Luke has written (Lk. 3¹⁵) to the Baptist's messianic preaching once more reflects Christian polemic against the Baptist sect. The additional proclamation of messianic judgement which Q gives (Matt. 3¹²; Lk. 3¹⁷), over and above what is in Mark, is likely to be original.

Mk. 1⁹⁻¹¹ par.: *The Baptism of Jesus.* Without disputing the historicity of Jesus' baptism by John,[2] the story as we have it must be classified as legend. The miraculous moment is essential to it and its edifying purpose is clear. And indeed one may be at first inclined to regard it as a biographical legend; it tells a story of Jesus. Admittedly it would not do to psychologize and talk of a 'call' story and reckon its content as a calling vision. It is characteristically different from calling stories like Isa. 6¹⁻¹³; Jer. 1⁵⁻¹⁹; Ez. 1 and 2; Acts 9¹⁻⁹; Lk. 5¹⁻¹¹; Rev. 1⁹⁻²⁰; Jn. 21¹⁵⁻¹⁷: not only is there not so much as a word about the inner experience of Jesus, but there is also no word of commission to the person called, and no answer from him, things

---

[1] That is evidently also the meaning of Acts 1⁵, 11¹⁶. For contrary to the views of W. Michaelis (*Taeufer, Jesus, Urgemeinde*, 1928, pp. 20–23) it has to be emphasized that Acts, like Paul, conceived of Baptism, as did Hellenistic Christianity, as the sacrament of the gift of the Spirit. The apparent exceptions actually go to prove that for Acts, baptism and reception of the spirit belong together. Acts 8¹⁴ᶠᶠ·, the baptism of the believing Samaritan has to be completed by the gift of the Spirit; 10⁴⁴ᶠᶠ·, the gift of the Spirit to Cornelius and his household convinced Peter that he would have to baptize them, cp. 11¹⁶ᶠ· Most of all the contrast of John's baptism with the Christian rite in 19¹⁻⁷ shows that for the latter the gift of the Spirit is characteristic. I might add in passing that I think that the characteristic of Apollos in Acts 18²⁵ (ἐπιστάμενος μόνον τὸ βάπτισμα 'Ἰωάννου) is a dubious addition of the author to his source, by which he meant to explain (on the pattern of 19¹⁻⁷) the unclear word ἀκριβέστερον in v. 26.

[2] I cannot share the scepticism of E. Meyer, *Ursprung u. Anfaenge d. Christent.*, I, 1921, pp. 83f. Indeed Acts 10³⁷ᶠ·, 13²⁴ᶠ· prove that the historical fact of Jesus' baptism is not necessary for linking the ministry of Jesus to John's; yet not that this linking must be made by the story of a baptism, or that it could only be made if the baptism of Jesus were not an actual historical fact. Cp. M. Goguel, *Jean-Baptiste*, pp. 139f.

which we normally find in proper accounts of a call. Nor is the passage concerned with Jesus' special calling to preach repentance and salvation, but the real subject is his being the messiah, or the Son of God,[1] and that cannot be described as a 'call'. If it is feasible to think of another word of the heavenly voice beside the σὺ εἶ ὁ υἱός μου κτλ it could only be perhaps an ἀκούετε αὐτοῦ addressed to men or to the Church (cp. Mk. 9[7]). The legend tells of Jesus' consecration as messiah, and so is basically not a biographical, but a faith legend.[2]

So it is inadmissible to read εἶδεν in Mk. 1[10] as if a vision were being reported—if, that is, one has also to insist that the subject of εἶδεν is Jesus and not the Baptist. Matthew and Luke are quite right to take Mark's story as the description of an objective happening and καὶ φωνὴ [ἐγένετο] in Mk. 1[11] displays the same idea.[3]

Gunkel[4] and Gressmann[5] interpret the story of the Baptism in terms of the type of the 'Call to Kingship Sagas' and suppose that the appearance of the dove in the former derives from a motif frequently found in fairy stories, in which the choice of a king is decided by a bird who selects the right aspirant out of a whole row. This motif indeed does occasionally turn up in later elaborations of the Baptism[6] but it

[1] Mk. 14[61] shows that for Mark, Son (of God) was understood as a title of the messianic king, especially if we compare it with 15[26]. Cp. also M. Dibelius, *R.G.G.*[2], I, Col. 1595: The voice from heaven 'still has an "adoptionist" ring, especially since the expression "Thou art my son" means in the language of oriental law acceptance as a son ("Thou shalt be as my son").' On adoption formulae, cp. e.g. Gunkel, *Die Psalmen*, 1926, on Ps. 2[7]. The characterization of the Baptism story is correct in M. Goguel, *Jean-Baptiste*, 1928, pp. 142–228.
[2] It is characteristic that the Church did not tell of a calling to the kingly office such as was elsewhere widespread: the king was called away from his everyday task of ploughing. Thus Saul, 1 Sam. 11[5ff.], and Cincinnatus, Liv., III, 26. There is the same motif in Slav legends. Cp. Hugo Winkler, *Geschichte Israels*, II (Voelker und Staaten des alten Orients 3), 1900, p. 156; also A. Jeremias, *Handbuch der altorientalischen Geisteskultur*[2], 929, p. 304.4.
[3] H. Rust, *Wunder der Bibel*, I, *Die Visionen des N.T.s*, 1922, pp. 37–40, manages to avoid the misinterpretation of εἶδεν, but deduces the visionary character of the event from the contents of the story: he certainly believes that this cannot be concerned with a 'calling' vision (though to be sure he thinks of the 'calling' to Messiahship to be one such!) but rather to a 'conversion vision' which he seeks to make intelligible psychologically. But the narrative does not justify this, rather contradicts its meaning. M. Goguel, *Jean-Baptiste*, p. 145 is right.
[4] H. Gunkel, *Das Maerchen im A.T.*, pp. 147–51. Examples of the fairy-story motif are in Antti Aarne, *Maerchentypen*, no. 567; Bolte-Polivka, op. cit., I, p. 325. Also *Neugriech. Maerchen*, edited by Kretschmer, p. 27 and W. Luedtke, *Nachrichten der Kgl. Ges. d. Wiss. zu Goettingen*, phil.-hist. Kl., 1917, pp. 746ff.
[5] H. Gressmann, *Die Sage von der Taufe Jesu, Ztschr. f. Missionskunde und Religionswiss.*, 34, 1919, pp. 86ff.; and esp. 'Die Sage von der Taufe Jesu und die vorderoriental. Taubengoettin', *Arch. f. R.-W.*, 20, 1920/1, pp. 1–40, 323–59.
[6] Von Soden draws my attention to an appearance of it in the reproduction of the Baptism in Heliand. There in 984–93 we read:

> . . . As he (Christ) the land bestrode
> Heaven's doors oped wide and down the Holy Ghost
> Came from th' Almighty one above on Christ,
> Full in the likeness of a beauteous bird,

is quite alien to the story of the Baptism in Mark, just as we never find in the early Christian Tradition any reflection that the choice of Jesus to be the messianic king was in any way a problem. This is not a matter where men have to choose, but where God determines. But another of Gressmann's suppositions is untenable—that the original ending of the story is lost, and that it told of John paying homage to Jesus as Messiah.[1]

In Gressmann's view the dove is certainly no simple figure from a fairy story but an incorporation of an original goddess, none other, indeed, than the dove goddess of the Near East worshipped as Ishtar in Babylon and Atargatis in Syria. Although his proof that these two goddesses were specially closely related to kingship may be regarded as given, any proof that they were said to have been used to choose a king is lacking.[2] To conclude from the one single fact that the Spirit in Mk. 1[10] appears in the form of a dove, that the Baptismal story must derive from a Near Eastern king-making saga in which a feminine deity, represented by its bird, the dove, adopts a man as her son or choses him for her lover[3]—that in my view is too great an audacity. Actually I think the puzzle of the dove is easy to solve; without doubt it can signify nothing else than the πνεῦμα, the divine

> A gracious dove, upon his shoulder sat
> And waited. Then a word from heaven came,
> From height serene, to greet the Saviour thus,
> The best of all kings, Christ: 'Him I begat
> From mine own kingdom; he delights me more
> Than all beside, the best and most loved Son.'

[1] Reitzenstein (*Iran. Erloesungsmyst.*, p. 263.1) rightly attacks this view: Gressmann's construction presupposes an ancient fairy-tale narrative which not only contradicts everything historical but also would have to be immediately weakened in the tradition. Moreover it is unbelievable that such a fairy story of the choice of a king could ever have been combined with the memory that Jesus was baptized by John.

[2] For the story in Diodor II, 4ff. (in Gressmann, *Arch. f. R.W.*, p. 334) told of Semiramis, that she was parted from her mother but was fed and protected by doves till she was found by some shepherds and taken to court, cannot possibly be taken as proof.

[3] Gressmann ventures the hypothesis that the text of the heavenly voice in Mark is a development from an older version: σὺ εἶ ὁ υἱός μου καὶ ὁ ἀγαπητός μου, ἐν σοὶ εὐδόκησα (so in syr[sin cur]), and that this text itself is due to the blending of two independent versions: (1) υἱός μου εἶ σύ, ἐγὼ σήμερον γεγέννηκά σε (Lk. 3[22] D, etc.), (2) σὺ εἶ ὁ ἀγαπητός μου, ἐν σοὶ εὐδόκησα (attested nowhere) of which the latter is the older and which on account of its high mythological content was very early superseded. This hypothesis is exceeded in fantasy only by H. Leisegang, *Pneuma Hag.*, pp. 80–95. He combines two apocryphal fragments which he ascribes, as usual, to the Gospel to the Hebrews, though their combination is highly doubtful (cp. A. Schmidtke, *Neue Fragmente u. Unters. z. d. judenchristl. Evangelien*, 1911), in order to establish his right to see the mother of Jesus in the *fons omnis spiritus sancti* which descended on Jesus at his baptism. She is the feminine member of a divine triad, a point which he proves by citing the fact that in the late Gnostic legend of the 'Report of Religious Strife in Persia', Mary, who is identified with Hera and Urania appears as πηγή. This divine triad is older than the gospels; so the Baptismal story must also be part of their background. (But if the first point be right—cp. D. Nielsen, *Der dreieinige Gott*, I, 1922—the second is not.) If in the gospels the Holy Spirit comes to Jesus as a dove, then, to be sure, the old myth is thrown into confusion and 'the Holy Spirit as the mother of Jesus is blended into a unity with the pneumatic Jesus'.

I

power which fills the (messianic) king. But the representation of the divine power, which fills kings in the form of a bird is found in Persia as well as Egypt,[1] and indeed we find the dove itself in Persia.[2] And nothing other than this conception and its corresponding figurative presentation, certainly not any fairy story or saga, is the presupposition of the form of the Baptismal story. In confirmation of this we may add that it would seem that the Holy Spirit is represented by the figure of a dove even in Judaism, and in particular the Targum on S.S. 212 interprets the 'voice of the turtle dove' as the 'voice of the Holy Spirit'.[3]

But there still remains something for the understanding of the legend, viz. the question how the tradition came to light on the baptism as the time for the consecration of the Messiah. One cannot say the choice is obvious; it is certainly not the oldest conception of the life of Jesus, for the oldest conception of it which almost completely dominates the Synoptics is not messianic. And in passages like Acts 2[36]; Herm., *Sim*, V, 2, 7, etc., and in the Church tradition behind Rom. 1[3f.] this older conception still comes to view, in which Jesus is exalted to be Messiah after his death and resurrection. This is confirmed by the story of the Transfiguration if this were originally (see below) an Easter story. If then the Church felt the understandable need to antedate the messiahship of Jesus to the days of his ministry—how could his Baptism be hit upon? For the tradition as it stood, of Jesus being baptized by John, was naturally an inadequate basis. It seems to me that the reason is to be found on the one hand in the consecration of the Messiah being thought of as the work of the Spirit (cp. Acts 4[27], 10[38]), and on the other hand in the conviction that Baptism bestows the Spirit (cp. 1 Cor. 6[11], 12[13]; 2 Cor. 1[22]; Acts 2[38], etc., p. 247, n.1). But since this conviction could naturally not be derived from John's baptism, but could only, in my view, grow up in a Christian, though first in an Hellenistic environment, it follows that the Baptismal legend is firstly Hellenistic in origin. The preceding

---

[1] For Persia cp. the collected evidence in Gressmann, *Arch. f. R.W.*, p. 38, which he simply puts, as I think, into a false perspective. For Egypt cp. *Altoriental. Bilder zum A.T.*[2], 1927, Table XLV, no. 104; Nechbet the imperial goddess of Upper Egypt is represented over Ramses II, with her ring and its inscription 'Give life'. Cp. Erman-Ranke, *Aegypten*[2], 1933, Abb. 196, p. 491; Wrescinski, *Atlas zur aegypt. Kulturgesch.*, I, Lfg. 13/14, Blatt 203.

[2] Cp. J. Scheftelowitz, *Die Entstehung der manich. Religion und des iran. Erloesungsmyst.*, 1922, p. 81.

[3] Strack-B. I, 124f. Cp. also I. Abrahams, *Studies in Pharisaism and the Gospels*, I, 1917, Chap. 5. The bird similitudes of the O.T. which illustrate the protecting power of God are not relevant here. To explain the dove in the Baptism by Gen. 8[8ff.], as H. von Baer attempts to do (*Der heil. Geist in den Lukasschriften*, 1926, pp. 58, 164) following Procksch: the dove is the ambassador of the new era of Grace which will follow the judgement, this seems to me too fantastic, and to have no basis in N.T. sayings.

idea, which it presupposes, that Jesus himself was the one who bore the Spirit, could already have been in circulation in the Palestinian Church, perhaps under the influence of prophecy (Isa. 42 ¹, 61 ¹); it answers the expectations of Jewish apocalyptic (Ps. Sol. 17 ⁴², 18 ⁸; EEn. 49 ³, 62 ²; Test. Lev. 18; Test. Jud. 24¹), though to be sure it is strikingly seldom voiced in the Synoptic Tradition.² The adoption formula in Mk. 1 ¹¹ par. (or Lk. 3 ²² D if this form is meant to represent an older type of text) could also have been applied to Jesus in the Palestinian Church, for it does not necessarily presuppose the metaphysical meaning of 'Son of God' (see p. 248, n. 1); of course if that were so it could not have had its place originally in the Baptismal scene. It has its parallel in Mk. 9 ⁷ and could, when all is said and done, in the last resort come from an Easter story. The use of τὸ πνεῦμα absolutely³ is a decisive pointer to the conclusion that Mk. 1 ⁹⁻¹¹ could not have come from the Palestinian Church. 'In Jewish literature it is so unheard of to speak of 'the Spirit' (הָרוּחַ) when the spirit of God is meant, that the single word 'spirit' would much rather be taken to mean a demon or the wind'.⁴ But finally the Hellenistic origin of the Baptismal legend is vouched for by the fact that Q obviously did not tell the story of the Baptism even though it had a section on the Baptist, including his sermon on repentance and his messianic message. At most Q could have recorded the fact of the Baptism; but without any doubt Q did not know of it as the consecration of the Messiah.⁵

If the Baptismal legend were so shaped by influence of the Christian cult, it is not to be wondered at that, under the same influence,

¹ That the Messiah is equipped with the Spirit corresponds to the fact that he is king. The anointed king has the Spirit of God; cp. e.g. 1 Sam. 16¹³; Isa. 11 ²; for this reason he can give oracles, Prov. 16¹⁰.

² The only clear case is Mk. 3 ²⁸, if this form of the saying be original. Goguel, *Jean-Baptiste*, pp. 192–200 thinks the Q form is original (see p. 132) and rightly takes Lk. 11 ²⁰ as more original than Matt. 12 ²⁸; and he shows that the idea of Jesus as the bringer of the Spirit is alien to the Synoptic Tradition. For Lk. 4¹⁸ᶠ·, 10²¹, 11⁽²⁾· ¹³ are naturally Lucan formulations, and πνεῦμα in Mk. 1 ¹² par. is an Hellenistic concept.

³ It is very characteristic that Matthew says: πνεῦμα θεοῦ, Luke τὸ πνεῦμα τὸ ἅγιον; both sense that Mark's style is unbiblical.

⁴ Dalman, *Sayings of Jesus*, p. 203. Similarly Schlatter, *Die Sprache und Heimat des vierten Evangelisten*, 1902, p. 28.1, who is mistaken only in thinking that the absolute τὸ πνεῦμα is Christian, and not a Graecism.

⁵ B. H. Streeter, *The Four Gospels*, p. 188 deduces from the fact that Q contained the Baptist's preaching and the Temptation that the Baptism must also have been in Q. But the conclusion is not warranted. For even it if be conceded that the Temptation was reported at the beginning of Q (and that is not certain, since its appearance in Matthew and Luke might be due to Mark) there is no inner connection between the Baptism and the Temptation even though Matthew and Luke seek to furnish one. But Acts 13²⁴ᶠ· with Matt. 11⁷⁻¹³ shows that the Baptist came into the Christian kerygma not because he baptized Jesus, but because of his place as the last of the prophets in the history of salvation. Neither is Acts 10³⁷ᶠ· about the Baptism of Jesus; the phrase ὡς ἔχρισεν αὐτὸν ὁ θεός does not refer to the Baptism but is to be understood in terms of Acts 2²¹; cp. Lk. 4¹⁸; Acts 4²⁷.

it was further developed, viz., that it should serve as the basis of the Christian rite of Baptism and so come to be a cult legend in the strict sense.[1] As happens elsewhere in the history of religion, the cultic mystery rests upon a first experience of it by the cult deity, is founded in his story; and as that is true of the Synoptic presentation of the Lord's Supper, so in the early Church the story of Jesus' Baptism was soon conceived of in this sense as a cult legend. Jesus was the first who received the Baptism of water and the Spirit, and by that inaugurated it as an efficacious rite for believers. Cp. Tertullian, *Adv. Jud.*, 8: *baptizato enim Christo, id est sanctificante aquas in suo baptismate. . . .*[2] So in the early Church the pictorial representations of Jesus' Baptism show it in the line of the one type as a Christian baptism, and it is possible to recognize it as the baptism of Jesus only by the dove depicted over him.[3] Do the Synoptics themselves show any traces of such a conception? The endowment of Jesus with the Spirit can hardly be cited as such, for, as we have shown, that is much more the primary thing on the basis of which the Baptism was chosen as the scene for the consecration of the Messiah. It is questionable whether the linking up of Baptism and Temptation can be traced to the cultic connection of Baptism with Exorcism.[4] But in any case that would not establish an influence of the cult upon the Baptismal story. For the connection of the Baptism with the Temptation is secondary; there is no inner connection between the consecration of the messianic

---

[1] Cp. A. Jacoby, *Ein bisher unbeachteter apokr. Bericht ueber die Taufe Jesu*, 1902; H. Windisch, 'Jesus und der Geist', *Studies in Early Christianity*, 1928, p. 224.

[2] Cp. further Ign Eph. 18[2]: ὁ γὰρ θεὸς ἡμῶν Ἰησοῦς ὁ Χριστός . . . ὃς ἐγενήθη καὶ ἐβαπτίσθη, ἵνα τῷ πάθει τὸ ὕδωρ καθαρίσῃ; also W. Bauer in *Ergaenzungsband zum Handbuch zum N.T.*; Tert., *De Bapt.*, I: *sed nos pisciculi secundum* Ἰχθύν *nostrum Jesum Christum in aqua nascimur.* Only by adopting this standpoint is Irenaeus able to defend the Baptism story against the Gnostics, III, 9.3: *spiritus ergo dei descendit in eum . . ., ut de abundantia unctionis eius nos percipientes salvaremur.* Cp. also W. Heitmueller, *Im Namen Jesu*, 1903, p. 279.1; W. Bauer, *Das Leben Jesu im Zeitalter der neutest. Apokryphen*, 1909, p. 141.

[3] I cite certain kinds of presentation from the *Dictionnaire d'Archéologie Chrétienne et de Liturgie*, II, 1910, pp. 346–80. (1) The laying on of hands: a picture in the sacramental chamber of Calixtus' Catacomb, Room A[2] (l. c. 352), further in the pictorial relief in l. c. 354. This is also attested in writing by Ephraim Arm. 39 = Auch.-Moes. 41f. (2) Sprinkling with water: in the sacramental chamber of Calixtus' Catacomb, Room A[3] (l. c. 352) also on reliefs. (3) Jesus praying: in the Coimeterion St. Peter and Marcellinus, *cubicul.* 54 (l. c. 353). (4) Angels portrayed by Jesus' side holding his clothes, which is characteristic of the oriental (Alexandrian) conception; also in the Pontius Catacomb in Rome, l. c. 368 and 374. We find this type in later times, e.g. in the painting by Masolino in Battistero Castiglione d'Olona. The representation of Jesus as a child (cp. the representations under 1 and 2 and H. Haas, *Das Scherflein der Witwe*, 1922, pp. 122f.) neither rests upon the Christian practice of infant baptism, nor as Leisegang (in Haas, op. cit., p. 125) thinks, on some mythological ground; but it rests on the traditional representations of baptism in the Mysteries where the person to be baptized is pictured as a small figure in contrast with the baptizing Godhead; cp. e.g. Table 1 in ΑΓΓΕΛΟΣ, 1, 1925, pp. 46–47. Cp. further J. Strzygowski, *Ikonographie der Taufe Christi*, 1885; M. Goguel, *Jean-Baptiste*, pp. 205–7.

[4] In the Early Church a connection of this kind would be accepted quite naturally. Cp. e.g. Cypr., *Ep.*, 69.15; Cyril Jer., *Cat.*, III, 12.

king and the Temptation. This means also that we can hardly explain the statement that Jesus fasted in Matt. 4² by reference to cultic fasting. On the other hand, Luke seems to have been influenced by the Christian cult, in having Jesus pray as he comes up out of the water (3²¹).

If, as is probable, Mark, as an Hellenistic Christian of the Pauline circle, already looked on Jesus as the pre-existent Son of God, his Baptismal story would be contradictory to his Christology. But of this he was no more aware than many believers after him as a conscious belief. With others it was admittedly conscious; thus Matthew by the other formulation given to the heavenly voice makes a proclamation of messiahship out of the consecration of the messiah,[1] and in John the Baptism serves as a recognition sign of the previously hidden Son of God. Matthew (3¹⁴ᶠ·) and the author of the passage that according to Jerome, *C. Pelag.*, III, 2, derives from the Gosp. Heb. have discerned another problem: how can Jesus undergo a baptism for the remission of sins? and each has tried, in his own way, to offer a solution. The residual peculiarities of Matthew and Luke may well depend on this.

Mk. 1¹²⁻¹³: *The Temptation.* It is clear that here we have the rudiments of an originally detailed legend,[2] or that if there were never any detailed legend of the Temptation, this is but the rudiments in the tradition of Jesus of a motif that has been fashioned in detail in some other tradition. And we learn from the Mark account neither what the temptations consisted of, nor what is meant that Jesus was μετὰ τῶν θηρίων. This means that we can hardly be clear whether the story in the end goes back to a nature myth of the kind that tells of Marduk's fight with the dragon of Chaos (so A. Meyer in the *Festgabe fuer H. Bluemner*, 1914, pp. 434–68; cp. also H. Gunkel, *Zum religionsgeschichtlichen Verstaendnis des N.T.*², 1910, pp. 70f.), or, which is indeed more probable, the story belongs to the type of the 'Temptations of the Holy Men' who are put to the test (by evil) and emerge victorious. Such stories are told about Buddha (cp. especially E. Windisch, *Mara und Buddha*, Abh. d. Kgl. sachs. Ges. d. Wiss., phil. hist. Kl., XV, 4, 1895; R. Garbe, *Indien und das Christentum*, 1914, pp. 50ff.; J. Aufhauser, *Buddha und Jesus*, Kl. Texte, no. 157, pp. 24–29) and about Zarathustra (*Sacred Books of the East*, pp. 206ff.) and later about Christian saints. Indeed it is tempting to regard the words πειραζόμενος ὑπὸ τοῦ σατανᾶ as an addition (of Mark in his

[1] Cp. M. Goguel, *Jean-Baptiste*, pp. 148f.
[2] A. Fridrichsen, *Le problème du miracle*, pp. 89f. and 123, n. 30, supposes that the third temptation in Q which has no organic relation to the first two, derives from a mutilated version of the tradition in Mark.

source?).[1] That would mean there was no temptation story in front of Mark, but a representation of Jesus as Paradisal Man, or as a Saint, who lived once more at peace with the beasts, with whom mankind has lived in enmity ever since the Fall.[2]

Matt. 4^{1-11}//Lk. 4^{1-12}: *The Temptation* (Q). The use of the text of Q by Matthew and Luke has been influenced by Mark, whence Matt. 4^{11} derives the angels who are absent from Luke. If they were however originally in Q they would be there as rudiments of an earlier form related to Mark. If their original function was to serve Jesus with food, and to do so throughout the whole forty days, their appearance is less well motivated in Matthew (and Q?) where Jesus hungered and fasted the whole forty days.[3] In the same way the forty days in Matthew and Luke (whether they come from Q or not) are not organic to the story, since the temptation itself starts only when the forty days are over. They are simply used as a basis for the first temptation.

For the rest, the Temptation in Q is a secondary formulation, and moreover as A. Meyer rightly recognized is scribal Haggada.[4] The dialogue between Jesus and the devil reflects Rabbinic disputations. There is a similar disputation in three stages, with the answer at each stage a quotation from scripture, in Sifre Deut., § 307 (in Fiebig, *Jued. Wundergeschichten*, pp. 43f.).[5] So this formulation would seem to come from apologetic and polemic. But what is defended? That, despite his humanity the earthly Jesus is Messiah?[6] But against that is the fact that the temptations are not specifically messianic.[7] Neither the first nor the second temptation (supposing Matthew's order to be

[1] N. Freese, *Die Versuchung Jesu nach den Synopt.*, Diss. Halle, 1922 (typewritten).

[2] This motif seems to lie behind Test. Napht., 8; Apoc. Mos. 10f.; cp. Fr. Spitta, *Z.N.W.*, 5, 1904, pp. 323–6; also *Z.N.W.*, 8, 1907, pp. 66–68. Further R. Reitzenstein, *Hellenist. Wundererzaehlungen*, 1906, p. 82.1; Athanasius, Life of St. Anthony, S.B. Heid. Ak. phil.-hist. Kl. 5, 1914, pp. 12, 38f.; *Historia Monach. u. hist. Laus.*, 1916, pp. 5, 177ff.; L. Troje, *ADAM und ZΩH*, S.B. Heid Ak. phil.-hist. Kl. 17, 1916, p. 30.3; S. Eitrem, *Die Versuchung Christi*, 1924, p. 21.2. In the Ps. Gosp. Matth. the motif has found its way into the stories of Jesus' childhood. Chap. 18^{19} (Tischendorf, *Evang. Apokr.*, pp. 85f.). There are grotesque fictional uses of the motif in Ac. J., Chap. 6of.; Ac. Thom., Chaps. 39–41, 68–81.

[3] M. Albertz, in his reconstruction of the Q form of the Temptation (*Die synopt. Streitgespraeche*, p. 165), omits both the angels and the forty days.

[4] Cp. Bousset, *Schriften des N.T.s*, I[3], 1917, p. 245: 'Jesus defeated the biblically ingenious devil with his falsely assumed weapons. He is no less a scribe than the other!'

[5] Other examples of Rabbinic disputations where question and answer are made with scriptural quotations are to be found in: Shek. 5. 49b, 2 (A Rabbi disputes with the Lord of the demons!;) Sanh. 43b; Yom. 56b; Tanh. B. בראשית § 20 (8a) in Strack-B. I, 391; II, 417; III, 103, 846. Also see above pp. 44f.

[6] This is the view, e.g. of M. Albertz, op. cit., p. 43, that the story is the sharpest criticism of the Jewish idea of the supernatural Son of God. But Schlatter in *Der Evangelist Matth.*, p. 104 rightly points out that Jesus' answer in Matt. 4^4 retains the idea of miracle.

[7] This has been emphatically stressed by Schlatter in *Die Theol. d. N.T.s*, I, 1909, pp. 356f. and in *Der Evangelist Matth.*, pp. 95–112.

original) is in any special way related to his messianic role, as if the temptations signified something like this: to provide a miraculous satisfaction of all hunger and misery on earth, and the securing of messianic dignity by a miracle. Not only does nothing of all this appear in the text, but manifestly Jesus' 'Way to Messiahship' was never a problem for the Church, but at the most only its time and character. So some particular way to Messiahship could never have been thought of as a temptation by the devil. Moreover, how could the Church, which saw the chief evidence for Jesus' Messiahship in his miracles, have come to say that the way of miracles was a temptation of Jesus by the devil! For this reason it is impossible to find in early Christianity any contention against the idea that miracles are characteristic of the messiahship of Jesus. Miracle as such never yields to criticism; but it is possible for a problem to arise on that basis, the problem that divine and demonic miracles are sufficiently alike to be mistaken for each other. (Mk. 3²² par.; 1 Cor. 12³; 2 Cor. 11¹⁴), and that even Antichrist comes ἐν πάσῃ δυνάμει καὶ σημείοις καὶ τέρασιν (2 Thess. 2⁹; Mk. 13²²). How then can the ψεῦδος of a satanic miracle be detected? No external criterion can be advanced, nor is one advanced in the Temptation narrative.[1] The idea Jesus uses to reject the temptation is simply that a miracle which does not happen in obedience to God, but defies him, is satanic. But that means that the issue in the Temptation story is not 'How can I recognize a miracle as divine or demonic?' but 'What sort of miracle is recognized by Jesus and his Church?' In other words, Jesus is distinguished from a magician, and Christian miracle working from magic. For magic serves human purposes, but Jesus and his Church serve the will of God. This is also the basis for the fact that the miracles in the first and second temptations are particularly characteristic of magic.[2] One can only remain undecided whether the Temptation story is more apologetically turned on to the Church's enemies who said Jesus was a magician, or was meant as a warning to the Church against thinking too much of miracles and against using them for its own self-centred purposes.[3]

But the third temptation clearly goes on quite other lines than the

[1] This remains true, even if the miraculous formation of bread and the casting down from the Temple are specifically magic acts, as S. Eitrem shows, op. cit., p. 271.1. For it is not the 'what' of the miracle that is rejected.

[2] Cp. Eitrem, op. cit., and before him, G. P. Wetter, *Der Sohn Gottes*, 1916, pp. 64ff., esp. 73ff. and 85–89, 139f.: Bousset, *Kyr. Chr.²*, pp. 54f.

[3] The former view is taken by Eitrem: the latter is the surely more probable judgement of Fridrichsen (*Le Problème du Miracle*, pp. 87–89). In his comment on Eitrem's work Fridrichsen has seen the particular motive of the Temptation story in the prèsentation of Jesus as the type of believers, who, in being tempted by Satan just as they are, has shown them the way to victory. This certainly cannot be excluded.

first two, since every pretence has disappeared and as a result it cannot begin with the usual εἰ υἱὸς εἶ τοῦ θεοῦ, and it is in no sense messianic. For it stands to reason that the Messiah will secure world dominion, and the way to it commended here—worshipping the devil—cannot be a temptation for the Messiah: but every idea of 'world' dominion or 'worldly' power such as that with which Syr[sin] begins Matt. 4[8] is read into the story. Probably the third temptation which does not properly fit in with the first two comes from some mythological or legendary tradition.[1] Together with the two preceding temptations it gives expression to the general idea that obedience to God demands exclusiveness (αὐτῷ μόνῳ) and illustrates it by Jesus who will not surrender that obedience even for the sake of world dominion. So none of the three temptations is specifically messianic, but is such as, fundamentally, every believer knows. And the Temptation story shows how obedient submission of the will to God characterizes Church and Messiah alike—particularly in regard to the problem of miracle.[2] Schlatter then is right in emphasizing, as he says from the very beginning, that the story of the Temptation only criticizes the popular idea of the Messiah in so far as the contrast is not in the domain of dogma, but in the realm of ethics. Moreover Schlatter is also right in finding in the Temptation narrative the piety of the 'Anawim'.[3]

The fact that this point of view found expression right away in a Temptation story is evidently due to the tradition offering it an older Temptation story actually as obnoxious and perhaps equally sparse in content as was that of Mark. The work of Christian scribes made the story in Q and gave it the form of a controversy dialogue on the Jewish model (see p. 254, n. 5). And as A. Meyer has supposed, perhaps the O.T. passages with which Jesus fought, viz. Deut. 8[3], 6[16, 13] had been already brought together, along with the events of the Wilderness that went with them, Exod. 16[14ff.], 17[1–6, 32] (cp. I Cor. 10[1–10]; Wis. 16[20, 26]). But there is no clue why these three events were told as three temptations of the Son of God, i.e. the people of God, and that this was the basis for them being ascribed to Jesus; for the Jewish

---

[1] Cp. p. 251, n. 2. Satan asks for worship from Nimrod as the price of rescue from the fire in the Jewish legend of Abraham: A. Wuensche, *Aus Israels Lehrhallen*, I, 1907, p. 29. The motif of the mountain from which all the world can be seen comes from the world of fairy-tales; cp. H. Willrich, *Z.N.W.*, IV, 1903, pp. 349f.; F. Pfister, *Berl. phil. Wochenschr.*, 1913, pp. 919f.; A. Meyer, op. cit.; H. Gunkel, *Das Maerchen im A.T.*, pp. 50f.; Klostermann on Matt. 4[8].

[2] According to Schlatter the three temptations show the submission of the will in faith, obedience and love (i.e. to God)—*Der Evangelist Matth.*, pp. 108, 112. Cp. Fridrichsen, op. cit., p. 88; the scriptural quotations which repel the tempter, demand '*la patience, l'humilité et la submission à la volonté de Dieu*'.

[3] *Festgabe f. A. Juelicher*, 1927, p. 10.

tradition, though it certainly knew stories of temptation by Satan,[1] knew of none about the temptation of Messiah, nor could it ever have recounted anything of the kind.

On the basis of its form the Temptation story in Q belongs to the sphere of the Palestinian Tradition, which indeed also indicates its belonging to Q. Yet the character of the Temptation story distinguishes it from the rest of the Q material, for that almost throughout gives only an indirect expression to the messiahship of Jesus, and only refers to it clearly in very few places, such as Matt. 11^{2-6} par., $23^{34-36, 37-39}$ par. and particularly Matt. 11^{25-30} par. But since this last passage shows manifest signs of Hellenistic influence (see pp. 159f.), similar signs might be traceable in the Temptation story in Q, namely in presupposing the idea of a υἱὸς τοῦ θεοῦ of whom miracle is characteristic. That does not befit the Jewish messianic conception of the Son of God, but much more the Hellenistic.[2] Judaism certainly anticipated miracles in the Messianic Age (Matt. 11^{2-6} belongs here too) but had no notion of the figure of Messiah as a miracle worker.[3] In the actual course of Jesus' ministry the possibility arose of appropriating to him the Hellenistic concept of the Son of God, which the Temptation story presupposed.

Mk. 8^{27-30} par.: *Peter's Confession.*[4] This passage is to be characterized as legend. In no sense does the naming of a place in v. 27a ensure the historical character of what is told, since the note belongs to the previous section and corresponds to v. 22a (see pp. 64f.); ἐν τῇ ὁδῷ is a typical Mark comment serving to introduce the piece of traditional material into his design (cp. $10^{17, 32}$, $9^{33f.}$).

The fact that Jesus takes the initiative with his question itself suggests that this narrative is secondary (see p. 66 and esp. Mk. 12^{35}), as does the content of the question altogether. Why does Jesus ask about something on which he is bound to be every bit as well informed as were the disciples?[5] The question is intended simply to

---

[1] Cp. Strack-B. I, 140f. esp. GnR 56 (35c).

[2] G. P. Wetter, *Der Sohn Gottes*, pp. 64ff.

[3] Cp. A. Schweitzer, *Quest of the Historical Jesus*, 1913, pp. 294f.; A. Froevig, *Das Selbstbewusstsein Jesu*, 1918, pp. 68–72; *Das Sendungsbewusstsein Jesu*, 1924, pp. 121f.; Strack-B. I, 593f.

[4] Cp. my essay in Z.N.W., 19, 1919/20, pp. 165–74; contrary views in W. Mundle, Z.N.W., 21, 1922, pp. 229–311.

[5] Mundle's objection, that questions like this do arise in everyday life, especially in the dealings of teachers with their disciples, does not meet the point; and the reference to Socrates' pedagogical question is quite out of place. The scene is not from everyday life, nor is the question pedagogical. The dialectic of Socratic questioning is as foreign to the Synoptic as to Jewish dialogues. Besides it is the disciple, not the teacher who poses the questions in Rabbinic dialogues. There is a general analogy which may be quoted from Herod III, 34 in the question put by Cambyses to Prexaspes: κοῖόν μέ τινα νομίζουσι Πέρσαι εἶναι ἄνδρα τίνας τε λόγους περὶ ἐμέο ποιεῦνται; but the difference of situation between Cambyses and Jesus indicates the different significance the question has.

provoke the answer; in other words, it is a literary device. Once more the disciples appear here as a medium between Jesus and the people (see pp. 48f.), i.e. the disciples represent the Church, and the passages give expression to the specific judgement which the Church had about Jesus, in distinction from that of those outside. This then is a legend of faith: faith in the Messiahship of Jesus is traced back to a story of the first Messianic confession which Peter made before Jesus. The historical Peter would indeed have had to confess Jesus as the *future* Messiah! And it would then be necessary to suppose, according to Reitzenstein's precedent, that Jesus understood himself in terms of the myth of the archetypal man, and that Peter had seized on this understanding too.

But we must add the following considerations: the narrative is fragmentary, since it must originally have contained an account of the attitude Jesus himself took to the confession he had stimulated.[1] The instruction to keep silent and the prophecy of the Passion, together with the rejection of Peter in vv. 31–33 are formulations by Mark, and parts of what follows need not, in my view, be considered as the original continuation of the Confession. I think that the original conclusion has been retained in Matt. 16[17–19]. Mark has dispensed with it, and has on top of that introduced a polemic against the Jewish-Christian point of view represented by Peter from the sphere of the Hellenistic christianity of the Pauline circle (8[32f.]).[2] At the least Matt. 16[17–19] goes back to an old Aramaic tradition (see pp. 138ff.). The words can hardly have been formulated in any other

---

[1] Mundle's question whether the fact of Jesus' question and Peter's answer (their historicity being supposed) would not have been important enough for the earliest Church, 'even if Jesus' answer was no longer known' completely misunderstands the character of the tradition. The Church should have preserved such a fragment! What the appearance of a complete story should be like, in which a man recognizes the Godhead and makes confession to him, is shown in Lk. 5[1–11]: the Missionary command follows the confession; cp. also Jn. 21[15–19].

[2] This answers the question put to me by K. Holl (*Urchristentum und Religionsgeschichte*, 1925, p. 26): 'And who, in the early Church would have presumed to rebuke the celebrated Κηφᾶς as Satan?' Of course I would say precisely that—that the early Church did celebrate Peter as μακάριος (Matt. 16[18f.]), and that Hellenistic Christians did carry on an opposition against him. K. G. Goetz's demand for more references where Matthew represents a better tradition than Mark and Luke, cannot be answered easily but that is also no refutation. We can always point out that in Matt. 15[21–28] Matthew has also corrected the text of Mark on the basis of a like tradition (see p. 38). And why could he not have had a special source for the important Confession of Peter, as he had for the Lord's Prayer? If Goetz (*Petrus*, p. 8) and Mundle do not find polemic against Peter anywhere else in Mark, that does not necessarily imply that—that the plain polemic in 8[33] is to be disputed, and the same applies to the story of the denial (see below). Naturally Peter's place in the early Church was too well known and his position in the tradition too secure for Mark completely to eliminate him or degrade him. If he be attacked in 8[33], he is attacked as the leader of a group being directed another way: but that is not to attack his position as leader. For the rest see Gal. 2 and the rivalry between Peter and the Beloved Disciple in John.

place than in the Palestinian Church, where Peter was looked up to as the founder and leader of the Church and the blessing of Peter was put into the mouth of the risen Lord. For it is doubtless the risen Lord who speaks in Matt. 16[17-19]; and if the supposition be correct, that Matt. 16[17-19] is the original conclusion to the story of the Confession, that but expresses the view that Peter's experience of Easter was the time when the early Church's messianic faith was born;[1] indeed we should then have to reckon the whole narrative as an Easter story, which had been (perhaps for the first time in Mark) carried back into the ministry of Jesus. Just as Jn. 20[22f.] is a parallel to Matt. 16[19] so the whole story of the Confession has a clear parallel in the Easter story in Jn. 21[15-19].

Mk. 9[2-8] par.: *The Transfiguration*. It has long since been recognized that this legend was originally a resurrection story.[2] What the voice from heaven says, οὗτός ἐστιν ὁ υἱός μου ὁ ἀγαπητός is clearly the proclamation of Jesus as Messiah, and the words ἀκούετε αὐτοῦ are not only addressed to the three disciples present, but are simply general. So then the mountain to which Jesus leads the disciples is basically the same as the mountain in Matt. 28[16]. But it remains uncertain whether one can make the same claim for the peculiar dating μετὰ ἓξ ἡμέρας in v. 2[3] (such a dating is found nowhere else outside the Passion narrative). In any event the sixth day is traditionally the day of the Epiphany;[4] was the reckoning originally

[1] For a discussion of this cp. F. Kattenbusch, 'Die Vorzugstellung des Petrus und der Charakter der Urgemeinde in Jerusalem', *Festgabe f. Karl Mueller*, 1922, pp. 322ff.; 'Der Spruch ueber Petrus und die Kirche bei Matth.', *T.S.K.*, 1922, pp. 96ff.

[2] Wellhausen and Loisy, ad loc.; Bousset, *Kyrios Christos*[2], pp. 61, 282.2; G. Bertram, *Festg. f. A. Deissmann*, 1927, p. 189. With detailed justification K. G. Goetz, *Petrus*, pp. 76–89; M. Goguel, *Jean-Baptiste*, pp. 210–18. In my view the author of 2 Pet. knew the story as a resurrection appearance; for λαβών . . . τιμὴν καὶ δόξαν in 1[17] can only refer to the Resurrection, or Ascension. The verses, 9f., following the story in Mark, also read as if the story were originally an Easter story: before the Resurrection the heavenly nature of Jesus was hidden. Goetz tries to make more probable the view that an older version of the Transfiguration story, which was unmistakably an Easter story, lies behind the version of it in Eth. Apoc. of Peter 15–17. However it seems to me that this version is but a mixture of the older type of the Greek version in the Akhmim fragment with the Synoptic Transfiguration story. Following E. Meyer (*Urspr. u. Anf. d. Christent.*, I, pp. 154–6) Harnack (S.B. Preuss. Ak., phil.-hist. Kl., 1922, pp. 62–86) has attempted to take the story back to a vision which Peter had during the ministry of Jesus, which in turn became the basis of the Easter vision. But that does not shed much light, quite apart from any question of the interpreting of details, for the reason that a visionary experience of Jesus while he was bodily present is hardly credible. That, as Meyer says 'similar things have often happened on innumerable occasions in every age' is something quite unknown to me. Acts 6[15] e.g. or the visions of Joan of Arc which Meyer cites are entirely different. It would be better to refer to monastic stories, where the πνεῦμα that fills those given to the spiritual life becomes visible, particularly while they are at prayer, as a flame of fire (cp. Reitzenstein, *Hist. Mon. u. hist. Laus., passim*, esp. p. 56.6). But this idea is impossible in the case of the Transfiguration because of μετεμορφώθη.

[3] So M. Goguel, *Jean-Baptiste*, pp. 212–14.

[4] Cp. W. Bacon, *H.T.R.*, 8, 1915, pp. 94–120; W. A. Heidel, *Am. Journ. of Phil.*, 45.3, 1924, pp. 218ff.

started from the crucifixion (or the Resurrection? Klostermann)? Further it is not impossible that originally the story was told of Peter alone, and that the two other disciples were subsequently added as in Mk. 1[29] (see p. 212) and 14[33]. Antedating the incident in the ministry of Jesus was hardly in the first place an attempt to put Jesus' Messiahship back into the ministry,[1] since that was done more radically in the Baptismal story. It is much more likely to have been taken up by Mark to serve as a heavenly ratification of Peter's confession and as a prophecy of the Resurrection in pictorial form (cp. 8[31]). For in its literary context it is also secondary; it is with vv. 9f. inserted between vv. 1 and 11, whose connection it forces apart.

It is doubtful whether the legend of Exod. 24 has had any effect; the six days are explicable here and there from the tradition (see above); the three trusted friends do not there accompany Moses to the theophany itself, and the cloud is known to be a traditional form of a theophany.[2] In any case such a reference would by no means explain everything. The two figures that appear beside Jesus we may suppose to have been originally two unidentified heavenly beings (angels or saints), providing the accessories to the Lord who had ascended into the heavenly glory.[3] They have their parallels in the Akhmim Fragment of the Apoc. of Peter 6: 'And as we prayed suddenly there appeared two men standing before the Lord, upon whom we were not able to look. For there issued from their countenance a ray as of the sun, and their raiment was shining so as the eye of man never saw the like, for no mouth is able to declare nor heart conceive the glory wherewith they were clad and the beauty of their countenance. . . .' The figures were then (by Mark?), following a law of folk-lore, identified and differentiated (see below), and at the same time perhaps their appearance was intended to serve as a confirmation of the Messiahship of Jesus.[4]

The story is by no means an unity, even if we cannot make a literary analysis with complete certainty.[5] It is possible that

[1] Cp. H. Usener, 'Das Weihnachtsfest', *Religionsgesch. Unters.*, I[2], 1911, pp. 38–40; Bousset, *Kyrios Christos*[2], pp. 61, 268.2.

[2] M. Werner, *Der Einfluss paulin. Theol. im Mk. Evg.*, 1923, pp. 13–15, absolutely opposes any effect of Exod. 24.

[3] Cp. A. Meyer, *Festg. f. Bluemner*, p. 451 and *Die Auferstehung Christi*, 1905, pp. 57a, 342; J. Kroll, Beitraege zum *Descensus ad inferos* (Verzeichnis der Vorlesungen an der Akademie Braunsberg 1922/3, 1922, p. 35.2). It remains a question whether the two heavenly beings, as Goetz and Meyer suppose, can be identified as the two escorts who, in Iranian belief, took the souls of the pious into the world of light.

[4] Cp. Bousset, *Die Religion des Judentums im n.t. Zeitalter*[3], 1926, pp. 232f. Strack-B. I, 756–8; IV, 779–98. Besides this the names in Mark have been inserted into the Ethiopic version of the Apoc. Pet.; cp. *Z.N.W.*, XIV, 1913, p. 73.

[5] In *Z.N.W.*, 21, 1922, pp. 185–215, E. Lohmeyer has made an analysis and interpretation of the Transfiguration with which I cannot concur. He divides the texts into two parts:

originally v. 7 followed v. 4. Backdating the story in the ministry suggests making the disciples share not only as passive spectators but as active participants. In v. 6 we see the author's embarrassment at trying to do this: οὐ γὰρ ᾔδει τί ἀποκριθῇ· ἔκφοβοι γὰρ ἐγένοντο. In v. 7 αὐτοῖς refers to the persons named in v. 4 (unless we read αὐτῷ with syr[sin]) and not to the disciples of vv. 5f.

From the reproduction of the parallel reports we must mention that Luke felt the need to give some definition to the dialogue of Jesus with Moses and Elijah, and at the same time to call particular attention to the prophetic character of the story: Moses and Elijah talk to Jesus about his death in Jerusalem (9[31]). The disciples' sleep perhaps goes back to the fairy-tale motif of magic sleep (Gunkel, *Das Maerchen im AT*, p. 104).

Mk. 11[1-10] par.: *The Triumphal Entry.* In the first place the securing of an animal to ride on is, in this story, a manifestly legendary characteristic, indeed, like 14[12-16] it is a fairy-tale motif. But the rest of the story is also legendary or at least strongly influenced by legend. For there can be no doubt about the legendary character of the animal,[1] and the assumption that has to be made if we are to take the story as history, the assumption namely, that Jesus intended to fulfil the prophecy in Zech. 9[9] and that the crowd recognized the ass

---

(1) vv. 4, 5, (6), 7, 8 are a legend that has grown out of Jewish eschatological expectations, and presents Jesus as the Messiah greater than the figures of the O.T. To those who are privileged here it is assured: that the day of salvation has already come, and its continuance is guaranteed by the person of the Messiah. The presence of the End is demonstrated by the presence of Moses and Elijah. [But even if Judaism knew Moses as a figure of the End, it was without any relation to the Messiah being implied thereby; and if Elijah were a forerunner of Messiah, it was without any combination with Moses (this idea is not found before about A.D. 900); cp. Strack-B. I, 756.] Peter's statement in v. 5 further recognizes the eschatological character of the situation; for tents were to be the dwellings at the end. [But v. 6 does not accord with this, as though Peter had rightly grasped the situation! For it is not obvious that Peter's proposal is senseless just because salvation has already come; on the contrary!] Finally cloud and voice are characteristic of eschatological epiphany. [But not only for such! and here the cloud has clearly the one function of being the bearer of the voice, since the speaker in the vision must be hidden according to the rules of style!] (2) v. 3 is a metamorphosis of Jesus, to be understood in terms of Hellenistic Mysteries; this story was added to that of the Jewish Messiah. [But is it conceivable that there should be an isolated handing on of v. 3, which in any event is no story?] Apart from particular considerations it seems to me inadmissible to separate v. 3 from v. 4. Even in vv. 4f. Jesus is clearly represented as 'one transformed' when the heavenly figures talk with him and Peter wants to build a tent for him as for them. Lohmeyer found the starting-point for his analysis in Peter's saying in v. 5; but even if it be right to take the meaning of a story from a saying spoken in it, it must be a saying characteristic of it, containing the point of the story. But that is not Peter's saying in v. 5, which can hardly be interpreted with any certainty, but the heavenly voice in v. 7; and this explains v. 3 just as surely as Mk. 1[11] explains v. 10 or Lk. 2[10] explains v. 9.

[1] That we are dealing with an animal not hitherto used for riding shows clearly that the entry into the city is not conceived as a secular occurrence; cp. the proofs in Klostermann. The Mount of Olives has probably Messianic significance as well, for there Yahweh's eschatological appearance was expected, and in popular belief Messiah would himself come there (Jos., *Bell.*, II, 13.5: § 262; *Ant.*, XX, 8.6 = 169).

as the Messiah's beast of burden, is absurd. There can only be one question. Was the Entry as such historical, but made a Messianic one by legend, or has it developed completely out of the prophecy?[1] Actually the passage in Zech. not only mentions the Ass, but also the Entry (Behold, thy king cometh unto thee) and the acclamation (Rejoice greatly, O daughter of Zion; shout, O daughter of Jerusalem). But it is conceivable that in the Synoptics it was not the inhabitants of Jerusalem that made up the shouting crowd, but the pilgrims going up to the feast, or alternatively, the disciples. And the report of Jesus' entry into Jerusalem with a crowd of pilgrims full of joy and expectation (at the Kingdom of God that was now coming) could provide the historical basis which became a Messianic legend under the influence of Zech. 9[9].[2]

(b) *The Passion Narrative*

Mk. 14[1f.,][10f.] par.: *Conspiracy and Judas' Betrayal.* Mk. 14[1f.,][10f.] could hardly have been an independent tradition at any time, but is a passage that from the start was written to fit a larger context. But we still have to consider whether these verses were written for a context itself made by bringing different pieces together or was the beginning of an originally coherent narrative.

The verses can in any case hardly be said to contain historical narrative. For apart from the fact that Judas' betrayal at least as it is actually presented belongs to legend,[3] there is no authentic record of the authority's decision preserved for us, but it has been inferred from the events themselves. There has been some attempt to find a chronology in vv. 1f. which contradicts that in vv. 12–16, and which is held to be old; Jesus' execution must have taken place before the Passover. If this latter view be right, we can hardly claim Mk. 14[1f.] in support. According to B the text of v. 2 reads: . . . μὴ ἐν τῇ ἑορτῇ, μήποτε ἔσται θόρυβος τοῦ λαοῦ. At first sight the meaning seems to be: Jesus must be arrested (or executed)[4] before the Feast. But that

---

[1] In Justin, *Apol.*, c. 32.73d the story is even more rounded off with prophetic proofs by the statement that the ass (following Gen. 49[11]) was tied up to a vine.

[2] H. Gressmann, *Z.f.K.*, N.F.3, 1922, p. 189 asks whether the story told in Jos., *Bell.*, II, 17.8f. = § 433ff. of the entry of the political Messiah Menahem ben Hiskia has been transferred to Jesus. But I see no basis for this; if a messianic entry were possible for Menahem, why not for Jesus?

[3] W. Wrede, *Vortraege und Studien*, 1907, pp. 127–46; G. Schlaeger, *Z.N.W.*, XV, 1914, pp. 50–59; M. Plath, *Z.N.W.*, XVII, 1916, pp. 178–88; J. M. Robertson, *Jesus and Judas*, 1927 (penetrating in criticism, but fantastic in its positive assertions: the betrayer Judas is an invention of Gentile Christians in order to discredit Jewish Christians, and an invention indeed on the basis of a figure in the Mystery Drama which lies behind the Passion story).

[4] So M. Dibelius, *Th.R.*, N.F.1, 1929, p. 193.1.

is in reality nonsensical; for the time—two days before the Feast, is much too short, and the crowd is already there. Is it possible then to understand: 'After the feast'? This decision would in that case have been accidentally upset by the unexpected betrayal of Judas who made it possible for a secret arrest to be made.[1] But that is never so stated afterwards (vv. 10f.). And would the Tradition really have preserved a decision that was never carried out? Is it not far more likely that it inferred the decision from the events? So in spite of the suspicions which underlie the variant readings in D, I can take its text as the original: μήποτε ἐν τῇ ἑορτῇ ἔσται θόρυβος τοῦ λαοῦ. The meaning is: Jesus must be arrested so that he should not excite an uproar during the Feast, i.e. only the arrest itself, not its actual time, was decided.[2] Admittedly I cannot explain how the B text arose.

The expansion of Mk. 14[1f.] in Matt. 26[1-5] is significant for the history of the Tradition: (1) In respect of form: Mark's report has been turned into direct speech by Jesus; (2) In matters of substance: a new prophecy is put into Jesus' lips, and the plot of the authorities is reported in greater detail.

Similarly Mk. 14[10f.] is expanded in Matt. 26[14f.]: (1) Direct speech has been made out of a report; (2) The amount of blood money is inferred from prophecy. Luke has omitted the obscure consideration in Mk. 14[2], while John in 11[47-53], who is more concerned with the connection of events than the Synoptics, takes no account of Mark.

Mk. 14[3-9] par.: *The Anointing at Bethany*. The story is alien to the plan of the Passion Story which underlies Mark, for it is evidently an insertion between vv. 1f. and 10f.[3] Particularly is it clear that vv. 8 and 9 (apart, say, from the words ὃ ἔσχεν ἐποίησεν in 8a) by which they were related to the Passion in the first place are secondary. They give the story, which has its own point in vv. 6f., a new point, and weaken it in doing so.[4] Down to v. 7 the story can be classed as an apophthegm without detracting from its legendary character; editorial work has thereafter turned it fully into a biographical legend.

Mk. 14[12-16] par.: *The Preparation of the Passover*. This is a variant of 11[2-6]. Jesus' foreknowledge is reminiscent of 1 Sam. 10 where

---

[1] So Dalman, *Jesus-Jeschua*, 1922, p. 91.

[2] For this conception there is also Jos., *Bell.*, I, 43 = § 88: ... ἐπανίσταται τὸ Ἰουδαϊκὸν ἐν ἑορτῇ· μάλιστα γάρ ἐν ταῖς εὐωχίαις αὐτῶν στάσις ἅπτεται. Cp. also *Ant.*, XX, 5.3 = § 105ff.

[3] According to W. Bussmann, *Synopt. Studien*, I, 1925, pp. 35–37 the story is secondary even in Mark.

[4] So also L. v. Sybel, *Z.N.W.*, 23, 1924, p. 185. If one sees vv. 6f. as a secondary addition as G. Bertram does (*Die Leidensgeschichte Jesu und der Christuskult*, 1922, pp. 16–18) the story becomes quite pointless. For vv. 4f. have to be taken as secondary along with vv. 6f. and what is left, vv. 2f. can no longer be taken in any way as an independent story in the tradition.

Samuel foretells whom Saul will meet on his way. Yet in the end the basis is a fairy-tale motif, where some creature (mostly an animal) precedes the traveller and so shows him his way.[1] It is clear that Mk. 14[12-16] cannot be an independent unit of the tradition; it presupposes a story of the Passover meal as its continuation, and it could well have been a secondary composition to fit it. The time reference in v. 12 is quite impossible in Jewish usage,[2] and must come from Mark unless one supposes that the whole section is an Hellenistic formulation. But that is hardly possible because here it is still the Passover that is presupposed, the Passover that the Hellenistic Eucharist replaced.

Mk. 14[17-21] par., or Lk. 22[21-23]: *The Foretelling of the Betraval.* From Ps. 40[10], which Jn. 13[18] expressly quotes, has been drawn the motif of Jesus being betrayed by a table companion, and this motif has found its formulation in a scene where Jesus reclines at table with the Twelve and foretells the awful thing.[3] The story can be found in a clearly more original form in Luke, at least in Lk. 22[21]; for v. 22 and in all probability v. 23 too were fashioned by Luke on the basis of Mark. We can no longer tell whether this meal was thought to be the last, for vv. 17–21 is manifestly an originally independent unit of the tradition, as the parallel preserved elsewhere in Luke indicates. Nor is it stated in this section of the tradition that the meal is actually the Passover; indeed it cannot possibly be the Passover; for at the Passover every participant has to have his own dish in front of him, whereas Mk. 14[20] presupposes that the participants are eating out of a common dish.[4]

Matthew and John were the first to say quite clearly that Judas was marked out as the traitor in this scene; Mark left it to the reader to gather it from the context in which he set the passage. But originally

---

[1] Cp. O. Gruppe, *Griechische Mythologie und Religionsgesch.* (Handb. d. klass. Altert. Wiss. V 2), II, 792.8; O. Boeckel, *Die deutsche Volkssage*[2], 1914, p. 87; H. Gunkel, *Das Maerchen im A.T.*, pp. 32f.; H. Guenther, Die christliche, *Legende des Abendlandes*, pp. 81f.

[2] The πρώτη ἡμέρα τῶν ἀζύμων is the 15th Nisan; ὅτε τὸ πάσχα ἔθυον refers to Nisan 14 'No law-abiding Jew would have spoken of the first day of the Feast if he had been meaning the Day of Preparation for it.' Dalman, *Jesus-Jeschua*, 1922, p. 97. On the other hand it is known to this section of the Tradition that the Passover meal had to be eaten in Jerusalem; cp. Dalman, op. cit., pp. 99f.; Strack-B. IV, 41f.

[3] Cp. G. Bertram, *Die Leidensgesch. Jesu*, pp. 32f.

[4] Strack-B. I, 989; IV, 64. It is an impossible suggestion that the scene in Mk. 14[17-21] did not take place at the Passover itself, but at the eating of the first dish, and that the text indicates the two parts of the meal by the repetition in v. 22 of the words καὶ ἐσθιόντων αὐτῶν. Either v. 18 or v. 22 would have to be made a more exact statement. The double ἐσθιόντων αὐτῶν shows the joining of two units of tradition. Cp. in addition to Wellhausen esp. E. Schwartz, *Z.N.W.*, VII, 1906, p. 23.1 and L. v. Sybel, *T.S.K.*, 1923, pp. 116f. I cannot think that the different attempts are successful which try to locate the whole scene of the meal in Bethany; cp. A. Loisy on Mk. 14[3-9]; W. Haupt, *Worte Jesu und Gemeindeueberlieferung*, 1913, pp. 132f.; K. G. Goetz, *Z.N.W.*, 20, 1921, pp. 169f.

there was no indication of any particular disciple, as C. H. Weisse, *Die evang. Geschichte*, 1838, I, pp. 601ff. recognized. The legendary character of the scene also follows from the presupposition that it is self-evident that there are twelve disciples,[1] as from the fact that the announcement of the betrayal is not followed by any practical consequences, but by the woe which comes from the theology of the Church in Mk. 14²¹. John was the first to notice that Judas' exit ought to be recorded.

Mk. 14²²⁻²⁵ par., or Lk. 22¹⁴⁻¹⁸: *The Institution of the Lord's Supper*. After the work of Eichhorn[2] and Heitmueller[3] I do not need to prove that a cult legend lies behind Mk. 14²²⁻²⁵. I simply point, as in the Baptismal story, to features in the way the section has been formulated which betray the influence of the cult. Representations of the Last Supper make their appearance late in Christian art (they were preceded by pictures of the Feast of the Blessed); the first known instance is the picture in Cod. Rossanensis (6/7 century) which is reproduced in Plate XVIII of O. Wulff, *Altchristliche und byzantinische Kunst*, I, 1914 (Handbuch der Kunstwissenschaft edited by Fr. Burger); it is quite simply a picture of the celebration of the cult,

From the tension between ἐσθιόντων αὐτῶν in Mk. 14²² and ἀνακειμένων αὐτῶν καὶ ἐσθιόντων in v. 18 it follows first that vv. 17–21 and vv. 22–25 were not originally contiguous. But it is not possible in some way to reject vv. 17–21 and take vv. 22–25 as the original continuation of vv. 12–16; for vv. 22–25 does not mention the Passover meal for which vv. 12–16 is a preparation.[4] Rather is it clear that vv. 22–25 is the cult legend of the Hellenistic circles about Paul made to serve as an organic continuation of vv. 12–16 by recounting the Passover meal. Indeed it is plain that vv. 22–25 have been inserted into a narrative already available, since it lacks any introduction of its own. And apparently Mark has preserved a fragment of this displaced account in v. 25; this can be seen in Lk. 22¹⁴⁻¹⁸, where the

---

[1] Cp. J. Wellhausen, *Einleitung in die drei ersten Evangelien*², 1911, 138ff.
[2] A. Eichhorn, *Das Abendmahl im N.T.* (Hefte zur Christl. Welt 36), 1898.
[3] W. Heitmueller, Article 'Abendmahl' in *R.G.G.*, I, 20–52.
[4] One may simply compare the artificial efforts of Strack-B. IV, 74–76 and Dalman, *Jesus-Jeschua*, pp. 98–166 to interpret the Synoptic story as the report of a Passover meal. Let us suppose that the use of ἄρτος instead of the necessary word ἄζυμα is but carelessness; let us not make too much of the difficulty of drinking from one cup (which Strack-B. 58 feels but not however Dalman, p. 140): no reader can discover from Mark's narrative that v. 22 is about the introduction of the Passover meal, or v. 23 about its conclusion (the 'cup of blessing'). Apart from that the main thing about the meal, the Passover lamb, is never even mentioned. Strack-B. and Dalman get into fresh difficulties with the Luke narrative, which Dalman avoids by a critical rejection of Luke's narrative, while Strack-B. wants to equate the cup in Lk. 22¹⁷ with the first cup of the Passover meal! For a criticism cp. Wellhausen, Loisy and E. Schwartz, *Z.N.W.*, 7, 1906, pp. 23f.; also Bertram, *Die Leidensgeschichte Jesu*, pp. 30f. and L. v. Sybel, *Theol. Stud. u. Krit.*, 1923, pp. 118f

older Tradition has been preserved in a more complete form, as has the original connection with the preparation of the meal (Lk. 22^{7-13}).[1] Here, apart from v. 17 where Mark's version (λάβετε κτλ) has clearly influenced Luke—there is no liturgical, cultic element at all. But that certainly does not immediately establish the historicity of the scene, but rather shows that there lay behind Luke too a biographical legend, as the reference to the passion clearly shows.

We may now attempt to get a little further behind the Luke text. We observe namely: (1) that the parallelism of Passover meal and cup is not convincing since the cup is but one part of the Passover meal; (2) that with the cup there is no reference to Jesus' death, and absolutely none to his person; the saying over the cup is much rather just a pointer to the coming Kingdom of God.[2] We may also suppose that originally bread was mentioned instead of the Passover, and that there was no reference to the Passion. The section was then turned into an account of the Passover in editorial revision and furnished with a legendary introduction vv. 7–13 (Mk. 14^{12-16}). It had originally been told how Jesus at a (ceremonial? the last?) meal expressed the certainty of his eating the next (festival) meal in the Kingdom of God, and then expected it to happen in the immediate future. But with such guesses we pass to the realm of uncertain hypotheses, however valuable they might prove. We can only recall that Jn. 13 gives us an account of the Last Supper where it is not thought of as a Passover, and has no cult legend in it, so that we may well ask whether the author of John had a more primitive account of the Last Supper in front of him.[3]

Mk. 14^{26-31} par., or Lk. 22^{31-34}: *The Road to Gethsemane and the Foretelling of Peter's Denial.* Mk. 14^{26} with its ὑμνήσαντες links up with the description of the Passover that has been present ever since vv. 12–16 although it is admittedly different from the two sections vv. 17–21 and vv. 22–25;[4] it can thus lead us in the first place to suppose that vv. 26–31 is a further unit of the tradition that has already appeared in vv. 12–16. But we do not need to take v. 26 as an original part of the pericope, and vv. 27–31 could originally have stood independent of what preceded it, or, alternatively, could have begun with a brief indication of its setting now provided in v. 26. The

---

[1] I believe Lk. 22^{19-20} to be an interpolation in its entirety. But even if Luke himself wrote some part of v. 19 it would but have introduced a new unit of the tradition, and vv. 14–18 would then too have had to be intelligible on their own.

[2] At this point Mark's version may be more original, and Luke made the alteration because the drinking of wine in the Kingdom of God was offensive to him. Admittedly though Lk. 22^{30} betrays nothing of such an attitude.

[3] Cp. L. v. Sybel, *T.S.K.*, 1923, p. 119.

[4] Cp. Strack-B. IV, 72f., 75f.

Luke parallel supports this, for it is placed in another setting (see the same). But Mk. 14²⁷⁻³¹ must have been continued, and this in fact is found, as we shall show, not in vv. 32–42, but in vv. 43–52. The tradition behind Mk. 14²⁷⁻³¹ has to be classed as an historical account with legendary traits; it prepares the way for the Arrest and Denial. For the rest, within vv. 27–31, v. 28 is secondary, for it breaks up the coherence of the piece and points beyond the Denial to an even wider context. It will have been introduced by Mark himself, so as to prepare for the ending of the Gospel that is now lost, unless it is itself a later addition to the Gospel.[1]

In Lk. 22³¹⁻³⁴ it seems to me that we have in vv. 31f. a piece of the tradition underlying Luke, though vv. 33f. could be his own formulation (following Mk. 14²⁹ᶠ·). For vv. 33f. look out of place following on vv. 31f., since v. 32 ends with a forward look to the great part Peter will play, whereas vv. 33f. contains only the tragic obverse of all that. But Lk. 22³¹ᶠ· is important for two chief reasons: (1) It shows that many components of the Passion story had a separate tradition as well. (2) There is a presupposition in vv. 31, 32a that all the disciples except Peter desert when they are sifted: only his loyalty remains unwavering.[2] So this Tradition knows nothing of the Denial either. That applies also to v. 32b if I am right in supposing that ἐπιστρέψας is an addition by Luke, who wants to connect it up with the Denial. The ideas of πίστις and ἐπιστρέφειν are obviously counterparts in that πίστις means 'faith' and ἐπιστρέφειν means 'to turn over a new leaf', both in the sense of the language of Hellenistic Christian Missions.[3] But in v. 32a it is clear to see that πίστις must mean 'loyalty'; ἐπιστρέψας is thus a misunderstanding; in other words, ἐπιστρέψας is an addition.[4] For the rest the intransitive use of ἐπιστρέφειν occurs in the other synoptics in a figurative sense only in the LXX quotation in Mk. 4¹² par., though it occurs in Luke again at 17⁴ and eight times in Acts, and so can be said to be a characteristic of Luke's style.

Mk. 14³²⁻⁴² par.: *Jesus in Gethsemane.* This is originally an individual story of a thorough-going legendary character, which has

---

[1] It is very noteworthy that in the Fayum Pap. (Kl. Texte, no. 8², pp. 20.5ff.) which contains the section, v. 28 is missing. Does an older Mark text really lie behind the Pap.?

[2] Yet the imagery of σινιάσαι presupposes that not all the disciples fall away, and the formulation ἵνα μὴ ἐκλίπῃ ἡ πίστις σου not only says nothing about a passing desertion, but seems to exclude it.

[3] 'Επιστρέφειν ἐπὶ τὸν κύριον (or τὸν θεόν) is synonymous with πιστεῦσαι ἐπὶ τὸν κύριον; the former in Acts 9³⁵, 11²¹, 14¹⁵, 15¹⁹, 26²⁰; the latter in 9⁴², 11¹⁷, 16³¹, 22¹⁹. Cp. esp. Acts 11²¹: πολύς τε ὁ ἀριθμὸς ὁ πιστεύσας ἐπέστρεψεν ἐπὶ τὸν κύριον; further 13⁸: διαστρέψαι ἀπὸ τῆς πίστεως; 14²²: ἐμμένειν τῇ πίστει; 16⁵: στερεοῦσθαι τῇ πίστει.

[4] That is also why I do not believe that the right reading is D itvar syrsc ἐπίστρεψον καὶ στήρισον, which would of course drop all reference to the denial.

not survived intact in Mark. In the first place v. 42 can be easily separated out as an addition (by Mark) which fits the scene into its context. But v. 41b is also a secondary addition by Mark. The scene must originally have closed with the words ἀπέχει· ἦλθεν ἡ ὥρα v. 41a as its impressive climax. Moreover, v. 38 is in all probability a saying introduced from the language of Christian edification. At the beginning the full number of the disciples in v. 32 conflicts (whether τοῖς μαθηταῖς αὐτοῦ or αὐτοῖς is adopted as the reading) with the three selected ones in v. 33 and thereby also with the sayings in vv. 32b and 34. We have a choice between regarding vv. 33f. as a later addition, or v. 32 as a secondary passage meant to serve as a link with what has preceded. It is hardly possible to plead for the originality of v. 32 on the ground that the three disciples are not mentioned and that Luke therefore used a parallel source which knew nothing of the three. For here as often, it could be that some polishing has taken place in Luke's source; and the use of Mk. 14³⁸ in Lk. 22⁴⁰ is further clear evidence of Luke's editorial activity.[1] On the other hand we cannot claim originality for vv. 33f. (see 1st edition) on the grounds that generally the appearance of a small number of disciples is older than the appearance of the Twelve; for in v. 32 it is not the Twelve who are mentioned, but just μαθηταί in general. Since we can hardly attribute the mention of the place-name Gethsemane to Mark's editing, v. 32 would have been the original beginning of the pericope. And since in v. 32 ἔρχονται εἰς χωρίον . . . conflicts[2] with ἐξῆλθον εἰς τὸ ὄρος τῶν ἐλαιῶν in v. 26, we can see that vv. 32–41 is an individual story that was not originally meant for its present context in Mark. Finally, in vv. 35f. there are two variants of the prayer brought together: καὶ προσηύχετο ἵνα . . . and καὶ ἔλεγεν . . .; Matthew and Luke each corrects this in his own way. The second version where the prayer is given in direct speech is, according to the analogies, the secondary, see below. It is characteristic for the history of the tradition that Luke or his copyist has expanded the scene by the wholly legendary section Lk. 22⁴³f.

Mk. 14⁴³⁻⁵² par.: *The Arrest*. After the passage we have just considered this section originally constituted the sequel to vv. 27–31, and describes the fulfilment of the first part of Jesus' prophecy: πάντες σκανδαλισθήσεσθε. Even this piece of narrative is coloured by legend in the motif of the betrayal by a kiss and in what Jesus says in vv. 48f., which sounds very much like Church apologetics and dog-

---

[1] Naturally we cannot appeal to Justin, *Dial.* 99, p. 326a, where only the three disciples are mentioned.
[2] E. Meyer pointed this out in *Ursprung u. Anf. des Christent.*, I, p. 148.2.

matics. 'The reproach in vv. 48f. ill suits the officers' (Klostermann); hence Luke gives it another audience in 22⁵². Presumably vv. 48f. have displaced something original, which provided a better motivation for v. 50 than we now have. For who are the πάντες who flee in v. 50? In terms of the context it is the μαθηταί; but why is that not stated? Were others originally the subject? Why was Jesus the only one to be arrested? Was there no intention to arrest his companions, or did they frustrate that intention by flight? Like v. 50, v. 51 seems to be a fragment of an old Tradition; Matthew and Luke no longer understood it.[1]

Matthew and Luke show how the legendary element grows. Matthew has inserted in 26⁵²⁻⁵⁴ an edifying discourse by Jesus which is very much out of place; perhaps it makes use of a logion from the tradition; cp. Rev. 13¹⁰. Luke 22⁵¹ reports the healing of the ear that was cut off, and tells us it was the right ear. Lastly, we learn from John (18¹⁰) the name of the disciple who cut the ear off, and of his victim as well.

Mk. 14⁵³⁻⁵⁴, ⁶⁶⁻⁷² par. and Lk. 22⁵⁴⁻⁶²: *Peter's Denial*. Mark's account provides the fulfilment of the second part of the prophecy in vv. 27–31; it would have followed immediately on vv. 43–52 in an earlier stage of the tradition, as it does in Luke's order, who seems to have made use of an older tradition at this point alongside Mark. In any case Mk. 14⁵⁵⁻⁶⁴ has been inserted into the story of Peter. We can hardly say with any certainty how far Lk. 22⁵⁴⁻⁶² faithfully reproduces the older version, or how far he has allowed himself to be influenced by Mark, or how much he has added on his own. The appearance of the servants in vv. 58 and 59 could well be due to his editorial work; as perhaps could the feature in v. 58 that Peter did not leave the αὐλή; but, finally, we can be sure of the look of Jesus in v. 61. The story of Peter is itself legendary and literary. The tradition which lies behind Lk. 22³¹ᶠ·, as we have shown, was unaware of this legend.[2]

Mk. 14⁵⁵⁻⁶⁴ par.: *Trial and Judgement by the Sanhedrin*. I think the

---

[1] Hence it seems to me improbable that the scene comes from the proof of prophecy (Am. 2¹⁶); Matthew would at least have understood that. Naturally the feature of the young man leaving his cloak behind can be a 'popular flight motif' (Bertram, *Leidensgesch.*, p. 91.4); but that does not explain the origin of the episode about the young man.

[2] W. Brandt's argument (*Die evang. Geschichte*, 1893, pp. 32–35) is in my opinion untenable. He holds that the cock is unhistorical on the grounds of Rabbinic statements that the keeping of hens was forbidden in Jerusalem, but that the time indicated by the ἀλεκτοροφωνία is genuine. The story has been woven round the statement that Peter denied Jesus 'at cockcrow'. Strack-B. I, 992f. shows that the rearing of hens in Jerusalem was forbidden in Jerusalem in Jesus' lifetime, though it was usual elsewhere in Palestine. But 'the Sadducees and the people were hardly concerned about such regulations', Dalman, *Orte u. Wege Jesu³*, 1924, p. 299.9. That the cock's role comes from some superstition where it heralds misfortune (Petron. 74) can hardly be accepted.

whole narrative in Mark is a secondary explanation of the brief state-ment in 15 ¹. Its insertion into the close context of the story of Peter, its supposed absence from Luke's other source (see below),¹ the improbability of the procuring of witnesses and the proceedings by night all prove this,² even if we may not without further ado draw literary consequences from criticism of subject-matter. The account is not an unity in itself. The High Priest's question in v. 60: οὐκ ἀποκρίνῃ οὐδέν κτλ is unmotivated after v. 59 where the failure of the witnesses is established.³ Wellhausen amongst others thinks vv. 61b, 62 is a secondary addition and v. 63 must follow on from v. 61a and refer to the blasphemy of the saying about the Temple. But to base the view that Jesus' confession of his Messiahship could not have led to his condemnation on the grounds of a critique of subject-matter does not permit any literary consequences for itself alone. In the first place we have to ask: not, what can be thought of as historical? but: what is intelligible as tradition in the Christian Church? And this question must be put before or after the question as to historical possibility as each individual case requires. For the later Christian tradition, from which at all events this story comes, Jesus' Messianic claim, which was the chief issue between the Church and Judaism, could very well appear to be the ground of his condemnation. And other analyses are possible. We can be sure that the two charges in vv. 58 and 61 are doublets; and the fact that witnesses were not called for Jesus' Messianic claim as they were for his saying about the Temple seems, in my view, to show that the two accusations did not belong together originally. But, since vv. 57–59 is a particularization of v. 56, and since v. 59 is a feeble and senseless repetition of the motif of v. 56, I hold that vv. 57–59 are secondary,⁴ and believe that the story originally was intended to record that Jesus was condemned on account of his Messianic claim.⁵

¹ W. Bussmann, *Synopt. Studien*, I, p. 16 indeed believes that Mk. 14⁵⁵⁻⁶¹ᵃ was missing from the text of Mark used by Luke. But if Lk. 22⁷¹ reproduces Mk. 14⁶³ which in turn presupposes vv. 55–59, Luke would at least have read Mk. 14⁵⁵.
² It has often been shown that the description contradicts in all essential points the regulations for trials as modified in the Mishna, cp. esp. G. Hoelscher, *Sanhedrin u. Makkot* (ausgew. Mishnatraktate 6), 1910, pp. 33–35; Strack-B. I, 1020–4. Even if we do not know how far Mishnaic law obtained in Jesus' time, we must not even then underrate the contradiction. While Strack-B. criticizes the proceedings described in the Synoptics as 'wicked perversion of the law' from the standpoint of the Mishna, Dalman, *Jesus-Jeschua*, pp. 91–93 thinks it can be justified. Also H. Lietzmann ('Der Prozess Jesu', *S.B.A.*, 1931, XIV) thinks Mk. 14⁵⁵⁻⁶⁴ is a legend.
³ Cp. B. Bertram, *Leidensgesch.*, p. 58.
⁴ Cp. E. Wendling, *Entstehung des Markus-Evangeliums*, p. 173.
⁵ R. Reitzenstein proposes a quite new understanding of the transactions of the San-hedrin (*Das mand. Buch d. Herrn d. Groesse*, pp. 67–70) which makes Mark's story appear as an unity. The charges of speaking of destroying the Temple and of making Messianic claims can be understood as one charge on the basis of the belief in the 'Primordial Man'

Lk. 22⁶⁶⁻⁷¹ combines Mark's account of the Trial with his own source which appears in v. 66 (corresponding to Mk. 15¹)—Luke has no special source for the Trial; it is much more a matter of editorial work in this section. The phrase in v. 71 τί ἔτι ἔχομεν μαρτυρίας χρείαν shows clearly that Luke had at least read part of the section Mk. 14⁵⁵⁻⁶¹ᵃ which he does not reproduce; at most it is possible that the verses Mk. 14⁵⁷⁻⁵⁹ were absent from Luke's copy of Mark. Yet Luke could also have detected them for apologetic reasons, in the same way that he omits the motif of the prophecy about destroying the Temple (Mk. 15²⁹) in 23³⁵⁻³⁷.¹ The μαρτυρία in v. 71, the lack of context for v. 69, the fact that Luke has forgotten to report the condemnation—all these things indicate the editorial character of the section. Similarly the fact that there is no appearance of the High Priest, and that the question about Messiahship is formulated differently from Mark rest on editorial activity. In Matthew's editing it is characteristic that in 26⁶³ he should introduce an oath into his formulation of the High Priest's words.

Mk. 14⁶⁵ par. and Lk. 22⁶³⁻⁶⁵: *The Ill-treatment of Jesus.* This is a piece of the tradition that is somewhat scattered, and Mark has put it at a peculiarly unfortunate place. It must have been a part of an older narrative which Luke obviously makes use of from another source. In an earlier stage of the tradition it may have followed on the Arrest, where it still stands in Luke.² For the rest only v. 63 in Luke comes from his alternative source; v. 64 is due to Mark's influence (τίς ἐστιν ὁ παίσας σε is in all probability a wholly secondary conformation to Matthew) and v. 65 is Luke's own formulation (cp. 3¹⁸, 21³⁷f.).

---

which Reitzenstein thinks was an article of faith in the Baptist Sect, on the basis of a Mandaean Apocalypse: the heavenly 'Man' is precisely the one who will destroy the Temple at his 'appearing'. The basis of Jesus' condemnation was his admittedly not obvious confession of this belief in the 'Primordial Man'. Now I hold it possible for the saying about the destruction and rebuilding of the Temple to have come from the myth of the Son of Man (see p. 120). But this interpretation clearly is not behind the text of Mark. If it were, there would be no reason at all for putting in v. 59, and v. 60 would have to follow v. 58. Moreover the High Priest's question in v. 61a would not only refer to v. 58 (by something like δή or ἄρα) but above everything else would have to contain the term ὁ υἱὸς τοῦ ἀνθρώπου as Bousset, *Kyrios Christos*², p. 39 has rightly emphasized. But finally the story as we have it puts the first charge as part of the false witness, while it admits the second! So for this reason it is not even probable that the conceptual unity of Temple Destruction and Primordial Man was dominant for the interpolator of vv. 57–59. Rather is it at most possible that vv. 57–59 is a protest against the application of the Baptist idea of Man to Jesus; cp. Bousset, op. cit. and M. Goguel, *Jean-Baptiste*, pp. 128–35. Cp. H. Lietzmann, op. cit., p. 6.

¹ Cp. M. Goguel, *Jean-Baptiste*, pp. 130–2.

² I doubt whether it is right to accept the view that the motif of προφήτευσον derives from an Hellenistic custom of mocking slaves (G. Rudberg, *Z.N.W.*, 24, 1925, pp. 307–9). More probably there is some custom of a game behind it. Cp. W. C. van Unnik, *Z.N.W.*, 29, 1930, pp. 310f.

Mk. 15$^{1-27}$ par.: *Delivery to Pilate, Sentence and Crucifixion*.[1] This is by no means an unitary composition. In vv. 1–5 there is a tension, as has been seen for a long time, between v. 2 and vv. 3–5, and v. 2 is secondary too. The purpose of this addition is clear: as in the secondary narrative in 14$^{55-64}$ the description has to be presented from the standpoint that Jesus was executed for his Messianic claims.

Moreover the episode of Barabbas is obviously a legendary expansion, the extent of which cannot be quite precisely determined (about vv. 6–15a); it exhibits (v. 12) the same outlook as the editorial material in vv. 2 and 26.[2] Finally the mocking in vv. 16–20a is a secondary explanation of v. 15b (φραγελλώσας) to which some traditional military custom lent some colour.[3]

Of the decisive Trial by the Sanhedrin Mark has preserved no older account than that in 15^{1} and perhaps the parallel in Lk. 22^{66} is even older. But for the trial before Pilate Luke has not preserved an older account, but simply produces an edited version of Mark which is principally governed by the feeling that the hierarchy would have had to advance a proper accusation against Jesus. Matthew also offers us a revision of Mark, enlarged by a few legendary features: 27^{19} Pilate's wife, 27^{24} Pilate's washing of his hands.

Apart from this Matthew and Luke introduce some more extensive and likewise purely legendary features: Matthew has introduced the death of Judas in 27$^{3-10}$, behind which lie Acts 1$^{8f.}$ and variants in the well-known Papias fragment. Matthew's version has perhaps taken shape by the transferring of an aetiological saga to Judas, and in any case under the influence of Zech. 11$^{12f.}$.[4] Its literary form may well be due to Matthew; I do not think it necessary to postulate a

---

[1] G. Aicher, *Der Prozess Jesu*, 1929, has no importance because it is without any critical sense.

[2] There is no evidence in either Jewish or Roman law for the custom to which Mk. 15^{6} refers. The custom at Roman lectisternia to which Hugo Grotius referred as an analogy, is not relevant, chiefly because that was concerned with mass pardons. Cp. esp. J. Merkel, *Z.N.W.*, 6, 1905, pp. 293–316. Naturally it is possible that a Governor would pardon a particular criminal because of the acclamation of the people (there is an example in Pap. Flor. 61.59ff. in A.D. 85, in Deissmann, *Light from the Ancient East*, 267). W. Brandt in *Die Evang. Geschichte*, 1893, pp. 102–5 had already conjectured that some historical incident of this kind had been joined with the Church's Tradition of Jesus' condemnation. Cp. Klostermann.

[3] H. Reich, 'Der Koenig mit der Dornenkrone', *Neue Jahrb. f. Phil.*, 1904, pp. 705ff.; P. Wendland, 'Jesus als Saturnalienkoenig', *Hermes* 33, 1898, pp. 175ff.; H. Vollmer, *Jesus und das Sacaeenopfer*, 1905; J. Geffcken, 'Die Verhoehnung Christi durch die Kriegsknechte', *Hermes* 41, 1906, pp. 220ff. The literature up to 1905 is cited in H. Vollmer, 'Der Koenig mit der Dornenkrone', *Z.N.W.*, 6, 1905, pp. 194ff.; also 8, 1907, pp. 320f. More recent literature in Klostermann; also T. Birt, *Aus dem Leben der Antike*^{3}, 1922, pp. 189–202, and *Philologus* 77, 1921, pp. 427f.; G. Bertram, *Die Leidensgeschichte Jesu*, pp. 72f.; L. Radermacher, *Arch. f. R.-W.* 28, 1930, pp. 31–35.

[4] Cp. Klostermann and F. K. Feigel, *Der Einfluss des Weissagungsbeweises u. anderer Motive auf die Leidensgeschichte*, 1910, pp. 43–46.

semitic original as the source of particulars like κορβανᾶς in v. 6 and
ἀπελθών in v. 5. The episode of Herod and Pilate which Luke introduces (23 ⁶⁻¹⁶) is a legend that has developed out of Ps. 2 ¹ᶠ·, in which
Herod and Pilate are seen as representing the βασιλεῖς and ἄρχοντες
who in the Psalm plot against the Lord's anointed; cp. Acts 4 ²⁷.¹

In Mark's story of the Crucifixion there is a legendary editing of
what is manifestly an ancient historical narrative to which we may
trace back vv. 20b–24a. We have already discussed v. 26 (p. 272),
and v. 24 (from καὶ διαμερίζονται onwards) comes from prophecy
(Ps. 21 ¹⁹). The time reference in v. 25 will be due to Mark's editing;
καὶ ἐσταύρωσαν αὐτόν is a doublet of σταυροῦσιν αὐτόν in v. 24. (D
corrects this in v. 25, cp. Matt. 26 ³⁶.) I do not presume to say
whether v. 28 also comes from prophecy (Isa. 53 ¹², cp. Lk. 22 ³⁷ᵃ).
Under the influence of prophecy (Ps. 68 ²²) Matt. 27 ³⁴ changes the
statement about wine and myrrh in Mk. 15 ²³. Luke has added (see
pp. 37f., 115f.) to the story of the road to the cross by the legendary
item in 23 ²⁷⁻³¹ (The Women of Jerusalem). Finally in a series of
manuscripts of Luke the Crucifixion itself is adorned by a legendary
feature (the intercession for his enemies 23 ³⁴).²

Mk. 15 ²⁹⁻³² par.: *The Mocking of the Crucified.* This is a legendary
formulation on the basis of a prophetic proof (Ps. 21 ⁸; Lam. 2 ¹⁵).
Indeed v. 29 and v. 31 are doublets, v. 31 being the later; for these
elements are characteristic. (1) The appearance of ἀρχιερεῖς and
γραμματεῖς who are typical opponents of Jesus in the secondary
tradition (see pp. 52f.). (2) Jesus being mocked as Messiah, which is a
further expression of the outlook of secondary tradition that he was
crucified as the Messiah. Matthew and Luke had the Mark story
before them with only immaterial editorial changes.

Mk. 15 ³³⁻³⁹ par.: *The Death of Jesus.* This account is strongly dis-
figured by legend. Clearly v. 34 is a secondary interpretation of the
cry of Jesus in v. 37 (πάλιν is missing in v. 37 though Matthew adds
it!) on the basis of Ps. 21 ². That in turn shows that vv. 35, 36b is
secondary. We can leave undecided whether v. 36a is an earlier or a
later addition;³ in any case this section is legendary, and is based upon
Ps. 68 ²². On the other hand vv. 33 and 38 go together: the τέρατα at
the death of Jesus and their impression on the Gentile onlookers. We

---

¹ M. Dibelius, 'Herodes und Pilatus,' *Z.N.W.*, 16, 1915, pp. 113ff.
² Cp. besides Klostermann: G. Bertram, *Die Leidensgesch. Jesu*, pp. 87f. Merx thinks
that an agraphon was inserted in v. 34: at least an ancient Jewish Christian saying could
be the basis of it. Cp. Dalman, *Jesus-Jeschua*, p. 177, and Strack-B. II, 264. On the problem of textual criticism cp. Harnack, *S.B.A.*, 1901, pp. 251ff and B. H. Streeter, *The Four
Gospels*, p. 138.
³ According to W. Bussmann, *Synopt. Studien*, I, pp. 19f. vv. 34–36 were lacking in
Ur-Mark.

cannot view this as ancient report, but only as Christian legend. It may be supposed that v. 39 originally went with v. 37 because ἰδὼν . . . ὅτι οὕτως ἐξέπνευσεν refers to ὁ δὲ Ἰησοῦς . . . ἐξέπνευσεν. But what is meant by οὕτως is in all probability the τέρας in v. 33 (and v. 38?),[1] so that v. 39 is also part of the legendary development. The time reference in vv. 33, 34 is the editorial work of Mark, as it is also in v. 25. It is impossible to say whether the one neutral v. 37 ever had a place in an older (relatively) legend-free tradition. Again the legendary features are intensified in Matthew by the increase in the number of the τέρατα (27[51b–53]). Luke was offended by the cry of dereliction based on Ps. 21[2] and replaced it in 23[46] by Ps. 30[6], while John gives it a different interpretation.

Mk. 15[40–41] par.: *The Women as Witnesses*. As at the Resurrection women are here named as witnesses. And here they are as little historical as there. They are necessary because the disciples who had fled could not be made to appear. Mk. 15[40f.] has to be taken as an isolated piece of tradition. In Matthew's reproduction at 27[55f.] the mother of Zebedee replaces Salome, just as she is also introduced into Mark's text in Matt. 20[20]. Luke omits the women's names, since he had already stated who the Galilean women were.

Mk. 15[42–47] par.: *The Burial*. This is an historical account which creates no impression of being a legend apart from the women who appear again as witnesses in v. 47, and vv. 44, 45 which Matthew and Luke in all probability did not have in their Mark. It can hardly be shown that the section was devised with the Easter story in mind. The first indication of that cannot be seen before the note in v. 46 that a stone was rolled in front of the entrance to the tomb, though that can also be simply a descriptive touch. The age of the tradition here preserved cannot of course be established.

Matthew makes Joseph of Arimathea a rich man and at the same time a disciple, thinking thereby to interpret Mark's ἦν προσδεχόμενος τὴν βασιλείαν τ. θ. Luke has given an even more detailed description of Joseph and emphasized in particular that he was not a party to the resolution of the Sanhedrin. With his ending of this story Luke has contrived a better connection with the story of Easter morning. Finally Matt. 27[62–66] attaches the legend of the sepulchre guard for apologetic reasons.

---

[1] This is in any case the way Matthew interprets it, for he makes the σεισμός, which he inserts into Mark's text in 51b–53, the occasion of the exclamation of the Centurion and those who were with him. Cp. however Plut., *Cleom.*, c. 39, p. 823e: The information about the τέρας at the crucifixion of Cleomenes has the effect of the executed man being taken for a son of the Gods. (ὡς ἀνδρὸς ἀνηρημένου θεοφιλοῦς καὶ κρείττονος τὴν φύσιν . . ἥρωα τὸν Κλεομένη καὶ θεῶν παῖδα προσαγορεύοντες.)

The History of the Tradition of the Passion

Before I analyse the remaining tradition of legends I will first review the history of the Passion tradition. It cannot be maintained that the Passion story as we have it in the Synoptic gospels is an organic unity. Even here what is offered us is made up of separate pieces. For the most part, though it does not indeed apply to them all, they are not dependent upon their context in the Passion narrative. Thus e.g. the story of the anointing, of the prophecy of the betrayal, of the Last Supper, of Gethsemane, of Peter's Denial. That such stories could be handed down as isolated elements is shown by 1 Cor. 11 23ff.; no context is necessary to understand it; all the necessary information is given in the brief introduction: ἐν τῇ νυκτὶ ᾗ παρεδίδετο, and this presupposes only that the hearer knew the fact of the παραδοθῆναι of Jesus. For such particular stories, once they were joined together into a whole, it was essentially the nature of the facts that determined a particular order. Another set of particular stories admittedly consists of supplementary embellishments of individual moments in a narrative that had already been knit together, as e.g. the stories of the Preparation of the Passover, the Hearing before the Sanhedrin, and of Herod and Pilate. Moreover Mark was not the first to make a continuous narrative from the individual stories available to him, but he had already before him a Passion story that was a continuous narrative. The analysis of the Johannine Passion story will show that John also made use of an older, connected Passion narrative.[1]

Unlike other material in the tradition the Passion narrative was very early fashioned into a coherent form; indeed it can almost be said that the coherence was the primary fact in this case. For what led to a coherent narrative, with which every story of the first group was bound up, and which stories of the second group embellished, was above all the Kerygma, as we know it in the prophecies of the Passion and Resurrection in Mk. 8 31, 9 31, 10 33f. and in the speeches in Acts. We have to reckon this Kerygma as the earliest connected tradition of the Passion and Death of Jesus. But close to it, as the analysis has shown, was a short narrative of historical reminiscence about the Arrest, Condemnation and Execution of Jesus. We must take account of all these four moments in accounting for the emergence of the Synoptic Passion story. Ecclesiastical art at this point bears a certain analogy: the Christian sarcophagi, which carry pictorial representations of a series of biblical (or other) scenes, show no

[1] Cp. M. Dibelius, *Th.R.*, N.F.1, 1929, pp. 192f.

particular order in any cases other than the passion, but make an arbitrary selection. The passion sarcophagi alone have a closed cycle of individual pictures.[1]

The argument for this is provided by the analysis. The first proof that individual stories constitute the main ingredient of the Passion story are the *doublets*: (*a*) The announcement of the betrayal is preserved in two versions: Mk. 14[17-21] and Lk. 22[21-23]. (*b*) Two descriptions of the Last Supper are preserved in Mk. 14[22-25] and Lk. 22[14-18]; and in addition we may note the conflict in Mark between Mk. 14[22-25] and 14[17-21]. (*c*) The foretelling of the disciples' desertion (and Peter's denial) is preserved in two versions: Mk. 14[27-31] and Lk. 22[31f.] (*d*) The trial before the Sanhedrin is preserved in the short note in Mk. 15[1] or Lk. 22[66] and in the fuller report of Mk. 14[55-64]. It is doubtful whether we can reckon as doublets (*e*) the mocking in Mk. 14[65] or Lk. 22[63] and Mk. 15[16-20a].[2] But it is very characteristic that (*f*) Mark in three successive stories mentions by name (and with differences in detail at that!) the women who are eyewitnesses. 15[40f.,] [47], 16[1]. This clearly shows that individual stories have been brought together here.

The second proof is, that Matthew and Luke *introduce new individual items*. This does not take into account the fact that Luke introduces different complexes of dominical sayings (22[24-30] and 22[35-38]), which is always a sign of the looseness of the design. In the same way I pass over the smaller additions which Matthew and Luke have made to the text of Mark. The following are important: (*a*) Matthew has introduced the death of Judas 27[3-10]. (*b*) Luke has divided the trial before Pilate (with a genuine feeling for a real jump in Mark) by inserting the Herod episode in 23[6-16]. (*c*) Luke has added to the journey to the Cross by the story of the women of Jerusalem 23[27-31]. (*d*) Matthew has appended the setting of the sepulchre guard in 27[62-66]. But we must also include the negative moment here as well, that Luke occasionally omits some unit, and so provides us with documentary evidence that Mark's Passion story is not an organic whole. The anointing of Mk. 14[3-9] is lacking in Luke, as is the hearing of the witnesses from Mk. 14[56-61] and the mocking of Jesus from Mk. 15[16-20a].

Now let us ask ourselves whether we are not obliged to apply the conclusion about Matthew and Luke to Mark, and conclude viz.

---

[1] Cp. H. v. Campenhausen, *Die Passionssarkophage*, 1929.

[2] It is characteristic of the interweaving of motifs in the tradition that in the fourth century the Hall where Jesus was beaten was shown on the ostensible site of the Palace of Caiaphas, although, according to the Synoptic account, Jesus was whipped in the Praetorium and not before Caiaphas (G. Dalman, *Orte u. Wege Jesu*[3] ,p. 347).

that he too had a narrative before him and expanded it by additions.[1] And we may seek to discern what can be validly accepted as a more original draft from such an *analysis of* Mark. (*a*) No doubt 14^{3-9} is an insertion, which interrupts the context, and contains a story specially made to fit the context. (*b*) The institution of the Lord's Supper in 14^{22-25} has been recognized as a secondary cult legend inserted into an older context, and in all probability it has displaced an older account. (*c*) As we have seen, the scene in Gethsemane marks (14^{32-42}) itself off from its context; it can then be dropped by John without damage to his general plan. (*d*) The detailed report of the trial before the Sanhedrin in 14^{55-64} breaks into the story of Peter. (*e*) The Barabbas episode in 15^{6-15a} is distinct from the trial before Pilate. (*f*) The mocking of Jesus in 15^{16-20a} is an insertion which expounds the motif of φραγελλώσας in 15^{15b}. If this section were partly or wholly absent from 'Ur-Mk' that would but confirm the judgement. Apart from these individual instances it is significant that the story of Peter's denial is not organically related to the overall design. Of course its following on the arrest is appropriate enough; it also comes absolutely to an end with 14^{72}. But if it were really organic with the context of the Passion story, it would have to be stated where Peter stayed. Did he still remain secretly close at hand? Did he flee to Galilee? That gives rise to further questions: Did Peter not try to meet the other disciples? Where did they stay? By rights their flight to Galilee, which, on the basis of 14^{28}, 16^{7} cannot be doubted, should have been reported.

If we ask *whether what remains constitutes a narrative complete in itself*, the answer is strictly negative. Mk. $14^{1f.,\ 10f.}$ has admittedly been handed down as an individual unit, but it presupposes a continuation. This is not to be found in vv. 12–16 and 17–21 because (1) otherwise we should have to be told why the arrest was so delayed that Jesus could celebrate the Passover after all, as vv. 12–16 presupposes. Because (2) in vv. 17–21 the betrayal has not yet taken place, Judas is still thought of as a table companion, and his departure is not recorded. But neither does $14^{1f.,\ 10f.}$ find any organic continuation in the following units. As the betrayer appears in Gethsemane in $14^{43f.}$ there is no reference to vv. 10f., but he is introduced as εἷς τῶν δώδεκα! It might also perhaps be expected in an organic narrative to find the appointment of a sign narrated in connection with vv. 10f. So Mk. $14^{1f.,\ 10f.}$ has to be taken as a secondary introduction to a collection of stories which Mark admittedly had before him and into which he inserted vv. 3–9.

[1] So, rightly, A. Meyer, *Festg. f. A. Juelicher*, pp. 47f.

The *Last Supper* forms the mid-point of a specific complex; certainly not Mk. 14[22-25], but a narrative displaced by it, which Luke 22[14-18] has better preserved and is echoed in Mk. 14[25]. Around this centre-piece are grouped the preparation Mk. 14[12-16], the foretelling of the betrayal 14[17-21] and the journey to Gethsemane with the prophecy of the disciples' desertion and Peter's denial in 14[26-31]. But this complex is not an organic unity. In this first place 14[17-21] stands out as an originally separate unit of the tradition, as it occurs in Luke in another place (22[21-23]) and further, as has been shown, Mk. 14[27-31] is only joined to the Last Supper by the transition verse of the editor. So outside the supper itself there remains only 14[12-16], which cannot have been an independent unit, but was composed for the sake of what followed. But if the position adopted on pp. 266f. above is right, that the Last Supper was not, as vv. 12–16 presupposes, a Passover meal, a position which has strong reasons of another kind to support it, then vv. 12–16 is an additional introduction composed for the Last Supper, and so at the beginning of the literary process there stands a particular individual unit which recounted the story of the Last Supper. It is a secondary question how far the whole complex was already in front of Mark. In my view it cannot be answered with any certainty. It is possible that he had the whole section as we know it (ὑμνήσαντες in v. 26 supports that, as it presupposes a preceding Passover celebration which had not been recounted in vv. 22–25) and that he only put vv. 22–25 in the place of an older report.

A connected piece consists of Mk. 14[53f., 66-72]: *Peter's Following and Denial*. But this could not originally have belonged organically to the Passion Narrative, for, as shown on p. 269, it is well enough linked with what precedes, but not at all with what comes after it. Moreover Lk. 22[31f.] shows that the legend of the betrayal did not always belong to the Passion story (p. 267); and lastly, the Peter episode would hardly have taken up so much space in an old presentation of the Passion and death of Jesus. But Mk. 14[27-31] goes with this passage (though naturally the secondary v. 28 is not included) since it contains the prophecy of the denial. While that does not exhaust the contents of vv. 27–31, it serves at the same time as an introduction to the *Arrest* in vv. 43–52. In turn this is a necessary presupposition to vv. 53f., 66–72, which must have been already current, and the common introduction vv. 27–31 must have been written at the time of its combination with the Petrine story. But is the arrest itself an independent narrative, or did it from the beginning form part of a larger context? As far as its beginning is concerned an introduction is not necessary; it could well have begun: 'As Jesus, on the night he was betrayed, was on the Mount of Olives, Judas came . . .'

But it is highly probable that the arrest originally had a sequel in which *Jesus was taken away and sentenced*. This could well have been contained in 14^{53a} and also perhaps 14^{65} and in any case in the original basis of 15^{1-5}. The end of the trial before Pilate has been displaced by the Barabbas episode; v. 15b will be a residual piece of the original. To this would be attached the story of the leading away to the crucifixion and the execution itself in vv. 15, 20b–24a and perhaps (27 and) 37. All these items are not stories as such, but an historical narrative that is told in short statements.

So I assume that there was a *primitive narrative* which told very briefly of the arrest, the condemnation by the Sanhedrin and Pilate, the journey to the cross, the crucifixion and death. This was developed at various stages, in part by earlier stories that were available and in part by forms that had newly appeared. It was enlarged by the story of Peter and furnished with one introduction preparing the way for both elements; Mk. 14^{27-31}. Further, it was joined (through Mk. 14^{26}) with a complex of stories that gathered around the Last Supper, and then received a further introduction in Mk. $14^{1f.}$, $^{10f.}$ Still later Mk. 14^{3-9}, $^{32-42}$ and in all probability vv. 55–64 were inserted. It is no longer possible to say at what stage the account of the crucifixion was fashioned, or the closing section in $15^{40f.}$, $^{42-47}$ was added.

Since Luke seems in many places to be following another source, the attempt can be made to see whether a similar basic narrative can be constructed from his material.[1] At first Luke follows Mark completely. For the Last Supper in 22^{14-18} he has another and indeed an older report than Mark and the question must be asked whether he had this report in a context like that in which it appears in Mark. But that can hardly be so, for in the preparation of the Supper (22^{7-13}) he obviously follows Mark, and so in all likelihood read this passage in his special source, from which he derived 22^{14-18}, without such an introduction. Further, the prophecy of the betrayal did not even precede the Supper here, but had absolutely no connection with it at all, for the connecting word πλήν (22^{21}) is a specifically Lucan linking formula (cp. 6^{24}, ^{35}, 13^{33}, 18^{8b}, etc.). Mark has been the cause of Luke combining this unit of tradition with the Last Supper but Luke has more skilfully subordinated it to the description of the Supper itself. No sure decision is possible about the following items:

[1] H. Lietzmann disputes the view that Luke contains any sort of special tradition (op. cit. pp. 3f.).

vv. 24–30 (Sayings about Precedence), vv. 31–34 (Prophecy of Disciples' Flight and Peter's Denial) and vv. 35 to 38 (Saying about the Sword); yet it is probable their placing is due to Luke's editing, though in doing that he relied on Mark again for the second item. As his custom was he has put into the Supper what can be put there, i.e., apart from the sayings of Jesus, items which have their parallels in Mk. 14$^{17-21, 27-31}$. Hence in 22^{39} (following Mk. 14^{26}) he can make Jesus arrive straightaway at the scene of the arrest. Then following Mark he places the scene in Gethsemane next, 22$^{40-46}$. This is as little a special Lucan report alongside Mark as is the arrest in 22$^{47-53}$. On the other hand in 22$^{54-71}$ he has joined another report to his Mark source: the Peter episode is not divided by the trial before the Sanhedrin by night; the ill treatment of Jesus is rightly placed on the following morning. But again the report of the trial is admittedly influenced by Mark. The story of Pilate Luke has so altered by his own editing and by introducing new material that it can no longer be determined to what extent he had another ancient source alongside Mark. There may well be other reasons why Mk. 15$^{16-20}$ is missing. Nor do the differences in the story of the crucifixion prove anything of a special Lucan source.

So Luke is more useful in confirming certain critical observations in the analysis of Mark than in reconstructing an older Passion narrative. In addition to Mark he had before him as individual elements of tradition accounts of the Last Supper, and the prophecy of the betrayal as of the disciples' flight (22$^{14-18, 21, 31f.}$). Besides these he used in addition to Mark, an account of Peter's denial and of the trial before the Sanhedrin. This must have gone back to include the arrest and continued to include Pilate's condemnation and the crucifixion. Nevertheless since no source can be discovered parallel to Mark the most probable thing is that Luke made use, alongside Mark, of another—and probably older—edition of the Passion narrative used by Mark. This is supported by the close relationship between Luke's and Mark's accounts of the denial.

We may summarize by noting the most important motifs that have made up the legend of the Passion story.[1] In the first place there is the *proof from prophecy*; as that had to help the Church solve the problem of a crucified Messiah, so it helped to fashion the telling of the Passion story. I can quote only the most important instances here.[2]

---

[1] For this G. Bertram's book, *Die Leidensgeschichte Jesu und der Christuskult*, 1922, is the most important. Unfortunately the author has a too imprecise concept of cult, and fails to distinguish the different motifs adequately.

[2] Cp. besides F. Strauss, *Leben Jesu*, esp. F. K. Feigel, *Der Einfluss des Weissagungsbeweises und anderer Motive auf die Leidensgeschichte*, 1910; K. Weidel, 'Studien ueber den Einfluss des

The story of the betrayal has at the least been enriched from the O.T. and possibly undergone quite radical development. From Zech. 11^{12} Matthew has taken the amount of blood-money, and tells the story of Judas' death (26^{15}, 27$^{3-10}$) under the influence of Zech. 11$^{12f.}$ But previously the announcement of the betrayal in Mk. 14^{18} had been affected by Ps. 40^{10} (cp. Jn. 13^{18}, where the passage is actually cited); even if the fact that Jesus was betrayed by an individual whose name might be Judas was not derived from this quotation from the Psalm, at any rate there came the idea of the betrayer having been one of Jesus' table companions and one of the Twelve. And even about Judas' kiss we have to ask whether it did not originate from 2 Sam. 20^9 (Prov. 27^6). The mocking in Mk. 14^{65} seems to have been coloured by Isa. 50^6. The episode of Pilate and Herod is the fulfilment of Ps. 2$^{1f.}$ (Lk. 23$^{6-12}$). And most of all, the picture of the crucifixion has been enriched with features drawn from the O.T. The statement that Jesus was crucified between two criminals (Mk. 15^{27}) may have been derived from Isa. 53^{12} (cp. Lk. 22^{37a}). In any case Mark derives the lottery for the garments (15^{24}) from Ps. 21^{19} (a verse which Jn. 19$^{23f.}$, taking the *parallel. membrorum* more literally, develops into a differential treatment of the ἱμάτια and the χιτών); the mocking of the passers-by (15^{29}) from Ps. 21^8, the interpretation of Jesus' last cry (15^{34}) from Ps. 21^2; the drinking of vinegar (15^{36}) from Ps. 68^{22}. In Matthew the influence of the O.T. goes still further. Even in 27^{34} before the crucifixion he has Jesus offered myrrh and wine, on the basis of Ps. 68^{22}; his account of the mockery of the hierarchy (27^{34}) is coloured by Ps. 21^9. Luke formulated Jesus' last cry (23^{46}) on the basis of Ps. 30^6, and added the γνωστοί of Jesus to the women who were at the cross (23^{49}), following Ps. 37^{12}, 87^9. It is not possible to ask about any of these features whether they grew up on Palestinian or Hellenistic soil. Without doubt proof from prophecy already figured in the Palestinian Church; and just as surely it would have been used in the Hellenistic Church.

If the features taken from the O.T., in so far as they are meant to prove the fulfilment of prophecy, are thus in a certain sense apologetic and dogmatic—though we should at the same time recognize their edifying and novel-like character—there are also legendary characteristics of another kind which have a specifically *apologetic motive*. The prophecy of the betrayal and the story of the sepulchre guard in Matt. 27$^{62-66}$ are due to the apologetic motive. And here and there

Weissagungsbeweises auf die evangelische Geschichte', *T.S.K.* 23, 1910, pp. 83–109, 163–194; 25, 1912, pp. 167–286; v. Ungern-Sternberg, *Der traditionelle alttest. Schriftbeweis 'De Christo' und 'De Evangelio' in der alten Kirche*, 1913; W. Bousset, *Juedisch-Christlicher Schulbetrieb in Alexandrien*, 1915, pp. 302f.

K

we find smaller elements with an apologetic interest. Such are Mk. 14[48f.]: the reproach for the arrest by night; Matt. 26[52-54]: the forbidding of armed defence and the emphasis on Jesus' voluntary surrender (a motif which is expressed even more strongly in Jn. 10[18], 18[7], 19[11]). Further apologetic grounds underlie those features which acquit the Romans and place all responsibility on the Jews;[1] this is found as early as Mark in the report of Pilate's struggle against the Sentencing of Jesus. Luke is even more emphatic in making Pilate emphasize the innocence of Jesus (23[4, 14, 20, 22]; Herod has to affirm it too 23[15]); Pilate tries to let Jesus off with a mere flogging (23[16-22]) and finally we read in 23[25]: τὸν δὲ Ἰησοῦν παρέδωκεν τῷ θελήματι αὐτῶν. Matthew too has added similar touches: Pilate's wife's dream 27[19];[2] Pilate's handwashing, including the Jews' cry: 27[24f.]: τὸ αἷμα αὐτοῦ ἐφ᾽ ἡμᾶς καὶ ἐπὶ τὰ τέκνα ἡμῶν. The last instance, the accusation and the ominous prophecy of retribution, Luke has put into an independent section 23[27-31].

Besides this we can discern some *pure novelistic motifs*. To this class belong the τέρατα accompanying Jesus' death, Mk. 15[33, 38]; Matt. 27[51b-53]. To what extent these τέρατα are of Jewish- or Hellenistic-Christian origin can perhaps be decided when the history of τέρατα has been more accurately studied. Many parallels to the synoptic τέρατα have frequently been quoted from Hellenism.[3] But Judaism itself told of miraculous happenings at the death of Rabbis and recounted prodigies which announced the destruction of the Temple.[4] The motif of the centurion by the cross in Mk. 15[39] has its parallels in the literature of martyrdom.[5] Some of Luke's material belongs here too; admittedly Lk. 22[43f.] (Jesus' strengthening by an angel) may well be a later insertion into Luke's text; and the same applies to 23[34] (the prayer for his executioners). But the healing of the

---

[1] Cp. H. Lietzmann, op. cit., pp. 11f.

[2] Behind this concise story there is manifestly a more extensive legend, for 'the Christian who first told the story of Pilate's wife, naturally knew about the content of the dream, and perhaps also about the result of the intervention'. (M. Dibelius, *Th.R.*, N.F.1, 1929, p. 207.)

[3] Material is given in the commentaries; cp. Wetstein. There is a host of prodigies from A. Gercke in Fleckeisen's *Jahrb. f. klass. Phil.*, Suppl. XXII, 1896, pp. 205ff. There is a wealth of material from the history of Religion in general (including the Jewish and Christian Traditions) in P. Saintyves, *Essais de Folklore Biblique*, 1923, pp. 423–63; according to Saintyves the motif of '*émoi des élements*' is characteristic of the death of the cosmic god; but the author clearly goes too far in ascribing to the synoptics the idea of Christ as the '*âme du monde*'.

[4] Cp. Strack-B. I, 1040f., 1045f.; G. Dalman, *Jesus-Jeschua*, p. 198; P. Fiebig, *Jued. Wundergesch.*, pp. 28f., 57–59; Saintyves (see preceding note), p. 431.

[5] The attitude of Rabbi Hanina b. Teradion at his martyrdom so overcame his executioner, that he went with him to his death in the flames: cp. Fiebig, *Jued. Wundergesch.*, pp. 41–43; Strack-B. I, 223. Examples of the conversion of executioners by Christian martyrs are cited in Harnack, *Militia Christi*, 1905, p. 75, and of the acclamation of the public at a martyr's death in E. Peterson, Εἷς θεός, 1926, pp. 184f. See above, p. 274, n. 1.

ear cut off from the servant of the High Priest goes back to Luke himself (22⁵¹, still more detailed in D), Jesus' moving glance at Peter in the story of the denial 22⁶¹, the forgiveness of one of the thieves 23³⁹⁻⁴³ and the scene in 23⁴⁸: 'And all the people that came together to that sight, beholding the things that were done, smote their breasts and returned,' which gets expanded in the manuscript tradition in various ways. As the textual tradition itself shows the growth of the legend, so do the later gospels. John knows in 18¹⁰ that it was Peter who drew his sword in Gethsemane, and that his victim was called Malchus; in 19³⁷ he knows the exact quantities of myrrh and aloes that were used at the embalming of Jesus. The Gospel of Peter e.g. has developed the motif of the two thieves and the theme of the sepulchre guard, etc.; in short the tendency of the tradition is plain. But the scene of Judas' kiss in Mk. 14⁴⁴ᶠ· must also be dealt with here, a scene which was evidently demanded by the need to envisage the infamous betrayal in a concrete way. For the same reason Mark has to make the three disciples sleep in 14³⁷ᶠᶠ·; the contrast between their dullness and Jesus' anxiety about death comes in this way to its highest point. A similar climax in contrast is reached in the Barabbas episode: The people, faced with the choice, decided in favour of the criminal and handed Jesus over to the executioner, Mr. 15⁶ᶠᶠ· So it is quite understandable that from the at first general description of the betrayer as the one ἐσθίων μετ' ἐμοῦ (Mk. 14¹⁸) should have developed the story of the prophecy at the meal. And the replacement of the more general ὁ ἐμβαπτόμενος μετ' ἐμοῦ (Mk. 14²⁰) by ὁ ἐμβάψας (Matt. 26²³) is a clear demonstration of the tendency to fill out the concrete act.[1] A decree of Hypatius of Ephesus ($Z.N.W.$, 26, 1927, p. 213) refers to a Παράδοσις in which the body of Jesus was thrown away naked and unburied before Joseph of Arimathea gave it burial.

Many of the passages now treated serve incidental *paraenetic* purposes, as Matt. 26⁵² (Forbidding Resistance) and Lk. 23³⁴ (Prayer for the Executioner) Lk. 23⁴⁰⁻⁴³ is the example of repentance at death. The fashioning of the Prophecy of the Betrayal can also be dealt with here: the question μήτι ἐγώ; should be a point of self-examination for every Christian. The motif finds independent expression in the addition of Mk. 14³⁸ to the Gethsemane story: γρηγορεῖτε καὶ προσεύχεσθε κτλ.

Dogmatic motifs are of particular importance. As it produced particular stories, the faith of the Christian Church brought the whole

---

[1] Cp. also F. K. Feigel, *Der Einfluss des Weissagungsbeweises und anderer Motive auf die Leidensgeschichte*, 1910, pp. 104ff.

Passion under the regulative idea that Jesus suffered and died as the Messiah. And it is particularly interesting to see how this motif took effect in a gradual development. As Mk. 14³²⁻⁴² (Gethsemane) and 14⁵⁵⁻⁶⁴ (Trial before the Sanhedrin) belong to a later stage of the tradition we can see the story continually getting enriched by gradual stages with correspondingly particular features. In the trial before Pilate Mk. 15² is an inserted verse where Jesus affirms that he is the βασιλεὺς τῶν Ἰουδαίων (Jn. 18³³⁻³⁷ has the theme in further stage of development) and it is in these terms that the inscription on the cross is formulated in Mk. 15²⁶. Even the secondary items in Mk. 15⁶⁻¹⁵ᵃ (Barabbas) and 15¹⁶⁻²⁰ (The Mocking) exhibit this same feature (cp. vv. 12 and 18); and lastly in Mark the centurion's cry in 15³⁹ is of this order. In Matt. 26⁵³ Jesus proves himself the Son of God at his arrest (a theme further developed in Jn. 18⁶). A smaller instance of the same kind is also found in Matthew's insertion of 26⁶⁸ into the mocking of Jesus: Χριστέ, τίς ἐστιν ὁ παίσας σε; This point of view comes out clearly in the addition of Matt. 27⁴³: εἶπεν γὰρ ὅτι θεοῦ εἰμι υἱός. We can perceive the same tendency in Lk. 23³⁹⁻⁴³ where the first thief mockingly says: οὐχὶ σὺ εἶ ὁ Χριστός; and Jesus promises to receive the second into Paradise. And when Lk. 23⁵³ tells us that Jesus was laid in a grave 'wherein never man before was laid' (ditto in Jn. 19⁴¹; cp. Matt. 27⁶⁰: ἐν τῷ καινῷ αὐτοῦ μνημείῳ) that is as much meant to show the 'cultic' character of his person as was Mk. 11² in telling of the entry into Jerusalem on an as yet unridden animal.

The Dogmatic stands in close relationship to the *Cult*. But the cultic motif in the proper sense of the word comes out in the story of the Last Supper, and there in a peculiarly double fashion. According to an older report that has been displaced in the main story (see pp. 265f.) the Last Supper was a Passover feast. As this estimation of the Last Supper has a secure place only in the legendary passage Mk. 14¹²⁻¹⁶, the idea that the Last Supper was a Passover may rest on the cult legend of the Jewish Christian Church which used it to explain their retention of the old Passover customs.[1] But what is certain is that in Mk. 14²²⁻²⁵ the story of the Last Supper has become a cultic legend of the κυριακὸν δεῖπνον.

(c) *The Easter Narratives*

Mk. 16¹⁻⁸ par.: *Easter Morning*. The story of the women on Easter morning is a quite secondary formulation which originally neither went with the preceding sections of Mark—for otherwise, after

[1] So E. Schwartz, *Z.N.W.*, 7, 1906, pp. 23f.

15⁴⁰, ⁴⁷ the women in 16¹ would not have been named again, and their intention to embalm the body does not agree with 15⁴⁶ where there is never so much as a thought that the burial was incomplete or provisional[1]—nor, in my view, with the supposed end of Mark which must have recounted the appearance of Jesus in Galilee. The statement οὐδενὶ οὐδὲν εἶπαν can originally have referred only to the discovery of the empty grave and 'to give an answer to the question why the women's story of the empty tomb remained unknown for so long' (Bousset). But immediately after v. 7 he makes a reference to v. 7, so that it must be inferred that the women did not carry out the angel's instructions. In my view that can be neither the original meaning of the whole story nor have accorded with the intentions of v. 7. So v. 7 is just as much as 14²⁸ a footnote put by Mark into the passage from the tradition, to prepare the way for a Galilean appearance of Jesus.[2] For the rest it seems to me that the secondary character of v. 7 follows also from its manifest presupposition that the disciples remained in Jerusalem after the catastrophe. But I have no doubt that the old tradition told of their flight to Galilee, and placed the appearances of the risen Lord there. But if the flight into Galilee be dispensed with, it is necessary to have the disciples artificially despatched to Galilee in order to achieve congruity with the old

---

[1] In Z.N.W., 7, 1906, pp. 30f. E. Schwartz has rightly pointed to the contradiction that the women who in 15⁴⁷ witnessed the closing of the tomb, first wondered on the way there (16³): τίς ἀποκυλίσει ἡμῖν τὸν λίθον; In particular he emphasizes the impossibility that the women meant to embalm the body, which had already been in the grave for two nights and a day. He concludes that the story could not have been told in this form before Sunday had been given its place as the day of the Resurrection; originally the embalming of the body by the women was reported along with the entombment. This latter point seems very doubtful to me; I believe that from the very beginning the story of the women was a story of an empty tomb, but a story that was originally not devised with the chronology controlling Mark in mind (Death on the παρασκευῇ, Resurrection on the μιᾷ τῶν σαββάτων). So Bousset, Kyrios Chr.², pp. 64f.

[2] It is by no means as incomprehensible as E. Meyer maintains, for the original end of Mark to have been lost. (E. Meyer, Ursprung u. Anf. d. Christent., I, pp. 17f.) It would be more understandable if this lost end had been in strong contradiction to the later Easter legend. This question, whether the end of Mark is missing, whether, that is, Mark originally contained a report of the appearance of the risen Lord in addition to the empty tomb, must be sharply distinguished from the question whether the pericope in 16¹⁻⁸ is complete, and has its original and organic conclusion in v. 8. This distinction has been emphasized by L. Brun, Die Auferstehung Christi in der urchristlichen Uberlieferung, 1925, pp. 9–11, and he has rightly answered the second question in the affirmative. But the observations of O. Lindton, Theol. Blaetter, 8, 1929, Cols. 229–34 do not take us further when he seeks to show that in 16⁸ not only the pericope but the whole of Mark comes to an end. His contention that for primitive Christian feeling the prophecy of an appearance in Mk. 16⁷ was as good as the appearance itself, contradicts the legend formulation which was in the sources of the other evangelists, as does the fact that 16⁸ was not treated as a conclusion but was added to. And if ἐφοβοῦντο were such an excellent finish, giving the point of the story in the impression of the overpowering appearance and the words of the angel it would at least have to read: ἐφοβοῦντο καὶ οὐδενὶ οὐδὲν εἶπαν. Instead of this ἐφοβοῦντο (even if 'numinous effect' be meant) serves as the reason (γάρ) for οὐδενὶ οὐδὲν εἶπαν, and is therefore manifestly apologetic in character.

Easter Tradition, and this actually happened in the editing of Mk. 16[7] and 14[28].

Yet Mark's presentation is extremely reserved, in so far as the Resurrection and the appearance of the risen Lord are not recounted. His construction is impressive: the wondering of the women v. 3, the surprised sight of the rolled-away stone and the appearance of the angel vv. 4f., the masterly formulated angelic message v. 6 and the shattering impression in v. 8. In Matthew and Luke the legend has already developed further. In particular Luke has to alter the angel's saying, because he does not give any account of an appearance of the risen Lord in Galilee. In 28[2-4] Matthew gives a still reserved description of the miraculous occurrence (which is later greatly expanded in the Gospel of Peter), and adds to it in vv. 9f. an appearance of Jesus to the women.

Of the *other Easter* stories only Lk. 24[13-35], The Walk to Emmaus, has the character of a true legend. Concerning it cp. H. Gunkel, *Zum religionsgeschichtlichen Verstaendnis des N.T.*, p. 71: 'Christ appears here as the unknown traveller—in the way that God of old liked to walk among men, in simple human form dressed as a traveller—and revealed his secret divine nature by peculiar characteristics; but, as soon as he was recognized, he disappeared. This outline of the story is strictly analogous to the oldest stories of the appearance of God; it could, so far as its style is concerned, appear in Genesis.'[1]

The other units in Matt. 28 and Lk. 24 give the impression of being self-conscious literary work and at least in part have to be styled editorial. Matt. 28[11-15], *The Deception of the Hierarchy*, is an apologetic legend that goes with 27[62-66].[2] The last *appearance of Jesus* in Matt. 28[16-20] is a sort of cult legend in virtue of the appended instruction to baptize. The appearance to the disciples in Lk. 24[36-49] seems to be an edited passage having as its basis an older legend which included an appearance in Galilee; vv. 44–49 is obviously in its entirety a literary production of Luke. Similarly Lk. 24[50-53] Jesus' Farewell is also a literary creation, which Luke may have had on hand. The Ascension was not yet recounted as a legend by the Synoptics. The editor of Acts has introduced an ascension legend into Acts; there is another in

[1] Gunkel refers to the story of Hagar in Gen. 16[7ff.], of the three men who visited Abraham, Gen. 18[1ff.] and others like them—*Kommentar zur Genesis*[3], pp. 193f. Dibelius (33 Beih. der *Z.A.W.*, 1918, p. 137) recalls the Homeric Demeter Hymn, 275ff. (The attendant changed herself into the goddess) and on the story of Epidaurus' healing, *Ditt. Syll.*[2], 803, pp. 26ff. (the unknown traveller reveals himself after the healing in Asclepius). Finally I would refer to two Chinese parallels in the Chinese Fairy Tales edited by R. Wilhelm in Die Maerchen der Weltliteratur, 1917, p. 73 and esp. p. 55.

[2] On Cumont's attempt (*R. Hist.*, 163, 1930, pp. 241–66) to connect an inscription found in Nazareth, a Διάταγμα Καίσαρος where theft of corpses is dealt with, with Matt. 28[11-15] cp. M. Goguel, *R.H.Ph.R.*, 10, 1930, pp. 289–93.

the *Epist. Apost.* (ed. C. Schmidt, p. 154): 'And as he said this, there was thunder and lightning and earthquake, and the heavens were rent asunder and there appeared a bright cloud which bore him up. And (there sounded) the voices of many angels, who rejoiced and gave praise and said "Gather us, O priest, to the light of glory". And as they drew near to the firmament we heard his voice: "Go in peace!"'

The Easter stories have been subjected to a form analysis, and to a study in the light of the history of the tradition by M. Albertz (*Z.N.W.*, 21, 1922, pp. 259–69) and in particular by Lyder Brun (*Die Auferstehung Christi in der urchristlichen Ueberlieferung*, 1925). Following their suggestions I will summarize what I take to be the most important motifs of the Easter stories and their history in the tradition, while only occasionally (or even not at all) paying attention to the extra-Synoptic material or the kerygmatic formulation of the Easter message.

The Easter stories we have looked at above fall into two groups— stories of the empty tomb and stories of the appearance of the risen Lord, though there are stories that combine them both (Matt. 28^{1-8} + $^{9f.}$; Jn. $20^{1, 11-18}$).

1. *Stories of the Empty Tomb:* Mk. 16^{1-8}; Matt. 28^{1-10} $^{(11-15)}$; Lk. 24^{1-11}; Jn. $20^{1, 11-18}$. Since Matt. 28^{11-15} is an apologetic legend that goes with 27^{62-66}, and Jn. $20^{1, 11-18}$ is a late formulation,[1] and since further the accounts in Matthew and Luke derive from Mark, the material reduces itself to the one story in Mk. 16^{1-8}. The purpose of the story is without doubt to prove the reality of the resurrection of Jesus by the empty tomb. It is a reflection of that purpose that this point is expressed in the words of the *Angelus interpres* (Mk. 16^6; Matt. $28^{5f.}$; Lk. 24^{5-7}). But in Mark what the angel says has a second point, to charge the women to send the disciples to Galilee where the risen Lord will appear to them (Mk. 16^7; Matt. 28^7; missing from Luke, see above). We have already shown that this second point is secondary, and it now becomes perfectly plain that it is so: it conflicts with the dominant motif of the passage. If now by this second part of the angel's message the story of the empty tomb is connected with the story of the appearance of the risen Lord in Galilee, then it becomes clear that the two stories had an independent origin. To be sure, we can from this fact draw no conclusion whether the story of the empty tomb is the older, since the reference to the appearance was no part of the original text of the story of the empty tomb. Other considerations will take us further.

[1] It is necessary simply to mention e.g. that the two angels in Jn. 20^{12} have become 'stage furniture' of no significance.

2. *Stories of the Appearance of the Risen Lord:* Matt. 28[9f.], [16-20]; Lk. 24[13-35], [36-49] (-[53]); Jn. 20[14-18], [19-23], [24-29], 21[1-14], [15-17]. From 1 Cor. 15[5-7] Albertz concludes that 'every ancient Tradition joined two stories together, the one a single spiritual Christ-experience, and the other a summary appointment to the Apostolate by the κύριος' (op. cit., 266). And Brun sees in this inseparableness of 'individual' and 'group' appearances the 'dominant pattern' of the Easter appearances. I do not think we can speak of such a 'dominant pattern', at least not if one understands thereby a concept of form which the tradition fashioned as such. It belongs to the very nature of things that the Easter appearances or visions should have been told in the first place of individuals and then of all the Apostles, and that obviously was the actual course of events; and in the same way, it is natural that the evangelists, as they collected and combined the traditions, should put at the end a story of an appearance to all the apostles.[1] So it is self-evident that Luke had to put the Emmaus story before the appearance in 24[36-49] ([53]); and it follows from 28[9f.] being but an appendix to the story of the empty tomb that Matthew had to place the appearance to the women in 28[9f.] before the story of 28[16-20].

But it is right to distinguish the two types of story, or better the two motifs—which separately or combined find expression in the stories: (*a*) The motif of proving the Resurrection by the appearance of the risen Lord. This is dominant in Lk. 24[13-35]; Jn. 20[1, 11-18] (in combination with the story of the empty tomb); 20[24-29], 21[1-14]. It is but faintly developed in Matt. 28[9f.], because here we do not have an independent story at all, but only an appendix to the story of the empty tomb. (*b*) The motif of the *missionary charge of the Risen Lord*: This is dominant in Matt. 28[16-20]; Jn. 20[19-23]. But just as the first motif can enter into Matt. 28[17] (οἱ δὲ ἐδίστασαν) and Jn. 20[20] (ἔδειξεν καὶ τὰς χεῖρας καὶ τὴν πλευρὰν αὐτοῖς), so both motifs are combined in Lk. 24[36-49] (a: vv. 36-43; b: vv. 44-49) and Acts 1[3-8] (a: v. 3; b: vv. 4-8). It is obvious that the first motif should fit appearances to individuals, but by no means necessarily so, as Lk. 24[36-43]; Matt. 28[17]; Jn. 20[20] show. Likewise it is obvious that the

---

[1] Albertz and Brun (the latter following Harnack, *S.B.A.*, 1922, pp. 62f.) believe that 1 Cor. 15[5-7] combines two traditions, both built on the same plan (appearance of Christ to one person—to all): (1) vv. 5 (6) (*a*) appearance to Peter, (*b*) to the Twelve, (*c*) to the five hundred. (2) v. 7 (*a*) to James, (*b*) to all the apostles. I greatly doubt whether this analysis and the consequences that follow it, are right—that in this Kerygma the rival traditions of Peter and James are combined. But be that as it may, in any case the appearances mentioned here, to Peter and to James are not from the same stage of the tradition as Matt. 28[9f.] and Lk. 24[13-35], as if one could find the 'plan' of 1 Cor. 15[5-7] in Matthew and Luke. Cp. also M. Goguel, *R.H.Ph.R.*, 6, 1926, pp. 183f.

second motif came out in stories of an appearance to all the apostles. But again that is not in any way necessary, as we can see from Jn. 21[15-17] where the context presupposes that the other disciples are present, but where actually the story is concerned only with what happens between Jesus and Peter. The same applies to Mk. 8[27-30], if it be right to think that behind it lies an old Easter story (see pp. 258f.). But the primary historical fact is not that the risen Lord gave his charge to the whole body of the apostles; for just as certainly as the appearance to Paul contained in itself a missionary charge to him, so also for Peter too who was the first to see the risen Lord (1 Cor. 15[5]; Lk. 24[34]) the appearance of Christ certainly implied a charge (Lk. 22[32], see p. 267).

It is now quite clear that the fashioning of the second motif in Matt. 28[16-20]; Lk. 24[44-49]; Acts 1[4-8] with all the Johannine stories, is a quite late achievement of Hellenistic Christianity (if not also in part of Hellenist Jewish-Christianity). For these stories presuppose the universal mission, as something authorized by a command of the risen Lord. The primitive Church knew nothing of this, as Gal. 2[7] clearly shows.[1] We can indeed hardly conceive of an earlier form of such a charge for the primitive Church as that of a mission to the Jews. For even if the task of preaching to Israel were given to the primitive Church in the certainty of the Resurrection, and found its expression in the Instruction Address (see pp. 145f.) there could hardly have been a story of an appearance in which this charge was expressly given. For this missionary task could not be experienced as something surprising, needing express authorization, but was self-evidently given in the certainty that Jesus was risen from the dead and that as the risen Lord he was the coming Messiah. And this and nothing else must have been the content of the oldest stories of the Easter appearances, just as it was the content of Paul's vision on the Damascus road. This is also shown in the stories of Peter's confession and of the Transfiguration (see pp. 145f.). We can never now know whether the lost end of Mark contained a story in which this was clear.

But even the stories which are fashioned by the first motif no longer with one exception contain their original idea; in particular Lk. 24[36-43]; Jn. 20[24-29] are late apologetic formulations. It is only in the Emmaus story that the basic thing is still the knowledge that the certainty of Jesus' Resurrection is identical with the certainty ὅτι αὐτός ἐστιν ὁ μέλλων λυτροῦσθαι τὸν Ἰσραήλ (Lk. 24[21]). In its form it is like the oldest of the Synoptic resurrection stories, and it is the only one which expressly refers to the fundamental appearance to

---

[1] Fascher, Z.N.W., 26, 1927, pp. 9f. appears not to have thought of this passage.

Peter (24³⁴). Thus the original Easter happenings are almost as good as overlaid by legend; that basic appearance which we read of in 1 Cor. 15⁵ has its only echoes in the Transfiguration, and the dominical saying in Lk. 22³²,[1] apart from Lk. 24²⁴ and to some degree the special mention of Peter in Mk. 16⁷.

The story of the empty tomb is completely secondary. It is misleading to oppose it as an 'angelophany' to the 'Christophanies', because ἐπιφάνεια means different things in the two contexts. The point of the story is that the empty tomb proves the Resurrection: the angel has no significance in himself, but simply plays the part of the *angelus interpres*. The story is an apologetic legend, as Mk. 16⁸ (see above) clearly shows. Paul knows nothing about the empty tomb, which does not imply that the story was not yet in existence, but most probably that it was a subordinate theme with no significance for the official Kerygma. The same point is suggested by the speeches in Acts.[2] That is finally established by the fact that originally there was no difference between the Resurrection of Jesus and his Ascension; this distinction first arose as a consequence of the Easter legends, which eventually necessitated a special story of an ascension with heaven as an end of the risen Lord's earthly sojourn. But the story of the empty tomb has its place right in the middle of this development, for in it the original idea of exaltation is modified already.[3]

Dogmatic and apologetic motifs have also vitally affected the Easter stories. Novelistic motifs have also affected the formulation here and there, especially in the Emmaus story. We can ask whether there has been any influence of the primitive Christian cult in the strict sense of

---

[1] On the displacement of Peter's vision cp. L. Brun, op. cit., pp. 50–52; over against Brun's doubt I would affirm that there was originally a genuine Easter story about Peter. Mk. 8²⁷⁻³⁰, 9²⁻⁸ seem to me to afford proof thereof.

[2] Cp. Fascher, *Z.N.W.*, 26, 1927, pp. 10ff. I fail to understand why Albertz, op. cit., p. 267 thinks that the stories (in reality there is but one story) of the appearance to the women is a genuine ancient tradition. His contention that in the main point the tradition has reduced the women's experience of Christ to the appearance of angels contradicts the fact that Matt. 28⁹ᶠ· and Jn. 20¹⁴⁻¹⁷ are developments of Mark 16¹⁻⁸; the case is therefore quite the opposite.

[3] So rightly G. Bertram, *Festgabe f. A. Deissmann*, 1927, pp. 187–217, who uses the very paradoxical title 'The Ascension of Jesus direct from the Cross and the belief in his resurrection' to deal with the contrast between the idea of Resurrection = Ascension and that of the empty tomb. E. Bickermann's essay on the Empty Tomb in *Z.N.W.*, 23, 1924, pp. 281–92 is highly instructive; he rightly emphasizes the contrast of the appearances of the risen Christ with the empty tomb, though he wrongly classes the latter among the 'Removal' stories. But the story of the empty tomb is without any doubt not a 'Removal Legend', but an Apologetic Legend, as ἠγέρθη is meant to show, as is plain from Mk. 16⁶. It is erroneous to think that the empty tomb presupposes an immediate Ascension; the very opposite is the case, as the motif of the stone rolled away indicates. Cp. O. Weinreich, *Genethliakon W. Schmid*, 1929, p. 311, n. 48a, who rightly says that in the story of the empty tomb it is not the 'how' but the 'fact' of the Resurrection that is decisive.

the term. That this has happened in the presentation of the Gospel to the Hebrew (Jer., Vir. Inl., 2; Kl. Texte, 8, p. 8) can hardly be doubted: James' funeral fast which is brought to an end when the risen Lord appears to him, is an obvious reflection of the ecclesiastical custom of an Easter fast.[1] When a meal plays a part in an appearance of the risen Lord in two of the Synoptic Easter stories (Lk. 24 $^{30, 41-43}$; also Acts 1 ^{4}? 10 ^{41}; Jn. 21 $^{12f.}$; Mk. 16 ^{14}: ἀνακειμένοις αὐτοῖς . . . ἐφανερώθη) we are led to think 'how the coming of the Lord was expected and experienced at the Lord's Supper in the Early Church'[2] and to find the motif of the presentation in that. The most important question, and the most difficult, is whether the dating of the Resurrection on Sunday rests upon a previous fixing upon Sunday as the day for the cult. If that be the case, the dating of the Crucifixion on a Friday would be explained, for it would have to be made the day of the Crucifixion because of the scriptural motif (τῇ ἡμέρᾳ τῇ τρίτῃ κατὰ τὰς γραφάς 1 Cor. 15 ^{4}). However the question can only be posed here, for it cannot be answered without a detailed study of the chronology of the Passion, the rise of the Christian observance of Sunday and of the motif of τῇ ἡμέρᾳ τῇ τρίτῃ.[3]

(d) *The Infancy Narratives, etc.*

Matt. 1 $^{18-25}$: *The Birth of Jesus.* This story seems to have been in Matthew's source, though the quotation inserted at vv. 22f. will have come from him, and in addition he could have formulated the introduction. In v. 21 the name of Jesus has to be translated in order to make the reason for αὐτὸς γὰρ σώσει κτλ intelligible. This tends to suggest that an originally Semitic report is the basis of the story. Admittedly this could not have then contained the motif unheard of in a Jewish environment, of a virgin birth.[4] It was first added in the transformation in Hellenism, where the idea of the generation of a

[1] Cp. L. Brun, op. cit., p, 46.
[2] Cp. L. Brun, op. cit., p. 74.1 and G. P. Wetter, *Altchristliche Liturgien*, I, 1921.
[3] Cp. E. Schwartz, *Z.N.W.*, 7, 1906, pp. 29–33.
[4] So also Klostermann. The idea of divine generation from a virgin is not only foreign to the O.T. and to Judaism, but is quite impossible to them. Philo's allegorical interpretation of O.T. birth stories in terms of the mystical ἱερὸς γάμος is only one piece of evidence. Cp. H. Leisegang, *Der Heil. Geist*, I, 1919, pp. 234f.; *Pneuma Hagion*, 1922, pp. 43–55. The idea of the Virgin Birth of the Messiah in particular is foreign to Judaism; cp. Strack-B. I, 49f. ('As against Jewish thought Matt. 1 ^{18} is something completely new'). The views of H. v. Baer, *Der Heil. Geist in den Lukasschriften*, 1926, pp. 114–24, I can only regard as a mishandling and attenuation of the text; they also tend to the very modest conclusion, 'that we have to assume some accompaniments of the birth which, perhaps straight away or perhaps later, in connection with the miraculous appearance of Jesus, were regarded by the relatives as a miracle wrought by God'. In the same way R. Asting, *Die Heiligkeit im Urchristentum*, 1930, pp. 119f. seems to me to water down the meaning of the text.

king or a hero from a virgin by the godhead was widespread.[1] The old story had simply told how an angel promised Joseph that his son would be Messiah. This is supported by the fact that Joseph is expressly addressed as 'υἱὸς Δαυείδ' and that in v. 21 we may well read with syr[sc]: 'She will bear thee a son.' Similarly the antenatal naming of the child, with the associated prophecy, is a traditional motif of O.T. and Jewish literature.[2]

Matt. 2[1-23]: *The Adoration of the Magi, The Flight into Egypt, The Slaughter of the Innocents, and The Return from Egypt.* In the first place this complex is independent of the legend in 1[18-25]; it does not presuppose it. But neither is it entirely an unity in itself. A. Dieterich has illuminatingly shown[3] that the joining of the story of the Magi with that of the Slaughter of the Innocents is secondary. On the other hand his tracing back of the story of the Wise Men to the journey of Tiridates to pay homage to Nero is not very illuminating. Here it seems more likely that use has been made of a folk saga or a fairy-tale motif. Indeed, it is not impossible that the story of the Adoration of the Magi had its origin in the Arabian cult of Dusares, which had its shrines in Petra and Hebron, and perhaps also in Bethlehem.[4] The feast of the birth of the God from his virgin mother was celebrated (on December 25th?) with the presentation of gifts such as money, ointments and incense.[5] That would lead to conceiving the rise of the story in this way: 'that, when in reliance on O.T. prophecy, the birthplace of Jesus was sought in Bethlehem, there was found the information about the Arabian Magi who celebrated the feast of the virgin goddess's son by presenting gifts for sacrifice'. Wetstein had

---

[1] Cp. H. Petersen, *Die wunderbare Geburt des Heilandes*, 1909; H. Gunkel, *Zum religionsgeschichtl. Verstaendnis des N.Ts.*[2], 1910, pp. 65f.; H. Usener, *Das Weihnachtsfest, Religionsgesch. Unters.*, I[2], 1911, pp. 71, 78; A. Steinmann, *Die Jungfrauengeburt und die vergleichende Religionsgeschichte*, 1919 (catholic); W. Bousset, *Kyrios Christos*[2], 1921, pp. 268–70; H. Leisegang, *Pneuma Hagion*, 1922, pp. 14–72; E. Norden, *Die Geburt des Kindes*, 1924, esp. pp. 76–116; C. Clemen, *Religionsgeschichtl. Erklaerung des N.Ts.*[2], 1924, pp. 115–21; J. G. Machen, *The Virgin Birth of Christ*, 1930 (apologetic). Novelistic Tradition treated in W. Gemoll, *Das Apophthegma*, 1924, pp. 64f.

[2] Cp. the promise of Ishmael's birth in Gen. 16[11] (by the ἄγγελος κυρίου); of Isaac Gen. 17[19]; of Solomon 1 Chr. 22[9]; of Josiah 1 Kings 13[2]. The motif is applied to Moses by Josephus in *Ant.* II, 9.3 = § 210–16. The references in Strack-B. I, 63 indicate how important the motif was to the Rabbis. Homer, *Od.* XI, pp. 248ff. is not a true parallel. The announcement of the name of someone called to play a special role is found in the Egyptian story of Setme Chamois (G. Moeller in H. Gressmann, Abh. d. Kgl. Akad. d. Wiss. zu Berlin 1918, phil.-hist. Kl. no. 7.63, see under Lk. 2[40-52]) and of King Cheops (A. Erman, *D. Lit. d. Aeg.*, pp. 74f.). In fairy-tales we can find the prophecy of birth with the naming in H. Schmidt and P. Kahle, *Volkserz. aus Palaestina*, I, 1918, pp. 147, 157 (as a fluctuating motif, ibid., II, 1930, p. 187); *Kaukasische Maerchen* (Maerchen der Weltlit.), p. 236.

[3] *Z.N.W.*, 3, 1902, pp. 1–14.

[4] Cp. G. Frenken, *Wunder u. Taten der Heiligen* (Buecher des Mittelalters I), 1925, pp. 186–91.

[5] On the Magi's gifts cp. also L. Troje, ΑΔΑΜ und ΖΩΗ (Sitzungsb. d. Heid. Ak. d. W. phil.-hist. Kl. 1916, no. 17, p. 51.1 and C. Clemen, *Religionsgeschichtl. Erkl. d. N.T.*[2], p. 195.

already collected ancient parallels to the motif of the star which announced the hero's birth, and to the motif of a star which pointed the way to the birth of a king; the material has been increased in more recent commentaries, e.g. by Klostermann in Lietzmann's Handbook.[1] The story of Herod who seeks to destroy the new-born king has a similar series of parallels. Possibly the Babylonian tradition already recounted a corresponding story about Sargon.[2] The Rabbinic does the same for Abraham.[3] The tradition has been preserved in an obscured form in the Moses saga (Exod. 2); it reappears quite clearly in Josephus, *Ant.*, II, 9, 2 and in the Rabbinic tradition (Strack-B. I, 88): Pharaoh is provoked to order a slaughter of children by the prophecy of the birth of an Israelite ruler. The motif is similarly to be found in Greek and Roman antiquity, whether in the form of the old ruler who sets traps for his new-born future rival and dethroner (e.g. Cyrus, Romulus and Remus) or in conjunction with the motif of child slaying (Suetonius, *Aug.*, 94 and *Nero*, 36; both in Klostermann).[4] Finally the motif has been used in various ways in fairy-tales.[5] Whether it was originally mythical is no longer important for our purposes; it can be found, e.g. in the Egyptian myth of Hathor and Horus, in the Greek myth of the birth of Apollo, and it re-emerges, from such a background, in Rev. 12.[6]

For the literary shaping of Matt. 2[1-23] Matthew is in all probability himself responsible. But it is difficult to tell how far he made use of oral or written tradition. It could thus well be the case that Matthew found the Flight into Egypt and the Return already in his

---

[1] Cp. also C. Clemen, *Rel. gesch. Erkl. d. N.T.s*[2], pp. 192–4. The fact that the star shows the way is a novelistic usage or a combination of the main motif with another. The star whose rise the Magi saw was originally a man's heavenly double, which rose with his birth and set at his death. Cp. F. Boll, *Z.N.W.*, 18, 1917–18, pp. 40–48, esp. pp. 43f. Cp. *Maerchen aus Turkestan u. Tibet* (Maerchen d. Weltlit.), p. 70 and the literature there cited on p. 305. But a guiding star is an idea to be met with in the tradition of antiquity, cp. the parallels in Klostermann on v. 10 and Clemen, op. cit., p. 194. Against reckoning the star astrologically cp. Boll, op. cit. In *Joh. Buch der Mandaeer*, II, pp. 75f. Lidzb. the star motif is transferred to John. For other omens at the birth of a hero see e.g. E. Norden, *Die Geburt des Kindes*, pp. 153ff.; W. Weber, *Der Prophet u. sein Gott*, 1925, pp. 6f.

[2] H. Gressmann, *Moses und seine Zeit*, 1913, pp. 77ff. The tradition, reproduced in Aelian, *Hist. An.*, XII, 21, reports it of Gilgamesh.

[3] B. Beer, *Das Leben Abrahams nach der jued. Sage*, 1875; A. Wuensche, *Aus Israels Lesehallen*, I, 1907, pp. 14–45; Strack-B. III, 34f.

[4] Cp. E. Norden, *Die Geburt des Kindes*, p. 158.

[5] Cp. Wundt, *Voelkerpsychologie*, pp. 308ff.; Bolte-Polivka, I, pp. 276ff.; V. Telle, Das 'Maerchen vom Schicksalskind', *Ztschr. d. Vereins f. Volkskunde*, 29, 1919, pp. 22ff. Further examples: *Maerchen aus Turkestan u. Tibet* (Maerchen d. Weltlit.), pp. 230f.; *Franzoes. Maerchen* (ibid.), I, pp. 119f.; further n. p. 311. In connection with the motif of child-slaughter see v. Hahn, *Griech u. alban. Maerchen*, 1864, p. 114. Finally cp. P. Saintyves, *Congrès d'Hist. du Christian.*, I, p. 249.

[6] It is hardly possible to prove that the motif had already been transferred to the Messiah in Jewish Messianic expectations (cp. Clemen, *Rel. gesch. Erkl. d. N.Ts.*[2], pp. 192–201).

source in some form. It is difficult to suppose that this story was originally intended as a polemic against the sort of defamations we read in Origen, *C.C.*, I, 28 and the Talmud (e.g. Sab. 104b). Has it really grown out of the proof from prophecy?[1] Or is the Flight into Egypt a motif of the tradition? The explanations to be found in Matthew in all probability are due to Matthew himself; so also is the awkward combination of the historical tradition of Nazareth as Jesus' home town with the messianic dogma of his birth at Bethlehem.

Lk. 1: *The Birth of John the Baptist and the Annunciation.* In the first place we may establish that there is *no primary connection between Lk. 1 and 2.* The Baptist and his parents have no further part to play in Lk. 2. Even more important is: (1) The motif of the angel's promise in 1 $^{30-33}$ has no sequel in Lk. 2, but is rather in contradiction to the angelic message in 2 $^{11-14}$; (2) The marriage of Joseph and Mary contemplated in 1 ^{27} is simply presupposed in chap. 2, whereas it had to be reported in the previous chapter. (3) Chap. 2 is not only fully intelligible on its own without Chap. 1, but every section of it is opposed to any combination with an introductory story.[2]

Thus in Chap. 1 we have a secondary combination of the antecedents to the Baptist with the prophecy of Jesus' birth. The Annunciation plays so small a part in Chap. 1 that we cannot avoid the conclusion that the Baptist's antecedents were originally an independent unity. The two stories are linked at two points. (1) Elizabeth's pregnancy at her advanced age is a sign to Mary that the angel's promise to herself will be fulfilled (vv. 36f.). But this motif is nullified by what Mary says in v. 38: γένοιτό μοι κατὰ τὸ ῥῆμά σου before she had learnt of the other sign; and when she visits Elizabeth no reference is made to this saying, which means that vv. 36f. have to be regarded in their context as secondary. (2) The meeting of Elizabeth and Mary brings the two mothers and their unborn sons into a direct relationship vv. 39–56; and certainly this part of the Baptist's story can be removed without any visible effect.

The Baptist's antecedents originally had no relation to a coming Messiah; the Baptist was rather one who was to prepare a way for God himself vv. 14–17. Whence Luke derived it is difficult to say, but in any case he took it, as the interpolations show, from a literary

---

[1] E. Meyer, *Urspr. u. Anf. d. Christent.*, I, p. 60: 'The child had to be brought to a place of safety somewhere, and the prophecy provided a suitable place.' The Jewish accounts of Jesus' stay in Egypt (Strack-B. I, 84f.) are obviously polemical fables.

[2] For an analysis see esp. D. Voelter, *Die evang. Erzaehlungen von der Geburt u. Kindheit Christi*, 1911; H. Gressmann, *Das Weihnachtsevangelium*, 1914; E. Norden, *Die Geburt des Kindes*, pp. 102–5 and Klostermann's Commentary (Handbuch zum N.T.[2]), 1929.

source, and naturally it would come from some Baptist sect.[1] The motifs of the legend are traditionally Jewish. (1) The announcement of the birth and the name, see on Matt. 1[18-25]; (2) The long infertility of the Mother, cp. Gen. 15ff.; Jdg. 13[15f.]; 1 Sam. 1f.; 2 Kings 4[8-17]. (3) The reception of a sign; cp. apart from Lk. 1[36f.], 2[12]; Gen. 15[8]; Jdg. 6[36ff.]; 1 Sam. 10[2]; 2 Kings 20[8]; also Isa. 7[10ff.]; Jn. 1[33].[2] But since the Baptist sect had no doubt spread to Hellenistic soil, as Acts and John show, it was possible for Luke to have found his legend of the Baptist in a Greek version. And that appears probable from the very start; for Luke was hardly in a position to provide himself with a Palestinian tradition in the Semitic tongue. But whether the Baptist legend had already reached its literary form in a Semitic environment, or whether it first received it in Hellenistic Baptist circles, can now no longer, in my view, be decided.

In the prophecy of the Birth of Messiah in 1[26-38] I take vv. 34–37 to be a secondary addition, in all probability made by Luke himself. It has long since been objected that Mary's question in v. 34 is an absurd one for a bride. Gunkel and Gressmann seek to escape this by ascribing it to a basic Semitic form, from which 'thou shalt receive' (namely at this moment) is falsely rendered into the future συλλήμψη (v. 31). But (1) Mary's saying does not become possessed of meaning by such retranslation; for we have to suppose either that it contains within itself the account of the conception in which case the clause ἐπεί κτλ. is quite meaningless. Or that it does not contain it, in which case the situation is no better, for then she may well ask: πῶς ἔσται τοῦτο, but is not able to explain her astonishment by the fact that she has had no sexual intercourse, since she has only just been told that she will conceive without it. Finally the future tense in v. 35, which cannot be changed with any show of plausibility, presupposes that συλλαμβάνειν is itself future. And (2) vv. 36f. are in any case an insertion (see above), and with them, that is to say, with the indication of the σημεῖον, we must suppose v. 34 to be an addition as well, since it contains the question which occasioned the sign.[3] In all

---

[1] It is a possible view that the story of the Baptist contained a scene in which Gabriel foretold the birth of a son to Elizabeth, which was replaced in the Christian Tradition by the Annunciation. The view finds support in the fact that it was Elizabeth who originally recited the Magnificat. Cp.Klostermann on v. 46a. But I think this hypothesis is uncertain; it is held by Voelter, op. cit.; E. Norden, *Die Geburt des Kindes*, p. 103 and Klostermann. I have stated my case against Norden in *Th.L.Z.*, 49, 1924, Cols. 322f. M. Goguel, *Jean-Baptiste*, pp. 69–75 does not examine the question but contents himself, as in the text above, with pointing out the existence of a Baptist source dealing with the Baptist's antecedents.

[2] The motif of the belief-quickening sign in Judaism: Strack-B. I, 640f., 726f.; in fairy stories: *Indische Maerchen* (Maerchen der Weltlit.), pp. 218f.

[3] J. G. Machen, *The Virgin Birth of Christ*, 1930, p. 138 is quite right to emphasize the close connection of v. 34 and vv. 36f. But for the rest I do not think he has succeeded in defending the integrity of the birth story (op. cit., pp. 119–68).

probability the editor (Luke) has followed the same pattern as in vv. 18–20: just as Zacharias raised a question about the angel's message, Mary has to do so here; and just as the former received a σημεῖον so also here. Originally v. 38 followed immediately on v. 33.[1] So the verses which contain the reference to the Virgin Birth are a Christian addition and derive from the same Hellenistic Christian sphere as Matt. 1[18–25] (see p. 291, n. 1).

The Meeting of Elizabeth and Mary: 1[39–45] was in the source Luke used; for if it were his own composition one would have expected a reference to vv. 36f. which he had inserted: Mary would have to confirm that the sign had been fulfilled. Then we should also conclude that the two sets of antecedents were already joined together for Luke; for only in such circumstances would a story like 1[39–45] have any point.[2]

Finally, the *two psalms*, 1[46–55] and 1[67–69] are originally independent units, and indeed Jewish eschatological hymns.[3] The first— whether in Luke's view it should be sung by Mary or Elizabeth—is artificially inserted into its context by the addition of v. 48 which gives the relationship to the actual situation (perhaps μοι in v. 49 must in like manner be ascribed to the editor). The second psalm vv. 67–79 is particularly obviously an insertion, for v. 66 brings the preceding story to a close, and vv. 65f. has already left the story of the circumcision behind. In the psalm itself, which is in any case constructed in the style of a hymn, v. 76 is a Christian or a Baptist addition, relating the psalm to the actual situation; and similarly perhaps, vv. 77–79.[4] Both psalms, of Jewish origin and in all probability composed in Aramaic (or Hebrew), had possibly already been introduced into the original Jewish form of the story of the Baptist; the Magnificat—which would then naturally be sung by Elizabeth—would be

---

[1] I admit that in my view this critical analysis cannot be supported by textual criticism (B. H. Streeter, *The Four Gospels*, pp. 267f.). For the rest cp. C. Clemen, *Rel. gesch. Erkl. d. N. Ts.*[2], pp. 115f.

[2] L. Radermacher (*Arch. f. R. W.*, 28, 1930, pp. 36–41) thinks that, because Elizabeth is inspired by the leaping of the child in the womb, the story of the meeting of Elizabeth and Mary is one of a type of ancient stories in which when one person meets another, he is inspired by some special sign (like the flight of an eagle) to prophesy about the future. But since there is no prophecy of the future in what Elizabeth says in vv. 42–45, he believes that Luke stopped short of it, because he had already recorded the angel's prophecy. This means that the story of the Annunciation and that of the meeting of the two women are two reports Luke had before him about one prophecy concerning Mary. This is an untenable position to adopt.

[3] Cp. H. Gunkel, *Festgabe f. A. v. Harnack*, 1921, pp. 43–60; J. Marty *R.H.Ph.R.*, 9, 1929, pp. 371f. For a contrary view J. G. Machen, *The Virgin Birth of Christ*, 1930, pp. 87ff.

[4] Gunkel, op. cit., pp. 58–60 believes vv. 76–79 are an addition, and that is inevitable if τοῦ δοῦναι in v. 77 is regarded as dependent on προπορεύσῃ in v. 76, a thing which is intended in the present text. However if v. 76 is taken out, τοῦ δοῦναι in v. 77 could be parallel to the same verb in v. 73, and then vv. 77–79 would belong to the prophecy spoken in vv. 74f. Goguel (op. cit., p. 74) also takes vv. 76–79 as an addition.

more appropriately placed after v. 25 than in its present position.

Lk. 2¹⁻²⁰: *The Birth of Jesus and the Announcement to the Shepherds.* The linking of the story to the Census is secondary and is due to the editor, i.e. to Luke himself, who makes use of the census motif to combine the historical and the legendary traditions—Nazareth and Bethlehem—together, and at the same time to put the Gospel story into the framework of world history.[1] In all probability of course the form of the story which Luke knew told of the parents' journey to Bethlehem or their presence there. Gressmann has pointed out a whole series of difficulties in the story, of which the chief are the following: (1) The announcement to the shepherds has no proper point, since it should be said at the end that the shepherds pay homage to the new-born child as the σωτήρ. (2) Why is the birth of the saviour of the world announced to the shepherds and not to his parents or the Jewish people? (3) The σημεῖον of the manger is only properly motivated if the child is only to be found by means of this particular sign; that is to say, he is a foundling, and we may conclude that in an earlier form of the story the shepherds were much more closely related to the royal foundling, but that they are now replaced by the parents. But against that it has to be pointed out: (1) The shepherds not only see the child, but spread abroad what the angel said about him, and praise God for what they had experienced, and this must surely be regarded as the proper organic conclusion to the Shepherd story. (2) The shepherds represent the people, who could not be brought into action in their entirety. Why it was precisely the shepherds who were chosen as the people's representatives of course requires an explanation, but it by no means justifies postulating a form of the story where the shepherds play a quite different role. (3) The most important thing is: the σημεῖον of the manger is admittedly intelligible only if the child is recognizable in terms of this σημεῖον only; but that does not necessitate him being a foundling. Rather is this unusual situation the means by which he is to be recognized among the many little children in Bethlehem (and the shepherds are so instructed in v. 12, cp. 16). Gressmann's opinion that the manger must be a quite particular manger to be found at a quite particular place, is utterly false, since if the child has to be found at some particular place the σημεῖον loses its point completely.[2]

Gressmann's conclusion, that a pre-Christian birth legend that had been transferred to Jesus lay behind Lk. 2¹⁻²⁰, and that in it the shepherds were replaced by the parents, seems to me quite

---

[1] Cp. M. Dibelius, *Th.R.*, N.F.1, 1929, p. 206.1.
[2] Cp. also C. Clemen, *Rel. gesch. Erklaerung d. N.Ts.*, pp. 202–9.

untenable.[1] It also seems to me quite impossible to suppose that even a pre-Christian Jewish legend of the birth of Messiah underlies the story (and naturally it would in turn rest upon Gentile influences). How could it have been told so long as Messiah was still expected? Of course the question remains whether particular motifs are of a pre-Christian origin. We have already remarked in reference to Matt. 1[18-25] that the motif of a prophecy about the birth of a hero is old and widely diffused; the Osiris legend Plut., *Is. et Os.*, 12 offers a parallel[2] to the proclamation of the birth in the proclamation of the birth of the μέγας βασιλεύς and εὐεργέτης. Further, as E. Norden (*Die Geburt des Kindes*, 91) has shown, the σήμερον of the angelic message in Lk. 2[11] has its analogy in the liturgical formula from the festival of the birth of Aion as used in Alexandria: ταύτῃ τῇ ὥρᾳ σήμερον ἡ κόρη ἐγέννησε τὸν Αἰῶνα. The σημεῖον of the child in the manger could also be a borrowed one, though no parallels are known to me. It is also possible that the shepherds' reception of the angel's message could be bound up with the Jewish expectation that the Messiah would be born at the shepherds' tower in Bethlehem (Targum Ps. Jonathan, Gen. 35[21]).[3] Yet according to Geffcken Vergil's well-known 4th Eclogue is also the proclamation and adoration of a miraculous child by a shepherd; Vergil is represented as a shepherd and the poem demands 'the assumption of a shepherd company listening to the announcer of joyful tidings'.[4] It is extremely doubtful whether shepherds played any part in the legends of Mithras' birth.[5] It can hardly be taken as a parallel that in the saga which according to Diodorus II, 4ff., Ktesias relates,[6] Semiramis, cast out by her mother, was found by some shepherds and brought up by them.

[1] It is all the more natural to try to discover the original in the Egyptian legend of the birth of Osiris; the most important motif (the σημεῖον) is not only not demonstrated in this case but according to Plut., *Is. et Os.*, 12, could hardly have been there at all; for in this legend Kronos hands the divine child over to the water carrier Pampyles (ἐγχειρίσαντος αὐτῷ τοῦ Κρόνου). But the chief motif, proclamation of the birth, is too widespread to allow a conclusion as to dependence; see following note.

[2] Cp. the preceding note. Further also the papyrus translated in Brugsch, *Religion und Mythologie der alten Aegypter*, pp. 627f.: 'Hail, Osiris Chenti Imenet (First in the West, or the Land of the Dead), thy mother Nut bore thee in Thebes, thou becamest a tiny boy. A joyful shout resounded at thy birth on earth as a child; Ra heard it in heaven his dwelling place'; quoted by Beth, *T.S.K.*, 89, 1916, p. 197; ibid., pp. 198f. are further Egyptian parallels. We may also compare the way in which in the Buddha legend of Asket Asita (cp. on Lk. 2[22-40]) heard in heaven the rejoicing that accompanied the birth of Buddha.

[3] Cp. C. Clemen, *T.S.K.*, 80, 1916, p. 252 who also refers to Edersheim, *The Life and Times of Jesus the Messiah*, I[3], 1892, p. 186.

[4] Geffcken, *Hermes* 49, 1914, pp. 321ff.

[5] Against Geffcken, who (op. cit.) represents this point of view and takes Poseidonios as the mediator, is J. Kroll, *Hermes* 50, 1915, pp. 137ff. On the whole question see also Gressmann, op. cit., p. 32; C. Clemen, *Rel. gesch. Erkl. d. N.Ts.*[2], p. 203; Millet, Syria 7, 1926, pp. 142ff.; in addition Gressmann, *Z.A.W.*, 44, 1926, p. 294.

[6] H. Gressmann, *Arch. f. R.-W.*, 20, 1920/21, pp. 334f.

Ought not the role of the shepherds in the gospel story (and in such-like parallels) to rest on the fact that they are the most suitable representatives of a new humanity which, by the birth of the Saviour-God, is to be taken back to the original state of Paradise? For the conventional way of thinking about Paradisaical existence is to conceive of it as some sort of shepherd life.

Whether the Christian legend of Lk. 2$^{1-20}$ grew up in Palestinian or Hellenistic Christianity has to be answered in my view by deciding for the second; the terms εὐαγγελίζεσθαι (v. 10) and σωτήρ (v. 11) are Hellenistic. Nor would that be altered even if we had to assume an Aramaic source for the formulae of praise and salvation in v. 14: for they could well have been taken from older liturgical material.

Lk. 2$^{22-40}$: *The Presentation in the Temple.* The distinctive motif of the story, the prophecy of the two exemplars of piety about Jesus, must have been current before the version used by Luke. For there is an artificial motivation for bringing the child Jesus into the Temple, the scene of the prophecy. And indeed it is twofold: (1) The sacrifice of purification as prescribed in Lev. 12; of course this requires only the mother to appear in the Temple; hence is added (2) the παραστῆσαι required by Exod. 13, which is interpreted by the author as a presentation of the child in the Temple, which in reality it neither had meant nor could mean, though it had to serve here as a motive to bring the parents with the child into the Temple. Possibly the end of v. 22 (from παραστῆσαι on) and v. 23 were added later; v. 24 follows on v. 22 (except the end). It is also possible that the original form of the story has been enlarged by a number of additions (cp. Klostermann) and in particular, as Loisy conjectures, by the section from the end of v. 28 to the beginning of v. 34; that would mean that in vv. 28–32 a universalist prophecy was added to one applying to Israel alone (v. 34).

The prophecy, which is the chief motif, is given in a double version: Simeon and Anna are doublets, which is made clear by the fact that there is really nothing for Anna to say after Simeon has spoken. The motif itself appears also in the legend of the Buddha, where it is said that the aged ascetic Asita, instructed by divine knowledge, came to the palace belonging to the father of the new-born child, and took the child into his arms and foretold the great role he would play, which he himself, nearing the end of his life, would not live to see. I do not think the relationship is sufficiently close to assume any dependence of the Christian legend on the Buddhist. Moreover the legend is too little characteristic to justify tracing back its every appearance to some source. It could have been more widespread in

Hellenism.[1] E. Meyer (*Ursprung und Anfaenge des Christentums*, I, p. 65), believes that the double prophecy of Simeon and Anna 'is reminiscent of the way in which, in Callisthenes,[2] when the oracle of Ammon reveals Alexander's divine origin, the revived oracle of Branchidae and the Sibyl Athenais of Erythrae announce at the same time his generation by Zeus; only what in Callisthenes is a conscious literary device appears here as naïve legend'.

For the rest, it is clear that Lk. 2²²⁻⁴⁰ is, like 2¹⁻²⁰, in origin an independent individual story. Simeon's prophecy gives the right impression only when it is the first. And as a matter of fact v. 33 also tells of the parents' astonishment, which has a proper motive only if nothing had previously been said to them about their child becoming the cause of Israel's σωτηρία.

Lk. 2⁴¹⁻⁵²: *Jesus in the Temple*. This is also originally an independent story, which does not presuppose those that precede it, as vv. 48 and 50 in particular show, for in them the parents still have no idea of the real importance of their child. The section has a double point: (1) the surprising wisdom of the youthful Jesus (v. 47); (2) his tarrying in the Temple, which makes known his religious destiny. Yet the two motifs are so closely related that there is no need to assume that they once existed apart in a literary form. There are many parallels to the first motif. Similar material can be found in Jos., Ant., II, 9, 6 = § 230f.; and Philo, Vit. Mos., I, 21 about Moses; Jos., Vit., 2 = § 9 actually of himself. Herodotus (I, 114f.) reports similarly of Cyrus, Plutarch, Alex., 5 of Alexander; and Philostratus, Vit. Apoll., I, 7 of Apollonius. The motif is also to be found in Chinese legend, cp. R. Wilhelm, *Chinesische Volksmaerchen* (1917), p. 287.[3] The oldest example is actually found in the Egyptian story of Setme Chamois. 'In the very damaged introduction it is related how Setme Chamois, son of King Ramses II and High Priest of Ptah of Memphis, and his wife Meh-Usechet were for a long time childless. One day Meh-Usechet dreamt that she would become pregnant after partaking of a certain fruit. She acted accordingly. Immediately

---

[1] The Buddhist text in J. Aufhauser, *Buddha and Jesus* (Kl. Texte, no. 157), 1926, pp. 9–11. Cp. according to others, R. Garbe, *Indien und das Christentum*, 1914, pp. 48–50, who argues for the dependence of the Christian legend on the Buddhist. Otherwise K. Beth, *T.S.K.* 89 (1916), pp. 192–202, who also refers to admittedly even less relevant Egyptian parallels. Against this dependence also E. Windisch in 'Aufsaetze zur Kultur- und Sprachgeschichte, vornehmlich des Orients', *E. Kuhn zum 70. Geburtstage gewidmet*, 1916, pp. 1–13; C. Clemen, *Rel. gesch. Erkl. d. N.Ts.*[2], pp. 209–11.

[2] In Strabo, XVII, 1.43. E. Meyer, op. cit., 68, discovers in the prophecy directed to Mary in v. 35a a reminiscence of the originally heathen saying, that was later adopted by the Jewish Sibyl: ῥομφαία γὰρ διελεύσεται διὰ μέσον σεῖο (Sib., III, 316, to the Egyptians).

[3] There combined with the motif found in the story of Moses of the saving of a hero in childhood in a basket entrusted to the river. The theme frequently appearing in fairy stories of a youth strong in body is of course only a distant analogy.

following on this Setme dreamed that a god commanded him to call the expected child Si-Osire. The youth, as we learn at the end of the story, was a dead person who had returned to the world, Hor, son of Penesh, a magician, who had lived a millennium and a half previously, and now, on his own request to Osiris the god of the dead, had been sent back to life, to keep the Egyptian magicians from the disgrace of being overcome in their art by a negro.'[1] Then in the text we read: 'The child grew and waxed strong. He was sent to [school]; [quickly he outstripped] the scribe entrusted with his education. . . . [Then when the] child Si-Osire attained the age of twelve, he had reached so far that no [scribe or sage could equal him] in reading the books of magic.' There is a parallel to the second motif in the story of R. Eliezer ben Hyrcanus, who ran away from his father to study the law, and was found in the law school by his father who came to Jerusalem to disinherit him.[2] There is also a parallel in the Buddha legend: During an excursion with some young people the young Gautama left his companions, and alone under a tree got lost in pious meditation in which spirits paid homage to him. Meanwhile the king had missed his son, and instituted a search for him. He was found under the tree, whose shadow had not moved round with the sun; and his father, overwhelmed with what he saw, praised his son.[3] Obviously there is no question of this story being a source, though it is a very instructive analogy.

SUPPLEMENT

Mk. 6[14-29] par.: *The Death of the Baptist*. This is a legend exhibiting no Christian characteristics. We cannot know from what tradition Mark has taken it. But since it could hardly have had a place in the Christian tradition from the very beginning,[4] it would seem probable that Mark took it over from Hellenistic Jewish tradition. This is also made feasible by the fact that there are heathen parallels.[5] The story is then perhaps an indication of a branch of Baptistry on Hellenistic soil. Mark introduced the story so as to fill the gap

[1] G. Moeller in H. Gressmann, *Abh. d. Kgl. Akademie d. Wiss. zu Berlin*, 1918, phil.-hist. Kl. no. 7, pp. 62–68; cp. Griffith, *Stories*, I, pp. 11ff.; H. Gressmann, *Protestantenblatt*, 1916 no. 16; L. Radermacher, *Rhein. Mus.*, 73, 1920, pp. 232–9; G. Roeder, *Altaegypt. Erzaehlungen u. Maerchen*, 1927, pp. 158ff.
[2] Bin Gorion, *Der Born Judas*, II, pp. 18–24 (two variants).
[3] G. A. Van den Bergh van Eysinga, *Indische Einfluesse auf evangelische Erzaehlungen* (Forschungen zur Religion und Literatur des A. und N.Ts. 4), 1904, pp. 26f. and G. Faber, Buddhistische und neutestamentliche Erzaehlungen (*Untersuchungen zum N.T.*), 1913, pp. 39–41; C. Clemen, *Rel. gesch. Erkl. d. N.Ts.*[2], p. 212.
[4] According to W. Bussmann, *Synopt. Studien*, I, pp. 30–34, Ur-Mark did not contain it.
[5] Herod., IX, 108–13; Livy, XXXIX, 43; Plut., *Artax*, 17. H. Windisch, *Z.N.W.*, XVIII, 1917, pp. 73ff., tries, in vain I think, to argue for the historicity of the story.

between the sending out of the disciples and their return. In v. 14 (where we should read ἔλεγεν) he has used a piece of the tradition as introduction, and this may have had a different sequel originally. Yet all conjectures how this may have run (cp. especially Wellhausen, ad loc. and on Matt. 6³⁰⁻³³) are incapable of proof. Vv. 15f. come from Mark himself, and indeed he took the motif of v. 15 from the tradition used in 8²⁸. V. 16 only takes v. 14 up again, and gives ἀκούσας a different object from ἤκουσεν in v. 14, namely, what has just been said: ὅν ἐγὼ κτλ is formed out of the story which follows.[1]

2. Concerning the History of the Material

From the survey of the material it can be seen straightaway that it is not an unity. The legendary motifs are of diverse origin and have found their present form in diverse circumstances. One section exhibits specifically Jewish features and the influence of the O.T. The section on the antecedents of the Baptist in Lk. 1 is as a whole borrowed from Judaism, or alternatively from the Jewish Baptist community, even if it existed in an Hellenistic environment. The two psalms in Lk. 1⁴⁶⁻⁵⁵ and 1⁶⁷⁻⁷⁹ (pp. 296f.) are also of Jewish origin. The prophecy of the birth of Messiah in Lk. 1²⁶⁻²⁸ (without vv. 34–37, pp. 295f.) exhibits Jewish characteristics, though the story in this instance has not been taken over from Judaism, but has some Jewish-Christian original behind it. The story of the Temptation in Q (Matt. 4¹⁻¹¹ par., pp. 254ff.) is fashioned in the spirit of Judaistic Christianity, even if we may not regard the basic motif of the Temptation as specifically Jewish. Similarly the Presentation in the Temple Lk. 2²²⁻⁴⁰ (pp. 299f.) is painted with Jewish or O.T. colours without the motif itself being characteristically Jewish. The story could have grown up in Hellenistic-Christian circles of Jewish origin. And the same applies to the story of Jesus in the Temple (Lk. 2⁴¹⁻⁵², pp. 300f.) and of the disciples on the way to Emmaus (Lk. 24¹³⁻³⁵, pp. 286 and 289f.). It is characteristic of all these stories that they arise out of the spirit of messianic hopes and intuitions and that in them the Christ-myth of Hellenistic Christianity of the Pauline sort has no influence at all, and that Christ does not have the place of a cultic deity. On the other hand it is unnecessary and indeed not probable to suppose in regard to these passages that they had already been given their form or

---

[1] M. Goguel, Jean-Baptiste, 1928, pp. 46–49 thinks v. 14 is editorial, though the motif does not come from Mk. 8²⁸ but from an older Tradition. This latter is quite possible. But in contrast to Goguel I believe that we have to infer from v. 14 that there were more reports of miracles by the Baptist. And precisely that gave rise to the question whether Jesus were the resurrected Baptist (cp. pp. 23f.). For the rest, the conclusion follows, that in contrast to the presentation in John, the ministry of Jesus did not begin until after the death of John the Baptist.

alternatively taken over by the Palestinian Church. Their literary character is such that one has to assume their formation in a more developed form of Christianity than the Palestinian Church attained —apart, that is, from Q's narrative of the Temptation.

Even if it can be said in general that the Messianic outlook had little significance in Hellenistic Christianity, but that the figure of Jesus was conceived of in mythical and cultic categories, it would still be wrong not to take account of the high proportion of Hellenistic Christianity which came out of Jewish-Hellenistic circles. Unfortunately the picture of *Jewish-Hellenistic Christianity* is still very obscure and its exploration has hardly begun. It is certain that there was a strong Jewish-Hellenistic Christianity, and a chief proof is the fact that the history of the Synoptic tradition appears in a Greek dress. I do not believe it is possible to state sufficiently sharply the contrast in the N.T. Canon with the Synoptic Gospels on the one hand and the Pauline letters and later literature on the other. It must still be a puzzle to understand why Christianity, in which Pauline and post-Pauline tendencies played so dominant a role, should also have the motives which drove it to take over and shape the Synoptic tradition out of the Palestinian Church. And this puzzle can only be solved by recognizing that there were strata of Hellenistic Christianity of which so far little is known, and on the further working out of which everything must depend. This will enable an important place to be given to the Jewish-Hellenistic element. Yet it is characteristic that the N.T. writing which shows the clearest marks of relationship to Jewish Hellenism, the Epistle to the Hebrews, is also the N.T. writing which more than any other— apart from the Synoptics—has the greatest interest in the life of Jesus. The infancy narratives in Luke seem to me particularly important sources of this Jewish-Hellenistic Christianity.

Possibly we should include the Baptism here. If it exhibits an Hellenistic quality in its combination of Spirit and Baptism (as explained on pp. 250f.) it belongs, as a legend of the dedication of the Messiah, to the circle of Messianic ideas.

Of course not every influence of the O.T. indicates a Jewish-Christian origin. The proof from prophecy played an important role right away in the Hellenistic Church, and this by no means only in circles of Jewish origin. We have already seen on pp. 281f. how important it was for the Passion story itself. Here it would be manifestly absurd always to be asking whether the origin were Palestinian, Jewish-Hellenistic or purely Hellenistic, as it would, e.g. be foolish to assume on the basis of Isa. 1[3] a Jewish Christian influence as the origin of the part played in later Christian tradition by the ox and the ass in the story of the nativity.

In the passages so far considered it is necessary sometimes to distinguish between the basic motif and its actual shape or form. The same origin need not be assumed for both. Indeed there is no occasion for the distinction in the stories of the Baptist's antecedents, in the prophecy of Messiah's birth, or in the two psalms in Lk. 1. But with the other opening stories of Luke we have to ask whether the basic motif has been taken over from pagan Hellenism, e.g. in the story of the Presentation (Lk. 2$^{22-40}$, pp. 299f.) and of Jesus in the Temple (Lk. 2$^{41-52}$, pp. 300f.). In that case the medium by which the stories came into the Christian tradition would be Hellenistic Judaism. Perhaps that may be assumed for the story of the Temptation in Mk. 1$^{12-13}$ (pp. 252f.). In Q this motif is edited under the influence of Hellenistic-Jewish scribes (Matt. 4$^{1-11}$ par., pp. 253ff.). This indubitably means affirming that the source Q, which in its basic form was incontrovertibly a Palestinian document, contained also Hellenistic elements. An Hellenistic editing of Q has to be assumed in any case on other grounds; on this, see below.

It seems clear to me that an Hellenistic origin has to be assumed for the motif of the Virgin Birth, Matt. 1$^{18-25}$ and Lk. 1$^{34f.}$ (pp. 295f.). Admittedly this motif could have entered Palestinian Judaism in pre-Christian times and could also have been taken over by the Palestinian-Christian tradition. But all attempts to prove this seem to me to have been unsuccessful so far; so I think it much more likely that the idea was taken over from an Hellenistic environment. I draw the same conclusion about the stories of the Magi and the Slaughter of the Innocents in Matt. 2$^{1-23}$ (pp. 291f.); the motifs are probably of Hellenistic origin: they evidently received their form in some stage of Hellenistic study of the scriptures, i.e. in a Christianity of Hellenistic-Jewish origin, or of an Hellenistic-Jewish tone. It is highly unlikely that such stories had already been taken over by a pre-Christian Hellenistic Judaism, or that they were told in that environment about the Messiah. How could such stories be told of a Messiah who had yet to come? Finally to this cycle there belongs the story of the birth at Bethlehem, Lk. 2$^{1-20}$ (pp. 297ff.), where Jewish motifs—the dogma of the birth at Bethlehem, the angels—are mixed with Hellenistic—the ideas of σωτήρ, εὐαγγελίζεσθαι, and the shepherds?

From the remaining legendary tradition many individual motifs could have been adopted from pagan Hellenism—such as the miraculous draught of fishes Lk. 5$^{1-11}$ (pp. 217f.); the mocking of

Jesus by the soldiers Mk. 15^{16-20a} (pp. 271f.), etc. Further research could throw more light on this.

Another group of legends is of a quite different kind. Their motifs have grown up within the Christian tradition itself. Indeed we must seek their *origin in Christian faith and Christian worship*, or alternatively in the unconscious tendency to depict the life of Jesus from the standpoint of faith and of cultic ideas. Of course it is also possible here for alien motifs to have influenced the formulation, and in particular we leave out of consideration at this point that Christian faith and Christian worship themselves contained both Jewish and Hellenistic motifs. So here we are concerned only to establish that certain sections of the Gospel story are not to be understood in terms of Jewish or Hellenistic story motifs, but have grown up out of Christian faith and worship.

To this class most particularly belong the Easter stories (see pp. 284–290). It was only natural for belief in the resurrection of Jesus to find immediate expression in such stories; and doubtless such stories were already in circulation in the Palestinian Church. They then grew rapidly and were developed in various ways, and the Easter stories which we now read in the Synoptics have all received their form in the Hellenistic Church. The old Easter story with which Mark closed is unhappily lost; another early Easter story lies behind the story of the Transfiguration and in all probability goes back to Palestinian tradition. By being antedated to take place during the ministry of Jesus it has become a story of an epiphany: The one who has come from heaven appears in his heavenly form (Dibelius, *Formgeschichte*, p. 85). And this antedating would certainly first be undertaken in an Hellenistic environment; possibly it was the work of Mark himself (see pp. 259f.). The story of the Entry into Jerusalem Mk. 11$^{1-10}$ (pp. 218f.) is a messianic legend which had perhaps already grown up in Palestinian Christianity. Finally the account of the proceedings before the Sanhedrin in Mk. 14$^{55-64}$ (pp. 269ff.) must be reckoned as a faith legend, for it is meant to show that Jesus was put to death as the Messiah, which also finds expression in the legendary editing of the story of the Crucifixion. Of course the scene does not arise out of the Messianic dogma—and to this extent it is particularly distinguishable from the stories of the antecedents of the Messiah—but from the common *Christian* belief in the Messiah, and the scene is thus completely in line with the legendary prophecies of the Passion.

The story of the Last Supper in the version of Mk. 14$^{22-25}$ (pp. 265ff.) does not in the first instance derive from the faith of the Church, but from its cult; it is the cult legend for the specifically Hellenistic celebration of the Lord's Supper as we know it in the Hellenistic Christianity established by St. Paul. We have indicated (pp. 250f.) how the story of the Baptism quickly became a cult legend in the Hellenistic Church. We must in the same way also recognize the command to baptize in Matt. 28[16-20] (p. 286) as a cult legend. Finally we must mention the story of Gethsemane in Mk. 14[32-42] (pp. 268f.) in this connection, since, at any rate in its secondary meaning, it has to be reckoned as a faith- or cult-legend. It takes that motif of the Christ-myth formulated by Paul in Phil. 2[8]: γενόμενος ὑπήκοος μέχρι θανάτου and brings it to a perceptual form, and so it could well have originated in an Hellenistic Christianity of a Pauline sort.

It is further possible to reckon among the faith legends those that are due to *apologetic motives*: the prophecy of the betrayal (Mk. 14[17-21] or Lk. 22[21] (pp. 264f.)), the flight of the disciples and the denial in Mk. 14[27-31] or Lk. 22[31f.] (pp. 266f.) and the stories about the sepulchre guards Matt. 27[62-66], 28[11-15] (pp. 275, 286), and a number of small features in the Passion narrative, see pp. 281f. Other legendary portions are better classified as novelistic. The Barabbas episode Mk. 15[6-15a], the mocking by the soldiers Mk. 15[16-20a], Peter's denial Mk. 14[53f.], [66-72] or Lk. 22[54-62], the death of Judas Matt. 27[3-10] (pp. 270-3) are to be counted as such, along with the incident of the women of Jerusalem Lk. 23[27-31] (pp. 37f.). In addition there are smaller novelistic features in the Passion narrative, see pp. 282f.

So one has to say, taking everything into account, that the legendary portions of the Gospel tradition overwhelmingly express the Christian faith and the Messianic circle of ideas, in part being derived directly from them, but in part making use of Old Testament, Jewish or Hellenistic motifs. In comparison with these the cultic motifs have little effect at first, and myth also has no great part to play. This latter applies in reference to the individual stories; for in the Evangelists' work seen as a whole, the Christ-myth of course plays a very great part, particularly in Mark and later in John, in so far as they present the life of Jesus as an epiphany—admittedly veiled in part—of the heavenly Son of God. That only applies to the individual stories in so far as they acquire a new significance in the framework of the Gospel, as is manifestly the case in the story of the Transfiguration in Mk. 9[2-8]. In the same way Mark will have conceived of the story of the Baptism as an epiphany, and Mark and the other evangelists have seen the miracle stories in the same light.[1] The fact that the figure of Jesus is seen in the light of faith, of cult and of myth is also the reason why he is not made the subject of any specific

[1] Cp. M. Dibelius, *Formgeschichte des Evangeliums*, pp. 84–88.

'legend of the saints'. There are no stories depicting him as the pattern of the life of devotion, or which make divine guidance concretely manifest at particular points of his life. There is no interest in his βίος in a purely historical sense, nor in the form of the veneration paid to the saints. The only exception is the story of the child Jesus in the Temple when he was twelve years old Lk. 2 $^{41-52}$ (pp. 30f.), and we may detect a certain tendency in this same direction in the infancy narratives generally, particularly those of Luke, even though they are much more expressions of belief in Jesus as Messiah or σωτήρ.[1]

SUPPLEMENT

Summary of the Technique of the Story

We have dealt with the form of the Apophthegm on pp. 61–69 of the Similitude on pp. 179–192, and of the Miracle Story on pp. 218–244. We must now expand what has already been said by some observations which apply to all narrative sections of the Gospel literature.

The first observation about the Apophthegm was on the great *conciseness of the story*, and this applies throughout. Apart from the Passion narrative there is no part of the story covering more than about two days' activity; only short incidents are reported, that would have occupied no more than a few minutes or hours. It is only when isolated incidents are joined or boxed together that there is an appearance of events stretched out over a longer period of time as in Matt. 2 and Lk. 1 or Mk. 11–13. Further the stories are all constructed out of one theme; whether events are outward or inward, no two are ever reported together if they occur together, e.g. we are not told what the ruler of the Synagogue thought or felt, who had summoned Jesus to his sick daughter, while on the way to his house or during the interruption by the woman with an issue of blood, Matt. 5 $^{21ff.}$ Similarly we are not told what happened among the rulers of the Jews between Mk. 14 $^{1f., 10f., 43ff.}$

Throughout the law of *scenic duality* operates. Apart from Jesus and

---

[1] M. Dibelius, *Th.R.*, N.F.1, 1929, pp. 206f., rightly refers to the absence of any proper 'legends of the saints'. He also emphasizes the fact that there is likewise no such legendary interest in the subordinate figures; even in their case we can find only tendencies like Lk. 23 $^{39-43}$ (The Penitent Thief). Other material, which must have once been recounted at greater length, like the story of Pilate's Wife (see above, p. 282, n. 2) has certainly been suppressed. For the rest, this attitude of the Synoptic Tradition corresponds to the Jewish attitude to legend. If the Jewish Tradition tells the stories of Adam and the Patriarchs (especially Abraham), of the Exodus from Egypt, of the Giving of the Law and the Wandering in the Wilderness, and decks them out with legendary incidents, if it reports the wonders of the Tabernacle and Temple, of the cult and of Jerusalem, if it recounts legendary novels like Daniel and Tobit and the martyrs, the interest nevertheless fastens not on the βίος of the holy man or the θεῖος ἄνθρωπος, but on God, his law, his sanctuary, his city, and on his guidance of his people.

his interlocutor (or a group of interlocutors) many more people can appear on the scene—even if the number be still limited—but almost always it is only Jesus and the interlocutor who share in the significant action, though, of course, the other party can be a group. Thus in the discussion in Mk. 2$^{5-10}$ the paralytic is quite disregarded. Or the tax-gatherer in Mk. 2$^{15-17}$ is but a non-participant figure at the feast; the Pharisees address the disciples, but even they are immediately forgotten, and Jesus answers his opponents. And if the disciples are thought of as being present at the conflict dialogues, they are also not participants. And even if several persons are necessary for the story, they appear one after another. The story of Peter's denial in Mk. 14$^{53f., 66-72}$ or Lk. 22$^{54-62}$ is thoroughly characteristic. Here the narrator has not managed to have Peter in the middle of a crowd of servants and maids and show how he was attacked from several quarters and vainly tried to defend himself, but the story is laid out in three small scenes following one upon another. This primitive technique, as this example shows, can reach the heights of artistic effect. On the other hand there is nothing but the impression of primitivity when in Mk. 5$^{21-43}$ the story of the Woman with the Issue of Blood is simply intruded into the Raising of Jairus' daughter. In the same way, when the Jewish elder and the friends of the Centurion come to Jesus one after the other in Lk. 7$^{1-10}$ the former are at once forgotten as soon as the latter appear on the scene. It is already a secondary stage of development when in the Matthew version of the story of the Syro-Phoenician woman the disciples speak as well as Jesus and the woman (Matt. 15^{23}). Similarly Matthew has brought the mother into the story of the Sons of Zebedee, but he drops her out right away. There are only very few incidents where three persons really have an equal standing alongside each other, thus Lk. 7$^{36-50}$ (The Woman at the Feast) and Lk. 10$^{38-42}$ (Mary and Martha).

As we have said, instead of an individual person we may find *a group*, though then, conforming to primitive style, it is treated as an unity: The Pharisees, the Disciples, the Relatives, the People of Nazareth, etc. The groups speak either as a choir (Mk. 2$^{16, 24}$, 9^{11}, etc.) or by their representative; thus Peter speaks for the Disciples (Mk. 8^{29}, 9^{5}, 10^{28}, etc.), the High Priest for the Sanhedrin (Mk. 14^{60}). It is almost never possible to detect a differentiation inside a group, the most notable case being in the Easter story in Matt. 28^{17}: οἱ ἰδόντες αὐτὸν προσεκύνησαν, οἱ δὲ ἐδίστασαν. Otherwise the disciples appear as an unitary group even in the Easter stories, sharing both doubt and joy (Lk. 24$^{11, 37}$). It is clearly a sign of a more developed style when individuals are singled out of the group in John, when, e.g. in the Feeding of the Five Thousand (6^{5-9}) and in the story of the Greeks (12^{20-22}) Philip and Andrew come forward, or when in the last discourse Thomas (14^3) and Judas (14^{22}) ask questions. In the same way it is secondary when doubt about the Resurrection, which in Matt. 28^{17} is represented by a group among the disciples, finds an individual representative in the Fourth Gospel in the person of Thomas (20^{24}). It is characteristic that in the Apocryphal tradition *Epist. Apost.* 11 (ed. C. Schmidt, pp. 42f.) Peter should put his hand into the nail-prints of Jesus' hand, Thomas into his side and Andrew into his foot-print.

Such a *tendency to differentiation and individualization* can be found frequently in the history of popular tradition. Where two or more persons appear one after the other, they were not differentiated at the primitive stage. There is no differentiation—apart from the individualizing giving of names—in the call of the two pairs of disciples in Mk. 1^{16-20}, nor in the story of the Sons of Zebedee in Mk. $10^{35ff.}$, or in the story of the Samaritan village in Lk. $9^{51ff.}$ Differentiation is a sign of secondary formulation; the story of the calling of the disciples in Jn. 1^{35-51} shows disciples who were first called in all their individual differences. Similarly Mark (and following him Matthew) does not differentiate between the criminals who were crucified with Jesus; in Lk. 23^{39-43} the differentiation has begun. With this we may compare how in the story of Arion in Herod, I, 24 the whole crew of the ship is determined to kill Arion, while in Plut. Conv. Sept. Sap. 18 the coxswain has separated from the group and sides with Arion. Similarly with the Dionysus saga in C. Jul. Hyginus, Poet. Astr. 2, 17 and in Apollod., Bibl. III, 5.3, pp. 117, 21ff. (Wagner) the coxswain does not appear, though he plays a part in Homer Hymn VII and in Ovid, Metam. III, 600ff. Similarly in Gen. $37^{18ff.}$ Reuben, or Judah takes the side of Joseph against his unfriendly brethren; unfortunately in this instance there has not been preserved the earlier stage of the story in which all Joseph's brethren were opposed to him. In the same way out of the originally undifferentiated mass of the 'Army of the Dead' (the 'Wild Hunt') the individual figure of a speaker raises itself.[1] The differentiation of a duality, at any rate by the giving of individual names can be seen in the story of the Transfiguration Mk. 9^{2-8}: The originally anonymous holy ones (see pp. 26of.) were differentiated and individualized as Moses and Elijah. Similarly the disciples who were sent

[1] Cp. Fr. Ranke, *Die Deutschen Volkssagen* (v. d. Leyen, Deutsches Sagenbuch, IV[2], 1924, pp. 113f.).

out to prepare the Passover were still anonymous in Mk. 14¹³ though in Lk. 22⁸ they are cited as Peter and John.¹

Even without any purpose of differentiation, *the tendency to individualize by naming* is manifestly strong. That has already been shown to be true in the cases of apophthegms and miracle stories (pp. 67f., 241f.); it applies also to the other stories to which names were added in later texts, or in later reproductions of the Synoptic stories. While in all three Synoptics the name of the disciple who drew his sword in Gethsemane and that of the High Priest's servant remain unknown, John 18¹⁰ knows the former as Peter and the latter as Malchus. It is the same thing when Jn. 18²⁶ identifies the δοῦλος who argues with Peter as a kinsman of Malchus. The thieves on the cross have been given different names in different texts and in the Gospel of Nicodemus: Zoathan and Hammata, or Dysmas and Gestas, etc. The captain of the sepulchre guard is called Petronius in the Gospel of Peter. The Magi in Matt. 2¹ff· have as Three Kings of Orient likewise been given individual names in the tradition of the Church.² The mount of the Temptation is named Tabor in the Gospel to the Hebrews, though elsewhere that is the name for the Mount of Transfiguration (Jerome, Ep. 46, 108) and in Cod δ 30 the mountain of Matt. 28¹⁶ is also called Tabor. To illustrate the process, it is sufficient to remember that the fruit which Adam tasted in Paradise was identified in different branches of the tradition as an olive, a fig, an apple, etc.³

It has already been shown in regard to apophthegms and miracle stories pp. 62f., 219f. that the *motives and feelings* of Jesus and the other participants are very seldom referred to. Now and again of course motives and feelings can be clearly recognized; they are in such cases indicated indirectly by actions and words. There is no mention of Peter's repentance, simply the words: ἐπιβαλὼν ἔκλαιεν (Mk. 14⁷²)· The High Priest tears his vestment (Mk. 14⁶³); but of his own feelings and those of the rest of the Sanhedrin there is no word. In Mk. 15⁴⁰ the women stand afar off at the crucifixion, but all that is said is: θεωροῦσαι. In Mk. 16¹ff· they come to the sepulchre, without a word being used to describe their mood; the only thing mentioned is their wondering question: τίς ἀποκυλίσει ἡμῖν τὸν λίθον ἐκ τῆς θύρας

---

¹ Cp. how in the ancient tradition the Muses and Graces were individualized at a secondary stage by being named.

² Cp. A. Meyer in E. Hennecke, *Neutest. Apokryphen*², 1924, pp. 78–80.

³ When in *Epist. Apost.*, 5 (ed. C. Schmidt, p. 31), it is not Peter but just 'one of the disciples' who appears in the story of the Temple tax, it is possible that an older tradition than Matt. 17²⁴ff· is showing through at that point. Nevertheless it is probably of some importance that here the whole body of the disciples reports ('since we had no money'.. 'let one of you cast the fish hook into the deep').

τοῦ μνημείου; Nothing is told of the motive of Joseph of Arimathea (Mk. 15 ⁴³ᶠᶠ·). It is only what the centurion at the cross said, not his feelings, that is reported; it was Matthew (27 ⁵⁴) who first says of him and his companions that they ἐφοβήθησαν σφόδρα. It is of course a quite secondary reflection when Jerome (Ep. 65.8 *Ad Principiam*) writes: *nisi enim habuisset (Jesus) et in vultu quiddam oculisque sidereum, nunquam eum statim secuti fuissent apostoli nec, qui ad comprehendendum eum venerant corruissent*; or when, in *Comm. in Matth.*, 9, 9 he speaks of the *fulgor ipse et majestas divinitatis occultae, quae etiam in humana facie relucebat*, or comments on the Cleansing of the Temple (on Matt. 21 ¹²): *igneum enim quiddam atque sidereum radiabat ex oculis eius et divinitatis majestas lucebat in facie.*[1] All such personal descriptions are, of course, far removed from the Synoptic mode of story telling.

Now and again however there are some small specially evident traces of the need for a plastic presentation. This is so when in Mk 10. ⁴⁹ᶠ· it is said of the blind man: ὁ δὲ ἀποβαλὼν τὸ ἱμάτιον αὐτοῦ ἀναπηδήσας ἦλθεν πρὸς τὸν ᾽Ιησοῦν, or when Luke (7 ¹⁴) remarks of the coffin-bearers: οἱ δὲ βαστάζοντες ἔστησαν. Similarly Mk. 4 ³⁸ tells us that Jesus: ἦν ἐν τῇ πρύμνῃ ἐπὶ τὸ προσκεφάλαιον καθεύδων. Such traces are very rare. The novelistic interest which dominates them, only comes really to life in the later development of the tradition. See for the apophthegms, pp. 68f.; for the Passion narrative, pp. 282f. There is an example of this sort of thing in the Clementine Liturgy, where there is a descriptive recitation of the Eucharistic words: ἐν ᾗ γὰρ νυκτὶ παρεδίδοτο, λαβὼν ἄρτον ταῖς ἁγίαις καὶ ἀμώμοις αὐτοῦ χερσὶ καὶ ἀναβλέψας πρὸς σέ, τὸν θεὸν αὐτοῦ καὶ πατέρα, καὶ κλάσας ἔδωκε τοῖς μαθηταῖς, εἰπών . . . ὡσαύτως καὶ τὸ ποτήριον κεράσας ἐξ οἴνου καὶ ὕδατος καὶ ἁγιάσας ἐπέδωκεν αὐτοῖς λέγων κτλ (Lietzmann, Kl. Texte, no. 61, pp. 18f.).

Such *novelistic tendencies* also show themselves in small details: The young man of Nain is the only son of his mother and she is a widow Lk. 7 ¹². That this is a typical feature of a legend is shown, e.g. by Lk. 9 ³⁸, where the epileptic boy is made the only son of his father, a matter about which Mk. 9 ¹⁷ is ignorant. Similarly Lk. 8 ⁴² where the daughter of the ruler of the synagogue has become his only daughter in contrast to Mk. 5 ²³. Still more innocuous, but methodically of interest, is the ear which was cut off from the servant in Gethsemane. In Lk. 22 ⁵⁰ it is the right ear, a fact which was not yet known to Mk. 14 ⁴⁷; in the same way the withered hand which Jesus healed has become the right hand in Lk. 6 ⁶ in contrast to Mk. 3 ¹. The same unconscious need of special verisimilitude appears here as in the

[1] Cp. A. Schmidtke, *Neue Fragmente*, etc., p. 286.

relationship of Matt. 5²⁹, ³⁰ to Mk. 9⁴³, ⁴⁵, ⁴⁷; while Mark speaks generally of hand, foot and eye, Matthew specifically mentions the right eye and the right hand. It is the same thing when in most manuscripts of Matt. 5³⁹ the reference is to a slap on the right cheek, whereas Lk. 6²⁹ mentions cheek in general. The question whether Jesus meant a slap with the inside or the back of the hand[1] is as without taste as it is lacking in understanding of the plastic art of popular speech.

In this connection there is the use of another means of popular speech—the *use of direct speech*. We have already indicated how it serves for reproducing motives and feelings; moreover we have shown on pp. 190f. how favourite an instrument it is in the telling of a similitude. But now there appears in the Tradition a further tendency to produce new sayings of the person engaged, in part as a continuation and expansion of sayings already there, in part as a transposition of an earlier report into direct speech. Of course it is not possible to speak of a natural law here; it also happens that a saying in direct speech is put into indirect, but the opposite tendency is remarkable everywhere.

Peter's ἐπιτιμᾶν in Mk. 8³² is interpreted in Matt. 16²² by the direct saying: ἵλεώς σοι, κύριε, οὐ μὴ ἔσται σοι τοῦτο, and the invective of Jesus in v. 23 contains the addition of σκάνδαλον εἶ ἐμοῦ. The request for the interpretation of the παραβολή in Mk. 7¹⁷ appears in direct speech in Matt. 15¹⁵, as does the request of the Phoenician woman in Matt. 15²², ²⁵ by contrast with Mk. 7²⁶; and the command to silence in Matt. 17⁹ in distinction from Mk. 9⁹. Instead of the indirect report of the quarrel among the disciples in Mk. 9³³f.; Matt. 18¹ says that the disciples came to Jesus with the question: τίς ἄρα μείζων ἐστὶν ἐν τῇ βασιλείᾳ τ. οὐρ. The report in Mk. 14¹: ἦν δὲ τὸ πάσχα καὶ τὰ ἄζυμα μετὰ δύο ἡμέρας becomes a direct saying of Jesus in Matt. 26¹f.: . . . οἴδατε ὅτι μετὰ δύο ἡμέρας τὸ πάσχα γίνεται. From ἔπιον ἐξ αὐτοῦ πάντες in Mk. 14²³, Matt. 26²⁷ makes πίετε ἐξ αὐτοῦ πάντες. Whereas in the scene of Judas' betrayal there is no word of Jesus reported in Mark at all, Matthew (26⁵⁰) and Luke (22⁴⁸) know of a saying on this occasion (naturally each his own). We may compare with this the fact that Luke has Jesus make a speech on the way to the cross (23²⁸⁻³¹) though here a saying from the tradition has been used (see pp. 37f.). Whereas in Mk. 14¹⁰ Judas goes to the High Priest ἵνα αὐτὸν παραδοῖ αὐτοῖς, Matt. 26¹⁵ tells us that he said: τί θέλετέ μοι δοῦ ναι καὶ ἐγὼ ὑμῖν παραδώσω

---

[1] J. Weismann, *Z.N.W.*, XIV, 1913, pp. 175ff.; K. Bornhaeuser, *Die Bergpredigt*, 1913 p. 95.

αὐτόν. Mk. 14⁶⁴ gives the verdict of the Sanhedrin in the form of a report: in Matt. 26⁶⁶ the judges say: ἔνοχος θανάτου ἐστίν. This process is generally particularly noticeable in the Passion narrative.

The same thing appears in the relationship of Luke to Mark. We have already referred to Lk. 22⁴⁸ and 23²⁸⁻³¹. Further, the injunction to the five thousand to sit down in Chap. 9¹⁴ is, in contrast to Mk. 6³⁹ given in direct speech (the same is true of Jn. 6¹⁰ where the collection of the fragments 6¹² is also consequent upon a direct command of Jesus). And whereas we are told in Mk. 5³⁰f. that when Jesus was touched by the woman with an issue of blood he felt τὴν ἐξ αὐτοῦ δύναμιν ἐξελθοῦσαν and then asked, τίς μου ἥψατο τῶν ἱματίων; Luke gives the whole incident in direct speech: ἥψατό μού τις· ἐγὼ γὰρ ἔγνων δύναμιν ἐξεληλυθυῖαν ἀπ' ἐμοῦ.

Examples increase in the later tradition. In the reproduction of the story of the woman with an issue of blood in the *Epist. Apost.* (ed. C. Schmidt, p. 30) the woman's answer is likewise given in direct speech: 'O Lord, I touched thee.' A number of texts add to Lk. 23⁴⁸ some actual words spoken by the crowds who had been shaken by the τέρατα on the cross. The gospel of Peter also reports such words in § 25. In § 6 the Gospel of Peter gives the words used by the soldiers who maltreated Jesus, etc. A clear example is Peter's lament after his denial, in Heliand vv. 5013–22.

The opposite tendency can be observed only very occasionally. Luke sometimes turns Mark's direct speech into a report (Lk. 8²⁹, ³² for Mk. 5⁸, ¹²) in the interest of the smoother telling of the story, and the same has to be said of the relationship of Matt. 24¹ and Lk. 21⁵ to Mk. 13¹.

So it is in fact possible to talk of something like a law and to judge particular references in terms of it. Thus ἐσπλαγχνίσθη ἐπ' αὐτούς in Mk. 6³⁴ is more original in form than σπλαγχνίζομαι ἐπὶ τὸν ὄχλον in Mk. 8² even if 8² is more original in so far as the compassion of Jesus is directed to the physical needs of the crowd (see pp. 216f.). When two versions of the prayer in Gethsemane are found side by side, an indirect form in Mk. 14³⁵ and a direct form in Mk. 14³⁶, the first must be taken as primary. In the same way Jesus' cry in Mk. 15³⁴ (ἐλωΐ κτλ) is a secondary interpretation of 15³⁷, where it is simply the occurrence of a loud cry that is recorded. Further, in the Charge in Lk. 10¹¹ the sayings about the on-going missionaries are to be reckoned as a secondary formulation over against Matt. 10¹⁴, where all that is retained is the instruction to depart from the unheeding town and to shake its dust from the foot.

Already in reviewing the style of the similitudes, pp. 188–192, we

L

have referred to certain laws of popular story telling, which we must refer to again here. *The law of repetition* can be seen in such instances where either a commission or a command is expressed in the same words, or where analogous actions are said to follow one another, very likely with the same or almost the same phraseology. The second instance is in Q's story of the Temptation (Matt. 4[1-11] par.). In the story of the denial, at any rate in Lk. 22[54-62], there is what almost amounts to a parity of scenes. In the story of Gethsemane Jesus is said indeed to pray and return to his disciples three times in succession, though the same expressions do not recur. The other form of repetition—commissioning a messenger—can be expected in the reports of the preparations for the triumphal entry and for the last supper. Yet it is only hinted at in Mk. 11[2-6], though Lk. 19[30-34] has a more strongly stylized account by his repetition of ὁ κύριος αὐτοῦ χρείαν ἔχει.

Numbers play a special part in popular story telling. We have already referred on p. 191 to the use of the *number three* in the similitudes. It can be found elsewhere: Jesus was three times tempted by the devil (Matt. 4[1-11] par.), he prayed three times in Gethsemane (Mk. 14[32-42]); Peter thrice denied his master (Mk. 14[53f., 66-72] or Lk. 22[54-62]). Perhaps we may also mention the thrice repeated prophecy of the passion (Mk. 8[31], 9[31], 10[33f.]); and possibly also the three privileged disciples Mk. 5[37], 9[2], 14[33]. From the apocryphal literature I would refer to *Epist. Apost.*, 10 (ed. C. Schmidt, pp. 38–41): Martha and Mary tell the disciples about the resurrection the one after the other, without meeting with any belief; the disciples themselves do not believe until Jesus himself comes the third time. Later Tradition speaks of three shepherds who were 'shone round about by the glory of the Lord' at Bethlehem.[1]

But the *number two* is specially important. Twice two disciples are called in Mk. 1[16-20]. Jesus sends the disciples out two by two in Mk. 6[7], Lk. 10[1]. Two disciples are the centre of the question asked by the sons of Zebedee Mk. 10[35ff.], as in the story of the inhospitable Samaritans Lk. 9[51ff.]. Two disciples take the walk to Emmaus in Lk. 24[13ff.]. Of special interest are those occasions when the two persons are plainly just nominal figures. Such nominal figures are found in Mk. 11[2] and 14[13] (the sending of the two to prepare for the triumphal entry and the last supper); two holy ones appear with Jesus in the resurrection story which lies behind the account of the transfiguration in Mk. 9[4]; two thieves were crucified with Jesus, Mk. 15[27].

[1] Arkulf (*circa* 670) in Geyer, *Itinera* 258 (cited in G. Dalman, *Orte u. Wege Jesu*[3], 1924, p. 49).

It would be plainly false to trace this number two to some mythical motif, as Rendel Harris (Dioscurismus)[1] or Clifford Pease Clark[2] want to do. It is much more likely that here we meet a completely popular folk motif, in all probability resting on the demands of comprehension, or symmetry.

The nominal figures can be envisaged as on the left and right of the hero, the altar, the door, etc.; the symmetrical grouping of a stage photo comes to mind (as when the king is accompanied by two pages or two knights). There are many examples of this sort of thing in folk poetry, e.g. 'Two snow white doves fly o'er my house' or in the song 'And now we ride outside the gate', the verse:

> 'And then inside the room he stepp'd.
>   By pale twin lights espying
> Twin maidens who their vigil kept
>   For the dead bride a-crying.'

And further:

> 'Evenings, when I go to sleep
> Fourteen angels vigil keep.
> Two keep watch at my right hand,
> Two mount guard at my left hand,
> Two join wings about my head,
> Two protect at foot of bed,
> Two do cover me up quite,
> Two will wake me when it's light,
> Two are there to make me wise
> To the way to Paradise.'[3]

From ancient times I recall the two serpents which approached the infant Hercules (Vergil, *Aen.*, 8, 288; Pind., Nem., 1, 66; Theocr., 24, 26) and the two serpents which strangled Laocoon and his sons (in spite of the three human beings involved! Vergil, *Aen.*, 2, 200ff.). In *Aen.*, 8, 697 Vergil tells of two serpents belonging to Cleopatra, whereas prose authors tell of only one. Clark, op. cit., cites a number of examples from Vergil, whose weapons, presents, etc., are stated to to be in pairs. More interesting as comparisons with the Synoptics in the passage already quoted from Wetstein in Mk. 16[5] who in turn cites Dionys. Hal., *Ant.*, VI, 13: ἐν ταύτῃ λέγονται τῇ μάχῃ . . . ἱππεῖς δύο φανῆναι κάλλει τε καὶ μεγέθει μακρῷ κρείττους, ὧν ἡ καθ' ἡμᾶς φύσις ἐκφέρει . . . καὶ μετὰ τὴν τροπὴν τῶν Λατίνων . . . ἐν τῇ Ῥωμαίων

---

[1] *Boanerges*, Cambridge, 1913.
[2] *Numerical Phraseology in Vergil*, Princeton, 1913.
[3] Cp. on the *number two* the contributions of Fr. Neumann and E. Mogk in H. Haas, *Das Scherflein der Witwe*, 1922, pp. 118, 120, 155ff.

ἀγορᾷ τὸν αὐτὸν τρόπον ὀφθῆναι δύο νεανίσκοι λέγονται . . . μήκιστοι καὶ κάλλιστοι καὶ τὴν αὐτὴν ἡλικίαν ἔχοντες . . . οὓς μεταχωρήσαντας ἐκ τῆς ἀγορᾶς ὑπ᾽ οὐδενὸς ἔτι λέγουσιν ὀφθῆναι.

From the Christian and Jewish traditions may be mentioned the two angels at the ascension Acts 1[10]; similarly two angels appear in 2 Macc. 3[26] and 3 Macc. 6[18]. Two 'men' carry up the heavenly old man in Herm., *Vis.*, I, 4, 2. In the Apocalypse of Peter (Akhmim-text, § 6) two holy ones appear alongside the risen Lord. In Acts 10[7] Cornelius sends two messengers to Peter, and in the story quoted in Fiebig, *Juedische Wundergeschichten*, pp. 19f., *Der Erzaehlungsstil der Evangelien*, p. 105, R. Gamaliel sends two pupils to R. Haninah b. Dosa. Here belong the two olive-trees which stand on the right and left of the lamp in Zech. 4[3], and which are called the two sons of oil that stand as servants by the Lord of the whole earth; perhaps also the two Ethiopians who kneel by Adam before God (*Vit. Ad. et Ev.*, 36) and are then called the sun and the moon.[1] Finally perhaps we can trace back to this same motif the two μάρτυρες in Rev. 11[3ff.] to which Bousset, *Der Antichrist*, 1895, p. 139.1 offers some parallels; meanwhile I would not suppose that in individual cases other special mythological motifs have not occasioned the use of the number two.[2]

That it is possible to talk of some sort of law of this mode of presentation can be seen from those cases where originally there was only one nominal figure, but in the next stage we find two reported. In Mk. 16[5] there is one angel at the tomb; this has become two in Lk. 24[4]; the Gospel of Peter §36 also states that two angels come from heaven to open the tomb of Jesus, and similarly Cod. Bobb. at Mk. 16[4]: *et descenderunt de caelis angeli et surgit in claritate et viri duo simul ascenderunt cum eo*. Correspondingly Luke's statement Lk. 7[19] that the Baptist sent two messengers to Jesus is without doubt a development of the Q version retained in Matthew: πέμψας διὰ τῶν μαθητῶν αὐτοῦ. The same conclusion must manifestly be drawn when Matt. 8[28ff.] makes two out of the possessed man of Mk. 5[1ff.], and Matt. 20[29ff.] mentions two blind men instead of the one in Mk. 10[46ff.]; the healing of the two blind men in Matt. 9[27ff.] is told under the influence of the same art of story telling. A similar judgement can be passed on the Nazarean edition of Matthew in the story of the rich young ruler (see p. 68), if the fragmentary character of the tradition does not prohibit a confident judgement.

Quite outstandingly instructive are the parallels from plastic art.

[1] Cp. A. Meyer, *Die Auferstehung Christi*, 1905, pp. 342f.
[2] Cp. C. Clemen, *Rel. gesch. Erkl. d. N.Ts.*[2], pp. 114–6. The 'two' typical of the appearance stories (cp. J. Kroll, *Beitr. zum Descensus ad inferos*, Verz. d. Vorl. an d. Akad. zu Braunsberg, 1922, p. 35.3) has however to be understood in the sense indicated above.

In his *Altorientalischen Symbolik*, H. Prinz has dealt with a whole series of representations in which one figure, which one would expect to see once only, is portrayed twice in terms of the 'law of formal reduplication which dominates Babylonian art' (p. 102; cp. pp. 102–8 and the examples on p. 61ff.: two bull-men who hold the stake on which the sun's disc rests; 92: the deity standing on two beasts lying turned in opposite directions from each other).[1] In ancient Christian art there is on a sarcophagus a representation of Daniel flanked by two lions (*Dictionnaire d'archéologie chrétienne et de liturgie*, II, pp. 357f.), and on carved ivory of the twelve-year-old Jesus between two scribes (ibid., pp. 363f.). Two mosaics in Ravenna portray the Baptism of Jesus in this way, since Jesus is depicted as between the Baptist and the river god (ibid., pp. 361f.); correspondingly on an ivory plastic Jesus is found between the Baptist and a bearded man (ibid., p. 366) and between the Baptist and an angel holding his raiment, in a fresco of the Pontius catacomb (ibid., pp. 367f., 374). Some examples from a later time can be added: two angels have been made out of the one at the Annunciation in the paintings of Filippo Lippi in the Munich Pinakothek and of Andrea del Sarto in the Pitti gallery at Florence. The martyrdom of St. Sebastian by Pollaiuolo (National Gallery, London) is a typical example: everything appears both left and right: two executioners, putting their arrows to their bows, two taking aim, and two at just the moment after shooting. Just as the two angels underneath the Virgin in Raphael's Sistine Madonna are present to everyone, so we find two such angels in a great number of pictures of the Adoration: two angels escort Mary to St. Bernard, and two follow her (Filippino Lippi in the Badia Gallery, Florence); there are two angels in Verrocchio's Baptism of Christ (Academia, Florence), and two accompany Mary to St. Bernard (Perugino, Munich, Old Pinakothek). Corresponding to this there are two women sitting at the feet of St. Fina, as St. Gregory tells of her death (Chirlandajo, in S. Gimignano). Most of the examples quoted and many other examples can be found conveniently in R. Hamann, *Die Frueh-Renaissance der italienischen Malerei*, 1909.

Of course the contrast of two types which is often to be found in the similitudes is something quite different (p. 192). From the narrative material in the Synoptics we may refer to Mary and Martha (Lk. 10[38–42]) and the differentiation in Lk. 23[39–43], demonstrably secondary, between the two thieves crucified with Jesus, the one being impenitent and the other contrite.

[1] Cp. further Otto Weber, *Altoriental. Siegelzylinder*, I, 1920, pp. 17.23ff., 28f., 112. M. Dibelius, *Die Lade Jahves*, 1906, pp. 84f.

III. The Editing of the Traditional Material

THERE is no definable boundary between the oral and written tradition, and similarly the process of the editing of the material of the tradition was beginning already before it had been fixed in a written form.[1] In so far as we have dealt with the history of the traditional material in the preceding sections, we have also been dealing with its editing. From that standpoint what we have done was essentially to recognize a certain tradition-law as going right back to the earliest possible form of the material, and what still remains to be done is to describe the editorial process in summary fashion, though with certain restrictions. Thus we shall not consider every change which the material of the tradition has undergone in the course of its history, but only such editorial changes as are due to the assembling of the material; that is, the history of that editorial work which, as far as we are concerned has come to a palpably substantial conclusion in the composition of the Synoptic Gospels. Thus our chief interest will now be the composition of the Gospels. But since it involves nothing in principle new, but only completes what was begun in the oral tradition, it can only be considered in organic connection with the history of the material as it lay before the evangelists. But for this reason the enquiry can be conducted without any special source theory. I presuppose only the so-called two-source theory. I have no doubt that Mark himself used written sources, and that Matthew and especially Luke had access to written sources other than Mark and Q,[2] but I do not propose to count on these as actual entities, for it matters little whether this or that editorial process peculiar to the written tradition took place before the Gospels were formed, or in them, even if there are differences in particular cases. Besides this I shall make another limitation in not attempting to be comprehensive. Comprehensiveness in this matter

[1] See pp. 6, 48, 88.
[2] Cp. M. Albertz, *Die synoptischen Streitgespraeche*, 1921, B. S. Easton, *The Gospel before the Gospels*, pp. 71f., and especially A. Meyer, 'Die Entstehung des Markus-Evangeliums', *Festg. f. A. Juelicher*, 1927, pp. 35–60. As Albertz rightly supposes that Mark knew a collection of conflict stories (I leave open whether in one or two collections) the question must be asked whether he knew a collection of miracle stories. In any case John used a σημεῖα-source. For analogies: cp. E. Groos, *Das Vilâjet-Nâme des Haǧǧt Bektasch* (Tuerk. Bibliothek 25), 1927, esp. pp. 208ff.

would demand special enquiries for each Gospel, that is to say, it would be a task of exegesis. Here I am concerned only to make the chief points clear, and to offer some illustrations.[1]

A. The Editing of the Spoken Word

1. THE COLLECTION OF THE MATERIAL AND THE COMPOSITION OF SPEECHES

IT has been shown already how early the editing of the speech material began, when one mashal was joined to another and small groups were formed. There is a natural limit to such groupings in the oral tradition, even if it cannot be precisely defined, a limit which can be exceeded for the first time in the written tradition. But even in the written collections the principles on which larger units are formed are at first no different from what they were in the oral tradition, i.e. it is simply a quite primitive process of adding one small unit to another, and in this similarity of content or some outward likeness (the use of some catchword) is the guiding principle, though now and then pure chance takes a hand. In some such manner as this we can account for comparatively extensive 'speeches' i.e. collections of particular units, and in such collections some sort of conceptual development in the 'speech' could give some sort of guidance. But we cannot in this way account for organic compositions, speeches that are a real unity, dominated by a specific theme and systematically arranged, unless the peculiar character of the ancient traditional material has been completely altered. Happily that did not take place in the Synoptic Gospels. Where it has to a certain extent taken place, as in the Fourth Gospel, it is no longer simply a question of a development of the older tradition, but something quite new comes to light as well.

The primitive stage of *serializing the dominical sayings without reference to their context* is clearly recognizable in our Synoptic Gospels.

Sometimes sayings were put into series without any sort of indication. Thus Mk. 9[43-48] is added on to the preceding verses with a simple γάρ; then v. 49 follows with a γάρ and v. 50a with a δέ, while v. 50b is without any conjunction. So also Mk. 10[31] is connected with its context by δέ.

---

[1] F. Strauss had already conceived the problems rightly (*Leben Jesu*, I, 1835, § 80, pp. 677–86). A wealth of important observations, though not from the standpoint of Form Criticism, can be found in the statistical collection on the way the individual evangelists worked, in W. Larfeld, *Die neutestamentl. Evangelien*, pp. 251–344.

Sometimes καὶ ἔλεγεν serves to indicate such a connection. It is possible that originally καὶ ἔλεγεν or λέγει ὁ 'Ιησοῦς stood there, as it does in the sayings collected in *Pap. Ox.*, I. If a collection like this had been taken up into a Gospel it would have been natural for ὁ 'Ιησοῦς to have fallen out, and the present tense to have been turned into the past, and that some word like αὐτοῖς should have been added to fit the context. This formula can be found frequently in Mk. 2²⁷, 4²¹, ²⁴, ²⁶, ³⁰, 6¹⁰, 7⁹, 9¹ and somewhat expanded in 7¹⁴, 8³⁴.

Sometimes perhaps even ἀμὴν λέγω ὑμῖν, which in many ways of course originally belonged to the saying concerned, can be a mark of such a connection, e.g. Mk. 3²⁸; at least it seems not to have belonged to the Q version of the saying, according to Lk. 12¹⁰. The same question may be asked about Mk. 10¹⁵, 11²³, 13³⁰, where the least that can be said is that in each case a new dominical saying is added on. It seems quite certain to me that διὰ τοῦτο λέγω ὑμῖν in Mk. 11²⁴ is a connecting formula of this kind.

Luke also makes use of these primitive connecting formulae:

5³⁶: ἔλεγεν δὲ καὶ παραβολὴν πρὸς αὐτούς, similarly 12¹⁶, 13⁶.

11⁵: καὶ εἶπεν πρὸς αὐτούς.

11⁹: κἀγὼ ὑμῖν λέγω.

12²²: εἶπεν δὲ πρὸς τοὺς μαθητὰς αὐτοῦ, cp. 17²².

12⁵⁴: ἔλεγεν δὲ καὶ τοῖς ὄχλοις.

14¹²: ἔλεγεν δὲ καὶ τῷ κεκληκότι αὐτόν etc.

In such cases Matthew has tried better to preserve the fiction of a connected speech, by using the following expressions for making connections:

δέ: 6¹, 10¹⁷ (originally ?), 11¹² (originally ?), 12⁴³, 18¹⁵, 25³¹.

γάρ: 6¹⁴.

τότε: 25¹.

οὖν: 5²³, 6⁹, 7¹² (originally ?).

διὰ τοῦτο: 6²⁵ (διὰ τοῦτο λέγω ὑμῖν), 12³¹, 18²³.

πάλιν: 13⁴⁵, ⁴⁷.

More circumstantial formulations: 24⁴³ (ἐκεῖνο δὲ γινώσκετε ὅτι); 25¹³ (γρηγορεῖτε οὖν . . . γάρ following Mk. 13³⁵).

Even if the particles were sometimes inserted by copyists they are not on that account any less characteristic.

Let us cite some examples of the motives which accompanied the making of such a series of sayings.

1. *The ordering of the material.* As early as Q it is manifest that all sorts of small units with any reference to the Baptist had been

assembled together: Matt. 11$^{2-19}$//Lk. 7$^{18-35}$, a group which is afterwards expanded by both Matthew and Luke. In Q the sayings about retaliation and loving one's enemy were joined with those about wealth (Lk. 6$^{27-42}$ par.), and then followed the sayings about bearing fruit, about serving by deeds and by the similitude of house building (Lk. 6$^{43-49}$ par.). As early as Q the conflict with the Pharisees was joined with the saying about the unclean spirit (Lk. 11$^{14-26}$), etc.

In Mark too this assembly of material can be detected. The sayings about outward observance of the law (7$^{9-13}$) and inward defilement (7$^{14-16}$ [$^{-23}$]) are added to the controversy about purity (7$^{1-8}$). Sayings about riches (10$^{23-27}$) and about rewards (10$^{28-31}$) have been added to the conversation with the rich young man (10$^{17-22}$). Mark has attached the similitude of the fig tree (13$^{28f.}$) to his little apocalypse (13$^{3-27}$) as well as varied sayings about the parousia (13$^{30-37}$), etc.

In the antitheses on legal piety in Chap. 5, Matthew, following the principle of subject arrangement, has put the exhortation to forgiveness (vv. 23f.) immediately after the theme of killing; similarly the sayings about temptation in vv. 29f. are joined to the theme of adultery. The Lord's Prayer is made to follow the sayings about prayer in 6$^{9-13}$ and those in turn follow the saying about forgiveness (6$^{14f.}$), etc.

Luke for example has composed a section on the theme of prayer: 11$^{1-4}$ the Lord's Prayer, 11$^{5-8}$ the parable of the importunate friend, 11$^{9-13}$ exhortation to intercession. He has also brought together the saying about inheritance, the story of the rich fool and the sayings about Anxiety in 12$^{13-34}$, and in 12$^{35-59}$ a number of passages concerned in various ways with eschatology.

Such groupings would have been made in different ways with the different types of speech material. If the 'logia' (in the narrower sense) were of the mashal sort, that is in its nature unassimilable into a group, the prophetic sayings in accordance with their nature would more easily be brought together in groups related by their content, provided that sections of assembled units were not primary in this instance. Matthew and Luke found a collection of Beatitudes already in Q, which Matthew enlarged with parallels and Luke with antithetical formulations. In the same way the woes against the Pharisees in Q constitute a group of sayings that belong together, and which Matthew and Luke have shaped differently. Mark has also taken the basis of his eschatological discourse from an older source. Also among the sayings about the law there would have been some primarily connected groups, or at the least groups that were formed very early. Thus behind Matthew 5²¹⁻³⁷ lies a complex of antitheses on legal piety, which Matthew then expanded; similarly the sayings about spiritual exercises in 6¹⁻¹⁸ were already connected, and were then enriched by additions. Similarly the missionary charges were very early or originally in a connected group, from which Mark has made excerpts, while Lk. 10²⁻¹² accurately reproduces Q and Matt. 10⁹⁻¹⁶ joins Q and Mark, and in the course of doing so Luke like Matthew adds all kinds of similar material.

2. *Association by formal relationship.* The similitude section in Mk. 4¹⁻³² is formed on this principle, and the basis seems to be a small collection already known to Mark.[1] Then Matthew in Chap. 13 considerably expands the section by adding new similitudes. Alongside similarity of content there is also a formal relationship in the collection of eschatological similitudes in Matt. 24⁴³–25³⁰ (⁴⁶). This formal relationship is also clearly operative in many smaller sections; thus the saying about judging in Lk. 6³⁶⁻³⁷ᵃ is not joined to the following pieces in 6³⁹ᶠ· (Blind Leaders of the Blind, Disciples and Master) simply because of their associated contents, but also by means of the formally related vv. 37b and 38 (imperative with καί consec.).

3. *Association by catchword.* The use of catchwords which was familiar in Israelite and Jewish literature, can frequently be found, as has long been recognized, in early Christian proverbial literature.[2] This is particularly prominent in Mk. 9³³ᶠᶠ·, see pp. 149f. Similarly in Mk. 4²¹ᶠᶠ·: the addition of the saying about light in vv. 21f. to the parable of the sower is due to the use of the catchword μόδιος, and this in turn has involved the addition of the saying about the measure in v. 24. In any case we then have attached to v. 24 after the catchphrase καὶ προστεθήσεται ὑμῖν—or, if we omit with D, after μετρηθήσεται ὑμῖν—the saying about having and getting in v. 25. In Lk. 14⁷⁻²⁴ there is assembled a series of passages linked by a quite external relationship to a 'feast'—vv. 7–11 (the order of seating),

---

[1] In my view Mk. 4¹⁰⁻¹² is an editorial formulation of Mark (see p. 199) concealing the transition which in Mark's source had led on from the similitude of the Sower to its interpretation. There is a question in v. 10 concerned with the telling of parables in general, and vv. 11f. constitutes the answer. But v. 13 presupposes that the question has been concerned with the parable that has just been told. So the question in the source must have read very much as Lk. 8⁹. In v. 10 we find the original questioners as the subject, οἱ περὶ αὐτόν, to which Mark has added σὺν τοῖς δώδεκα; and of course ὅτε ἐγένετο κατὰ μόνας also derives from Mark, see below.

[2] The Roman Catholic theologian Thadd. Soiron has examined the Synoptic proverbial material from this standpoint, and his book, *Logia Jesu*, 1916, in spite of many excesses and false conclusions contains many sound observations. Some comparable Jewish material is assembled there on pp. 159–63.

vv. 12–14 (the true guests), vv. 15–24 (parable of the Feast). In Lk. 11 [34–36] the saying about the eye as the light of the body is added to the metaphor of light simply *ad vocem* λύχνος, etc. We have shown on pp. 95ff., 129f. how *the original meaning of a saying is often distorted* or made unrecognizable by such editing.

Further, in such an editorial process the collectors have sometimes added *intensifications and explanations*. They are not frequent in Mark; it is possible to ask, e.g. whether the expression ὃς ἔχει ὦτα ἀκούειν ἀκουέτω has been added by Mark. The tendency for the tradition to attach such expressions is in any case quite clear; some manuscripts also add it after Mk. 7 [16] (as it is also found in several at Lk. 12 [21]). Likewise in Mk. 9 [48] ὅπου ὁ σκώληξ αὐτῶν κτλ is already found inserted in some manuscripts as an intensifying conclusion after vv. 43 and 45. Finally we may refer to ἀκούετε in Mk. 4 [3] and ἀκούσατέ μου πάντες καὶ σύνετε in 7 [14].

Matthew has introduced more of such editorial expressions. At 21 [33] in the allegory of the wicked husbandmen he has followed Mark's example and inserted ἀκούσατε. He has attached ὁ ἔχων ὦτα ἀκούειν ἀκουέτω to the saying about the Baptist as Elijah in 11 [15], while in 13 [43] he has added it to the interpretation of the similitude of the tares. Similarly he has introduced the phrase ἐκεῖ ἔσται ὁ κλαυθμὸς καὶ ὁ βρυγμὸς τῶν ὀδόντων in various places: 8 [12], 13 [42, 50], 22 [13], 24 [51b], 25 [30]. He has added to the saying about the coming of the Son of Man in 16 [27] (cp. Mk. 8 [38]) the continuation: καὶ τότε ἀποδώσει ἑκάστῳ κατὰ τὴν πρᾶξιν αὐτοῦ, and in the polemic against the Pharisees in 23 [33] a threat on the pattern of 3 [7] (Q). He has many times fashioned an explanation: at 16 [11] for the saying about the yeast; 12 [40] for the sign of Jonah; 23 [28] for the saying about whited sepulchres. To the phrase ἀλλ' οἷς ἡτοίμασται which he borrowed from Mark he has added (20 [23]) as a commentary ὑπὸ τοῦ πατρός μου. (Similarly the command to keep silent from Mk. 8 [30]: ἵνα μηδενὶ λέγωσιν περὶ αὐτοῦ is explained at 16 [20] with the phrase: ἵνα μηδενὶ εἴπωσιν ὅτι αὐτός ἐστιν ὁ Χριστός. We may also compare instances like 26 [68], where to Mark's προφήτευσον is added: Χριστέ, τίς ἐστιν ὁ παίσας σε; and 26 [73] where instead of καὶ γὰρ Γαλιλαῖος εἶ Matthew says: καὶ γὰρ ἡ λαλιά σου δῆλόν σε ποιεῖ.)

Luke has also furnished the speech material with emphases and explanations. Smaller additions are insignificant, like the frequently, added πλήν; the ὑποδείξω ὑμῖν at 6 [47], 12 [5]; the λέγω ὑμῖν at 12 [4f., 8, 51] 14 [24], 15 [7, 10], 19 [26]—expressions which cannot of course always be confidently attributed to Luke. To the saying ἄφες τοὺς νεκροὺς θάψαι τοὺς ἑαυτῶν νεκρούς he has attached in 9 [60]: σὺ δὲ ἀπελθὼν διάγγελλε τὴν βασιλείαν τ. θ. and has correspondingly paraphrased ἵνα κἀκεῖ κηρύξω in Mk. 1³⁸ into: εὐαγγελίσασθαί με δεῖ τὴν βασιλείαν τ. θ. in 4⁴³. Cp. further Lk. 9², ¹¹ with Mk. 6⁷, ³⁴ and Lk. 18¹¹, 21³¹ with Mk. 10²⁹, 13²⁹. The phrase εἰς μετάνοιαν which is used as a comment on (οὐκ) ἐλήλυθα καλέσαι in 5³² belongs to the same stage of editing. The gift of God's goodness which in Q (Matt. 7¹¹) is described in general terms as ἀγαθά is given specific definition by Luke as the πνεῦμα ἅγιον.¹ Instead of Q's μὴ θησαυρίζετε ὑμῖν θησαυροὺς ἐπὶ τῆς γῆς (Matt. 6¹⁹) Luke has a positive form in 12³³: πωλήσατε τὰ ὑπάρχοντα ὑμῶν καὶ δότε ἐλεημοσύνην. He also comments on the warning of the leaven of the Pharisees in Luke 12¹. To the metaphor of the kingdom divided against itself he adds in 11¹⁸ᵇ: ὅτι λέγετε ἐν βεελζεβοὺλ ἐκβάλλειν με τὰ δαιμόνια. Similarly the phrase in the polemic against the Pharisees in 11⁴⁸ᵇ could well be Luke's work: ὅτι αὐτοὶ μὲν ἀπέκτειναν αὐτούς, ὑμεῖς δὲ οἰκοδομεῖτε. At 17²⁵ he has inserted between two sayings about the suddenness of the parousia: πρῶτον δὲ δεῖ αὐτὸν πολλὰ παθεῖν καὶ ἀποδοκιμασθῆναι ἀπὸ τῆς γενεᾶς ταύτης. In 20³⁴⁻³⁶ he has filled out the answer to the Sadducee's question with all sorts of explanatory additions. Finally in the eschatological discourse he has introduced all sorts of explanatory material: 21⁸ (καὶ ὁ καιρὸς ἤγγικεν), v. 11 (multiplication of signs), v. 15 (the operation of a spirit-endowed defence), vv. 20–24 (reference to events of the Jewish War), v. 26 (the fear of the earth's inhabitants), v. 28 (a word of encouragement), etc.

In this review I have mentioned only those additions and modifications that can be regarded in the narrower sense as editorial, and can be regarded with considerable certainty as the work of the evangelists; comparison may also be made with examples mentioned earlier (see pp. 87–95, 130f.). I have not dealt with explanatory additions to the similitudes at this point (see pp. 185f., 197f.), nor with the alterations made in the speech material for various reasons that cannot be classed as editorial in the strict sense. These have been previously considered (see pp. 93f., 126f., 147f., 151).

We can do no more than infer the extent of the stages in collecting *the speech material* that went on before Matthew and Luke; yet the collection of sayings called Q which was used by Matthew and Luke does permit of a fairly accurate reconstruction.² For our purposes

---

¹ On this alteration by Luke cp. H. v. Baer, *Der Heilige Geist in den Lukasschriften*, 1926, p. 152; I do not hold that the alteration is 'insignificant'.
² Cp. in addition to Holtzmann's and Juelicher's Introductions to the N.T.: E. Weizsaecker, *Untersuchungen ueber die evang. Geschichte*², 1901; P. Wernle, *Die synoptische Frage*, 1894: A. Harnack, *Sprueche und Reden Jesu*, 1907; G. H. Mueller, *Zur Synopse* (Forschungen zur Religion und Literatur des Alten und Neuen Testaments 11), 1908; J. Wellhausen, *Einleitung in die drei ersten Evangelien*², 1911; B. H. Streeter, *The Four Gospels*, 1924, pp. 271–292.

there is no point in narrowly defining its extent or order, once the sort of collection, within which Q represents one stage, has been made clear. The one point that might be emphasized is that Q obviously concluded with some eschatological-apocalyptic sayings. I further recall what has been freely and frequently said, that such a source, in view of its character, would easily lend itself to enlargements, and would certainly be developed in different versions. Above all there is one thing that must not be forgotten: such editorial work took on a quite new character once it was undertaken on Hellenistic soil. We have to conclude that Q, which originally appeared in an Aramaic version, was variously translated into Greek, because it obviously was known to Matthew and Luke in different versions.[1] As with the translation, so do we have to take into account a certain amount of editing; and in the speech material which in overwhelming proportions derives from the Palestinian Church we find some Hellenistic material from time to time. Matt. 11^{25-27}//Lk. $10^{21f.}$ seems to me at least in part to be a leading example of this (see pp. 159f.). I would make the same conjecture about the story of the Temptation—for its motif seems to be characteristic of Hellenistic Christianity (see pp. 253–7). We may add that the story of the Temptation does not fit in stylistically with its framework in the Q collection of sayings. The story of the centurion from Capernaum in Matt. 8^{5-13}//Lk. 7^{1-10} may also belong to this group. For the rest I would merely refer to the earlier consideration of the Palestinian or Hellenistic origin of the speech material (see pp. 47f., 54f., 59f., 154ff., 163).

Matthew and Luke are known to have proceeded alike in joining the speech material from Q with what they found in Mark. But they differ in that Matthew as a rule simply inserted his material from Q into the Marcan outline and thus by joining the speech material from Q and Mark fashioned the large speech units such as the Missionary Charge, the Parable Discourse, the Discourse on the Pharisees, etc. Matthew further adds to such complexes some floating sayings from other sources, so that the long discourses of Jesus are a characteristic feature of his gospel. By contrast Luke as a rule has kept his material from Mark and Q apart, and so has two Missionary Charges, two Discourses on the Pharisees, etc. But this is only a matter of degree; for the composition of speeches is not wanting in Luke either; such e.g. are the discourse at the feast 14^{7-24}, the discourse on discipleship 14^{25-35}, on the lost 15^{1-32} and the compositions in 12^{13-34} (attitude to possessions in this world) and 12^{35-59} (eschatological units), etc.

---

[1] Cp. A. Juelicher, *Einleitung in das N.T.*[7], 1931, pp. 340f.; J. Wellhausen, *Einleitung in die drei ersten Evangelien*[2], 1911, pp. 59f.

2. The Insertion of the Speech Material into the Narratives

The insertion of the speech material into the narrative sections was done in different ways, and in doing it the speech material again underwent some alterations. The apophthegms, which constitute one section of the speech material, were ideally suited to take their place in a narrative presentation of the ministry of Jesus once the need had been felt to preserve them. For in the apophthegms there were sayings of Jesus that had been spoken in specific historical situations and so could easily be introduced into an historical narrative. Other sayings were not so easy to make use of; for them *some situation had to be found in the life of Jesus* where they could severally be given a fixed time and place.[1] As we have indicated, Matthew has frequently done this by inserting the speech material into situations he found in Mark; yet sometimes he has himself created a situation, as at 5[1] for the Sermon on the Mount, and at 9[35] for the charge to the disciples. Luke particularly has recourse to this means, since he does not treat his sources like Matthew, but uses Mark, Q, and whatever other sources he makes use of, one after another. But this method of creating a situation for the speech material is observable even in Mark, and was doubtless customary before him, and indeed this can itself be done in different ways. We have already shown on pp. 6off. the importance of the apophthegm in this respect, in that unattached speech material was partly added to available apophthegms, and partly made into new apophthegms by an analogous process. Now that the basic points have been made clear, we may describe the individual procedures of the three Synoptists.

(a) Mark

Added to apophthegms that plainly belong to the Tradition:

2[21f.] (Metaphor of cloth and wine) to 2[19] (Fasting).

2[27f.] (The Sabbath) to 2[23-26] (Plucking corn).

3[27] and 3[28f.] (The strong man, blasphemy against the Spirit) to 3[22-26] (Beelzebub divided).

7[9-13] (corban) to 7[1-8] (handwashing).

10[23-27] (riches) to 10[17-22] (rich young man).

Elsewhere independent scenes are created which are of course in part but supplements to given apophthegms. Thus in 7[14] we read: καὶ

---

[1] M. Kaehler saw this clearly; cp. *Der sog. histor. Jesus und der geschichtliche, biblische Christus*, p. 192.1.

προσκαλεσάμενος πάλιν τὸν ὄχλον ἔλεγεν αὐτοῖς. The same note appears in 8³⁴. Similarly Mark having broken off the beginning of the apophthegm in 3²² (see pp. 10f.) has to make an introduction for the sayings in vv. 23ff., and it reads: καὶ προσκαλεσάμενος αὐτοὺς ἔλεγεν. Finally this same formula is used in 10⁴² to link the saying about service with the story of the sons of Zebedee. There is an analogy in 10²³: καὶ περιβλεψάμενος ὁ Ἰησοῦς λέγει τοῖς μαθηταῖς αὐτοῦ. 9³⁵ is not clear: καὶ καθίσας ἐφώνησεν τοὺς δώδεκα, where the motif of calling to him has been superseded by another introductory motif.

This last instance belongs to a group of sayings peculiar to Mark, of instruction to the disciples, which attach to apophthegms and other stories, or are given quite independent formulation. In part they consist of logia, in part of other speech material, namely esoteric instructions.

Such incidents are sometimes introduced by *questions put by the disciples*:

4¹⁰⁻¹³: καὶ ὅτε ἐγένετο κατὰ μόνας, ἠρώτων αὐτὸν . . . τὰς παραβολάς (see p. 325, n. 1).

7¹⁷⁻²³, after the saying about purity: καὶ ὅτε εἰσῆλθεν εἰς οἶκον . . . ἐπηρώτων αὐτὸν οἱ μαθηταὶ αὐτοῦ . . .

9²⁸ᶠ·, after the healing of the epileptic boy: καὶ εἰσελθόντος αὐτοῦ εἰς οἶκον οἱ μαθηταὶ αὐτοῦ κατ' ἰδίαν ἐπηρώτων αὐτόν . . .

10¹⁰⁻¹², after the controversy about divorce: καὶ εἰς τὴν οἰκίαν πάλιν οἱ μαθηταὶ περὶ τούτου ἐπηρώτων αὐτόν . . .

13³ᶠᶠ·: καὶ καθημένου αὐτοῦ εἰς τὸ ὄρος τῶν ἐλαιῶν . . . ἐπηρώτα αὐτὸν κατ' ἰδίαν Πέτρος . . .

To these belong also the disciples' questions in 9¹¹⁻¹³ (on the way down from the mount of Transfiguration) and 10²⁸ (Peter's question about the rewards of discipleship), only with this difference, that no new incident with the disciples begins at these two points.

At other places a *dialogue or controversy between disciples* is used as the occasion for adding some logia:[1]

9³³ᶠᶠ·: καὶ ἐν τῇ οἰκίᾳ γενόμενος ἐπηρώτα αὐτούς· τί ἐν τῇ ὁδῷ διελογίζεσθε; . . .

8¹⁶⁻²¹: καὶ διελογίζοντο πρὸς ἀλλήλους ὅτι ἄρτους οὐκ ἔχουσιν . . .

10⁴¹: The argument about the request of the sons of Zebedee serves as a transition.

We may add 10²⁶: after the saying about riches the phrase οἱ δὲ

[1] This editorial device appears very frequently in the Buddhist tradition, somewhat in the form: 'One day the monks in the classroom began a discussion. . . . Then the Master came and asked. . . .' Examples are in *Buddhist. Maerchen* (Maerchen d. Weltlit.), pp. 31, 234, 293, 297, 308, 315, 332, 347.

περισσῶς ἐξεπλήσσοντο λέγοντες πρὸς ἑαυτούς . . . serves as the introduction point of a new saying.

Very often a conversation or a saying of Jesus is introduced by a question put by Jesus himself:

8²⁷ᵇ⁻³⁰: καὶ ἐν τῇ ὁδῷ ἐπηρώτα τοὺς μαθητὰς αὐτοῦ λέγων αὐτοῖς· τίνα με λέγουσιν οἱ ἄνθρωποι εἶναι;

9³³ᶠᶠ· combined with the motif of a dialogue between the disciples (see above).

12³⁵⁻³⁷: Introduction to the question of David's Son.

The scenes which contain pure esoteric instruction, like the prophecies of the passion, are introduced *without any special cause* being assigned:

8³¹: καὶ ἤρξατο διδάσκειν αὐτοὺς ὅτι . . .

9³⁰⁻³²: κἀκεῖθεν ἐξελθόντες παρεπορεύοντο διὰ τῆς Γαλιλαίας . . . ἐδίδασκεν γὰρ τοὺς μαθητὰς αὐτοῦ . . .

10³²⁻³⁴: ἦσαν δὲ ἐν τῇ ὁδῷ ἀναβαίνοντες εἰς Ἱεροσόλυμα . . . καὶ παραλαβὼν πάλιν τοὺς δώδεκα ἤρξατο αὐτοῖς λέγειν . . .

To these belong also the introduction to the injunction to keep silent after the Transfiguration: 9⁹: καὶ καταβαινόντων αὐτῶν ἐκ τοῦ ὄρους διεστείλατο αὐτοῖς . . .

In addition there are in Mark some scenes which are in the *highest degree formulations analogous to the apophthegms*; they are due in part to Mark, and in part to his predecessors. They have already in part been analysed.

2⁶⁻¹⁰: A miracle story from the tradition is used as a frame for the saying about the right to forgive sins.

2¹⁵⁻¹⁷: The scene of the meal with the tax-gatherer as the introduction to the saying about the physician.

6⁷⁻¹³: καὶ προσκαλεῖται τοὺς δώδεκα καὶ ἤρξατο αὐτοὺς ἀποστέλλειν as the introduction to the Missionary discourse.

8¹¹⁻¹³: καὶ ἐξῆλθον οἱ Φαρισαῖοι καὶ ἤρξαντο συνζητεῖν αὐτῷ . . . as the introduction to the refusal of a sign.

8¹⁴: καὶ ἐπελάθοντο λαβεῖν ἄρτους . . . as the introduction to the saying about leaven.

12³⁷ᵇ, ³⁸ᵃ: καὶ ὁ πολὺς ὄχλος ἤκουεν αὐτοῦ ἡδέως as the introduction to the polemic against the Pharisees.

The motifs for the differing introductory formulations are in part *borrowed from apophthegms in the Tradition*. The introductions in 2⁶ᶠᶠ·, ¹⁵ᶠᶠ·, 8¹¹ᶠᶠ· are drawn from the Traditional idea of the conflict with the Pharisees. Two motifs are used in 9³³ᶠᶠ·: (1) The motif of dispute over precedence, drawn from 10³⁵ᶠᶠ· and (2) The motif of a child, taken from 10¹³ᶠᶠ· This gives the whole incident a certain lack of clarity, in so far as we are able to rely upon the text, which has been much emended.

Quite often such formulations need a summary at the end, or some retrospective linking at the beginning, though there is very little of it in Mark.

3³⁰: ὅτι ἔλεγον· πνεῦμα ἀκάθαρτον ἔχει.

4³³ᶠ·: The end of the parable discourse.

6¹²ᶠ·: The result of the missionary charge.

In all these cases we are dealing with *Mark's* (*or his predecessors'*) *editorial work*, which continues the process already noticed of formulating new apophthegmatic items, and edits the partly traditional and partly new-formed speech material in a way that makes it suitable for insertion into a story of the life of Jesus. In such statements about situations we must not look for ancient tradition; and that is quite clear when, as is methodologically necessary, we do not treat individual cases in isolation, but study them along with analogous instances. For the rest Mark has abstained from large-scale editorial work on the traditional material; on certain editorial remarks which are not concerned with the insertion of speech material into the narrative see p. 326. Mark has made some observations on the esoteric instructions about the misunderstanding of the disciples, 9¹⁰, ³² and has formed this motif into a symbolic dialogue between Jesus and Peter in 8³².

It is useful to note that a fixed terminology operates in such editorial activity. In the following review I have put in brackets the passages when the expression concerned appears in an editorial passage of another kind.

προσκαλεῖσθαι: the disciples as object: (3¹³), 6⁷, (8¹), 10⁴², (12⁴³).

A different object: 3²³, 7¹⁴, 8³⁴.

φωνεῖν: 9³⁵ (the disciples are the object).

παραλαμβάνειν: (9²), 10³², (14³³), cp. *Pap. Ox.*, V, 840, 7 (Kleine Texte, 31, 4). Similarly 10²³: περιβλεψάμενος and 10²⁷ ἐμβλέψας; these terms are borrowed from the ancient tradition: 3⁵, ³⁴, 10²¹ where identical phrases serve as introductions to sayings of Jesus; yet 3³⁴ may well be an editorial formulation. In the dramatic art of Mark the house is the typical scene, either before or after some scene with a crowd, for some secret teaching to the disciples: 7¹⁷, 9²⁸, 10¹⁰ (otherwise in editorial passages 2¹⁵, 7²⁴, 9³³). On the other hand 2¹, 3²⁰ in all probability belong to the ancient tradition.

The road is the scene in 8²⁷, 10¹⁷, ³² and is a secondary motif at 9³³. In this case situation indicators are found in παρα- or διαπορεύεσθαι (2²³), 9³⁰; alternatively ἀνα- or καταβαίνειν: 10³², 9⁹.

It is characteristic that in the old apophthegms the cause of Jesus' speaking is something happening to him, whereas in the secondary formulations it is for the most part Jesus himself who takes the initiative. Cp. 9³³ with 10³⁵; 9³⁶ with 10¹³; 7¹⁴ with 7⁵; 10²³ with 10¹⁷; further 8²⁷, 12³⁵ and the esoteric instruction in 8³¹, 9⁹, ³⁰, 10³². Nevertheless the old form of apophthegm is retained in the form of the disciples' question (see pp. 61f., 65f.).

(b) *Matthew*

Matthew has carried the editing of the speech material further. He reproduces the *questions of the disciples* save for Mk. 10¹⁰. But at 24¹ (Mk. 13¹) he makes all the disciples ask the question instead of one only, and at 15¹⁵ (Mk. 7¹⁷) he uses Peter instead of the μαθηταί. He formulates some questions by the disciples on his own account 15¹², 19¹⁰ (with Mk. 10²⁴, ²⁶ as the pattern) and 18²¹ (with Peter as the questioner). On one occasion he fashions a question for Jesus himself: 13⁵¹.

Other Introductory Scenes

5¹: Introduction to the Sermon on the Mount. Some small introductory phrase must have existed already in Q, naming the disciples as the audience, as is shown by Lk. 6²⁰ and the fact that Matt. 5¹ also mentions the μαθηταί, although in Matthew after 7²⁸ the ὄχλοι come to the fore as the audience. But the circumstantial introduction and the reference to the mountain plainly derives from Matthew (cp. Lk. 6²⁰).

9³⁵f.: Introduction to the Missionary Charge (very likely with the use of Mk. 6⁶ᵇ, ³⁴).

11²⁰: Introduction to the woes on the Galilean towns.

Transition Passages

10⁵ᵃ: τούτους τοὺς δώδεκα ἀπέστειλεν ὁ Ἰησοῦς κτλ (Resumption of 10¹ = Mk. 6⁷ after the intervening list of Apostles).

10²⁶: μὴ οὖν φοβηθῆτε αὐτούς joining two sections of a source.

15¹⁴: ἄφετε αὐτούς as a transition to a new saying.

Terminal Formulations

7²⁸f.: The impression of the Sermon on the Mount. (With some use of Mk. 1²².)

11¹: Conclusion of the Missionary Charge (καὶ ἐγένετο ὅτε ἐτέλεσεν ὁ Ἰησοῦς διατάσσων τοῖς δώδεκα μαθηταῖς αὐτοῦ . . .).

12⁴⁵: οὕτως ἔσται καὶ τῇ γενεᾷ ταύτῃ τῇ πονηρᾷ as the end of the saying about the unclean spirit.

13⁵¹ᶠ·: End of the parable discourse with a logion attached by means of a question.

15²⁰ᵇ: End of the discourse on purity.

17¹³: End of the discourse after the Transfiguration; the disciples recognize that Jesus sees the Baptist as Elijah.

Best known of all are the typical end-formulae which Matthew uses as a transition back to the Mark-text, after having reproduced some speech material from Q: καὶ ἐγένετο ὅτε ἐτέλεσεν ὁ Ἰησοῦς τοὺς λόγους τούτους 7²⁸, 13⁵³, 19¹, 26¹ (cp. already 11¹).[1]

(c) Luke

In part Luke follows the old method of attaching speech sections to *Traditional apophthegms*. Thus the story of the rich farmer in 12¹⁶⁻²¹ is attached to an apophthegm, and the apophthegm about repentance, in 13¹⁻⁵ is the introduction to the parable of the unfruitful fig tree and the question about the greatest commandment in 10²⁵ᶠᶠ· is the framework for the story of the Good Samaritan (see pp. 22f.).

But for the most part Luke has fashioned *his own introductions* independently, whose motifs he often simply borrows from the sayings he wants to reproduce. Just as he formed an introduction (the popular agreement that the Baptist was the Messiah) to the subsequent sayings of the Baptist from the sayings themselves, he did the same thing later on with the sayings of Jesus. According to this recipe he provided (10¹) Q's Missionary Charge with an introduction, and the return of the disciples in 10¹⁷ then had to serve as the occasion for some new logia. As a background of the Lord's Prayer in 11¹ we have the situation in which Jesus prayed and the request of the disciples which it prompted. The Pharisaic discourse from Q is introduced in 11³⁷ by the situation at the feast and the motif of handwashing (following Mk. 7¹ᶠᶠ·?). The situation of a journey and the question εἰ ὀλίγοι οἱ σωζόμενοι provide the background for the saying about the narrow gate in 13²². The feast in 14¹ᶠᶠ· has to serve as the situation for the healing of the dropsical man, for the sayings about order of precedence, the true guests, and for the parable of the great feast; again a journey provides the situation for the sayings about discipleship in 14²⁵. The similitudes about lost things are introduced in 15¹ᶠᶠ· by recording the crowd of publicans and sinners

[1] Evidently Matthew found this formula in Q as a transition from the Sermon on the Mount to the story of the Centurion; for Matt. 7²⁸ corresponds to Lk. 7¹; cp. B. H. Streeter, *The Four Gospels*, p. 262; E. v. Dobschuetz, *Z.N.W.*, 27, 1929, p. 341.

and the indignation of the Pharisees that Jesus ate with them (! following Mk. 2¹⁶). The disciples' request πρόσθες ἡμῖν πίστιν in 17⁵ introduces the saying about faith. The saying about the coming of the reign of God is introduced in 17²⁰ in the manner of Greek philosophical apophthegms. In 18¹ff· the statement of aim—πρὸς τὸ δεῖν πάντοτε προσεύχεσθαι αὐτοὺς καὶ μὴ ἐγκακεῖν—leads, to be sure on the basis of a false generalization, to the parable of the unrighteous judge. And before the story of the Pharisee and the Publican, at 18⁹ we read: εἶπεν δὲ καὶ πρός τινας τοὺς πεποιθότας ἐφ' ἑαυτοῖς ὅτι εἰσὶν δίκαιοι καὶ ἐξουθενοῦντας τοὺς λοιποὺς τὴν παραβολὴν ταύτην. And the parable of the Talents in 19¹¹ is introduced by the note that Jesus was nigh to Jerusalem, and that people supposed that the Kingdom of God was immediately to appear; just as Luke here uses the expression ἀκουόντων δὲ αὐτῶν ταῦτα, he alters Mark's simple introduction (12³⁸) to the Pharisaic discourse at 20⁴⁵ to ἀκούοντος δὲ παντὸς τοῦ λαοῦ εἶπεν . . . Luke has to make a new introduction to the warning against ambition 22²⁴ since he does not repeat the question asked by the sons of Zebedee, and he borrows the motif from 9⁴⁶ (= Mk. 9³³f·). Perhaps 22³⁵, the introduction to the saying about the swords, is also a creation of Luke; if so it would be a product of his own perplexity.

It is only with difficulty that we can distinguish introductions from transition formulations. We have shown on p. 323 that Luke still frequently used the primitive connective formulae. But alongside them there are more artificial constructions. The saying about the blessed eyes in 10²³ is joined to the preceding sayings by the expression: καὶ στραφεὶς πρὸς τοὺς μαθητὰς κατ' ἰδίαν εἶπεν. At 11²⁹ we read as the connection: τῶν δὲ ὄχλων ἐπαθροιζομένων ἤρξατο λέγειν . . . There is a similar formulation to lead from the Pharisaic discourse in 12¹ to the warning against the leaven of the Pharisees. The transition from the apophthegm about inheritance to the story of the rich fool has been made by the dominical saying in 12¹⁵ (warning against πλεονεξία). A question by Peter in 12⁴¹ leads from the similitude of the thief to that of the wise and the unfaithful stewards. The remark that Jesus had observed the behaviour of the guests leads from 14¹⁻⁶ to 14⁷⁻¹², vv. 12–14 are then linked on by ἔλεγεν δὲ καὶ τῷ κεκληκότι αὐτόν, and as a transition to the parable of the Great Feast we find in 1 ¹⁵ a saying from the tradition (μακάριος ὅστις φάγεται ἄρτον ἐν τῇ βασιλείᾳ τ. θ.), which is put into the mouth of one of the guests. The polemical saying against the Pharisees in 16¹⁵ is introduced by the report in 16¹⁴ of the Pharisees' grumbling about the Mammon saying which preceded. In 17³⁷ a disciples' question provides the transition from the eschatological discourse to the saying about the body and the eagles (on this see also p. 91).

As this review shows, *certain motifs are typical of such formulations*; I shall enumerate them, and add for the sake of completeness the analogous situation indicators which Luke has also used for other than speech material.

Jesus praying: 6[12], 9[18], 11[1] (following Mk. 1[35]).

The situation of a feast (except for 5[29] where Luke is reproducing Mk. 2[15]): 7[36], 11[37], 14[1], and in these Jesus is always at table with a Pharisee. The schematic character of the statement is quite plain; for the situation given to the conflict sayings against the Pharisees in 11[37] is most unsuitable, and moreover 11[37], 14[1] take place, according to Luke's outline, in Samaria.

Jesus in the Synagogue (apart from the places where Luke is reproducing Mark): 4[15], 13[10].

Jesus on journeys through cities and villages: 5[12], 7[11], 8[1], (10[1]).

Jesus on the journey to Jerusalem: 9[57], 10[38], 13[22], 14[25], 17[11], 18[35], 19[1, 11] (Mk. 9[30], 10[17, 32, 46] have been more or less a pattern for these).

The motif of question and answer, where it is not invariably the rule for the disciples to speak: the disciples report, request or ask something: 10[17], 11[1], 12[41] (Peter), 17[5, 37].

What others have said as the stimulus: 11[45], 13[23], 14[15], 15[2], 17[20]. Further for the speech section in 3[11-14] a question addressed by the crowd to the Baptist is prefixed as an introduction in 3[10].

Jesus surrounded by the multitude: 5[1], 7[11], 8[4] (expansion of Mark's original); 11[27, 29], 12[1], 14[25], 19[48], 20[1], 21[38].

The thoughts or behaviour of those present provide the stimulus, without any formulation being given in direct speech: 11[38], 14[7], 16[14], 18[9], 19[11], 22[24].

It is characteristic of Luke, that the introduction available in the tradition proves inadequate for him, because it will not serve as a link with the larger context he has in mind. In such a case he expands the introduction. For example, at 4[1] he adds to the introduction to the story of the Temptation that Jesus returned from the Jordan full of the Holy Spirit. (Correspondingly he alters the editorial passage in Mk. 1[14f.], which is placed between the Temptation and the public ministry at 4[14f.], by going back to 4[1] and anticipating 4[18]: πνεῦμα κυρίου ἐπ' ἐμέ, and saying: καὶ ὑπέστρεψεν ὁ Ἰησοῦς ἐν τῇ δυνάμει τοῦ πνεύματος . . .).[1] For the question from John the Baptist he depicts Jesus at his messianic work, 7[21]. For

---

[1] Cp. H. v. Baer, *Der Heil. Geist in den Lukasschriften*, pp. 67f.

Luke, Jesus' question is not an adequate introduction to Peter's confession; he adds the motif of Jesus at prayer. At 20²⁰ he has significantly expanded the Mark source (Mk. 12¹³) so as to expose the Pharisees' intention to trap Jesus by questioning him about the tribute money, and to prepare for the betrayal of Jesus to the Romans.

Something peculiar to Luke is that in two places there is interruption of a speech, which Luke has inserted to give the reader a sense of the concrete situation. Thus at 11⁴⁵ the Pharisaic discourse is interrupted by one of the listeners saying: διδάσκαλε, ταῦτα λέγων καὶ ἡμᾶς ὑβρίζεις. Similarly the cry of the audience μὴ γένοιτο is inserted at 20¹⁶ᵇ before using the allegory of the wicked husbandmen.

Finally, Luke of course wrote some conclusions as well as introductions. Thus at the end of the Baptist's preaching in 3¹⁸ we read: πολλὰ μὲν οὖν καὶ ἕτερα παρακαλῶν εὐηγγελίζετο τὸν λαόν. The impressions of the Pharisees are described at 11⁵³ᶠ·: the rage and evil intentions of men who have been rebuked. After the question about the tribute money at 20²⁶ Mk. 12¹⁷ is intensified: καὶ οὐκ ἴσχυσαν ἐπιλαβέσθαι αὐτοῦ ῥήματος ἐναντίον τοῦ λαοῦ. The conclusion to the Sermon on the Plain is in all probability modelled on Q: ἐπειδὴ επλήρωσεν πάντα τὰ ῥήματα αὐτοῦ εἰς τὰς ἀκοὰς τοῦ λαοῦ . . . (cp. Matt. 7²⁸).

B. The Editing of the Narrative Material and the Compositions of the Gospels

THE editorial activity we have examined to some extent treated the speech material on a par with narrative elements, and even took it, in part, past the stage of an individual story and adapted it to a connected narrative. In this latter sense, however, all the material, even the narrative element, had to be edited. For even if it consisted indisputably of particular situations, which were useful for insertion into a story of Jesus' life, yet it was primarily made up of individual elements for which no connecting passages existed. Successful editing at this point would thus go hand in hand with binding the whole of the material into a coherent presentation and it is for this reason that this last part of our enquiry attempts a description of the gospels as wholes. The description in what follows is in the first instance literary-historical. But since the work of the Evangelists was not that of producing a scientific biography but rather to give to 'the

Kerygma a definite place and task', we shall have to make clear in what follows the theological character of Gospels.[1]

1. THE GOSPEL ACCORDING TO ST. MARK

In Mark we can still see quite clearly, and most easily in comparison with Luke, that the most ancient tradition consisted of individual sections, and that the connecting together is secondary. K. L. Schmidt has shown that in detail by a careful analysis.[2] Here I shall only try to fasten on the fundamental, the typical phenomena and describe the regular characteristics of the development; particular analysis has been already done, for the most part, in previous sections. But the analysis of course cannot always be carried out with certainty. The original situation-indicators are often so closely tied up with the editorial introductions and postscripts that it is no longer possible to make a clear division between them. The pointers which are necessarily presupposed by the subsequent story generally belong to the basic material. Others, especially connecting pointers, are the work of an editor. Sometimes the task of analysis is made easier when the introduction contains two motifs which can be explained as the survival of traditional and editorial elements; thus Mk. 6[45f.] (see p. 216). In other cases the introduction contradicts the story that follows, as in Mk. 8[22] the indication of καὶ ἔρχονται εἰς Βηθσαϊδάν; for the following story after v. 23 takes place outside a village. It is difficult to judge in what cases a concrete geographical note belongs to the fundamental basis of the tradition. Generally speaking the geographical scene is a matter of indifference to the story and would hardly have been bound up with it originally. On the other hand perhaps not all geographical statements are editorial conjectures; some may well have been found in the ancient tradition and transferred from it to other stories (see p. 64f., 242f.). By contrast notices of time which are as good as never really presupposed by any story, are always the work of an editor. Finally it is uncertain which editorial links belong to Mark himself and which to some earlier stage of the tradition. We have to reckon with the existence of some such links, as is quite clear in some instances. But to decide this point is for the most part not a matter of fundamental importance; the main thing is to recognize the way in which the editing has been done on the whole. And in every case analysis shows that Mark has nowhere used a source which itself had already portrayed a thoroughly coherent life of Jesus which could have been described as a Gospel. Finally it is

---

[1] Cp. J. Schniewind, *Th.R.*, N.F.2, 1930, pp. 151–8.
[2] *Der Rahmen der Geschichte Jesu*, 1919; cp. also A. Meyer, *Festg. f. A. Juelicher*, pp. 35–60.

also of no major importance whether the text of Mark later suffered occasional editorial changes in some of its details.

The presuppositions which underlie the expositions of individual elements, and the notes of situation and time have been dealt with on pp. 63–66, 242–244. On the basis of the facts yielded in this way Mark has dealt with the traditional material in the following way:[1]

1. *Simple linking in succession.* This is indicated by the simple use of καί: 1¹⁶ (here especially striking, because it is the first story of the ministry: Matthew discerns this muddle and makes Jesus move to Capernaum 4¹³), 1⁴⁰, 2²³, 3²⁰, 7¹, ³². Sometimes καί is intensified by εὐθύς, which brings out a sort of temporal link: 1¹², ²¹ (if the beginning of the verse καὶ εἰσπορεύονται κτλ. belongs to the previous section); 6⁴⁵. Sometimes πάλιν is added, though not usually as indicating 'for the second time in reference to some specific earlier occasion but simply as a succession formula for the Aramaic תוב: 2¹, ¹³, 3¹, 4¹, 11²⁷.'[2]

2. *Place Connection:* In the first place this is very primitive in that it merely says that Jesus went 'from thence' to the scene of the following story. The verb ἐξελθεῖν is frequently used for this purpose: 1²⁹, 2¹³, 6¹,³⁴, 7³¹, 8²⁷, 9³⁰, 11¹², or ἀπελθεῖν: 1³⁵; 6³², ⁴⁶, 7²⁴, 8¹³, or even simply ἐλθεῖν or alternatively ἔρχεσθαι: 5¹, 6⁵³, 8¹⁰, ²², 10¹, ⁴⁶, 11²⁷, 14³². Further ἐκπορεύεσθαι 10¹⁷, ⁴⁶, 31¹ and ἀναχωρεῖν 3⁷. Twice we find διαπερᾶν 5²¹, 6⁵³.

Moreover the connection is made even closer by turning the transitional verb into a *participium coniunctum*, e.g. 1²⁹ (ἐξελθόντες ἦλθον), 6³⁴, 7¹³, 9³⁰, etc. We also find the semitic ἀναστάς (ἐξῆλθεν) on some occasions: 1³⁵, 7²⁴, 10¹.

Sometimes this sort of connection is made with a *genitivus absolutus*: 1³², 5², ²¹, 6⁵⁴, 10¹⁷, ⁴⁶, 11¹², 13¹, ³. Instead of or alongside it we can find an ὅτε clause 1³², 4¹⁰, 7¹⁷, 11¹, 14¹².

The word ἐκεῖθεν is typical, sometimes with such verbs of motion, sometimes without: 6¹, 7²⁴, 9³⁰, 10¹. It appears elsewhere in the Text tradition (as 1¹⁹). Occasionally instead of ἐκεῖθεν we find a more precise *indication of the starting-point*, as in 1²⁹: ἐκ τῆς συναγωγῆς; 7³¹: ἐκ τῶν ὁρίων Τύρου; 11¹²: ἀπὸ Βηθανίας.

Wherever we meet these and similar expressions we are finding what are plainly editorial formulations. This joins up with the statement of destination which sometimes of course was already in the tradition available to Mk. (1²⁹: εἰς τὴν οἰκίαν Σίμωνος κτλ; 6¹:

[1] I take into account in the following review all individual elements, even those that are *entirely* the products of editorial work.
[2] That the readings sometimes vary makes no essential difference.

εἰς τὴν πατρίδα αὐτοῦ; 6⁴⁶: εἰς τὸ ὄρος), but which for the most part is a result of the work of editing:

1³⁵: εἰς ἔρημον τόπον.   7³¹: εἰς τὴν θάλασσαν τῆς Γαλιλαίας.

2¹³: παρὰ τὴν θάλασσαν.   8¹⁰: εἰς τὰ μέρη Δαλμανουθά(?).

3⁷: πρὸς τὴν θάλασσαν.   8¹³: εἰς τὸ πέραν.

5¹: εἰς τὸ πέραν, also 5²¹.   8²²: εἰς Βηθσαϊδάν.

6³²: εἰς ἔρημον τόπον κατ' ἰδίαν 8²⁷: εἰς τὰς κώμας Καισαρίας τῆς
(the naming of the ἔρημος τόπος   Φιλίππου.

does not necessarily make it a   10¹: εἰς τὰ ὅρια τῆς Ἰουδαίας πέραν
part of the original tradition,   τοῦ Ἰορδάνου.

as 8¹ shows, but it could have   10⁴⁶: εἰς Ἰεριχώ.

been derived from it).   11²⁷: εἰς Ἱεροσόλυμα.

6⁵³: εἰς Γεννησαρέτ.   14³²: εἰς χωρίον οὗ τὸ ὄνομα Γεθση-

7²⁴: εἰς τὰ ὅρια Τύρου.   μανεί.

3. In all these instances the spatial link is also a *temporal* one. This expresses the temporal sequence, which in certain circumstances can indicate a material link as well.

1⁹: ἐν ἐκείναις ταῖς ἡμέραις; similarly 8¹.

2¹: καὶ . . . δι' ἡμερῶν.[1]

The temporal link in 4³⁵ᶠ· is particularly precise, and the editor has here bound the separate elements together not only with ἐν ἐκείνῃ τῇ ἡμέρᾳ but also with ὡς ἦν (ἐν τῷ πλοίῳ) so as to establish the connection with 4¹ᶠᶠ· (see pp. 215f.). Mk. 6³⁰⁻³³ displays a special interest in the context, on the one hand by indicating the connection with the sending out of the disciples reported in 6⁷⁻¹³, and on the other by supplying what is presupposed for the following story of the feeding of the five thousand. The disciples' need for rest is used as the motive for finding an ἔρημος τόπος, and the crowd which is necessary for the feeding is brought to the place at the right time in a very circumstantial manner. The actual placing of certain stories is another example of this sort of linking together, as 3²²⁻³⁰ is put between 3²⁰ᶠ· and 3³¹⁻³⁵ (see pp. 12f., 29), 5²⁵⁻³⁴ between 5²¹⁻²⁴ and 5³⁵⁻⁴³ (pp. 214f.), 6¹⁴⁻²⁹ between 6⁷⁻¹³ and 6³⁰ᶠᶠ· (pp. 301f.), 11¹⁵⁻¹⁹ between 11¹²⁻¹⁴ and 11²⁰ (pp. 217f.), 14³⁻⁹ between 14¹ᶠᶠ· and 14¹⁰ᶠ· (pp. 262f.).[2]†

The only instance of close linking together over a larger portion of narrative is to be found in the story of the Passion. Editorial formula-

---

[1] Such formal expressions are typical and occur in popular literature of a similar kind; cp. K. L. Schmidt, *Eucharisterion* (f. H. Gunkel), II, 1923, pp. 84f., 110.

[2] E. v. Dobschuetz, *Z.N.W.*, 27, 1928, pp. 193–8 draws attention to such devices in Mark's art of story telling.   † See page 367.

tions like 14$^{1f.,}$ $^{10f.}$ link episodes together. Prophecies like 14$^{17-21,}$ $^{27-31}$ prepare for events about to take place. Jesus' last ministry in Jerusalem is somewhat awkwardly compressed along with the Passion itself into a sequence of seven days, and the several components of the last act are divided among the hours of the day: the first watch of the night (ὀψίας γενομένης) starts at 14^{17}; 14$^{27ff.}$ take up the second, 14$^{66ff.}$ the third, and the fourth (πρωί) begins at 15^1. From 15^{25} onwards there are three hourly notes of time: 15^{25} is the third hour, 15$^{33f.}$ the sixth and ninth, 15^{42}: ὀψίας γενομένης. But the end had already been foreshadowed in the story of the life of Jesus, and so the gospel as a whole is held together by some sort of primitive linking up of the parts. Apart from the predictions of the Passion such links can be seen in the editorial comments at 3^6; 11^{18}; 12^{12}.

In such a way Mark has been able to give his collection the appearance of a story coherent geographically, chronologically and in part also materially. He further sometimes betrays a feeling of the inadequacy of putting stories one after another or joining them together, and of the need for proper descriptions. Some are partly only expanded transitions or *situation indications*. Among these I would put the descriptive notices of Jesus' teaching such as we find in 1^{22,} ^{39}, 2$^{1f.}$ (here the editorial work can no longer be clearly distinguished from the tradition); 2^{13} (καὶ πᾶς ὁ ὄχλος ἤρχετο πρὸς αὐτὸν καὶ ἐδίδασκεν αὐτούς); 10^{1b} (καὶ συνπορεύονται πάλιν ὄχλοι πρὸς αὐτόν, καὶ ὡς εἰώθει πάλιν ἐδίδασκεν αὐτούς); 4$^{1f.,}$ $^{33f.}$ are also in this class. We must also refer to the end formulations, which recount the impression Jesus made or the effects of his teaching, as 1^{28} (καὶ ἐξῆλθεν ἡ ἀκοὴ αὐτοῦ εὐθὺς πανταχοῦ εἰς ὅλην τὴν περίχωρον τῆς Γαλιλαίας); 1^{45}, 12^{34b,} ^{37b}.

The editorial formulations which describe the healing activity of Jesus in detail go much further than this: 1$^{32-34}$, 3$^{7-12}$, 6$^{53-56}$. In the same sort of way Mark prefixed to the account of Jesus' ministry a summarizing description of his preaching of repentance (under the influence of the terminology used in Christian missionary preaching) in 1$^{14f.}$ Finally in this connection there is the appointment of the Twelve for which Mark finds a motive in their continuing in company with Jesus (ἵνα ὦσιν μετ' αὐτοῦ) as in their being sent out (ἵνα ἀποστέλλη αὐτούς κτλ).

On the other hand there was no need yet for Mark—as for Luke and the author of the gospel quoted in Epiph. Haer. 30^{13}—to introduce his heroes and to preface their appearance with a general indication of the date. The Baptist, like Jesus, appears in Mark without any preparation, and this is where it can be seen especially clearly that the author brings individual stories together, whose characters were known to the Church, but were not thought of against a wider literary background.

The total picture of the ministry of Jesus which results is something like this: The ministry fundamentally took place in Galilee. Capernaum, which seems firmly established in the tradition, and the Sea of Galilee which most certainly was, are the centre of it. Before the journey to Jerusalem the boundaries were only crossed occasionally, and the names of Bethsaida, Caesarea Philippi and Decapolis are not securely attached to any particular unit but were already linked up with the tradition before Mark; the same applies to Tyre, which is certainly, however, an editorial construction. In this geographical area were the scenes which provided the dramatic material for the art of Mark and his predecessors, scenes of the *lake and the lakeside*, and they were transferred from stories where they essentially belonged to others, as need arose.[1] If Mark were given the motif of lakeside scenery by an earlier editing, in $4^{1f.}$, $5^{21f.}$ then he transferred it to 2^{13}, 3^{7}. The transference of the motif of a boat from 4^{1} to 3^{9} is especially a mechanical device. The crossing of the lake which is bound up with the nature of the material in $4^{35ff.}$ and $6^{45ff.}$ has been made use of on several occasions: 5^{21}, $6^{31f.}$, 5^{3}, 8^{10}, $^{13f.}$. We have mentioned the *house and the road* as the scenery of apophthegmatic formulations on p. 332. We may add the *Synagogue* in 1^{21}, 3^{1}, 6^{2} here in all likelihood found by Mark already in the tradition at each point, but then used by him at 1^{39}. He found a *mountain* in his source at 9^{2} and perhaps also at 6^{46}, but at 3^{13} he makes it the place for the choice of the apostles, and at 13^{3} where because of the Jerusalem setting it has to be the Mount of Olives he makes it the place of secret instruction to the disciples. The editorial sections mention journeying, or alternatively preaching and healing in villages and cities in $1^{38, 45}$, $6^{6b, 56}$, 8^{27}.

Jesus is thought of as teaching and healing. Outside the dialogues and parable discourse the teaching activity is referred to quite schematically $1^{21f.}$, $2^{2, 13}$, $6^{2, 6, 34}$, 10^{1}, 12^{35}. But Jesus as teacher remains a persistent picture; cp. 12^{14}: . . . ἐπ' ἀληθείας τὴν ὁδὸν τοῦ θεοῦ διδάσκεις, and 14^{49}: καθ' ἡμέραν ἤμην πρὸς ὑμᾶς ἐν τῷ ἱερῷ διδάσκων. The same is true of Jesus as healer, as the healing stories and summaries show him 1^{32-34}, 3^{7-12}, 6^{53-56}, as well as remarks such as 1^{39}, $5^{27f.}$, 6^{5}. As a teacher Jesus is pictured sitting down (4^{1}, 9^{35}, 12^{41}, 13^{3}) with the crowd in a circle round him (3^{34}). Otherwise

---

[1] H. v. Soden also speaks of typical instead of concrete indications of place, in *Das Interesse des apost.-Zeitalters an der evg. Geschichte*, 1892, p. 140.

he is said to περιπατεῖν (1¹⁶), περιάγειν (6⁶) or παράγειν (2¹⁴).¹
Finally we must refer to the motif of Jesus at prayer, which is to be
found at 1³⁵, 6⁴⁶, 14³²ff. It is useful in this way to realize what were
the typical ideas of Jesus which Mark and his circle made use of; and
it is important to make clear that the features which constitute this
picture belong to the editorial process.

It is further a part of the picture that the *crowd* streamed to him and
surrounded him, and this is constantly described in typical hyper-
bolic terms:

1³²f.: καὶ ἦν ὅλη ἡ πόλις ἐπισυνηγμένη πρὸς τὴν θύραν.

2²: καὶ συνήχθησαν πολλοί, ὥστε μηκέτι χωρεῖν μηδὲ τὰ πρὸς τὴν θύραν

2¹³: καὶ πᾶς ὁ ὄχλος ἤρχετο πρὸς αὐτόν.

3⁹: ἵνα πλοιάριον προσκαρτερῇ αὐτῷ διὰ τὸν ὄχλον ἵνα μὴ θλίβωσ
     αὐτόν.

3²⁰: καὶ συνέρχεται πάλιν ὁ ὄχλος, ὥστε μὴ δύνασθαι αὐτοὺς μηδὲ
     ἄρτον φαγεῖν.

4¹: καὶ συνάγεται πρὸς αὐτὸν ὄχλος πλεῖστος, ὥστε αὐτὸν εἰς πλοῖον
     ἐμβάντα καθῆσθαι ἐν τῇ θαλάσσῃ.

5²¹: συνήχθη ὄχλος πολύς ἐπ’ αὐτόν.

5²⁴: καὶ ἠκολούθει αὐτῷ ὄχλος πολύς, καὶ συνέθλιβον αὐτόν; cp. v. 31.

6³¹: ἦσαν γὰρ οἱ ἐρχόμενοι καὶ οἱ ὑπάγοντες πολλοί, καὶ οὐδὲ φαγεῖν
     εὐκαίρουν.

6⁵⁵f.: περιέδραμον ὅλην τὴν χώραν ἐκείνην κτλ.

8¹: πάλιν πολλοῦ ὄχλου ὄντος.

In 3⁷f. there followed him from every quarter a great crowd, which
is always presupposed as being there: 7¹⁴, 8³⁴, 9¹⁴f., 10¹, ⁴⁶, 11¹⁸,
12¹², ³⁷ᵇ. All the sick are brought to Jesus: 1³², 3¹⁰, 6⁵⁵f. (and the
individual stories). This is clearly a case of a schematic presentation,
of editorial activity. And for this reason it is impossible to infer from
Mark anything about the historical attitude of Jesus to the people,
or about the development of his relationship to them.

How schematic the *appearance of the opponents* is, who appear just
when the author needs them, we have shown on pp. 52ff. in dealing
with the conflict dialogues. The *appearance of the disciples* who accompany Jesus is similarly schematic and editorial. Of course the disciples have their place in the older tradition. This is so not only at
9¹⁴ff. where the point of the pericope lies in the contrast of Master
and disciple, but elsewhere too when they are used as foils for Jesus:
in the stories of stilling the storm, 4³⁵ff., walking on the water, 6⁴⁵ff.,
blessing the children, 10¹³f., or in a subordinate part at the feeding

¹ The MSS. vary a great deal in such expressions.

and at 5^{31} in the crowd. Naturally it has to appear in certain conflict dialogues: $2^{(18-20),\ 23-26},\ 7^{1-8}$.

Besides this, individual disciples belong to some units of the tradition: 1^{29-31} (Peter's mother-in-law); 5^{37} (escorts to the daughter of the ἀρχισυνάγωγος); 9^{2-8} (transfiguration); 9^{38-40} (the unknown exorcist); 10^{35-40} (the sons of Zebedee); 14^{33} (Gethsemane); and of course the stories of their calling $1^{16-20},\ 2^{14}$.

In later tradition, and indeed in essence by Mark himself, it is everywhere presupposed that the disciples—apart from the passages dealing with their calling, mission and return $3^{13-19},\ 6^{7-13,\ 30-33}$— always accompany Jesus as a group and this is how we must understand $2^{15f.},\ 3^{7},\ 4^{10,\ 34},\ 6^{1,\ 53f.}$ (indicated by the plural verb); 8^{22} (plural verb), $8^{27},\ 10^{46}$, and also the last week in Jerusalem at $11^{12,\ 19,\ 27a}$, etc. That this is a schematic presentation follows from the fact that the disciples have not been introduced into a large number of individual stories from the tradition, and then Jesus appears alone: $1^{40ff.},\ 2^{1ff.},\ 3^{1ff.},\ 7^{24ff.}$ (Matt. 15^{23} adds the disciples); $7^{32ff.},\ 8^{22ff.}$ More particularly however at the beginning of the story Jesus is sometimes named as the only subject (or the verb is singular), whereas according to editorial connections we should expect both him and the disciples to be mentioned (or the verb in the plural). This sometimes leads to a conflict of plural and singular which points to a mixture of tradition and editing.

1^{21}: καὶ εἰσπορεύονται εἰς Καφ.· καὶ εὐθὺς . . · . εἰσελθὼν (?) . . . ἐδίδασκεν (then v. 29 at the end reads: καὶ εὐθὺς . . . ἐξελθόντες ἦλθον).

5^{1}: καὶ ἦλθον εἰς τὸ πέραν . . . καὶ ἐξελθόντος αὐτοῦ ἐκ τοῦ πλοίου.

$5^{18,\ 21}$: καὶ ἐμβαίνοντος αὐτοῦ εἰς τὸ πλοῖον . . . καὶ διαπεράσαντος τοῦ Ἰησοῦ.

10^{46}: καὶ ἔρχονται εἰς Ἰεριχώ· καὶ ἐκπορευομένου αὐτοῦ ἀπὸ Ἰεριχώ— and now follows an obvious editorial expansion: καὶ τῶν μαθητῶν αὐτοῦ, whereas we would have expected: καὶ ἐκπορευομένων αὐτῶν, and without ἀπὸ Ἰερ. at that.

11^{15}: καὶ ἔρχονται εἰς Ἱεροσόλυμα· καὶ εἰσελθὼν εἰς τὸ ἱερὸν ἤρξατο . . .

11^{27}: καὶ ἔρχονται πάλιν εἰς Ἱεροσόλυμα· καὶ ἐν τῷ ἱερῷ περιπατοῦντος αὐτοῦ.

What really happened can be seen perfectly clearly in the work of the copyist, who, under the constraints of schematic presentation at one time turns a singular verb into the plural, and at another smooths out a juxtaposition of plural and singular by turning the plural into a singular, and so reveals what could have gone on in the treatment of pericopes when the story was separated from their context and told as isolated stories of Jesus.[1] Thus the original text of Mk. 9^{14} (D syr^{sin}) obviously read: καὶ ἐλθὼν . . . εἶδεν, while most witnesses read: καὶ ἐλθόντες . . . εἶδον. Perhaps at 8^{22} also ἔρχεται (ℵ * ΑΓ al) is to be preferred to ἔρχονται (ℵ^c BCD al). Other instances of D and syr^{sin} reading the singular are: 10^{46}, 11$^{1,\ 12,\ 15,\ 20,\ 27}$. Of course we cannot always be certain of our judgements.

Finally this reading of the situation is confirmed by observing later developments: it has always been self-evident that the disciples were constant companions of Jesus. Thus they appear with him, e.g. in *Pap. Ox.*, V, 840, 22 (Kleine Texte, 31, 5). Matthew and Luke are considered below. Then this emphasis became dogmatic: as the constant companions of Jesus the Twelve are the authoritative witnesses to the gospel (Acts 1$^{21f.}$, 10$^{39f.}$). Then they themselves affirm such authority frequently in *Epist. Apost.* (ed. C. Schmidt, pp. 28.13, 35.10f., 36.1f.).

Indeed when Mark speaks of the μαθηταί as a group he obviously has the Twelve in mind (in all probability naïvely and without any reflection, even in the passages before their appointment 2$^{15f.}$, 18^{23}, 3$^{7,\ 9}$). The δώδεκα are expressly mentioned—apart from 3$^{13-19}$, 6$^{7-13}$—at 4^{10}, 9^{35}, 10$^{32-41}$ (οἱ δέκα, D οἱ λοιποί); 11^{11}, 14^{17} and in addition Judas is called εἷς τῶν δώδεκα 14$^{10,\ 20,\ 43}$. All these references are the secondary editorial work of Mark, and indeed may be partly of later copyists.[2] But where the old tradition and the stages of the tradition before Mark speak of the μαθηταί the probability is that the Twelve were not meant, certainly not a limited circle of disciples, but a changing circle of followers, such a circle as was about Jesus in 3^{34} (see pp. 67f.). It is very typical that Matt. 12^{49} refers to μαθηταί instead of περὶ αὐτὸν κύκλῳ καθήμενοι (Mk. 3^{34}), and clearly means the Twelve; so here we have an idea, which Mark was responsible for introducing into the material of the tradition as a whole, now brought into an individual story.

Without prejudice to what has been said on p. 310 about the secondary tendency to individualize by the giving of names, I think it probable that those sections of the tradition which use the names of individual disciples come from an earlier time when the idea of the Twelve as Jesus' constant companions had not yet been formed or successfully carried through. I further think that in the following passages the naming of the disciples is original: 5^{37}, 9^{38}, 10^{35} and probably 13^3 as well. In 1^{29} (p. 212) and 9^2 (p. 260) only Peter

---

[1] K. L. Schmidt: *Rahmen der Geschichte Jesu*, p. 276.
[2] Cp. Wellhausen, *Einleitung in die drei ersten Evangelien*[2], p. 139, especially clear is 4^{10}, see p. 351.1.

M

would have been named originally; the other three names were added under the influence of 1¹⁶⁻²⁰, and in 1²⁹ are due to a copyist of Mark, for they are not found in either Matthew's or Luke's reproduction. From the tradition outside Mark perhaps Luke 9⁵⁴ also belongs to the same sections of the tradition. It is quite natural that the original would tell of an indefinite circle of μαθηταί that often surrounded Jesus; and yet that when some particular thing was related about such μαθηταί one or the other should be actually named. Then there arose first the idea of the twelve, and the later novelistic improvisation brought one or another into prominence out of the circle of the Twelve as need arose, yet without doing it any injury.

The editorial activity of Mark (and his predecessors) which we have described essentially rests upon literary motifs, even though they are mixed with dogmatic motifs in the picture of Jesus as the constantly attacked teacher and healer, and in the idea of the Twelve. But apart from this Mark is influenced by dogmatic motives in his composition, and I must refer to them, though I can deal with them very briefly in view of the interest that has long been shown in them, particularly by Wrede, Wellhausen, M. Dibelius and A. Fridrichsen. Dibelius' characterization of Mark as the book of secret epiphanies[1] is just right. On the one hand the life of Jesus is represented as a series of revelations. Baptism and Transfiguration are alike epiphanies in Mark's view: the stories of the stilling of the storm and of the walking on the water report epiphanies just as much as the feeding stories. So do the healings wrought by the Son of God, especially the exorcisms of the demons which by their supernatural powers recognize the Son of God. In addition to this Jesus reveals himself to his own in the esoteric instruction of the disciples, and just as the exalted one truly appeared to them (9²ᶠᶠ·) so he also spoke as such to them (8³⁴, 13⁹⁻¹³). Yet on the other hand a veil of secrecy is drawn over the revelations: the demons must be silent, those who are healed must not talk about the miracle. Jesus sought solitariness and concealment; he told parables in order to conceal the secret of the Kingdom of God. The fear which originally characterized the impression of the miracle (p. 226) also described the impression of the teaching.[2] The disciples must not speak about what they have seen and heard until his resurrection, indeed they cannot yet themselves enter properly into the secret of his Messiahship; the incapacity to under-

---

[1] *Formgeschichte des Evangeliums*, p. 64.
[2] θαμβεῖσθαι Mk. 10²⁴; ἐκπλήττεσθαι Mk. 1²², 6², 10²⁶, 11¹⁸; Matt. 7²⁸, 22³³; Lk. 4³²; cp. Acts 13¹²; θαυμάζειν Matt. 22²²; Lk. 20²⁶. Cp. E. Peterson, Εἷς θεός, p. 195.

stand lay like some sorcerers' ban on them all. The dogmatic element in all these features has long been recognized. For the author they are the means of writing a life of Jesus as the Messiah, in so far as he was able to do so on the basis of the tradition available to him and under the influence of the faith of the Church, in which he stood.[1] We can leave for the present undecided the question whether the theory of the Messianic secret is to be explained as apologetic—i.e. as an answer to the question why Jesus was not universally recognized as Messiah—or as a veiling of the fact that faith in Jesus' Messiahship begins from belief in his resurrection. I hold the second view to be right, and Wrede thought the same.[2] In any case the author has succeeded by making use of the means available to him, in setting the tradition in a certain light, in impressing it with a meaning such as it needed in the Hellenistic Churches of Paul's persuasion; in linking it with the Christological Kerygma of Christendom, in anchoring the Christian mysteries of Baptism and Lord's Supper in it and so giving for the first time a presentation of the life of Jesus which could rightly be called εὐαγγέλιον Ἰησοῦ Χριστοῦ (Mk. 1¹). I do not think M. Dibelius' judgement[3] right when he says that Matthew is the first 'Gospel' in the strict sense, while the description 'Gospel' cannot be applied to Mark. Mark could well have been the normal Gospel for Pauline Hellenistic Christianity, and it is the joining together of Mark and the speech material in Q rather than the word 'Gospel' which is inappropriate in this connection.[4]

This in fact marks the purpose of the author: *the union of the Hellenis-*

---

[1] The characterization given by M. Dibelius, *Formgeschichte des Evangeliums*, pp. 57–66 I wholeheartedly agree with, apart from his remarks on literary criticism.

[2] Cp. my arguments in *Z.N.W.*, 19, 1919/20, pp. 165–9. E. Bickermann (*Z.N.W.*, 22, 1923, pp. 122–40) makes Mark's messianic secret analogous to the secret which is a widespread feature in the Lives of the Prophets, where, in the case of the hero, divine revelation (or alternatively the divine calling) precedes his public appearance. In such a case the first period of the prophets' activity must be in secret and in such lives we find the motifs of the command to keep silence and of the disciples' misconceptions (op. cit., pp. 125f., 128f.). But there is no analogy as a whole, for the confession of messiahship is certainly not the turning-point from which Jesus' public appearance begins, and the injunction to silence persists after it (8³⁰, 9⁹). The corresponding event to the turning-point in such lives of the prophets would much more properly be the resurrection! Even the Baptism cannot be classed as a prophet's calling, and Jesus did not, as Balaam did, receive a command to make revelations. A. Fridrichsen (*Le Problème du Miracle*, pp. 76–82) though he admittedly does not examine the problem in all its bearings, thinks that the command to the demons and the healed persons to keep silent grew up for apologetic reasons, being directed against the insinuations that Jesus was a magician and a self-advertising thaumaturgist. But I do not find this very satisfying, either.

[3] *Formgeschichte des Evangeliums*, p. 81.

[4] M. Werner has rightly shown that Mark is not a product of Pauline theology (*Der Einfluss paulinischer Theologie im Mk-Evg.*, 1923). But as he fails to distinguish between tradition and editorial matter, or between the traditional stories in Mark, he does not positively determine to what sort of Hellenistic Christianity Mark belonged. That it was the same sort as Paul's can in any case be seen as the result of the enquiry conducted by B. W. Bacon, *The Gospel of Mark*, 1925, in his discussion with Werner.

tic kerygma about Christ, whose essential content consists of the Christ myth as we learn of it in Paul (esp. Phil. 2 [6ff.]; Rom. 3 [24]) with the *tradition of the story of Jesus.* It is only natural that he should make use of apophthegms and miracle stories for this purpose, collecting them and putting them together. It would have been far too paltry a thing to have confined the work to miracle stories. And since his whole enterprise is explicable only in terms of the importance which the tradition itself had it would have been quite unintelligible if he had left out one whole component part like the apophthegms. But on their side the apophthegms were the bridge to the sayings of Jesus, of which evidently Mark offers a selection. M. Dibelius[1] has rightly seen that the question must not be put in this way: Why had Mark only a selection of dominical sayings to offer?, but rather: Why did he accept some at all? Since the dominical sayings were originally collected for instructional purposes, the reason for their incorporation into the Gospel is not self-evident. But once a composition had been made out of miracle stories and apophthegms, it would have been unnatural in the long run to have kept the dominical sayings out. They had to be brought in, and they had to be approximated, as we have seen, to the apophthegmatic form.

It must be emphasized that these considerations which are meant to discover the motives for the composition of Mark, have all the time an eye on the Gospel as a *phenomenon in the history of literature.* By this of course I do not mean that by this historical-literary process the apophthegms and dominical sayings were first brought within the framework of the Christian proclamation of Jesus Christ, within the sphere of the 'gospel' in the wider sense. The situation is much more that the process of literary history is in the last resort comprehensible only on the basis of the fundamental presupposition that in all the sayings of Jesus which were reported, he speaks who is recognized in faith and worship as Messiah or Lord, and who, as the proclamation makes known his works and hands on his sayings, is actually present for the Church.[2] From this point of view even the theory of the 'messianic secret' is no longer a merely literary phenomenon, but the actually necessary expression of faith in a Messiah for whom an incognito was characteristic. But we cannot pursue that here.[3]

The fact that Mark—so far as we can see—was the first to try to write a εὐαγγέλιον that would be at the same time a presentation of the life of Jesus corresponds to the fact that the mythical element is

---

[1] *Formgeschichte des Evangeliums,* p. 77.
[2] Cp. J. Schniewind, *Th.R.,* N.F.2, 1930, pp. 142, 158f.
[3] Cp. J. Schniewind, op. cit., pp. 186f.

stronger in Mark than in either Matthew or Luke. For if in these two gospels the miraculous element is heightened and new mythical elements are in fact introduced, nevertheless in the whole outline the Christ myth recedes in favour of the picture of the earthly ministry of Jesus; in Matthew, because he portrays Jesus at far greater length as the Teacher: in Luke, because he thinks of his task from the very beginning quite as much as an historian's as an evangelist's. The only essential element of the Christ myth not yet adopted by Mark is the pre-existence of Jesus. This dogmatic idea clearly does not lend itself so easily to a presentation of the life of Jesus; John was the first who was able to use it in this way. Yet Mark has also written the beginning of his book under the dominating standpoint of epiphany: for him the Baptist is not the preacher of repentance; his role is to introduce Jesus; and the Baptism is the first story that Mark tells of Jesus.[1]

For the rest *Mark's selection of material* cannot have been determined by the mythical foundation of the Kerygma. The chronological outline was what was given him, i.e. the representation of Baptism, the first appearance and ministry up to the time of the journey to Jerusalem and to the Cross. In individual cases the question of order is not easy to solve, and it will not be treated of here. I will but select this—that the ordering of the material is often determined by quite accidental grounds, namely by what smaller collections were already available to Mark. Such a group comes into view in the group of stories in 1^{16-39}, the collection of conflict dialogues in Chaps. 2 and 3 (but which Mark has, however, expanded from another tradition and by editorial additions); further, the group of stories in $4^{35}-5^{43}$, etc. But I do not propose to burden my work with source theories, but only to emphasize that when one tries to determine the leading ideas of Mark's arrangement of his material one has to take into account the collections of material that he had in front of him.[2] Just as in making such collections some part was played by the arrangement of the material in order (Chap. 2^3) so Mark has frequently worked on the same principle. So it is a misconception to infer from Mark's ordering of his material any conclusions about the chronology and development of the life of Jesus,[3] but it is for the same reason also false to point out, with very few exceptions, what Mark's leading ideas were. Wrede himself rightly recognized that it was impossible to speak of epochs in Mark's presentation. That conflicts between

[1] Cp. M. Dibelius, *Formgeschichte des Evangeliums*, p. 65.
[2] See p. 321, n. 2.
[3] This has been rightly and, in my view, conclusively shown by K. L. Schmidt (*Der Rahmen der Geschichte Jesu*).

Jesus and the leaders of the people are recounted in 2^1–3^6 (or alternatively 2^{35}) is quite accidental and does not depend on any sort of pragmatism in Mark; he produces similar scenes in Chaps. 7, 8 and 10 as well. That such conflicts are placed in tighter sequence in Chaps. 11 and 12 is due only to an historicizing reflection; they appear as appropriate preparations for the final catastrophe. Even the assumption that 3^7–6^{13} can be regarded as expounding the theme: Jesus' ministry among the people and their rejection of him, I take to be true only in so far as the theme applies to his whole life. I think it quite illusory to believe that the selection and ordering of the material in this section was specially influenced by this point of view; Jesus' ministry and the attitude of the people are the same from beginning to end of Mark's gospel. I do not even think it correct to entitle 6^{14}–8^{26} as Jesus' ministry in Gentile country; for that simply expresses the wish to have an overall title for a section, a wish which in its embarrassment clings to some insignificant geographical notes, which Mark partly found in his sources and partly added himself on his own conjecture, but which always has but one purpose—to give an individual story a situation, and which therefore admits no further consequences to be drawn.

Mark is not sufficiently master of his material to be able to venture on a systematic construction himself. The one actual section—apart from the preface and the period in Jerusalem—is the confession of Peter in $8^{27\text{ff.}}$ Of course, not in the sense that the ministry as a whole was given a new turn (in this Wrede is quite right) but only in so far as the esoteric instruction about the new conception of Messiahship began at this point. So it is an epoch for the reader only, not for the life of Jesus; for Mark has neither depicted the recognition of Jesus as something newly won by him, as the fruit of his ministry or of his estimate of the outward and inward situation, nor has he pictured the recognition by the disciples as the outcome of some development. Nor have the new revelations any consequences for the conduct of Jesus or the disciples, save that Mark is now able for the first time naturally to introduce a story like that of the sons of Zebedee. The fact that the disciples play a greater part in this section is grounded simply in their being the natural objects of the teachings. They thus represent the reader, i.e. the Church. The author is not interested in the disciples as historical persons or their relationship to Jesus. Finally in the tradition material which Mark uses in 8^{27}–10^{52} there is hardly any difference from what has gone before: the people and the opponents appear in precisely the same way as before; at the most Mark consciously makes use of some proverbs in Chaps. 8 and 9, which before that would not have been intelligible. To a restricted degree it is also true to say that 8^{27}–10^{52} occupies a special place in Mark: here Christian dogma has attained its point of greatest influence on the presentation.

2. The Gospel according to St. Matthew

In Matthew we also find from time to time the *simple connection of passages* with καί, e.g. 4^{23}, $8^{14, 19}$, 9^{35}, 14^{22}, 16^1. Sometimes the καί is intensified by ἰδού, e.g. $8^{2, 24}$, 9^2, 12^{10}, 15^{22}. There is also the use of δέ to join passages together, e.g. 4^{18}, 11^2.

But for the most part Matthew is intent on stronger links, particularly on calling attention to *temporal connections*. This is done in a quite primitive and schematic way by a word so characteristic of Matthew: τότε, e.g. 2^{16}, 3^{13}, 4^1, 9^{14}, $12^{22, 38}$, 15^1. The end-formula mentioned on pp. 333f. also provides such a connection, and Matthew generally uses it at the transition from a Q Tradition passage to a Mark passage: καὶ ἐγένετο ὅτε ἐτέλεσεν ὁ 'Ιησοῦς τοὺς λόγους τούτους and similarly: 7^{28}, 11^1 (here between two Q passages); 13^{53}, 19^1, 26^1. Such connections also are used for the formulae which introduce most of the Mark passages, as:

ἐν τῇ ἡμέρᾳ ἐκείνῃ 13^1, 22^{23}, in the plural 3^1.
ἐν ἐκείνῳ τῷ καιρῷ 12^1, 14^1, 11^{25} (Q passage).
ἐν ἐκείνῃ τῇ ὥρᾳ 18^1, 26^{55}.

Geographical contexts are given by the well used ἐκεῖθεν, e.g. $9^{9, 27}$, $12^{9, 15}$, $15^{21, 29}$.

Matthew also effects a *close connection of individual stories* without such formulae, so that a temporal and geographical context is supplied. Thus he frequently uses the absolute genitive that is sometimes already in Mark, e.g. 9^{18}: ταῦτα αὐτοῦ λαλοῦντος; 12^{46}: ἔτι αὐτοῦ λαλοῦντος; cp. $2^{1, 13, 19}$, $8^{1, 5, 28}$, 9^{32}, $17^{22, 24}$. In the same way we find the *participium coniunctum* which establishes a connection by reference to what has gone before, e.g.:

ἰδὼν δέ (ὁ 'Ιησοῦς) 5^1, 8^{18}.   ἐξελθὼν ὁ 'Ιησοῦς 13^1, 15^{21}.
ὁ δέ 'Ιησοῦς γνούς 12^{15}.   μεταβὰς ἐκεῖθεν 12^9, 15^{29}, etc.
ἀκούσας δέ ὁ 'Ιησοῦς 4^{12}, 14^{13}.

The participle is in the dative, e.g. at 8^1, 9^{27}.

Sometimes out of such a formulation a small scene takes shape; thus 8^{18}, when Matthew makes a transition from the summary of the healings of the sick in $8^{16f.}$ to the apophthegm about discipleship, and uses the clause: ἰδὼν δὲ ὁ Ἰησοῦς πολλοὺς ὄχλους περὶ αὐτὸν ἐκέλευσεν ἀπελθεῖν εἰς τὸ πέραν.

By such and similar means Matthew ensures that the gaps which often separate the individual sections of Mark are filled up, and so a picture of a more established context grows up. We may compare some transition expressions from Mark and Matthew.

Mk. 1¹⁴: μετὰ δὲ τὸ παραδοθῆναι τὸν Ἰωάννην ἦλθεν ὁ Ἰησοῦς εἰς τὴν Γαλιλαίαν.	Matt. 4¹²: ἀκούσας δὲ ὅτι Ἰωάννης παρεδόθη, ἀνεχώρησεν εἰς τὴν Γαλιλαίαν.
Mk. 1⁴⁰: καὶ ἔρχεται πρὸς αὐτὸν λεπρὸς παρακαλῶν αὐτὸν καὶ γονυπετῶν . . .	Matt. 8¹: καταβάντι δὲ αὐτῷ ἀπὸ τοῦ ὄρους ἠκολούθησαν αὐτῷ ὄχλοι πολλοί. καὶ ἰδοὺ λεπρὸς προσελθὼν προσεκύνει αὐτῷ.
Mk. 4¹: καὶ πάλιν ἤρξατο διδάσκειν παρὰ τὴν θάλασσαν.	Matt. 13¹: ἐν τῇ ἡμέρᾳ ἐκείνῃ ἐξελθὼν ὁ Ἰησοῦς ἐκ τῆς οἰκίας ἐκάθητο παρὰ τὴν θάλασσαν.

How much the *picture of continuity is but appearance* is shown, as is well known, at the point where the end of the narrative of the Baptist's death is linked to the continuing story of Jesus, and Matthew in 14¹²ᵇ, ¹³ᵃ has forgotten the parenthetic nature of the story of the Baptist. The connection in 5¹ is similar, for after a summary description of the crowds following Jesus, we read: ἰδὼν δὲ τοὺς ὄχλους ἀνέβη εἰς τὸ ὄρος as though some specific crowd were coming to him. The same effect is produced by τότε in 12²².

How illusory the picture is can also be seen if we take Matthew's time references seriously: one day stretches from 5¹ to 8¹⁷, and so includes the Sermon on the Mount, the healing of the leper, of the Centurion's son and of Peter's mother-in-law. The next day is also far too fully packed, reaching as it does at least from 8¹⁸ to 9⁹ and containing the apophthegms about discipleship, the stilling of the storm, the demon exorcism in Gadara, and, after repeated sea crossings the healing of the paralytic and the call of Matthew. If we make a new day begin at 9¹⁰—and that is not so much as hinted at—it will last until 9³⁴, and so include the meal with the Taxgatherer, the question from John's disciples, the healing of the woman with an issue of blood, and the raising of the daughter of the ἄρχων, the healing of the two blind men and of the demonpossessed mute. Both Sabbath stories in 12¹⁻⁸ and ⁹⁻¹⁴ which Mark joins with a simple πάλιν in 3¹, take place in Matthew on *one* day (καὶ μεταβὰς ἐκεῖθεν ἦλθεν . . .). One day stretches from 12²² to 13⁵² and so comprises the dispute with the Pharisees, the demand for a sign, the saying about the unclean Spirit, the episode about the true kinsmen and the whole set of parables.

Like Mark, Matthew makes some pure editorial sections, general descriptions looking past the present moment to recall the whole ministry of Jesus, as in 9^{26} there is a report on the widespread fame that Jesus had won. Most of all there are summarizing notes: 4^{13} Jesus' removal from Nazareth to Capernaum; 4$^{23-25}$ The teaching and healing of Jesus and the following of the people (based on motifs from Mk. 1^{39}, 3$^{7-12}$); similar descriptions appear at 9$^{35-36}$ (making use of Mk. 6$^{6,\ 34}$) and 15$^{29-31}$ (using Mk. 7$^{31-37}$, though in substitution for the healing of the deaf mute recounted in Mk. 7$^{31-37}$). Here too belongs the description of Jesus' ministry of healing in the Temple, at 21^{14}, a form in which Matthew has joined at vv. 15ff. with a passage from the tradition.

But the *whole outline of the life of Jesus* in Matthew is not basically different in form from that of Mark.[1] Admittedly Matthew undertook some transpositions in Mark's outline, of which the most important is that in 8^{1}–9^{34} he gives us a collection of miracle stories and in doing so brings together from Chaps. 1, 2, 4 and 5 of Mark stories that are separated there and in a different order. But neither is it an essential alteration when, for reasons no longer discernible, he omits certain stories from Mark (Mk. 1$^{21-28}$, 7$^{32-36}$, 8$^{22-26}$, 9$^{38-40}$, 12$^{41-44}$).[2] Neither is it when, as he frequently does, he abbreviates Mark's stories by omitting small novelistic features. He is not always apt in doing this, as e.g. in 9$^{1-8}$ (the healing of the paralytic) where in consequence of omitting Mk. 2$^{2,\ 4f.}$, the words ἰδὼν ὁ Ἰησοῦς τὴν πίστιν αὐτῶν in v. 2 is left unmotivated; or in 8$^{28-34}$ where it is unintelligible why the spirits from the two demoniacs should pass into the whole herd of swine, because Matthew has omitted the saying about Legion (Mk. 5$^{9f.}$); or finally in 9$^{20-22}$, where the main feature of the story about the woman with the issue of blood has been lost, viz. her being healed by a secret touching of Jesus' garments. Such abbreviations have deprived the miracle stories of their purity of form without of course changing them into another literary genus. Dibelius believes: they were dematerialized, christologized.[3] I think it fits the facts better to say: they are less Hellenistic; in this editorial work Matthew's Jewish-Christian quality is brought to light.

But the chief differences are as follows: (1) Matthew has *joined the*

---

[1] Cp. Burkitt's statement quoted by Streeter (*The Four Gospels*, p. 159): 'Matthew is a fresh edition of Mark, revised, rearranged, and enriched with new material; ... Luke is a new historical work made by combining parts of Mark with parts of other documents.'

[2] Perhaps they were not all to be read in his text of Mark.

[3] *Formgeschichte des Evangeliums*, p. 55.

sayings of Q to the presentation of Mark.[1] But in view of the fact that for the most part he has placed the speech material in situations which he found already in Mark (missionary charge, discourse to the disciples Chap. 18, pharisaic discourse, eschatological discourse) or in situations easily introduced into the Mark outline (the Sermon on the Mount, the baptismal discourse) the picture as a whole is not really changed.

(2) Matthew has added *legendary material* of all kinds. Within the ministry of Jesus this is admittedly quite inappreciable. There are indeed only two instances: 14^{28-31}, Peter on the water, and 17^{24-27} the coin in the fish's mouth. The Passion narrative is more strongly coloured with legendary material, and in addition the original and now lost end of Mark has been replaced by a legendary Easter story. Above all, however, there are the infancy narratives which together with the genealogy prefixed to them not only contain the motifs of dogmatics and legend about Christ, but also answer some sort of biographical demand, so that in this respect Matthew represents an advance on Mark.

In spite of all this however the *picture of the life of Jesus* remains, on the whole, unaltered. The two halves of Mark's portrait: The Galilean Ministry and the time in Jerusalem with the Passion, is the ground-plan also in Matthew. It is of little moment that Matthew does not keep to the daily happenings in the Passion week; he reproduces the passing of the hours at the crucifixion almost completely. Inside the Galilean period the confession of Peter is admittedly no longer such a clearly defined section, since in Matthew Jesus has already been hailed as Son of David by the two blind men 9^{27} and the Syro-Phoenician woman 15^{22}, and in 14^{33} the disciples have paid him homage as the Son of God. The Sermon on the Mount and the missionary charge also present Jesus as the Messiah when he speaks of being persecuted for his sake and of imitating him (5^{10-12}, $10^{17-22, 26-33}$). Nevertheless on the whole the section corresponding to Mk. $8^{27}-10^{45}$ (Matt. $16^{13}-20^{28}$) has also preserved its esoteric character that so distinguishes it from the rest of the Galilean period; the one large insertion which Matthew has made in 18^{10-35} accordingly has the form of esoteric instruction of the disciples, and 18^{15-20} especially contains sayings in which the risen Lord addresses the Christian Church.

Even Mark's *geography* is unaltered. Just as in Mark, the ministry essentially takes place in Galilee with Sea of Galilee as the middle point and Capernaum regarded more specifically as the actual centre.

[1] Cp. B. H. Streeter, *The Four Gospels*, p. 166.

Bethsaida and Decapolis are only indirectly mentioned in the saying against Chorazin and Bethsaida 11²¹, and not as places on Jesus' journey. But Matthew has also found it necessary (15²¹) to keep the journey to the neighbourhood of Tyre (and Sidon) for the sake of the story of the Phoenician woman; and in Matthew Peter's confession also takes place at Caesarea Philippi (16¹³). There are no new geographical notes beyond the questionable Μαγαδάν in 15³⁹ for the equally questionable Δαλμανουθά of Mk. 8¹⁰. The last journey to Jerusalem, following Mk. 10¹ begins at 19¹, and the reminder about the passion on the way to Jerusalem in 20¹⁷ is parallel to Mk. 10³². Matthew also makes Jesus go east of Jordan and by Jericho, and places the healing of the blind man as Jesus leaves Jericho, 20²⁹ᶠᶠ. The geography of Jerusalem is just the same as Mark's, save that apparently Bethany has been replaced by Bethphage in the story of the triumphal entry in 21¹; elsewhere it is mentioned, as in Mark, at 21¹⁷, 26⁶. Jesus makes no excursions from Jerusalem.

The notes on scenery are the same as in Mark, even if sometimes Matthew treats the Mark text freely in making transpositions. Thus in 9¹ Jesus comes from crossing of the sea to heal the paralytic, and so the seashore naturally has to disappear from 9¹⁸. Since he is not interested in Mark's theory of a Messianic secret, he has for the most part not used a house as the scene of his stories; it is not used in the instruction of the disciples 15¹⁵, 17¹⁹, 19⁹ and similarly 9¹, 12²², 15¹, 18¹. In contrast to this Matthew has himself introduced a house in 13³⁶ (interpretation of the parable of the tares) and 17²⁵ (temple tax). He reproduces πορεύεσθαι or ἀνα- and καταβαίνειν from Mark, but has no interest in making the road a piece of real scenery, and leaves out the mention of ὁδός at 16¹³, 19¹⁶, though he adds at 21¹⁹ that the fig tree stood ἐπὶ τῆς ὁδοῦ. Following Mark the Synagogue is the scene for incidents at 12⁹, 13⁵⁴ and in the summaries at 4²³ (cp. Mk. 1³⁹) and 9³⁵ it is mentioned as the typical place for Jesus to teach. The mountain is mentioned, as in Mark, at 14²³, 17¹, 24³ and is omitted only at 10¹, though Matthew introduces it himself as a new scene in 5¹, 15²⁹ (28¹⁶). Matthew also makes Jesus go through all Galilee (4²³), through villages and cities (9³⁵, 11¹, ²⁰).

As in Mark *Jesus is thought of as healer and teacher.* The editorial comments which Matthew adds to Mark speak of Jesus' διδάσκειν: 4²³, 5², 7²⁹, 9³⁵, 11¹, 21²³ which are for the most part Matthew's own formulations. In teaching, Jesus sits, as Mark reports: 13², 24³, and besides 13¹, 15²⁹, 26⁵⁵, or, as in Mark, he is walking about: 4¹⁸, 9⁹, and in addition 4²³, 9²⁷, ³⁵. Matthew adds healings on his own account: 14¹⁴, 19², 21¹⁴.

The *crowds* flock to Jesus. In his editorial comments Matthew keeps on referring to the ὄχλοι πολλοί (he likes the plural) e.g. $4^{25f.}$, 7^{28}, 8^1, ^{18}, 9^8, ^{33}, ^{36}, 12^{46}, 15^{30}, 23^1. Sick people are brought to Jesus: 4^{23}, 9^{35}, $15^{30f.}$ And as in Mark the portrait is unified and schematic; there is no story of any development in the relationship of the people to Jesus.

The *disciples* have the same part to play as in Mark. It is obviously of no significance that Matthew often expressly mentions the μαθηταί where their presence is only presupposed in the Mark text. But sometimes he brings them in where Mark was not thinking of them: 9^{19}, 12^{49}, 23^1. In editorial additions he will make them speak to Jesus, or Jesus to them: 15^{23}, $26^{1f.}$, or fashion some question for a disciple to serve as the introduction to a logion: 15^{12}, 19^{10}. Twelve is for him a self-evident number, and it is typical that in the Transfiguration scene and in the dialogue afterwards he should simply say οἱ μαθηταί (17^{6}, ^{10}, ^{13}); he seems to have forgotten that according to 17^3 only the three privileged ones were present, as he does when at v. 14 he differs from Mk. 9^{14} and says that they came πρὸς τὸν ὄχλον instead of πρὸς τοὺς μαθητάς; and similarly the eschatological discourse at 24^3 is said to be given not just to the four privileged ones, but to the μαθηταί altogether.

If, in spite of this conservative attitude to Mark's outline and the schematic character of his portrayal Matthew's gospel on the whole makes a very different impression from Mark's, and if it has served a special purpose in the Church, that is not solely due to the expansion of Mark's material from Q and other sources, but is essentially because by his gentle transpositions and his dexterous insertion of the speech material Matthew has created an order which combines with Mark's chronological-geographical outline an impressive grouping of material to give his Gospel the strongest impression of a Catechism or Teaching Book. The description of the Ministry proper he begins after the preparatory material at 4^{12-25} with the great programmatic Sermon on the Mount, by which alone he wins the day against his competitors. Then he goes on to the great series of miracles in 8^1-9^{34}, where he has changed the order of Mark to suit his purpose, and on this follows the disciple section in $9^{35}-10^{42}$ where Matthew has skilfully joined Mark and Q passages. Then follows a somewhat looser section on the Baptist and the populace 11^{1-30} after which come the conflicts and disputes of 12^{1-50} for which Matthew has saved the most important conflict dialogues from Mk. 2 and 3, and joined them with corresponding passages from Q. The chapter of Parables (13) is again expanded with related material. Beyond this

Matthew follows Mark fairly accurately, only expanding the instruction of the disciples in Chap. 18 from Q and other Traditions, and finally in the same way adding to the pharisaic and the eschatological discourses in Chaps. 23 and 24–25. Other insertions are of a more occasional kind. But all this has frequently been noticed and needs no further elaboration here. Yet from it all it is clear that Matthew is less dependent than Mark upon the chance arrangement of his sources and, even if not without some exceptions, is much more the master of his material. It remains only to mention that the accumulation of material seems now and again to be determined by a special liking for significant numbers. No doubt the twice seven structure of the three parts of the genealogy in 1 [2–17] does not originate with him, and the Pharisaic discourse would also have had its seven woes already in Q. But he seems to have given sevenfold form to the Beatitudes (the blessedness of the πραεῖς is secondary in the text of Matthew) and similarly to the petitions of the Lord's Prayer. He made the similitudes in Chap. 13 number seven and has brought together ten miracles in 8[1]–9[34].

The note of *ecclesiastical piety* which pervades the Gospel affects the arrangement too. Nevertheless Matthew's portrayal is not so consciously motivated by the Christian Church's outlook as was Mark's. It is much more an unconscious influence in Matthew, and that is why the literary form of his work is not to the same extent as Mark's dependent on this outlook. And that is why it is also unnecessary to pursue the point here in detail; we need to draw attention to a few points only. Just as the Sermon on the Mount in Matthew gives less the impression of prophetic preaching than of a Church Catechism, so Matthew has taken sayings from the tradition which have a specifically ecclesiastical interest: 16[17–19], 18[15–20], and he puts into the mouth of the risen Lord the Church's baptismal formula and the command to teach and make converts (28[18–20]). An ecclesiastical interest and a consequent universal standpoint is also expressed in the Matthew version of the similitudes of the tares and the fish net. This ecclesiasticism is not opposed to the view that Matthew obviously comes from Jewish rabbinical circles (cp. his emendations of Mark, pp. 18 and 27) and uses Jewish (or Jewish-Christian) tradition. He can even turn a Jewish ecclesiastical motif to the service of the Christian Church as 16[17–19] and 18[15–20] show. And for the same reason he can make use of specifically Jewish-Christian sayings from Q which Luke has evidently passed by (e.g. 5[17–19], 10[5]). So for him the proof that in Jesus prophecy has been fulfilled is particularly important (see below). The use of characteristically Rabbinic formulae like βασιλεία τῶν οὐρανῶν instead of βασιλεία τοῦ θεοῦ, like παρεκτὸς λόγου πορνείας (5³²), the sublime address to God in prayer (6⁹), the quotation of the O.T. from the Hebrew text and other characteristics show that the author of the Gospel must be reckoned as a Jewish Christian, indeed as one who was previously a Jewish scribe.[1]

Along with the ecclesiasticism there goes the *Christianizing of the portrait of the disciples*, the substitution of the blessing in 13¹⁶ᶠ. (from Q) for the reproof of Mk. 4¹³, and the omission of the censure for their misunderstanding and little faith of Mk. 4⁴⁰, 6⁵².[2] In this sort of thing he is by no means consistent, but he often effects a change by a small modification.

Finally he raises the stature of *Jesus into the divine* by using the appropriate expressions. The infancy stories serve this purpose. We have already remarked how at 14³³ the disciples have already said, before Peter's confession that ἀληθῶς θεοῦ υἱὸς εἶ. In Matthew Jesus is naturally unable to decline the title addressed to him by the rich young man, διδάσκαλε ἀγαθέ, as Mark can; Jesus' reply in 19¹⁷ has been inaptly amended. And it is particularly characteristic that while in Mark Jesus only infrequently assumes the features of the exalted one (8³⁴, 9²⁻⁸, 13⁹⁻¹³) in Matthew sayings of the exalted one are much more frequently put into the mouth of the human Jesus, apart from the parallels to the passages in Mk. at 5¹¹ᶠ., 10³²ᶠ. (by changing the original), 11(²⁵) ²⁷⁻³⁰, 16¹⁷⁻¹⁹, 18¹⁵⁻²⁰. Moreover in being given words of 'Wisdom' to speak, Jesus speaks as the exalted one: 23³⁴ᶠ., ³⁷⁻³⁹. So even the trifle is characteristic, that men worship (προσκυνεῖν) Jesus, a thing which appears in Mark only at 5⁶, but is recounted ten times in Matthew (2², ⁸, ¹¹, 8², 9¹⁸, 14³³, 15²⁵, 20²⁰, 28⁹, ¹⁷).[3]

Finally we must dwell on one peculiarity of Matthew, which gives his Gospel a certain temper, and is part of its literary historical character: The *reference to the fulfilment of prophecy*, which pervades the whole book and derives from the author's theological as well as his apologetic anti-Jewish interest. With the introduction τοῦτο δὲ (ὅλον) γέγονεν ἵνα πληρωθῇ τὸ ῥηθὲν ὑπό . . . (the quotation follows): 1²², 21⁴ (without a quotation 26⁵⁶). Introduced simply by ἵνα πληρωθῇ τὸ ῥηθὲν ὑπό . . . (the quotation follows): 2¹⁵, 4¹⁴, 12¹⁷, or alternatively ὅπως πληρωθῇ . . . 8¹⁷, 13³⁵ (without quotation 2²³).

---

[1] Cp. E. v. Dobschuetz, *Z.N.W.*, 27, 1928, pp. 338–48. Abundant proofs in detail in A. Schlatter, *Der Evangelist Matthaeus*, 1929.

[2] Cp. H. v. Soden, *Das Interesse des apost. Zeitalters an der evg. Gesch.*, pp. 137f.

[3] With these views, cp. esp. Wellhausen, *Einleitung in die drei ersten Evangelien*², pp. 49–52, 61–63.

τότε ἐπληρώθη τὸ ῥηθὲν διά ... (the quotation follows): 2^{17}, 27^9.

οὕτως γὰρ γέγραπται διά ... (the quotation follows): 2^5.

οὗτος γάρ ἐστιν ὁ ῥηθεὶς διὰ 'Ησαΐου τοῦ προφήτου λέγοντος (the quotation follows): 3^3.

καὶ ἀναπληροῦται αὐτοῖς ἡ προφητεία 'Ησαΐου ἡ λέγουσα (the quotation follows): 13^{14}.

These passages contribute to the unified character of the Gospel. The uniformity of mood (in spite of a certain contradiction of individual sayings of Jesus), the joining together of Mark's account with the wealth of speech material from Q constitute above all the distinctiveness of Matthew's Gospel and are the basis of its special effectiveness in the Church.

3. The Gospel according to St. Luke

Luke sometimes simply places one piece of speech material after the other (see p. 323) and he sometimes deals with the narrative material in the same way, sometimes with καί 4^{16}, 7^{18}, 10^{25} (καὶ ἰδού), 11^{14}, 18^{18}, etc., or with δέ 7^2, ^{36}, 8^{19}, 9^7, 10^{17}, 13^{10}, ^{23}, 14^{25}, 15^1, etc. But for the most part he is concerned to produce a well-knit context, and this he does in two ways:

1. Luke emphasizes the *immediate temporal continuity* of a scene with the one that preceded it.

Now and again it happens that he fuses two scenes into one. Thus at $5^{33ff.}$ he transfers the question on fasting into the preceding story of the meal with the tax-gatherer, and makes the Scribes and Pharisees, to whom Jesus gave the answer about the physician and the sick, put the question about fasting: οἱ δὲ εἶπαν πρὸς αὐτόν. ... In the same way he combines the question from the Sadducees with the one about the Son of David at $20^{41ff.}$, though here Jesus puts the question about the Messiahship of David's Son at v. 39 to the applauding Scribes: εἶπεν δὲ πρὸς αὐτούς. Luke has in the same way left out the change of scene in Mk. 13^3 and so made the prophecy of the destruction of the Temple and the eschatological discourse into one incident, $21^{5ff.}$.

Elsewhere the expressions used by Mark and Matthew serve Luke too for indicating temporal connections:

10^{21}: ἐν αὐτῇ τῇ ὥρᾳ

13^1, ^{31}: ἐν αὐτῷ τῷ καιρῷ

5^{27}, 10^1: μετὰ ταῦτα

The somewhat more circumstantial: καὶ ἐγένετο ὅτε ἐτέλεσεν ταῦτα τὰ ῥήματα λαλῶν ἦλθεν in 7 ¹ D is in all probability derived from the source Q.

Sometimes the immediacy of the temporal connection is brought out by the use of the infinitive:

11 ²⁷: ἐγένετο δὲ ἐν τῷ λέγειν αὐτὸν ταῦτα . . .

11 ³⁷: ἐν δὲ τῷ λαλῆσαι . . .

Further 8 ⁴⁰ (B), 10 ³⁸.

Unusually frequent is his use of the *participium coniunctum* in making transitions:

4 ³⁸: ἀναστὰς δὲ ἀπὸ τῆς συναγωγῆς εἰσῆλθεν . . .

6 ¹⁷: καὶ καταβὰς μετ' αὐτῶν ἔστη ἐπὶ τόπου πεδινοῦ . . .

9 ¹: συνκαλεσάμενος δὲ τοὺς δώδεκα ἔδωκεν αὐτοῖς . . .

19 ²⁸: καὶ εἰπὼν ταῦτα ἐπορεύετο . . .

21 ¹: ἀναβλέψας δὲ εἶδεν τοὺς βάλλοντας . . .; 18 ³¹, 22 ³⁹, etc.

Luke frequently uses the genitive absolute too:

3 ¹⁵: προσδοκῶντος δὲ τοῦ λαοῦ καὶ διαλογιζομένων πάντων . . . ἀπεκρίνατο . . .

7 ²⁴: ἀπελθόντων δὲ τῶν ἀγγέλων Ἰωάννου ἤρξατο λέγειν . . .

8 ⁴: συνιόντος δε ὄχλου πολλοῦ καὶ τῶν κατὰ πόλιν ἐπιπορευομένων πρὸς αὐτὸν εἶπεν . . . 4 ⁴⁰, 9 ⁴³, ⁵⁷, 11 ²⁹, 12 ¹, 19 ¹¹, 20 ⁴⁵, etc.

2. Yet it is more characteristic of Luke that he can sense how false a picture is given if all the units are indifferently placed into one immediate temporal context, as happened in Mark at first, and was then further developed by Matthew. Luke knows that the few stories that have been passed on do not completely fit the course of events, but are only examples and illustrations; and so he frequently draws attention in some introductory phrase to the fact that the following section is really within a larger context. For this purpose he chooses a familiar formula from the LXX, καὶ ἐγένετο, which is particularly used in Luke for introducing many stories from Mark.

So without any connection with what has immediately preceded, and with a mention of the appropriate place:

(1 ⁵: ἐγένετο ἐν ταῖς ἡμέραις Ἡρῴδου βασιλέως τῆς Ἰουδαίας . . .)

1 ⁸: ἐγένετο δὲ ἐν τῷ ἱερατεύειν αὐτόν . . .

3 ²¹: ἐγένετο δὲ ἐν τῷ βαπτισθῆναι ἅπαντα τὸν λαόν . . .

5 ¹: ἐγένετο δὲ ἐν τῷ τὸν ὄχλον ἐπικεῖσθαι αὐτῷ . . .

5 ¹²: καὶ ἐγένετο ἐν τῷ εἶναι αὐτὸν ἐν μιᾷ τῶν πόλεων . . .

5 ¹⁷: καὶ ἐγένετο ἐν μιᾷ τῶν ἡμερῶν . . .

Further 8 ²², 9 ¹⁸, ⁵¹, 11 ¹, 14 ¹, 17 ¹¹, 18 ³⁵, 20 ¹, etc.

Also, though with a link with what has preceded:

2¹: ἐγένετο δὲ ἐν ταῖς ἡμέραις ἐκείναις . . .

6⁷: ἐγένετο δὲ ἐν ἑτέρῳ σαββάτῳ . . .

6¹²: ἐγένετο δὲ ἐν ταῖς ἡμέραις ταύταις . . .

7¹¹, 8¹: καὶ ἐγένετο ἐν τῷ (καθ') ἑξῆς . . .

9³⁷ (B): ἐγένετο δὲ τῇ ἑξῆς ἡμέρᾳ . . .

Further 8⁴⁰ (D), 9²⁸. Some closing formulae serve the same purpose, see below.

Many of the transition formulae, especially those with καὶ ἐγένετο not only serve to establish a connection with the preceding story, but also contain at the same time notes on the situation for the one following. They often give a fairly detailed description of a situation characteristic of the life and ministry of Jesus. Such indications of situations have been enumerated already on pp. 335f.

More extensive are the formulations which bring the new situations together in factual connection with what has gone before. Among them we can count the transition formula at 3¹⁵ which introduces the Baptist's messianic preaching. προσδοκῶντος δὲ τοῦ λαοῦ καὶ διαλογιζομένων πάντων ἐν ταῖς καρδίαις αὐτῶν περὶ τοῦ Ἰωάννου, μή ποτε αὐτὸς εἴη ὁ Χριστός, ἀπεκρίνατο λέγων . . . The connection between the Baptism and the Temptation is made even more strongly than in Mark at 4¹: Ἰησοῦς δὲ πλήρης πνεύματος ἁγίου ὑπέστρεψεν ἀπὸ τοῦ Ἰορδάνου καὶ ἤγετο ἐν τῷ πνεύματι ἐν τῇ ἐρήμῳ . . . And correspondingly we read at 4¹⁴ after the Temptation: καὶ ὑπέστρεψεν ὁ Ἰησοῦς ἐν τῇ δυνάμει τοῦ πνεύματος εἰς τὴν Γαλιλαίαν καὶ φήμη ἐξῆλθεν καθ' ὅλης τῆς περιχώρου περὶ αὐτοῦ, καὶ αὐτὸς ἐδίδασκεν ἐν ταῖς συναγωγαῖς αὐτῶν, δοξαζόμενος ὑπὸ πάντων. The appearance of Jesus in Capernaum is linked to the preceding incident at Nazareth 4³⁰ᶠ· in the simplest way: αὐτὸς δὲ διελθὼν διὰ μέσου αὐτῶν ἐπορεύετο καὶ κατῆλθεν εἰς Καφαρναούμ. Similarly Luke has written the following sentence in 5²⁹ to fill the gap between the calling of Levi and the meal with the tax-gatherer (Mk. 2¹⁵): καὶ ἐποίησεν δοχὴν μεγάλην Λευεὶς αὐτῷ ἐν τῇ οἰκίᾳ αὐτοῦ . . . It is the same kind of thing when in 9⁵¹ Luke clearly marks the transition from the Galilean ministry to the journey to Jerusalem: ἐγένετο δὲ ἐν τῷ συμπληροῦσθαι τὰς ἡμέρας τῆς ἀναλήμψεως αὐτοῦ καὶ αὐτὸς τὸ πρόσωπον ἐστήρισεν τοῦ πορεύεσθαι εἰς Ἱερουσαλήμ.

Luke takes over Mark's *concluding formulae*, though he occasionally transforms and expands them: 5²⁶, 6¹¹, 19⁴⁷ᶠ·, 20¹⁹, ²⁶, ³⁹ᶠ·. He adds some new ones: 9⁴³ᵃ (after the healing of the epileptic boy): ἐξεπλήσσοντο δὲ πάντες ἐπὶ τῇ μεγαλειότητι τοῦ θεοῦ; 13¹⁷ (after the healing of the crooked woman): καὶ ταῦτα λέγοντος αὐτοῦ κατῃσχύνοντο πάντες οἱ ἀντικείμενοι αὐτῷ, καὶ πᾶς ὁ ὄχλος ἔχαιρεν ἐπὶ πᾶσιν τοῖς ἐνδόξοις τοῖς γινομένοις ὑπ' αὐτοῦ ; 18⁴³ (after the healing of the blind man): καὶ πᾶς ὁ λαὸς ἰδὼν ἔδωκεν αἶνον τῷ θεῷ. By contrast the closing formula in Mk. 4³³ has to disappear from Luke, because he has changed the whole situation of the parable discourse.[1] In the last week at Jerusalem Luke manages to make the individual stories look like fragments of a fuller occasion by using such conclusion formulae, although he otherwise disturbs Mark's arrangement of the days. So in 19⁴⁷ᶠ· we read: καὶ ἦν διδάσκων τὸ καθ' ἡμέραν ἐν τῷ ἱερῷ . . . ὁ λαὸς γὰρ ἅπας ἐξεκρέμετο αὐτοῦ ἀκούων, and in consequence the question in 20¹ᶠᶠ· about authority looks like a mere episode. Correspondingly 21³⁷ᶠ· closes this activity in Jerusalem with the comment: ἦν δὲ τὰς ἡμέρας ἐν τῷ ἱερῷ διδά σκων, τὸς ὲ νύκτας ἐξερχόμενος ηὐλίζετο εἰς τὸ ὄρος τὸ καλούμενον ἐλαιῶν, καὶ πᾶς ὁ λαὸς ὤρθριζεν πρὸς αὐτὸν ἐν τῷ ἱερῷ ἀκούειν αὐτοῦ.

Finally we must mention here Luke's editorial formulations, which bring the events related into *connection with secular history*. That happens as early as the brief introductory formula in 1⁵: ἐγένετο ἐν ταῖς ἡμέραις Ἡρῴδου βασιλέως τῆς Ἰουδαίας. Luke has given to the Christmas story in 2¹ᶠᶠ· a similar link with world history—the census of Quirinius. He has fixed the appearance of the Baptist by a sixfold synchronism at 3¹ᶠᶠ· And at 3¹⁹ᶠ· he remarks: ὁ δὲ Ἡρῴδης ὁ τετράρχης, ἐλεγχόμενος ὑπ' αὐτοῦ . . . κατέκλεισεν τὸν Ἰωάννην ἐν φυλακῇ.

What sort of total picture of Jesus' ministry do we then get from Luke? Like Matthew he has added to material from Mark from his source Q, and further drawn upon other traditional material. But he carries out the intercalation of sources very differently from Matthew.[2] He does not take the Mark outline as his basis and then add speech material at suitable points. But on the whole his method is to alternate his sources, to put them alongside one another; and in this way he recounts two missionary charges, two Pharisaic discourses, etc. After the infancy narratives and the introductory history he simply follows Mark in essentials from 4³¹ to 6¹⁹ (Mk. 1²¹–3¹⁹), and then adds some passages from Q in 6²⁰–8³ which he has expanded from his special source at 7¹¹⁻¹⁹, ³⁶⁻⁵⁰, 8¹⁻³, after which he continues in 8⁴–9⁵⁰ with Mk. 3³¹–9⁴⁰ leaving out Mk. 6⁴⁵–8²⁶.[3] This is followed by 9⁵¹–18¹⁴, the Great Interpolation in Mark's story, and of this section 9⁵¹ (alternatively v. 57)–13³⁰ is the basis into which

[1] Rightly explained by K. L. Schmidt, *Rahmen der Geschichte Jesu*, pp. 134f.
[2] Cp. B. H. Streeter, *The Four Gospels*, pp. 167f.
[3] I shall not discuss the question whether Luke deliberately left out the section Mk. 6⁴⁵–8²⁶ or, as appears probable to me, it was not in his copy of Mark. Cp. W. Bussmann, *Synopt. Studien*, I, 1925.

material from the special source is intercalated, while in 13^{31}–18^{14} the special source is dominant and passages from Q are inserted into it.[1] From this point on Luke again follows Mark completely, though in the Passion narrative he seems occasionally to have made use of another source, and in the concluding stories he has considerably expanded Mark from another tradition.

In all this his use of Mark's arrangement is more conservative than that of Matthew. He does not alter the Mark groupings in any considerable way. This means that he has not, like Matthew, made his account subservient to some systematic interest. Rather does he directly continue the method developed in Mark because he is interested in an *historically continuous and connected presentation*, whose demands of course he realizes much more comprehensively than Mark. The editorial material we have reviewed serves this purpose, and from this point of view we can understand some of the occasional small transpositions of the text of Mark. The most important of these is his displacement of Jesus' visit to Nazareth at the beginning of his ministry and its reshaping to a programmatic entrance in 4$^{16-30}$. Similarly he takes the story of the calling of the disciples, told very differently by him and places it later at 5$^{1-11}$ because it is psychologically more probable that Jesus had been active for some time before he called any disciples. The transposition of Mk. 3$^{7-12}$ and 3$^{13-19}$ in Lk. 6$^{12-16}$ and 6$^{17-19}$ is a triviality by which Luke ensures that there is an audience for the discourse that follows.[2] The correlation of 4^{13} and 22^3 is also characteristic of the interpretation of the story of Jesus as an unity: Satan leaves Jesus for the time being, so as to usher in the catastrophe at the end.

The fundamental change by which, in spite of a wholly conservative attitude, Luke has transformed the whole plan of Mark is that in using his sources by turns he has introduced a completely new period into the life of Jesus with the *report of journeying* that begins at 9^{51}. He probably felt the need not to leave the journey to Jerusalem so much in the dark as Mark had done, and found in it at the same time a background well adapted to receive all kinds of situationless units. So he emphasized, as we have shown on p. 336, the journey situation in his editorial notes. But he was not very skilful; for though Jesus was journeying, by Luke's statement through Samaria, he was still

---

[1] I cannot convince myself that there is a fragment of a special Gospel incorporated into Lk. 9^{51}–18^{14} (Schaarschmidt, *T.S.K.*, 101, 1929, pp. 357–80).

[2] L. Brun has shown (*Symb. Osl.*, 9, 1930, pp. 38–50) that in the composition of Luke the tendency already evident in his sources (cp. A. Meyer, *Festg f. A. Juelicher*, pp. 35–60) to put related sections together in pairs, shows itself again. But in my view it is not possible to speak of a consciously accomplished principle of composition.

surrounded by the same audience, and questioned by the same opponents as he had been in Galilee.[1] The fact that Jesus is here also invited to dine with the Pharisees (11 ^{37}, 14^{1}), goes into the Synagogue (13^{10}), that Antipas sought his life (13 $^{31ff.}$) and that Jesus in the end, in Luke as in Mark, comes to Jericho—shows particularly that Luke has not been able to sustain the fiction of a Samaritan journey. It is very difficult to say whether the idea of making the journey go through Samaria came to him because the piece from the tradition in 9 $^{52-56}$ contained this background or whether he thought of it himself and only then placed 9 $^{52-56}$ in Samaria.

One consequence of this dismemberment of the Mark-context is that the esoteric portion of Mark (8 ^{27}–10^{45}) loses its meaning in Luke. It is cut in two: Peter's Confession and the first and second announcement of the Passion come before the journey (9 $^{18-22}$, $^{43b-45}$); the third announcement of the Passion comes at the end of the journey (18 $^{31-34}$). Luke has omitted the Zebedee debate, and he puts his parallels to Mk. 10^{45} into the Last Supper (22 ^{27}). On the other hand Jesus announces his Messiahship in his first sermon at 4 $^{16ff.}$, and Luke reports an epiphany of the κύριος in 5 $^{1-11}$, so that Peter's Confession cannot be epoch making as it is in Mark.

For the rest, Luke's *geography* for the Galilean ministry is throughout the same as Mark's: Capernaum, we read in 4 ^{30} is the starting-place of Jesus' ministry, it is the scene of the story of the centurion (7 ^{1}) and is mentioned yet again in the woes at 10^{15} (from Q). Luke follows Mark in introducing the Sea of Galilee in 5 $^{1ff.}$, 8$^{22ff.}$ Journeys outside the confines of Galilee are unthinkable for Luke, apart from that in 8 ^{26} to the χώρα τῶν Γερασηνῶν, and this is due to the omission of the section Mk. 6 ^{45}–8^{26}. Similarly Decapolis (apart from an indirect reference in 10^{13}) and Tyre are not here the scenes of Jesus' ministry. The mention of Bethsaida in 9^{10} is quite fragmentary. Caesarea Philippi is not named as the place of Peter's confession. The only additional geographical detail is Nain 7^{11}. After the journey through Samaria Luke again comes back to Mark's geography, so that, as we have said, Jesus arrives at Jericho 18^{35}. The stay in Jerusalem gives essentially the same picture as Mark; in Luke too Jesus goes to Jerusalem via the Mount of Olives (19^{29}). Bethany plays no further part except in 19 ^{29} where it seems to be mentioned along with Bethphage as a stage of the journey. It is the Mount of Olives that is rather spoken of as the nightly lodging-place (21 ^{37}), and this I would not trace back to any special tradition, but regard as a combination of Luke's on the basis of Mk. 14^{26}.

[1] Cp. Wellhausen, *Einleitung in die drei ersten Evangelien*[2], p. 53.

The *notes on the scenes* correspond pretty well with Mark's. The sea-shore of course is less used, as Luke puts the parable discourse else-where—Luke (5³) has changed the motif of Jesus' teaching from a ship (Mk. 4¹ᶠ·)—and the section Mk. 6⁴⁵–8²⁶ where it occurs more than once, is missing from Luke. Neither is it specially stressed in 8⁴⁰ (Mk. 5²¹) and is missing from 5²⁷ (Mk. 2¹³) and 6¹⁷ (Mk. 3⁷), where in its place we find τόπος πεδινός. The feeding in 9¹⁰ᶠᶠ· does not happen on the shore, but at Bethsaida. So the sea and sea journeys come only at 5¹ᶠᶠ· (the calling of the Disciples); 8²²ᶠᶠ· (stilling of the storm) and 8²⁶, ³⁷ (the Gerasene). There is no teaching of the dis-ciples in a house at all, and it is mentioned only as the place where guests are received: 10³⁸ (Mary and Martha) and 19⁵ (Zaccheus) which were already in the tradition, and 7³⁶, 14¹, also indirectly 11³⁷ in Luke's editorial passages. The Way provides the scene in the editorial introduction 9⁵¹, and we have said on p. 336 that the motif of Jesus' journeying and going up to Jerusalem frequently provides the background. At the same place we have cited the passages in which (apart from those parallel to Mark) Jesus teaches in the Synagogue. And as the Synagogue is mentioned in the summarizing formula in 4¹⁵, so is it expressly stated in 4¹⁶ that Jesus went there κατὰ τὸ εἰωθὸς αὐτῷ. The mountain is referred to in 6¹², 9²⁸, following Mark, but is missing from the parallel to Mk. 13³ and of course there is no parallel to Mk. 6⁴⁶. The meals which are peculiar to Luke have been referred to on pp. 335f.

As in Mark Jesus is thought of as *teacher and healer*. Luke mentions Jesus' διδάσκειν in addition to Mark's editorial passages and in his own editorial formulations at 4¹⁵, 5³, 6⁶, 13¹⁰, ²², 19⁴⁷, 20¹, 21³⁷ (cp. 13²⁶, 23⁵). Jesus sits to teach in the Synagogue 4²⁰ and in the ship 5³. Luke himself introduces Jesus' healing into the source material at 5¹⁷, 7²¹ (cp. 8²), 9¹¹, and in the same way makes him heal the ear that had been cut off the servant of the High Priest (22⁵¹). The people gather to listen to Jesus: 5¹, ¹⁵, 6¹⁷, 15¹, 19⁴⁸, 20⁴⁵, 21³⁸ and to be healed by him: 5¹⁵, 6¹⁷ᶠ· So Luke constantly emphasizes how the people flock to him, and surround him, and how Jesus speaks to the crowds; cp. the enumeration of the editorial for-mulations on p. 336.

It is self-evident that the *disciples accompany Jesus*, and they are expressly called the δώδεκα at 8¹ and 9¹² (so also following Mark at 9¹, 18³¹) and Luke understands the Twelve by the term ἀπόστολοι at the Last Supper 22²⁴, as he does by the term μαθηταί at 9¹⁸ᶠᶠ· (Peter's confession and the first announcement of the Passion) and 22³⁹, ⁴⁵ (Gethsemane). But elsewhere by μαθηταί Luke means a larger following: it is from the μαθηταί that Jesus chooses the Twelve 6¹³; at 6¹⁷ there is an ὄχλος πολὺς τῶν μαθητῶν αὐτοῦ about him, and it is to these μαθηταί that we must understand that the discourse of 6²⁰ff. is addressed. Similarly the μαθηταί to whom Jesus directs his sayings in 10²², ²³f. are the seventy, who return to him at 10¹⁷; and at 19¹⁷ ἅπαν τὸ πλῆθος τῶν μαθητῶν rejoice as he enters into Jerusalem. This is quite in keeping with the concept of μαθητής in the sayings about discipleship in 14²⁶f., ³³. At other places one can be uncertain whether Luke means the Twelve or some larger circle when he uses μαθηταί: 7¹¹, 11¹, 12¹, ²², 16¹, 17¹, ²², 20⁴⁵, in the same way the idea of ἀπόστολοι in 17⁵ is uncertain. The disciples approach Jesus with news and questions (see p. 336). When the tradition provides the names of individual disciples, Luke repeats them, except for the characteristic passages in 21⁷ and 22⁴⁰: for him the eschatological discourse seems in no way to be confined to the disciples (cp. 21⁵; καί τινων λεγόντων), and in the story of Gethsemane he presupposes that the whole Twelve accompany Jesus. On his own account Luke mentions individual disciples at 12⁴¹ (Peter as the questioner) and 22⁸ (Peter and John as messengers to prepare for the Last Supper).

Luke's *chief interest is literary*. His ambition was to write his story in a way that would impress even his cultured Greek readers, and he had a special concern to reproduce the right τάξις, i.e. an evidently historical sequence (1¹⁻⁴). His work is actually above the level of Mark and Matthew in this respect. But even he was unable to portray a real development or realize an inner connection between the works and the destiny of Jesus. We can recognize the indications of an 'external' development when Jesus is first made to appear in his own town of Nazareth, then to continue his ministry in Galilee, and finally in Samaria and Jerusalem. For all that the naming of the different places is not joined up with any real conception of growth in Jesus' ministry itself; the picture of the ministry remains the same schematic one throughout. We can speak of leading ideas in Luke's presentation only to a very limited extent. It is clear that Luke has thought of the story of Jesus and that of the Apostles as an unity, even if it be a manifest overstatement to say that the specific stimulus of his work lay in the second part (Acts) to which the Gospel was but an indispensable preliminary.[1] Luke was not successful in achieving an unity of historical action; yet for him all the events he recorded exhibited a spirit-produced unity. Just as the Spirit was the funda-

---

[1] E. Meyer, *Urspr. u. Anf. des Christent.*, I, 1921, p. 2. He rightly stresses the unity of Acts and Luke; M. Dibelius rightly warns against overestimating the unity as a literary phenomenon. *Eucharisterion* (fuer H. Gunkel), II, 1923, pp. 28f.

mental basis of Jesus' life and ministry (Lk. 1^{35}, 3^{22}, $4^{1, 14, 18}$, 10^{21}), so he also founded and guided the Church and its mission (Acts 1^8, $2^{1ff.}$, $13^{2, 4}$, 15^{28}, etc.).[1] But Luke's literary ability does not rise above a certain technique. In some ways he is even more dependent on his sources than Matthew, even if in particular cases he deals with his material more freely and gives it linguistically a more independent form.[2] This is a good thing for the worth of his book as a source, as is the fact that he does not permit his dogmatic conceptions to exercise any essential influence on his work. That can hardly be called meritorious, for he has obviously not adopted a strongly marked position with specific tendencies. It is possible to point out some favourite themes: a liking for the poor and the despised, a sentimental trait with which we may join a certain predilection for women.[3] These traits are of course just as much due to the tradition which Luke used. What is peculiar to him is the apologetic tendency which appears in the Passion narrative. Luke's universalism and his attitude to the Parousia are less characteristic of himself than of his circle and his age. So is the heightening of the miraculous, the tendency to legend, the raising of the person of Jesus to the divine, which has its external manifestation in his calling Jesus κύριος in the days of his flesh. All this has been noted often, and has often been put forward,[4] and we need add nothing now. For our purposes it is essential to recognize that the Gospel of Luke is the climax of the history of the Synoptic Tradition in so far as the development which the tradition had undergone from the beginning has attained its greatest success in Luke: the editing and connecting of isolated sections into a coherent continuity.

[1] Cp. H. v. Baer, *Der Heil. Geist in den Lukasschriften*, 1926; also J. Schniewind, *Th.R.* N.F.2, 1930, pp. 155f.

[2] Cp. A. Fridrichsen, *Le Problème du Miracle*, pp. 32f.

[3] A. Fridrichsen classes Luke's picture of Jesus in this connection under the Hellenistic idea of εὐεργέτης (op. cit., p. 42). But it would be more correct in most of the relevant passages to see an expression of the piety of the Anawim, cp. J. Schniewind, *Th.R.*, N.F.2, 1930, pp. 157f.

[4] Cp. esp. the characteristics in Wellhausen, *Einleitung in die drei ersten Evangelien*[2], pp. 52–57, 60, 61, 63–64; further V. O. Janssen, *Der literarische Charakter des Lukas-Evangeliums* (Diss. Jena, 1917), pp. 43–58.

Conclusion

THE outcome of the development we have exhibited is the Gospel, which we meet first of all in the three forms of the Synoptists. What can we say about it from the point of view of the history of literature?

The motives that have led to its formation are plain. *The collection of the material of the tradition began in the primitive Palestinian Church.* Apologetic and polemic led to the collection and production of apophthegmatic sections. The demands of edification and the vitality of the prophetic spirit in the Church resulted in the handing on, the production and the collection of prophetic and apocalyptic sayings of the Lord. Further collections of dominical sayings grew out of the need for paraenesis and Church discipline. It is only natural that stories of Jesus should be told and handed down in the Church—biographical apophthegms, miracle stories and others. And just as surely as the miracle stories and such like were used in propaganda and apologetic as proofs of messiahship, so is it impossible to regard any one interest as the dominant factor; as it is generally not right to ask question about purpose and need only; for a spiritual possession objectifies itself also without any special aim.

With all this the Church did not itself create new literary genres but took over traditional forms that had long been used in Judaism, and which—so far as dominical sayings are concerned—Jesus himself had also used. That such forms were ready to hand encouraged the relatively rapid precipitation of a somewhat fixed tradition. Yet with all this the type of the Gospel was not yet formed, but only in preparation. For these methods served only for the handing down of isolated sections. And when such sections were finally collected and fixed in written form and in this way underwent naturally enough some process of editing—as we must suppose took place for the speech material in Q, and for the shorter collections of apophthegms and miracle stories which Mark used—then the result was only some enumerations and summings up. Such collections have their analogy in the collections of Rabbinic traditions, which are also a threading together of individual elements of the tradition without making any organic unity. But of course a collection from the Jesus-tradition must differ from the very start from a Rabbinic collection in that it does not gather together the voices of different authorities, but isolates the Jesus-tradition alone.[1] No doubt this is a preparation for the Gospel, but it is not yet a making of the Gospel. For the idea of an unified presentation of the life of Jesus, knit together by some dominant concept, which first constitutes the Gospel, was obviously far removed from the Palestinian Church. This fits the picture which we have to form of the character of this eschatological community, as it does the analysis of our earliest Gospel, Mark.

It is in Mark that *the Gospel type* is first to be met. In no way is any one of his sources to be called a Gospel. Of course we cannot prove that there was no one alongside him, or before him, whose work could, like his, be termed a Gospel; but it is hardly likely. For neither Matthew nor Luke has used such a work; both take the outline of Mark as basic. At all events the Gospel is a product of the Hellenistic Church. Its origin thus rests on two factors: (1) On the Hellenistic Church taking over the Palestinian tradition. (2) On new motives in the Hellenistic Church which produced the shaping of the traditional material into a Gospel.[2]

1. *The taking over of the Palestinian Tradition* is part of a problem which is not simple to solve. Yet this much can be said: The taking of it over is intelligible not only because the first missionaries were Christian Jews, but also because the Jewish Christian element at first constituted a large percentage of the Hellenistic Church. The need to take over the Tradition can hardly have been equally great in all parts of the Hellenistic Church; but that churches of the Pauline type stood in need of this tradition to some extent is shown by Paul's appeal to dominical sayings—we need refer only to 1 Cor. 7[25], 9[14]. This need would naturally grow in the course of time; Jesus would have to be made obviously a διδάσκαλος to Gentile Christians, in spite of his primary cultic significance.[3] Moreover it is not possible to do without stories of Jesus indefinitely. For if the κύριος was essentially a cultic deity for the Hellenistic Church as well, then, in order to retain the peculiar character of Christian faith—the union of the cultic deity with the historical person of Jesus—a tradition about the story of Jesus was necessary; and the analogy of Hellenistic saviours about whom stories were related could not but help to further the demand for and consequently the taking over of the tradition.

[1] This has been rightly emphasized by G. Kittel, *Die Probleme des palaestin. Spaetjudentums und das Urchristentum*, 1926, pp. 63–69.

[2] Cp. B. H. Streeter, *The Four Gospels*, pp. 495–7.

[3] Cp. Justin, *Apol.*, I, 6: τὸν παρ' αὐτοῦ (sc. τοῦ θεοῦ) υἱὸν ἐλθόντα καὶ διδάξαντα ἡμᾶς ταῦτα; 13: τὸν διδάσκαλόν τε τούτων γενόμενον ἡμῖν καὶ εἰς τοῦτο γεννηθέντα 'Ιησοῦν Χριστόν. Cp. G. Baldensperger, *R.H.Ph.R.*, 2, 1922, p. 115.

In this regard it is difficult to say what specific items of the tradition played a part in the concrete situations of the Church's life. Dominical sayings of course were needed in preaching, paranesis and Church discipline. I do not myself think as M. Dibelius does, that apophthegms played any part in preaching. Nor were the themes of the conflict dialogues exactly existential for Hellenistic Christians, nor is any such use made probable by the sources. I think that the apophthegms had here a quite essentially literary existence. Besides, they could have been told in some uncontrollable form of the tradition. The same can be said of the miracle stories, for which Dibelius postulates a class of story-tellers;[1] but in addition they played a special part in missionary preaching as Acts 2^{22}, 10^{38} show. The more the proof from prophecy was developed, the more the need for stories of Jesus was felt in connection therewith, especially of the Passion narrative. For the rest it is that the sheer weight of the extant tradition availed for its propagation even though there was no longer any concrete need for many of its constituent sections.

2. It is possible to hold that a coherent presentation of the life of Jesus on the basis of a tradition of separate sections and small collections had to come at some time. The more the wealth of the oral tradition dried up, the more the need would grow of a collection as full and definitive as possible. And it seems but natural that the tradition which had an historical person at its centre should have been conceived in the form of a coherent, historical, biographical story. But this consideration by no means suffices to explain the peculiar character of the Synoptic gospels. Indeed their lack of specifically biographical material, their lacunae in the life story of Jesus are due to their presentation being based on the then extant tradition. But their own specific characteristic, a creation of Mark, can be understood only from the *character of the Christian kerygma*, whose expansion and illustration the gospels had to serve. The primitive Christian kerygma that grew up on Hellenistic soil is represented by many passages in the Pauline letters, which depend upon the Church tradition (Rom. $1^{3f.}$, $6^{3f.}$, 10^9; 1 Cor. 11^{23-26}, 15^{3-7}, Phil. 2^{6-11}), as by the equivalent passages in Acts (2^{22-24}, 3^{13-15}, 10^{37-41}, 13^{26-31}).[2] The Christ who is preached is not the historic Jesus, but the Christ of the faith and the cult. Hence in the foreground of the preaching of Christ stands the death and resurrection of Jesus Christ as the saving acts which are known by faith and become effective for the believer in Baptism and Lord's Supper. Thus

---

[1] *Formgeschichte des Evangeliums*, p. 36.
[2] Ibid., pp. 7–14.

the kerygma of Christ is cultic legend and the *Gospels are expanded cult legends.*[1] I Cor. 11^{23-26} (Lord's Supper) and 15^{3-7} (Resurrection) show that the motifs of the kerygma required more illustration; Acts $10^{37f.}$, $13^{24f.}$ show how the ministry of the Baptist and the Baptism of Jesus served as a starting-point of the expanded kerygma, and by this means the earthly life of Jesus was at one and the same time removed from the sphere of secular events and brought into the context of the divine plan of salvation; finally Acts 2^{22}, 10^{38} evidence the need to see the earthly life of Jesus illustrated as proof of the divine equipment of the Lord. Which all amounts to this: The tradition had to be presented as an unity from the point of view that in it he who spoke and was spoken of was he who had lived on earth as the Son of God, had suffered, died, risen and been exalted to heavenly glory. And inevitably the centre of gravity had to be the end of the story, the Passion and Resurrection.[2] Mark was the creator of this sort of Gospel; the Christ myth gives his book, the book of secret epiphanies, not indeed a biographical unity, but an unity based upon the myth of the kerygma. The Passion story, which is anticipated in allusions like $2^{19f.}$ and 12^{1-11}, and the esoteric instruction of the disciples as at 8^{31}, 9^{31}, $10^{33f.}$ gains weight in importance; the Easter story, in any case prepared for in the same esoteric teaching and at the Transfiguration (9^{2-10}), constitutes the end of the life that had been introduced by the Baptism as a messianic consecration and interspersed with miracles, and whose secret had been known from the beginning by the spirits for whom this life spelt judgement. Matthew and Luke strengthened the mythical side of the gospel at points by many miracle stories and by their infancy narratives and Easter stories. But generally speaking they have not really developed the Mark type any further, but have simply made use of an historical tradition not accessible to Mark but available to them. There was no real development of the type of Gospel created by Mark before John, and there of course the myth has completely violated the historical tradition.

Are such observations adequate, or must we look around for analogies to the explanation of the form of the Gospel? What analogies can be suggested? There are none in the *Greek Tradition*; for

[1] Cp. H. v. Soden, 'Die Entstehung der christlichen Kirche', *Geschichte der christlichen Kirche*, I, 1919, p. 72.

[2] Cp. M. Kaehler, *Der sog. histor. Jesus*, p. 80.1: 'One could say somewhat challengingly that the Gospels are Passion Narratives with circumstantial introductions.' A. Schlatter, *Der Glaube im NT*[4], p. 477: 'For each of the Evangelists the Gospel was the story of Jesus' way to the Cross.' Cp. also R. Guardini, *The Spirit of Liturgy* (Ecclesia Orans I)[6, 7], 1921, p. 41, where the individual stories in the Gospels are interpreted out of their context in the Mass.

there is no point in considering either the Memoirs which Justin (Apol., I, 66) might have been thinking with his reference to ἀπομνημονεύματα, or the Hellenistic biography.[1] There is no histori-cal-biographical interest in the Gospels, and that is why they have nothing to say about Jesus' human personality, his appearance and character, his origin, education and development; quite apart from the fact that they do not command the cultivated techniques of composition necessary for grand literature, nor let the personalities of their author appear. The literature of *memoirs and lives of the philoso-phers* are related to the Gospels at the most in that they, like the Gos-pels, gather together in somewhat looser form dialogues and episodes from the lives of important men; but as they lack any link with myth and cult, so the Gospels lack any interest of a scientific-historical kind.

The Gospels bear some analogy to many books of *lesser literature*, where we find collections of episodes and dialogues of a popular hero like Aesop or of a miracle worker like Apollonius of Tyana, a literature which was later continued in certain lives of Christian monks and saints. There is apparently a still closer analogy with *popular oriental books*, of which admittedly only one example has been preserved for us: the Ahikar Story. 'Yet this one example suffices to show that popular books like Aramaic gospels circulated in pre-Chris-tian times; but the Ahikar story had the same literary character: the peculiar combination of proverbial wisdom (proverbs, fables, parables) with a story; it is immaterial at this point whether such a combination were a pure adventure story (Ahikar) or a half-historical biography interspersed with miracle stories (the Gospels).' This judgement of Gressmann,[2] attractive at first, proves to be untenable. For while the analogy of Ahikar may well explain the small collec-tions that preceded Mark, it cannot explain the type of the Gospel; for this presupposes a Christ myth and cult and is a creation of Hellenistic Christianity. For the same reason the analogy of other popular collections of the sayings and doings of well known and favourite persons from various cultures takes us no further.[3] Such collections (like the Tradition of Francis of Assisi, the Story of Dr. Faust, the Hassidic Legend of the great Maggid) admittedly also lack scientific character and a developed technique of composition,

[1] Cp. O. Staehlin, in Christ-Schmidt, *Geschichte der griechischen Literatur*, II, 1924, p. 1161; A. Fridrichsen, *Le Problème du Miracle*, p. 116; C. W. Votaw, 'The Gospels and Contemporary Biographies,' *A.J.Th.*, 19, 1915, pp. 45–73, 216–49.

[2] Abh. der Berliner Akad. d. Wiss., 1918, phil.-hist. Kl. 7, p. 4.

[3] Cp. K. L. Schmidt, 'Die Stellung der Evangelien in der allgemeinen Literatur-geschichte' (from *Eucharisterion*, II, pp. 50–134), 1923; further references to literature are given there.

interest in chronology, factual connections and psychological motivations; but the Gospels differ—apart from a lack of anything romantic —from them in this—that they do not tell of a much admired human personality, but of Jesus Christ, the Son of God, the Lord of the Church, and do so because they have grown out of Christian worship and remain tied to it.[1] 'The facts of the case really are that the formation of our Gospels, indeed of the forms that preceded them, is comprehensible only because there is a kerygma which proclaims a man who lived "in the flesh" as the "Lord".'[2]

Finally it seems to me that Hans v. Soden's view[3] that the literary form of the Gospels had its *origin in the Apocalypse* is quite untenable. As there was prefixed to Jewish apocalyptic an historical story put into the future in order to provide some assurance as to the correctness of the prophecy about the end, so to Christian prophecy of Jesus as the coming Messiah, there was a prefix of his life, written as an already completed fulfilment of the prophecy, to serve as a guarantee. But against this view we must remember that there is not the slightest trace in the Christian tradition that the Life of Jesus was ever written in the future tense, and moreover that it was only at first a gradual process—beginning with the Passion—that put the life under the standpoint of fulfilled prophecy. Also it is not the history of the Messiah that precedes the end in the Apocalypses, but the history of the αἰὼν οὗτος, or alternatively the history of the nation subjected to the sufferings of this aeon; moreover, if the Messiah had been the object of such prophecy he would not have been to so great a degree the subject giving it, as is the case in Mark and the other Synoptics. I will not put too much stress on the fact that the Synoptics do not end with an eschatological prognosis, since the lost end of Mark could possibly so have closed. One ought rather to take Q as an analogy to apocalyptic writings such as Ethiopian Enoch and the Didache; like them, Q embraced both paraenesis and eschatological prophecy, and clearly ended in an eschatological prognosis. But this analogy seems to me inapplicable to the type of the Gospel.

It seems to me that while we need analogies for understanding the individual components of the Synoptic Tradition we do not need them for the Gospel as a whole. The analogies that are to hand serve only to throw the uniqueness of the Gospel into still stronger relief. It has grown out of the immanent urge to development which lay in the tradition fashioned for various motives, and out of the

[1] Cp. *R.G.G.*, II[2], Cols. 418–22; also J. Schniewind, *Th.R.*, N.F.2, 1930, p. 146.
[2] J. Schniewind, op. cit., 183; generally pp. 178–188.
[3] H. v. Soden, *Die Enstenhung der christlichen Kirche*, p. 66.

Christ-myth and the Christ-cult of Hellenistic Christianity. It is thus an original creation of Christianity.[1] Can it be described as an unique literary genus? In my view we are entitled to use the concept of a literary genus in the light of its history, where alone a literary genus as such can establish itself. For only history can decide whether the form of a literary work is an accident or a developable form with a life of its own. In the Synoptic Gospels the literary form as such did not achieve a life of its own. These works are completely subordinate to Christian faith and worship. And what we know of the Apocryphal gospels does nothing to change the picture; they are but legendary adaptations and expansions. The situation could admittedly be quite different with the Gnostic gospels, but the remnant available does not suffice for a judgement to be made. For us it is only the Gospel according to St. John that can show how a literary history of the Gospel could have become possible. Its authors saw that the type created by the Synoptists was a developable literary form, which had served as a receptacle for their polemic and revelatory material, had indeed forced itself upon them, and which they had to use. So a literary history of the Gospel became possible, in which the form of the Gospel could have developed new possibilities of giving form to spiritual contents. That this did not happen is due to the canonization of our four gospels, which cut short the development of Gospel writing. So it is hardly possible to speak of the Gospels as a literary genus; the Gospel belongs to the history of dogma and worship. If anyone is looking for the history of the Gospel as a literary genus, the modern stories of the life of Jesus are the nearest thing that he can find.

[1] Cp. C. G. Montefiore, *The Synoptic Gospels*, I[2], pp. xxviif. C. A. Bernoulli also recognizes the originality of the Gospel, in *Johannes der Taeufer und die Urgemeinde*, 1918, p. 420, even if I am unable to follow him in his psychological characterization of this originality.

RUDOLF BULTMANN

THE HISTORY OF THE SYNOPTIC TRADITION

SUPPLEMENT
(revised 1962)

FOREWORD

WHAT was said in the Foreword to the second edition of the main volume remains valid for this third edition. I have only to add my repeated thanks to W. Baumgartner for many amplifying references; and to my colleague W. G. Kümmel I am greatly indebted for help in many ways. Above all I have to thank most warmly Ph. Vielhauer who has shared with me the work on this supplement. The literature on the Synoptic Gospels which has appeared since the second edition of 1931 is so enormous that it is quite impossible for an individual to have complete command of it and so in spite of the unselfish labours of Ph. Vielhauer completeness has still not been achieved. We would be grateful for any omissions which are brought to our notice.

Marburg, 1958   RUDOLF BULTMANN

ABBREVIATIONS

Bibl.Z.	=	*Biblische Zeitschrift*
Coniect. Neot.	=	*Coniectanae Neotestamentica*
D.S.D.	=	*Dead Sea Book of Discipline*
Ev. Th.	=	*Evangelische Theologie*
H.T.R.	=	*Harvard Theological Review*
J.B.L.	=	*Journal of Biblical Literature*
J.T.S.	=	*Journal of Theological Studies*
Nov. Test.	=	*Novum Testamentum*
Nt. St.	=	*New Testament Studies*
OLZ	=	*Orientalische Literaturzeitung*
R.A.C.	=	*Reallexikon für Antike und Christentum*
R.B.	=	*Revue Biblique*
R.H.Ph.R.	=	*Revue d'Histoire et de Philosophie religieuses*
R.G.G.	=	*Die Religion in Geschichte und Gegenwart*
S.B.	=	*Sitzungsberichte der . . . Akademie der Wissenschaften*. The name of the Academy, e.g. Berlin, Heidelberg, is given as needed; the reference is always to *Abhandlungen der phil.-hist. Klasse.*
Strack-B.	=	L. H. Strack und P. Billerbeck, *Kommentar zum NT aus Talmud und Midrasch*
St. Th.	=	*Studia Theologica*
Th.Bl.	=	*Theologische Blätter*
Th.L.Z.	=	*Theologische Literaturzeitung*
Th.R.	=	*Theologische Rundschau*
Th.St.Kr.	=	*Theologische Studien und Kritiken*
ThWB	=	*Theologisches Wörterbuch zum NT*
Th.Z.Basel	=	*Theologische Zeitschrift* of the theology faculty of Basel.
Wünsche	=	K.Aug. Wünsche, *Neue Beiträge zur Erläuterung der Evangelien aus Talmud und Midrasch.*
Z.A.W.	=	*Zeitschrift für die Alttestamentliche Wissenschaft*
Z.N.W.	=	*Zeitschrift für die Neutestamentliche Wissenschaft*
Z.syst.Th.	=	*Zeitschrift für systematische Theologie*
Z.Th.K.	=	*Zeitschrift für Theologie und Kirche*

To save space I have frequently made use of abbreviations for works which I have cited frequently in the references. The following are the most important:

As *Background* is cited the Festschrift for C. H. Dodd, *The Background of the N.T. and its Eschatology*, 1956.

Matthew Black, *An Aramaic Approach to the Gospels and Acts*, is quoted as *Aram. Appr.* and the references are to the second edition 1954.

Herbert Braun, *Spätjüdisch-häretischer und frühchristlicher Radikalismus*, vols. I and II, 1957, is often quoted as *Radik*.

Martin Dibelius, *Die Formgeschichte des Evangeliums*, is usually cited as *Formg.* with reference to the second edition 1933.

C. H. Dodd, *The Parables of the Kingdom*, is usually cited as *Parables* and the references are to the tenth edition 1950.

Joachim Jeremias, *Die Abendmahlsworte Jesu*, is cited as *Abendmahslw.* and the references are to the second edition 1949.

— — *Die Gleichnisse Jesu*, is cited as *Gleichn.* and the references are to the fourth edition 1956.

Wilfred L. Knox, *The Sources of the Synoptic Gospels*, I, 1953, is cited as *Sources*.

W. G. Kümmel, *Verheissung und Erfüllung*, is cited as *Verh. u. Erf.* and the references are to the second edition.

References to Ernst Lohmeyer's Commentaries on Mark and Matthew (in Meyer's Commentary) are generally indicated by ad. loc. When detailed references to legends are not given, the reference is always to a volume of Märchen der Weltliteratur published by Diederichs formerly in Jena and now Düsseldorf-Köln.

References to the Festschrift for M. Goguel, *Aux Sources de la Tradition chrétienne*, 1950, are given as *Aux Sources*.

Other abbreviations should be quite clear.

COMMENTS AND SUPPLEMENTARY NOTES

Page 3, n. 3. *Add:* In the meantime the question of the Synoptic sources has no\ been finally answered. Following B. H. Streeter (see n. 4), Vincent Taylor has tried to reconstruct Proto-Luke (*Behind the Third Gospel*, 1926). P. Thielscher's attempt to discover the Synoptic sources (*Unser Wissen von Jesus*, I, 1930) is very arbitrary, as is R. Thiel's reconstruction of three sources for Mark (*Drei Markus-Evangelien*, 1938). The most complicated reconstruction, and the least convincing, is that of Em. Hirsch, expressly directed against form-criticism (*Frühgeschichte des Evangeliums*, I, 1941, ²1951; II, 1941). Even less convincing is the development of Hirsch's reconstruction by Heinr. Helmbold (*Vorsynopt. Evgelien*, 1953). Nor is L. Vaganay's source-theory convincing (*La Problème Synoptique*, 1954). In addition I would mention the critical literary analysis of Mark by J. M. C. Crum (*St. Mark's Gospel. Two Stages in its Making*, 1936) and by A. T. Cadoux (*The Sources of the Second Gospel*, 1953); of Matthew by G. D. Kilpatrick (*The Origin of the Gospel according to Saint Matthew*, 1946). For the rest I refer readers to Introductions to the New Testament.

Page 5, n. 3. *Add:* Cp. P. Benoit, *R.B.*, 53, 1956, pp. 481–512, who criticizes the methods of form-criticism from the standpoint of Roman Catholic supernaturalism.

Page 6, n. 1. *Add:* From the literature since 1929 I would mention: C. H. Dodd, 'The Framework of the Gospels', *Expository Times*, 43, 1932, No. 9; R. H. Lightfoot, *History and Interpretation in the Gospels*, 1934, pp. 27–56; J. Baruzi, 'Problèmes d'Histoire des Religions', *Nouvelle Encyclopédie Philosophique*, V, 1935; Kendrick Grobel, *Formgeschichte und synopt. Quellenanalyse*, 1937; Olof Linton, 'Formkristna evengeliecitat i traditionshistorik belysning', *Svensk exegetisk Arsbok*, II, 1937, pp. 107–36; F. C. Grant, *The Earliest Gospel*, 1943; P. C. Grant, *The Gospels, their Origin and Growth*, 1957. Cp. also the section on form-criticism in Alfr. Wikenhauser, *Einleitung in das N.T.*, 1953, pp. 182–99.

Page 7. *To the end of the first paragraph add:* Vincent Taylor (*The Formation of the Gospel Tradition*) criticizes form-criticism without nevertheless questioning its legitimacy. W. L. Knox (*The Sources of the Synoptic Gospels*, I, 1952, II, 1957) is also critical in his attitude, holding that the Synoptic sources are not individual stories but collections of such, which had been given a fixed form at an early stage. But is this really an objection to form-critical research? More serious is the criticism of Harald Riesenfeld (*The Gospel Tradition and its Beginnings*, 1957). The 'life-situation' of the Tradition lies neither in Church nor missionary preaching. The Tradition was not formed by some anonymous community, but by teachers who handed on in fixed form and as a 'Sacred Word' the sayings and works of Jesus so that they could be recited in the assemblies of the church. But their origin was with Jesus himself, who like some new Moses taught the inner circle of the disciples as a Rabbi, having the interval between his death and parousia particularly in mind. This position seems untenable to me.

Some more recent works have taken a positive attitude to form-criticism, and have developed it. Their interest has been directed to the actual composition of the Gospels, in order to determine the historical and theological characteristics of the individual evangelists. On Mark, W. Marxsen, *Der Evangelist Markus*, 1956; on Matthew, Krister Stendahl, *The School of St. Matthew*, 1954; Günther Bornkamm, 'Enderwartung und Kirche in Mt-Evg.' (in *The Background of the NT and its Eschatology, Festschr. f. C. H. Dodd*, 1956, p. 222–60); see also G. Bornkamm, G. Barth, H. J. Held, *Überlieferung u. Auslegung im Mt.-Evg.*, 1960; on Luke, H. Conzelmann, *Die Mitte der Zeit*³, 1960; N. A. Dahl, 'Die Passionsgeschichte bei Mt,' *Nt. St.*, II (1955–56), pp. 17–32. G. Schille, in his *Bemerkungen zur Formgeschichte des Evg.*, tries to explain the structure of the three Synoptic Gospels by reference to their catechetical and missionary motivation; I 'Rahmen u. Aufbau des Mk.-Evg.', *Nt. St.*, IV (1957–58), pp. 1–24; II 'Das Evg. des Mt. als Katechismus', ibid., pp. 101–14; III 'Das Evg. als Missionsbuch', ibid., V (1958–59), pp. 1–11. In general, questionable—in spite of several good observations. D. Daube wants to explain the structure in terms of the Jewish Haggadah and its liturgy: 'The Earliest Structure of the Gospels', *Nt. St.*, V (1958–59), pp. 174–87; very questionable. On the Gospel's origin in the Kerygma see O. A. Piper, 'The Origin of the Gospel Pattern', *J.B.L.*, 78 (1958–59), pp. 112–24. Contributions by various authors in *La Formation des Evangiles. Problèmes Synoptiques et Formgeschichte*, Bruges, 1957. D. E. Nineham criticizes Form Criticism in *J.T.S.*, N.S. 9 (1958), pp. 13–25, 243–52.

Page 12. *To the second paragraph add:* Dibelius (*Formg.*, pp. 94f.) reckons Lk. 13¹⁰⁻¹⁴ as a mixed form; the paradigm style has been influenced by that of the Novelle.

n. 1. *Add:* Also J. Sundwall (*Die Zusammensetzung des Mk-Evg.*), 1934 and M. Dibelius (*Die Formgesch.*², p. 42) consider v. 6 to be an editorial addition. Similarly Crum (see above, p. 3, n. 3), p. 20 (see also p. 67) who nevertheless also takes v. 5a as an addition (περιβλεψάμενος . . . καρδίας αὐτῶν). Lohmeyer proposes to retain v. 6 as the end of the pericope (*Das. Evg. d. Mk.*, ad. loc.) and needs only to delete the phrase οἱ Φαρισαῖοι μετὰ τῶν Ἡρῳδιανῶν, and J. Jeremias concurs, *Z.N.W.*, 36, 1937, p. 211.

Page 13, n. 3.   *Add:* Dibelius (*Formg.*, pp. 221f.) thinks that Mark had v. 22b (the accusation Βεελζεβοὺλ ἔχει) to v. 26 before him unattached to any particular situation, though it was perhaps already joined with v. 27 and vv. 28–30. According to Lohmeyer (*Evg. d. Mk.*, ad. loc) vv. 27 and 28 have been added to vv. 22–26. These two proverbs were already joined in the source Mark used; it has an appendix in v. 30.

Page 15, n. 1.   *Add:* Lohmeyer (*Evg. d. Mk.*, ad loc.) holds vv. 5b–10 as secondary within the passage 2¹⁻¹², and considers it was composed for the miracle story, though Sundwall (op. cit., pp. 12–15) considers vv. 5–9 to be an independent conflict dialogue to which v. 10 is a secondary addition. Moreover the final v. 12 is an addition, since the acclamation is stylistically unsuitable. Crum (op. cit.) considers that v. 10 alone is an insertion, while G. H. Boobyer (*H.T.R.*, 47, 1954, pp. 115–20) thinks that only v. 10a is an editorial addition (made before Mark?) directed to the Christian reader, or hearer. In consequence a καί or καὶ εὐθύς or τότε has been omitted before λέγει τῷ παραλυτικῷ.—M. Dibelius consistently defends the unity of the pericope (*Formg.*², pp. 63f.). R. T. Mead takes the same view as Dibelius in *J.B.L.* 80 (1961), pp. 348–54.

Page 16. *To the end of the first paragraph add:* In the view of J. Dupont (*Gnosis*, 1949, p. 196, n. 2) Matthew is earlier than Mark since in Matthew the scriptural proof proceeds in Jewish fashion *a maiore ad minus*, whereas in Mark David is simply instanced as an example of necessity leading to the infringement of the commandment. On the other hand H. Greeven (op. cit., pp. 65–78, see below, n. 1) has shown that Matthew has made use of our text of Mark, apart from the fact that in his text of Mk. τῷ παραλυτικῷ (v. 5) and ἆρον τὸν κράββατόν σου (v. 9) are lacking.

To line 16 add: Lohmeyer (*Evg. d. Mk.*, ad loc.) also thinks the section is a community product.

n. 1. *Add:* Similarly Greeven, 'Wort u. Dienst', *Jahrb. d. Theol. Schule Bethel*, N.F. 4, 1955, pp. 75f., and H. Riesenfeld, *Jésus Transfiguré*, 1947, pp. 326–30; though this is difficult to reconcile with their advocacy of a connection with the primitive Christian baptismal liturgy.

n. 2. *Add:* Crum (*St. Mark's Gospel*, pp. 19f., 103f.) thinks vv. 25f. and v. 28 are additions. Käsemann (*Z.Th.K.*, 51, 1954, pp. 145f.) takes v. 28 as an addition qualifying and weakening it. According to Lohmeyer (ad loc.) vv. 23–26 are a unity; vv. 27 and 28 are two further independent sayings about the Sabbath, the first affirming and the second denying the validity of the Sabbath. Although T. W. Manson in 1932 (*The Teaching of Jesus*², p. 214) held the view that ὁ υἱὸς τοῦ ἀνθρώπου in Mk. 2²⁸ meant simply 'man' (as in 2¹⁰) in 1947 (*Coniect. Neotest.*, XI, pp. 138–46) he interprets ἄνθρωπος in v. 27 as well as υἱὸς τοῦ ἀνθρώπου in v. 28 as Son of Man not as meaning an individual but (following Dan. 7¹⁸ff.) Jesus and his disciples. To the contrary J. Dupont, *Gnosis*, 1949, p. 196, n. 2, who, however, takes Matt. 12¹⁻⁸ to be more original than Mk.2 ²³⁻²⁸. Also against Manson, F. W. Beare, *J.B.L.* 79 (1960), pp. 130–6.

Page 17, n. 2. *Add:* Though Sundwall (op. cit., pp. 43f.) also takes vv. 6–8 as the original answer, M. Dibelius (*Formg.*, pp. 222f.) and W. G. Kuemmel (*Z.N.W.*, 33, 1934, pp. 122f.) think otherwise. I cannot think their argument convincing.

Page 18, n. 2. *Add:* According to M. Black (*Aram. Appr.*², 1954, pp. 18f.–37) the language indicates that Mk. 7¹⁻⁸ derives from the Palestinian church (πυγμῇ v. 3 and ἀπ' ἀγορᾶς in the partitive sense).

n. 3. *Add:* Lohmeyer (ad loc.) also believes that vv. 15f. are a scene designed for the Jewish Christian Church (ὅτι . . . ἐσθίει). There are two words in v. 17 neither of which fits the situation, which is fashioned on the basis of the second, since καλεῖν can mean 'called' as well as 'invited'. Sundwall (op. cit., pp. 15f.) takes the end of v. 15 to be an insertion (ἦσαν γὰρ . . . ἠκολούθουν αὐτῷ) and thinks that vv. 15f. and 17b belong together; v. 17a was added later. Crum (op. cit., p. 19) and Dodd (*Parables*, pp. 117f.) take the opposite view and regard v. 17b as secondary. W. L. Knox (*Sources*, I, p. 13) thinks vv. 15f. are an insertion into 2¹³⁻¹⁷. Yet in spite of that he admits the impossible—that 2¹³⁻¹⁷ may be regarded as an unity handed down in the tradition.

Page 19, n. 3. *Add:* Sundwall (op. cit., p. 16) and Lohmeyer (ad loc.) take καὶ οἱ Φαρισαῖοι and καὶ οἱ μαθηταὶ τῶν Φαρισαίων as late additions, and are in all probability right in doing so.

n. 4. *Add:* In addition Crum (op. cit., p. 19), Jeremias (*Gleichnisse*⁴, pp. 44, n. 2, 59), Kümmel (*Verheissung und Erfüllung*², p. 69), and Kraeling (*John the Baptist*, p. 173) think vv. 19b–20 are a secondary addition, while Lohmeyer (ad loc.) thinks that only v. 20 is an addition (and moreover, in two stages), a position to which C. H. Dodd also inclines (*Parables*¹⁰, p. 116, n. 2).

Page 20, n. 2. *Add:* For the connection of Mk. 11²⁷⁻³³ with the Cleansing of the Temple see also J. Jeremias, *Eucharistic Words of Jesus*, 1955, p. 64; but Goguel (*Vie de Jésus*, 1932, pp. 399–401) and Sundwall (op. cit., p. 719) link [καὶ] ἔρχονται πρὸς αὐτόν κτλ in 27b with 11¹⁶.

Page 21, n. 2. *Add:* M. Dibelius (*Formg.*², p. 111), who considers Lk. 7³⁶⁻⁵⁰ to be legend, leaves it undecided whether the parable in vv. 41–43 is an alien element in the story. According to M. Black (*Aram. Appr.*², pp. 139f.) v. 47 has been wrongly translated from the Aramaic, and should read: Therefore I tell you: the man to whom many sins are forgiven loves much, but the man to whom little is forgiven loves little. So v. 47 follows vv. 41–43 excellently as "a general statement of the moral of the parable". Cp. further J. Finegan, *Die Überlieferung der Leidens- u. Auferstehungsgeschichte Jesu*, 1934, p. 4, and E. R. Goodenough, *J.B.L.*, 54, 1945, pp. 154f.

Page 22. *At the end of the first section add:* Matt. 19²⁰ makes the rich man into a νεανίσκος (is this on the basis of ἐκ νεότητός μου in Mk. 10²⁰ which Matt. omits?). In Lk. 18¹⁸ the questioner is an ἄρχων (because of his wealth?).

n. 1. *Add:* Sundwall (op. cit., p. 66) holds that vv. 23b, 25 are an ancient double aphorism; v. 24 is another variant of the same logion inserted between these two. An ancient aphorism lies behind vv. 26f. Verse 28 is editorial transition, and if vv. 28–30 were actually joined originally on to vv. 21f. by the catch word ἀκολουθεῖν it has been separated from it by the editorial section in vv. 23–27. Crum (op. cit., pp. 63f.) takes an entirely different view, and holds that $10^{17, \; 21-23, \; 25, \; 28}$ are the original elements; the logion originally followed Matt. 19^{28}. This is probably but a fantasy. Herb. Braun (*Spätjüdisch-häretischer und frühchristlicher Radikalismus*, II, 1957, p. 75, n. 1) takes vv. 24, 26f. to be secondary.

Page 24. *At the end of the first paragraph add:* On Matt. 11^{7-19} par. see below, pp. 164f.

n. 1. Thus also C. H. Kraeling, *John the Baptist*, 1951, pp. 128–31, especially on the grounds that the Baptist, who proclaimed the 'Coming One' as a 'fire kindler', could not possibly ask whether Jesus were the 'Coming One'. Contrariwise W. G. Kümmel, *Verheissung u. Erfüllung*[2], 1953, pp. 102–4, defends the passage as 'ancient trustworthy tradition'.

n. 2. *Add:* Likewise Dibelius (*Formg.*, pp. 57f.), R. H. Lightfoot (*History and Interpretation in the Gospels*, 1934, p. 120, n. 1), H. Braun (op. cit., II, p. 105, n. 1) consider v. 38 to be a *vaticinium ex eventu*. Otherwise Kümmel (*Verh. u. Erf.*, pp. 62f.) and W. L. Knox (*Sources*, I, p. 71). While Sundwall (op. cit., pp. 68f.) makes an analysis identical with that in the text, Dibelius (*Formg.*, p. 48) wonders whether vv. 41 or 42ff. originally followed immediately after v. 37, and whether the story were not originally about some unnamed disciples—a suggestion which I think highly improbable. Lightfoot (op. cit.) also would link vv. 41–45 to v. 37.

Page 25. *To the third line from the top add:* Crum (op. cit., p. 25) also believes v. 40 to be an addition (deriving from Q).

Add to line 7 from the bottom: Conversely, W. Manson (*Jesus the Messiah*, 1943, p. 30.) thinks that the Markan context is historical, because the scene occurs near the Mount of Olives, and Jesus quoted Zech. 14^4 in the light of the saying about the Mount of Olives, whereas in Q the saying has become detached from its original situation.

Add to line 5 from the bottom: Even W. L. Knox (*Sources*, I, p. 82) acknowledges that vv. 23–25 are an attached logion.

Page 26. *At the end of the first paragraph add:* Likewise Dibelius (*Formg.*, pp. 41f.) thinks vv. 51, 52a constitute an introduction by Luke to an element of the Tradition, which probably referred to some unnamed disciples, and whose original conclusion has disappeared. In the same way H. Conzelmann (*Die Mitte der Zeit*[3], 1960, p. 58) believes v. 51 to be Lukan editing. He is mistaken in ascribing to me the view that the locating of the pericope in

Samaria is not original and pre-Lukan; I do not think that this is what is constructed, but rather the travel narrative itself.

To the end of the second paragraph add: There is a variant of interest for the history of the tradition in H. I. Bell and T. C. Skeat, *Fragments of an Unknown Gospel*, 1935, ll. 43–59. The introduction is constructed on the model of Jn. 3² with the use of Jn. 5³⁶ or 10²⁵. The formulation of the question is removed from its Jewish setting and universalized: ἐξὸν τοῖς βασιλεῦσ[ιν ἀποδοῦ]ναι τὰ ἀνήκοντα τῇ ἀρχῇ. Cp. Goro Mayeda, *Das Leben-Jesu-Fragment, Papyrus Egerton*, 2, 1946, pp. 37–51.

To line 5 from the top of the third paragraph add: Whereas Sundwall (op. cit., p. 74) makes the same analysis and rightly takes only the parenthesis in v. 18 (οἵτινες λέγουσιν κτλ) as editorial, Crum (op. cit., p. 25) erroneously reduces the original story to vv. 18a, 26f.

At the end of paragraph 3 add: According to W. L. Knox (*Sources*, I, p. 90) the divergences of the Luke version, especially the parallels in Lk. 20³⁴ᶠ·, show that Luke did not use the text of Mark but some independently circulating version.

To line 2 from the foot of the page add: Dibelius (*Formg.*, p. 223) also separates vv. 10–12 from the preceding. Verses 2–5 are the introduction to the middle section 6–9, which perhaps did not originally belong here, since the dialogue is artificial.

Page 27, n. 1. *Add:* Jeremias (*Jesus als Weltvollender*, 1930, p. 65) thinks Matthew's text original; for in Mark 'Jesus permits a question to be put which is never disputed by the Rabbis—no Rabbi doubted the admissibility of divorce which was anchored in the Law (Dt. 24¹).' But can this be a criterion? According to Lohmeyer (*Evg. des Mt.* ad. loc.) Mark presupposes listeners who do not have confidence in the Mosaic practice of divorce, whereas for the hearers of Matthew there is complete acceptance of the Mosaic laws of marriage and divorce. But this does not establish the priority of the text of Matthew.

n. 2. *Add:* J. Dupont, *Mariage et divorce dans l'Evang. Mt.* 19³⁻¹², 1959.

Page 28, n. 1. *Add:* Appropriately Dibelius (*Formg.*, pp. 108f.): 'Clearly what was in the tradition was simply the saying about "fishers of men" with an indication of those to whom it was addressed. The fact that Mark relates this and nothing more, and then adds from the tradition of the disciples' names the call of another pair of brothers, though without having a second call of Jesus to add—indicates that he created the scene of the calling of the disciples.' Lohmeyer (*Evg. d. Mk.*, ad. loc., and *Urchristl. Mystik in Neutest. Studien*, 1935, pp. 57–79) is quite wrong in taking vv. 16–18 as an epiphany story belonging to the cycle of 'Stories of the Son of Man'. For the contrary view see Marie Veit, *Die Auffassung von der Person Jesu im Urchristentum nach den neuesten Forschungen* (Diss. theol. Marb.), 1946, pp. 1–54. There are numerous parallels to the call story, where, to be sure, the chief figure is for the most part the person who is called. Saul and Elisha are called from the plough (1 Sam. 11; 1 Kings 19¹⁹ᶠᶠ·), Gideon from threshing (Jg. 6¹¹ᶠᶠ·). There is also the summons from the plough of Cincinnatus, etc., cf. A. Jeremias, *Handb. d. altoriental. Geisterkultur*², 1929, p. 304. For Bishops cf. Saintyves, *Essais de Folklore Biblique*, 1923, pp. 93f.

n. 2. *Add:* J. Manck, *Nov. Test.* 2, 1958, pp. 138–41, and C. W. F. Smith, *H.T.R.* 52, 1959, pp. 187–203.

n. 3. *Add:* The reference of 'Son of Man' to the true Israel by T. W. Manson, *The Sayings of Jesus*, 1949, pp. 72f., is also impossible.

Page 29, n. 4. *Add:* In his *Formg.*, p. 60, n. 1, Dibelius holds to his conception of vv. 34 and 35. For the rest his analysis is found on pp. 43f., and is as follows: at v. 31 an independent story begins, for which Mark has made preparation in vv. 20f., which are his creation. Otherwise, and correctly, Sundwall, op. cit., pp. 21f.: καὶ ἔρχεται [ὁ 'Ιησοῦς] εἰς οἶκον must belong to the traditional pericope, because it is presupposed by ἔξω στήκοντες in v. 31. In v. 31 ἔρχονται comes from the editor, being made necessary by the insertion of vv. 22–30; originally v. 31 followed v. 21 thus: καὶ ἡ μήτηρ αὐτοῦ καὶ οἱ ἀδελφοὶ αὐτοῦ ἔξω στήκοντες ἀπέστειλαν.

Page 31, n. 1. *Add:* Dibelius (*Formg.*, pp. 106f.) has modified his former opinions (*Formg.*¹, p. 78): 'Perhaps the story originally derived from a saying of Jesus, which must have been a twin saying' (like *Pap. Oxy.* I, 1:5). 'The latter half of this saying would then have been changed by the Tradition into the corresponding event.' But it is improbable that the whole pericope developed out of a saying since it contains too much distinctive material: the description of Jesus as a carpenter, the naming of his brothers and the mention of his sisters. But is not such material always available to fantasy? Is the description of Jesus as υἱὸς τῆς Μαρίας a sign of the relatively late origin of the story? Normal Semitic custom would name the son after the father, not the mother, even if the father were dead. R. H. Lightfoot (*Hist. and Interp.*, p. 187) therefore supposes that the mention of the mother's name is contemptuous. That would mean that Mary had already a bad reputation. But it is much more likely that she was already by this time revered as the mother of the Lord. Lk. 4²² reads: οὐχὶ υἱός ἐστιν 'Ιωσὴφ οὗτος;

n. 3. *Add:* According to W. L. Knox (*Sources*, I, pp. 47–49) the story originally told of Jesus' failure, but was modified by Mark. Highly improbable!

Page 32. *At the end of the second paragraph add:* O. Cullmann (*Die Tauflehre des N.T.*, 1948, pp. 70–72) thinks that the pericope was formulated at a time when the question of infant baptism was a live one. While J. Jeremias (*Hat die älteste Christenheit die Kindertaufe gekannt?*, 1938, pp. 26f.) had also found a reference to infant baptism in Mk. 10¹⁵, he now sees (*Z.N.W.*, 40, 1941, pp. 243–5) in this verse the condition for proselyte baptism.

n. 1. *Add:* Br. Violet (*Z.N.W.*, 37, 1938, pp. 251–71) accepts this as a translation from the Aramaic, and reconstructs the original meaning of v. 22 thus: 'And they all testified against him, and were aghast at the words of grace which came from his mouth.' In this way the unity of thought is restored. Similarly

Jeremias, *Jesu Verheissung für die Völker*, 1956, pp. 37–39. For Luke's version cf. Dibelius, *Formg.*, pp. 107f. and *Aufsätze zur Apostelgesch.*[2], 1957, p. 158; R. H. Lightfoot, *Hist. and Interp.*, pp. 199–205; H. Conzelmann, *Die Mitte der Zeit*, p. 24; W. L. Knox, *Sources*, I, p. 48.

n. 3. *Add:* So also Lohmeyer (*Evg. d. Mk.*, ad loc.). Crum (op. cit., p. 62) lifts v. 15 from the pericope and places it after 9^{33-36}. This is the context in 'Mk. I' which has been broken by 'Mk. II' (see below, p. 149). Sundwall takes a similar view, holding that the sayings in Mk. 10^{14}b; 10^{15}; 9^{37} were originally drawn in to the Tradition as key sayings. An apophthegm has been built around them, viz. $10^{13-16}+9^{36-37}$. Mark has divided up this context and made two separate elements of it. E. Percy argues for the unity of Mk. 10^{13-16} (*Die Botschaft Jesu*, 1953, pp. 31–37).

Page 33. *To line 3 from the top add:* From antiquity cp. esp. Horace, *Carm.*, III, 23. Dibelius (*Formg.*, p. 261) supposes (following Wendling, *Entstehung des Mk-Evg.*, pp. 153f.) that Mk. 12 $^{41-44}$ was originally a 'cautionary tale' told by Jesus.

To the end of paragraph 2 add: Dibelius (*Formg.*, pp. 115f.) even thinks that Lk. 10^{38-42} is a legend. The point, however, is not in the difference between the active and the contemplative life, but in Jesus' criticism of Martha's protest. Although the early Church evidently understood this in an ascetic sense, it must nevertheless be understood eschatologically. E. Laland (*St. Th.*, 13, 1959, pp. 70–85) disputes the view that this is a biographical apophthegm and regards the pericope as an instruction on the correct attitude towards peripatetic missionaries.

At the end of paragraph 3 add: According to Dibelius (*Formg.*, p. 117) Lk. 17^{11-19} is a legend, with Jesus at its centre: 'a story of the recognition of a Samaritan and his piety by Jesus'. According to W. L. Knox (*Sources*, II, p. 106) the story comes from Palestinian sources which Luke has hellenized.
To line 3 from the bottom of the text add: H. Braun (op. cit., II, p. 27) also accepts v. 8 as a moralizing addition.

n. 1. *Add:* L. Szimonides (*Nieuw theol. Tijdschr.*, 24, 1935, pp. 46–52) holds that the story is one which Jesus borrowed from Indian tradition. He adds other fantasies as well.

Page 34. *At the end of paragraph 1 add:* According to Dibelius (*Formg.*[2], p. 115), Lk. 19^{1-10} is a true personal legend and W. L. Knox (*Sources*, II, p. 112) regards the story as containing historic memories.

Page 35. *To the end of paragraph 1 add:* Lohmeyer (*Kultus u. Evg.*, 1942, pp. 64f.; cp. *Evg. d. Mt.*, ad loc.) takes Matt. 17^{24-27} as a community product. For Hirsch (*Die Auferstehungsgeschichte u. der christl. Glaube*, 1940, p. 21) the story was originally an Easter story, going back to a visionary experience of Peter—scarcely credible!

n. 3. *Add:* Cp. W. Aly, *Volksmärchen, Sage u. Novelle bei Herodot.*, 1921, p. 90; Dibelius, *Formg.*, p. 97, n. 2.

n. 4. *Add:* As Wellhausen, so Goguel, *Vie de Jésus*, p. 333; H. Lietzmann, *Geschichte der Alten Kirche*, I³, p. 47; Rud. Meyer, *Der Prophet aus Galiläa*, 1940, p. 159, n. 74 (cp. also p. 121); W. L. Knox, *Sources*, II, p. 82; G. Bornkamm, *Jesus von Nazareth*, 1956, p. 142. Dibelius (*Formg.*, p. 163) merely remarks: 'Here too the introduction is in all probability the work of the evangelist'. Kümmel (*Verh. u. Erfül.*, p. 65) while thinking the connection of vv. 32 with 33 not original, sees in both verses original sayings of Jesus where he is dealing with his forthcoming death. Black (*Aram. Appr.*², pp. 152f.) retains the traditional text and by translating back into Aramaic obtains a parallelism:

(32) Behold I cast out demons, and I do cures day by day,
    But one day soon I am perfected.
(33) But day by day I must needs work,
    Then one day soon pass on.

Cp. also H. Conzelmann, *Die Mitte der Zeit*, p. 183.

Page 36. *To lines 2–3 from the top add:* Yet Sundwall (op. cit., pp. 71f.) connects the pericope originally with v. 16, to which 11²⁷b⁻³⁰ follows (see above, p. 20), whereas Dibelius (*Formg.*, p. 42) believes v. 18 to be the original conclusion.

To the end of paragraph 1 add: Lohmeyer says (*Evg. d. Mk.*, ad loc.) that the story 'can hardly be called an historical narrative, but rather a parenetic example with some teaching added' (p. 237) 'fashioned for catechetical purposes' (p. 235). For the interpretation cp. also Lohmeyer, *Th. Bl.*, 20, 1941, cols. 257–64, and *Kultus u. Evangelium*, 1942, pp. 44–51. Cp. further E. Haenchen, *Z.Th.K.* 56 (1959), pp. 34–42; C. Roth, *Nov. Test.* 4 (1960), pp. 174–81.

Page 37. *To paragraph 2 line 3 add:* Dibelius (*Formg.*, p. 203.1) believes that in 23²⁷⁻³¹ a traditional logion has been used.

To the end of page add: Goguel (*Z.N.W.*, 31, 1932, pp. 292f.) sees good tradition in the scene. According to Cullmann (*Der Staat im N.T.*, 1956, pp. 38f.), who thinks the scene historical, the subject of ποιοῦσιν in v. 31 is the Romans.

n. 1. *Add:* As Klostermann and Lohmeyer (both ad loc.) rightly see, vv. 8 and 9 are different additions (only v. 8 has its counterpart in Jn. 12⁷). Jeremias, in *Z.N.W.*, 35, 1936, pp. 75–82, thinks that v. 8 was the original basis of the pericope, because it rests on the rabbinic distinction between 'alms' and 'acts of love' and then proceeds to interpret καλὸν ἔργον as the 'act of love' which is the burial of the dead. Although he here explains v. 9, for very good reasons, as an hellenistic addition,

he tries (like Lohmeyer, ad loc.) to make probable its Palestinian character and
its original place as the end of the pericope in *Z.N.W.*, 44, 1952/53, pp. 103-7,
and in *Jesu Verheissung für die Völker*, 1956, p. 19. The verse is to be understood
tschatologically: '. . . when they (the angels) proclaim the good news of victory
to the whole world, then what she has done shall also be told before God, that he
may remember her (at the last judgement).' This does not make sense to me!
According to H. Sahlin (*St. Th.* 13, 1959, pp. 172-9) the Pericope gives an account
of Jesus' messianic consecration, and should come after Mk. 8²⁶. On v. 4 cp. John
Bauer, *Nov. Test.* III (1959), pp. 54-56; there is a parallel to it in Plautus, *Pseudolus*,
438-41.

n. 3. *Add:* According to Klausner (*Jesus von Nazareth*, 1930, p. 489) the legend grew
up because of the Jewish custom of giving those led out to execution wine to drink
mixed with incense as a narcotic, a custom which women especially used to observe.

Page 38. *To line 7 of paragraph 1 add:* Lohmeyer (*Evg. d. Mk.*, ad
loc.) takes the healing as a secondary motif, which has grown on
to the original dialogue (request for healing and its gratification).
Similarly Dibelius, *Formg.*, p. 261 (see below, pp. 38f).

To line 6 of paragraph 2 add: Just as in the case of Mk. 7²⁴⁻³¹ (see
above), Dibelius (*Formg.*, pp. 245 and 261.3) supposes that in 8⁵⁻¹³
the primary element in the story was the dialogue, and the healing
a secondary feature. E. Haenchen, in *Z. Th.K.*, 56 (1959), pp. 23-28,
comes to a different conclusion.

n. 3. *Add:* Dibelius (op. cit., p. 261, n. 3) also believes that v. 24 is introduced
from Matthew.

n. 4. *Add:* M. Black (*Aram. Appr.*², pp. 116ff.) conjectures that ἄνθρωπος ὑπὸ ἐξουσίαν
(τασσόμενος) in Matt. 8⁹ and Lk. 7⁸ is a wrong translation for ἄνθρωπος ἔχων ἐξουσίαν
(so syrsin). G. Zuntz (*J.T.S.*, 46, 1945, pp. 183-90) supposes (on the basis of
syrsin and syrcur) that the original text was ἄνθρωπός εἰμι ἐν ἐξουσίᾳ.

Page 41. *To the end of paragraph 1 add:* Dibelius (*Formg.*, pp. 64f.)
disputes my right to call the passages I have so denominated 'controversy dialogues', because there is in them no theme developed and
unfolded by statement and counter-statement. The dialogue form is
unquestionably not the decisive feature of the class, for there is no
movement to and fro in the dialogue, nor does the opponent ever
once have to resort to verbal attack. The interest fastens on the
saying or action of Jesus alone.

I do not think this position to be right. For even if the 'controversy
dialogues' contain no dialogue in the sense of the Greek διαλέγεσθαι,
the question is still one of statement and counterstatement. And just
as in these elements of the Tradition a saying or an act of Jesus can
have the significance of a saying (e.g. Mk. 3⁵; 2¹⁵) and so be the
(silent) decision of a dispute, so can the lurking silence of the

opponent (Mk. 3²). Of course the point is found in the final saying of Jesus; but (in a real conflict discourse) this is always a saying which resolves a question, not some unrelated truth. The stories are the reproduction of a *debate*, and it is immaterial how many turns of the discourse are reported; indeed, it were surely sufficient originally that *one* question should be posed and *one* answer given. Rabbinic discourses with a number of turns are more artificial. Moreover Dibelius, op. cit., pp. 141f., fails to analyse the form of the rabbinic paradigms and ignores the analogies I have cited on pp. 41ff.

Page 53, n. 1. *Add:* In the same way F. J. Leenhardt, 'Aux Sources de la Tradition Chrétienne' (*Festschr. f. M. Goguel*), 1950, p. 136, makes a Pharisee out of the lawyer in Lk. 10²⁵.

Page 54. *To the end of paragraph 2 add:* G. Bornkamm (*The Background of the N.T. and its Eschatology*, p. 249) rightly points out that there is no account of any real discussion of Jesus with the disciples.

To line 9 from the top of paragraph 3 add: According to J. Klausner, *Jesus von Nazareth*, 1930, p. 218.1, Pilate was confused with Archelaus, and what was referred to was the event reported by Jos. *Ant.*, XVII, 11:2, when Archelaus had 3,000 men killed in the Temple, among them many Galileans.

n. 1. *Add:* N. A. Dahl (*Das Volk Gottes*, 1941, p. 313; n.22 on p. 176) believes that he may thus conclude that this tendency is most active in Matthew, that the process came to its completion in the Palestinian environment, and reflects the actual situation of the primitive Church. In my view he is wrong.

Page 57. *To the end of paragraph 2 add:* On the calling of disciples or pupils in the life of the philosopher and θεῖος ἀνήρ see L. Bieler, ΘΕΙΟΣ ΑΝΗΡ I, 1923, p. 123. Ibid., pp. 123f. for the motif of conversion (renunciation of family and the like). For Mk. 3³³ cp. also Mand. *Ginza*, 432:40ff.: 'In the house of life thou canst not put thy trust in father or mother, in brother or sister, in gold or silver. . . . Thy brothers are Uthras of the Kuštā, and thy sisters faithful Škīnās'; cp. also *Ginza*, 390:21f.

Page 58, n. 1. *Add:* On the motif of laughing and weeping, see also W. Wichmann, *Die Leidenstheologie*, 1930, p. 62 (also n. 20).

Page 60. *To the end of paragraph 2 add:* On Mk. 14³⁻⁹ see above, p. 28.

Page 61. *To line 10 of paragraph 2 add:* Thus in Jn. 13 the evangelist had before him the story of the Foot-washing, 13⁴ᶠ·, ¹²⁻¹⁵, to which vv. 16 (17) and 20 had already been added, into which he himself then inserted vv. 18f.

To line 5 from the top of paragraph 3 add: Nevertheless Mk. 3¹³⁻¹⁹ seems to be a part of the Tradition, into which the evangelist has inserted vv. 14b–15 (ἵνα ὦσιν κτλ). V. 16 takes up again from καὶ ἐποίησεν δώδεκα in v. 14a. But possibly v. 13 is also some of the evangelist's editorial work; that would leave only v. 14a (καὶ ἐποίησεν δώδεκα) and v. 16 (καὶ ἐπέθηκεν κτλ) to v. 19 as before the evangelist. But is the text sound? The words καὶ ἐποίησεν τ. δώδεκα are missing from K D Θ pl latt syr, and instead φ sah have the words πρῶτον Σίμωνα only. According to M. Goguel (*L'Eglise primitive*, 1947, pp. 92f.), Mk. 3¹³⁻¹⁹ is an editorial composition made from a traditional list of Apostles and a piece of tradition which told of Peter's (and the Zebedees') change of name. Ed. Meyer's analysis is unconvincing (*Ursprung u. Anfänge des Christentums*, I, 1921, p. 436); he thinks that vv. 13, 14a derive from a 'Disciple-source', into which vv. 14b–19 have been inserted from a 'Source of the Twelve'. The analysis of W. L. Knox is also unconvincing (*Sources*, I, pp. 18–21); he believes that he can see in 3⁷⁻¹⁵ the beginning of 'The Source of the Twelve' or one of its sections, to which Mark has added the list in vv. 16–19 from some other source. I have no belief in either a 'Disciple-source' or a 'Twelve-source'.

Page 63, n. 1. *Add:* C. H. Turner, to whom R. H. Lightfoot (*Hist. and Interpretation,* p. 35, n. 1) refers, reminds us (*J.T.S.*, 1924, pp. 378ff.) that the indefinite 'they' with which many elements of the Tradition began (e.g. Mk. 10¹³, καὶ προσέφερον αὐτῷ παιδία) represents an Aramaic passive, which Matthew and Luke frequently replace when they have no definite subject to introduce. In the same way Turner (ibid., 1925, p. 226) draws attention to the fact that Mark seldom says 'Jesus' in his story, though the copyist repeatedly inserts it (e.g. Mk. 12⁴¹). Further Matthew adds ὁ Ἰησοῦς some forty times, while Luke more frequently uses αὐτός.

Page 64. *To line 2 from bottom of paragraph 1 add:* (This is also true of V. Blinzler's historical reconstruction in *Nov. Test.* 2, 1959, pp. 24–49.)

Page 65. *To the end of paragraph 1 add:* (On indications of place see R. H. Lightfoot, *Hist. and Interp.*, pp. 99f., and H. J. Ebeling, *Das Messiasgeheimnis und die Botschaft des Mk.-Evangelisten*, 1939, pp. 211ff. On Mk. 7³¹ in particular see ibid., p. 210. W. L. Knox (*Sources*, I, p. 59) believes that the indications of place in Mk. 7³¹ had been given in the miracle story of 7³¹⁻³⁶; for it is on this account that Mark has to bring Jesus back from Tyre (7²⁴) into Decapolis.)

Page 66. *To line* 10 *in paragraph* 2 *add:* (On Mk. 12³⁵⁻³⁷ see below, pp. 137f.)

Page 67. *In line* 3 *of paragraph* 2 *add:* (cp. the versions of the story of Jehuda ben Tabbai, or Jehoschua ben Perachja in J. Klausner, *Jesus von Nazareth*, pp. 26f., esp. n. 35.)

In line 10 *of paragraph* 2 *add:* (The disciples' question in 9¹¹: ὅτι λέγουσιν οἱ γραμματεῖς has formal correspondence to Jesus' question in 12³⁵: πῶς λέγουσιν οἱ γραμματεῖς ὅτι . . .)

Page 68. *To the end of paragraph* 2 *add:* On the naming of persons originally unnamed see also Dibelius, *Formg.*, p. 111. On the disclosure of proper names in Rabbinic exegesis cp. Jos. Bonsirven, *Exégèse Rabbinique et Exégèse Paulinienne*, 1939, pp. 66f., e.g. Akiba fills up by combination a name lacking in the O.T. text (Schlatter, *Der Glaube im N.T.*⁴, p. 52). In Echa Rabbati the mother of the seven Maccabean martyrs (2 Macc. 7; 4 Macc.) is named Miriam (H. W. Surkan, *Martyrien in jüd. u. frühchristl. Zeit*, 1938, p. 53). The man whom Jesus summoned to discipleship in Matt. 8²¹ᶠ· was an apostle, according to Tertullian, and identified as the apostle Philip by Clement of Alexandria (W. Bauer, *Das Leben Jesu im Zeitalter der neutest. Apokryphen*, 1909, pp. 517f).

Page 69. *To the end of paragraph* 1 *add:* Mk. 1⁴⁰ᶠ· appears in *Fragments of an Unknown Gospel*, by H. I. Bell and T. C. Skeat, 1935, p. 28, in this form: 'And behold, there cometh unto him a leper and saith: Master Jesus, journeying with lepers and eating with them in the inn, I myself also became a leper. If therefore thou wilt, I shall be clean.' (Goro Mayeda, *Das Leben-Jesu-Fragment Pap. Egerton 2*, 1946, pp. 8 and 32.)

Page 70. *To the end of paragraph* 1 *add:* Cp. W. Baumgartner, *T.R.*, N.F.5, 1933, pp. 274–6. C. F. Burney (*The Poetry of Our Lord*, 1925) distinguishes four kinds of parallelism: Synonymous, antithetic, synthetic and climactic.

Page 79. *To line* 9 *from the bottom add:* W. Manson (*Jesus the Messiah*, 1952, p. 31) believes that the Matthew version is nearest to the Aramaic original because of the reminiscence of Isa. 50⁶⁻⁸.

To line 3 *from the bottom add:* Cp. Dibelius, *Botschaft u. Geschichte*, I, 1953, p. 114.

Page 81. *To lines* 12/13 *from the top add:* (So also Dibelius, *Botschaft u. Geschichte*, I, p. 109.)

To line 5 *from the bottom add:* F. Perles (*Z.N.W.*, 25, 1926, p. 163) takes v. 6b as an explanatory gloss on the Greek text, not as an original constituent of the logion.

n. 1. *Add:* J. M. C. Crum (*The Rhythmical Sayings of Our Lord*, 1950) tries to demonstrate the poetic form of the logion.

Page 83. *To line* 4 *from the top add:* A. Fridrichsen (*Coniect. Neotest.*, II, 1936, p. 1) takes the saying about self-denial in Mk. 8[34] as a pleonastic expansion.

To line 3 *of paragraph* 3 *add:* So also Dibelius, *Botschaft u. Geschichte*, I, p. 114.

Page 84. *To line* 4 *of paragraph* 2 *add:* W. Pesch, 'Zur Exegese von Mt. 6[19-21] und Lk. 12[33, 34]', *Biblica* 40 (1960), pp. 356–78.

Page 86. *To line* 14 *from the top add:* Jeremias (*Jesus als Weltvollender*, 1930, p. 21, n. 1) indeed admits that the trilogy of hand, foot and eye befits the style of Jesus (see below, p. 314.)

n. 1. *Add:* On the development or alternatively the re-creation of dominical sayings see esp. H. Köster, *Z.N.W.*, 48, 1957, pp. 223ff.

n. 2. *Add:* Has a gnostic saying been adopted in v. 11f., into which only because of the context οὖν and μαμωνᾶ are introduced? Cp. the antithesis of τὰ ἐπίγεια and τὰ ἐπουράνια in Jn. 3[12], and also Hippol. El., vv. 8, 39–44; further the antithesis τὰ ἀλλότρια—τὰ ἴδια, Iren. I, 21, 5; also the Johannine dualistic meaning of ἀληθινός.

Page 87. *To the end of paragraph* 2 *add:* Cp. also on the saying about light, Jeremias, *Z.N.W.*, 39, 1940, pp. 237–40.

Page 88. *To line* 10 *from the top add:* So also Dibelius, *Botsch. u. Gesch.*, I, p. 109. On v. 48 see also E. Fuchs, *Neutest. Studien f. R. Bultmann*, 1954, pp. 130–6.

Page 89. *To line* 1 *add:* (Cp. the development of Diog. Laert. VI. 60 in Stob. IV. 31b, 48, p. 750,6 W; see Rudberg, *Arb. u. Mitt. aus dem neutest. Seminar zu Uppsala*, IV, 1936, p. 42.)

To the bottom line add: (On the textual and traditional history of Matt. 17[20] and its parallels cp. J. Duplacy, *Memorial A. Gelin*, 1962, pp. 273–87.)

Page 90. *To line* 12 *from the top add:* On Matt. 10²⁵ᵇ see H. Braun, *Spätjüd.-häret. u. frühchr. Radikalismus*, II, p. 106, n. 1.

Page 91. *To line* 12 *from the top add:* πίστις θεοῦ = belief in God only here (otherwise in Rom. 3³). It is not O.T. Jewish, but derives from the missionary usages; cp. πίστις πρὸς or ἐπὶ τὸν θεόν, 1 Th. 1⁸; Heb. 6¹.

To line 19 *from the top add:* Also H. Braun (op. cit., I, p. 80, n. 6) thinks that Matt. 5³⁴⁻³⁷ is secondary.

Page 92. *To line* 13 *from the top add:* E. Percy (*Die Botschaft Jesu*, 1953, pp. 233–6) renews the plea for the originality of Mk. 2¹⁹ᵇ⁻²⁰; he is not convincing.

To line 19 *from the top add:* In addition Crum (*St. Mark's Gospel*, p. 19) and C. H. Dodd (*The Parables*¹⁰, pp. 117f.) think Mk. 2¹⁷ᵇ to be secondary. Sundwall (op. cit., pp. 15f.) on the contrary believes that v. 17b originally belonged to the story in vv. 15–17, and that 17a is an unattached logion that has been inserted.

n. 2. *Add:* Clem. *Hom.* 11, 33 adds to Matt. 12⁴²: καὶ οὐ πιστεύετε, and in the same way to Lk. 11³²: καὶ οὐδεὶς πιστεύει.

Page 93. *To line* 7 *from the top of the last paragraph add:* So too H. Braun in *Libertas Christiana* (*Festschr. f. Delekat*), 1957, p. 11.

To line 5 *from the bottom add:* (H.-W. Bartsch, *Th. Z.* Basel 16, 1960, pp. 5–18.)

Page 95, n. 1. *Add:* It is intended that Lk. 12², as v. 1 shows, should be a warning against ὑπόκρισις: secrecy is of no avail to the hypocrite.

Page 96. *To line* 4 *from the bottom add:* The interpretations of Dodd (*Parables*¹⁰, pp. 136–9) and Jeremias (*Die Gleichnisse Jesu*⁴, pp. 32f.) are the same as this.

Page 97. *To line* 6 *of paragraph* 1 *add:* (Cp. here E. Käsemann, *Z.Th.K.* 51 (1954), pp. 147f. and 57 (1960), pp. 176–8; cp. also his *Exeget. Versuche und Vorarbeiten* I, 1960, p. 209. K. is concerned to show the paradoxical transformation or re-interpretation of Wisdom-sayings into statements of prophetic eschatology; this can only be partially right.)

n. 1. *To the quotation of Ps. Phokyl. add:* Theogn. 662ff.:

    . . καί τε πενιχρὸς ἀνήρ
αἶψα μαλ' ἐπλούτησε· καὶ ὃς μάλα πολλὰ πέπαται
ἐξαπίνης πάντ' οὖν ὤλεσε νυκτὶ μιᾷ.

Page 98. *To line* 6 *from the top of the second paragraph add:* Dodd (*Parables*, pp. 138–42) sees that the saying about salt has been given a paranetic application; originally it was a lament that the Jewish people had lost what was their most valuable asset. Jeremias (*Gleichn.*, pp. 103f.) thinks that the saying about light being put under a bushel means extinguishing the light and translates accordingly: 'One does not light a lamp in order to put it out again immediately.' Jesus uttered the saying in reference to his mission, as if he were warned about dangers ahead. He must not spare himself; the light must shine. This is very doubtful to me.

To line 9 *from the top of the second paragraph add:* It is by no means clear that the ἱμάτιον in Mk. 2²¹ is the garment of the world (Jeremias, *Jesus als Weltvollender*, pp. 24–27, and *Gleichn.*, pp. 100f.)

To line 14 *in second paragraph add:* Dodd (*Parables*¹⁰, pp. 123f.: 'The Ministry of Jesus is an eschatological event') and Kümmel (*Verh. u. Erf.*, pp. 100f.: the meaning of Mk. 3²⁷ is 'that the rule of God has begun to be effective') both interpret in this sense. Jeremias (*Gleichn.*, pp. 105f.) interprets the binding of the 'strong man' as Jesus' victory over temptation.

To line 2 *from the bottom add:* Matt. 15¹³ (with no parallel in Luke!) is an isolated saying inserted by Matthew. The disciples' question in v. 12 is answered in v. 14. The saying is directed to the Pharisees only with artificiality. Whence does it come? Does it belong to the context of the contemplation of plants which is to be found in Ignatius, in the Od. Sol., among the Mandæans, etc.? See H. Schlier, *Religionsgesch. Unters. zu den Ign.-Briefen*, 1929, p. 53, n. 1; Ph. Vielhauer, *Oikodome*, 1939, pp. 42–45 (and see also n. 100, pp. 179f.); H. Hommel, *Theologia Viatorum*, V, 1953–4, pp. 322f.

n. 2. from p. 97. *Add at end:* Cp. esp. further Theogn. 725ff.; Solon, Fr. 14 (Diehl); Eur., *Suppl.*, 775ff.

n. 1. *Add:* Cp. Br. Snell, *Die Entdeckung des Geistes*², 1955, pp. 271f.: '. . . where Homer (sc. Od. 18, 130ff.) comes closest to the discovery of the soul . . . he says quite clearly that the beast is more persistent and protected than man.'

Page 99. *To line* 16 *of paragraph* 1 *add:* Dodd (*Parables*¹⁰, p. 88) recognizes that the original meaning of Matt. 24²⁸ is not recoverable.

Page 101. *To line* 3 *from the top of last paragraph add:* On the question of genuineness see the excellent work of F. C. Grant, *Neutest. Studien f. R. Bultmann*², 1957, pp. 137–43.

Page 103, n. 1. *Add:* W. L. Knox (*Sources*, I, p. 15) defends the genuineness of Lk. 5³⁹ in the sense that Jesus has used a proverbial saying.

n. 2. *Add:* F. Perles (*Z.N.W.*, 25, 1926, pp. 163f.) retranslates: 'Do not put a ring on a dog, and lay no pearl on the snout of a swine.' Cp. also M. Black, *Aram. Appr.*, pp. 146f. Perhaps a Parthian proverb; cp. G. Widengren, *Iranisch-Semitische Kulturbegegnung in parthischer Zeit*, 1960, p. 36.

n. 3. *Add:* Cp. J. Klausner, *Jesus von Nazareth*, 1930, p. 551.

Page 104. *To line 6 add:* Dibelius (*Formg.*, p. 249) thinks that Lk. 14⁷⁻¹¹ was originally a parable, and indeed an eschatological warning, intended to avoid false claims of self-righteousness before God. This is very doubtful in my opinion.

To the end of paragraph 3 add: H. Braun (op. cit., II, p. 74, n. 2) makes a different judgement: The opposition of earthly and heavenly treasures was not known in late Judaism; the negative attitude to possessions is nevertheless characteristic of the sects (sc. the Qumran Texts, etc.).

Page 105, n. 2. *Add:* Cp. H. Braun in *Libertas Christiana* (Festschr. f. Delekat 1957), pp. 9f.: Rabbin. parallels. Also in his *Spätjüd. häret. u. frühchristl. Radikalismus*, II, 1957, p. 36, n. 1: doubts as to the genuineness of Matt. 8³⁵.

n. 3. *Add:* Mk. 10³¹ could be an ancient proverb, as Schniewind (*Das N.T. Deutsch*, ad loc.) and Jeremias (*Gleichn.*, p. 26) suppose; the sense being roughly: 'How human destiny changes!' Lohmeyer (*Evg. des Mk.*, ad loc.) thinks, on the contrary, that the saying has an eschatological meaning. On Matt. 22¹⁴ see H. Braun, *Spätjüd. . . . Radik.*, II, p. 41 (n. 1 on p. 40): the opposition of κλητοί to the ἐκλεκτοί is not late Jewish apocalyptic; 'if it is not a genuine saying of Jesus, it is in any event a formulation quite *sui generis*'.

Page 106, n. 1. *Add:* Cp. J. Klausner, *Jesus von Nazareth*, pp. 534–7.

Page 107. *To the end of paragraph 1 add:* On Matt. 7³: Petron., *Cena Trimalchionis*, 57, 8. *In alio peduclum vides, in te ricinum non vides=* You see your neighbour's lice, but not the cattle-tick on your own skin.

n. 1. *Add:* Cp. also the proverbs set out in Mand. Ginza (ed. Lidzb.), pp. 376.13ff.

Page 108, n. 1. *Add:* But cp. Leo Haefeli, *Sprichwörter u. Redensarten aus der Zeit Christi*, 1934; E. Littmann, *Morgenländ. Spruchweisheit. Arabische Sprichwörter u. Rätsel*, 1937.

n. 2. *Add:* On Lk. 10¹⁸ see below, p. 161.

Page 109. *To line 3 from the bottom add:* It is improbable that Isa. 61

should be, as W. Manson believes, the basis of the beatitudes, as of the whole Sermon on the Mount in Q. (*Jesus the Messiah*, pp. 8off.).

n. 2. *Add:* According to Kümmel (*Verh. u. Erf.*, pp. 104f.) there is expressed in Lk. 10²³ᵗ· par. the conviction of 'the presence of messianic fulfilment of salvation in the words and works of Jesus'. E. Käsemann (*Z.Th.K.* 57 (1960), pp. 170f.), who regards all beatitudes as community formulations, takes Matt. 13¹⁶f· (preferring the δίκαιοι of Matt. to the βασιλεῖς of Lk.) as the expression of the Palestinian-Syrian communities' understanding of themselves, in that they regard themselves as prophets and righteous men. Scarcely illuminating!

n. 3. *Add:* Cp. also G. Erdmann, *Die Vorgeschichten des Lk.- u. Mt. Evg.*, 1932, p. 45.

n. 4. *Add:* For the originality of the second person in Luke as over against the third person in Matthew: Dibelius (*Formg.*, p. 248; *Botsch. u. Gesch.*, I, pp. 111f.), T. W. Manson (*The Sayings of Jesus*, p. 47), E. Percy (*Die Botschaft Jesu*, pp. 82–84; see also pp. 40–45).

Page 110. *To line 6 from the bottom add:* (Cp. the interpretation of the Matthaean form in E. Käsemann, *Z.Th.K.* 57 (1960), pp. 172f. and in G. Braumann, *Nov. Test.* 4 (1960), pp. 253–60.)

Page 111. *At the end of paragraph 2 add:* (On the authenticity of Lk. 12³² as a Saying of Jesus, see W. Pesch, *Biblica* 41 (1960), pp. 25–40.)

n. 1. *Add:* On the fire of judgement cp. Bousset-Gressmann, *Die Religion des Judentums*³, p. 279; P. Volz, *Die Eschatologie der jüd. Gemeinde*, pp. 318f., 335f. There is a detailed discussion of the question in C. H. Kraeling, *John the Baptist*, 1951, pp. 58–63, 114–18. He understands the πνεῦμα of baptism as the (fiery) breath of the eschatological judge (cp. Isa. 11⁴; 2 Th. 2⁸, etc.). To avoid misunderstanding of πνεῦμα as the spirit bestowed in Christian baptism (already referred to in Mark with the addition of ἅγιον), πνεῦμα and πῦρ are combined in Q and should be understood as an hendiadys.

Page 112. *To the end of paragraph 2 add:* It is certainly secondary that Mk. 8³⁸ and Lk. 9²⁶ are missing in some (western) texts. Dodd (*Parables*¹⁰, pp. 93f.) takes the Q form as original, where there is no reference to the 'coming' of the Son of man. According to Käsemann (*N.T. Stud.*, I, 1955, pp. 256f.) the I-saying in Matthew is secondary compared with Mark's reference to the Son of man, and yet ὁμολογεῖν and ἀρνεῖσθαι in Matthew and Luke are primary rather than Mark's stylish ἐπαισχύνεσθαι. The saying cannot be traced back to Jesus, as the content shows, 'since it takes confession of Christ (!) as the criterion for the last day. The form of the sentence has the same implication'. Similarly Vielhauer (*Festschr. f. G. Dehn*, pp. 68f.): The saying presupposes the persecution of the disciples for the sake of Jesus. For the rest it is no longer possible to establish what was the original wording; it is 'just as possible that Son of man has been inserted into Lk. 12⁸ as it is for it to have been deleted from Lk. 12⁷'. According to E. Käsemann too (in *Z.Th.K.* 51 (1954), pp. 150 and 57 (1960), p. 182) Mk. 8³⁸ (or Matt. 10³²) is a saying to be attributed to Christian post-Easter prophecy.

To the end of paragraph 3 add: (Käsemann also regards Matt. 10²⁰⁻²⁴ as a saying typical of early-Christian prophecy: *Z.Th.K.* 57 (1960), p. 178.)

Page 113. *To line 10 of paragraph 2 add:* (Lk. 11⁴⁸//Matt. 23³¹ must also have been in Q in all probability, if the variant ὑμεῖς (δὲ) οἰκοδομεῖτε (Luke) for (ὅτι) υἱοί ἐστε (Matthew) comes from different translations of אתון בבין אתון, as Black, following Torrey, supposes (*Aram. Appr.*², pp. 11f.).

Page 114. *To line 6 of paragraph 1 add:* E. Haenchen (*Z.Th.K.*, 48, 1951, pp. 38–63) gives an excellent analysis of Matt. 23. He shows that the material used for composing the address comes in essentials from the Jewish Christian community, to which the Scribes and Pharisees constitute an united opposition. Cp. F. Heinrichs, *Die Komposition der antipharis. und antirabbin. Wehereden bei den Synopt.*, 1957.

n. 1. *Add:* Cp. Haenchen, op. cit., pp. 52ff.: Since Luke lets the hearer be addressed in v. 48 in the second person, while v. 49 reads εἰς αὐτούς, the third person would have stood in his source. In v. 34 Matthew has changed it into πρὸς ὑμᾶς because in this gospel it is Jesus, and not 'Wisdom' who speaks. For the rest cp. T. Arvedson, *Mysterium Christi*, 1937, pp. 209–12; Rud. Meyer, *Der Prophet aus Galiläa*, 1940, pp. 48–50; H. J. Schoeps, *Die jüdischen Prophetenmorde. Symb. Bibl. Uppsal.*, II, 1943.

Page 115, n. 1. *Add:* According to Haenchen (*Z.Th.K.*, 48, 1951, p. 56), Matt. 23³⁷⁻³⁹ par. cannot have been the continuation of 23³⁴⁻³⁶; for in 23³⁴⁻³⁶ 'Wisdom' looks prophetically into the future, while in 23³⁷⁻³⁹ she looks back on the mission of the Prophets as something past. Similarly Kümmel (*Verh. u. Erf.*, pp. 73–75) who thinks that 23³⁷⁻³⁹ is probably 'an independent saying of Jesus coming from the oldest tradition'. Verse 39 is the original ending, though Rud. Meyer (*Der Prophet aus Galiläa*, p. 50) and Haenchen (op. cit., p. 57) consider v. 39 to be a Christian addition.

n. 2. *Add:* W. L. Knox (*Sources*, II, p. 82) takes the view that by ἕως κτλ. Matthew has in mind Jesus' return in glory, and that Luke by contrast thinks of Jesus' entry into Jerusalem. The saying derives from an early stage of Jesus' ministry, when he hoped to go to Jerusalem when it was ready to receive him. This is in the highest degree improbable! Lyder Brun (*Segen u. Fluch im Urchristentum*, 1932, p. 55) and Kümmel (op. cit., pp. 74f.) relate the saying to Jesus' coming at his Parousia. Haenchen (op. cit., p. 57) takes the same view; yet that is the meaning of the

Christian additions in v. 39, while the quotation in vv. 37f. completes a proclamation of judgement without any mention of Messiah.

n. 4. *Add:* O. Michel (*Th.W.B.*, V, pp. 127.2ff.) points out that according to O.T. and Jewish usage the 'House' can be the Temple, Jerusalem, or the Jewish people. Haenchen (op. cit., p. 55) decides in favour of the Temple.

Page 116, n. 2. *Add:* H. Greeven (*Gebet u. Eschatologie im N.T.*, 1931, p. 62) also takes the Luke-form as original, but thinks that κύριε, κύριε refers to the exalted Lord. W. L. Knox (*Sources*, II, pp. 31f.) takes the Matthew-form for the original.

Page 117. *To line 5 of paragraph 2 add:* (On the other hand, E. Käsemann, *Z.Th.K.* 57 (1960), p. 163, regards Matthew as more original than Luke).

At the end of the second paragraph add: (According to Käsemann, op. cit., pp. 163f., the Saying is directed against the enthusiastic piety of a particular group of the post-Easter community.

To the end of paragraph 3 add: Dodd (*Parables*[10], p. 87) also asks whether the connection between Matt. 24^{37-39} and 24^{40} is original. If not, then vv. 40f. are a metaphor whose meaning is undecided; it may have referred to the selective effectiveness of Jesus' call. For the rest, Kümmel (*Verh. u. Erf.*, p. 32, n. 63) and Vielhauer (*Festschr. f. G. Dehn*, p. 66) rightly take the view that in vv. 37 and 39 Matthew has introduced the term παρουσία instead of 'Day (or of the day) of the Son of man'.

To line 7 from the bottom add: (Otherwise Lohmeyer, *Das Urchristentum*, I, p. 18, n. 2 and *Evg. d. Mt.* ad loc., and Kraeling, *John the Baptist*, p. 197, n. 4.).

Page 118. *To the end of page add:* Jeremias (*Gleichn.*, pp. 45–47) believes that Lk. 12^{35-38} and Mk. 13^{33-37} are parallels. Behind them is a parable of Doorkeepers, which is decked out by both Mark and Luke with allegorizing additions which adapt the original parousia parable to the situation where the parousia has been deferred. Kümmel (*Verh. u. Erf.*, pp. 48f.) does not agree that the problem of the delayed parousia really belongs to the text. Dodd (*Parables*[10], pp. 160–7) says the parables give a warning to be awake and ready in view of the threatening dangers which have been occasioned by the crisis initiated by Jesus—a point of view which I think improbable.

n. 1. *Add:* A. Vögtle, *Synopt. Studien* (*Festschr. f. A. Wikenhauser*), 1954, pp. 230–77, has made a detailed study of the saying about the sign of Jonah with a wealth of discussion of the literature. Yet cp. in addition O. Cullmann, *Die Christologie des N.T.*, 1957, pp. 61f.; O. Betz, *Nov. Test.* 2, 1958, pp. 131ff.

n. 2. *Add:* Jeremias (*Gleichn.*, pp. 91, 154, n. 2) and Kümmel (*Verh. u. Erf.*, p. 61) both think Matt. 12⁴⁰ and Lk. 11³⁰ secondary; whilst Cullmann (op. cit.) is undecided. Vögtle (op. cit.) thinks that Lk. 11³⁰ and Matt. 12⁴⁰ are the community's interpretation, Luke's being the more relevant. Yet cp. Kraeling (*John the Baptist*, p. 137), who interprets the sign of Jonah in terms of the Baptist's preaching of repentance—also P. Seidelin, *St. Th.*, V, 1952, pp. 119–31.

Page 119. *To line 11 from the top add:* Jeremias (*Gleichn.*, pp. 47–50) looks behind Matt. 24⁴⁵⁻⁵¹//Lk. 12⁴²⁻⁴⁶ for an original parable which has been adapted by Matthew's and Luke's editing to the situation of a parousia deferred. Originally this was a threatening rally to the leaders of the people, or, alternatively, to the Scribes. So also Dodd (*Parables*¹⁰, pp. 158–60).

To line 7 from the bottom add: Dodd (*Parables*¹⁰, pp. 155f.) points to the affinity with 1 Th. 5²⁻⁸; probably some paranetic tradition is behind both passages.

Page 120, n. 1. *Add:* Cp. esp. M. Simon, op. cit., pp. 247f.

Page 121. *To the end of paragraph 1 add:* The questions as to the meaning and genuineness of the saying about the destruction of the Temple has been fully discussed by Ph. Vielhauer, *Oikodome*, 1939, pp. 62–70; W. G. Kümmel, *Verh. u. Erf.*, 1953, pp. 92–97; G. Harder in *Theologia Viatorum*, 1952, pp. 72–74; M. Simon in *Aux Sources de la Tradition Chrétienne*, 1950, pp. 247–57. Most scholars in my view rightly understand the saying as an eschatological prophecy in the manner of Jewish apocalyptic, which was then reinterpreted by the Christian Church, the new Temple being interpreted as the Christian Community of the Body of Jesus (Jn. 2²¹). Only a few scholars, e.g. Schlatter (*Markus, der Evangelist für die Griechen*, 1935, p. 239) and Dodd (*Parables*¹⁰, pp. 60–62), think that the prophecy of the destruction of the Temple refers to a forthcoming historical event (on this matter further material in Kümmel, op. cit., p. 94, n. 47). While Hölscher (*Th. Bl.*, 12, 1933, col. 193) takes the prophecy as a *vaticinium ex eventu*, most scholars believe it to be a genuine saying of Jesus, even though the original wording cannot be established any longer with certainty: thus Goguel, *Vie de Jésus*², pp. 399ff.; Lohmeyer, *Evg. d. Mk.*, ad loc; Vielhauer, op. cit.; Dodd, op. cit.; Kümmel, op. cit.; O. Cullmann, *Petrus*, 1952, pp. 222f., while Rudolf Meyer (*Der Prophet aus Galiläa*, 1940, pp. 17f.) argues for the genuineness of Mk. 13², which nevertheless militates against that of Mk. 14⁵⁸.

To the end of paragraph 2 add: Detailed discussion of the saying in Kümmel (*Verh. u. Erf.*, pp. 19–22), who rightly rejects Dodd's reinterpretation (*Parables*[10], pp. 42, 53f.), and interprets it as a prophecy of the future coming of God's rule, and in such a way that the futurity is itself limited. He thinks the saying belongs to the oldest and most genuine tradition. To the contrary, and rightly, G. Bornkamm (*In Memoriam Ernst Lohmeyer*, 1951, pp. 116–19). The saying is a community formulation. In addition to Kümmel and Bornkamm, cp. also W. Marxsen, *Der Evglist. Markus*, 1956, p. 140, n. 1.

n. 1. *Add:* The interpretation of Mand. Joh., Book ch. 76, is very dubious; see E. Percy, *Untersuchungen über den Ursprung der joh. Theologie*, 1939, p. 254, n. 29.

Page 122. *To line 2 add:* Like other scholars W. Kümmel (*Verh. u. Erf.*, pp. 26–29, with ample references to other literature, p. 29, n. 54) understands ἐντὸς ὑμῶν (at least as most probably) meaning 'among you', and in the particular meaning 'that the rule of God has come into effect in advance in Jesus and the present events occurring around his person'. Bent Noack ('Das Gottesreich bei Lukas, Eine Studie zu Lk. 17²⁰⁻²⁴', *Symb. Bibl. Uppsal.*, 10, 1948) provides a history of the exposition of the saying and a proper interpretation. He understands ἐντός as 'inter' and ἐστίν as a real present tense. C. H. Roberts (*H.T.R.*, 41, 1948, pp. 1–8) understands ἐντός, in the light of two papyrus examples, as 'at the disposal of' or 'available'. Extensive discussion of Lk. 17²⁰f. by Aug. Strobel, in *Z.N.W.* 49 (1958), pp. 157–96 (in addition *Z.N.W.* 51 (1960), pp. 133f.) and by Alex. Rüstow, ibid., pp. 197–234).

To line 6 from top of page add: (Matthew's formulation, which introduces the idea of παρουσία, is secondary to Luke's; see above, p. 117.)

To the end of paragraph 2 add: Vielhauer (*Festschr. f. G. Dehn.*, pp. 67f.) thinks that Lk. 17²³ is a community product, because it presupposes the equation of Messiah with the Son of man, and their identification with Jesus.

To line 22 from top add: (On the tradition of persecution sayings see D. W. Riddle, *Z.N.W.*, 33, 1934, pp. 271–89. On Mk. 13¹⁰ see Jeremias, *Jesu Verheissung für die Völker*, 1956, pp. 19f.)

To the end of line 23 add: There is complete unanimity among scholars that the discourse in Mk. 13⁵⁻²⁷ contains material from Jewish apocalyptic under Christian editing. Verses 7, 8, 12, 14–20, 24–27 are almost unanimously thought to be such material. Some

scholars believe the section is adapted from a written source; thus
Hölscher (*Th. Bl.*, 12, 1953, cols. 193–202), who thinks that such a
source originated in the period 39/40–40/41, when Caligula's order to
display his portrait in the Temple was due to be carried out. Sundwall (op. cit., pp. 76–78) takes the same view, and believes that the
source has been combined with a collection of Christian sayings
which included vv. 2, 5f., 9, 13a, 11, 23, 30. Other scholars do not
assume a coherent written source, but rather that individual sayings
or groups of sayings underlie the discourse; thus Kümmel (*Verh. u.
Erf.*, pp. 88–97) and G. Harder (*Theol. Viatorum*, 1952, pp. 71–107).
W. Marxsen holds the same views (*Der Evglist. Markus*, 1956,
pp. 101–40) though he wants to prove the unity of the composition
that Mark has created out of these materials. F. Busch (*Zum Verständ-
nis der synopt. Eschatologie: Mk. 13 neu untersucht*, 1938) rejects an analysis which separates traditional from editorial matter. Kümmel and
Marxsen dispute his point of view. On J. W. Bowman and A.
Feuillet who both question the apocalyptic-eschatological significance of Mk. 13, see Kümmel, op. cit., p. 90, n. 37. On Mk. 13 [9f.]
see espec. G. D. Kilpatrick. He wants to take εἰς πάντα τὰ ἔθνη with
what precedes rather than with what follows, and defends this view
(already propounded in 1955 in *Studies in the Gospels: Essays in Memory
of R. H. Lightfoot*) in *J.T.S.*, N.S. 9 (1958), pp. 81–86, against
objections from A. M. Farrer and C. F. D. Moule.

To line 2 from bottom add: Yet in all probability Matt. 24[10–12] also
derives from Jewish tradition, cp. *Did.* 16.7f., and see below, p. 126.
On Matt. 10 [23] see Kümmel, op. cit., p. 35, and for a contrary view
Vielhauer, *Festschr. f. G. Dehn*, pp. 59–61, and H. E. Tödt, *Der
Menschensohn in der synoptischen Überlieferung*, 1959, pp. 56f.; H. Schürmann, *Bibl. Z.*, N.F. 3, 1959, p. 82–88, disputes the connection of the
legion with the primitive Christian mission, and attempts to show
that in the history of the tradition this 'apocalyptic comfort-saying'
belongs together with Lk. 12 [11f.] (= Matt. 10 [19]), that in Q they were
originally next to each other, that Lk. omitted it as no longer necessary, and that Mk. replaced it with Mk. 13 [10]. Cp. also J. Dupont,
Nov. Test. 2, 1958, pp. 228–44. On the editing of Matthew reflecting
the missionary situation of the Church see Marxsen, op. cit., pp.
135–9.

n. 1. *Add:* I have stated a fuller case for my view that Lk. 17 [25] is secondary in *Th.
Bl.*, 20, 1941, col. 278. Also against its genuineness, H. Conzelmann, *Die Mitte der
Zeit*, p. 106, n. 1. For its genuineness, Kümmel, *Verh. u. Erf.*, pp. 63f., and M. Buber,
Pro Regno pro Sanctuario, 1950, pp. 71–78.

Page 123. *To the end of paragraph* 1 *add:* On the editing of Luke as treating eschatological prophecy as an eschatological interpretation of history, see Harder, op. cit., *passim*, and Marxsen, op. cit., pp. 129–35. On Luke cp. also Aug. Strobel, *Z.N.W.*, 47, 1956, pp. 72–75, L. Gaston, *Th.Z.Basel* 16, 1960, pp. 161–72, and also P. Winter, *St.Th.* 8, 1954, pp. 138–55.

To the end of paragraph 2 *add:* The Parable of the Fig Tree could be a parallel to Lk. 12[54–56]. So also Dodd, *Parables*[10], p. 137, n. 1. He, like Jeremias (*Gleichn.*, pp. 102ff.), thinks that the parable in its context has a secondary function as a warning reference to the terrors of the End, though it originally referred to the signs of the present time of salvation, though this seems doubtful to me. Kümmel (*Verh. u. Erf.*, pp. 14–16) is probably right in stressing the parallelism with Lk. 12[54–56] as well: ταῦτα refers to the signs of the end, and the parousia must be understood as the subject of ἐγγύς ἐστιν.

To the end of paragraph 3 *add:* Kümmel (*Verh. u. Erf.*, p. 54) rightly defends the interpretation of ἡ γενεὰ αὕτη as 'this generation' against misinterpretations such as 'the (Jewish) people' (Schnie-wind) and 'this kind' (Michaelis).

To the end of paragraph 4 *add:* Kümmel (op. cit., p. 85) argues, to my mind wrongly, for the genuineness of Mk. 13[31].

To the end of paragraph 5 *add:* Kümmel (op. cit., pp. 34–36) sees the difficulty of taking the saying as a genuine saying of Jesus (the absolute ὁ υἱός appears here only in Mark, and only at Matt. 11[27] elsewhere in the Synoptics) yet comes to the conclusion 'that the saying has not gone undistorted in its wording, but is nevertheless in regard to its main idea a saying properly reproducing the most primitive tradition'—further support for this position is noticed on p. 36, n. 79.

Page 124. *To line* 11 *from the top add:* Cp. esp. L. Ginza, III, 59, p. 591 Lidzb.

To line 5 *from the bottom of paragraph* 1 *add:* (Jeremias' opinion, *Jesu Verheissung für die Völker*, p. 41, n. 164, is, in my view, against the weight of the evidence of analogies from the history of religion.)

To the end of paragraph 1 *add:* Jeremias (*Gleichn.*, p. 174) also admits that Matt. 25[31–46] displays characteristics of a secondary kind. According to Dodd (*Parables*[10], p. 85, n. 1) the judgement scene has been constructed in order to provide a lively dramatic setting for dominical sayings like Matt. 10[40–42]; Mk. 9[37]. Vielhauer (*Festschr. f. G.*

Dehn, pp. 57f.) thinks that v. 31 derives from Matthew, who has introduced the Son of man, whereas the following verses are about 'the king', i.e. God. This is also the view of Sh. E. Johnson (*J.B.L.*, 74, 1953, p. 39), though he understands the king as the Messiah. J. A. T. Robinson's analysis (*N.T. Studies*, 2, 1955–56, pp. 225–37) is much too ingenious: Matthew has combined (1) a parable about a shepherd (vv. 32f.); (2) an allegorical interpretation (contained in vv. 34–40); (3) dominical sayings (vv. 35–40). The specifically Christian content of the passage does not lie in the moral, but, as H. Braun (*Spätjüd. häret. u. frühchristl. Radik.*, II, p. 94, n. 2) rightly says, in the identification of the person of the judge with the needy. (Cp. further A. Wikenhauser, *Die Liebeswerke in dem Gerichtsgemälde Mt. 25*[31–46]. *Bibl. Z.*, 20, 1932, pp. 366–77.)

To line 2 from bottom add: Also Lightfoot (*Hist. and Int.*, p. 92) links 9[11–13] with 9[1].

Page 125, n. 1. *Add:* Lohmeyer (*Evg. d. Mk.*, ad loc.) also regards v. 12b as a gloss, while others seek help in transposition. Thus Sundwall (op. cit., p. 57) proposes the order 11–12b, 12a, 13; F. C. Grant (*The Earliest Gospel*, p. 101; cp. pp. 114f.) 11, 12a, 13b, 13ab, 12b. Neither is satisfying. Cp. also W. Trilling, *Bibl.Z.*, N.F. 3, 1959, pp. 279ff.

Page 126. *To line 6 from the top add:* (On Matt. 24[10–12] cp. the parallels in *Did.* 16.7f.)

Page 127. *To line 3 from the top of the last paragraph add:* (On Christian formulations cp. D. W. Riddle, *Z.N.W.*, 33, 1944, pp. 271–89, and F. C. Grant, *Neutest. Studien f. R. Bultmann*, pp. 137–43.)

Page 128. *To n. 1 add:* and also H. Schürmann's extensive investigation of the 'Christ-language' in *Bibl.Z.*, N.F. 2, 1958, pp. 54–84.

Page 130. *To line 2 from end of paragraph 2 add:* Vielhauer (*Festschr. f. G. Dehn*, pp. 56f.) thinks that Lk. 17[22] is an introduction to the following passage.

Page 131. *To line 13 from the bottom add:* W. L. Knox (*Sources*, I, pp. 56f.) believes Mk. 8[14f] is good ancient tradition, which reaches back to a time when memory was held to, without serving any edifying purpose. The meaning of the saying in v. 15 is to warn against *agents provocateurs* who sought to get information from the disciples so as to use it against Jesus. I think this is improbable to an extraordinary degree.

n. 1. *Add:* Lyder Brun (*Segen u. Fluch im Urchristentum*, p. 117) rightly opposes

Fridrichsen's interpretation. For the priority of the Mark version see also T. W. Manson, *The Teaching of Jesus*, pp. 216f; H. Braun, *Spätjüd.-häret. u. frühchristl. Radik.*, II, p. 27, n. 3; G. Bornkamm, *The Background of the N.T. and its Eschatology*, pp. 243f. Bornkamm interprets the Q version thus: Blasphemy against the Son of man may be forgiven in the time before Pentecost; after Pentecost for the first time 'blasphemy is an unforgivable sin, for the one who speaks in the Spirit is the self-revealing, exalted Lord'. Conzelmann (*Die Mitte der Zeit*, p. 155, n. 2) agrees. Similarly C. K. Barrett, *The Holy Spirit and the Gospel Tradition*, 1947, pp. 103ff.: The forgivable sin is the blasphemy against the Son of man committed in an heathen condition; the unforgivable sin is the blasphemy against the Spirit in the Church; that constitutes apostasy. G. Fitzer (*Th.Z.*, 13, 1947, pp. 161–82), who thinks the Q form is secondary, reconstructs the following as the original text of Mk. 3²⁸: πάντα ἀφεθήσεται τῷ υἱῷ τοῦ ἀνθρώπου [τὰ ἁμαρτήματα καὶ αἱ βλασφημίαι], ἐὰν δὲ βλασφημήσῃ κτλ, and relates the 'Son of man' to Jesus, and thinks the saying had already become unintelligible to Mark, and was corrected on dogmatic grounds by the alteration of an original singular 'Son of man' into a plural. Fitzer discovers the meaning of the original saying from the context: if the Son of man, whose works are done in the Holy Spirit, blasphemes the Spirit, i.e. denies the source of his power and might, he would make himself guilty of an eternal sin; but since to state it thus is to expose its impossibility, the foolishness of the charge that he has an unclean spirit is proven. Yet Fitzer himself admits that Jesus' opponents could hardly have understood this argument, and that the presuppositions of this interpretation—the possibility of sin and the forgiveness of sin for the Son of man, and further, the association of the title Son of man with the Holy Spirit—are very problematical indeed. According to E. Käsemann, *Z.Th.K.* 57 (1960), p. 180, Matt. 12³² is directed against the opposition experienced by the Christian mission, which regarded itself as determined by the Spirit. In general on pp. 131ff. cp. Käsemann, op. cit., pp. 171ff.

Page 132. *To line* 12 *from foot add:* On the text of Mk. 10¹¹ᶠ·, etc., see esp. F. C. Grant, *The Earliest Gospel*, p. 117.

Page 133. *To line* 15 *from the top add:* Schlatter (*Der Evglist. Matth.*, p. 205) also takes Matt. 6⁷⁻¹⁵ as an 'intrusion into a coherent series of sayings'.
To line 22 *from the top add:* (Cp. E. Lohmeyer, *Das Vaterunser²*, 1947, and K. G. Kuhn, *Achtzehngebet und Vater Unser und der Reim*, 1950.)

Page 134, n. 1. *Add:* H. Braun (*Radikalismus*, II, pp. 24–25, n. 9) takes v. 22b (or alternatively 22bc) as a later casuistical interpretation, while Lohmeyer (*Evg. d. Mt.*, ad loc.) thinks that two sayings have grown together: vv. 21b, 22a and v. 22bc. For the rest, κρίσις in v. 21 does not mean 'judgement' (in the sense of a court of justice) as it does in v. 22, but 'punishment' as in Rev. 18¹⁰; Heb. 10²⁷ and elsewhere. According to Dalman, *Jesus-Jeschua*, pp. 66f., ἔνοχος can stand only for the Aramaic מִתְהַיַּב: 'with additional penalty'. On Matt. 5²¹ᶠ· as 'evidence for the sacral administration of justice in the primitive community', cp. M. Weise, *Z.N.W.* 49 (1958), pp. 116–23.

Page 135. *To line* 15 *from the top add:* (Since καὶ μισήσεις κτλ. is not a quotation from the O.T., H. Braun (*Radikalismus*, II, p. 58 (n. 1 from p. 57)) asks whether this is not an emphatic expression of opposition to the teaching of hate among the 'sects'.)

To line 10 from the bottom add: (On the secondary character of Luke's version cp. Dibelius, *Botschaft u. Geschichte*, I, pp. 113f.)

Page 135, n. 1. *Add:* The first three examples fit with difficulty into the context. Why does not the antithesis confine itself to μή ὁμόσαι ὅλως and to v. 37? Clearly the antithesis means: The distinction between sayings which have to be true (statements on oath) and those which do not need to be true is a false distinction; the demand for truth applies to all statements. But the four examples seem to set this idea aside, and to suggest that there are statements which have less obligatory power; thus the sacredness of an oath seems to be intensified, as in Matt. 23¹⁶⁻¹⁹ (or, 22; see pp. 133f.). In the actual context the meaning can only be: any protestation of truth is forbidden in the prohibition of oaths, for every statement is in fact an oath. Lohmeyer (*Evg. d. Mt.*, ad loc.) also perceives that this group of sayings has no original unity; it seems 'to have grown together in the tradition itself'.

Page 136, n. 1. *Add:* Cp. V. Hasler, *Th.Z.Basel* 15, 1959, pp. 90–106.

n. 2. *Add:* Cp. the analysis in W. L. Knox, *Sources*, II, pp. 20–25.

Page 137. *To the end of the page add:* Lohmeyer (*Evg. d. Mk.*, ad loc.), Jeremias (*Jesu Verh. f. d. Völker*, p. 45), and O. Cullmann (*Christologie des N.T.*, p. 87) dispute the view that Mk. 12³⁵⁻³⁷ is a community formulation. Lohmeyer indeed understands the saying as the scriptural proof advanced by Jesus that the Messiah is not, as the scribes maintain, a Davidic figure, but a transcendent Lord, the Son of man. Jeremias thinks that Jesus poses an Haggadah-question, i.e. one which refers to a contradiction between two passages of scripture (this was already the view of D. Daube, *J.T.S.*, N.S. 2, 1951, p. 48). The answer is: Both passages are right, but refer to different things, 'David's Son' to the earthly appearance of the hidden Messiah, 'David's Lord' to the enthroned being of whom Ps. 110² speaks. (But there is no quotation of two passages of scripture!) This is also the position of G. Bornkamm (*The Background*, p. 242). According to Cullmann (op. cit., pp. 132f.) Jesus does not dispute the Davidic sonship of the Messiah, but rather the political ideal of Messiahship. Presumably Jesus' knowledge of his being Son of God remains in the background, and over against that sonship his Davidic descent is not disputed but rather depreciated. R. P. Gagg (*Th. Z.*, 7, 1951, pp. 18–30) postulates an introduction consisting of a question by an opponent, and understands the saying of Jesus in vv. 35–37 as a riddle without theological significance. In the tradition the opponent's question disappeared, because the

Church was no longer interested in the status of Messiah as a son of David; and that led to the pericope becoming an expression of Jesus' dignity as the Lord. This is quite incredible. According to N. A. Dahl, *Kerygma und Dogma* I (1955), p. 164, the historicity of the saying cannot be proved.

Page 138. *To the end of paragraph* 1 *add:* The same judgement is shared by H. Braun (*Radikalismus*, II, 8, n. 2 to p. 7; p. 11, n. 2) about the pericope. E. Schweizer (*Th.L.Z.*, 77, 1952, Cols. 479–84) tries to show that vv. 18f. are a piece of tradition of which v. 18 at one time circulated alone, as Lk. 16¹⁷ indicates. Matthew has inserted ἕως ἂν πάντα γένηται into v. 18, and vv. 17, 20 are also his formulations. In them he takes up the thesis of the conservative tendency of the primitive Church, though reinterpreting it by saying that as the one who brings the new law with its content of loving one's neighbour, Jesus is fulfilling the Law and the Prophets. In Knox's view (*Sources*, II, p. 19) v. 19 did not originally go with vv. 17f. but, together with v. 20, formed an introduction to vv. 21ff., which Matthew obtained from another source. Lohmeyer (*Evg. d. Mt.*, ad loc.) takes a similar view (apart from the question of sources). According to E. Käsemann, *Z.Th.K.* 57 (1960), pp. 165f., even v. 18d (ἕως . . .) may be a comment of Matthew's, certainly however v. 20. The traditional v. 20 is formulated in prophetic style on the pattern of the holy right (cp. *Nt. St.* 1, 1954/5, pp. 248–60) and is directed against the Hellenistic Christians. On v. 19 see H. Schürmann, *Bibl. Z.*, N.F., 1960, pp. 238–50.

To line 6 *from the bottom add:* (O. Linton (*Das Problem der Urkirche in der neueren Forschung*, 1932, pp. 157–74) gives a detailed account of research in this field. So do A. Oepke, *St. Th.*, II, 1950, pp. 110–65; H. Clavier, *N.T. Studien f. R. Bultmann*, 1954, pp. 94–100, who gives a review of the interpretation of Matt. 16¹⁸ from the Early Church to the present time. There is a careful examination in a critique of the most recent research in A. Vögtle, *Bibl. Z.*, 1957, pp. 252–72; 1958, pp. 85–103). P. Obrist, *Echtheitsfragen und Deutung der Petrusstelle Mt.* 16¹⁸ᶠ· *in der deutschen protestantischen Theologie der letzten* 30 *Jahre*, 1961.

Page 139, n. 1 from p. 138. *To line* 6 *from the top add:* L. Brun (*Segen und Fluch in Urchristentum*, 1932, pp. 93–100) interprets the verbs in terms of disciplinary authority, as does Jeremias, Art. κλείς, *Th.W.B.*, III, pp. 749–51.

n.i. from p. 138. *Add at end:* L. Brun (op. cit., p. 96) is also against the identification of ἐκκλησία and βασιλεία τοῦ οὐρανου.

n. 1. *Add:* On the word play Πέτρος-πέτρα see also H. Rheinfelder, *Bibl. Z.*, 24, 1938/39, pp. 139–63, esp. pp. 157ff.; further H. Clavier, op. cit., pp. 101–9.

n. 2. *To line 11 from the bottom add:* R. Eppel (*Aux Sources de la Trad. Chrét.*, pp. 71–73) thinks that πύλαι is a mistranslation of שַׁעֲרֵי = πυλωροί. By these are meant personal demonic powers (as in Slav. En., 42.1). G. Bornkamm (*The Background*, p. 255, n. 1) recalls the travail and distress which would precede the appearance of the Son of man.

Page 140, n. 2 from p. 139. *To line 6 from the top add:* Cp. Eric Burrows in *The Labyrinth, Further Studies . . .* Ed. S. H. Hooke, 1935, pp. 53ff. M. Seller, *Die Pforten des Hades*, 1959.

n. 2 from p. 139. *Add at end:* R. Otto (*Reich Gottes und Menschensohn*[2], 1940, pp. 295f.) accepts Harnack's hypothesis. Goguel (*Bulletin de la Faculté libre de Théol. Prot.*, 4, 1938, No. 15) does not.

n. 1. *To line 3 add:* On the metaphor of a building see also P. Vielhauer, *Oikodome*, 1940, pp. 16ff., 70ff.

Page 141. *To the end of paragraph 1 add:* L. Brun (*Segen u. Fluch*, pp. 93ff.) thinks that Matt. 18[18] is a church regulation appended as an illustration of v. 17, especially to indicate the possibility of the lifting of the excommunication in v. 17 (if penitence were shown). Pertinent material on Matt. 18[15–19] is to be found in von Campenhausen, *Kirchl. Amt.*, pp. 138–40.

To the end of paragraph 2 add: On Matt. 18[15–17] see L. Brun, op. cit., pp. 92f. No saying of the historical Jesus is behind the section, but only a rule of Church discipline from the Jewish Christian community. Similarly von Campenhausen, see above. H. Braun, *Radikalismus*, II, p. 26, n. 4: 'The last two instances (two witnesses, and the whole company) could have come from the sects.'

n. 2 from p. 140. *Add at end:* L. Rost, *Die Vorstufen von Kirche u. Synagoge im A.T.*, 1938, p. 133: 'Jesus would have said nothing especially exciting if he had only held out the prospect of his K'nischta. He would then have made himself out as the founder of a new sect only.' Against the genuineness of Matt. 16[18–19], cp. e.g. further, Bultmann, *Th.Bl.*, 20, 1941, cols. 265–79, Kümmel, 'Kirchenbegr. u. Geschichtsbew. in der Urgemeinde u. bei Jesus', *Symb. Bibl. Uppsal.*, I, 1943, pp. 37–41, and *St. Th.*, VII, 1953, pp. 1–27; Strathmann, *Z. Syst. Th.*, 20, 1943, pp. 223ff.; O. J. F. Seitz, *J.B.L.*, 69, 1950, pp. 329–40; von Campenhausen, *Kirchl. Amt. u. geistl. Vollmacht*, 1953, pp. 141–3; G. Bornkamm in *The Background*, pp. 245f. Others try to defend the genuineness of the verses, e.g. H. D. Wendland, *Die Eschatologie des Reiches Gottes bei Jesus*, 1931, pp. 164–87; A. Oepke, *St. Th.*, II, 1950, pp. 110–65; N. A. Dahl, *St. Th.*, V, 1951, pp. 160–6, and O. Cullmann, *Petrus*, 1952, pp. 176–238, who is of the opinion that they really belong to the scene of Jesus' farewell to his disciples, and have been wrongly attached by Matthew to the scene of Peter's confession of the Messiah in Mk. 8[27–30]. According to Vögtle (op. cit.) vv. 18f. are a piece of tradition inserted by Matthew; he leaves quite open the question as to the possible place of origin, exactly when the promise was made to Peter. See below, p. 258, n. 1.

Page 142. *To line 8 from the top add:* On v. 19 see H. Greeven, 'Gebet u. Eschatologie im N.T.', *Neutest. Forsch.*, 3.1, 1931, p. 70.

To line 8 from the bottom add: Rightly also Sundwall, op. cit., p. 61; H. Braun, *Radikalismus*, II, p. 86, n. 3. But O. Michel (*Th. St. Kr.*, 108, 1937/38, pp. 401–15) on the contrary would interpret μιϰροί as a designation of the disciples. Kümmel (*Verh. u. Erf.*, pp. 86f.) rightly rejects this view, though he is admittedly wrong to identify the 'little ones' with 'the poor' of Matt. 5³. Käsemann, *Z.Th.K.* 57 (1960), pp. 169f., 173, regards Matt. 10⁴¹ as a primitive Christian prophetic statement of the 'holy right', which is at once invalidated in v. 42.

n. 2. *Add:* Crum (*The Rhythmical Sayings of Our Lord*, 1950) reconstructs an original composition from Matt. 18¹⁰; Mk. 9³⁷⁻⁴¹; Lk. 17¹, ². On the relation of the sayings about σϰανδαλίζειν and the μιϰροί see Jeremias, *Z.N.W.*, 29, 1930, p. 149, n.1.

Page 144. *To the end of paragraph 3 add:* J. Schniewind (*Das Evg. nach Matt.*⁴, 1950, p. 288) considers Matt. 23⁸⁻¹⁰ as a community formulation. So does E. Haenchen (*Z.Th.K.*, 48, 1951, pp. 43f.) who believes them to be the sayings of a Christian prophet. Similarly Käsemann (*Z.Th.K.* 57 (1960), pp. 164ff.), who sees in the saying a protest against a 'community-order forming (itself) in the manner of a Christian Rabbinical hierarchy'. Cp. also S. T. Townsend, *J.T.S.*, N.S. 12 (1961), pp. 56–59.

Page 144, n. 1. *Add:* Jeremias (*Judaica*, 3, 1947/8, pp. 249–64) takes a different view, and maintains the priority of Mk. 10⁴⁵ and its Palestinian origin. But even if Mk. 10⁴⁵ does derive from a Palestinian tradition, it is a secondary saying compared with Lk. 22²⁷; Jeremias tries to avoid this conclusion by challenging any literary connection of the two passages and assigning Lk. 22²⁷ to a special source, in which Jesus is presented as ready for the footwashing (op. cit., p. 260). Ed. Lohse (*Märtyrer und Gottes-Knecht*, 1955, pp. 116–22) sees in Mk. 10⁴⁵ a kerygmatic formula of the primitive Palestinian church; the indications he lists of the Hellenistic origins of Lk. 22²⁴⁻²⁷ apply to vv. 24–26 only, but not to v. 27. H. W. Wolff (*Jesaja 53 im Urchristentum* (Diss. Halle), 1942, pp. 52–57) seeks to defend the genuineness of Mk. 10⁴⁵. Also for its genuineness is O. Cullmann, *Christologie des N.T.*, p. 64. Kümmel is sceptically against in *Verh. u. Erf.*, pp. 66f.

Page 145. *To the end of line 2 from the top add:* Cp. p. 142 on Mk. 9³⁷, ⁴¹.

To the end of paragraph 2 add: J. Héring (*Aux Sources*, pp. 95–102) sees in this the ancient Christian concept of the child.

To the end of paragraph 3 add: E. Lohmeyer (*Urchristentum*, I, 1932, p. 21, n. 1) thinks otherwise. So does Kraeling (*John the Baptist*, 1951, p. 197, n. 4); and Percy (*Die Botschaft Jesu*, 1953, pp. 9f.) seeks to trace Lk. 3¹⁰⁻¹⁴ back to the Baptist tradition. In the judgement of von Campenhausen (*Universitas*, 12, 1957, p. 1149, n. 3), 'we must note that the text does not refer to Christian soldiers, though its use in Luke is not without certain apologetic motives, in order to dispose of any political apprehensions about the new movement'.

Page 145, n. 1. *Add:* See Käsemann, *Nt. St.* 1 (1954/5), pp. 248–60, on expressions of holy right in the N.T., and also in *Z.Th.K.* 57 (1960), pp. 166f., 173, 181, specifically on Matt. 10⁵ᶠ·: here one hears 'the voice of the strictest kind of Jewish Christianity'.

Page 147. *To line 13 from the top add:* (Wellhausen's hypothesis, *Einleitung in die drei ersten Evangelien*², p. 27, that καθάρισον in Matt. 23²⁶ and δότε ἐλεημοσύνην in Lk. 11⁴¹ are variants deriving from the Aramaic *dakkau* or *zakkau*, is confirmed by Black, *Aram. Appr.*², p. 2. This means that an ancient tradition lies behind this passage.)

To line 3 from the bottom add: Matt. 5²³ᶠ· could have been taken over from Jewish tradition; for, according to Jeremias, *Z.N.W.*, 36, 1937, pp. 150–4, the meaning of the saying corresponds to the Jewish idea that the sacrifice is effective only on condition of repentance, which has to be demonstrated in the purging of fraternal relationships. Yet Jeremias believes that Matt. 5²³ᶠ· is an authentic saying of Jesus. Lk. 17³ᶠ· is in any event in the line of Jewish tradition, see G. F. Moore, *Judaism*, II, pp. 152f.

Page 148. *To line 14 from the bottom add* (after Matt. 5³²; 19⁹): (cp. H. Baltensweiler, *Th. Z. Basel* 15, 1959, pp. 340–56).

Page 149, n. 1. *Add:* Sundwall (op. cit., pp. 60–63) thinks that Mk. 9³³⁻³⁵ᵃ and ³⁶ are an editorial introduction. Crum gives a very bold analysis (*St. Mark's Gospel*, pp. 62f.): A hidden incident lay behind Mk. I, 9³³⁻³⁶; 10¹⁵, which was expanded by Mk. II (in Mk. I, 10¹³ᶠ·, ¹⁶ followed 10¹⁵). Only the introduction in 9³⁵ is ancient: καὶ καθίσας ἐφώνησεν τοὺς δώδεκα; then v. 36 follows.

Page 153. *To line 2 from the bottom add:* (Kümmel, *Verh. u. Erf.*, p. 63, is against the assumption of a *vaticinium ex eventu*.)
n. 1. *Add:* Cp. H. E. Tödt, *Der Menschensohn in der synopt. Überlieferung*, 1959; Ed. Schweitzer, *Z.N.W.* 50 (1959), pp. 185–209 and *J.B.L.* 79 (1960) pp. 119–29.

Page 154. *To the end of paragraph 2 add:* (In Black's view, *Aram. Appr.*², p. 89, τί θέλω is an aramaism.)

n. 1. *Add:* Jeremias (*Jesus als Weltvollender*, 1930, p. 70, n. 11) believes that it is the cosmos and not Jesus that is the object of baptism in v. 50. But that is not the case! R. Otto (*Reich Gottes u. Menschensohn*[2], p. 311) accepts Lk. 12[50] as genuine and sees in it a 'true prophetic presentiment'. Schniewind (*Rechtgläubigkeit u. Frömmigkeit*, I, 1938, p. 93) believes that Lk. 12[50] and Matt. 10[38] presuppose that John's baptism was a symbol of death. Similarly O. Cullmann (*Christologie des N.T.*, p. 66), who thinks that for Jesus 'to be baptized' meant the same as 'to die'.

Page 155. *To the end of paragraph 2 add:* So also Jeremias, *Gleichn.*, p. 139, n. 1.

To the end of paragraph 3 add: Lohmeyer (*Evg. d. Mk.*, ad loc.) thinks otherwise, and holds that Mk. 1[35-38] is a piece of Tradition, and v. 39 for an addition by Mark.

To line 3 from the bottom of page add: (Jeremias (*Jesu Verh. f. d. Völker*, p. 23) argues for the genuineness of Matt. 15[24].)

Page 156, n. 2. *To line 2 from the bottom add:* Examples from Greek literature for ἦλθον or ἥκω (Subj. a divinity): Hom. *Iliad*, 1.207; Eur. *Bacch.* 1f.; *Ion*, 5; *Or.* 1628. In prophetic style ἔρχομαι Pind. *Pyth.* 2.3f. Because Matt. 5[17] derives from the Jewish-Christian community, ἦλθον cannot be a sign of the Hellenistic language, if it is not introduced by translation; cp. *Pap. Egerton*, 10ff.: μὴ δ[οκεῖτε ὅ]τι ἐγὼ ἦλθον κατηγορῆσαι [ὑμῶν] with Jn. 5[45]: μὴ δοκεῖτε ὅτι ἐγὼ κατηγορήσω ὑμῶν. According to Käsemann (*Z.Th.K.* 57 (1960), p. 167), all sayings which begin with the words 'I have come' are secondary, they let one 'hear the exalted Lord through the mouth of the prophet'.

Page 157. *To line 7 from the bottom add:* (For the rest see below, p. 286.)

Page 158. *To line 16 from the bottom add:* (In the judgement of R. Otto, *Reich Gottes u. Menschensohn*, v. 19 characterizes the 'charismatic type', which possessed exemption from injuries.)

Page 159, n. 1. *Add:* There is no parallel to Lk. 22[30a] in Matthew and it could be an insertion by Luke, intended to assimilate the saying to the circumstances of a meal (Klostermann).

n. 4. *Add:* The saying is accepted as genuine, e.g. by Kümmel, 'Kirchenbegr. v. Geschichtsbew.', *Symbl. Bibl. Upsal.*, I, 1943, pp. 30f., 56; also *Verh. u. Erf.*, pp. 41, 81; by A. Fridrichsen, *The Apostle and his Message*, 1947, p. 18. From this, Fridrichsen infers that Jesus contemplated the thousand years Messianic kingdom; for the messianic kingdom under the rule of the twelve tribes cannot be thought of as the eternal age of salvation. R. Otto (*Reich Gottes u. Menschensohn*, pp. 228–33) also accepts the saying as genuine, and moreover believes Lk. 22[29f.] is the original continuation of 22[17-19a] (22, 28 are editorial transitions to assimilate the inserted sections (19b–20, 21–23, 24–27); nothing is thereby implied as to the relationship to Matt. 19²⁸! Yet the words ὑμεῖς οἱ ἀκολουθήσαντές μοι are confirmed by Luke's ὑμεῖς δέ ἐστε οἱ διαμεμνηκότες, and Matt. 19²⁸ shows that the saying was freely in circulation; why did Matthew wrest it from its real context? Against Otto see Dibelius, *Gött. Gel. Anz.*, 1936, p. 213. Against the genuineness of the saying, Vielhauer, *Festschr. f. G. Dehn*, pp. 61–64.

n. 5. *Add:* For questions concerning text criticism see Kümmel, *Verh. u. Erf.*, p. 35, n. 71: Percy, *Botschaft Jesu*, pp. 260–3; J. Bieneck, *Sohn Gottes als Christusbezeichnung der Synoptiker*, pp. 79–82, and esp. P. Winter, *Nov. Test.*, I, 1956, pp. 112–48.

Page 160. *To line 2 from the top add:* (Cp. J. B. Bauer, *Th. Z. Basel* 17, 1961, pp. 99–106, who produces interesting Babylonian parallels to vv. 28–30 and regards the short form of the saying in the Gospel of Thomas, Logion 90, as possibly the original one.)

To the end of paragraph 1 add: The sayings in Matt. 11²⁵⁻³⁰ are treated as genuine, e.g. by: W. Grundmann, *Jesus der Galiläer und das Judentum*, 1940, pp. 209–23; J. Bieneck, op. cit., pp. 75–87; E. Stauffer, *Background*, pp. 295f.; Percy, op. cit., pp. 259–71; O. Cullmann, *Christologie des N.T.*, pp. 292–4. Dibelius (*Formgesch.*², pp. 279–84) thinks that the three 'strophes' in Matt. 11²⁵⁻³⁰, notwithstanding their obviously divergent origins, constituted an unity in Q, combining both a self-commendation and sermonic demand; but that 'is the typical sign of a divine or semi-divine revealer in Hellenistic piety, that is to say, a mythical figure'. Kümmel (*Verh. u. Erf.*, p. 27) in my opinion rightly disputes the genuineness of Matt. 11²⁷ as a saying of Jesus. Dinkler (*Neutest. Studien f. R. Bultmann*, pp. 115–17) supports the view that Matt. 11²⁸⁻³⁰ derives from Jewish Wisdom Literature and so cannot be accounted a genuine saying of Jesus. Black (*Aram. Appr.*², pp. 140f.) tries, like others before him, to reconstruct the original Aramaic of these verses. T. Arvedson (*Das Mysterium Christi*, 1937) has failed in his interesting attempt to discover in Matt. 11²⁵⁻³⁰ the Liturgy of a Mystery with the Enthronement of Christ as its centre.

n. 1. *Add:* See in addition what has been added above to the text. J. Dupont (*Gnosis*, pp. 58–62) tries to interpret Matt. 11²⁷ in terms of Jewish apocalyptic.

n. 3. *Add:* E. Percy (*Botschaft Jesu*, p. 169) also supports the priority of Luke. T. W. Manson (*Teaching of Jesus*, pp. 237–43) supposes, hardly aright, that two different translations of the same Aramaic original lie behind Matthew and Luke.

Page 161, n. 1. *Add:* (1) On 'carrying the cross' see Percy, *Botschaft Jesu*, pp. 170–4; but most esp. see Dinkler, *Neutest. Studien f. R. Bultmann*, pp. 110–29, who offers a completely new interpretation. The saying in Lk. 14²⁷ par. is not a community formulation, but a saying of Jesus, which is linked to the cultic significance of

o*

Tau or Chi (τ or χ). Jesus demands 'the eschatological seal of the elect' and 'thereby leads his disciples back as his own or as his "sheep" into the absolute kingdom of God or of the "Shepherd" ' and thus makes them his followers. (2) On ἔρχεσθαι ὀπίσω see M. Smith, *Tannaitic Parallels to the Gospels*, 1951, p. 30 and n. 100–2, p. 44. On the literal sense of ἔρχ. ὀπ. cp. also L. Köhler, *Der hebräische Mensch*, 1953, p. 141. (3) On ἀπαρνεῖσθαι see A. Fridrichsen, *Coniect. Neotest.*, II, 1936, pp. 1–8; VI, 1942, pp. 94–96; ἀπαρν. ἑαυτόν is in all probability the Greek substitute for μισεῖν τὴν ψυχήν.

n. 2. *Add:* Similar to Windisch is R. Otto, *Reich Gottes u. Menschensohn*, p. 80. Much better is O. Perles, *Die Wunderüberlieferung der Synoptiker*, 1934, p. 20: Lk. 10^{18} is a parallel to Mk. 3^{27} (The Binding of the Strong Man). In the same way Kümmel (*Verh. u. Erf.*, pp. 106f.) believes that some visionary experience lies behind the formulation.

Page 162, n. 1. *Add:* On ἐν δακτύλῳ, see T. W. Manson, *The Teaching of Jesus*, pp. 82f. Cp. also, on Matt. 12^{28} par., Kümmel, *Verh. u. Erf.* pp. 98–101.

Page 164, n. 1. *Add:* According to A. Fridrichsen, *Coniect. Neotest.*, II, 1936, p. 45, the passage comes from the debate of the early church with the Jews on the question of exorcism of demons by Jesus. On the linguistic problems see H. S. Nyberg, ibid., pp. 22–35.

Page 165, n. 1. *Add:* Lohmeyer (*Urchrist.*, I, p. 19, n. 1) thinks that v. 11b is an addition by the Church, as it was reported of John's disciples that they called themselves 'great' (Ps. Clem. Rec., I, 59). F. Dibelius (*Z.N.W.*, 10, 1910, pp. 190–2) has argued for the interpretation of the early Church that the μικρότερος in v. 11 is Jesus. This is again repeated by O. Michel, *Th. St. Kr.*, 108, 1937/8, pp. 412–15, and O. Cullmann, *Coniect. Neotest.*, XI, 1947, p. 30, and *Christologie des N.T.*, pp. 23 and 31. The meaning is: 'He who is less (sc. Jesus, i.e. as pupil) is greater than he (sc. John) in the Kingdom of heaven.' The verb βιάζεται is taken by most exegetes as a passive, and then the βιασταί can be the demonic powers (M. Dibelius) or the Jewish opponents (so, e.g., Schrenk, *Th.W.B.*, I, 610) or the Zealots (so Cullmann, *Der Staat im N.T.*, 1956, p. 14) or the Baptist community (so A. Fridrichsen, *Th.Z.*, II, 1946, pp. 470f.), or the question may be left open (so Kümmel, *Verh. u. Erf.*). Percy (*Botsch. Jesu.*, pp. 191–7) reads βιάζεται as a middle: 'makes its way'; the βιασταί are then the men who fight with their utmost strength to attain the kingdom of God. Percy has a detailed discussion of the different points of view. Käsemann, in *Z.Th.K.* 51 (1954), p. 149 or in *Exeget. Versuche und Besinnungen* I, 1960, p. 210, regards Matt. 11$^{12f.}$ (and parallels) as an authentic saying of Jesus. He understands the βιασταί as 'men of force', without further comment. Cp. also G. Baumann, *Z.N.W.* 62 (1961), pp. 104–9; W. Trilling, *Bibl. Z.*, N.F. 3, 1959, pp. 275–9; O. Betz, *Nov. Test.* 2, 1958, pp. 125–8; on the parallel Lk. 16^6, see Fr. W. Danker, *J.B.L.* 77 (1958), pp. 231–45 and E. Bammel, *H.T.R.* 51, 1958, pp. 101–6, who makes out a case for a Baptist-origin for v. 16 (and 17f.).

Page 166. *In line 4 from the top of paragraph 2 add:* (Especially cp. M. Black, *Aram. Appr.*^{2}, 1954.)

In line 9 from the top of paragraph 2 add: P. Winter (*Nov. Test.* 1, 1956, pp. 112–48) disputes the view that Matt. 11[27]/Lk. 10[22] is a Hellenistic formulation, and reconstructs the original Hebrew text.

In line 4 from the bottom add: (Cp. A. Fischer, *Ausdrücke* per Merismum *im Arabischen*, Streitberg-Festgabe, 1924, pp. 46–58; Joh. Pedersen, *Rev. H. Ph. Rel.*, 1930, p. 352.)

Page 167, n. 1. *Add:* R. Eisler ('Ἰησοῦς βασιλεύς, II, 1930) wants (as K. Furrer, *Zeitschr. f. Missionskunde u. Religionswiss.*, 1890) to read 'well' for 'eye' (both עַיִן) and interprets: He whose well-house is so much in decay that a whole beam has fallen into the water has no right to object to the splinter floating in his neighbour's well.' This is as grotesque as the hypothesis of G. B. King, *H.T.R.*, 26, 1953, pp. 73–76, who supposes that there has been a mistranslation; the splinter is the splinter between the brother's teeth.

Page 170. *To the end of paragraph 5 add:* Cp. H. Greeven, 'Wort und Dienst', *Jahrb. d. Theol. Schule Bethel*, N.F.3, 1952, pp. 86–101, esp. p. 96.

n. 1. *Add:* Jeremias (*Die Gleichnisse Jesu*[4], 1956, pp. 195–8) contains a list of the abundant literature in the parables. Special attention must be paid to C. H. Dodd, *Parables*[10], 1950. The most I can add to this is the contribution of R. Pautrel, '*Les canons du* mashal *rabbinique*', *Rech. de science rel.*, 26, 1936, pp. 5–45; 28, 1938, pp. 264–81.

Page 171. *To the end of paragraph 1 add:* Jeremias (*Gleichn.*, p. 94, n. 1) (with reservations) and H. Braun (*Radikalismus*, II, p. 33, n. 9) also think that Lk. 14[33] is a secondary addition.

To line 4 of paragraph 2 add: Cp. H. Greeven, op. cit., pp. 97f.

To the end of paragraph 2 add: On the relationship of Matthew to Luke who has retained the original meaning, see Jeremias, *Gleichn.*, pp. 28–31; in Luke the parable is directed to the Pharisees and Scribes, but in Matthew to the disciples.

To the end of paragraph 3 add: Jeremias (*Gleichn.*, pp. 40f.) seeks to retain the originality of the parable (which was occasioned by an insurrection which shortly followed it) at the cost of eliminating the Son of man in v. 40, or replacing him with the eschatological catastrophe. Against this view Vielhauer (*Festschr. f. G. Dehn*, p. 66) rightly says: 'the warning presupposes the postponement of the Parousia and proves that the parable is a Church formulation'.

To the end of paragraph 4 add: See above, p. 119.

Page 172. *To the end of paragraph 2 add:* Cp. Jeremias, *Gleichn.*, pp. 32f.: while the parable is in Luke a parable of crisis ('before very long you will appear before the judge') Matthew has changed it into paraenesis—a view already advanced by Dodd, *Parables*[10], pp. 136–9. W. L. Knox (*Sources*, II, pp. 74f.) seeks to interpret the passage as also a warning to come to terms with the Roman authority, a position which I think absurd.

To the end of paragraph 4 add: In the judgement of R. Leivestad, *J.B.L.*, 71, 1952, pp. 178–81, σοφία in Luke is the divine wisdom, while in Matt. 11[19], who preserves the original, σοφία is used ironically and signifies the wisdom of the Jews.

To the end of paragraph 5 add: Lohmeyer (*Evg. d. Mk.*, ad loc.) thinks that Mk. 4[30-32] combines two variants of the same parable—which is not convincing. Dodd (*Parables*[10], pp. 189–91) thinks the Q version preserved intact by Luke is original and believes that the parable speaks of the growth of God's kingdom which has now reached its fulfilment. So too W. L. Knox (*Sources*, II, p. 79, n. 1). Kümmel (*Verh. u. Erf.*., pp. 122–4) rightly points out to the contrary: the point of the parable is not the growth or development, but the contrast of the small beginning and the great end, as the Matthew-version shows, and which is more original than the Q version. Jeremias accepts the same interpretation (*Gleichn.*, pp. 127–30).

To the end of paragraph 6 add: Jeremias (op. cit., p. 68) and Kümmel (op. cit., p. 124) maintain that the parables of the mustard seed and the leaven originally belonged together. Dodd (op. cit., p. 192) doubts this. So too H.-W. Bartsch, *Th. Z. Basel* 15, 1959, pp. 126–8, who tries to prove that Mk. 4[30] is a quotation of Isa. 40[18] and as such makes clear the general significance of parabolic language.

n. 1. *Add:* Streeter is followed by Sundwall (op. cit., p. 28), Schniewind (ad loc.), and Lohmeyer (ad loc.). R. Otto (*Reich Gottes u. Menschensohn.*, p. 88) has an original but unconvincing view: Mk. 4[26-29] is the continuation of vv. 3–8, whose point is first made in the continuation.

Page 173. *To the end of paragraph 1 add:* R. Harder (*Theologia Viatorum*, 1948/9, pp. 51–70) deals with Mk. 4[26-29] in detail and with reference to interpretations since Jülicher.

To the end of paragraph 4 add: Dodd (*Parables*[10], pp. 187–9) and Jeremias (*Gleichn.*, p. 72) think that the application in vv. 49f. is an addition by Matthew. Kümmel (*Verh. u. Erf.*, pp. 129f.) admits that the formulation might derive from Matthew but thinks that vv. 49f. are the actual end of the parable, while Dodd holds that the parable is improperly turned into an eschatological one by these verses. Originally they referred to the mission of the disciples (as 'fishers of men') in reaction to whose preaching the division came about of which the parable speaks. Against this Kümmel (op. cit.) rightly says: the division takes place at the last judgement. Jeremias (pp. 189–91) also interprets the parable eschatologically, and furthermore takes it as going with Matt. 13[24-30] to form one double parable.

To line 2 from the bottom add: On the question whether Mk. 13[28-29] is a parallel of Lk. 12[54-56] see above, p. 123.

Page 174. *To the end of paragraph 1 add:* As to whether Mk. 13[34-37] and Lk. 12[35-38] are parallels see above, p. 119.

Page 175. *To the end of paragraph 2 add:* On this form see H. Greeven, *Wort und Dienst*, 1952, pp. 86–101, esp. pp. 91f., 97.

To the end of paragraph 3 add: Kümmel (*Verh. u. Erf.*, p. 52) and Jeremias (*Gleichn.*, pp. 133–6) uphold the view that vv. 6–8a were originally part of the parable, and the latter would include also v. 8b. W. L. Knox (*Sources*, II, pp. 112f.) disputes the originality of vv. 6–8, and indeed thinks that vv. 6 and 7 are the later edited form of the original conclusion, but that by contrast v. 8 is an appended dominical saying.

To line 6 from foot of page add: Dodd (*Parables*[10], pp. 120–2) and Jeremias (*Gleichn.*, pp. 37–40, 56–59) also believe that Matt. vv. 11–14 and Lk. vv. 22f. are additions, the latter also including vv. 6f. Jeremias sees in vv. 11–14 an originally independent parable. It is improbable, as T. W. Manson (*The Teaching of Jesus*, p. 85) holds, that in Matt. v. 6 there is hidden what remains of a lost parable related to the parable of the vineyard. On the interpretation of the parable see E. Linnemann, *Z.N.W.* 51 (1960), pp. 246–55, and W. Trilling, *Bibl. Z.*, N.F. 4, 1960, pp. 251–65.

Page 176. *To the end of paragraph 1 add:* Dodd (*Parables*[10], pp. 30f.) and Jeremias take the verses 8b–12 as additions, giving different interpretations. Dodd thinks that possibly v. 8a is the original end of the parable, and Jeremias that it is certainly so, as seems probable to me. Percy (*Botsch. Jesu*, pp. 166f.) rates vv. 8 and 9 as original, and W. L. Knox (*Sources*, II, pp. 93f.) at least v. 8. An analysis and interpretation of the parable by J. D. M. Derrett, *Nt. St.* 7 (1960/61), pp. 198–219.

To the end of paragraph 2 add: Dodd (*Parables*[10], pp. 146–53) and Jeremias (*Gleichn.*, pp. 50–55, 144) both think that the parable was originally directed against the Pharisees or the Scribes, who failed to make the treasure entrusted to them productive. Matthew, like Luke, turned it into an eschatological parable, and this is clear from the allegorical verses 21, 23, 30 in Matthew, and in Luke from its being combined with the allegory of the 'Pretenders to the throne' (which, according to Jeremias, was originally an independent parable. The paraenetic verses Matt. 25, 29 = Lk. 19, 26 had already grown on to the parable as Matthew and Luke knew it. According to Black (*Aram. Appr.*[2], pp. 2f.) there is an Aramaic version behind the text, as the variants Matt. 25[21f.] and Lk. 19[17] show.

To the end of the page add: Verse 13 cannot be original; for in vv. 1–12 it is not being asleep, but lack of due preparation that is censured. Dodd (*Parables*[10], pp. 172f.) and Jeremias (*Gleichn.*, pp. 43–45) think that Matt. 25[1–15] was not originally an allegory with the theme of a (postponed) parousia of the Son of man, but a 'parable of crisis', a 'summons in face of the imminent eschatological crisis'. Against this view is G. Bornkamm (*In Memoriam Ernst Lohmeyer*, pp. 119–26): Matt. 25[1–12] is a Church formulation in view of the postponement of the Parousia. F. A. Strobel, *Nov. Test.* 2 (1958), pp. 199–227, explains the parable as the expression of the Quartodecimans' Passover-expectation.

n. 1. *Add:* The term 'Son of Light' has now been found in heretical Judaism, as the texts from the Dead Sea show; see H. Braun, *Radikalismus*, II, p. 391, n. 1.

n. 2. *Add:* Cp. esp. G. Bornkamm, *In Memoriam Ernst Lohmeyer*, p. 121.

Page 177. *To the end of paragraph 1 add:* Dodd (*Parables*[10], pp. 183–6), Jeremias (*Gleichn.*, pp. 189–91) and Kümmel (*Verh. u. Erf.*, pp. 125–8) take the same view. Jeremias believes that Matt. 13[24–30] belong together in one double parable; see above, p. 173, on Matt. 13[47–50]. W. L. Knox (*Sources*, II, p. 130) thinks that Matt. 13[24–30] is the edited form of an older parable. He proposes the deletion of Matt. 13[25, 27, 28a] and the changing of αὐτῷ in 28b to τῷ οἰκοδεσπότῃ.

To the end of paragraph 3 add: Dodd and Jeremias also think Matt. 20[6] is an addition (especially in some textual traditions of 6b). W. L. Knox (*Sources*, II, pp. 134f.) believes that the original parable has been adapted to the theory of the five ages of the world (see Jeremias); originally there could have been but two, and at most three hirings.

To the end of paragraph 4 add: Dodd, like Jeremias, contests the view that Mk. 12$^{1-9}$ is an allegory, even if the section already contained some traces of allegory by the time of Mark, and was further allegorized by Matthew and Luke. Kümmel rightly opposes this (*Verh. u. Erf.*, pp. 75f., and in *Aux Sources*, pp. 120–31); The section is Church formulation, an allegorical presentation of the history of salvation. The secondary character of Mk. 12$^{10f.}$ is also maintained against Jeremias by Vielhauer (*Oikodome*, p. 60). On the appendix Matt. 21$^{43f.}$ see R. Swaeles, *Nt. St.* 6 (1959/60), pp. 310–13.

To line 2 from foot of page add: Jeremias also takes Matt. 21^{32} as a secondary addition, but one which Matthew found in his source, a point which G. Bornkamm (*The Background*, p. 236, n. 2) doubts. A different view is taken by A. Schlatter (*Jahrb. d. Theol. Schule Bethel*, II, 1931) who relates the parable to Lk. 15$^{11-32}$ in the history of the tradition.

Page 178. *To the end of paragraph 2 add:* A mistaken analysis of the parable of the Good Samaritan by H. Binder, *Th. Z. Basel* 15 (1959), pp. 176–94.

To the end of paragraph 3 add: Dibelius (*Formgesch.*, p. 258) also reckons Lk. 12^{21} as a secondary addition.

Page 179. *To line 2 from top add:* Dibelius (*Formgesch.*, p. 254) also takes Lk. 18^{14b} to be a secondary addition.

n. 1. *Add:* On introductory formulae see Jeremias, *Gleichn.*, pp. 85–88.

Page 181. *To end of paragraph 1 add:* On the question of τίς ἐξ ὑμῶν (Matt. 7^9; Lk. 17^7), which has no rabbinic parallels, see H. Greeven, 'Wort u. Dienst', *Jahrb. d. Theol. Schule Bethel*, 1952, pp. 86ff.; G. Bornkamm, *Jesus von Nazareth*, 1956, pp. 63f.

n. 1. *Add:* Metaphors or parables in interrogatory form, e.g. also in Job 6$^{5f.}$; 8^{11}; Hebr. 12^{7b}; Lucr., *De Rerum Natura*, III, 6–8. In the judgement of Fridrichsen, *Symb. Osl.*, 12, 1934, pp. 40ff., Lk. 11$^{5-7}$ as a whole is to be understood as a question.

Page 183. *To line 9 from the bottom add:* There are Egyptian examples in Theod. Hopfner, *Plutarch über Isis und Osiris*, I, 1940, pp. 112f.; K. Ranke, 'Die Zwei Brüder', *Folklore Fellows Communications*, 114, 1934, p. 252; Grimm, *Kinder- u. Hausmärchen*, No. 135.

Page 185. *To line 14 from the bottom add:* Examples of the use *e contrario* may be found, e.g. in Homer, *Il.*, 14, 394ff.; Vergil, *Aen.*, 12, 921ff.; Rückert, *Die Weisheit des Brahmanen*, II, p. 4; Hölderlin, 'Froh kehrt der Schiffer heim. . .' .

Page 186. *In line* 1 *add:* See Jeremias, *Gleichn.*, pp. 88–96, on the tendency of the tradition to attach an application to parables having no interpretation, or to change or enlarge upon a given interpretation, especially by adding generalizing sayings as conclusion

Page 187. *To the end of paragraph* 2 *add:* Dodd (*Parables*[10], pp. 181f., 183f.) and Jeremias (*Gleichn.*, pp. 65–67, 69–72) consider Mk. 4^{13-20}; Matt. 13^{36-43} secondary. On the secondary character of Matt. 13^{36-43} see also Kümmel, *Verh. u. Erf.*, pp. 125f.

n. 3. *To line* 1 *add:* (So Dodd, Jeremias and G. Bornkamm in *The Background*, p. 253, n. 4).

Page 192. *To line* 2 *from the bottom add:* (According to W. L. Knox, *Sources*, II, p. 112, Lk. 19^{11} was in Luke's source and was the reason for his putting the parable at this place in the gospel.)

Page 193. *In line* 4 *from the top add:* (see above, p. 178, n. 2.)

In line 5 *from the bottom of paragraph* 1 *add:* Yet perhaps Mark used an ancient piece of tradition; see above, pp. 173f.

To the end of paragraph 1 *add:* Jeremias (*Gleichn.*, p. 84) and W. L. Knox (*Sources*, II, p. 67) have the same judgement on Lk. 12^{41}.

In line 3 *from the top of paragraph* 2 *add:* (On the secondary context, editorial pointers to the situation and transitions, see Jeremias, *Gleichn.*, pp. 81–84.)

Page 196. *In line* 12 *from the bottom add:* While in Ed. Schweizer's opinion (*Th.Z.*, 4, 1948, pp. 469–71) Lk. 15^{11-16} semitizes, according to Jeremias (ibid., 1949, pp. 228–31, and then again to the contrary Schweizer, ibid., pp. 231–3) and W. L. Knox (*Sources*, II, pp. 90–92) the whole parable is full of Semitisms. Jeremias (*Gleichn.*, pp. 115f.) holds that the emphasis is on the second half of the parable, where 'the justification of the good news becomes a reproach and a plea in the hearts of its critics'.

n. 1. *To line* 3 *from the top add:* Cp. also Isidore Lévy, *La Légende de Pythagore de Grèce en Palestine*, 1927, pp. 310–12. *To the end of the note add:* Cp. the analysis and interpretation of J. D. M. Derrett, *Nt. St.* 7 (1960/61), pp. 364–80.

Page 197. *In line* 2 *from the bottom of paragraph* 1 *add:* Jeremias thinks that the emphasis is on the second half. While the first part teaches the reversal of destinies in the other world, the second provides a basis for the rejection of the request for a sign. But these two themes nevertheless do not form a unity!

n. 3. *Add:* Cp. also Ginza L., III, 53, p. 583, 15ff. Lidzb.

Page 198, n. 2. *Add:* In such cases it seems pointless not to say confusing to me to talk of 'semi-allegorical forms' (Dibelius, *Formg.*, pp. 256f.).

Page 199. *In line 4 from the bottom of paragraph 1 add:* The genuineness of Mk. 4^{10-12} can be maintained only on the presupposition that they contain a mistranslation from the aramaic which turns the original meaning into its opposite. This was the view of T. W. Manson (*The Teaching of Jesus,*[2] 1935, pp. 75–80) who by referring to the relationship between v. 12 and the Targum version of Isa. $6^{9f.}$ postulated a positive meaning for v. 12 and accepted οἵ instead of ἵνα as the correct translation. Jeremias (*Gleichn.*, pp. 7–12) has developed this thesis and tried to show that μήποτε in v. 12 means 'unless', that vv. 11f. did not originally refer to the parables but to Jesus' preaching generally, characterizing it as 'puzzling', and that it was put into its present context on the basis of a wrong association of sayings. Catholic scholars have tried in a number of investigations to establish the genuineness of Mk. 4^{10-12} and to contest the theory of 'secrecy' and 'hardening' which was condemned as a 'modernist' error by the decree 'Lamentabili' of 3. vii. 1907 (Denziger, *Enchiridion*, 2013); cp. the comprehensive essay by U. Holzmeister, *Biblica*, 15, 1934, pp. 321–64.

To end of paragraph 1 add: Jülicher's merit in recognizing allegories or allegorical traces as secondary is acknowledged by Dodd, as well as by Jeremias (cp. esp. Jeremias, *Gleichn.*, pp. 74f.). Lohmeyer's attempt (*Z. Syst. Th.*, 15, 1938, pp. 319–46) to question the distinction between parable and allegory altogether I can only regard as a failure. The particular difference in the understanding of parable represented by Dodd and Jeremias from that of Jülicher is not concerned with the contrast of parable and allegory, but consists in the criticism that Jülicher finds universal religious or moral truths illustrated in the parables, instead of seeing in them answers to questions arising on occasion out of the concrete historical situation of Jesus or his hearers. The parables are to be understood in the light of Jesus' eschatological message and the problems it aroused. For Dodd they are evidence of a 'realized eschatology', for Jeremias of an eschatology realizing itself. Cp. esp. Dodd, op. cit., pp. 24–26,

Jeremias, op. cit., pp. 12–16. Further, N. A. Dahl, *Stud. Theol.*, V, 1951, pp. 132–6. However the interpretation of parables in terms of the ministry of Jesus need not in any way contradict the interpretation which sees them expressing universal religious or moral truths, for the concrete situation could have given many an opportunity to imprint them on the mind.

Page 200, n. 1. *Add:* Jülicher is right: Lk. 16$^{1-8}$, like Lk. 11$^{57-59}$, teaches the proper use of time in the last moment. It is a mistake to interpret only through vv. 9–12 as if the parable taught the proper valuation of earthly goods. Jeremias (*Gleichn.*, pp. 24–36, 149f.) is right. Gerda Krüger (*Bibl. Z.*, 21, 1933, pp. 170–81) takes vv. 8b, 9 into the parable and sees its point in a *conclusio a minori ad maius* from the unjust steward to the 'sons of light'. H. Preisker (*Th.L.Z.*, 74, 1949, pp. 85–92) seeks to interpret the parable in terms of a correlation with Lk. 15^{11} and 16^{16} as a warning against the deceitfulness of riches.

n. 2 *Add:* On the parables about seed cf. Dahl, op. cit. He seeks to prove that Jesus (like the O.T. and N.T. in general) has the idea of the organic growth of seed, and so made it possible to interpret all seed parables in conformity with the eschatological teaching of Jesus, which proclaimed at one and the same time the future kingdom of God and its secret present reality. But is it possible to think of the apocalyptic idea according to which many events should happen before the eschatological fulfilment, as an organic growth? It is only thanks to this interpretation that Dahl secures his proposition of the present reality of the Kingdom of God in the ministry of Jesus.

n. 3. *Add:* Jeremias (*Gleichn.*, pp. 127–30) and Kümmel (*Verh. u. Erf.*, pp. 122–5) rightly refuse to see in the parables of the mustard seed and the leaven any idea of development and find the point in the contrast of small beginning and great end. But it is doubtful to me whether it is right to see the beginning in the small group of Jesus' disciples and the great end the universal people of God in the final time of salvation (which is the understanding of Jeremias). But in any case I hold Dahl's interpretation (op. cit., pp. 147–9) to be wrong, that namely, the parables are intended to show the organic unity between Jesus' ministry in Israel and the future Kingdom of God. See also above, pp. 172f.

n. 4. *Add:* Cp. esp. also Eccl. 10^1 or (so Budde) 9^{18b}, 10^1.

n. 5. *Add:* Jeremias (*Gleichn.*, pp. 132f.) and Kümmel (*Verh. u. Erf.*, pp. 120–2) see in Mk. 4$^{26-29}$ an express reference to the sure coming of the Kingdom of God ('when the eschatological measure is fulfilled'—so Jeremias). While in Jeremias the parable exhorts to patience, in Kümmel it is meant to console. See also above, p. 173.

Page 202, n. 1. *Add:* On Matt. 6^{24} see E. Johannsen and P. Döring, 'Das Leben der Schambala, beleuchtet durch ihre Sprichwörter', *Zeitschr. f. Kolonialkunde*, V, 1915, No. 365, p. 48: 'One mouth cannot taste two sorts of broth at the same time'; No. 516, p. 61: 'Eating and flute-playing do not agree'.

Page 203. *In line 3 of paragraph 2 add:* (Jeremias sees an original complete parable in Matt. 22$^{11-13}$; see above, p. 175.)

Page 209. *In line 3 from the bottom add:* (Lohmeyer, ad loc., thinks v. 28 is the original.) On the meaning of the speech cp. Ed. Schweizer, *Festschr. f. J. Jeremias, B.Z.N.W.* 26, 1960, pp. 90–93, and Frz. Mussner, *Bibl. Z.*, N.F. 4, 1960, pp. 285f., who reach similar conclusions.

n. 1. *Add:* H. J. Ebeling (*Das Messiasgeheimnis u. die Botschaft des Marcus-Evangelisten,* 1939, pp. 127f.) is right to dissent from Lohmeyer who (ad loc.) thinks of the demon's speech as 'indeterminate'.

Page 210, n. 2. *Add:* Dibelius (*Formg.*, p. 70) is in all probability right in holding v. 17 as the original end of the story; vv. 18–20 come from Mark. R. H. Lightfoot (*Hist. and Interp.*, pp. 88f.) thinks that v. 15 is the original conclusion; v. 16 serves to bind it with the following story, and vv. 18–20 are a further addition. Sundwall (op. cit., p. 31) proposes to put v. 8 after v. 10. Crum (*St. Mark's Gospel,* p. 21) takes both vv. 6–8 and vv. 18–20 as editorial additions. W. L. Knox (*Sources*, I, p. 40) sees v. 8 as an unhappy addition by Mark to his source.

n. 3. *Add:* The evil is sent into natures where it generally has a home. Swine reckon as demonic animals. Hence we find in Franconian the command to the gout: 'Go into the swine, free me from my pain!' in Eugen Fehrle, *Zauber u. Segen*, 1926, p. 16.

Page 211. *To the end of paragraph 1 add:* On the words ἦλθες . . . πρὸ καιροῦ added by Matthew to 8^{29} see G. Bornkamm, *Mythos u. Legende in den apokr. Thomas-Akten*, 1933, pp. 41f.

In line 6 from the bottom add: (Sundwall (op. cit., pp. 58–60) thinks that only vv. 20–27 are a story from the tradition; vv. 14–19, with 28, are editorial additions by Mark. H. J. Ebeling (op. cit., pp. 172f.) wrongly resists separation of the narrative by literary criticism.

n. 5 from p. 210. *Add at end:* Dibelius (*Formg.*, pp. 85–87) rejects the interpretation of the story by a fairy-tale motif. The passage of the demons into the swine is only meant to demonstrate the reality of the miracle, and the name 'Legion' to illustrate its greatness. In the view of W. L. Knox (*Sources*, I, p. 39) the basis of the story is an originally heathen aetiological myth, explaining how swine (or other sacrifice) were thrown from a rock into a lake or river as a purificatory sacrifice. Not very likely! There is a story about a herd of swine hunted by a demon in No. 507 of Jos. Müller, *Sagen aus Uri*, II, 1929.

Page 212. *To line 2 from the top add:* Dibelius (*Formg.*, p. 77, n. 1) shows how Matthew has edifyingly restyled the narrative by omitting the prescription of Mk. 9^{29} and introducing a saying about having faith like a grain of mustard seed in v. 20 = Matt. 17^{20}//Lk. 17^{6}.

n. 2. *Add:* Dibelius (*Formg.*, p. 70) also thinks that the injunction to keep silent originally belonged to the story: The healing first became valid when the priestly requirements had been met and the sacrifice made. On the contrary Lohmeyer (ad loc.), who takes v. 44 as belonging to the ancient story, interprets εἰς μαρτύριον αὐτοῖς for a(n accusing) testimony against the unbelieving priests, while Strathmann (*Th.W.B.*, IV, pp. 509, 8ff.) interprets it as a piece of prosecutor's evidence of the unbelief of the people.

Page 213. *In line 2 from the bottom of paragraph 2 add:* (According to Dibelius, *Formg.*, p. 72, Mark is also the source of v. 37.)

In line 5 of paragraph 3, after 'Bethsaida certainly is not' *add:* So also Lohmeyer, ad loc.

In line 8 of paragraph 3 add: (Otherwise Lohmeyer, ad loc., and H. J. Ebeling, op. cit., pp. 140f.)

In line 7 from the bottom of page add: (On the question of localization see Dibelius, *Formg.*, pp. 49f., and P. Ketter, *Biblica*, 15, 1934, pp. 411–18.)

In line 3 from the bottom of page add: Sundwall (op. cit., p. 69) tries to unravel the original story. The details of the pericope are clearly worked out by Lohmeyer (ad loc.).

Page 214. *To the end of paragraph 2 add:* Sundwall (op. cit., pp. 32f.) believes that v. 21 is editorial and thinks that the original introduction to the story of the woman with the issue of blood is v. 24. Otherwise he separates vv. 37 and 43a from the rest and considers that ἀκούσασα-ἐλθοῦσα in v. 27 is in all probability an insertion. H. J. Ebeling (op. cit., pp. 134f.) wants to retain v. 43a.

n. 1. *Add:* Against A. Meyer: Dibelius, *Formg.*, p. 220, n. 1. Sundwall (op. cit., p. 35) also thinks that Mark has interwoven the two stories together.

Page 215. *In line 5 from the top of paragraph 3 add:* Dibelius (*Formg.*, p. 71) thinks that v. 13 is an addition by Luke, as is the end of v. 15: καὶ ἔδωκεν κτλ.

To the end of the section add: W. L. Knox (*Sources*, I, p. 41, n. 2) contests the Hellenistic character of the story on account of the semitic parataxis.

n. 2. *Add:* Dibelius (*Formg.*, p. 76, n. 1) cites a modern example (report of a healing at Lourdes).

Page 216. *To the end of paragraph 1 add:* G. Bornkamm ('Wort u. Dienst', *Jahrb. der Theol. Schule Bethel*, NF1, 1948, pp. 49–54) shows that the Matthew version does not depend upon an older Mark text, but owes its form to Matthew who from theological motives has turned the stilling of the storm from a nature miracle into a type of discipleship by modifying the Mark text and transposing it into another context; the substitution of 'men' for disciples in Matt. 8²⁷ is explained by the men being the representatives of those to whom the story applied in preaching. The symbolic meaning of the pericope is also treated by G. Bornkamm in *The Background (Festschr. f. Dodd)*, p. 239.

In line 17 *from the top of paragraph* 2 *add:* (J. Leipoldt (*Th.L.Z.*, 1948, p. 741) is in all probability right in thinking that Mk. 6⁴⁸ᶠᶠ· originally described a manifestation of the risen Lord.)

In line 19 *from the top of paragraph* 2 *add:* Dibelius (*Formg.*, p. 77) also traces v. 52 back to the evangelists, whereas H. J. Ebeling (op. cit., pp. 150f.) proposes that it be kept as an integral element of the story.

Page 217. *To the end of paragraph* 1 *add:* K. Petersen (*Z.N.W.*, 32, 1933, pp. 217f.) seeks to support the oft-repeated idea that the feeding stories were influenced by the account of the Last Supper. G. H. Boobyer (*J.T.S.*, N.S. 3, 1952, pp. 161–71) rightly opposes the view that they just symbolically represent the eucharist.

To the third line of paragraph 2 *add:* G. Ziener (*Bibl. Z.*, N.F. 4, 1960, pp. 282–5) tries to find a reason for the two-fold elaboration of the history of the feeding in the pre-Markan tradition.

Page 218. *To the end of paragraph* 2 *add:* The view that the story—perhaps grown out of a parable—gives a symbolic representation of the judgement on Jerusalem and the Temple or, alternatively, the Jewish people, is adopted e.g. by L. Brun, *Segen u. Fluch im Urchristentum*, pp. 75f.; R. H. Lightfoot, *Hist. and Interp.*, p. 86, n. 2; Dodd, *Parables*, p. 63, n. 1; Dibelius, *Botschaft u. Gesch.*, I, p. 351; W. L. Knox, *Sources*, I, p. 82. The last author believes that the story arose from the parable in Lk. 13⁶⁻⁹. Another view in Lohmeyer, ad loc. Yet cp. W. H. P. Hatch, 'The Cursing of the Fig Tree', *Journ. Pal. Or. Soc.*, III, 1923, pp. 7–12. C. W. F. Smith, *J.B.L.* 79 (1960), pp. 315–27.

n. 1. *Add:* On the relationship of Lk. 5¹⁻¹¹ to Jn. 21¹⁻¹⁴ see further L. Brun, *Symb. Osl.*, XI, 1932, pp. 35–54; Goguel, *H.T.R.*, 25, 1932, pp. 21–25; Dibelius, *Formg.*, p. 110. All these scholars think that Lk. 5¹⁻¹¹ was not originally a resurrection story, projected by Luke into the ministry, which, however, I think probable (*Das Evg. des Joh.*, p. 545).

n. 2. *Add:* Cp. Rud. Meyer, 'Der Ring des Polykrates, Mt. 17²⁷ u. die rabbin. Uberlieferung', *Oriental. Lit. Z.*, 40, 1937, pp. 665ff.

n. 3. *Add:* Cp. further: Otto Perels, *Die Wunderüberlieferung der Synoptiker in ihrem Verhältnis zur Wortüberlieferung*, 1934. Alan Richardson, *The Miracle Stories of the Gospels*, 1942. Lawrence J. McGinley, *Form Criticism of the Synoptic Healing Narratives*, 1944 (directed against Form Criticism). Georges Crespy, *La Guérison par la foi*, 1952.

Page 219, n. 1. *Add:* Cp. of course Acts 10³⁸: ὃς διῆλθεν εὐεργετῶν κτλ, and alongside it Acts 2²²: Ἰησοῦν τ. Ναζ., ἄνδρα ἀποδεδειγμένον ἀπὸ τοῦ θεοῦ εἰς ὑμᾶς δυνάμεσι καὶ τέρασι καὶ σημείοις.

n. 3. *Add:* Cp. also Ludwig Bieler, ΘΕΙΟΣ ΑΝΗΡ, I, 1935, pp. 113–16.

Page 220, n. 3. *Add:* Cp. Rud. Herzog, 'Die Wunderheilungen von Epidauros', *Philol. Suppl.*, 22, 1931; R. Nehrbass, 'Sprache u. Stil. der Jamata von Epidauros', *Philol. Suppl.*, 27, 1935.

n. 4. *Add:* In the 2nd Edition of his *Formgeschichte* Dibelius has much expanded the section on the topic of the miracle stories: pp. 78–88. Ibid., pp. 169–72 on the scheme of the miracle stories of Epidauros and their analogies to the synoptic miracle stories.

Page 221. *To line* 13 *from bottom add:* Cp. Schweiz., *Arch. f. Volkskunde*, 43, p. 302.

n. 1. *Add:* Strack-B., II, pp. 15–17 (on Mk. 7³³); Scheftelowitz, *Altpaläst. Bauernglaube*, pp. 120f.

Page 222. *To the end of paragraph* 2 *add:* On ἐφίστασθαι see also *Fab. Aesop.*, 90b, p. 44, Halm; Lucian, *Icarom.*, 13.

To line 9 *from the bottom add:* On the gesture of touching see *R.A.C.*, III, cols. 404–21 s.v. Contactus, esp. cols. 416–19. On touching the garment: T. Canaan, *Journ. Pal. Or. Soc.*, 7, 1927, p. 41.

Page 223. *To the end of paragraph* 2 *add:* Eur., *Iph. T.*, 1337f. (κατῆδε βάρβαρα μέλη μαγεύουσα). Cp. also Dibelius, *Formg.*, p. 81.

n. 2. *Add:* On demon exorcism see also G. Bornkamm, *Mythos u. Legende in den apokr. Thomas-Akten*, 1933, pp. 39f.

Page 224. *In line* 5 *of paragraph* 1 *add:* Cp. *Sagen aus Baselland*, 1938, p. 136: A spirit expelled from a bottle was able to choose his own dwelling, and chose it under a great wine cask.

To line 4 *from bottom add:* On the secrecy of the miracle see also Dibelius, *Formg.*, pp. 91f.

Page 225. *In line* 3 *from the top add:* On healing by stages cp. G. Jungbauer, *Böhmerwald-Sagen*, 1924, p. 234.

To the end of paragraph 4 *add:* On *IG*, IV, 951, pp. 105f. see Rud. Herzog, *Die Wunderheilungen v. Epidauros*, pp. 100ff., esp. p. 103.

In line 5 *of paragraph* 5 *add: Act. Petr. c. Sim.* 11 (The demon exorcised in Rome by Peter damaged a statue of the emperor).

Page 226. *To the end of paragraph* 1 *add:* On the impression of the miraculous cp. Hymn. Hom. *in Venerem*, 83, 181f.; Pindar, *Pyth.* IV, 57f. On θαυμάζειν see Dibelius, *Formg.*, p. 78, n. 1 (and further Lucian, *Philops.* 12 conclusion). Χαίρειν and εὐχαριστεῖν also in Hellenistic miracle stories; see O. Weinreich, *Antike Heilungswunder*, 1909, pp. 108f. On δοξάζειν, ἐπαινεῖν and εὐχαριστεῖν at the end of miracle stories see E. G. Gulin, *Die Freude im N.T.*, I, 1932, p. 100, n. 1. Dibelius thinks that he can detect the acclamation formula also in Lk. 7[16].

Page 229. *To the end of paragraph* 1 *add:* Cp. also W. L. Hertslet, *Der Treppenwitz in der Weltgeschichte*[2], 1927, where many examples of travel stories can be found.

Page 231, n. 1. *Add:* On Rabbinic miracle stories see P. Fiebig, *Z.N.W.*, 35, 1936, pp. 308f., and esp. Dibelius, *Formg.*, pp. 142–9.

Page 232. *To the end of paragraph* 3 *add:* For the healing of the blind cp. the excursus on Jn. 9[1–34] in W. Bauer, *Das Joh. Evg.* (Handb. z. N.T., 6), 1933. L. Szimonidesz (*Nieuw. theol. Tijdschr.*, 24, 1935, pp. 233–9) wants to trace the healing of the blind man in Mk. 8[22–26] (symbolically understood) to a Buddhist parable. Fantastic!

Page 235, n. 1. *Add:* Cp. Also Iamblichus, *Vit. Pythag.*, §§ 14–27; further K. Kerényi, *Die Griech.-oriental. Romanliteratur*, 1927, p. 101, n. 29.

Page 237, n. 1. *Add:* On the motif of walking on water see however Apollon. Rhod., *Argon.*, I, pp. 182ff. Cp. also G. Bertram, *Rev.H.Ph.Rel.*, 1927, pp. 516–40; J. B. Aufhauser, *Schutzpatrone gegen See- und Kriegsnot*, 1935; L. Bieler, ΘΕΙΟΣ ΑΝΗΡ, I, 1935, pp. 96f. (on other nature miracles, ibid., pp. 103f.).

n. 2. *Add:* Dibelius (*Formg.*, p. 277, n. 2) rejects the borrowing from Buddhist tradition.

Page 238. *To the end of paragraph* 2 *add:* On the miraculous draught of fish see L. Bieler, op. cit., pp. 105–8.

To the end of paragraph 3 *add:* Cp. A. Meyer, *Das Weihnachtsfest*, 1913.

n. 1. *Add:* Cp. rather *Hymn. Hom. in Apoll. Pyth.*, 221ff., esp. 255ff. Further *Act. Petr. c. Sim.* 5, p. 51, 10f. Lips.; *Südseemärchen*, p. 273; *Buddhist. Märchen*, p. 45; *Plattdeutsche Volksmärchen*, I, p. 223.

Page 241. *To the end of paragraph* 1 *add:* Dibelius (*Formg.*, p. 148) thinks that the difference between the Synoptic and Rabbinic miracle stories is greater than their affinity. Above all the latter are in no sense 'epiphanies' as they are in the Synoptics. But that however means: the synoptic miracle stories point to the Hellenistic sphere where the idea of an epiphany belongs.

Page 244. *To line* 9 *from the bottom of the first section add:* There is an hypothetical reconstruction of the introduction, Mk. 6³⁴, in Sundwall, op. cit., p. 39.

Page 245, n. 1 from page 244. *Add:* Dibelius (*Formg.*, p. 102) rightly points out that in the Synoptics there are no strictly personal legends which describe the life and death of any 'holy' man.

Page 245, n. 3. *Add:* Cp. also Ludw. Köhler, *Kleine Lichter*, 1945, pp. 79–86. H. Sahlin, *St. Th.* 13, 1959, pp. 167–72.

Page 246, n. 2. *Add:* As the fire with which the coming one is to baptize is throughout fire of judgement, which is understood by many at the same time as a purifying fire (C. H. Kraeling, *John the Baptist*, pp. 58–63; E. Percy, *Die Botschaft Jesu*, p. 6; N. A. Dahl, *Norsk Teol. Tidsskr.*, 1935, pp. 36–52), πνεῦμα and πῦρ are, according to Kraeling, an hendiadys. The Christian interpretation given to πνεῦμα is secondary. Similarly Dahl who points out that the community of the Qumran texts also expected an eschatological purification through the spirit (*D.S.D.*, 3:6–8; 4:20f.). L. W. Barnard, *J.T.S.*, N.S. 8 (1957), p. 107; J. E. Yates, *Nt. St.* 4 (1958), pp. 334–8; E. Best, *Nov. Test.* 4 (1960), pp. 236–43; J. A. T. Robinson, *H.T.R.* 50, 1957, pp. 175–91. On the general idea of a baptism of fire see C-M. Edsman, *Le Baptême de Feu*, 1940 and *Ignis Divinus*, 1949.

Page 247, n. 1. *Add:* The same view is held by E. Käsemann, *Z. Th.K.*, 49, 1952, pp. 150f. See also G. Bornkamm, *Th.Bl.*, 1938, col. 48.

n. 2. *Add:* Paul Guénin (*Y a-t-il un Conflit entre Jean-Baptiste et Jésus*, 1933, pp. 144ff.) contests the view that Jesus was baptized by John. Kraeling (op. cit., p. 131) to my mind rightly pleads for the historicity of the narrative.

Page 248, n. 1. *Add:* Dibelius (*Formg.*, pp. 270f.) and Lohmeyer (ad loc.) give the same interpretation to the baptismal story, even if with different nuances in detail. Cp. further Arvedson, *Mysterium Christi*, pp. 124f. Joachim Bieneck (*Sohn Gottes als Christusbezeichnung der Synoptiker*, 1951, pp. 48f., 58–60) in my view wrongly contests the messianic significance of the title 'Son of God'.

n. 4. *Add:* Dibelius (*Formg.*, p. 272, n. 1) also considers it probable that some fairy-tale motif is basic. Cp. also L. Bieler, ΘΕΙΟΣ ΑΝΗΡ, I, pp. 110f.: animals witness to the θεῖος ἀνήρ.

n. 6. *Add:* Cp. also Protev. Jac., 9.1, p. 18 Tisch: The choice of Joseph as a husband for Mary by a dove. The conjecture of Ludw. Köhler, 'Ehrfurcht vor dem Leben', *Festschr. f. A. Schweitzer*, pp. 77–81, that περιστερά derives from πυρὸς τέρας is not illuminating.

Page 249, n. 3. *Add:* Cp. Friedr. Sühling, *Die Taube als relig. Symbol im christl. Altertum*, 1930. See W. Bauer, *Th.L.Z.*, 1931, Cols. 175–7. On the epiclesis ἐλθὲ ... ἡ ἱερὰ περιστερά *Act. Thom.*, 50, p. 166.12f. Bonnet, see G. Bornkamm, *Mythos u. Legende in den apokr. Thomas-Akten*, pp. 96f. On Selma Hirsch, *Taufe, Versuchung u. Verklärung Jesu*, 1933, pp. 53ff., who seeks to understand the baptism as a figure of the Shekina, see Dibelius, *Formg.*, p. 272, n. 1. On δόξα represented as a bird see Aug. v. Gall, Βασιλεία τοῦ θεοῦ, 1926, p. 107, n. 2. Cp. also P. Guénin, op. cit., pp. 130–5.

Page 250, n. 3. *Add:* Cp. also P. Guénin, op. cit., pp. 130–5.

Page 251. *To the end of paragraph 1 add:* T. Arvedson (*Mysterium Christi*, pp. 123–6) sees Jesus' baptism as his enthronement as messianic king and in particular in the traditional oriental sense of a royal enthronement to death and revival. Similarly G. Bornkamm, *Th. Bl.*, 17, 1938, cols. 44f.; O. Cullmann, *Die Tauflehre des N.T.*, 1948, pp. 15f., and *Die Christologie des N.T.*, 1957, pp. 65–67, like Joach. Bieneck, *Sohn Gottes*, pp. 61f., conceive the voice from heaven in Mk. 1¹¹ as a quotation of Isa. 42¹: Jesus is here summoned as the Son to take up the task of the Servant of Yahweh. I think this fantastic. For the rest cp. on the baptismal narrative: D. Ploij, 'The Baptism of Jesus' in *Amicitiae Corolla* (Festschr. f. Rendel Harris), 1933, pp. 239 ff.; Jos. Kosetter, *Die Taufe Jesu*, 1936.

n. 1. *Add:* Cp. H. Gressmann, *Der Messias*, 1929, pp. 2–6, on the consecration of kings and priests; W. Staerk, *Die Erlösererwartung in den östlichen Religionen* (Soter II), 1938, p. 296, n. 1.

Page 252, n. 1. *Add:* Jos. Thomas, *Le Mouvement Baptiste en Palestine et Syrie*, 1935, p. 390.

n. 2. *Add:* H. Braun, *Z.Th.K.*, 50, 1935, pp. 39–43.

Page 253. *In line 1 add:* (Dibelius (*Formg.*, p. 272) rightly says: Q provided a dialogue between Jesus and the devil and Mk. 1¹²ᶠ· gave Matthew and Luke an opportunity to record the dialogue here.)

To the end of paragraph 1 add: Dibelius (*Formg.*, p. 272) holds that by mentioning Jesus' prayer Luke has changed the narrative into the class of personal legend.

To the end of paragraph 2 add: Kraeling (*John the Baptist*, pp. 312–5) and G. Bornkamm (*The Background*, p. 245) oppose the view that the motif of Matt. 3¹⁴ᶠ· is the problem of the sinlessness of Jesus.

Kraeling thinks the question is: How can the higher be baptized by the lower?, and Bornkamm: How can the messianic baptizer be baptized with a baptism which is outdated? O. Cullmann (*Christologie des N.T.*, p. 66) thinks that the meaning of Matt. 3¹⁴ᶠ· is: Jesus is baptized not for his own sins, but for those of his people. Cp. also the motif in the life of the θεῖος ἀνήρ, where the teacher recognizes the surpassing greatness of his pupil; see L. Bieler, op. cit., I, pp. 37f.

In line 2 from the bottom add: Lohmeyer (ad loc.) believes that the story belongs to the Son of Man series; the opposition of Jesus and Satan shows Jesus as a divine figure whose victory over temptation goes without saying; in the testing of Jesus what is tried is not himself but the eschatological destiny of man and of the world, which he must fulfil. M. Veit (*Die Auffassung von der Person Jesu nach den neuesten Forschungen*, Diss. Theol. Marburg, 1946, pp. 3f.) is right in taking the contrary view.

n. 2. *Add:* J. Dupont (*Nt. St.*, 1957, pp. 287–304) thinks that Mk. 1¹²ᶠ· is the rudimentary base of the more fully preserved temptation narrative in Matthew and Luke. Dibelius (*Formg.*, p. 129, n. 1) thinks Mk. 1¹²ᶠ· is not such a rudimentary base: Mark has 'described a stage in the life of Jesus in accordance with the laws of legendary biography of the saints, but has not reproduced in outline some lost legend.' Lohmeyer (ad loc.) also denies that Mk. 1¹²ᶠ· is a rudimentary basis. J. Jeremias (*Die Abendmahlsworte Jesu*, 1949, p. 63) thinks that Mark deliberately wrote 'in the veiled language of symbol'.

Page 254, n. 1. *Add:* G. Erdmann (*Die Vorgeschichten des Lk.- u. Mk.-Evg.*, 1932, p. 122, n. 4) takes πειραζόμενος ὑπὸ τ. σατ. as a secondary addition and sees in v. 13 the basis of a childhood story with affinities to the Anthropos myth.

n. 2. *Add:* J. Jeremias (*Th.W.B.*, I, p. 141) thinks that Mk. 1¹³ rests upon the Adam–Christ typology. Just as Adam was reverenced in Paradise by the beasts and ministered to by the angels, so now was Jesus after undergoing the temptation. W. Staerk (*Erlösererw.*, p. 9) holds that the angels in Paradise trembled before Adam and the beasts were in awe of him. F. C. Grant (*The Earliest Gospel*, 1943, p. 77) holds that the wild beasts represent Satan as embodiments of demons. Jesus is thus depicted as a martyr analogous to the Roman martyrs who came into the arena with the wild beasts. See L. Bieler, op. cit., pp. 104–11, on animal miracles in the life of the θεῖος ἀνήρ.

n. 5. *Add:* Cp. A. Marmorstein, 'The Background of the Haggadah', *Hebr. Union Coll. Annual*, VI, 186, 1929, p. 46.

n. 7. *Add:* J. Schniewind (in *Das N.T. Deutsch*, ad loc.) seeks to understand the temptations messianically. J. Jeremias (*Gleichn.*, pp. 105f.) believes that the three temptations in Matthew and Luke originally had a separate existence but that they all three have as their object the tempting of the political Messiahship. Lohmeyer (ad loc.) makes it more complicated: in the first and third temptations Jesus is tempted as the Son of man, in the second as the Messiah. Cp. to the contrary Dibelius (*Formg.*, p. 274): the dialogue in Q 'is meant first of all to make clear that Jesus did not perform a certain miracle, and why: not the miracle of helping himself, not a miracle for display . . . It is meant to make clear that he did nothing to obtain power by human means. All that comes from the devil—this is what the dialogue teaches, and so gives an exhortation to Christian people.' Cp. also G. H. P. Tompson, *J.T.S.*, N.S. 11 (1960), pp. 1–12.

Page 257. *To the end of paragraph 2 add:* On the history of the interpretation of the Temptation see Erich Fascher, *Jesus u. der Satan* (Hallische Monographien 11), 1949.

To the end of paragraph 3 add: Sundwall (op. cit., p. 54) thinks that v. 27 is also editorial, and H. J. Ebeling (*Das Messiasgeh.*, pp. 211f.) that at least the localization in Caesarea is; also v. 27a.

n. 5. *Add:* Cp. Lucian, *Icarom.*, 24 (Zeus to Menipp.): εἰπέ μοι, Μένιππε, ἔφη, περὶ δὲ ἐμοῦ οἱ ἄνθρωποι τίνα γνώμην ἔχουσι. As an exception in Rabbinic didactic dialogue see Pirq. Ab. 2:9 where, however, the issue is about a type of catachesis.

Page 258, n. 1. *Add:* R. Otto (*Reich Gottes u. Menschensohn*, pp. 314f.) also thinks that Mark has broken off the original ending, and simply because it was there prophesied to Peter that he would not die. H. J. Ebeling (op. cit., pp. 217f.) believes that the pericope is finished with Peter's confession, which is the point of the story; the following injunction to secrecy is only an underlining of the fact that a mystery had been declared. Like J. Weiss, Wendling and A. Meyer, Sundwall tries to interpret vv. 32b, 33 as the original continuation of v. 30. W. L. Knox (*Sources*, I, p. 63) holds that in Mark's source $9^{2f.}$ followed 8^{27-30}, so that no one could miss the attitude Jesus took to Peter's confession. Then 8^{31}–9^1 was inserted from anjoher source. O. Cullmann (*Petrus*, pp. 176–238; cp. also *Christologie des N.T.*, pp. 122f.) thinks very differently. He thinks Mk. 8^{27-33} is an unitary pericope, with its point in vv. 31–33. In Matt. 16^{17-19} the evangelist has inserted a passage which has a more likely origin in the context of the farewell discourse, such as the dialogue in Lk. 22^{31-34}. Cullmann's psychologizing interpretation which accepts Mk. 8^{27-31} and Matt. 16^{17-19} as genuine historical accounts I cannot myself regard as right. M. Goguel (*Bull. de la Fac. Libre de Théol. Protest. de Paris*, 1938, No. 15) also thinks that Matt. 16^{17-19} has been inserted from a source unknown to Mark, though the verses did not originate until after A.D. 70. O. J. F. Seitz (*J.B.L.*, 69, 1950, pp. 329–40) thinks that Matt. 16^{17-19} derives from a resurrection narrative transported back into the ministry of Jesus. His reconstruction of the original wording of the saying is anyhow very questionable. A. Vögtle, who has carefully examined the composition of Matt. 16 $^{13-23}$ par. with copious reference to the literature (*Bibl. Z.*, 1957, pp. 252–72; 1958, pp. 85–103), holds the view that Matt. 16^{17-19} is an addition by Matthew to the Mark narrative, though even so he separates v. 18 from v. 17. The beatitude in v. 17 is a formulation by Matthew to be understood as a response to Peter's confession; but the promise in vv. 18f. is a dominical saying taken by Matthew from the tradition, possibly the tradition about the risen Lord. Cullmann's hypothesis is rejected. Cp. also above, p. 140, n. 2.

n. 2. *Add:* R. Bultmann, *Th.Bl.*, 20, 1941, cols. 265–79. On O. Cullmann, see above, addition to n. 1. It is noteworthy that Matt. 16¹⁷⁻¹⁹ appears as an Easter tradition in Shahrastâni, *Religionsparteien u. Philosophenschulen*, tr. by Th. Haarbrücker, I, 1850, p. 261.

Page 259. *In line 1 of paragraph 2 add:* (On the literature: J. Blinzler, *Die neutestamentlichen Berichte über die Verklärung Jesu*, 1937; J. Höller, *Die Verklärung Jesu*, 1937; E. Dabrowski, *La Transfiguration de Jésus*, 1939; U. Holzmeister, *Biblica*, 21, 1940, pp. 200–10; G. H. Boobyer, *St. Mark and the Transfiguration Story*, 1944; H. Riesenfeld, *Jésus Transfiguré*, 1947; A. M. Ramsey, *The Glory of God and the Transfiguration*, 1949.)

n. 2. *Add:* The Transfiguration is envisaged as originally a resurrection story also by O. J. F. Seitz, *J.B.L.*, 69, 1950, p. 339; Morton S. Enslin, *Jewish Quart. Rev.*, 43, 1952, pp.44f. F. C. Grant, *The Earliest Gospel*, pp. 154f. is undecided. The contrary view is held by e.g. H. J. Ebeling, *Das Messiasgeheimnis*, pp. 195f.; E. Percy, *Die Botschaft Jesu*, pp. 300–7; further E. Lohmeyer, ad loc., who rejects the view that the Transfiguration was originally a resurrection story by maintaining that the risen Lord had not yet been glorified; but Acts 3¹³ is against this. H. Riesenfeld abandons the *quaestio facti* and interprets the background of the story in terms of the history of its motif as the cultic-eschatological scheme of a Messianic enthronement transferred to Jesus, and sees the story as in part a premonstration of this enthronement, though lacking for its fulfilment the suffering and the entry into the eschatological 'rest'. He is wrong in rejecting the view that the Transfiguration was in origin a resurrection story, for to the oldest Christian way of thinking the resurrection of Jesus meant his institution into his Messianic dignity (Rom. 1³f.; Acts. 2³⁶, 3¹³). Riesenfeld's analysis of particular motifs is frequently fantastic, and his contention that the Jewish Messianic enthronement and the Transfiguration of Jesus are related to the feast of booths is untenable; cp. W. G. Kümmel, *Symb. Bibl. Uppsal.*, 11, 1948, pp. 47–56; E. Percy, *Die Botschaft Jesu*, pp. 300–7. He argues convincingly against Boobyer's thesis that the Transfiguration is a premonstration of the Parousia. Boobyer's thesis is restated with unessential modifications by A. M. Ramsey (op. cit., pp. 112ff.).

n. 3. *Add:* Cp. also Höller, op. cit., pp. 10–21. It is most unlikely that the six days derive from Exod. 24¹⁶, as is suggested by Dibelius, *Formg.*, p. 275, n. 5, and H. J. Schoeps, *Theologie u. Geschichte des Judenchristentums*, 1949, p. 95, n. 5, for there the six days refer to the veiling of the mountain by the cloud while Moses was on it. Riesenfeld (op. cit., pp. 276f.) connects the six days with the six days between the Day of Atonement and the Feast of Tabernacles. Arvedson (*Myst. Christi*, pp. 131f.), thinks that the six days were the traditional interval between the first and second Mystery consecration. Crum (*St. Mark's Gospel*, p. 69) is fantastic. W. L. Knox (*Sources*, I, p. 68) holds that the six days were originally reckoned as from Mk. 8²⁷⁻³⁰.

Page 260, n. 2. *Add:* On the cloud motif cp. Riesenfeld, op. cit., pp. 130–45, 248–50; W. Staerk, *Erlösererwartung*, p. 323. On the description of the glistening raiment, cp. *Hymn. Hom. in Ven.*, pp. 86f.

n. 4. *Add:* It cannot be proved that Elijah and Moses as prototypes and forerunners of the Messiah were thought of in late Judaism as sufferers, or that they did not for the first time provide a reference to the Passion in Lk. 9[31] but in the original Transfiguration story (so J. Jeremias, *Th.W.B.*, II, pp. 941ff.; IV, pp. 877f., and Riesenfeld, op. cit., pp. 262f.). On the typology of Moses and Elijah see also H. J. Schoeps, op. cit., pp. 95f. P. Dabbeck (*Bibl.*, 23, 1942, pp. 175–89) thinks that in the early Christian tradition Moses represents God the Father and Elijah the Holy Ghost! Probably Moses and Elijah are mentioned because, according to Jewish tradition, they were the only ones who did not die, but were taken into heaven; see Schlatter, *Der Evglist. Matth.*, on Matt. 17[3].

Page 261. *In line 5 paragraph 2 add:* (On the Luke version see H. Conzelmann, *Die Mitte der Zeit*, pp. 170f.: 'Thus the passion is interpreted beforehand and interpreted as the path to Glory.' Cp. also ibid., pp. 45–47). Cp. further: A. Feuilliet, 'Les perspectives propres à chaque evangéliste dans les récits de la transfiguration', *Biblica* 39 (1958), pp. 281–301. J. Manek, *Nov. Test.* 2, 1958, pp. 8–23, seeks to prove that ἔξοδος (Lk. 9[31]) does not refer to the Passion and death, but to the Resurrection.

n. 5 from p. 260. *Add at end:* In his commentary on Mark, Lohmeyer has retracted his analysis and described the text as a literary unity and as purely Jewish in its place in the history of religion. So far as vv. 5f. are concerned, Dibelius (*Formg.*, pp. 275f.) and Lohmeyer (ad loc.) are right: Peter's statement means that the time of fulfilment is dawning or has begun; this is actually said to be false in v. 6. Yet the story can still be understood as an unity. In this sense vv. 5f. would very well fit with an Easter story. A different analysis is made by H.-P. Müller, *Z.N.W.* 51 (1960), pp. 56–64. He thinks (but is unlikely to be right) that two motifs have been combined in Mk. 9[2-8]—v. 2ab, 7, (9): the appearance of the cloud, and v. 2c–6, 8: Jesus' transformation into a figure of light. H. Baltensweiler, *Die Verklärung Jesu*, 1959, seeks to prove the historicity of the narrative.

n. 1. *Add:* W. L. Knox (*Sources*, I, pp. 77f.) points out that Mark, like Luke, and unlike Matthew, speaks of ὄνος and also does not use Matthew's quotation from Zechariah. G. Erdmann (*Die Vorgeschichten des Lk- und Mt-Evg.*, p. 61) thinks that the Legend derives from the Moses-Messiah typology, which has the ass as the beast on which Moses and Messiah ride.

Page 262. *To the end of paragraph 2 add:* (From the literature on the Passion narrative I would mention: A. C. J. Germanus, *Passionis Domini Nostri J. Christi Praefationes Historicae*, 3 vols., 1933–6; J. Finegan, *Die Überlieferung der Leidens- und Auferstehungsgeschichte Jesu*, 1934; J. M. Vosté, *De Passione et Morte J. Christi*, 1937,; El. Bickermann, 'Utilitas Crucis', *Rev. d'Hist. des Religions*, 112, 1935, pp. 169–241; K. H. Schelkle, *Die Passion Jesu in der Verkündigung des N.T.*, 1949). On the chronology of the history of the Passion see James A. Walther, *J.B.L.* 77 (1958), pp. 116–22.

P

Page 263. *To the end of paragraph* 1 *add:* Nevertheless Mk. 14[1f.] has to be seen as a witness for the arrest taking place before the Passover. For the motivation is admittedly nonsensical; but the report will rest on the simple fact that Jesus was arrested and condemned before the feast. The idea that the arrest followed the feast is only put into the verses of Mk. 14[12–16, 26], which make the Last Supper appear to be a Passover meal (see below). So also R. H. Lightfoot, *Hist. and Interpr.*, pp. 130–41; similarly J. Finegan, op. cit., p. 62. G. Bertram (*Die Leidensgeschichte Jesu u. der Christuskult*, p. 13) and Jeremias (*Die Abendmahlsworte Jesu*, pp. 40–42) suggest taking ἐν τῇ ἑορτῇ not as a time reference but as meaning 'in the festival crowd'. Dibelius (*Formg.*, p. 181, n. 2) rightly opposes this.

To the end of paragraph 3 *add:* On Matthew's version see also Dibelius, *Botschaft u. Geschichte*, I, p. 250, n. 2; on Luke's version see M. Goguel, *La Vie de Jésus*, p. 461, n. 1; Finegan, op. cit., p. 6.

To the end of paragraph 4 *add:* Finegan (op. cit., pp. 63f.) and Lohmeyer (ad loc.) also think that vv. 8f. are secondary.

n. 3. *Add:* Finegan (op. cit., pp. 63f.) also thinks that Mk. 14[3–9] is really an independent pericope out of harmony with its context, which comes best after 11[19]. The naming of the otherwise unknown Simon favours its historicity.

Page 264. *To the end of paragraph* 1 *add:* Dibelius (*Formg.*, pp. 182, 189f.) rightly sees that Mk. 14[12–16] is put first as an introduction to the narrative of the Last Supper, and that by this means the Last Supper becomes a Passover meal. Ed. Schweizer is also right: Mk. 14[12–16] cannot have been an item in the ancient Passion narrative. Jeremias (*Die Abendmahlsworte*, pp. 52f.) also believes that Mk. 14[12–16] belongs to a tradition other than that of 14[1].

In line 8 *of paragraph* 2 *add:* (Finegan (op. cit., pp. 9f.) is in all probability right in opposing this: there is only the text of Mark behind the text of Luke.)

n. 1. *Add:* R. Söder, *Die apokr. Apostelgeschichten u. die romanhafte Literatur der Antike*, 1932, pp. 110f.; G. Bornkamm, *Mythos u. Legende in den apokr. Thomasakten*, 1933, p. 33.

n. 2. *Add:* In the opinion of Jeremias, *Die Abendmahlsworte Jesu*, pp. 11f., 52f., Mk. 14[12] refers to Nisan 14: τῇ πρώτῃ ἡμέρᾳ τῶν ἀζύμων is a wrong translation which should read 'on the day before the ἄζυμα'. Black (*Aram. Appr.*[2], p. 100, n. 3) takes the same view.

Page 265. *To the end of paragraph* 1 *add:* On the legendary character of Mk. 14[17–21] see also Finegan, op. cit., pp. 65f. G. Bertram

(*Leidensgesch.*, pp. 34f.) and H. W. Surkau (*Martyrien in jüdischer und frühchristlicher Zeit*, pp. 84f.) rightly point to the fact that v. 21b i. the transformation of a universal proposition. (Matt. 18⁷//Lk. 17¹)s Cp. further L. Bieler, op. cit., I, pp. 42ff.: the θεῖος ἀνήρ has to have an opponent, who is painted in the blackest colours.

In line 2 from top of paragraph 2 add: (On the narrative of the Lord's Supper see the survey of research by E. Lohmeyer, *Th.R.*, N.F. 9, 1937, pp. 168–227, 273–312; 10, 1938, pp. 81–99; Ed. Schweizer, *Th.L.Z.* 79, 1954, cols. 577–92; *R.G.G.*², I, cols. 10–21; Hans Lessig, *Das Abendmahlsproblem im Lichte der neutestamentl. Forschung seit 1900* (Diss. theol., Bonn), 1953. H. Schürmann, *Neutest. Abh.* 19, 5 (1953); 20, 4 (1955); 20, 5 (1957); N. Turner, *J.T.S.*, N.S. 8 (1957), pp. 108–11; S. Temple, *Nt. St.* 7 (1960/61), pp. 77–85. On Lk. 22¹⁸ see esp. C. K. Barrett, *J.B.S.*, N.S. 9 (1958), pp. 305–7.

To the end of paragraph 2 add: Cp. the portrayal of the Last Supper in the Fresco from Wadi Sarya (fifth–sixth century) in the British Museum.

In line 3 from top of paragraph 3 add: (so, e.g. also Dibelius, *Formg.*, p. 207, n. 2, and W. L. Knox, *Sources*, I, pp. 119f.).

n. 4. *Add:* Jeremias (*Die Abendmahlsworte Jesu*) seeks to advance proof that the Last Supper was a Passover meal. Critically opposed to this position are: Ph. Vielhauer, *Z. deutsch. Paläst.-V.*, 69, 1953, pp. 188–90; N. Turner, *J.T.S.*, N.S. 8, 1957, pp. 108–11; less emphatically Ed. Schweizer, *Th.L.Z.*, 79, 1954, cols. 582–4, and *R.G.G.*³, I, cols. 17f. In discussion with Jeremias, K. G. Kuhn (*Ev. Th.*, 1950/1, pp. 516–18) shows that in any event Mk. 14²²⁻²⁴ contains no reference to a Passover meal.

Page 266, n. 1. *Add:* For the originality of Lk. 22¹⁹⁻²⁰ there are: Dibelius, *Formg.*, pp. 210–12; Jeremias, op. cit., pp. 67–79; Kuhn, op. cit., p. 515, and *Th.L.Z.*, 75, 1950, col. 404; B. H. Throckmorton, *Anglic. Th. Rev.*, 3, 1948, pp. 55f.; H. Schürmann, *Biblica*, 32, 1951, pp. 364–92, 522–41: Schweizer, *Th.L.Z.*, 1957, cols. 573f. Against its originality: G. D. Kilpatrick, *J.T.S.*, 47, 1946, pp. 49–56; P. Benoit, *J.T.S.*, 49, 1948, pp. 145–7; H. Chadwick, *H.T.R.*, 50, 1957, pp. 249–58, who (in discussion of Jeremias and Schürmann) takes Lk. 22¹⁵⁻¹⁸ as an independent unit of tradition taken over by Luke and to which Lk. 22¹⁹ᵃ has been added from Mark by way of expansion. On Lk. 22¹⁶ see Black, *Aram. Appr.*², pp. 165–72.

n. 2. *Add:* Lohmeyer (ad loc., pp. 303f.) also accepts the originality of Mk. 14²⁵.

n. 3. *Add:* Loisy ('Les Origines de la Cène Eucharistique' in *Congrès d'histoire du Christianisme*, I, 1928, p. 30) takes the same view.

Page 267. *To the end of paragraph 2 add:* Dibelius (*Formg.*, p. 201), Goguel (*H.T.R.*, 25, 1952, pp. 3f., and *Vie de Jésus*, pp. 470f.),

Greeven (*Gebet u. Eschatologie im N.T.*, pp. 50f.) see in Lk. 22³¹ᶠ· a logion that has nothing at all to do with the story of the denial, though without drawing the consequence of the unhistoricity of the denial itself. Against my interpretation are: von Campenhausen, op. cit., p. 44, and W. L. Knox (*Sources*, I, p. 124). Finegan (op. cit., pp. 14f.) believes Lk. 22³¹⁻³⁴ to be an wholly Lukan construction. On the tradition of the denial within the context of the Passion see G. Klein, *Z.T.K.* 68 (1961), pp. 294–8.

n. 1. *Add:* Cp. Jeremias, *Abendmahlsw.*, pp. 29f.: there was no Hallel at the end of ordinary meals; this 'can refer only to the second half of the Passover Hallel'. A comprehensive treatment of Lk. 22³¹ᶠ· by G. Klein, *Z.T.K.* 68 (1961), pp. 298–311, who shares the view expounded in the text.

n. 3. *Add:* Sundwall (op. cit., p. 80), Finegan (op. cit., p. 69), Lohmeyer (ad loc.), and H. von Campenhausen ('Der Ablauf der Osterereignisse u. das leere Grab' (*S. B. Heidelb.*, 1952, 4), p. 35, n. 116) also deem Mk. 14²⁸ to be an intrusion into the context to prepare for 16⁷. So too Kümmel (*Verh. u. Erf.*, pp. 70–2) who rightly rejects Lohmeyer's conception of 14²⁸ as the promise of a Parousia to be waited for in Galilee. C. F. Evans, *J.B.L.*, 55, 1954, pp. 3–18 wants to interpret the verse allegorically as directing the disciples to the Gentile mission. Dibelius (*Botschaft u. Gesch.*, I, pp. 250f.) thinks that the verse comes from an older narrative. On the historicity of the prophecy of the flight of the disciples see M. Goguel, *H.T.R.*, 25, 1952, pp. 2f.

Page 268. *To the end of paragraph 1 add:* While Lohmeyer (ad loc.) and Ebeling (*Messiasgeheimnis*, pp. 174–8) think that the story is an unity, K. G. Kuhn (*Ev. Th.*, 1952/3, pp. 260–85) takes it to be a combination of two narratives: A=vv. 32, 35, 40f.; B=vv. 33f., 36–38; editorial additions by Mark are v. 39 and the words πάλιν in v. 40, καὶ ἔρχεται τὸ τρίτον in v. 41, and, finally, v. 42. A has its point in the Christological saying about the hour of the Son of man in v. 41, while B has its point in the paraenetic saying about temptation in v. 38. W. L. Knox (*Sources*, I, pp. 125–9) explains the difficulties of Mark's text and the differences between Mark and Luke by the change of sources used, though he also takes editorial activity into account. Cp. further the analysis by Finegan (op. cit., pp. 70f.) and Rud. Meyer (*Der Prophet aus Galiläa*, pp. 34f.). Without giving a literary analysis (apart from taking the separation of the three intimates in v. 33 as an addition by Mk.) Dibelius (*Formg.*, pp. 212–14 and *Botsch. u. Gesch.*, I, pp. 258–71) gives an excellent characterization of the motifs of the Gethsemane story, which he certainly does not take to be an originally unattached individual narrative. Its dominant motif, the lament and prayer of Jesus, takes him back to the primitive Christian idea which comes to light in Heb. 5⁷, that the wrestling in prayer is proof of the Messiahship of Jesus, in that he thus fulfils prophecy (to be found in the Psalms). On the reproduction of the text in Matthew and Luke see also Dibelius (*Botsch. u. Gesch.*, I, pp. 268–70). Like L. Braun (*Z.N.W.*, 32, 1933, pp. 265–76) he thinks Lk. 22[43f.] to be genuinely Lukan. Rightly he opposes the view of K. G. Kuhn (op. cit., pp. 268–70) that the original for Luke's Gethsemane scene (Lk. 22[40–42, 45f.]) comes from a special source.

Page 269. *In line 1 add:* Surkau (op. cit., p. 86) finds the martyr motif active in this scene: the martyr is superior to those who arrest him.

In line 2 from the top add: Goguel (*Vie de Jésus*, p. 484) also questions the historicity of vv. 48f. According to Finegan the original basis, i.e. vv. 43 (without the transition), 46, 50, is historical tradition.

To the end of paragraph 1 add: On Matt. 26[50] see F. Rehkopf, *Z.N.W.* 52 (1961), pp. 109–15; a different view is taken by W. Eltester, *Neotestamentica et Patristica*, Festchsr. f. O. Cullmann, 1962, pp. 70–92; Surkau (op. cit., pp. 88f.) sees in Matt. 26[52–54] the motif of angel hosts who guard the devout.

In line 4 of paragraph 2 add: (According to H. Kosmeta, *Nov. Test.* 4, 1960, pp. 3ff., v. 52 is a quotation from the Targum on Isa. 50[11].)

In line 4 from bottom of page add: Finegan (op. cit., p. 23) rightly disputes the view that Luke made use of an older tradition alongside Mark. On the other hand P. Winter, *Z.N.W.* 50 (1959), pp. 222–6, produces good reasons for holding the opposite view. A discussion of the question is found in G. Klein, *Z.Th.K.* 68 (1961), pp. 290ff.

To the end of paragraph 3 add: Goguel (*H.T.R.* 25, 1932, pp. 1–27, and *Vie de Jésus*, pp. 470–7) also thinks Peter's denial unhistorical, while Dibelius (*Formg.*, pp. 215–18) though thinking it historical, holds that it has been given a novelistic form.

n. 1. *Add:* Dibelius (*Formg.*, p. 183, and *Botsch u. Gesch*, I, p. 252) thinks that the unnamed young man was the eyewitness from whom the original narrative derived. The contrary view is held by H. Lietzmann, *Z.N.W.*, 30, 1931, p. 214. Goguel (*Vie de Jésus*, pp. 485f.) thinks that vv. 47 and and 51f. are the rudiments of a tradition in which the followers of Jesus tried to resist his arrest.

n. 2. *Add:* J. Jeremias (*Jerusalem zur Zeit Jesu*, I, 1923, pp. 53f.) thinks it probable that hens were sold in the market at Jerusalem. Cp. also G. Stuhlfaut, *Die apokr. Petrus-Geschichten in der altchristl. Kunst*, 1925, pp. 27f.; Olof Linton, *Das Problem der Urkirche in der neueren Forschung*, 1932, pp. 96–101. P. Winter, *Z.N.W.* 50 (1959), pp. 226f., brings out the exhortatory purpose of the history of the denial: Peter, in his denial, is contrasted with Jesus, steadfast in his suffering.

Page 270, n. 2. *Add:* Lietzmann, appealing to Jean Juster (*Les Juifs dans l'empire romain*, II, 1914, pp. 123ff.), thinks that the Jews in the time of Jesus had the right to execute judgement in capital trials; since Jesus was condemned by the Roman authorities he could not also have been sentenced by the Jewish Sanhedrin. A voluminous discussion has followed on the question of competence. Cp. Fr. Büchsel, *Z.N.W.*, 30, 1931, pp. 202–10; Lietzmann, ibid., pp. 211–15, and 31, 1932, pp, 78–84; Goguel, ibid., pp. 289–301; Fr. Büchsel, ibid., 33, 1934, pp. 84–87; H. J. Ebeling, ibid., 35, 1936, pp. 290–5; J. Jeremias, ibid., 43, 1950/1, pp. 145–50 (with a further bibliography). Cp. further: Finegan, op. cit., p. 72; R. H. Lightfoot, *Hist. and Interpr.*, pp. 142–51; J. Lengle, *Hermes*, 70, 1935, pp. 312–21; K. L. Schmidt, *Judaica*, I, 1945/6, pp. 1–40; J. Blinzler, *Der Process Jesu*[2], 1954; G. D. Kilpatrick, *The Trial of Jesus*, 1953; Ph. Vielhauer, *Festschr. f. G. Dehn*, pp. 64f.; O. Cullmann, *Der Staat im N.T.*, 1956, pp. 28–33; T. A. Burkill, 'The Trial of Jesus', *Vigiliae Christianae* 12 (1958), pp. 1–18; P. Winter, *The Trial of Jesus*, 1961, and *Z.N.W.* 50 (1959), pp. 14–33, 221–52. There is a detailed discussion of the legal problem in E. Bickermann, 'Utilitas Crucis', *Rev. d'Hist. des Religions*, 62, 1935, pp. 169–241; T. A. Burkill, *Vigiliae Christianae* 10 (1956), pp. 80–96. Winter (*Z.N.W.* 50, 1959, pp. 22–33) and Blinzler (*Z.N.W.* 52, 1961, pp. 54–65) explain the contradiction with the Mishna's legal procedure on the grounds that at the time of Jesus it was the Sadducean legal code that was valid, whereas the Mishna represents the Pharisaic. There is an estimate in Dibelius, without considering the legal problem (*Formg.*, pp. 192f., and *Botsch. u. Gesch.*, I, pp. 254f.). He thinks that the report of a trial before the Sanhedrin is legendary; it has grown up out of the traditional saying of Jesus against the Temple. He perceives that the narrative is not an unity, as does W. L. Knox (*Sources*, I, pp. 132–4), who explains it as a contamination of the sources. F. C. Grant (*The Earliest Gospel*, p. 68) thinks that Mk. 14[62b] (καὶ ὄψεσθε κλτ) is an addition to ἐγώ εἰμι. O. Cullmann (*Christologie des N.T.*, pp. 118–21) holds that ἐγώ εἰμι is a false rendering of the Aramaic אֲמַרְתְּ which Matthew has rightly translated as σὺ εἶπας, and has been confirmed by Luke who has preserved the proper reminiscence, that Jesus answered the High Priests' question with neither 'yes' nor 'no'. Kümmel (*Verh. u. Erf.*, pp. 42–44) thinks otherwise, though apart from this he defends the historicity of this scene.

n. 5. *In line 4 from the bottom add:* The analogy tells against Lohmeyer (*Das Evg. des Mk.*, pp. 327ff., 330), who on the basis of his conception of the Son of man maintains that the sayings about the Temple and about the Son of man belong together, and misinterprets v. 59; the examples advanced by him on p. 327 fail to prove what they ought to prove; and precisely if v. 59 expresses the judgement of the narrator is there an hiatus opened between v. 58 and vv. 61f. On the interpretation of Mk. 14[62] see H. K. McArthur, *Nt. St.* 4 (1957/8), pp. 156–8; T. F. Glasson, ibid. 7 (1960/1), pp. 88–93.

Page 271, n. 2. *Add:* Dibelius (*Formg.*, p. 193, n. 1) is opposed to Rubberg and van Unnik: the word προφήτευσον is the 'scornful demand of the so-called man of God "give a divine utterance about yourself!"' The scene rests upon the fulfilment of a prophecy (Isa. 50[5f.]). The same view is taken by Lohmeyer (ad loc.).

Page 272. *In line 2 of paragraph 3 add:* Finegan (op. cit., p. 24) is nevertheless probably right in thinking that Lk. 22[66] is a conflation of Mk. 14[53b] and 15[1].

To the end of paragraph 3 add: On Pilate's wife in the history of exegesis see E. Fascher, *Hallische Monographien*, 20, 1951, pp. 5–31.

n. 1. *Add:* P. Winter, *Z.N.W.* 50 (1959), pp. 250f., argues for the historicity of the inscription on the cross, as does N. A. Dahl, in *Der histor. Jesus u. der kerygmat. Christus*, 1960, pp. 189f.

n. 2. *Add:* Goguel (*Z.N.W.*, 31, 1932, p. 296) conjectures that the Barabbas episode displaced another story which contradicted the Christian conception of Pilate's good will.

n. 3. *Add:* L. Dürr, *Ursprung u. Ausbau der Israelit.-jüd. Heilandserwartung*, 1925, p. 142; W. Staerk, *Erlösererwartung*, pp. 27, n. 2 and 515.

n. 4. *Add:* Cp. G. D. Kilpatrick, *The Origin of the Gospel according to St. Matthew*, p. 81. P. Benoit ('La Mort de Judas', *Synopt. Studien f. A. Wikenhausen*, 1953, pp. 1–19) tries to discern a Jerusalem tradition behind the narrative in Matthew. Cp. also Dibelius, *Botsch. u. Gesch.*, I, pp. 272–7.

Page 273. *In line 3 from top of paragraph 2 add:* In v. 21 (Simon of Cyrene) which has been neglected, like 14[51] by Matthew and Mark, there is plainly the rudiments of ancient tradition. So Dibelius, *Formg.*, p. 183, and *Botsch. u. Gesch.*, I, pp. 252f.; Finegan, op. cit., p. 75; Lietzmann, *Z.N.W.*, 30, 1931, pp. 214f.

In line 3 from top of paragraph 3 add: (So also Lohmeyer, ad loc., though he will not recognize in this literary construction any strata of a different age.)

In line 2 from the top of last paragraph add: (Cp. Dibelius, *Formg.*, pp. 194–6.)

In line 5 from top of last paragraph add: On v. 34's traditional history see J. Guilka, *Bibl. Z.*, N.F. 3, 1959, pp. 294–7.

n. 3. *Add:* The peculiar parallelism of Mk. 14[55–64] with 15[2–5] makes G. Braumann conclude that Mark edited two parallel traditions. *Z.N.W.* 52 (1961), pp. 273–8.

Page 274. *In line 10 from the top add:* Cp. H. Riesenfeld, *The Resurrection in Ezekiel XXXVII and in the Dura-Europos Paintings*, 1948, pp. 35ff.

To the end of paragraph 3 add: While H. von. Campenhausen 'Der Ablauf der Osterereignisse', (*S.B. Heidelb.*, 1952–4), pp. 33f., sees an apologetic motive at work in Mk. 15[43–45] (against the suspicion that Jesus was only apparently dead), Finegan (op. cit., pp. 78–80) finds at this point an ancient narrative independent of the following story about the empty tomb. On the historical events behind the sepulchre stories see G. Baldensperger, *Rev. H. Ph. Rel.*, 1932, pp. 413–43; 1933, pp. 105–44; 1934, pp. 97–125. J. Spencer Kennard (*J.B.L.*, 74, 1955, pp. 227–38) seeks to defend the historicity of the sepulchre stories.

To last line of text add: (On. Matt. 27[62–66] see Hans Grass, *Ostergeschehen u. Osterberichte*, 1956, pp. 23f.)

n. 1. *Add:* See also below, p. 282, n. 5.

Page 276. *To the end of paragraph 2 add:* Dibelius (*Formg.*, pp. 178–83) is at one with me in thinking that the passion narrative originally contained a series of isolated units that were in circulation, but is probably right to question whether Lk. 22[14–18] and 22[21–23] are doublets of the corresponding passages in Mark (Finegan, op. cit., pp. 9f., holds the same view in respect of 22[21–23]); they are much more likely to be edited versions of the Mark text.

In line 4 of paragraph 3 add: (Finegan's hypothesis, op. cit., p. 16, that Lk. 22[35–38] is not a piece of tradition, but a literary creation of Luke, seems untenable to me.)

To line 3 from bottom add: (On the editing of Mark's text by Matthew see N. A. Dahl, *Nt. St.*, 2, 1955, pp. 17–32.)

Page 279. *To the end of paragraph 3 add:* Compare with the analysis given here the different attempts to work out the oldest strata of the Passion tradition and their editing by the evangelists, esp. Mark: Dibelius, *Formg.*, pp. 178–218, and *Botsch. u. Gesch.*, I, pp. 248–57; Sundwall, op. cit., pp. 8off.; R. H. Lightfoot, *Hist. and Interpr.*, pp. 126–81; F. C. Grant, *The Earliest Gospel*, pp. 175–87; Finegan, op. cit., p. 82; K. G. Kuhn, *Ev. Th.*, 1952–3, pp. 261f.; Jeremias, *Abendmahlsw.*, pp. 50–55; W. L. Knox, *Sources*, I, pp. 115–47. See especially P. Winter, *The Trial of Jesus*, 1961 and *Z.N.W.* 50 (1959), pp. 14–33, 221–52. His analysis agrees almost exactly with that given above.

Page 280. *To the end of paragraph 1 add:* The view that Luke had some other source besides Mark available for the passion narrative shows itself untenable, as has been already frequently shown in the supplements to the preceding analyses, esp. in connection with Finegan. Cp. also N. A. Dahl, op. cit., pp. 2of. On the other hand P. Winter produces good arguments for the opposite view in *Z.N.W.* 50 (1959), pp. 221–6. Cp. also J. B. Tyson, *Nov. Test.* 3, 1959, pp. 249–58.

n. 1. *Add:* Cp. further, Dibelius, *Formg.*, pp. 21f., and *Rev. H. Ph. Rel.*, 1933, pp. 30–45; Goguel, *Vie de Jésus*, pp. 448f. T. A. Burkill, *Nov. Test.* 2, 1958, pp. 254–71.

Page 281, n. 2. from p. 280. *Add at end:* Dibelius, *Formg.*, pp. 187–9. Chr. Maurer (*Z.Th.K.*, 50, 1953, pp. 1–38, esp. pp. 6–28) tries to show—and indeed with some powerful exegesis—that the theological basis of the Passion narrative in Mark is a '*de facto* scriptural proof' that Jesus was the servant of God in Second Isaiah.

Page 282, n. 1. *Add:* On the apologetic motif, cp. W. Bauer, *Das Leben Jesu im Zeitalter der neutest. Apokryphen*, 1909, pp. 181–209; Goguel, *Vie de Jésus*, pp. 450f.

n. 2. *Add:* Cp. Dibelius, *Formg.*, pp. 113f.; R. H. Lightfoot, *Hist. and Interpr.*, p. 160; esp. E. Fascher, *Th.L.Z.*, 72, 1947, cols. 201–4 (and see above, p. 272); A. Oepke, ibid., 73, 1948, cols. 743–6.

n. 3. *Add:* Dibelius, *Botsch., u. Gesch.*, I, pp. 37f.; G. Erdmann, *Die Vorgeschichten des Lk- und Mt-Evg.*, pp. 129f.; W. Staerk, *Erlösererwartung*, pp. 27, n. 2, 479; R. Söder, *Die apokr. Apostelgesch.*, pp. 70ff.; L. Bieler, ΘΕΙΟΣ ΑΝΗΡ, I, p. 47. Cp. also L. Brun, *Segen u. Fluch*, pp. 76–78.

n. 5. *Add:* On the influence of the martyr-motif see Dibelius, *Formg.*, pp. 202–5, and *Botsch. u. Gesch.*, I, pp. 263f., 269f.; Surkau, *Jüd. u. frühchristl. Martyrien*, passim; Lightfoot, *Hist. and Interpr.*, pp. 176–9; H. von Campenhausen, *Die Idee des Martyriums in der alten Kirche*, 1936, pp. 58f.

Page 283. *In line 10 from the top add:* (cp. N. Krieger, *Nov. Test.* 2, 1958, pp. 73f.)

Page 284. *To the end of paragraph 2 add:* G. Schille (*Z.Th.K.*, 52, 1953, pp. 161–205) tries to make out that the Passion (and Easter) tradition which came to Mark had their 'Sitz im Leben' (life situation) in the cultic activity of the Church; not only the narrative of the Last Supper, but the whole story of the last night is an 'anamnesis' and comes from an Agape held on the anniversary of what was reported. The narrative of Good Friday has in all probability, as the mention of the three prayer hours in Mk. 15$^{25, 33f.}$ permits us to suppose, derived from and for the three hours' service in which, at least on the anniversary of Good Friday, there is meditation on the events (sometimes at the same hours of the day). The burial legends owe their origin to an early celebration of Easter, possibly corresponding to a celebration at the tomb of Jesus. But Schille's arguments are so problematical that they fail to carry conviction.

Page 285, n. 1. *Add:* Cp. also Lohmeyer, *Evg. d. Mk.*, pp. 351f.

n. 2. *Add:* On the question whether Mark ended with 16$^{1–8}$ see the bibliography cited by W. Bauer in *Th.W.B.* under φοβέω. That the original ending has been broken off is maintained by Finegan, op. cit., p. 107; W. L. Knox, *H.T.R.*, 35, 1942, pp. 12–23. The contrary view that Mk. 16$^{1–8}$ is the original conclusion is held by Dibelius, *Formg.*, p. 190; Lohmeyer, *Galiläa u. Jerusalem*, pp. 10–14, and *Evg. des Mk.*, pp. 356–60; W. Michaelis, *Die Erscheinungen des Auferstandenen*, 1944, pp. 5–8; J. M. Creed, *J.T.S.*, 1930, pp. 135ff.; R. H. Lightfoot, *Locality and Doctrine in the Gospels*, 1938, pp. 1–48 (detailed discussion of the problem); Jeremias, *Abendmahlsw.*, p. 63; W. C. Allen, *J.T.S.*, 47, 1946, pp. 46–9; 48, 1947, pp. 201–3; L. J. D. Richardson, ibid., 49, 1948, pp. 144f.; M. S. Enslin, *Jew. Quart. Rev.*, N.S., 43, 1952, pp. 28f.; W. Marxsen, *Der Evglist. Mk.*, pp. 51–59; H. Grass, *Ostergeschehen u. Osterberichte*, pp. 16–19. H. von Campenhausen ('Der Ablauf der

Osterereignisse u. das leere Grab', pp. 24f., 34f.) is undecided. He thinks that v. 7 is not an insertion and explains v. 8 as apologetically motivated; against suspicions such as those reported in Matt. 28[13-15] it had to be established that the disciples had no connection with the empty tomb. Lohmeyer, like Michaelis, interprets v. 7 not as a promise of an appearance of the risen Lord, but as a promise of the Parousia. Kümmel (*Verh. u. Erf.*, pp. 70–2) rightly rejects this view.

Page 286. *To the end of paragraph 2 add:* Grass (op. cit., pp. 25–28) also thinks that Matt. 28[2-4, 9f.] is legend. Matthew and Luke both correct Mk. 16[8] (the silence of the women). In 24[1-11] Luke has not used a special tradition alongside Mark (so, rightly, Grass, op. cit., pp. 32–35).

To the end of paragraph 3 add: Dibelius (*Formg.*, p. 191) thinks that in Lk. 24[13-35] vv. 21b (or 22)–24 are an addition which has to be joined to the other traditional material. The same view is held by F. C. Grant, *J.B.L.*, 55, 1937, pp. 285–307, and M. S. Enslin, *Jew. Quart. Rev.*, 43, 1952, pp. 38–40. Paul Schubert (*Neutest. Stud. f. R. Bultmann*, 1954, pp. 174f.) thinks that the original story edited by Luke consists of vv. 13, 15b, 16, 28–31.

In line 6 from the top of paragraph 4 add: On Matt. 28[11-20] see Dibelius, *Formg.*, p. 285; Lohmeyer, *Galiläa u. Jerusalem*, pp. 15–17; T. Arvedson, *Mysterium Christi*, pp. 135f.; H. W. Bartsch., *Ev.Th.*, 1947/48, pp. 120–6; O. Michel, ibid., 1950/51, pp. 16–26; Grass, op. cit., pp. 28–32.

In line 2 from bottom add: While Finegan (op. cit., p. 92) thinks that Lk. 24[50-53] is Lukan for reasons of style, Menoud (*Neutest. Studien f. R. Bultmann*, pp. 148–56) thinks, perhaps rightly, that the section is an interpolation. The same view is expressed by H. Conzelmann, *Die Mitte der Zeit*, pp. 79, 177, n. 2.

n. 2. *Add:* On Διάταγμα Καίσαρος see Stephen Lösch, *Diatagma Kaisaros*, 1936.

Page 287. *To the end of paragraph 2 add:* Recent literature about the Easter story is surveyed by W. G. Kümmel, *Th.R.*, N.F., 17, 1948/49, pp. 16–19. Particularly noteworthy are M. Goguel, *La Foi à la Résurrection de Jésus dans le Christianisme Primitif*, 1939; E. Hirsch, *Die Auferstehungsgeschichten u. der christl. Glaube*, 1940; H. Michaelis, *Die Erscheinungen des Auferstandenen*, 1944. From literature that has appeared since then: H. von Campenhausen, 'Der Ablauf der Osterereignisse u. das leere Grab', (*S.B. Heidelb.*, 1952/54); M. S. Enslin, *Jew. Quart. Rev.*, N.S. 43.1, 1952, pp. 27–56; H. Grass, *Ostergeschehen u. Osterberichte*, 1956.

Page 288. *In line 8 of paragraph 2 add:* (The attempt by Michaelis, op. cit., pp. 121f., to find good ancient tradition in Matt. 28⁹f. is not satisfying.)

To line 3 from bottom add: Lohmeyer (*Galil. u. Jerus.*) joins the two motifs to the two localities, Jerusalem and Galilee. The Easter stories, which demonstrate the fact of the resurrection and its scriptural character, are tied up with Jerusalem; the Galilean stories are not intended to provide this proof, but to report a new and greater revelation, which follows the former, and eschatologically fulfils it. The basis of this construction is the interpretation of ὄψεσθε in Mk. 16⁷ as the promise of the Parousia; see above, p. 235, at the end of note 2. On the question as to the localization of the Easter events see esp. the comprehensive and careful enquiry by Grass, op. cit., pp. 113–27. He maintains, in my opinion rightly, the priority of the Galilean appearances, particularly in criticism of Lohmeyer and von Campenhausen.

n. 1. *Add:* On I Cor. 15⁵⁻⁷ see Jeremias, *Abendmahlsw.*, pp. 95–97, and for the rest Lietzmann-Kümmel in *Handb. zum N.T.*

Page 290, n. 3. *Add:* Cp. further J. Leipoldt, *Th.L.Z.*, 73, 1948, cols. 737–42, which gives the material from the history of religions. While Finegan recognizes the legendary character of the stories about the tomb (only the flight of the disciples hinted in Mk. 14²⁸, 16⁷ is historical), H. von Campenhausen ('Der Ablauf der Osterereignisse u. das leere Grab', *SB Heidelb.*, 1952, 4) tries to offer proof for the historicity of the empty tomb. Michaelis (op. cit., pp. 73–96) understands all Christophanies as appearances of Jesus from heaven and interprets the Ascension as a resurrection appearance, which has been given the characteristics of a farewell appearance because its presentation is directed towards the idea of the parousia.

Page 291, n. 3. *Add:* Finegan (op. cit., pp. 105f.) thinks that the day of the resurrection was actually a Sunday; the fixing on the 'third day' followed on the basis of scriptural proof, and it was on that ground that Friday came to be reckoned as the day of the crucifixion.

n. 4. *Add:* In his paper 'Jungfrauensohn u. Krippenkind' (in *Botsch. u. Gesch.*, I, pp. 1–78) Dibelius has shown that in Hellenistic Judaism there was a theologumenon of the generation of holy men by God to the exclusion of the natural father, and in all probability, under the influence of Hellenistic (Egyptian) ideas, that the spirit of a God begat a son in a mortal spouse, which is something to be distinguished from the marriage of a God with a mortal wife. There is evidence for the birth of a child of God from a virgin in Hellenistic Egypt. The motif of the abstinence of the bridegroom until the birth is specifically pagan (on this see also G. Erdmann, *Die Vorgeschichten des Lk.- u. Mt.-Evg.*, p. 56). Dibelius (as Erdmann), in reference to Matt. 1¹⁸⁻²⁵, emphasizes the apologetic motif: the virgin birth is defended (cp. also *Formg.*, p. 125). The appeal to Isa. 7¹⁴ is not in accord with the Palestinian–Jewish understanding of the text, but rather with the Hellenistic. W. L. Knox (*Sources*, II, p. 122) reconstructs a more original form of the story.

Page 292. *In line 4 from top of paragraph 2 add:* (So also Dibelius, *Formg.*, pp. 125f.; Erdmann, op. cit., p. 56; and Knox, *Sources*, II, pp. 122f.)

n. 1. *Add:* Wilh. Weber, *Der Prophet u. sein Gott*, 1925, pp. 121f.; L. Bieler, ΘΕΙΟΣ ANHP, I, pp. 24–28; W. Staerk, *Erlösungserwartung*, pp. 300–61. On the infancy narratives etc. in Matthew see esp. E. Käsemann, *Z.Th.K.* 51 (1954), pp. 134f.: the narrative's motifs are (1) prophetic proof, and (2) the parallelism with the Moses Haggadah. This is transferred to Jesus, because he is the eschatological saviour. The presupposition is the primitive Christian eschatology. According to K. Stendahl, *Festschr. f. J. Jeremias*, *B.Z.N.W.* 26, 1960, pp. 94–105, Matthew's intention is not to give an 'antecedent history' in narrative form, but rather an apologetic and scriptural answer to the question who Jesus is (Matt. 1), and where he is from (Matt. 2).

n. 3. *Add:* E. Kornemann (*Weltgesch. des Mittelmeerraumes*, II, 1949, p. 92) thinks that the prototype was the embassy of homage to Rome by Tiridates in A.D. 64. W. Staerk (op. cit., pp. 368–71) believes that the idea of homage belongs to the motifs found in the ancient near east, of the myth of the birth of the divine king, who would usher in the new age. According to Geo. Widengren the star-motif comes from Iranian sources; originally the star was itself the redeemer, ('the great king'), as Dibelius supposed. (*Iranisch-semitische Kulturbegegnung*, 1960, pp. 67–86.)

n. 4. *Add:* Dibelius (*Botsch. u. Gesch.*, I, pp. 76f.) supposes that the tradition to which Justin witnesses, that Jesus was born in a cave, had its ground in the fact that in or near Bethlehem there was a sacred cave, which had been a cultic sanctuary of Tammuz or Adonis.

n. 5. *Add:* Staerk (op. cit., p. 28) believes that they are the gifts which Adam had received in Paradise.

Page 293, n. 1. *Add:* On the star motif cp. H. Gressmann, *Der Messias*, 1929, p. 37; H. Wagenvoort, *Vergils vierte Ekloge u. das Sidus Julium* (Mededeel. d. Koninkl. Akad., Afd. Letterkunde, Deel 67, Serie A, No. 1, Amsterdam), 1929; Andr. Alföldi, *Hermes*, 65, 1930, pp. 372f. (the royal star on coins); W. Staerk, *Erlösungserw.*, pp. 366f.; Lohmeyer, *Th. Bl.*, 17, 1938, cols. 289–99 (the narrative rests on the story of Balaam, Num. 22–24). Dibelius (*Botsch. u. Gesch.*, I, p. 42, n. 68) supposes that first of all it was related in a myth that the Saviour would appear as a star, 'only when it was changed into the form of an actual story was the star which was the Saviour turned into the star which announced his birth'.

n. 4. *Add:* W. Weber, *Der Prophet u. sein Gott*, p. 98; L. Bieler, op. cit., I, pp. 40f.; Staerk, op. cit., pp. 371–4.

n. 6. *Add:* Staerk, op. cit., pp. 371f., 401f., the motif back to the myth; cp. also H. Gressmann, *Der Messias*, p. 439.

Page 294. *To the end of paragraph 1 add:* Dibelius (*Formg.*, p. 126, n. 2) rightly says that vv. 22f. are not legendary, but were added by Matthew with the intention of introducing Nazareth as the home of Jesus.

To the end of paragraph 3 add: Very similar to this is Dibelius' analysis (see addition to p. 294, n. 2) who in any case thinks that vv. 36f. and vv. 39–56 are insertions by Luke into his source.

In line 2 from bottom add: (So also Dibelius, *Botsch. u. Gesch.*, I, pp. 4f.)

n. 1. *Add:* Cp. Erdmann, op. cit., pp. 6of.: The 'flight into Egypt' derives from Jewish typology: as the first deliverer came from Egypt, so must the last. Staerk (op. cit., p. 372, n. 1) on the other hand explains it in terms of a mythological scheme: Egypt is the underworld, or Chaos, out of which the deliverer rises.

n. 2. *Add:* G. Erdmann, *Die Vorgeschichten des Lk.- u. Mt.-Evgs.*, 1932; M. Dibelius, 'Jungfrauensohn u. Krippenkind', in *Botsch. u. Gesch.*, I, 1953, pp. 1–78, esp. pp. 1–17; Fr. Dornseiff, *Z.N.W.*, 35, 1936, pp. 129–34; P. Winter, *Nov. Test.*, I, 1956, pp. 184–99.

Page 295, n. 1. *Add:* Dibelius (*Formg.*, p. 121, and *Botsch. u. Gesch.*, I, pp. 2f.) thinks that the story of the Baptist is of Jewish, not Christian origin. It comes from Baptist circles according to Erdmann, op. cit., pp. 19ff.; Rud. Meyer, *Der Prophet aus Galiläa*, 1940, p. 82; C. H. Kraeling, *John the Baptist*, 1951, pp. 16–23; P. Winter, *Nov. Test.*, I, 1956, pp. 184–99 (he revives Völter's hypothesis). P. Benoit (*Nt. St.*, 3, 1957, pp. 169–94) on the other hand tries to show that the story of the Baptist is a Lukan composition from oral tradition, modelled on biblical prototypes and enriched by an ancient Jewish-Christian hymn (Lk. 1[68–79], see below). Whereas Dibelius (*Botsch. u. Gesch.*, I, p. 8) concludes from the Semitic character of the language that the story was originally circulated in Aramaic, Winter (*Nt. St.*, I, 1954/55, pp. 111–21) tries to prove that, like the birth narrative of Jesus, it was translated from an Hebrew source. R. N. Turner (ibid., 2, 1955–6, pp. 100–9) rightly states the contrary view. For the Palestinian-Jewish character see again Winter, *St. Th.* 12 (1958), pp. 103–7. He comments on particular verses out of Lk. 1 and 2 in *Z.N.W.* 49 (1958), pp. 65–77. Erdmann (op. cit., pp. 9ff.) thinks that the story of John's birth was originally an independent legend and provided the pattern (on the principle of syncresis) for the birth story of Jesus. Dornseiff (op. cit.) offers confirmation for this view. As regards the question of the source(s) of Lk. 1 and 2 cp. further M. D. Goulder and M. S. Sanderson, 'St. Luke's Genesis', *J.T.S.*, N.S. 8 (1957), pp. 12–30; R. Laurentin, *Structure et Théologie de Luc I–II*, 1957, replied to by M. D. Goulder in *J.T.S.*, N.S. 9 (1958), pp. 358–60.

n. 2. *Add:* P. Winter (op. cit.) thinks that the story derives from the version of the stories of the births of Samson and Samuel as they are preserved in the pseudo-philonic 'Liber Antiquitatum Biblicarum'. On confirmatory signs see also Hom. *Od.*, 11, 127; 23, 293; Verg. *Aen.*, 8, 42ff.

n. 3. *Add:* J. Gewiess explains v. 34 as a literary device which Luke uses to heighten the significance of v. 35, *Bibl. Z.*, N.F. 5, 1961, pp. 221–54.

Page 296. *To the end of paragraph 1 add:* Dibelius (*Formg.*, p. 121, and

Botsch. u. Gesch., I, pp. 12–14) consider v. 36f. to be secondary, and wants to take vv. 34f. as original, rejecting ἐμνηστευμένην ἀνδρὶ ᾧ ὄνομα Ἰωσήφ in v. 27 as an addition by the evangelist, to serve as a link between chs. 1 and 2. Erdmann (op. cit., pp. 11f.) also thinks vv. 34f. are original: 1²⁶⁻³⁸ is a literary composition of Luke on the pattern of the Baptist legend in 1⁵⁻²⁵; the virgin birth of Jesus has to surpass the birth of the Baptist. A. Fridrichsen (*Th.L.Z.*, 60, 1935, p. 399) rightly rejects this. Further, Selma Hirsch (*Die Vorstellung von einem weiblichen Pneuma Hagion*, 1927, pp. 1–16) will have nothing to do with any hypothesis of an interpolation, though less enlighteningly thinks that the narrative is a combination of two sources.

To the end of paragraph 2 add: Dibelius (*Formg.*, p. 122, and *Botsch u. Gesch.*, I, pp. 13f.) thinks otherwise and takes vv. 39–45 (or even 56) for Luke's own composition. Without deciding on this issue, C. H. Kraeling (*John the Baptist*, pp. 125f.) shows that Lk. 1³⁹⁻⁴⁵ is a Christian product from the controversy between the Baptist and the Christian community. (According to Torrey, followed by Black, *Aram. Appr.*², p. 11, εἰς πόλιν Ἰούδα in v. 39 is a mistranslation for εἰς τὴν χώραν τῆς Ἰουδαίας.

n. 2. *Add:* Dibelius (*Botsch. u. Gesch.*, p. 13, n. 15) is also against Radermacher. On the leaping of the child in the womb see Dornseiff, op. cit., p. 132, who refers to Callimachus, *Hymn.*, 4.162ff.

n. 3. *Add:* Against Gunkel is Erdmann, *Vorgeschichten*, pp. 31–33: the psalms were composed *ad hoc*, and the Magnificat indeed belongs to the Baptist tradition, while the Benedictus was composed by Luke after the pattern of the Magnificat. Also against Gunkel is Dornseiff, op. cit., p. 133, who however opposes Erdmann's view that the Benedictus was composed on the pattern of the Magnificat. P. Winter (*Bull. Rylands Library*, 37.1, 1954) tries to show that vv. 46–55 and vv. 68–75 (on vv. 76–79 see below, p. 296, n. 4) were Maccabean psalms that had already been introduced into Luke's source; the δούλη in v. 48 was originally Israel personified. Cp. also P. Winter, *St. Th.* 12 (1958), pp. 104f. Harnack (*S.B. Berlin*, 1900, pp. 538–56) thinks that the Magnificat should rightly be sung by Elizabeth, as does Kraeling, *John the Baptist*, pp. 170f. The contrary view is stated by Dibelius, *Botsch. u. Gesch.*, I, p. 14.

n. 4. *Add:* Rud. Meyer (*Der Prophet aus Galiläa*, p. 154) and P. Winter (op. cit.) (see above, on n. 3) think that vv. 76–79 are a Christian addition. For the unity of vv. 76–79, in all probability correctly, Erdmann, *Vorgesch.*, p. 10, and especially Ph. Vielhauer, *Z.Th.K.*, 49, 1952, opp. 255–72.

Page 297, n. 1. *Add:* On Augustus' census see Dibelius, *Botsch. u. Gesch.*, I, pp. 53f.; he thinks the statement is an addition by Luke to the traditional story. (Dibelius also thinks that τῇ ἐμνηστευμένη αὐτῷ in v. 5 is also an addition by Luke and in all probability ὅς ἐστιν Χριστὸς κύριος in v. 11 as well.) Eb. Nestle (*Z.N.W.*, 11, 1910 p. 87) thinks that perhaps ἀπογραφή has come from Ps. 86⁶. Gressmann

(*Der Messias*, p. 49) explains the dating in the year of Quirinius by the fact that this was the year in which Judas of Galilee arose. Cp. also L. Bieler, op. cit., I, p. 28. The birthplace of the θεῖος ἀνήρ can be unusual. According to Iamblichus, *Vit. Pyth.*, 7, Pythagoras was born while his parents were on a journey; cp. ibid., II, p. 96.

n. 2. *Add:* On the shepherds and the child in the manger see most especially (against Gressmann) Dibelius, *Botsch. u. Gesch.*, I, pp. 57–60, and esp. pp. 60–77.

Page 298, n. 2. *Add:* On the Osiris legend see Dibelius, *Botsch. u. Gesch.*, I, p. 66. Further, W. Staerk, *Erlösererw.*, pp. 325f. Ibid., pp. 363, 368–71, for the proclamation, the angelic message and the homage. Cp. also E. Abegg, *Der Messiasglaube in Indien u. Iran*, 1928, pp. 81f.; W. Weber, *Der Prophet u. sein Gott*, p. 122.

n. 3. *Add:* Cp. also Dibelius, *Botsch. u. Gesch.*, I, pp. 65f.

n. 5. *Add:* On the problem of the shepherd scene on the Mithras monuments see Dibelius, *Botsch. u. Gesch.*, I, pp. 67–72.

Page 299. *To the end of paragraph 2 add:* Jeremias (*Z.N.W.*, 28, 1929, pp. 13–20) has shown the liturgical character very strongly by his translation back into Hebrew; G. von Rad (ibid., 29, 1930, pp. 111–15) criticizes his translation. M. Black (*Aram. Appr.*[2], p. 125) provides a retranslation into Aramaic, which yields a good example of paronomasia. Cp. further J. Wobbe, *Bibl. Z.*, 22, 1934, pp. 118–52, 224–45, and ibid., 23, 1935/36, pp. 358–64. On the Hellenistic character of the story see Dibelius, *Botsch. u. Gesch.*, I, pp. 61, 63, 73.

Page 300. *To the end of paragraph 2 add:* (Similarly the characterization of Lk. 2[22–40] in Dibelius, *Formg.*, pp. 122–4.)

In line 4 from the top of paragraph 3 add: This is alien to the characterization of the story in Dibelius (*Formg.*, pp. 103–5) who rightly takes v. 49 as the original ending of the story. Erdmann (op. cit., pp. 19–22) is not enlightening with his idea that the story is an edited legend about the Baptist. Black (*Aram. Appr.*[2], p. 3) supposes that the section derives from an Aramaic source. B. van Jersel (*Nov. Test.* 4, 1960, pp. 161–73) seeks to show that the story belongs to a primitive stage of the earliest Christian tradition, and that its origins are in the catechetical instruction.

In line 8 from the end add: Cp. further *Hymn. Homer. in Apoll. Del*, 127ff.; *in Herm.*, 17f.; Eur., *Iphig. Aul.*, 1249ff.; Callimachus, *in Jovem*, 55ff.

n. 1. *Add:* Cp. further W. Staerk, *Erlösererw.*, p. 404; Erdmann, op. cit., pp. 13f. (also Fridrichsen, *Th.L.Z.*, 60, 1935, p. 400, and Dibelius, *Formg.*, p. 123, n. 2); W. Weber, *Der Prophet u. sein Gott*, p. 123.

n. 2. *Add:* Cp. Erdmann, op. cit., pp. 13f.; also Dibelius, *Formg.*, p. 123, n. 2.

n. 3. *Add:* Cp. further Dibelius, *Formg.*, pp. 104f.; Staerk, *Erlösererw.*, pp. 374–6; L. Troje, AΔAM *und* ZΩH (*S.B. Heidelb.*, 1916, 17, p. 78, n. 2; L. Bieler, ΘΕΙΟΣ ANHP, I, pp. 30, 34f., 38f., 76.

Page 302. *To the end of paragraph 1 add:* H. Ljungvik (*Z.N.W.*, 33, 1934, pp. 90–92) thinks that ἔλεγον should be read in v. 14; καὶ ἔλεγον represents the place of an accusative clause (καὶ instead of an expected ὅτι) to ἤκουσεν. It is what the people thought that is stated in v. 14. This view is adopted by Lohmeyer, ad loc., and Jeremias, *Th.W.B.*, II, p. 938, n. 64.

n. 1. *Add:* While Lohmeyer offers no critical analysis of the text, Rud. Meyer (*Der Prophet aus Galiläa*, pp. 38–40) has an analysis as above. He thinks that the original sequence must have been Herod's decision to proceed against Jesus as against the Baptist, and he appeals to Mk. 8[15] and Lk. 13[31-33]. Cp. further J. Thomas, *Le Mouvement Baptiste*, pp. 110f.; H. J. Ebeling, *Das Messiasgeheimnis*, pp. 214–16.

Page 310, n. 3. *Add:* Cp. W. L. Hertslet, *Der Treppenwitz in der Weltgesch.*[4], 1927, pp. 10f.

Page 312. *To the end of paragraph 2 add:* Sayings in direct speech in miracle stories which belong essentially to them are of course not to be understood as secondary material (cp. O. Perels, *Die Wunder- überlieferung der Synoptiker*, p. 14).

n. 1. *Add:* The side which, according to John 19[34], the spear entered, was the right—such is the Ethiopian tradition; similarly *Acta Pilati*, B 11, p. 311, Tischend. Also in the Liturgy of St. Chrysostom and elsewhere.

Page 313. *To the end of paragraph 1 add:* The words ὁσάκις κτλ. in I Cor. 11[26] are found as a saying of Jesus in *Const. Apost.* VIII, 12.37; see H. v. Soden, *Sakrament und Ethik bei Paulus*, 1931 (esp. p. 30; also p. 29, n. 2).

Page 314. *In line 3 from the top of paragraph 3 add:* (Yet in this case we must always remember that Rabbinic messengers were normally sent in pairs; see Rengstorf in *Th.W.B.*, I, 417.29 and n. 68.)

n. 1. *Add:* On the number three cp. Verg., *Aen.*, 6, 700f.; 8, 230f. The triplication in the sayings of Jesus discussed by Jeremias in *Jesus als Weltvollender*, 1930, p. 21, n. 1, is something different.

Page 315. *To line 3 of paragraph 2 add:* Cp. e.g. Hom., *Od.*, 21, 66: As Penelope comes into the room, ἀμφίπολος δ' ἄρα οἱ κεδνὴ ἑκάτερθε παρέστη.

n. 3. *Add* Cp. Two white doves in Grimm, *Kinder- u. Hausmärchen*, No. 33 (conclusion) and No. 76. Two white doves appear as messengers of Venus in Verg., *Aen.*, 6, 190.

Page 316. *To the end of paragraph 3 add:* In cases where two people appear in Matthew instead of one in Mark, Holzmeister, *Biblica*, 7, 1926, pp. 170–82, and P. Ketter, ibid., 15, 1934, p. 411, think that there is no development of the tradition, but that in the corresponding places in Mark and Luke there was in the numerical details the ancient *sensus praecisivus*, which would not exclude the healing of a second person.

Page 317. *In line* 16 *from top of page add:* A picture of Peter and Marcellinus in the catacombs shows Noah in the Ark with two doves flying to him from right and left with the olive branch (Wilpert, *Die Malereien der Katak. Roms.*, Pl. 98; H. W. Beyer in 'Von der Antike zum Christent.', *Festg. f. V. Schulze*, 1931, Ill. 2). The adoration of the Magi in the same catacomb shows Mary and the child in the middle and, to right and left, one of the Magi (Wilpert, Pl. 60; in Beyer, Ill. 5.)

Page 321, n. 2. *Add:* Sundwall (*Die Zusammensetzung des Markusevg.*, 1934, pp. 14f., 20, 75) shares Albertz's opinion that there was a collection of conflict dialogues, and tries to justify an original collection of miracle stories. J. M. C. Crum (*St. Mark's Gospel*, 1936) seeks to understand our present Mark text as the combination of Mk. i with Mk. ii. Dibelius (*Formg.*, p. 220) thinks that Mark had the cycle of Mk. 4^{35}–5^{43} in front of him, but is sceptical about earlier collections, though W. L. Knox (*The Sources of the Synoptic Gospels*, I, 1953; II, 1957) thinks that he can establish the existence of a whole series of them.

Page 323. *At the end of paragraph 1 add:* W. L. Knox (op. cit., *passim*) refers to this. To my mind it is a matter of secondary importance how far the evangelists found such formulae in their eventual sources, and how far they introduced them themselves.

Page 324. *At the end of paragraph 2 add:* On the discourse Mk. 13 see H. Conzelmann, *Z.N.W.* 50 (1959), pp. 210–21.

Page 325, n. 1. *Add:* Mk. 4^{10-12} bursts the frame. In v. 10 the situation of vv. 1f. is left behind; but vv. 33f. presuppose that it still obtains. Then v. 13 presupposes that a question was asked about the meaning of the parable that had just been told. Presumably Mark found the parable already in a setting, for v. 34 is a violent reinterpretation of v. 33. Like vv. 10–12, v. 34 comes from Mark. If v. 33 stood in the source then also v. 2, whereas v. 1 goes back to Mark and prepares for the link with vv. 35ff. Similarly, but somewhat differently, Dibelius, *Formg.*, pp. 229f., 237. Different attempts to discover a fundamental base behind

Mark are found in Sundwall, op. cit., pp. 25f.; R. H. Lightfoot, *Hist. and Interp.*, p. 38; W. L. Knox, *Sources*, I, pp. 35–38. Jeremias (*Gleichn.*[4], pp. 7–12) thinks that vv. 10–12 are an ancient logion inserted by Mark, which did not originally deal specifically with the parables, but rather with the preaching of Jesus generally. The secret was the present irruption of the reign of God. That fails to enlighten me. See above, p. 198. On the editing of Mk. 4[1-34] cp. also G. H. Boobyer, *Nt. St.* 8 (1961/2), pp. 59–70.

Page 327, n. 2. *Add:* Jeremias (*Z.N.W.*, 29, 1930, pp. 147–9) has argued against the existence of Q on the ground that the mnemonic collections of catchwords available in the linguistic material show that Matthew and Luke drew on oral tradition. W. Bussmann (ibid., 31, 1932, p. 23–32) rightly argues against this point of view.

Page 328. *To the end of paragraph 2 add:* Of course such compositions could have been available to Luke. W. L. Knox (*Sources*, II, pp. 39–118) tries to work out what they were by process of analysis. I do not think certainty is possible.

Page 329. *In line 6 from end of paragraph 1 add:* Dibelius (*Formg.*, pp. 220–7, 261f.) treats the methods of Mark in the same way.

To the end of paragraph 1 add: (Cp. C. H. Turner, *J.T.S.*, 1925, pp. 225–40; 1926, pp. 9–30; Max Zerwick, *Untersuchungen zum Markus-Stil*, 1937).

Page 333. *At the end of paragraph 3 add:* On the Sermon on the Mount see H. K. McArthur, *Understanding the Sermon on the Mount*, 1960. Cp. A. Descampes, 'Essai d'interprétation de Mt. 5[17-48]. "Formgeschichte" ou "Redaktionsgeschichte".' *Studia Ev.*, 1959, pp. 156–73.

Page 334. *In line 14 from bottom add:* (Cp. Dibelius, *Formg.*, pp. 161–3; also Jeremias, *Gleichn.*, p. 84.)

Page 337. *In line 6 from bottom of paragraph 3 add:* (W. L. Knox (*Sources*, I, pp. 101f.) conjectures that Lk. 11[53f.] was the end of the source used in 11[37-52].)

Page 338, n. 1. *Add:* From the extensive literature see esp. F. C. Grant, *The Growth of the Gospels*, 1933; R. H. Lightfoot, *Hist. and Interp. in the Gospels*, 1934, and *Locality and Doctrine in the Gospels*, 1938.

n. 2. *Add:* Cp. further E. Lohmeyer, *Galiläa und Jerusalem*, 1936; Lightfoot (see n. 1) with Lohmeyer sees Mark's plan in the opposition of Galilee as the land of eschatological fulfilment to Jerusalem. G. H. Boobyer, 'Galilee and the Galileans in St. Mark's Gospel', *Bull. Rylands Library*, 35.2, 1953, pp. 334–8. G. Hartmann,

Der Aufbau des Mk.-Evgs., 1936; J. M. C. Crum, *St. Mark's Gospel*, 1936; W. Marxsen, *Der Evangelist Mk.*, 1956. H. Riesenfeld (*Neutest. Studien f. Rud. Bultmann*, 1954, pp. 157, 164) shows how the tradition used by Mark is interwoven into his theological, or Christological arrangement.

Page 339. *In line 4 of paragraph 3 add:* Cp. καὶ γίνεται, 2¹⁵, καὶ ἐγένετο, 1⁹ (?); 2²³. To conclude from the repetition of such words as πάλιν that different sources were used, as W. L. Knox does (*Sources*, I, p. 19), is to me unjustifiable.

To end of paragraph 3 add: Cp. R. H. Lightfoot, *Hist. and Interp.*, pp. 36f.

To the end of paragraph 6 add: On the editorial ending with the genitive absolute see K. G. Kuhn, *Ev. Th.*, 1952/53, pp. 261f.

Page 340. *To line 3 from foot add:* 14⁵⁵⁻⁶⁴ between 14⁵³ᶠ· and ⁶⁶⁻⁷² (p. 269). In many instances the connection is made clearer by repetition of some word or expression, as Sundwall points out; e.g. 1¹² is connected with 1¹⁰ᶠ· by the word πνεῦμα, 2¹⁵ with 2¹⁴ by τελώνιον—τελῶναι, 9¹ with 8³⁸ by ἐλθεῖν ἐν τῇ δόξῃ—ἐλθεῖν ἐν δυνάμει.

Page 341. *To the end of paragraph 3 add:* See above, pp. 61f., on the analysis of 3¹³⁻¹⁹.

Page 342. *In line 15 of paragraph 2 add:* On Mk. 4¹ᶠ· see above, n. 1 on p. 325.

Page 343. *In line 4 of paragraph 2 add:* 1⁴⁵: καὶ ἤρχοντο πρὸς αὐτὸν πάντοθεν.

To end of paragraph 2 add: Corresponding to these are passages where he is removed from the crowds (H. J. Ebeling, *Messiasgeh.*, pp. 116f.), 3⁹; 4¹; 6³¹ᶠ·. Perhaps also 1⁴⁵ᵃ; 3⁷; 7²⁴; 9³⁰ᶠ··.

Page 346. *To the end of paragraph 1 add:* (On the μαθηταί, the Twelve and the Three, cp. also Lohmeyer, *Galiläa und Jerusalem*, pp. 59f.)

Page 347, n. 1. *Add:* Cp. in the second edition of the *Formg.*, esp. pp. 225f., 231–4, 278f., 297.

n. 2. *Add:* H. J. Ebeling (*Das Messiasgeh. u. die Botschaft des Marcus-Evangelisten* (1939) attacks both the apologetic theory and Wrede's interpretation. The secret in Mark is meant only to show the greatness of the mystery that is revealed and thus to heighten the blessing and responsibility of the hearers—or readers; this is an original but not very satisfying idea. Cp. further E. Sjöberg, *Der verborgene Menschensohn in den Evangelien*, 1955; G. H. Boobyer, *Nt. St.* 6 (1959/60), pp. 225–35; T. A. Burkill, *Z.N.W.* 52 (1961), pp. 189–213.

n. 3. *Add:* Cp. Dibelius, *Formg.*, pp. 237–9, 259–62: Mark provides but a selection from Jesus' teaching and does not intend to make a full selection of the material. The paraenesis comes into the tradition for reasons very different from those for Jesus' deeds. The question, once answered affirmatively by B. Weiss, whether Mark knew Q (and used it), is rightly rejected by Burton H. Throckmorton, *J.B.L.*, 67, 1948, pp. 319–29.

Page 349, n. 3. *Add:* G. Hartmann (*Der Aufbau des Markusevg.*) makes the attempt to prove that the construction of Mark is in seven main symmetrical divisions, but that seems not to be evident. Important for the question as to Mark's sources and his own editorial work: W. L. Knox, *The Sources of the Synoptic Gospels, I. St. Mark*, 1953; P. Parker, *The Gospel before Mark*, 1953; A. Kuby, *Z.N.W.* 49 (1958), pp. 52–64; J. P. Brown, *J.B.L.* 78 (1959), pp. 215–27; T. A. Burkill, *Z.N.W.* 51 (1960), pp. 31–46; S. G. F. Brandon, *Nt. St.*. 7 (1960/1), pp. 126–41; W. Karnetzki, *Z.N.W.* 52 (1961), pp. 238–72.

Page 355. *In line 8 from the top add:* (With this, cp. Jeremias, *Z.N.W.*, 35, 1936, pp. 280–2. Further literature in W. Bauer, *W.B.*⁴, col. 337f.)

Page 356. *In line 3 from the top add:* (R. H. Lightfoot (*Hist. and Interp.*, p. 20) observes that in Matthew the crowd always stands when Jesus teaches.)

In line 12 from the bottom add: Dibelius (*Formg.*, p. 263) explains the abbreviation of the narrative material taken from Mark as Matthew's tendency to assimilate narratives to Q and to make them approximate to teaching.

In line 6 from the bottom add: In 4²³⁻²⁵ Matthew has used the words κηρύσσειν and θεραπεύειν to indicate, so to speak, the arrangement of the following chapters: 5¹–7²⁹, treat of κηρύσσειν, 8¹–9³⁴ of θεραπεύειν. It is unlikely that the ten (?) miracle stories assembled in 8¹–9³⁴ correspond to the ten miracles of Moses in Egypt, as H. J. Schoeps maintains in *Theologie u. Geschichte des Judenchristentums*, p. 93.

Page 357. *In line 6 of paragraph 2 add:* (On this cp. G. Bornkamm in *The Background*, pp. 222–60.)

Page 358. *In line 4 of paragraph 3 add:* (On this cp. N. A. Dahl, *Das Volk Gottes*, 1941, pp. 184f.)

In line 5 *from the bottom add:* (Cp. K. Stendahl, *The School of St. Matthew*, 1954, pp. 39–317. W. L. Knox (*Sources*, II, pp. 126f.) believes that Matthew made use of a collection of testimonies.)

n. 1. *Add:* Cp. further K. Stendahl, *The School of St. Matthew*, 1954, pp. 11–35. K. Thieme (*Judaica*, 5, 1949, pp. 130–52, 161–82) indulges in fundamentally ypological triflings and fantastic numerical speculations. Cp. further L. Cerfaux, *L'Év. de St. Mt. Discours de Mission*, 1957; H. Ch. Waetjen, 'The transformation of Judaism according to St. Matth.', Diss. Tübingen, 1958; W. Trilling, *Das wahre Israel: Studien zur Theologie des Matthäusevg.*, 1959; Nepper-Christusen, *J.B.L.* 79 (1960), pp. 88–91.

Page 359. *Before line* 14 *add:* On the following, cp. esp. L. Brun, 'Zur Kompositionstechnik des Lukasevg.', *Symb. Osloenses*, 9, 1930 ; F. Dornseiff, 'Lukas der Schriftsteller', *Z.N.W.*, 35, 1936, pp. 129–55; esp. H. Conzelmann, *Die Mitte der Zeit*, 1954, who gives an interpretation of the composition of Luke in terms of the problems of the interval between the earthly life of Jesus and his Parousia. On Luke's theology cp. J. C. O'Neill, *J.T.S.* 10 (1959), pp. 1–10.

Page 360. *To the end of paragraph* 3 *add:* See A. J. Wensinck in *Bull. Bezan Club*, 12, 1937, p. 38, for καὶ ἐγένετο as an Aramaism.

Page 361. *To the end of paragraph* 3 *add:* On the connection of the content of 9^{51} with what precedes it see P. Schubert, *Neutest. Studien f. R. Bultmann*, 1954, pp. 183–5. On such far-reaching connections and on preparation for future narrative see R. H. Lightfoot, *Hist. and Interp.*, p. 170, n. 1 and 3.

Page 362, n. 2. *Add:* We shall not here consider the various Proto-Luke hypotheses; on this cp. K. Grobel, *Formgeschichte und Synoptische Quellenanalyse*, 1937. E. Schweizer (*Th.Z.Basel*, 6, 1950, pp. 161–85) seeks to trace a special hebraising source in Luke: (1) in material peculiar to him (Lk. 1f.; 5^{1-11}; 7^{11-17}; 7^{36-50}; 8^{1-3}; 9^{51-55}; $11^{27f.}$; 13^{10-17}; 14^{1-5}; 17^{11-19}; 19^{1-10}; $23^{50}-24^{53}$) and (2) in sections with parallels in Mark or Matthew (5^{12-26}; $8^{22-25,\ 40-56}$; $9^{18-22,\ 28-45}$; 11^{1-14}; 18^{35-43}; $19^{5,\ 29,\ 47f.}$; 20^1) and those which appear in two blocks in Matthew (Matt. $8^{1-9,\ 34}$ and $16^{13}-17^{23}$). Schweizer assumes that these narratives were already available to Mark, that their order in Matthew is original, that some forerunner of Luke combined this material with the special material cited, and that Luke often expanded and corrected Mark's outline and wording. Opposed to Schweizer is W. Michaelis, *St. Th.*, IV, 1951, pp. 86–93, and *Einleitung in das N.T.*, 1954, pp. 72f. Fr. Rehkopf's attempt to establish for the whole of Luke a source independent of Mark can scarcely be called successful ('Die Lukanische Sonderquelle'). But his observations concerning Luke's use of language are important. As regards the material peculiar to Luke, cp. the criticism of the Proto-Luke hypothesis by H. Montefiore, *J.T.S.*, N.S. 12 (1961), pp. 59f. H. F. D. Sparks thinks that Luke has sometimes rearranged passages from his Markan material (*Nt. St.* 3, 1956/7, pp. 219–23); the contrary view in J. Jeremias, ibid. 4 (1957/8), pp. 115–19.

Page 363. *In line 3 of paragraph 2 add:* (On Luke's transpositions see R. H. Lightfoot, *Hist. and Interp.*, p. 171, n. 1; H. F. D. Sparks, *Nt. St.*, 3, 1957, pp. 219–23.)

n. 2. *Add:* R. Morgenthaler seeks to establish a 'duality principle' as such a principle of composition (*Die lukanische Geschichtsschreibung als Zeugnis*, I, 1948). But K. Schürmann (*Z. Kath. Theol.*, 75, 1953, pp. 83–93) has shown that a tendency to avoid doublets is also in evidence in Luke.

Page 364. *To the end of paragraph 1 add:* On Luke's travel narrative see R. Otto, *Reich Gottes u. Menschensohn*, pp. 7f.; W. Gasse, *Z.N.W.*, 34, 1935, pp. 293–9; H. Conzelmann, *Die Mitte der Zeit*[3], pp. 60–66, 184f. W. Grundmann, *Z.N.W.* 50 (1959), pp. 252–70; W. M. C. Robinson, *J.B.L.* 79 (1960), pp. 20–31.

To the end of the last line add: On Luke's geography see esp. Conzelmann, op. cit., pp. 30f., and (treating of Jerusalem) pp. 60–65.

Page 366. *To line 11 from the top add:* In distinction from Mark and Matthew who distinguish between the ὄχλος (or the ὄχλοι) and the μαθηταί, Luke speaks also of the ὄχλος and the πλῆθος of the μαθηταί in 6[17]; 19[37].

In line 5 of paragraph 2 add: Since in composing his gospel Luke was relatively bound to the tradition that had already received its shape, he did not have the same literary freedom as he possessed in composing the Acts of the Apostles; while in Acts he lets individual people make speeches, in the gospel he puts no real address on the lips of Jesus. (Dibelius, *Aufsätze zur Apostelgesch.*, p. 158.)

n. 1. *Add:* Cp. also B. W. Bacon, *Rev.H.Ph.Rel.*, 1928, pp. 209–26. H. C. Snape, *H.T.R.* 55, 1960, pp. 27–46.

Page 367, n. 4. *Add:* Jeremias (*Jesus als Weltvollender*, p. 56, n.1) thinks that Luke intended to present Jesus as the Second Adam, who overcame the temptation to which the first Adam fell. Dibelius (*Formg.*, pp. 299f.) sees the distinguishing feature of Luke in that he writes his gospel, not as an epiphany story, but as legend. Lohmeyer (*Kultus u. Evg.*, pp. 66–68) holds that Luke has reduced the original opposition to the cultus and the temple, so that Jesus appears as 'the pious son of a people' who 'knows he is tied to God's holy dwelling places even in the special circumstances of his eschatological mission'. Conzelmann (*Die Mitte der Zeit*) shows how Luke interprets the history of Israel and the story of Jesus as he does his own time in terms of the deferred parousia. P. Schubert (*Neutest. Studien f. R. Bultmann*, pp. 165–86) shows how Luke's theology of 'proof from prophecy' has influenced his editing of his material. Cp. further G. W. H. Lampe, 'The Lucan Portrait of Christ', *Nt. St.*, 2, 1955/56, pp. 160–75.

Page 369, n. 2. *Add:* Taking Lohmeyer's idea further, G. Schille (*Nt. St.*, 4, 1957/58, pp. 1–24) tries to locate the motive leading to the composition of Mark's gospel in the needs of catechesis and he also seeks to explain the structure of Mark from the perspective of catechesis—which is a considerable exaggeration, in spite of many valid observations that he makes.

Page 370, n. 1. *Add:* In the Second Edition, p. 66.

n. 2. *Add:* Cp. C. H. Dodd, *The Apostolic Preaching and its Developments*[4], 1950. On Harald Riesenfeld, *The Gospel Tradition and its Beginning*, 1957, see above, p. 381.

Page 371. *In line* 13 *from the top add:* H. W. Bartsch, *Th.Bl.*, 19, 1940, cols. 301–8.

To the end of paragraph 1 *add:* (R. H. Lightfoot (*Hist. and Interp.*, pp. xiif., 220–4) also relates Mark and John in this way.)

n. 2. *Add to line* 4 *from the top:* Cp. F. C. Grant, *The Earliest Gospel*, pp. 58–75, and esp. pp. 76–88.

GENERAL INDEX

(For further information see the Table of Contents)